Portrait of Julian Ursyn Niemcewicz (1808), after his
return to Poland. From Alexander Kraushar, *Okruchy
przeszłości,* 1913.

UNDER THEIR VINE
AND FIG TREE

UNDER THEIR

UNDER THEIR VINE
AND FIG TREE

"But they shall sit every man under
his vine and under his fig tree."

Micah iv. 4

VINE AND FIG TREE

*Travels through America in 1797–1799, 1805
with some further account of life in New Jersey*

by JULIAN URSYN NIEMCEWICZ

*Translated and Edited with an Introduction and Notes
by* METCHIE J. E. BUDKA

Published as Volume XIV in the Collections of
The New Jersey Historical Society at Newark
by THE GRASSMANN PUBLISHING COMPANY, INC.
Elizabeth   *New Jersey*

The "Journey to Niagara, 1805" was first published in *The New-York Historical Society Quarterly,* the visit to Harvard College in Chapter VI was published in *The New England Quarterly* and the visit to Mount Vernon of Chapter IV in the *American Heritage Magazine.*

Winner of the First Annual
Doctoral Dissertation Award
of
The Kosciuszko Foundation

Acknowledgments

I wish to acknowledge my debt to Professor Wiktor Weintraub of Harvard. During the writing of my thesis on the American Diaries of Julian Ursyn Niemcewicz he gave his interest, guidance and advice without stint; and I thank him for all his generous and constant help during the preparation of this book for publication. I am deeply grateful to him for his teaching and criticism and that he shared with me his perception of the Polish American scene.

I wish to thank my many friends and associates in Poland. In the summer of 1956 I was awarded a grant to attend an international vacation course at the University of Warsaw for teachers of Polish. I am indebted to Mr. Wacław Zawadzki who first told me then that the original diaries of Niemcewicz had been found and who has since that time given me every help and assistance. I wish to record my thanks to the late Professor Emil Kipa whom I met in 1956 for his interest and encouragement. I am grateful to Mrs. Antonina Wellman-Zalewska, his associate, who prepared the Polish edition of Niemcewicz's *Travels,* and who made a copy available to me during my transcription of the Polish manuscript. This was of immeasurable help. I would like also to thank Dr. Jan Dihm.

I have incurred many debts and have had much encouragement from friends. I am indebted to Dr. Cecile Stora and Mme. Jacques Lewin who both read the transcripts for their great help in establishing the French text. I owe much to Dr. and Mme. Jacques Lewin. I am grateful to Mrs. James T. Flexner who advised me, after much fruitless search, of source material in early American music—to other colleagues and friends whose suggestions and help are acknowledged in the notes. I would like to thank the present and former staff of The New-York Historical Society for their help particularly Mr. Charles E. Baker, Mr. Arthur B. Carlson, Miss Theresa B. Czajkowska, Miss Betty J. Ezequelle, Mr. Michael Lazlo and Mr. Theodore J. Peruche. The library resources of the Columbia University Library, the New York Public Library and Widener Library at Harvard and other collections have been indispensable and I thank their staffs. I have been able to consult and to reproduce in this book many documents, manuscripts and drawings from both private and public collections for which acknowledgments have been made in the captions. In particular I want to thank in this respect Mrs. Richard C. Aldrich, Viscount Bolingbroke, the Reverend Edward B. Bunn, S.J., President, Georgetown University and Father W. C. Repetti, S.J., Archivist, Mr. Storer G. Decatur and the Hon. Hamilton Fish. Acknowledgment is due to the University of North Carolina Press and Professor William Peden for permission to quote from their edition of Jefferson's *Notes on the State of Virginia.* I thank Mr. Matthew Mirlocca for his work on the Meyer Map of Elizabethtown and Mrs. Theodore Thayer for her work on the Niemcewicz marriage certificate.

I thank Mr. Robert M. Lunny, Director of The New Jersey Historical Society for his help and valuable suggestions. I wish to thank too Mr. Howard W. Wiseman and the staff of the Society for their many kindnesses.

I thank Mrs. John Kean for an illuminating view into the collections of the Niemcewicz memorabilia at Liberty Hall and her gracious permission for their use in this book.

I am grateful to Mr. Edward J. Grassmann and the Hon. Robert Winthrop Kean for their generous help in making the publication of this book possible.

METCHIE J. E. BUDKA

New York, 1964

Foreword

It is a happy occasion for The New Jersey Historical Society to publish the Travels through America of Julian Ursyn Niemcewicz as Volume XIV of its *Collections*, in a superb translation from the original French and Polish and with an introduction specially written for this complete English edition by Metchie J. E. Budka.

In 1956 when the Polish Archives were opened Mr. Budka went to Poland to search for the American manuscripts of Niemcewicz taken there when he left our shores in 1807. By a fortunate happenstance the convulsions of war uncovered the complete diary of his American travels and Mr. Budka prepared a critical edition of the manuscripts. This study done at Harvard University received the first Kosciuszko Foundation Doctoral Dissertation Award.

It was Niemcewicz's intention to write a description of America for his fellow countrymen but the diary was never published in his lifetime. Niemcewicz was a highly cultivated, intellectual, witty and perceptive man, and his honest observations on his adopted country and its many prominent citizens whom he knew should be of considerable interest to all. Especially interested will be New Jerseymen in whose state Niemcewicz made his home, and also Americans of Polish background who honor the writer as a great Polish literary figure, patriot and lover of freedom who found so much to admire in America.

In 1800 Niemcewicz married Susan Livingston Kean, widow of John Kean and niece of William Livingston, the first governor of New Jersey in the new United States. It was this circumstance that led to the most happy joining of forces in the name of the Society.

Our Trustee and Patron the Hon. Robert Winthrop Kean, a direct descendant of Mrs. Niemcewicz, in keeping with the tradition in the Kean family to honor the virtue and accomplishments of this noble Pole, has offered his support for the publication of this diary. Our Trustee and Patron Mr. Edward J. Grassmann, because of his love of Elizabethtown where Niemcewicz found happy refuge, has joined his support.

The Society is grateful to them and is pleased to present this testament to America of a Pole who loved his adopted land but could not forget his own.

HARRY O. H. FRELINGHUYSEN
President

Preface

Preface

Niemcewicz's American diaries are one of the earliest and most important documents in the complex, fascinating and still largely unexplored story of American-Polish cultural relations. Two factors, above all, determined its specific course and import. Poland's desperate struggle to defend her independence came in the wake of the American war of independence. Since, unlike Polish attempts, it came off well, it became a source of inspiration for Poles, a constant reminder that it was possible to challenge successfully the established European political order. Later on, in the course of the nineteenth century, the United States became the haven for masses of peasants from overpopulated villages and for Polish Jews from equally overcrowded ghettos. Thus, the United States became for the Poles a country exotic, distant, widely different and, at the same time, emotionally close, a country having a serious impact on Poland's social and political history. Everybody who visited Poland recently knows that this attitude is to a large extent true today. The story is still to be told. Its early stage is nowhere as fully illustrated as in the case of Niemcewicz and his American stay.

But Niemcewicz's diaries are interesting also in their own right, outside the framework of American-Polish relations. If there ever existed a perfect extrovert, Niemcewicz was one. He travelled widely, by eighteenth-century standards, had tremendous gusto for life and a keen eye for life's minutiae. Everything interested him: the prices of foodstuffs, the conditions of prisons, specific fauna and flora of particular regions, good, or not so good, looks of ladies—the reader of the diaries would hardly guess that in this respect he was far from being a disinterested observer only—good, or bad, manners of children, the political climate of the country, the state of roads. Mostly on the move, always intellectually alert, curious about people, he had a great capacity for absorbing data. Thus, the diaries form an amusing, richly detailed, variegated, if not especially deep, chronicle of the American life by the end of the eighteenth century. Its value is enhanced by the fact that, owing to his social grace as well as connections, he was able to meet with a number of important people starting with no lesser a figure than George Washington himself. Settled in America and married to an American lady with whom he managed to establish excellent relations later, once they were separated by the width of the Atlantic, he was able to give an insider's and not just a casual tourist's story. At the same time, constant comparisons with so different Polish conditions give his descriptions of the American scene a special relief. Once the political situation in Poland changed for the better with the creation of the Duchy of Warsaw in 1806, he returned to his native country feeling that the place for him, both as a politician and a writer, was there. But he deemed it wise to retain his American passport. He became the prototype of the familiar figure on the Polish social scene, a re-emigrant from America.

Until recently, only parts of the text of the diaries were known, and the manuscript was considered to be lost. The Polish edition of the whole preserved text, with its French parts in Polish translation, appeared as late as 1959. The work on the present edition was started independently, at an earlier date. As befits an edition which could draw on the resources of American libraries, it surpasses its Polish counterpart in the richness and precision of its notes. Dr. Budka's patient and painstaking research—as his notes bear witness—has proved that Niemcewicz's diaries have the abiding virtue of a good historical document: they are reliable, factually accurate. And his translation, for being careful, manages to recapture the easy grace, the abandon of Niemcewicz's Polish and French jottings, and, thus, enables the reader to enjoy the diaries as good reading stuff.

WIKTOR WEINTRAUB

Contents

Part I

TRAVELS THROUGH AMERICA, 1797-1799

Contents

Part II
JOURNEY TO NIAGARA, 1805

Part III
UNDER OUR VINE AND FIG TREE

Notes to Text

Appendices

Bibliography

Index

Illustrations

Frontispiece, Portrait of Julian Ursyn Niemcewicz

Niemcewicz's Sketches in the Text

Introduction

JULIAN URSYN NIEMCEWICZ (1758-1841)

In the Introduction to his life of George Washington published in Warsaw in 1803 Niemcewicz wrote,

"This part is taken from the diary of my journeys in America; I did not judge this diary complete enough to place in the present collection; but when I am back there again, I will improve and enlarge it and thus make known to my compatriots in their own language this country which, after the loss of my own, I have taken as my fatherland." [1]

The diaries were neither improved nor enlarged, nor were they ever published in Poland in his time.[2] They were left in Warsaw when Niemcewicz departed hurriedly in 1831 on a mission to enlist English aid for the revolutionary government of the Congress Kingdom. In his memoirs written in exile in Paris Niemcewicz doubted that they had survived the "tempests and plunders" of the intervening years.[3] Happily they have survived tempests and plunders of which Niemcewicz could not have dreamed and provide an unexpected source of vivid and fresh information about America a century and a half ago.

Niemcewicz came to America in 1797 when he was 39 years old as companion to Tadeusz Kościuszko, the leader of the Polish insurrection of 1794 against Russia, with whom he had been captured after the defeat at the Battle of Maciejowice. Following their release by Paul I in 1796, on his accession, and after two years of imprisonment in St. Petersburg Kościuszko, a sick man suffering severe physical and mental anguish from his battle wounds, his defeat and the loss of his country, decided to return to America. He asked Niemcewicz to accompany him. Niemcewicz, a man of warm human compassion, agreed and he wrote of this moment, "Just as the shackles of my imprisonment were torn from me I put on the sweeter bonds of friendship." [4]

Niemcewicz's ten-year stay in America was a hiatus in a long life devoted to service to Poland as publisher, playwright, pamphleteer, politician, soldier, educator, statesman and poet. His is the diary account of America of this period of widest range; agriculture and architecture, botany, bridges and balls, coachmen and commencements, heroes and homesteads, magic and mining, prisons and politics, warships and waterfalls, all provoked his lively and informed interest.

Niemcewicz was born on 16 February 1758 into an old Polish noble family established for generations near Brest (Brześć-Litewski) in the Lithuanian part of the old Polish-Lithuanian Commonwealth.[5] The Polish nobility in spite of great differences in material prosperity had long enjoyed a peculiar equivalence of political power and social status. They elected through their Dietines (Sejmiki) deputies to the Diets (Sejms) who in turn legislated for the country. When Niemcewicz was born, Poland had essentially lost her political independence. The disastrous potential of each single Deputy's right of veto was fully realized in political chaos, at a time when Poland's neighbors, Austria, Prussia and Russia were developing strong central governments seeking territorial conquests. Internally there were abuses in individual interest, corruption and aggrandizement of power through economic and other means. Freedom had become anarchy and privileges were without the counterbalance of responsibilities. The peasants were no more than slaves, and the burghers, the inhabitants of the long neglected cities, were deprived of all civil status. Neighboring foreign powers interfered at will in Poland's internal affairs and exercised influence through the agency of a few large families.[5a]

Political disunities did not affect the domestic life of the well-to-do Polish nobleman. Niemcewicz's early life as he himself described it in his memoirs was a kaleidoscope of all the elements in the life of the Polish middle nobility at the end of the Saxon reign and the first years of the reign of Poland's last king, Stanisław August. Niemcewicz writes fondly of his happy childhood on the family estates, and his nostalgia is evident whenever he writes of life in the country. In describing his early years, however, he contrasts the good family life, the legendary hospitality, the old customs both of dress and manners, the high moral standards, the so-called Sarmatian virtues with the prejudices, superstitions, the lack of any real education or appreciation of the modern concepts of trade and industry. He pictures his father as an enlightened member of his class searching the archives for records of ancient history, thereby instilling in the young Niemcewicz a love for his country, but also as a man who allowed his religious piety to deteriorate into dogma and cult, who spent much time seeking to convert Jews and non-Catholics. Niemcewicz in his mature years spoke of "the prejudices of my childhood awakening in me." [6]

Niemcewicz's early education with a tutor, the usual one for his class and time, consisted in the memorization of long and incomprehensible Latin passages. When he was thirteen, he left home to attend the School for Knights (Szkoła Rycerska) in Warsaw. This school, a quasi-military academy, had been created by the King, Stanisław August, in 1765 in order to provide a cadre of gentry elite. It was the only lay school in Poland; the faculty were scholars of the highest caliber and its foundation signalized the new King's vigorous support of the teachings in the spirit of the Enlightenment. Niemcewicz's attendance at this school placed him in the center of the intellectual and cultural revolution then taking place in Poland, especially in Warsaw. The emphatic idea of the co-founder and commandant of the school, Prince Adam Kazimierz Czartoryski, that the basis of good moral behavior lies in an education for citizenship, a knowledge and understanding of the world, impressed Niemcewicz greatly, and exerted a lasting and decisive influence on him.

A poem written by Niemcewicz, while at school, attracted the attention of the Prince and after graduation in 1777 Niemcewicz was appointed his adjutant. The Czartoryskis, a powerful magnate family, took into their household and under their patronage many young men of promise. Of the Czartoryski family, the historian Handelsman has written,

"From the middle of the century there arose and developed in this house a tradition of bountifulness, promotion for science and art, consecration to public affairs and a readiness to support disinterestedly all good undertakings." [7]

Niemcewicz lived first in the Blue Palace in Warsaw. He took part in the social life of the city which was now both the capital of Poland and the growing and active center of culture and society. Niemcewicz enjoyed the forms, the graces and the trappings of fashion and society, and the apprenticeship he served here informed his life-long interests in manners and social life.

One of the first tasks the Prince set him was to translate into Polish some French historical romances, perhaps to improve his French or to establish his style. These, all of the school of Madame de La Fayette written with a multiplicity of detail to which Niemcewicz added historical commentary, conditioned the style of his later historical writings. Niemcewicz accompanied the Prince on long journeys to his vast domains in fabulous cavalcades of horses, camels and carriages. After the first partition of Poland he went with Czartoryski to Vienna to visit the Emperor Joseph II. The Prince later underwrote a prolonged two-year tour abroad which included journeys through Italy, France and England. He returned a "European knight" as his biographer Prince Adam Jerzy Czartoryski, son of his benefactor, described him. It was under the influence of these journeys that he began to write seriously, first a versified letter *An Account of a Journey to Podolia* (1782) and later *Travels to Italy* (1784) which the King was pleased to have read to him. The price exacted for the benevolent support of the Prince can be seen in some of his polemic and panegyric poetry written at this time. Niemcewicz went abroad again in 1787 to England and France, where he met Jefferson for the first time.

Niemcewicz was now thirty years old, discouraged, a dilettante interested in everything but firmly committed to nothing. There is reason to suppose that he would have gladly returned home to manage his father's estates if he had been encouraged to do so. As much as his life and activity so far had seemed unproductive and without purpose, so were his talents intensely engaged by the spirit of reform that characterized the ensuing period of the Four Year Diet.[8] His election to this famous reform Diet through the intercession of Prince Potemkin, the most powerful man in Russia, reflects only the complications of Polish politics and was a fact which Niemcewicz himself could never satisfactorily explain. Once elected he threw himself wholeheartedly on the side of the reform group. This group of "Patriots" lead by Ignacy Potocki hoped, with the Russian preoccupation with the Turks and with the aid of a Prussian treaty, to institute the desperately needed reforms. During the interval of the discussion of the reforms and the drafting of the new Constitution (the famous Constitution of the 3rd of May, 1791) much work had to be done, and that in some haste, to prepare the gentry to accept its provisions. This work Niemcewicz did. In the Diet he is known for his speeches in favor of granting civil rights to the burghers, in support of a permanent army and his warnings against shifting the burdens of taxation onto the peasants. Niemcewicz wrote lampoons and pamphlets and the first Polish political fables; he collaborated in publishing a newspaper, but his most famous work of this period, a comedy *The Deputy's Return* (1790), was written in a little over a month's time in order to prepare the gentry for the new elections to the Diet. It was enormously successful and Krasicki described it as the "first true Polish comedy." In all these activities, as a contemporary, Count Lawrence Engstrom, the Swedish Ambassador, has said of him, "My dear friend, Julian Ursyn Niemcewicz, at that time still young and keen, [was] active and enlightened and a bold and hot patriot who never feared to tell the truth." [9]

When the Targowica Confederation (1792) under the leadership of Ksawery Branicki, Seweryn Rzewuski and Szczęsny Potocki with

the help of Russia destroyed the work of the reform group, Niemcewicz left Poland with the other leaders of the group and went
abroad. Although historians may now interpret their actions differently, to Niemcewicz the Targowicans were traitors, destroying the
only reasonable chance for the regeneration of the Commonwealth. In
his American Diaries he likens them to Benedict Arnold. This was a
black moment for Niemcewicz with the new Constitution overthrown,
his King joining the traitors and Russian soldiers overrunning the
land. For the first time Niemcewicz had found a goal, a new future
for Poland which took all his efforts, demanded all his talents, and it
had turned to ashes. His anger and despair found expression in savage and bitter satires. Niemcewicz used the diplomatic pouch from
Vienna to smuggle some of them into Poland. After the second partition Niemcewicz wrote a sad and touching elegy, *Spring* (1793),
which reflected his despair.

"How hard it is to call Poland by another name."

Niemcewicz was in Italy when he learned of the Kościuszko insurrection. He hurried to Poland and joined Kościuszko in camp on June
16, 1794. Kościuszko had been made Supreme Leader and after a
short time he appointed Niemcewicz his adjutant and Secretary of
State. October 10, 1794, at the Battle of Maciejowice both men were
wounded and taken into captivity. The battle and the long imprisonment in St. Petersburg have been described by Niemcewicz in his
Notes sur ma Captivité à St. Pétersbourg en 1794, 1795 et 1796 written
in Elizabeth, N.J. in 1800 though not published until 1843 in Paris.
This is a vivid and evocative account of an imprisonment.

When the two men were taken, both had sustained wounds, Niemcewicz in his right hand, Kościuszko severe and critical wounds of
the head and thigh. It was at this time that Niemcewicz's servant, believing his master as an author would rather have his writings with him
than fresh linen, packed one of Niemcewicz's two trunks with some of
his more vituperative works. These were of course confiscated, and
it was to this circumstance that Niemcewicz ascribes his especially
severe imprisonment.

Kościuszko and Niemcewicz were separated, and the long journey
(under heavy guard until the Insurrection finally collapsed in November) took them to Kiev and then to St. Petersburg. There Niemcewicz
was placed in solitary confinement in a wooden prison where he remained for two years. In the beginning his imprisonment was especially harsh. His written answers to formal questions show him a man

of great spirit and strength of character.[10] He reminded Catherine of
Cossack atrocities and urged clemency for his country. His first request was that his servant be freed and that he be permitted to buy a
few books. He asked also for a knife and fork, which were never provided. When the conditions of his imprisonment were eased somewhat, he spent his time reading (a list of his books is available), writing and translating. It was at this time that he translated Johnson's
Rasselas and Pope's *The Rape of the Lock.* His biographer Prince
Czartoryski points to the writing of an amusing parody, "The Memoirs
of Bielawski," since lost, as an indication of the return, even in prison,
of Niemcewicz's natural ebullience and optimism. Bielawski was a
poet of sorts in Warsaw and the other writers all took turns to make
him a butt of their jokes.

The treatment given Kościuszko and other leaders of the Insurrection was in sharp contrast to that accorded Niemcewicz. Indeed
Catherine's generosity towards Kościuszko was, in keeping with Paul's
politics, made public only much later.[11]

When Kościuszko was freed by Paul I after Catherine's death in
1796, he inquired about the fate of his comrades. There was hesitation
about releasing Niemcewicz because of his restless and refractory
(bezpokojnavo i stroptivavo) character. He was finally released on
Kościuszko's earnest plea. Kościuszko, as were his comrades, was required to take an oath of allegiance to the Czar. Niemcewicz remembers this oath as one of the most hateful things in which he
ever participated. Kościuszko had decided that if he should be released
from prison, he would go to America. When he had the opportunity
to talk with Niemcewicz, Kościuszko confided in him his great despair,
told how he tried to kill himself on the battlefield, and asked Niemcewicz to accompany him to America.

They set out for Sweden on December 19, 1796, in an impressive
entourage provided by the Czar and laden with his gifts: money,
clothes, furs (there is a legend that the sable fur in which Jefferson
was painted by Rembrandt Peale (1805) is a part of this gift) and
servants. A Polish officer Libiszewski volunteered to accompany them
in order to carry Kościuszko when necessary as he still was unable to
walk. From Sweden Kościuszko and Niemcewicz went to England and
set sail from Bristol, arriving in America August 19, 1797.

Kościuszko was received in America with acclaim. During his stay
here he visited his old friends of the Revolutionary days, General
Anthony Walton White in New Brunswick and General Horatio Gates
in New York City. Apart from these visits he lived in Philadelphia

with his servant Dombrowski and his companion Niemcewicz. Niemcewicz's diary, which begins ten days after their arrival, describes this period in some detail.

On May 4, 1798, Kościuszko left Philadelphia to return to Europe. This sudden and, to Niemcewicz, unexpected departure presents problems. To Niemcewicz, personally, the manner of Kościuszko's departure, kept secret from him until the abrupt announcement at the last moment, the role he was assigned in concealing it, and the fact that Kościuszko had abandoned his intention of settling in America, were all deeply distressing. Niemcewicz was an aristocrat, proud and sensitive. His friendship and confidence had been casually set aside. His emotional involvement, seen in the account of this affair, contrasts with his accustomed cool and disciplined detachment. Niemcewicz did not at any time publicly discuss either Kościuszko's decision and its intent, or their apparent estrangement. He deleted from the published account of his visit to Washington all references to his discomfiture at lying on Kościuszko's behalf. They met briefly once again in Europe. On Kościuszko's death Niemcewicz wrote a eulogy.[12] Niemcewicz's generous silence does little to illuminate the questions, why did Kościuszko behave as he did toward Niemcewicz, why did he depart so soon and so precipitately after giving Niemcewicz and others reasons to believe that he was coming to America with the intention of settling here.

As a result of his leadership of the Insurrection, Kościuszko had become, even in his own time, a legend and has remained a legendary figure of Polish bravery and heroism. He attracted the confidence and inspired the whole-hearted admiration of his many friends. One cannot document a legend, certainly not in terms of the realities of a broken friendship.

The reasons for Kościuszko's departure may be contained in the reasons for his coming to America, and these reasons are obscured by the clouds of legend built about the man. Kościuszko appears to have considered coming to America early during his imprisonment. It was reported by his interrogator, Major Titov, that on December 14, 1794, Kościuszko promised, if released, to leave immediately for America and never to return.[13] On his release, Kościuszko, not a man to take defeat easily, burdened with the Czar's gifts and an oath of allegiance, and still seriously ill, may have sought rest in America and hoped with his American Revolutionary War monies to avoid using the Czar's gifts.

Many opinions have been advanced concerning the reasons for Kościuszko's departure to France: that he had become disenchanted by the complex conflicts and disagreements of America, a nation at peace, so different from the single-minded revolutionary fervor that he had known; that he went to France at the invitation of the Directorate; or that he went as an unofficial emissary of Jefferson to the French government. Certainly Jefferson knew of Kościuszko's decision and participated in and organized his departure. But there is no clear evidence for any or all of these reasons. There is one curious piece of evidence, a letter written by the French Consul Letombe describing an interview he had with Kościuszko who sent for him on August 20th, only one day after his arrival in America. If the letter accurately describes the events, it certainly shows that Kościuszko never had any intention of settling here. The terms of the reported conversation do more: they throw a most interesting light on Kościuszko and his actions. Letombe wrote,

> "The same Member of Congress came to tell me that General Kościuszko desired to speak to me, therefore I went to the General last night. He wants to go to France. He will go there immediately by a safe way. He is observed here. This Martyr of liberty cannot speak or act, but only with the greatest precaution. He is here only to mislead his enemies. He asked me, Citizen Minister, to inform you of these facts without delay." [14]

This suggests a man who saw himself not as a private citizen but still as the active leader of his people, the central figure in a conspiracy which was to turn defeat into victory, a man whose words and actions were at all times intentionally diversionary.

Kościuszko's decision not to confide in Niemcewicz may be explained by the differences between the two men. Niemcewicz was a democrat but he could not be described as a pure and zealous republican. Niemcewicz was not wholly sympathetic to the French revolutionaries. Their differences may have been sharpened by the advice Niemcewicz gave to Kościuszko on the disposition of the Czar's gift. When Kościuszko received his American monies, he wished to return the gift. In his memoirs Niemcewicz wrote that he had advised Kościuszko against returning the gift in consideration of the effect on the Czar's violent and arbitrary temper. It is known that Kościuszko's letter sent from France, which was aggressively unfriendly in tone, infuriated Paul I; many Poles were severely punished and Niemcewicz's family were forbidden to send him help or even to write to him.

If Kościuszko saw himself as an active Revolutionary leader; then the return of the monies and the denial of his oath were a necessary prelude to all renewed activity. Perhaps we have misread the evidence; perhaps Kościuszko sought to return the money and foreswore his oath because the burden was intolerable. Kościuszko remained imprisoned in his defeat.

> "And that one Talent which is death to hide,
> Lodg'd with me useless, . . ."

The departure of Kościuszko left Niemcewicz alone. The Polish officer, Libiszewski, who accompanied Kościuszko to America in order to assist him personally, was shortly after his arrival and even before Kościuszko's departure earning a meager salary playing in an orchestra. In one of Niemcewicz's accounts he records a loan to Libiszewski of thirty dollars from his own sparse funds.

Prevented by the restrictions of Paul I from returning to Poland under Russian rule, and without personal means Niemcewicz lived on in America largely on borrowed funds. He decided to settle in Elizabeth, N.J., because of the relative cheapness of living there as well as for its pleasant surroundings and its large European settlement.

The diaries which primarily describe his travels in America do not contain any details of his life in Elizabeth nor of his personal contacts with his friends here or abroad. His memoirs written in his old age and a journal of his return journey to America help to fill the gap.

In 1800 Niemcewicz married Mrs. Susan Livingston Kean,[15] a member of one of the leading families in Elizabeth and widow of John Kean, a war companion of Kościuszko. His marriage did not materially change his mode of life, but the unaccustomed labor of running their small farm helped him to forget his sad plight. As a condition of the marriage Niemcewicz renounced any rights to his wife's and her son's estate, though he worked hard to maintain and increase it. He undertook the education of his stepson, and between them there grew a bond of affection which remained unbroken until Peter Kean's death in 1828.

In 1802 Niemcewicz returned to Poland in order to settle his father's estate. Intellectual activity of sorts was allowed in partitioned Poland of that time, and in some cases encouraged. Warsaw was then under Prussian rule. Niemcewicz was elected a member of the Society of the Friends of Learning which had been founded in 1800, and was offered, through the intercession of Prince Adam Jerzy Czartoryski, the chair of Polish Literature at the University of Wilno. The obligations in America proved too strong and he returned here in 1804.

In the journal of his travels in Europe and his return to America in 1804 he describes his private and domestic life during this second stay in America. This rather uncharacteristically revealing account reprinted here was published in 1873 from a copy purportedly made from the original found in Warsaw.[16] It reveals a man enveloped in a surprised and reluctant melancholy. He appeared to enjoy his farming, grafting peach trees, planting maize, dealing with hired hands, but he ran afoul of his own image of domestic bliss. The safe harbor which he had described in the American diaries seemed not to be his in the reality of his own marriage. His wife was in poor health. She disliked his friends and liked neither entertaining nor being entertained. Niemcewicz missed the stimulation of being involved in political and professional affairs. He, an essentially gregarious man, was isolated in solitude, a solitude which ought to have been bliss but was not.

Only visits to relatives of his wife, the Livingstons, to Colonel Jonathan Williams, the Commandant of West Point, of whom he has left a pleasantly revealing portrait, and to the Biddles in Philadelphia broke up the monotony of his home life. Lord and Lady Bolingbroke,[17] who maintained a residence in Liberty Hall in Elizabeth, with whom he was to travel later to visit Niagara, were not congenial to his wife and his contact with them was less than he would have wished.

There is correspondence between him and the American Philosophical Society which shows him in the characteristic role of Polish patriot negotiating for an exchange of books between the Society and the University of Wilno. His correspondence with Jefferson was only on private affairs.[18]

In the notebooks bound with his Diary he has left an outline of his daily activities :

"1) Before breakfast, the Bible.

2) Ten to twelve. If *vena* writing my poem [*Four Seasons of Human Life*], if not then translating sermons.

3) Until two, chemistry or serious reading; just before dinner, Ariosto.

4) After dinner, voyages *and novels*, etc., etc."

In his literary work Niemcewicz shared in the lethargy that engulfed the Polish writers after the third partition and which had shut off the abundantly fruitful outpouring of the previous period. He wrote, of his first stay in America, "In the course of my five year stay in America, taken up by other work, literature concerned me least of all." [19] That period produced only *Notes sur ma Captivité* . . . written in the May before his marriage.

Although not a fruitful time by any standards and for one of the most prolific Polish writers an exceptionally sterile period, it is in this

American period that Niemcewicz began to imitate English balladry which, coupled with his earlier *dumy*, gives him the role of precursor of the genre in Poland. Adam Mickiewicz, Poland's greatest poet, credits him as his teacher in the form.[20] The English model of the ballad *Winter* included in the collection published in Warsaw in 1803 is found in the notebooks containing the Diaries. His *Alonzo and Helen*, in imitation of Lewis, was written on his sea voyage from America in 1802.[21]

The American notebooks also contain his translations of Hugh Blair's sermons started during his first stay here and continued until the February of the year when he left, 1807. Other notebooks of the period found in the family house in Skoki have in them writings from English authors such as Macpherson, Young, Beattie (*The Minstrel*), Moore, Cowley, Dyer as well as Delille.[22] There were only two major original works of this period; one the poem *Puławy* (1802-1804) was written in Poland, and the other, *Four Seasons of Human Life*, whose "verse [hard and unsmooth,] went for me as from a stone," [23] weighed down by the solitude of a foreign land.

In 1807, the formation of the Grand Duchy of Warsaw and the call of the Marshal of the old Constitution Diet, in which Niemcewicz had worked so hard, broke his attachments in America. His wife, reluctant to see him go, was finally persuaded. They maintained cordial relations during their separation and on her death in 1833 she left him an annuity.[24]

In a comment characteristic of Niemcewicz he recounts the impression America had made on him immediately on his return to Europe. In Dresden on being invited to dinner by the King of Saxony, who was to be the new Grand Duke of Warsaw, he hired a litter to carry him because it was raining.

"While I was being carried, I lost myself in thought and as I was thinking, it pained me to see how this sort of carriage savors of aristocracy. Why should two people turn themselves into animals in order to carry a third. Had I not just returned from America, truly a country of freedom and equality, I might have found this completely natural but here in the first instant, I must admit that it appears a bit savage." [25]

From 1807 to 1831, during the time of the Grand Duchy and of its successor the Congress Kingdom, Niemcewicz was ever present in the political activities of his country, an active publicist and one of the leading literary figures. Whether in his official positions as Secretary of the Senate and member of the Educational Commission or in his many unofficial roles, his single-minded and unswerving devotion to his country earned him the trust and respect of all. The measure of his popularity was his unanimous election as Senator-Castellan in 1830. This was an unprecedented honor in Poland for one in his position in the aristocratic hierarchy. The aura of patriotism that surrounded this honorable and sympathetic man has persuaded some scholars to ascribe a more leading role to him than he actually held. His influence, although large and pervasive, was essentially indirect as his biographer Prince Czartoryski has said.[26] His political philosophy had always been conservative and he continued to align himself with the more conservative group even as the division between conservatives and radicals became more sharp and violent both in Poland and later after the Great Emigration of 1831. Handelsman wrote of the time of the Congress Kingdom,

> "In relations with America, England and France, poet of the greatest fame, idol of youth, an authority of the salons; a scourge to all, whom he pursues, with wit and mischief, not considering the consequences, not even sparing the Grand Duke [Constantine] himself; interested and informing himself quickly and accurately, he was always a trustworthy source of pertinent information for Prince Adam about Warsaw, the authorities and the country." [27]

When Niemcewicz returned to Poland, the words dammed back by solitude poured out. As Niemcewicz lived, he wrote, and as he wrote, he lived. Not only his life but his writing was now bursting into manifold activities. Shortly after his return he wrote most of his *Historical Songs*, a project initiated by the Society of the Friends of Learning to instill into the youth of Poland, by the charm of song and the conciseness of poetry, at the earliest possible moment, a love of their country. As a member of the Education Commission Niemcewicz traveled about Poland, at his own expense, inspecting schools and wrote his impressions of these and later travels in his *Historical Travels over Polish Lands (1811-1828)* (1858). It was on these journeys that he began to search the archives as his father had done for manuscripts, medals and other mementoes of Poland's past glories. He believed that in knowing Polish history, succeeding generations might maintain the integrity of the nation even though her land be gone. This archival material was published by him later in six volumes, *A Collection of Historical Memoirs on Ancient Poland* (1822-1833). He wrote *Lithuanian Letters* (1812) an attempt to enlist the Polish landlords in the Lithuanian lands in Napoleon's campaign in Russia. This forced a hasty departure before the advancing Russian armies and an exile in Dresden, Leipzig and Prague until the intercession of Prince Czartoryski made it possible for him to return. His Diary of this period has been published. It is an interesting account of life during Napoleon's last campaigns.[28]

On his return to the Congress Kingdom Niemcewicz was again Secretary of the Senate and member of the Educational Commission. He published his *Historical Songs* (1816) that made him "poet of the greatest fame." The *Songs* were not of great literary merit but they had an enormous and immediate success and went quickly through many editions. Their essentially patriotic tone aroused the fears of the Austrians who in turn alerted the Russian government, and they had the books removed from school libraries in 1827.

Niemcewicz, always a prolific writer, produced in the period between 1815 and 1830 a tremendous volume of works over a tremendous range of forms, from fables to operas. Some of these were published but a great deal remains in manuscript or is lost. His publications include the novel in diary form, *Two Gentlemen Sieciech* (1815), *The History of the Reign of Sigismund III* (1819), and the historical novel, *John of Tenczyn* (1825). Niemcewicz put his considerable knowledge of Jewish life into a novel, *Levi and Sarah* (1821), where in the form of letters he contrasted the fanaticism of the older generation with the progressiveness of the new. Though not the first Polish writer to explore the general problem, his was the first novel to propose the social integration of the Jews in Poland. He was not wholly free of anti-semitism so common in Poland and wrote an account, *The Year 3333 . . .* (1821), describing Warsaw taken over by the Jews.

In 1817 Niemcewicz published, at considerable personal expense, his *Fables*. He tells how, in Poland at that time, with its lack of facilities for manufacturing paper and without the means of importing it, old paper from which ink had been washed was used. Niemcewicz's opera *Jadwiga*, the first in Polish, was performed on the 22nd of December 1814, and *Zbigniew*, a tragedy, with choral music written by Karol Kurpiński, was played on the 6th of November 1819.

With money earned from his writings he bought a farm near Warsaw which he called Ursynów. The place-name remains both in Warsaw and in Elizabeth, New Jersey, where his stepson Peter honored his stepfather by calling his property Ursino. It was a happy time for him. His farm was open to the young writers of the period. He encouraged and helped many of them. Niemcewicz, perhaps because of his long absence abroad, never belonged to the school of Warsaw classicism

which developed strongly at this time, and took no part in the polemics on the relative merits of classicism and the upsurging romanticism.

Niemcewicz was elected President (1826) of the now Royal Society
of the Friends of Learning. It is widely held that his counsel prevented the assassination of the Czar's family in 1829. This act has
been dramatized in Juliusz Słowacki's *Kordian:*

> "Wstrzymać ich, na Boga!
> Niech myśl młodych ciemnicy nie przestąpi proga,
> Niech spisek z czarną twarzą na świat nie wychodzi, . . .
> Bo mogę wezwać prochy królów za obrońce . . ."

(Hold them back for God's sake! Let not the thinking of youth cross
the threshold of the cell. Let not the conspiracy with the black face
go out into the world . . . For I can invoke the dust of kings in defense . . .) [29]

When the November Revolution occurred, Niemcewicz at first traveled to Cracow to prepare a place for the evacuation of the government and then as ambassador to Great Britain; and this forlorn old
man took his 73 years to work and fight for the support of his country.
He spent two years in ceaseless wanderings, organizing activities to
publicize the Polish cause. His diaries show him waiting on the English Prime Minister or in a newspaper office trying to place poems of
Mickiewicz's such as *Parade* or *Prayer of an Exile* which he had translated. When all hope faded for his country, he traveled about in the
interest of a Czartoryski project for an educational fund for the children of Polish emigrees. The diaries of this stay abroad effect in their
recounting of the events a tone of growing despair missing in the early
diaries of this essentially optimistic man.

Finally Niemcewicz went to France where most of the Great Emigration had settled. Here he continued his Diaries, wrote his Memoirs
a second time and arranged to have his unique collection of Polish
writings and memorabilia sold to the Raczyński family in Poznań.
There they served as the basis of one of the finest libraries in what
was once Poland and as a lasting testament to his country that he
loved so well.[30]

Niemcewicz died in Paris 21 May 1841, and is buried in Mont-
morency Cemetery beside his friend General Karol Kniaziewicz.

Niemcewicz has eluded the boundaries of literary criticism. In his
lectures as the first incumbent of the new chair of Slavic Literature
in France, Adam Mickiewicz, Poland's greatest poet, who loved and
esteemed Niemcewicz, spoke of the problem of the inextricable rela-

Fig. 2. Certificate of marriage between Julian Ursin Niemcewicz and Susan Kean, 2 July 1800. The handwriting is very faint, this copy slightly retouched. Courtesy of Mrs. John Kean.

Fig. 1. Susan Ursin Niemcewicz. From *Przyjaciel Ludu*, 1846.

Fig. 3. The home of Julian Ursyn and Susan Niemcewicz in Elizabethtown, New Jersey. The house stood on the street now named Elizabeth Avenue just west of West Scott Place. From a drawing by Zygmunt Vogel probably from a contemporary sketch by Niemcewicz. Courtesy of The Collections of the Graphic Arts Department, National Museum, Warsaw.

Fig. 4. Earliest known view of Liberty Hall or Ursino, so named in honor of Niemcewicz by his wife and stepson after his departure. Courtesy of Mrs. John Kean.

Fig. 5. Julian Ursyn Niemcewicz during his last exile in Paris. From Charles Forster, *La Vieille Pologne*, 1836.

Fig. 6. Portrait of Susan Ursin Niemcewicz, by an unknown artist. Courtesy of Mrs. John Kean.

Fig. 7. Tadeusz Kościuszko in London (1797); according to Niemcewicz, "the best likeness." From a painting by Richard Cosway. Courtesy of the National Museum, Warsaw.

Fig. 8. "Kościuszko and the Polish Nobles obtaining their Liberty through the generosity of the Emperor Paul I." Mezzotint from drawing by Aleksander Orłowski. According to Niemcewicz his likeness appears in this drawing. He has not been further identified. Courtesy of the National Museum, Warsaw.

Thomas Jefferson

A Philosopher a Patriote and a Friend

Dessiné par son Ami Tadée Kosciuszko.

Et Gravé par Mc. Sokolnicki

Fig. 9. Thomas Jefferson by Tadeusz Kościuszko. Original (now lost) drawn from life in Philadelphia, 1798. Courtesy of The Kosciuszko Foundation.

Fig. 10. Skoki, the Niemcewicz ancestral home. From Kraushar's *Okruchy przeszłości*, 1913.

tionship between Niemcewicz's role in Polish history and his literary work. He said,

"Tous les événements de sa vie et ses travaux littéraires sont liés aux faits historiques, de manière que, jusqu'à présent, la critique littéraire attaque quelquefois en Niemcewicz l'homme politique, et les partis politiques prennent la défense du littérateur." [31]

Mickiewicz honored Niemcewicz's patriotism as the prime well-spring not only of his writings, "L'art n'a pas été son idole; . . . Il s'est servi de ses ouvrages comme d'instrument pour combattre les ennemis de la Pologne;" but of his life. A man who led where others were to follow.

Other critics have recognized this problem. To Tarnowski, who found little artistic merit in Niemcewicz's work, "The life and influence of Niemcewicz belong much more to history than to the history of literature." [32] For Brückner Niemcewicz's role in literature was that of a teacher and innovator. He said of him, "Niemcewicz showed what is literature, Śniadecki, science; they both drew them into a continual service of citizenship." [33]

It is true that from the whole compass of his efforts and the variety of his forms no one of his political writings or his quasi-experimental works (frequently imitative and based on foreign models) has outstanding literary merit. The climate has changed, the moment has passed and the first Polish model has been forgotten in the triumphs of its successors. When placed together in that category whereby they reflect the author's desire to teach, to improve those things that would help and to hold up to scorn those that would hinder his country his writings, as his life, place him high in its history. He played a noble role in the eighteenth century intellectual rebirth of Poland which saved Poland as a nation even while it saw Poland lost as a country.

The memoirs and diaries, so long neglected, stand apart; unlike all others, written for the pleasure of recall, unexpectedly artistic in their intent, timeless in spite of their time-serving form and content; they are, "Undoubtedly the most valuable monument that Niemcewicz raised for himself." [34]

THE DIARIES

The account of a journey, written in diary form at the time it was undertaken, may include classic diary material—private or quasi-private communication between a man and himself. It will inevitably also include comments and observations on new sights and sounds, manners and incidents which a man would naturally wish to communicate to others. In Niemcewicz's diary there is very little private communication of the man with himself. The diaries are largely descriptions of people and places, comments and reflections on his experiences and observations. He brought to them all his talents as a writer, his perceptions as a mature man. Though of noble birth, he was not affronted by simplicity and rudeness of manners. Coming to America, perhaps to stay here permanently, he sought rapport with a people seeking to rule themselves and his humanity found eager sympathy with them.

The diaries begin 29 August 1797, ten days after his arrival, and continue almost day by day with only one major break to 8 November 1799. The diary of the *Journey to Niagara* which took place in October 1805 is bound with them.

In the American Diary Niemcewicz comments thus on one of the great pleasures of undertaking a journey.

". . . then I went away . . . leaving behind the luxury of visiting these wonders and even more the luxury, I say (for which almost all distant journeys are undertaken) of telling later that I had been so far and had seen things which no one or only a few have ever seen."

In the luxury of the telling Niemcewicz called upon his conceits as a historian and his habits as a writer. His picture of America, of men and their institutions emerges from a multiplicity of detail and his words flow quickly and artfully, at times eddying unexpectedly, without need for pondering and delay.

Writing of his American Diary Niemcewicz said, "I did not judge this diary complete enough . . . I will improve and enlarge it," and in the journal of his visit to Niagara he added,

"On the journey I have gathered together my observations rather poorly; always on the road, having time only to eat a bite, tired in the evening; in the midst of the noise of the taverns, not finding a quiet corner, I scribbled without order and in haste. It remains for me to glean them well and that is what I plan to do on my return journey."

But the American Diary was not improved or enlarged, nor is there a more polished version of the journey to Niagara. For to scribble and to write down in haste was the manner in which Niemcewicz wrote. Earlier he had written *Deputy's Return* in little more than a month's time. Niemcewicz published only one brief excerpt from the American

Diary, an account of his meeting with Washington and his visit at Mount Vernon, and this was virtually unchanged.[35]

Critics have deplored his reluctance to polish and to perfect as one of his major defects. The critic Józef I. Kraszewski, a voluminous and prolific writer himself, has made perhaps the most pertinent and apt comment. Writing in the Introduction to some of Niemcewicz's memoirs he said,

> "Whatever judgment is given by the esthetician and critic on Niemcewicz's works, written in haste, often unfinished, however always commanding a distinctive talent and unusual taste—the memoirs should be placed separately—they are of a genre most proper for his improvising disposition: for in it sincerity and facility are a virtue and not a defect." [36]

The Diaries contain virtually no erasures or interpolations. The remarkable talent to write down easily and in the moment the first impression of a scene or person or an idea and to build these parts into a satisfying whole is clearly evident in them. Indeed as one reads the American Diary and the Journey to Niagara it is difficult to dismiss them as merely notes taken for future writings. There is a changing rhythm of action, exposition and commentary which seems to be under the author's control. The response of the author is fresh and unpredictable and the choice of the events to be recorded frequently unexpected. Although the visit to General Gates begins with the sonorous, "Nous trouvâmes sur le seuil le vainqueur de Saratoga," it ends with General Gates shopping in the market place for meat, fish and vegetables.

Niemcewicz closes his lengthy description of the Shaker community with the unexpected comment,

> "If in Europe in spite of circumstances tending to change everything, orders of monks and nuns are destined to remain, would it not be a hundred times more useful if they had at least the arrangement that the society of Shakers have; that is, the nuns and monks according to their sex and strength would work together towards providing for both their societies. It seems to me that it would even be a step towards improvement if they were permitted to have intercourse with each other and have children."

Niemcewicz's writing takes full advantage of the diary form which permits discontinuities. More importantly his talent has broken through the evident trammels of this form which does not permit the luxury of hindsight. All this has been done without sacrifice to historical accuracy. The result is a magnificent impressionistic portrait of America.

The literary value of these diaries, the evident art is, at its best moments, close and akin to the art of the one unique *"Sentimental Journey."* Niemcewicz echoes Sterne most provocatively in his viewpoint, in the "angle of vision" so praised by Virginia Woolf whereby, "A girl may be more interesting than a cathedral, a dead donkey more instructive than a living philosopher." [37] Niemcewicz had read Sterne in prison and there are probably further echoes of Sterne in the discontinuities, the unexpected turns, and in the image fragments, the bird in the cage, the dance in praise of God and the moment's gallantry towards the attractive Mme. Delameter. To have realized, even occasionally, the power of so exacting and demanding a form and to have adapted it, at times, so brilliantly while "scribbling without order and in haste" was Niemcewicz's triumph.

Consider in contrast the *Travels* of the Duke de La Rochefoucault Liancourt. Liancourt wrote in the dedication to his *Travels,*

"If . . . I should not have written merely a journal of my travels, which I wish to do, that being the only kind of work which does not require greater talents than mine and where truth can be the principal merit . . ." [38]

La Rochefoucault Liancourt truly observed the limitations he set himself and his journals are a collection, an inventory of precise observations and information totally lacking in form.

Only during Niemcewicz's comparatively long stay in Philadelphia does his diary include much material listed under different headings such as Trade, Income, Taxes, containing information derived from books and earnest conversations, etc., and these accounts do not include any interpretive generalizations. In Philadelphia as elsewhere he was a careful reader of newspapers and they provided a ready source of information. The newspapers published the debates in Congress and vigorously aired many other questions of the day; some correspondence can be established between the appearance of certain newspaper items and comments in his diary. Niemcewicz carried a copy of Morse's *Geography* with him to the city of Washington and through the New England States, and there are indications that he consulted the book even before then. From time to time he refers directly to material in the *Geography* and once he innocently employed a fact in Morse so that, "A ship of 950 tons for the East India trade was lately built in this town [Providence] and fitted for the sea," is turned into, "A 950 ton vessel destined for the East Indies and fully loaded was sailing safely." [39] In general, however, Niemcewicz wrote from and about his own personal observations.

Niemcewicz was an empiricist in his writings and sought to provide details from which his readers might draw their own conclusions. His perceptions were acute and the breadth and comprehension of his vision large. To Niemcewicz multiplicity of detail was implicit in his intent, whether writing biography, diaries, memoirs or histories. In introducing his life of Washington Niemcewicz wrote, "They will quarrel with me that I go too much into minor detail, but it is just such details that paint the man," and later in his memoirs, "I however will not omit the smallest circumstances passed over as beneath the dignity of the historian for they often throw light on the state of mind and manners of the people." [40]

Niemcewicz's literary ability wove these skeins of detail into a luminous tapestry. Happily this gift was complemented by his complete concern for accuracy of detail and the substantial nature of his reporting.[41] Faÿ has said of some French writings about the United States,

"Un phénomène curieux se produit pour les écrivains qui ont des prétentions littéraires. Il leur parait que le sujet même, l'Amérique et sa révolution, est un peu bas et a besoin d'être relevé; ils s'y consacrent avec tant de soin qu'ils n'ont plus le moyen ni le loisir de rechercher l'exactitude. Il leur semble que le critérium par lequel le public jugera de leur sérieux sera la dignité du ton et la beauté des épisodes." [42]

Niemcewicz was nowhere guilty of these implied faults. In Niemcewicz the virtue of accuracy and of choice, places us in the America of those days and enlarges the penetration and scope of our view.

Niemcewicz traveled in company with Kościuszko from Philadelphia to New Jersey and New York and then back to Philadelphia where he spent the longest period of time (approximately five months) until Kościuszko left for France. Until this time the Diary was written in French and a transition from French to Polish occurs during the visit to George Washington. This is closely preceded by three very brief passages in Polish. In one of these a sentence begun in French is completed in Polish. Clearly Niemcewicz communicated with himself with necessary clarity in French although his French is a foreigner's French. Although the change from one language to another might suggest a major discontinuity in attitude or style, no such break is in fact detectable. The question, why the transition, is probably rather the question, why write in French at all. When Niemcewicz first arrived in America, he had been using French and he believed that he had come to America to settle here. He first began to write occasionally in Polish at Mount Vernon after Kościuszko's departure, and wholly in Polish after he received there his first replies from Poland on June 9th. Perhaps his enhanced loneliness provoked the final change, or perhaps he wrote always in the language in which he intended to publish and the letters had provided hope that the travels might be published in Poland. He returned to French in 1800 for the *Notes sur ma Captivité . . .* published in France and for the *Journey to Niagara* which he kept *"ad feliciora tempora."* [43]

After borrowing money for the purpose from Jefferson he completed a tour of Maryland, Pennsylvania, the New England states and New York, settling in Elizabeth, New Jersey, at the "ordinary" house of Lewis Rivers, the tailor. Obtaining some money from abroad he then took part in a month's natural history tour of the pine barrens of southern New Jersey and after revisiting the iron works at Boonton and his old acquaintances the Faesches, he returned to Elizabeth.

Niemcewicz's interests were many. Sometimes they can be ascribed to the circumstances of his life. A landsman, he remarks that whether on a short sail on Narraganset Bay or on the ocean a boat can make way no matter how adverse the wind, and it will with "time and patience" reach the destined shore. Bridges attract him very much and he describes nearly all of those he saw in great detail, sometimes giving their exact dimensions. When he was a boy and came to school in Warsaw, the ancient bridge across the Vistula no longer existed and one had to cross by ferry. In science Niemcewicz's interest was largely restricted to the bizarre—the wonders of science, a mammoth, a monster boy, and in this and in his knowledge of flowers, birds and fish, Niemcewicz was very much a man of his age. When he sought to describe a new form or to define the differences between European and American varieties of flora, his observations were exact and his accounts of them lucid.

Niemcewicz's interest in the legislative process, in elections, in all aspects of government was more than the comparative professional interest of an experienced politician. He came as a warm admirer of American democracy. He had said in 1791 in his much quoted speech urging the enfranchisement of the burghers,

"Courage and ability are not linked to a class or to a name; they are either a gift of nature, or the result of education, work and study; any man can possess them. . . . In no free and sensibly governed country is the door closed to service, to virtue or to ability . . . No one knows who Washington's father was, nor whom Franklin counted as his grandfather, but everyone knows and posterity will know that Washington and Franklin saved America." [44]

Niemcewicz wanted to see and to understand the workings of this democracy; as always Poland and Polish institutions were his reference points. He was fascinated by the success of the legislative process in the evolution of opinion, a process never completely worked out in Poland.

The Quaker-run prisons of Philadelphia were the cynosure of every European who came here. La Rochefoucauld-Liancourt wrote a book about them and, in its German translation under the name of Howard, it was used as the basis for prison reform throughout Europe. [45] Niemcewicz also approached the problem from the point of view of improving prison conditions. As a result of his observations in Philadelphia, recorded in his diary, and later in the prisons in New York, he published a work in 1818 on prison reform in Poland. [46] Because of his own two-year imprisonment in St. Petersburg he saw the prisons from the prisoners' point of view and not merely as a problem in reform and administration.

To the problem of slavery Niemcewicz brought human understanding rather than the doctrinaire approach of Brissot. When Niemcewicz describes the Negro who had been recaptured, bound in chains, he sees one man's suffering. He feels for the Negro as a man. It is this personal aspect of slavery that we see in his description of the white owner living in constant fear that his slaves will be subverted by visitors. Human slavery evoked his compassion; he saw it as an insult to individual human dignity. He did not look upon the slaves as an exploited class in the modern sense. He does not conclude that children are exploited in running cotton mills, but rather notes that the machines are easy enough for children to run. For a Polish nobleman the slaves, in the services they performed, were the peasants of American society. It was the intolerable and degrading conditions of their servitude, the idea of a man as property, which he hated. As a child he had wept to see his father's cook, a peasant belonging to the Pułaski family, taken away in chains.

One man, George Washington, stands out in the Niemcewicz diary, and Niemcewicz has given us the most warm and intimate portrait of Washington which exists. In introducing his account of the meeting with George Washington Niemcewicz writes of the details in Plutarch's *Lives*, which create an empathy between the reader and great men.

"Nous aimons dans Plutarque les détails, les anecdotes, les minuties même qu'il nous donne dans les vies des hommes illustres, tout cela nous intéresse tant la raison en est peut-être que l'homme rapporte tout à lui-même."

In seeking to portray a hero as an individual man Niemcewicz showed a development away from the concept of the ideal man of the 18th century,[47] a development which allowed him to consider writing a biography.

Niemcewicz's diary is thronged with people; not all have great names, some are nameless, but they are all individuals. When they speak, they speak with authentic American voices; they recall and recapture a man or a whole society.

In all of Niemcewicz's writings he tried to let the American speak for himself, and the scene evoke its own response. He stands by, detached; his own observations and reflections do not oppress and constrain our own judgments. Washington his hero is quoted a great deal. This device of bringing the reader directly into Washington's presence is only one of many he used in this instance to minimize the distance between the reader and Mount Vernon. Niemcewicz used direct quotation not only for this purpose but also to evoke a mood. When Niemcewicz and his friend Faesch arrive late at night in Boonton, we hear, "Mon père, est-il à la maison?" "Non, il est à Mount Hope," and Niemcewicz's comment: "Notre joie fût diminuée de moitié." The voices in the darkness at once accentuated human isolation and human community. The drama of the sudden departure of Kościuszko is also recorded in direct quotation.

At times it is easy to trace specific influences in Niemcewicz's imagery and descriptive manner. He was trained in the classical school but had undergone pre-romantic influences. His poet-predecessor in America (1783) Tomasz Kajetan Węgierski (1755-1787) has left his diaries of his stay here and they show in their description of the natural beauty of the land that Polish writers already knew and valued the Ossian Songs.[48] Niemcewicz's own descriptions of nature show him schooled in Rousseau. The emotional effects of nature are often described, his own thoughts on the lonely Newport shore, and the solace offered by nature to others. Thus the lovely Connecticut scene provides refuge for those fleeing danger; the hut at Harper's Ferry providing sanctuary for those violating the social customs of the day. The mountain scenery always threatens and frightens, and their description is of that kind which gives the "agréable effroi" of Delille.

The device of calling for the skill of a painter was also borrowed from Delille.[49]

All visitors to America were interested in its waterfalls, particularly Niagara, and Slavic writers in the romantic genre were to use the waterfall a great deal as a motif.[50] Niemcewicz himself did not engage in romantic description; his own descriptions would have provided material for future Romantics, as did those of Bartram for Coleridge, and Bartram and Charlevoix for Chateaubriand. Though his description of Niagara is not mechanistic as is that of Volney,[51] to whom Niemcewicz concedes "the greatest veracity and detail," it is perspicuous and direct with the phraseology of Classical description. He uses such phrases as "the glassy dome" and "the water escaping its prison." To Niemcewicz Niagara was a mobile force but not yet a personalized force. The legend of the Naiad Niagara imprisoned as a waterfall has been called commonplace by Krzyżanowski.[52] It may well be banal as an image, but it must be compared with Niemcewicz's version of the transformation of the nymph Salmacis dissolving in her own sweat, and read in the spirit of the Classical Joke. Krasicki, his own countryman, had achieved great success in a work in this spirit, *The Epic of the Mice* (1776) (*Myszeis*).[53] There is classical imagery in the idyll of Cupid goading the rural couple at the plow and in the bucolic scene in the Chesterfield Gorge.

Descriptions such as that of the funeral in Maryland and the graveyard in Connecticut are in the spirit of Young's *Night Thoughts* and show the pre-romantic influence on Niemcewicz, although later a similar funeral scene, described in the Journey to Niagara, evoked an entirely different "enlightened" response. Niemcewicz sees time and labor lost, with the event a holiday.

The pleasures of these diaries lie beyond the recognitions of analysis. There is the wit and charm of a traveler restrained in the Diaries by the melancholy of his loneliness reviving completely to enliven the vignette of a journey to Niagara in the company of dear friends. There is the poet and the soldier whose patriotic pose is at ease. And there is the familiar American scene itself with the intermediate of a hundred and sixty years.

Niemcewicz's American experiences did not directly inspire any of his later published imaginative works as did the experiences of Chateaubriand. It is not surprising for "Art was not his idol." A cursory survey of his works shows only minor allusions. In his poem *Meditations in Ursynów* he is an eye witness to Washington's role as Cincinnatus.[54] The name of Henry Gahn, his friend and companion in New York, is given to a character in *John from Tenczyn*. Recently a

poem by Niemcewicz about American Indians has been published.[55]
The immediate inspiration here was the reading of a book on America.
In his American Diary Niemcewicz often compares the conditions of
the peasant with that of negro slaves. The unpublished narrative, "The
Orphan Pretender or The Picture of the Times," enlarges on this
theme.[56]

In Paris in exile Niemcewicz recalled his American experiences to
place them in his Memoirs, excerpts from which are reprinted here.
The diaries which he had kept all his life were dispersed and he wrote
from memory. He regretted the loss of his American Diaries as he did
others from different periods. Indeed he says that of all the losses
suffered throughout his life, the loss of his diaries was not the least
painful. The question remains whether the Memoirs would have been
written in their present form if his diaries had been available to him,
for he incorporated into them completely unchanged the *Notes sur
ma Captivité.*

The Memoirs and the American Diaries differ in the long view of
the one and the immediacy of the other. The Memoirs are shaped
not by the rhythms of a journey but by the smoother flow of recollection. When Niemcewicz chose to describe in his Memoirs some incident which he had recorded in his diaries, then the two versions agree.
Niemcewicz had a prodigious memory; thus the description of the
hummingbird in the cage and the contredanse praising God by the
Shakers are, in both versions, accurately placed in their same setting
and give rise to like reflections.

On certain occasions Niemcewicz uses some incident in a different
context and for a different artistic purpose. There is a poetic phrase
in the diaries used by Niemcewicz to describe old ladies in the home
of Colonel Wadsworth in Connecticut: ". . . the second [half of the
day] they read the Bible, and while reading sometimes sleep, sometimes weep, but always believe." In his Memoirs a similar phrase,
". . . then they read the Bible, and while reading, doze but always
believe," is used to describe old ladies, but here the phrase is put
into the mouth of a farmer to show flippancy towards religion, an unusual trait in America just at that time.[57] Historical figures once
brought to the fore by intimate detail, now grown legendary or powerful, he foreshortens by personal anecdote. He tells of Louis Phillipe,
the king of the French, being cross because his dinner invitation in
America had been refused; or of shooting robins for Kościuszko's
lunch.[58]

The Memoirs and their exemplar the Diaries find an honored place
in his country's literature. They place Niemcewicz with Jan Chry-

zostom Pasek (c. 1636-1701) and Father Jędrzej Kitowicz (1728-1804) in the memoir-writing tradition so important in their country.

The historian may find more valuable source material in Liancourt's *Travels* and ignore their tedium, or in Moreau de St. Méry's *Journeys* [59] in spite of the easily wounded sensibilities of this petulant bourgeois; the philosopher may turn to Brissot,[60] but no more true, lovely, sympathetic or engaging account of America of this period will be found in all the canons of travel literature. The reader may now partake of their intelligence and their charm. America has always been better served by her aristocratic visitors.

THE MANUSCRIPTS

Twelve notebooks written by Niemcewicz in America are now (1963) in the National Library of Poland in the Krasiński Palace in Warsaw: B.N. BOZ 918. Niemcewicz took them back with him to Poland, since when they have been lost and discovered, lost again and rediscovered several times. They are presently bound together in hard covers with a leather back on which is lettered the title *Rękopisma własnoręczne. Podróże po Ameryce i Kazania* (*Manuscripts written in his own hand. Travels through America and Sermons*). The initials J.U.N. appear on the bottom of the spine. With one exception (the tenth) all the notebooks as measured in the binding are 6⅜ inches by 7¹⁵⁄₁₆ inches in size, the tenth being 5¾ inches by 7¼ inches.

The first seven of the notebooks in the binding, which are numbered consecutively II to VIII, form part of the Niemcewicz journals and cover the period 29 August 1797 to 8 November 1799, although without day to day continuity. The eighth notebook (unnumbered) is also a part of his diary and contains the account of his journey to Niagara in 1805.

The remaining four notebooks are not diaries. They contain manuscript translations of sermons of the Scottish divine Hugh Blair, records of songs, ballads and poems in French and English, notes on chemistry, recipes and a projected timetable for daily activities. Of these four notebooks the first is undated, but it contains the English prototype of the ballad *Winter*, published in 1803. The last page of the second notebook carries the notation in Niemcewicz's hand Jan: 30 1806 Eliz: Town. In the middle of the third notebook is written the date 16 List. [Nov.] E. T. Ameryka. There are two dates in the fourth and last notebook, 14 Grudnia [December] 1806 in the middle of the notebook and on the last page the date 13 Lutego [February] 1807. Elisabeth Town. This last page also bears the imprinted seal on which

are the words Ex Bibliotheca C: O: Zamoyski. These last four notebooks do not belong to the journal proper: they are probably bound
in chronological sequence.

Frontispiece. The frontispiece contains on the top right hand corner
the number 918. The title page written by hand, not that of Niemcewicz, reads:

Niemcewicza Juliana
Podróż
po Ameryce 1797-1799
1805-1807
własnoręcznie opisana.

(Julian Niemcewicz's Travel in America 1797-1799, 1805-1807; written
in his own hand.)

There is a note in Polish dated 1900 written and signed by W. M.
Kozłowski explaining why the date 1798 originally written was
changed by him to 1797. It is clear that such a change has been made.

There is no evidence whether the notebooks as bought by Niemcewicz had hard or soft covers. We shall refer to as the cover leaf, that
first page of the notebook now bound with the text. The front pages
of the cover leaves of all the eight notebooks of the journals carry
printed illustrations, and in two instances the printer's name.

First Notebook. This is identified top center as No. II in handwriting.

Illustration—Man on horseback (in color).

The cover leaf carries the inscription written large across the top.

Rękopisma własnoręczne
Podróże po Ameryce
Kazania
J.U.N.

(Manuscripts written in my own hand. Travels in America. Sermons.
J.U.N.) The hand is very similar to that of Niemcewicz in his diaries.[61]

There is a note in the bottom left hand corner in another hand (similar to that of Kozłowski): Brak zeszytu I-ego (First notebook missing). On the inside of the notebook cover are quotations and notes.
This page also carries the printed seal of the Zamoyski library.

There are 58 pages of text numbered 1, 3, 5, 7, etc. (not by Niemcewicz). The inside back cover leaf is blank. On the outside cover
leaf is a drawing (upside down) of the head of a man. The letters
Nie are written over the right ear. This drawing bears a striking
resemblance to certain portraits of Niemcewicz. See Figures 82 and
83.[62]

Second Notebook. This notebook was used back to front; the illustration is therefore at the end; it will be described as it occurs. The notebook is identified top center as No. III, the cover leaf is otherwise empty. At the top center of the first text page, No. 3 is written by Niemcewicz. There are 42 pages of text (numbered as before).

Illustration—Two pictures, a) of man carrying long reeds with printed legend "Old Chairs to mend, old Chairs to mend," b) of woman with basket on her head with printed legend "Fresh Cod dainty live Cod."

On the illustrated back cover is a list of clothing.

Third Notebook. This is identified top center as No. IV.

Illustration—Man leading horse with the legend underneath London. Pub. & Printed by W. G. Jones.

At the top center of the first text page, No. 4 is written by Niemcewicz. On the inside cover leaf is a note. The first leaf is unused. There are 42 pages of text (numbered as before). In this notebook Niemcewicz drew six sketches to illustrate the text.

Fourth Notebook. This is identified top center as No. V. Illustration—Animals with legend, "The Leopard and other Beasts No. 58."

There are 43 pages of text (numbered as before); the last text page is written on the inside cover leaf. There is a note on the outside back cover leaf.

Fifth Notebook. This is identified top center as No. VI. Illustration—Man leading horse with legend, "Duke of Bedford's Dragon."

There are 44 pages of text (numbered as before) and one sketch. There are numerical calculations on the outside back cover leaf.

Sixth Notebook. This is identified top center as No. VII. Illustration—Man on horseback with legend, "Major Erskine No. 24."

There is a note on the inside front cover leaf. There are 44 pages of text (numbered as before) with two sketches. There is a numerical calculation on the outside back cover leaf.

Seventh Notebook. This is identified top center as No. VIII. Illustration—Figure of man with legend, "A Turk No. 17." There is a note on the front and many notes on the inside front cover leaf. There are 37 pages of text, numbered as before anonymously 1, 3 . . . 29 and 1, 2, 4 . . . 8. On page 29 the text stops at the bottom of the page on June 14th [1799]. It resumes on November 1st—the enumerator here then changed the pagination to 1, 2, 4 . . . 8. There are three sketches in the text. There are notes on the inside back cover leaf.

Eighth Notebook. Illustration—Four prints with appropriate legends, "Autumn," "Winter," "Spring," and "Summer." There is printed, "Printed and sold by R. and W. Dean and Co., Manchester." There are 52 pages of text. There are some numerical calculations on the back cover leaf. There is one sketch.

Deciphering the Manuscript

Although I have examined the manuscript on several occasions, microfilm copies were used exclusively in this study. Notebooks numbered II, III, IV and the eighth notebook are largely written in French. The whole of this text was deciphered directly from the microfilm and a complete transcription was prepared. The handwriting is small in size and constant in form. The lines are evenly spaced and wide apart. There are very few interlineations and fewer deletions. Some interpolations are written in the margin. Such difficulties as the manuscript presented arose either from a few pages of very faint script or from the formation of the terminal letters in some words.

The Polish text begins eight manuscript pages before the end of notebook numbered IV. During the preparation from the microfilm of the transcript of the Polish text a copy of the Wellman-Zalewska (Polish) edition of the text was available to me. My reading of the Polish part of the manuscript was helped immeasurably by the printed version.

Editing the Manuscript

In our earlier study [63] the French text of the notebooks numbered II, III and IV was presented in the original language; the Polish text in notebooks IV (8 manuscript pages), V, VI and VII was translated into English. The notebook containing the Journey to Niagara was translated into English from the original French for our publication in the *Quarterly* of the New-York Historical Society. It is reprinted here unchanged.

The interpolation in French and Latin dated 1 fev. 1799 in notebook numbered VIII, manuscript pages 13-14 (between the writings on c. 3 November 1798 and 30 May 1799), concerning the treatment given by Charlevoix of the Indians and by Tacitus of the Germans has been removed to the Appendix. Notes, lists, quotations, expense accounts and calculations written either on the cover leaves or in the margin (or not a part of the text) are described and collected in the Appendix.

The modernized expanded method [64] as it applies to translation was used here for both the French and Polish texts. Efforts were made not to employ English words brought into the language after 1800. Whenever English words, or words in a language foreign to the text, were used these are shown printed in italics. No changes have been made in their spelling nor in the spelling of proper names and place names. Where a Polish translation of an English word or phrase was written down, repetition has been avoided. In the printed text manuscript page numbers have been placed as close as possible to their original positions. The text has been divided into chapters for ease of reading.

In a few instances Niemcewicz did not indicate where marginal notes were to be brought down into the line of the text. In these cases they were brought in where it was considered appropriate and a note was made to that effect. The author's special abbreviations, such as dol. for dollar, have not been expanded.

Niemcewicz's French was not perfect literary French. The syntax was frequently incorrect and the grammar on occasion in error. The text was not, however, difficult to translate except on the rare occasions, referred to in the notes, when Niemcewicz invented French translations of Polish words.

Niemcewicz's Polish presented no difficulty. He was a literary man and especially interested in the problem of regaining and preserving the purity of the Polish language. He was very much aware of this problem. The archaism in Niemcewicz's Polish is mostly in orthography, which had not been stabilized by that time. He employed on, em, om, etc., for the modern nasals ę and ą. He regularly used y for i, i for j, etc., and dialect forms in declensions and conjugations, for example widziemy instead of widzimy. Other spelling irregularities include the alteration p/b, łep for łeb [head] and puł for pół, and, as pointed out by St. Kot, ą/o characteristic for Lithuanians, niecą for nieco. Spelling such as examin for egzamin, however, presents no difficulty for an American reader. Uses of words such as prezentacya, monument, sytuacya, papier instead of their more indigenous Polish counterparts przedstawienie, pomnik, położenie, gazeta, obviously are in the same category. Polish words derived from foreign sources other than Latin did not present any special problems. However, it was important to be aware of the archaisms in Niemcewicz's usage, as for example his use of the noun przytomność for obecność (being present).[65] The dictionary of Bogumił Linde, written in this period, was especially helpful in resolving these problems.[66]

THE AMERICAN DIARIES IN EARLIER PUBLICATIONS—HISTORICAL COMMENTARY

The Writings of Niemcewicz

In his memoirs, written in his old age, Niemcewicz refers specifically to his American Diaries in their two major divisions, the period

1797-1799 and the journey to Niagara, 1805. Niemcewicz was equally specific about other diaries and writings pertaining to certain periods, beginning with the first written in verse to Józef Szymanowski, the diaries of his two trips to Italy, his imprisonment in St. Petersburg and others prior and subsequent to this period.[67]

During the writing of both versions [68] of his memoirs (1823-1825) in Warsaw and (1834-1838) in Paris, Niemcewicz states that the only journal or notes available to him were those on his imprisonment in St. Petersburg written in Elizabeth, N.J., in 1800. Niemcewicz regrets that the others were unavailable and presumes them to be lost.

In a letter to Count Edward Roger Raczyński dated 26 September 1835 Niemcewicz writes,

". . . Madame la Comtesse, dans sa dernière lettre, me propose l'achat de mes manuscrits pour 300 ducats. Je ne marchanderai pas avec mes amis, surtout lorsque ces documents si précieux doivent être conservés dans un musée aussi important que celui que vous avez fondé. J'en excepte cependant les manuscrits de ma main, que je désirerais déposer chez mon neveu Thadeé; . . ." [69]

At that time Count Raczyński was publishing many important Polish manuscripts and collecting memorabilia of Poland. Apart from his collections in the Rogalin Palace (his home) he had founded (1829) and donated (1832) to the city of Poznań a public library bearing his name. It is interesting therefore that in 1858 there is a published reference to certain folio copies, in the Rogalin library, of Niemcewicz's manuscript account of his journey to America.[70] There is a further published reference in 1928 to the presence in the Rogalin library of Niemcewicz's account of his journey to America; the author here does not, however, state whether he is referring to copies or to original manuscripts. Niemcewicz in his memoirs in describing his manuscripts as lost, himself suggested the Rogalin Palace as one of the places where some of them might possibly be found.[71]

The enigma of the number II written on the cover leaf of the American Diaries whereon is also written *Travels in America written in my own hand and Sermons,* J.U.N. (in Polish) both probably by Niemcewicz invites speculation. Was there a notebook numbered I, what did it contain, and why is it not bound with the others? Were the notebooks bound under Niemcewicz's direction and at what time? If, as is appears, the handwriting is that of Niemcewicz, then he must have been responsible for collecting the notebooks together sometime after 1807, the dating of the last material in them.

In 1858 an article entitled, "Diary of My Journey," with a subtitle,

"The Journey of Julian Ursyn Niemcewicz from Petersburg to America translated from the original French into Polish" appeared in *Przegląd Poznański* (*Poznań Review*), XXV (1858), 438-461. It covers Niemcewicz's journey from St. Petersburg to Stockholm. This diary, then in the Rogalin library, is now lost. It is possible, particularly in view of the subtitle, that the notebook which contained this diary also contained the diary of the continuing journey from Stockholm to America and that it was the missing notebook numbered I. Niemcewicz refers specifically in his memoirs to journals he kept throughout the whole journey from St. Petersburg through Stockholm and England to America including the ocean voyage.[72] Perhaps the notebook numbered I, bought earlier, was of substantially different size and not therefore bound with the rest. The notebook numbered I was not therefore necessarily lost to Niemcewicz at the time of binding.

Niemcewicz's one brief publication from the American Diaries, his biography of Washington, places the notebook numbered IV in Warsaw in 1803.

In 1873 there appeared a book with the title, *Pamiętniki Juliana Niemcewicza, Dziennik Drugiej Podróży do Ameryki, 1804-1807* (*Memoirs of Julian Ursyn Niemcewicz, Diary of the Second Journey to America*), with an introduction signed W.W. This was a transcription from a manuscript copy of a draft prepared purportedly from the original of a part of Niemcewicz's diary. This manuscript is now lost and the book together with a reprint of the article without the introduction in the *Przegląd Lwowski* (*Lwow Review*) is the only source. In this diary Niemcewicz said, "The diary of my trip to Niagara is written in a separate notebook and I will not repeat it here." [73]

The Writings Used by Others

In 1900 Władysław M. Kozłowski examined the manuscripts of the American Diaries and wrote, as noted earlier, that notebook numbered I was missing. Kozłowski's first publication from this manuscript material was an article entitled, "A Visit to Mount Vernon a Century Ago," and published in *The Century Magazine*, February 1902.[74] The work is subtitled, "A Few Pages from an Unpublished Diary of the Polish Poet, J. U. Niemcewicz," and in his introduction Kozłowski writes that the diary was never published and that "after painful researches" he succeeded in finding it in one of the libraries in Poland. Kozłowski does not state in which library he had found the manuscript and appeared unaware that Niemcewicz had published this same material.

In 1906 Kozłowski published a second translation into Polish of a part of Niemcewicz's diary. This extract is from the second notebook, No. III, and describes the departure of Kościuszko from America. In his introduction to the publication Kozłowski states that the diaries are in French except for a brief passage towards the end.[75] This leaves the impression that Kozłowski did not see some or all of the notebooks numbered IV, V, VI and VII, all of which are in Polish. If this were so, then clearly the notebooks were not bound together before 1906. In 1917 Kozłowski published a third translation from Niemcewicz's diary in *Bluszcz* (*Ivy*).[76] This is a very brief fragment (about one-tenth) from the whole account of the journey to Niagara from the eighth notebook.

In 1906 Korzon consulted Niemcewicz's diary and in the second edition of his biography of Kościuszko gives a long quotation from Niemcewicz's diary (notebook no. III) pertaining to the departure of Kościuszko in May 1798.[77]

The Polish edition of the American Diaries, *Podróże po Ameryce*, prepared by Antonina Wellman-Zalewska under the general editorship of Emil Kipa and recently published in Poland, is based completely on the original manuscript. It is the only recent authoritative publication in Polish from the diary material.

The Wellman-Zalewska edition includes not only the material in the seven notebooks numbered II-VIII and the eighth "Journey to Niagara" notebook but also reprints of the writings of Niemcewicz from earlier publications and the first publication, from the manuscript, of a letter from Niemcewicz to Prince Adam Kazimierz Czartoryski of 6 February 1798, summarizing the events of the American journey up to that time. That part of the diaries written by Niemcewicz in French is here translated into Polish, and the Polish section has been modernized.

The editing of the Polish manuscripts follows modern editorial practice. There are not very many differences between our readings of the text and those of any consequence are few. Perhaps most serious is her reading of Portland for Portsmouth. This gives the impression that Niemcewicz went further into Maine than just across the border. The editor, not having American sources available to her, makes certain errors in the identification of people.

In her Introduction Wellman-Zalewska's interpretation of Niemcewicz and the Niemcewicz-Kościuszko relationship differs substantially from ours.

We are unaware of any other publications based directly on manuscript material.[78]

NOTES TO THE INTRODUCTION

1. Julian Ursyn Niemcewicz, *Pism różnych wierszem i prozą*, ed. Tadeusz Mostowski, Wybór pisarzów polskich (Warsaw, 1803), I, iv.

2. The first complete publication is Julian Ursyn Niemcewicz, *Podróże po Ameryce 1797-1807*, ed. Antonina Wellman-Zalewska (Warsaw, 1959).

3. Julian Ursin Niemcewicz, *Pamiętniki czasów moich*, ed. Karol Ursin Niemcewicz (Paris, 1848), p. 333. These memoirs written in Paris cover the period from 1758 to 1829, and were published posthumously. An earlier version of his memoirs covering the period 1758 to 1796 was written by Niemcewicz in Warsaw and finished in 1825; this has recently been published together with a more carefully edited version of the Paris manuscript memoirs for the period 1796 to 1829. Julian Ursyn Niemcewicz, *Pamiętniki czasów moich*, ed. Jan Dihm, 2 vols. (Warsaw, 1957), II, 225; later cited as Niemcewicz, *Pamiętniki* I or II, or, to avoid ambiguity, as (Warsaw) I or II.

4. *Pamiętniki*, II, 172.

5. The principal biographical sources for Julian Ursyn Niemcewicz are the two editions of his memoirs and his biography by Prince Adam Jerzy Czartoryski, *Żywot J. U. Niemcewicza* (Berlin and Poznań, 1860). Since both the *Memoirs* and the biography are written by old men and the *Memoirs* are conscious works of art, the material must be used judiciously. To the sources mentioned one must add the biographical sketches by Jan Dihm in his introductions to recent editions of Niemcewicz's writings. See especially Jan Dihm, *Niemcewicz jako polityk i publicysta w czasie sejmu czteroletniego* (Kraków, 1928). This sketch is based partly on manuscript letters. Dihm does not always document his sources. Another biographical account is found in Karol Zbyszewski, *Niemcewicz od przodu i tyłu* (Warsaw, 1939), where the events as related by Niemcewicz in his Paris memoirs are interpreted in a highly amusing, sometimes colored manner.

5a. A dispassionate exploration of this complicated period in Polish history may be found in Herbert H. Kaplan, *The First Partition of Poland* (New York, 1962).

6. See "Wiadomość o rękopisach pozostałych po Julianie Niemcewiczu," *Przegląd Poznański*, XXVI (1858), 43.

7. Marceli Handelsman, *Adam Czartoryski* (Warsaw, 1948-1950), I, 7.

8. R. R. Palmer in his recent book devotes chapters to the Polish Democratic Revolution and comments on Niemcewicz's role in it; see his *The Age of the Democratic Revolution*, 2 vols. (Princeton, 1959, 1964).

9. See Ignacy Krasicki, *Pisma wybrane*, ed. Tadeusz Mikulski (Warsaw, 1954), IV, 300; and *Pamiętniki Wawrzyńca hr. Engeströma*, ed. and trans. Józef I. Kraszewski, Pamiętniki z ośmnastego wieku, XV (Poznań, 1875), p. 82.

10. Consider Niemcewicz's deposition: "Doprosy Kostiuškie, Niemcevič" i dr. i ich pokazanja," *Čtenja v Imperatorskom Obščestvje Istorii i Drevnostej Rossiskich pri Moskovskom Universitete*, Part IV, smes (1866), 188-202.

11. G. A. Vorobjev, "Razgovory Imperatora Pavla 1-go c Tadeusem Kostiuško v Peterburge," *Russkaja Starina*, CXXIV (1905), 394, 395.

12. The eulogy was delivered on 14 November 1817 in Warsaw; see Julian Ursyn Niemcewicz, *Dzieła poetyczne wierszem i prozą*, ed. Jan Nep Bobrowicz

(Leipzig, 1838-1840), XII, 161-168; Julian Ursyn Niemcewicz, "Kosciusco," trans. anon. in H. Niles, *Principles and Acts of the Revolution in America* (Baltimore, 1822), pp. 474-476.

13. S. M. Gorjainov, *Zatočenie T. Kostiuški v Kreposti* (1794-1795 gg.) (Moscow, 1912), p. 20.

14. See Frederick J. Turner, *Correspondence of French Ministers* (1791-1797), *Annual Report of the American Historical Association for the Year 1903* (Washington, D.C.), II, 1069; the letter is translated in Miecislaus Haiman, *Kosciuszko Leader and Exile* (New York, 1946), p. 46.

15. Susan Livingston Kean (1759?-1833), daughter of Peter Van Brugh Livingston and Mary, née Alexander; see Florence Van Rensselaer, *The Livingston Family in America* (New York, 1949), pp. 85, 95. Susan Livingston Kean was the widow of John Kean (1756?-1795), whom she married in 1786. John Kean was originally from South Carolina, delegate to the Continental Congress shortly after the Revolutionary War and Cashier of the first Bank of the United States in Philadelphia; see George Lockhart Rives, *Genealogical Notes* (New York, 1914), pp. 73-74.

16. *Pamiętniki Juliana Ursyna Niemcewicza 1804-1807. Dziennik drugiej podróży do Ameryki*, ed. anon. (Lwów, 1873), p. vi; this was reprinted in *Przegląd Lwowski*, V, VI (1873), and most recently in Wellman-Zalewska, ed., *Podróże po Ameryce*.

17. George Richard, 3rd Viscount Bolingbroke and 4th Viscount St. John (1761-1824), and Isabelle Charlotte Antoinette Sophia, Baroness Hompesch (d. 1848), niece of the last Grand Master of Malta, lived under the pseudonym of Belasise during their ten-year stay in America. They married in 1804 after the death of Bolingbroke's first wife in 1803 and returned to England in 1806. Burke's *Peerage* (101st ed., 1956). See also "A House with a History, 'Liberty Hall' and its Many Romantic Associations. The Episode of Lord Bolingbroke and His Beautiful Young Mistress," *The New York World*, 18 December 1876 and corrective letter of Julia Lawrence in *The New York Times*, 29 January 1877. See also "Journey to Niagara, 1805," trans. and ed. Metchie J. E. Budka, *The New-York Historical Society Quarterly*, XLIV (January, 1960), 72-113; reprinted here.

18. Published by W. M. Kozłowski, "Niemcewicz en Amérique et sa correspondance inédite avec Jefferson (1797-1810)," *Revue de Littérature Comparée*, VIII (1928), 29-45. A recent search for further correspondence has produced no significant new material; see Eugene Kusielewicz, "The Jefferson Niemcewicz Correspondence," *The Polish Review*, II, 4 (1957), 7-21. The Niemcewicz material, which includes correspondence about him, is catalogued and available in the Archives of the American Philosophical Society, Philadelphia. Two of his letters to the Society have been published; see Eugene Kusielewicz, "Niemcewicz in America," *The Polish Review*, V, no. 1 (1960), 74, 75.

19. Niemcewicz, *Pism różnych* (Warsaw, 1803), I, i.

20. Adam Mickiewicz, *Dzieła wszystkie* (Warsaw, 1933), XVI, 50.

21. The source of *Winter* is A *Winter Piece* by John Aikin, M.D. (1747-1822); see Metchie J. E. Budka, "The American Notebooks of Julian Ursyn Niemcewicz. An Early Source of the Polish Ballad," *The Slavonic and East European Review* (in press); see for Niemcewicz's relationship to the general problem of Polish balladry, Czesław Zgorzelski, *Ballada polska*, Biblioteka Narodowa, Ser. 1, No. 177 (Wrocław, 1962).

22. See in this connection, Leon Płoszewski, "Pierwsza redakcja 'Spiewów his-

torycznych' (z r. 1809)," Pamiętnik Literacki, XIV (1916), passim; see also Apolonja Załuska, *Poezja opisowa Delille'a w Polsce*, Prace Historyczno-Literackie, no. 44 (Kraków, 1934), pp. 103-114, esp. 113.

23. Niemcewicz, "Dziennik drugiej podróży do Ameryki," *Przegląd Lwowski*, VI (1873), 410, translated here. Linde ascribes this phrase to Horace, *Satires* 141. [sic]; probably *Satires* I, iv, 8.

24. Mrs. Niemcewicz's will left him six hundred dollars a year. Since the other heirs were minors, her son Peter having predeceased her, and because there were two wills, there was considerable misunderstanding and delay in payment. In his biography Czartoryski complained that the provisions of the will were not scrupulously carried out; see *Żywot*, pp. 249, 292, 316. Manuscript letters, however, in the Polish Library in Paris make it clear that the matter was eventually straightened out.

25. "Dziennik kieszonkowy J. U. Niemcewicza" [12 June 1807 –9 November 1807], ed. Antonina Wellman-Zalewska, *Miscellanea z doby oświecenia*, Archiwum Literackie, V (Wrocław, 1960), p. 509.

26. Czartoryski, *Żywot*, p. 155. For a sympathetic account of Niemcewicz's activity see Marjan Tyrowicz, "Działalność publiczna J. U. Niemcewicza w latach 1807-1813," *Ateneum Wileńskie*, VII (1930), 263-292. See also Ignacy Chrzanowski, "Pochwała Niemcewicza," *Literatura a Naród* (Lwów, 1936), pp. 97-108. See also Wacław Berent, *Zmierzch wodzów* (Warsaw, 1939), pp. 105-167 (reprinted in Rome, 1946), pp. 71-116; and the works of Jan Dihm.

27. Handelsman, *Czartoryski*, I, 123.

28. Julian Ursyn Niemcewicz, *Pamiętniki (1811-1820)* [Memoir period actually 1809-1820], introd. Józef I. Kraszewski (Poznań, 1871).

29. Juliusz Słowacki, *Dzieła*, ed. Julian Krzyżanowski (Wrocław, 1949), V, 222, line 148-153. Cf. Marjan Tyrowicz, "Juljan Ursyn Niemcewicz w dobie Królestwa Kongresowego i nocy listopadowej," *Przegląd Współczesny*, IX (October, 1930), 94-106; (November, 1930), 230-255.

30. See Czartoryski, *Żywot*, p. 407; Jan Pasek, *Pamiętniki*, ed. Roman Pollak (Warsaw, 1955), p. 47; see also Andrzej Wojtkowski, *Edward Raczyński i jego dzieło* (Poznań, 1929), pp. 105-107, 339, n. 74; see also *Miejska biblioteka publiczna im. Edwarda Raczyńskiego w Poznaniu* (Poznań, 1959), p. 5.

31. Mickiewicz on Niemcewicz in Lecture XXI printed in *Notes sur ma Captivité*, pp. 229-236. See Wiktor Weintraub, *Literature as Prophecy* (Hague, 1959), pp. 5-7, concerning the problems of reliability in the published texts of Mickiewicz's lectures. See Weintraub, *Literature*, passim, for analysis of the use of literary criticism as a creative force.

32. Tarnowski, who accorded to Niemcewicz a great talent as a publicist, deplored his careless facility in writing and his eclecticism and only reluctantly gave him credit for trying out new forms. See Stanisław Tarnowski, *Historya literatury polskiej*, 2nd ed. (Kraków, 1904), IV, passim, esp. 117, 362, 364.

33. Brückner aware of Niemcewicz's artistic shortcomings emphasizes his literary innovations as a part of his role as a good citizen and accords him an important role in the development of the novel form. See Aleksander Brückner, *Dzieje kultury polskiej* (Kraków, 1931-1946), III, 631, 651-653.

34. Julian Krzyżanowski, *W świecie romantycznym* (Kraków, 1961), p. 22.

35. In this publication an attempt was made at a biography of Washington, one of the earliest extant, to satisfy the great interest in Washington in Poland. The element from the Diary was prefaced by speeches by Washington and ad-

dresses to him plus Thomas Law's letter on the circumstances of Washington's death. First published as "Krótka wiadomość o życiu i sprawach generała Washington," *Pism różnych wierszem i prozą* (Warsaw, 1803), I, 209-328; later in *Dzieła poetyczne*, XI, 1-112.

36. *Pamiętniki* (*1811-1820*), II, xiv-xv.

37. Laurence Sterne, *A Sentimental Journey through France and Italy*, introd. Virginia Woolf, The World's Classics no. 333 (London, 1957), p. x.

38. La Rochefoucault Liancourt Duke de, *Travels through the United States of North America, the Country of the Iroquois and Upper Canada in the Years 1795, 1796 and 1797*, trans. H. Neuman, 2 vols. (London, 1799), I, xxi.

39. Niemcewicz used Jedidiah Morse, *The American Geography: or, A View of the Present Situation of the United States of America . . . and of Europe, Asia, and Africa*. A New Edition. Illustrated with 25 maps. 4to. (London, 1794). This is the only edition which corresponds exactly in pages and the map cited by Niemcewicz. See p. 345.

40. Niemcewicz, *Pism różnych* (Warsaw, 1803), I, iv; *Pamiętniki* (Paris), pp. 7, 47.

41. Study has shown, as the notes and the text display, not only that Niemcewicz was accurate in reporting "facts"—dates, places, etc., but also that his impressions and his judgments were true. Niemcewicz made a very few minor errors, e.g. "Journey to Niagara, 1805," p. 250, n. 64. In a brief introduction to the article by Kozłowski, "A Visit to Mount Vernon a Century Ago," *The Century Magazine*, LXIII (February, 1902), 510-512, Worthington C. Ford verified the dates of Niemcewicz's visit to Mount Vernon and other details by reference to Washington's diary. The introduction otherwise has many errors concerning Niemcewicz's own life. See also Edward Channing's comment on the Century magazine article, "Possibly the most interesting insight into Washington's home life is to be found in . . . Polish Poet Niemcewicz," *A History of the United States* (New York, 1920), IV, 58. There is no equivalent in Niemcewicz's diaries of the well-known mosquitoes of Isaac Weld, Jun. which bit through Washington's boot; see *Travels through the States of North America and the Provinces of Upper and Lower Canada during the years 1795, 1796 and 1797*, 4th ed., 2 vols. (London, 1807), I, 285.

42. Bernard Faÿ, *Bibliographie critique des Ouvrages français relatifs aux Etats-Unis* (*1770-1800*) (Paris, 1924), pp. 57-58.

43. "I have my whole diary of my journey which I shall keep for an appropriate moment," see letter of Julian Niemcewicz to Mrs. Katarzyna Potocki Kossakowski from Elisabeth Town, 23 November 1805, *Archiwum wróblewieckie*, ed. W. Tarnowski (Lwów, 1883), p. 28. The letter is reprinted here.

44. *Żywot*, pp. 271-272. Niemcewicz read Franklin's *Autobiography*; see Appendix II here.

45. See Thorsten Sellin, "Philadelphia Prisons of the Eighteenth Century," *Historic Philadelphia*, Trans. Amer. Phil. Soc., XLIII, Part 1 (1953), 330, n. 8.

46. Niemcewicz, "O więzieniach publicznych czyli domach pokuty rzecz krótka," *Dzieła poetyczne*, XI, 115 ff.

47. See Henry Steele Commager, "Leadership in Eighteenth Century America and Today," *Proceedings of the American Academy of Arts and Sciences*, XC (1961), 663.

48. Tomasz Kajetan Węgierski (1755-1787). Węgierski was a poet of great talent but was embittered by personal difficulties; he spent much time abroad. He

traveled to America in 1783 and wrote a diary in French of his trip there. For pre-romantic features in his descriptions of nature in this diary see Ignacy Chrzanowski, *Historja literatury niepodległej Polski* (965-1795) (London, 1947), pp. 587-588. The Węgierski diary was first edited for publication by Stanisław Kossowski, "Z życia Węgierskiego, pamiętniki i listy," *Przewodnik Naukowy i Literacki,* XXXVI (1908), 44 ff., and translated in part by Miecislaus Haiman, *Poland and the American Revolutionary War* (Chicago, 1932), pp. 115-148.

49. Załuska, *Poezja,* pp. 77, 112.

50. Dimitrij Cizevskij, *On Romanticism in Slavic Literature,* trans. D. S. Worth (The Hague, 1957), pp. 11-28.

51. Constantin-François Chasseboeuf Volney, *Tableau du Climat et du Sol des Etats-Unis d'Amérique* (Paris, 1803); trans. C. B. Brown (Philadelphia, 1804), pp. 80-94.

52. Krzyżanowski, *W świecie,* p. 23.

53. Ignacy Krasicki, "Myszeidos," *Pisma wybrane,* I, 1-59. Niemcewicz's idea of the classical joke is in the spirit of Ariosto, see Wiktor Weintraub, ed. *Wybór pism,* by Ignacy Krasicki (Jerusalem, 1944), pp. 31-32.

54. *Żywot,* p. 209. See also Niemcewicz, *List do Karola Kniaziewicza* (Paris, 1834).

55. Janusz Odrowąż-Pieniążek, "Un poèm canado-américain de J. U. Niemcewicz," *Études Slaves et Est-Européennes,* VII, 1, 2 (1962), 78-80.

56. Jan Dihm, "Nieznana powieść J. U. Niemcewicza," *Pamiętnik Literacki,* XXIX (1932), 216. The manuscript is in the Czartoryski Library in Cracow, *Czas,* no. 164 (1866); see also Zofia Libiszowska, *Opinia polska wobec rewolucji amerykańskiej w XVIII wieku* (Łódź, 1962), p. 133. For contemporary foreign comment on the state of Polish serfdom see *The Lee Papers,* Collections of the New-York Historical Society (1871), I, 40-41; see also Carl Knies, *Carl Freidrichs von Baden brieflicher Verkehr mit Mirabeau und Du Pont* (Heidelberg, 1892), I, 392-393.

57. Howard Mumford Jones, *America and French Culture, 1750-1848* (Chapel Hill, 1927), p. 391, passim.

58. *Pamiętniki,* II, 218, 223-224.

59. Moreau de Saint-Méry, *Voyage aux Etats-Unis de l'Amérique, 1793-1798,* ed. Stewart L. Mims, Yale Historical Publications, Manuscripts and Edited Texts (New Haven, 1913).

60. J. P. Brissot de Warville, *New Travels in the United States of America, performed in 1788,* trans. anon. (London, 1792).

61. The autograph of his initials on a manuscript letter in the American Philosophical Society library appears very similar to the initials as written here.

62. This portrait of Niemcewicz was identified and reproduced in *Podróże po Ameryce,* p. ii, as from the year 1795, from a copper engraving by J. Ligber now in the National Museum in Warsaw.

63. Metchie J. E. Budka, trans. and ed., *The American Diaries of Julian Ursyn Niemcewicz* (1797-1799, 1805) with an introduction and notes (Ph.D. thesis, Harvard, 1962).

64. Oscar Handlin, Arthur Meier Schlesinger, Samuel Eliot Morison, Frederick Merk, Arthur Meier Schlesinger, Jr., Paul Herman Buck, *Harvard Guide to American History* (Cambridge, Mass., 1955), p. 99, passim.

65. Stanisław Kot, ed., *Powrót posła . . . oraz wybór bajek politycznych z epoki Sejmu Wielkiego,* 6th ed., Biblioteka Narodowa, Series I, no. 4 (Wrocław,

1950), "Uwaga" ff. p. xli. For a list of the irregularities in Niemcewicz's spelling of Polish see *Podróże po Ameryce*, p. xxvii.

66. M. Samuel Bogumił Linde, *Słownik języka polskiego*, 3rd ed., photo-offset (Warsaw, 1951).

67. See Niemcewicz, *Pamiętniki*, I, 160, 165; II, 17, 63, 107, 119, 201, 207, 210, 225, 228-229, 250 n. 16, 256, 274, 303; see also *Pamiętniki* (Paris), pp. 2, 47, 89, 104, 220. Page references after 220 in the Paris Memoirs are omitted as the later writings here were based, as were the Warsaw Memoirs, on essentially the same manuscript materials, i.e., *Notes sur ma Captivité*, and MS. Pamiętniki Część III in the Biblioteka Polska (Paris); see *Pamiętniki* (Warsaw), I, 353. For specific allusions by Niemcewicz to separate diaries and notebooks see also Józef Tretiak, *Finis poloniae, Historja legendy maciejowickiej i jej rozwiązanie* (Kraków, 1921), pp. 47, 48, 51.

68. There has been speculation by both Dihm (*Pamiętniki* (Warsaw), I, 24) and Wellman-Zalewska (*Podróże po Ameryce*, p. xxii, n. 22) that Niemcewicz wrote a version of his memoirs while in America. This speculation is based on a garbled version of a newspaper account of a visit to the Kean house in Elizabeth, N.J., where some mementos of Niemcewicz and some of his letters are preserved. The actual article in *Nowy Świat—The Polish Morning World*, New York (June 19, 1938) states in free translation,

> "The greatest interest is aroused by a bundle of papers typewritten in 1918 in the English language . . . They are typed on 30 sheets of ordinary paper, as well as I could make out from a superficial perusal they frequently mentioned details from the history of Niemcewicz's stay in America."

The material to which the newspaper article referred is a typescript copy of an anonymous translation from the memoirs of Niemcewicz written in Paris. The translation is of the account of his American stay before 1802.

The legend on this typescript reads:

"Extract from Memoirs of Count Niemcewicz Relating to his Sojourn in the United States.

Transcribed from a copy (36 typewritten sheets, reduced to 30 herein) given me in 1918 by Henry Redmond, Esq., who had received it at Callendar House from his brother, Geraldyn Redmond, Esq. The copy has evidently been made from a MS by some one unfamiliar with both the subject and the handwriting. The spelling of proper names and of quotations from foreign languages is so faulty as in some cases to obscure the meaning, in at least one sentence, as on page 8, of this transcript (page 7 herein) it has not been possible to elucidate it.

S.M.F.W.

(Sarah Morris Fish Webster)

(Mrs. Sidney Webster, Newport, R.I.)"

The Redmonds were in some way related to the Livingstons.

Mrs. Webster's conclusion that the copy was made from a manuscript appears most reasonable. The names misspelled in the typescript are not misspelled in the published version. See *Pamiętniki czasów moich* (Paris, 1848), pp. 323-347.

Even without this evidence we would be reluctant to accept the suggestion that such a version of his memoirs was written. It would be completely alien to Niemcewicz's habits not to have made some reference to it in later writings.

69. Czartoryski, *Żywot*, p. 407.

70. *Czas* and *Przegląd Poznański* give the same information, "Book, 'in folio' which in two identical copies includes the travels of the author over America . . ." In *Przegląd Poznański*, XXVI (1858), 42, there is a quotation which is from the Diary (comparing Benedict Arnold with Potocki et al.); the Polish spelling has been modernized, perhaps for publication. *Czas* carries the further information that Count Edward Raczyński had all his manuscripts copied, and these copies were for the most part badly done; *Czas* no. 164 (1866), 2. Gubrynowicz says, "A few versions, in English, French and Polish have been preserved in the Rogalin Library and the Zamoyski Library in Warsaw. Kozłowski printed a few excerpts," see Bronisław Gubrynowicz, "W sprawie pamiętników i pism publicystycznych J. U. Niemcewicza," *Pamiętnik IV powszechnego zjazdu historyków w Poznaniu, 1925* (Lwów, 1925) p. 38; see also *Miejska biblioteka publiczna im. Edwarda Raczyńskiego w Poznaniu* (Poznań, 1959), p. 5.

71. Edward Maliszewski, *Bibljografja pamiętników polskich i Polski dotyczących (Druki i Rękopisy)* (Warsaw, 1928), p. 372; *Pamiętniki*, II, 201.

72. *Pamiętniki*, II, 207, 210.

73. *Pamiętniki . . . 1804-1807* (Lwów, 1873). The source of this publication was the Rogalin Library, see *Przegląd Poznański*, XXVI (1858), 43; see "Pamiętniki . . . 1804-1807," *Przegląd Lwowski*, VI (1873), 483.

74. *The Century Magazine*, LXIII, 510-522.

75. "Pobyt Kościuszki i Niemcewicza w Ameryce (w latach 1797 i 1798)," *Biblioteka Warszawska*, IV, no. 2 (1906), 241-284. In *Kwartalnik Historyczny*, XX (1906), Kozłowski uses the same diary material again.

76. W. Kozłowski, ed., "Niemcewicz u Niagary," *Bluszcz*, no. 28, 29 (1917).

77. Tadeusz Korzon, *Kościuszko biografia z dokumentów wysnuta*, 2nd edition (Kraków, 1906), p. lii.

78. Haiman has published translations into English from Niemcewicz's own published account of his visit to Washington, from Kozłowski's article in *Biblioteka Warszawska*, 1906, and from Niemcewicz's memoirs published in Paris, 1848; see Haiman, "Julian Ursyn Niemcewicz in America," *Poland and the American Revolutionary War* (Chicago, 1932), pp. 151-190. Some parts of the translations of Haiman and that of Kozłowski in the *Century* magazine have recently been reprinted by Kusielewicz and Krzyżanowski in *The Polish Review*. See Eugene Kusielewicz, Ludwik Krzyżanowski, "Julian Ursyn Niemcewicz's American Diary," *The Polish Review*, III, No. 3 (1958), 83-115; see esp. pp. 84, n. 1, 89, n. 7, 95, n. 22; also reprinted in *Julian Ursyn Niemcewicz and America*, ed. Ludwik Krzyżanowski (New York, 1961). For a good bibliography of Niemcewicz's works translated into English see Anne H. Sidwa and Marion Moore Coleman, *Niemcewicz an Anniversary Tribute* (Cambridge Springs, Pennsylvania, 1958), pp. 14-15.

Part I

TRAVELS THROUGH AMERICA, 1797-1799

Fig. 11. Autograph title page of Niemcewicz's notebooks containing the diaries of his Travels through America. From the manuscripts in the Krasiński Palace. Courtesy of the National Library, Warsaw.

Chapter I

PHILADELPHIA, JOURNEYS TO NEW BRUNS-WICK AND NEW YORK CITY. ELIZABETH-TOWN AND NEW BRUNSWICK

29 August. [1797] Before leaving Philadelphia I had the pleasure of seeing its Legislative Assembly.[1] At eleven o'clock in the morning the Governor [2] repaired to the Senate Chamber where the Senators and the members of the House of Representatives had gathered together. The Governor, having taken the place of the President of the Senate, made a speech in which he gave an account of the state of the Commonwealth of Pennsylvania, its finances, and of the steps and precautions that he had taken against the contagion raging at the time. He gave the reasons why he had not approved the last resolution of the Legislature. He recommended to the consideration of the two Houses statutes to be adopted, and above all the question of the schools and of education in general. His speech was clear, simple and appropriate, although without any rhetorical embellishments; such in a word that all magistrates, who have need neither to arouse feelings nor to flatter, might give everywhere. The appearance of the Assembly without being in any way imposing aroused respect. The Senators sat in the first row, the Representatives behind them; in front of the President's rostrum stood a large table with the Statutes and many papers on it; to the side were two secretaries. No one wore a sword and all were in everyday clothes. It was the Assembly of a new nation uncorrupted by luxury. There were farmers with white hair, some Quakers, etc., at least so they appeared. Those who have a more complete knowledge of the country claim that corruption, already very widespread especially in the big cities, does not accord with the simplicity which we admire in the Representatives.

The Governor, having finished his speech, bade farewell to the Assembly and retired. Immediately the Representatives went down to their own Chamber below. They are, as in the Senate, arranged in a semi-circle, each one having a chair and in front of him a table; the *Speaker* is on a slightly raised dais with a table and the secretary below. A member made a few remarks about the Governor's veto. Some others answered him showing that the Governor had acted only according to the rights given to him by the Constitution.

[2] The usher announced the Secretary of the Commonwealth. The barrier opened, he entered, greeted the Speaker of the House and stated the purpose of his mission: it is in this way that the Governor communicates with the two chambers. Having given the papers to the Speaker he left. A *bil* was read directing the application of ten thousand dollars for the relief of the sick poor. A committee of five was nominated to confer with the doctors, to investigate the hospitals, etc. After the reading of the *bil* the Speaker took it and asked *"does the house agree to the Resolution."* He repeated the question twice. Silence being a sign of approval, the Speaker then said, *"The bil agreed"* and returned it to the Secretary of the House. It is then brought to the Senate who after having approved it send it on to the Governor. He, by signing it, gives it his approval and the resolution then has the force of law; if he disapproves, he sends it back to the House with his comments. If after that two thirds of those in each House call for the same resolution, then it becomes law without the Governor's approval.

The subject of the debates was not of great importance, consequently everything took place very quietly. The Senate also sent to the House of Representatives a motion which had been passed there: whether it were not advisable in view of the sickness that ravaged the city to adjourn. As there was nothing of importance to do and as the time of the new elections was approaching, they adjourned *sine die*. Before they dispersed, the Speaker signed, for each one of the members present, an order on the Treasury: each member received three dollars for every day that he had attended the session and, besides, the money needed to return home. The evening of the same day I met several members returning home on horseback with a little portmanteau behind. One must say that, while this country has Representatives travelling in this way, there is nothing to fear neither from corruption nor tyranny. N.B. General Mifflin, Governor of Pennsylvania, [3] resembles our Zakrzewski [3] so closely that he might be mistaken for him.

Meanwhile *the Yellow fever*,[4] the debates on its origin, the disputes among the doctors about the best way to treat it, the proclamations of the government, the unseemly quarrels of the newspapers, all these afflicted Philadelphia in the most cruel fashion. The alarums were indeed greater than the disease. Thirty-six thousand inhabitants have left the city, the streets deserted or their emptiness interrupted by funeral processions. Doctor Rush⁵ urged Kośc[iuszko] to leave. General White⁶ and General Gates,⁷ his old friends, pressed him with letter after letter to come to see them. We decided to leave the city.

New Brunswick is only 65 miles from Philadelphia, which makes 16¼ miles, counting 4 English to one Polish mile.⁸ An agreement was finally reached with difficulty for a carriage with two horses at 32 dollars or 16 ducats. When it came to pay for the room, it was even worse. The agreement had been ten dollars per principal and five for the servant per week. Mrs. Lonsson⁹ found a way, however, to make us pay 50 dollars for 12 days. One can judge from this the excessively high prices of the country.

We left Philadelphia Wednesday morning at 6 o'clock, 30th of August. It is not by passing through a country in a carriage that one can know it or claim to give an exact description of it. I restrict myself to noting down here the impression which its appearance, in general, and a few objects in particular, have made on me. The cultivation of the land, the buildings, all in fact recall a recent era when civilized man first began to inhabit this country. Everything here is new; everything appears to have been made as if yesterday. The roads are not yet maintained by the government and their state, excellent or poor, depends on the seasons. The towns consist for the most part of only one street, more or less long. I saw there some craftsmen and some little shops stocked with basic commodities. It is also very common that *gentilmen* farmers have their houses in these little towns and supervise every day their farms which are situated only a short distance away. One sees a very large number of these country houses all around Philadelphia; they are for the most part of wood, built in a manner both light and elegant. All of them are [4] painted white, with green blinds which give them a very gay air. One never sees here as in England the lawns, the pretty gardens filled with flowers, the plants and the bushes, whose different shades of green have such a pleasing effect on the eye; neither does one see here that extreme care in their upkeep. Everything appears here to tend only toward usefulness; there are no parks; the houses are surrounded by orchards which lead to fields covered with Indian corn, wheat, buckwheat, etc.

Everywhere one sees with pleasure the astonishing and rapid progress of man's work and his industry. All here is the work of a century. Looking back beyond this the imagination sees only deserts and savages. You never see here, as in Europe, temples, towers, the remains of old Gothic castles, indeed any monuments which carry you back through past centuries and trace for you past eras of barbarism, of feudalism and indeed all those stages through which the human mind has traveled, step by step, until it came, in government as in the arts, to that degree of perfection in which we see it today. The traveler sees and exists only in the present, while in Europe a thousand objects transport his imagination into the past. There he finds much broader fields for remembrances and sweet reveries.

Aften ten miles we passed by Frankfort,[10] a little town of about 60 houses situated on a clear *creek*. The bridge [11] over it is rather pretty and well built. The houses are all new and of wood. Further on we stopped at Washington tavern [12] to refresh our horses. There we met a family driven from Philadelphia by the yellow fever, who had come to seek refuge. The innkeeper had profited greatly from their distress: he had charged them 50 piasters a week for only two small rooms not including food, etc. We continued on our way up to Bristol, passing always through flat country dotted with farms; the fields were covered with Indian corn more often than with any other grain. In the middle of wheat and buckwheat, they plant in alternate rows pear trees, peaches, but especially apple trees. During winter cider [5] is the common drink of the country, as water mixed with rum is during the summer. The immense and ancient forests with which this country was entirely covered before the arrival of the Europeans have given way to thickets. This is no longer a wilderness, but these are small and attractive woods—black woods as we call them.[13] I have not seen many fir trees; cedars appear to take their place. The most common tree is the oak, of which one can count at least ten species. There are some similar to ours, and others whose leaves are much longer, more slender and serrated—*rovera* [14] or green oaks, etc. After the oak, the *chesnoot* is the most common; all these trees are intertwined with festoons of wild vine.

We arrived for dinner in Bristol, a small town built on a high bank of the Dellavare. If the country through which we have passed up to now, covered completely with Indian corn and fruit trees which bound the horizon on every side, has not presented a single vista of any extent over which the eye might gaze; if the country was too overladen and consequently somber, nothing can be compared to the beauty and gaiety of the situation of Bristol. The Dellavare flows here in all its majesty. It is extremely wide and its waters are clear and limpid.

The town of Bourlingtown [Burlington] situated on the opposite bank in the state of New Jersey enlivens this countryside so rich, widespread, and varied. A few vessels of 60 tons were in port; several boats were crossing the river, their passengers, for the most part, those who had walked from Philadelphia, refugees, like so many others in the

Fig. 12. View of the bridge at Frankfort near Philadelphia in 1797. From Robert Gilmor, "Memorandums . . . 1797 with views from Pen-Sketches by the Author." By courtesy of the Trustees of the Boston Public Library.

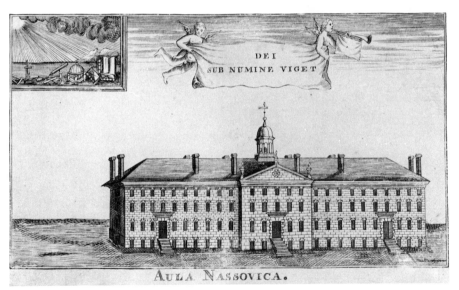

Fig. 13. Oldest known view (1760) of Nassau Hall, Princeton. Courtesy of Princeton University Library.

Fig. 14. View of New Brunswick (c. 1795). From an original pen and ink drawing by Archibald Robertson with his manuscript key. Courtesy of Manuscript Division, New York Public Library, Emmet, 2756.

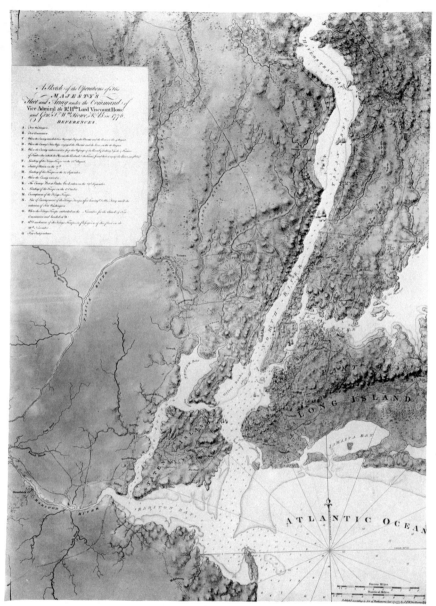

Fig. 15. Sketch of Operations of His Majesty's Fleet and Army (1776).
Courtesy of Prints Division, New York Public Library.

List of Votes for Members of the Legislative Council, Members of Assembly, and Sheriff, for the County of Essex.

FOR COUNCIL.

	John Condit.	Wm. Crane.
Newark,	903	763
Elizabeth-Town,	28	758
Acquackanonk,	315	54
Spring field,	812	80
Wessfield,	31	265
Total,	1390	1297

FOR ASSEMBLY.

	Baldwin,
Newark,	871
Elizabeth-Town,	775
Acquackanonk,	387
Spring field,	311
Wessfield,	138
Total,	2234

(Stanbery, Speer, Pennington, Wade columns)

	Baldwin,	Stanbery,	Speer,	Pennington,	Wade,
Newark,	871	778	175	173	
Elizabeth-Town,	775	36	771	752	
Acquackanonk,	387	97	122	37	
Spring field,	311	308	288	33	22
Wessfield,	138	14	16	289	152
Total,	2234	1328	1208	1304	1154

FOR SHERIFF.

	James Hedden.	Thomas Ward.
Newark,	313	720
Elizabeth-Town,	726	10
Acquackanonk,	75	88
Spring field,	30	307
Wessfield,	272	24
Total,	1466	1149

Whole number of votes in each township, viz. Newark, 1074; Elizabeth-Town, 816; Acquackanonk, 166; Springfield, 344; Wessfield, 393. Whole number of votes given in the county, 2701.

From the above it will be seen, that JOHN CONDIT, Esq. is chosen to represent this County of Essex in the Legislative Council of this state.—That JONAS WADE, WILLIAM S. PENNINGTON, & RECOMPENCE STANBERY, are elected Members of Assembly—and that JAMES HEDDEN is chosen Sheriff.

List of Votes for the same Officers in Morris County.

	Total;
Pequanock,	501
Roxbury,	899
Hanover,	
Mendham,	
Morris,	

Council.
Chilion Ford, 49 43 46 172 191—501
Ab. Kitchell, 271 121 281 187 187 59—899

Assembly.
Aar. Kitchell, 319 137 326 263 16—1232
Silas Condict, 272 176 28—851
David Welsh, 268 118 231 168 55—840

---

being his colleagues, although the lad was not run in the same ticket. The issue of the election in this county is another lesson to the republicans of the importance of the exertion of every individual on the day of election. It is through union we are too often beaten.—Exertion and union will always insure success.

FOR THE CENTINEL.

THE FREEDOM OF ELECTION.

A NEW SONG.

To the Tune of—The Battle of the Kegs.

NEW-JERSEY hail!—thrice happy state!
thy genius still befriends thee;
The Arts obedient round thee wait,
and Science still attends thee:
In freedom's cause you gain'd applause,
and nobly spurn'd subjection;
You're now the Oracle of Laws,
and Freedom of Election!

Let Democrats, with senseless prate,
maintain the foster fox, sir;
Should ne'er with politics of state
their gentle minds perplex, sir:
Such vulgar prejudice we scorn;
their fox is no objection:
New trophies shall our brows adorn,
by Freedom of Election!

What tho' we read, in days of yore,
the woman's occupation,
Was to direct the wheel and loom,
not to direct the nation:
This narrow-minded policy
by us hath met derision;
While woman's bound, man can't be free,
nor have a fair Election.

This ray of light, which shines so bright,
beam'd first upon that land, sir,
Where David lately prophesy'd,
and gave us God's command, sir;
He did declare, with solemn air,
Melovial state was near, sir!
Strange things, and new, should strike our view,
and lo! it doth appear, sir.

Oh! must parade those widows maid!
some marching cheek by jole, sir;
In flags, or chair, some beat the air,
and press'd on to the Pole, sir!
While men of rank, who play'd this prank,
beat up the widows' quarters:
Their hands they laid on every maid,
and scarce spar'd wives, or daughters!

This precious clause of faction laws
we shortly will amend, sir;
And woman's rights, with all our might,
we'll labour to defend, sir!
To Congress, to ...

A Mr. C. who was candidate for a member of the Assembly for Morris County, and a federal *republican*, happening in company with Messrs. B. and D. who are federalists *only*, D. observed to B. that he expected that C. would gain the ensuing election; why P demanded B. because, replied D. "all the negroes in our quarter are engaged for him, for they say he is in favor of freedom." "I perceive (says C.) that your negroes are more in favor of *freedom* than their masters."

Subscriptions for the relief of the poor of Philadelphia, are earnestly solicited by the commissioners, who have already expended the 10,000 dollars granted by the Legislature. Several individuals, we are happy to say, have contributed liberally. The compassionate belonging to that place, and remaining there, a few days ago presented to the commissioners for the use of the sick, near two thousand dollars, in addition to former donations. It is difficult to say why the distresses of that unfortunate capitol, the Athens of America, has not already claimed some attention for the relief of its sick, from the adjoining and sister states.

EXPLICIT AND IMPORTANT.

Letter from the Minister of the Marine and of the Colonies, to an American Merchant, dated the 10th Floreal, April 30, containing a solution of two questions on the decree of the 12th Ventose.

"I have examined, citizen, the questions which you have proposed to me by your letter of the 7th of last month. These questions are reduced to two, viz.

"1. Are American vessels good prizes when they have not on board the Role d'Equipage prescribed by the 9th article of the regulations of the 6th July, 1778?

"2. In case they are, is any thing but the vessel a prize?

"On the first question, the executive directory has many times, in a manner the most formal, promulgated for the affirmative, particularly by its decree of the 12th Brumaire last, in approbation of a report which was made by the minister of justice, on the capture of the ship Royal Captain, and this decision of the executive directory is in every point conformable to the stipulations of the treaty of the 6th of Feb. 1778, which the Americans may and ought to refer to.

"In effect, the articles 25 and 27 of this treaty require, that there ought to be found on board of every American vessel, a passport or sea-letter, conformable to the form which is joined to it, on constituting this form, it will there be seen, that the captain engages himself to deliver to the officers of the marine, in the ports where he may enter, a list, signed and affirmed to by witnesses, containing the names, surnames, and the places of birth and residence of the crew. Every American vessel ought therefore to have on board a passport ...

---

without merit, tools, adapted by nature to the burden of tyranny, are impatient under a want of decorum; and, from the bloody anti-chamber of Robespierre, have transferred themselves into the interest of the vagabond court of Louis 18th, watching for the moment when to renew their infamous guillotinings, robberies, and murders. These are the wretches who would transfer the majesty of the French people to an individual infect called a king. But France is alive to her real interests; and after having vanquished the universe, and broken the despotic chains of 14 centuries, she will not easily be allured into the bondage of Egyptian task-masters. They who count upon such a visionary event, will certainly be deceived. Royalty is vanished like a dream—Men wonder how they have been so long deceived.—The Republic is fixed on a firm basis, and, while virtuous, may it be eternal."

The latest accounts from Philadelphia average the deaths at about *fourteen* every 24 hours. The deaths in Baltimore, at the last dates, including the suburbs, did not exceed *five* or *six*, during the same term.

[From a New-London Paper.]

It is said that a certain reverend gentleman in this city, who has a short time since presented with a fine pair of twins, has in his possession a pumpkin, raised on his ground this season, which is eight feet in length. While his wine and fig-tree were so fruitful, who could desire an increase of salary?

TANGIERS, July 10.

The Emperor of Morocco, Muly Solyman, has marched for Rebat, with a body of sixty-three thousand cavalry, and is to be joined on his march by his brother, Prince Muley Taib, with another body of thirty-five thousand horse, when they are to proceed together to Morocco, with a view to depose their brother Bendrick. These *fraternal* visits are likely to occasion the effusion of much kindred blood.

ELIZABETH-TOWN, October 4.

KOSCIUSKO.

On Friday last arrived in this town, that warm friend to liberty and mankind, Gen. Kosciusko. He makes a stay of some time in this place.

By yesterday's Eastern Mail.

NEW-YORK, October 17.

PUBLIC ENTRY.

Agreeably to notice, a detachment of cavalry, and about 130 private gentlemen on horseback, rode out to Haerlem yesterday morning, and escorted JOHN ADAMS, President of the United States, into the town. This procession was joined at the Bull's Head, by a detachment of ...

TOO much credit cannot be given to the *Fœderal* ladies of Elizabeth, for the heroic virtue displayed on Wednesday last, in gallantly advancing in a body to the poll to support their favorite candidates. It is a pity that the singular influence of female patriotism should be attended with any ill consequences, but it is said that the husbands and sweethearts of these heroines begin to suspect that some motive other than a love of the federal cause excited the enterprize. It is to be hoped, that this suspicion will not create a resentment that will reach the honorable candidates, who were highly flattered by this Amazonic exertion; and Fortune must be a malicious jade indeed, after all to render it unsuccessful. The ex-ulting *labour* approaching is evident in the most careless observer. The alacrity with which the mourners, and even males, assembled, afforded a transient prospect of immediate relief, but, horrible reverse! aristocratic imbecility gave way to republican vigour, and the hope of the aspiring family was strangled in embryo—the abortion took place on Saturday, at 3 o'clock, P.M. amidst the sighs and groans of the disconsolate friends of good order and good government.

A Correspondent remarks, notwithstanding the impracticality of arbitrary power under which Essex county has for a long time laboured, it must now appear incontestably that they are the friends and patrons of *Equality*, since no less than seventy-five women were polled at the late election in a neighbouring borough. The *Rights of Man* have been warmly inlisted on by Tom Paine and other democrats, but we outstrip them in the science of government, and not only preach the *Rights of Women*, but boldly push it into practice—Madame Wolstonecrafte has certainly the merit of broaching this subject, and as women are now to take a part in the jurisprudence of our state, we may shortly expect to see them *take the helm* of government.

A Correspondent congratulates his fellow-citizens of Essex county upon the issue of the late election. For some years past the republicans of this county have not been represented in assembly, viz. they have not been represented by men of their choice. They will now have, is is presumed, a very satisfactory representation—William S. Pennington is a firm Republican; and we have good reason to believe, that Jonas Wade and Recompence Stanbery are worthy of government.

And welcome in the *peaceful* scene,
Of government in petticoats!!!

For the CENTINEL.

THE AUTUMNAL RACES.

NOW th' autumnal heats are past,
The fed'ral steeds the race have lost;
That flying shot, that random guess,
That fed'ral nags would win the race,
Was vainly made; the scribbler knew
That *Brigadier* would never do
To run the heats; he may be smart
When harness'd to a cartman's cart
To drag down loads of Irishmen,
Those voters, bought at Pautert..n,
To provide a keg of Yankee rum,
To treat them on their journey home.
Not long since, true fed'ral jolt,
Was coupled with a Yankee Colt;
In such foul play may act a part,
It's quite a vain, but fed'ral art.
Behold! *Mercantile Sandy Mane*,
Brought forward by the fed'ral train;
He ne'er could run New Market rout,
Without a halter to his snout;
His wind was poor, his keeper knew,
But vainly hop'd that he would do,
Tail'd fast behind old Col'nel Blue.
When True Blue's wind began to fail,
The presageing kidnap'd all females;
The fair ones came, with marshal pride,
On fix great nags, mounted astride,
Obedient to their leader's word;
A curious novel to record.
In th' autumnal heats, the four who won,
Were Democrat, Republican.
True Democrat, that active horse,
As ever started on the course;
He is of true Republic blood,
For Freedom he has always stood;
Bright gallant Roan, from Orange Dale,
Old one ey'd Bay, and Silver Tail;
Tho Silver Tail, cock-weather kind,
He tried his coat, so came behind.

* It is painful to remark, that the whole Borough of Elizabeth should be thus duped at elections by a few leading characters there.

The power and cunning of *teachers* are dangerous; they may imbibe *pernicious* political tenets into the tender minds of the rising generation. Something on this important subject, vide first page.

very simple principles; one, that every vessel which has not on board neither passport nor Role d'Equipage, is reputed an enemy: the other, that in the terms of the seventh articles of the third book, title nine, of the ordonnance of 1781, merchandizes belonging to neutral, or even Frenchmen, which are found in an enemy's vessel, are a good prize.

"Thus no doubt remains but the cargo of every American vessel, on board which, there shall not be found neither a passport nor Role d'Equipage in proper form, ought to be confiscated.—This opinion is, as I have stated before, conformably to what has been decided by the Executive Directory, and it is that of the minister of justice, whom I have particularly consulted on these two questions."   TRUGUET.'

His Holiness the Pope is said to have been immortalizing himself by giving his assent to the abolition of the inquisition in Spain.

A letter from a *respectable American, et Pour-deaux*, dated *August* 8, states the following information.

"That the Minister of the Interior had sent to the Municipality of Bourdeaux, intelligence of the expected arrival of two new envoys from America. That, in the event of their arriving at that port, every possible honor was to be shewn them, and their journey to Paris rendered every way convenient and agreeable."

Extract of a letter from Paris, dated August 6.

"The turn of observation in this capital cannot but smile, when they read in the English, and some American, papers, *serious apprehensions* of a revolution in this country, in favor of royalty. Men of influence and property, under the old government, no doubt wish and desire it, and it is perfectly natural for them so to do. They have sense enough, however, to see that a counter-revolution cannot now be effected without a profusion of blood; and it is beyond a doubt, that active counter-revolutionists would be the first victims on the occasion. The fact is, as I see things here, the whole energy of the present citizenship of France is to linked in with the cause of the revolution, and a republican form of government, that an effort no less than that of the *united nation* could overset the republican system. I see nobody here wishing, or wanting, a change of the government, but a parcel of harpies and vultures, bred in indolence, the drones of the hive, the burden of society, who wish to subsist on the labour of the industrious; and, as of old, be fed and supported from the spendthrift table of monarchy. These animals of royalty, born

says, in his communication, that his avocations were his premier duty: but yet, if it had been to defend the invaded liberties of his country, he would have turned out with the utmost alacrity.

MARRIED—Last evening, by the Rev. Dr. Macwhorter, Mr. NEHEMIAH WARD, of Bloomfield, to Miss LYDIA NUTMAN, of this town.

The MEDICAL LECTURES *in the University of Pennsylvania are postponed until the last Monday in November.*

LOST,

A SHORT time since, a bundle of EXE-CUTIONS. The most of which were granted by Robert Wade, Esq. and the remainder by John Lindlly, Esq. Whoever may have found them, and will return them to the subscriber, shall receive his thanks, and a reasonable allowance for his trouble.
JOSEPH ROBERTS, *Constable.*
Camp-Town, *October* 17, 1797.   55-3w.

Taken up astray,

ON Thursday morning last, in a field back of Col. Samuel Ogden's mill, in this town, a dark bay MARE, about fourteen hands high. She has a narrow white streak in her face, and the hair round her feet is black. She is supposed to be the mare that broke from a person at the Toll-house on the Newark bridge, on was on his way to New-York, the preceding evening. The owner (whoever he may be) is informed, that he can have his mare by proving her to be his, and paying the charges which have and may accrue.   JAMES ACKERMAN.
Newark, *October* 18, 1797.   55-tf

FOUR DOLLARS REWARD.

RAN AWAY from the subscriber about four weeks since, a boy by the name of MAT-THEW HARRISON: he had on when he went away, a white hat, long blue coat, a pair of gingham trowlers, and clasps in his shoes: He is of a dark complexion and has black hair, and was learning the Tanning and Shoe-making business. Whoever will take up the said boy and return him to the subscriber, or lodge him in El-fex goal, shall have the above reward, and be paid all reasonable charges.
JONATHAN KEEN.
Newark, *October* 18, 1797.   55 3w.

Fig. 17. New York from Hobuck Ferry House, New Jersey. Robertson-Jukes view, 1800. Courtesy of Prints Division, New York Public Library.

Fig. 18. State Prison on the Bank of the North River in Greenwich Village, New York. Courtesy of The New-York Historical Society, New York City.

Fig. 19. A Plan of the City of New York (1797). Courtesy of Prints Division, New York Public Library.

Fig. 20. A View of Broad Street, Wall Street and the City Hall (1797). Courtesy of Prints Division, New York Public Library.

countryside. I was angry to have missed Mr. Suttcliff [15] who had left
here only this morning. As compensation we had the company of the
Spanish Consul, an excellent conversationalist who has discovered that
there is no country in the world more free or happier than that of
Biscay. We dined with a former commissioner for supplies during the
Revolution. He recounted to us the adversities which he had met,
particularly of a violent wind which had held him back with 300 head
of cattle during three consecutive days without there being any way
of crossing the Dellavare, etc. The dinner without wine cost us two
dollars. We crossed the Dellavare at Trenton, capital of Jersey and famous for the victory which Gl. Washington [6] had won there over the
Hessians, a success which revived the hope and courage of the Americans disheartened by so many reverses. It is at Trentown that the
Dellavare ceases to be navigable. The passers-by can see there the
falls, which obstruct navigation.

Princetown is notable only for its college, which is a building
erected before the Revolution and rather large. We arrived at night
in Kingstown, a small market town of about 20 houses. We lodged
in a very good inn kept by a family of Dutch descent but who have
lost entirely the use of their mother tongue. Opposite was a rather
striking house. It belonged, so I was told, to an old sailor who, having
braved the seas for nearly 30 years, had finally the good sense to enjoy
the fruit of his labors in tranquility and retirement. He had bought a
house and nearly 300 acres for about 4,000 pounds sterling. This land
is worked by four men; to each he pays nearly 40 pounds sterling,
not counting provisions for them and their family. In the evening the
sailor's *parlor* was lighted and the shutters were opened; I could distinguish the whole family gathered in a room furnished with neatness
and taste. It consisted of a father, mother and four children, of whom
the eldest was already quite grown up. After the many storms, labors
and dangers that this man had faced, how sweet the rest, which he
enjoys there in the midst of his family, must appear to him. We had
a very good supper and a good lodging; all this for 1½ dollars.

31 August. The next day we continued our route and at ten o'clock
arrived at New Brunswick; we alighted and went into the house of
General White.

Brunswick is situated on very low ground. For this country the
town is rather large, far from the great cities and surrounded by a
countryside fairly well populated and fertile. Supplies are offered here
at a better price than elsewhere. The Raritan river, navigable for boats
of 60 tons, affords a convenient waterway. It empties its waters into
the sea at Amboy, 9 miles from Brunswick. Amboy, although very

well situated and in spite of the attentions of the government, has never become a commercial town; the too great proximity to New York will always be an impediment. All the commerce of Jersey is carried on therefore through the intermedium of New York and Philadelphia. It must, indeed, be considerable and the [7] agriculture flourishing, since the countryside everywhere shows well-cultivated land, towns growing rapidly, and the inhabitants living in the greatest comfort. This whole region contains countless iron mines; everywhere the ground is dark red. Even outstandingly good copper mines have been found, but the lack of hands and their excessive cost stands in the way of their exploitation. This will be so until there are more hands than the cultivation of the soil requires; at that time the excess of the population will turn towards industry, i.e., towards mills, factories, mining, etc. This period appears still far distant. Men appear here to prefer agriculture to all other means of existence. They prefer personal ownership to all other ways of making money, however profitable they may be. As a state becomes populous, the excess population go to seek settlement in the regions which are not yet cultivated. The North and the *West* offer them wild uncultivated tracts which in spite of the flood of emigrants from Europe will not be populated for a long time. In spite of this there are actually seven iron mines and two furnaces which produce annually 400 tons of iron and 540 of *bar Iron*. Along the sea coast, by digging down about fifty feet you come to *the Salt Marsh* or a swampy and salt terrain; there are often found there shells of enormous oysters as well as the skeletons of gigantic animals called Monmuth [Mammoth?].[15a]

Gl. White's house is situated on higher ground and at some distance from the town. The Gl. having become involved with a fraudulent speculator has lost a large part of his fortune. He lives, so they say, only on that of his wife. The poor state of his affairs has changed him from a man, formerly most lively and sociable, today, into one often very pensive and glum. Trouble has empoisoned his domestic bliss; his farm is considerably neglected and he gains from it only that needed for the maintenance of his family and of his slaves. In the house there is less order than one ordinarily sees in America. One sees everywhere a spirit of discontent and discouragement. So true is it that affluence, an income above one's needs, exerts the principal influence on the well-being of man.

Mrs. White, born in Charles Town in New Carolina, although nearly 30 years old, which is a great deal in this country, can still be taken for a beauty. She has the largest and the most beautiful black eyes that one could see. In them one sees shining all the fire of the south. Because she is tall, her plumpness, without being a detraction gives her a great air of majesty. [8] Her eyes shine with all the fires of the South. Her only daughter, Liza, five years old, is a spoiled child as are most American children. One hears her say sometimes to her mother, *"You damn'd bitsh."* The least inconvenience that she encounters makes unhappiness for the whole household. Mrs. White was asked on one occasion, if she had to choose between the two misfortunes to lose her husband or her daughter, which would she prefer, "to keep my daughter" she answered without hesitation and in the presence of her husband.

Can it be true that a single stallion that the General owns brings in perhaps more than his farm of 200 acres? He paid 1,800 dollars for it; he hires it out to cover and takes 10 dollars for each occasion. The stallion has served one hundred and more mares in a single summer; the income therefore is 1,000 dollars. He had another stallion which he sold for 2,000 dollars; such is the excessive costliness of good horses here. The one which remains with him is quite beautiful, white, and resembling more a Polish than an English horse.

3 7b. Sunday the 3rd September I was at divine service in the Presbyterian church. The bareness of Protestant churches always displeases me. Their form of worship is deprived of all that can touch the heart or strike the senses; no music, no pomp of any sort. The pastor indulges in many affectations, with his eyes closed and in a voice half quavering and half gasping with fervor, he says *let us pray.* He delivers a prayer of his own composition generally in imitation of the Psalms, but far from their sublime and moving simplicity. A Psalm is then sung, then they pray, he reads the gospel, again a Psalm, and again a prayer, and a sermon. All this lasts almost three hours. The sermon was more metaphysical than moral. I do not know if the preacher himself understood it very well.

In Brunswick as everywhere in America one does not see any poverty, for every man who wants to work is sure to earn enough to live on and still have something to put aside. Not only did I not see in the church one single person in rags as at home, but no one was even badly dressed. Equality ordained by the law is upheld as much as it should and can be, that is to say that the law is the same for everybody both as it protects and as it punishes. Wealth and public office give some distinction, that is to say the persons of this class better suited to each other by education and wealth keep together and mix little with the rest. However, [9] in the course of daily life everyone is on the most perfect footing of equality. The poorest farmer, the day worker, even the domestic never raise their hats to the richest man.

They always claim the title of *Sir*. In spite however of law and customs, vanity, the wish to be conspicuous, to raise oneself above one's equals breaks through even here. As there are no titles of Prince, Count, Baron, etc., they take great care to retain the military titles bestowed during the Revolution. One says then General such and such, Colonel, Major, etc., or in civil life, *Governor*, Judge, *Doctor such and such a one.*

The principal personages in Brunswick are Gl. White, Colonel Bayard,[16] Judge Patersson [17] and a lawyer named [blank]. All these families are related and live in close contact. They take turns in giving dinner parties and teas. I was invited to one such. The meal consists of the following. The first course, two or three roast capons with a sauce of butter, cooked oysters, etc., a roast beef, some boiled mutton, some fish or a ham. The second course a *Pouding* or tart or *Custards* or blanc-manger and some preserves. The tablecloth is removed and fruits, almonds, grapes, *chesnuts* and wine are then served. One drinks the health of the President, the Vice-President, and Congress. The ladies retire; the gentlemen remain for hours in order to chat and drink toasts. Finally they join the ladies and take coffee and tea.

I have begun to read the History of the American Revolution. There are two of them, one by Dr. Ramsay [18] very well written as to style, the other by Gordon [19] more voluminous, perhaps diffuse but full of very interesting anecdotes and containing all the facts. What thoughts they bring to the reader's mind! It appears that Providence and the stupidity of the English Generals strove more for the Americans than their own valor and zeal. One sees this particularly in all that took place on Long Island and New York Island. Gl. Washington, following the judgment of his council, undertook to defend Long Island. An army was sent there. Gl. Green,[20] who should have been the commander, fell ill. Gl. Sullivan [21] took the command. He let himself be surprised by the English. The army should have been entirely defeated in crossing the river in order to make their way to New York Island. A thick fog arose covering the retreat and at the moment when all the army and its baggage had passed, the fog lifted. Gl. Mifflin rendered the greatest service there. Gl. Howes,[22] instead of having the fleet and the army come down [10] by the North River and instead of closing the crossing at Kingsbridge, and consequently surrounding all the American forces on the Island of New York, thus terminating the war with a single blow, followed the Americans along the side of Long Island, amused himself by sniping at them and giving Washington time to cross into New Jersey. Gl. Howe sent Lord Cornwallis [23] in pursuit and ordered him not to push further than Brunswick. The

Americans were discouraged; the militia were deserting. Washington did not have 3,000 men. Cornwallis would have been able to wipe him out, but he could not go against his orders. At Trentown a boat that the English had hidden badly and which the Americans burned, slowed up their progress even more and completely delivered the Republicans from their final downfall. The surprise of the Hessians at Trentown gave them courage and caused the militia to return. The battles of Princetown and Germantown seasoned them. What cowardice, indifference, patience, and courage can one not find in the conduct of the Americans! At one time they fled at a single shot; at another they deserted their flags by thousands, and then one sees them fight as most hardened troops and endure the greatest labors, the greatest privations, misery, and hunger as true heroes. In the number of fortunate accidents for America must be counted the interception of a letter of the English minister containing the plan of attack on Charles Town.[24] They knew in time how to defend it.

Many of my mornings in Brunswick were devoted to the hunt. I rather like this exercise but having left the countryside at the age of 13 and seeing very little of it since, I have not had the occasion to follow it. It is very healthy for the body, distracts the mind; the upshot, we enjoy a pleasure bound up with the sensation of our own skill, etc. Hunting in America is very tiring because of the infinite number of hedges. All the properties, all the fields are protected by them as much to secure the ownership as to preserve them from damage by animals. All means are used to keep the latter out of the fields. All the pigs, sheep, what shall I say, even all the geese carry on their necks long sticks tied in triangles which prevent them from passing through the hedges.

One morning I visited Dr. Bitsh [Beach] [25] who lives four miles from Brunswick. [11] The road leading to his farm is the most picturesque that one could hope to see. There is, to the right, the Raritan river which continues on receding into the far distance. One sees at the far end a bridge and beyond that the river appears to lose itself in the bushy thickets of dark green. The two banks are covered with farms and orchards. The house of Dr. Bitsh is very simple and rustic, surrounded not simply by an orchard but a forest of peach, pear and apple trees. The good pastor took Lieut. Boot [26] and me there. We saw branches of peach trees which, overburdened by the weight of the fruit, had broken off and were strewn on the ground. What fecundity! The family of the pastor consisted of two or three young women of marriageable age. All appeared most happy in their retreat.

9 7br. We left Brunswick Saturday 9th of September to go to Gl.

Gates. We passed through flat countryside, cultivated and inhabited as that [illegible] on the way from Philadelphia. Springfield, Elizabeth Town and Newark are the little towns that one comes to along the way; I shall speak at greater length of these on our return. After having crossed the salt marsh and a dike many miles long we arrived very late at night in Hobock.[27] We found the inn filled with sailors and other gentlemen, vagabonds, all a little drunk and in very good spirits. They were dancing in a room below. I saw a dance absolutely identical to that of our Polish Jews. We had to go without supper for everything had been eaten, to sleep in bad beds, and the next day to pay exorbitantly.

Sunday morning the 10th of September the view of the beautiful North River, the towers of the city of New York recompensed me a little for the bad lodging. Thanks to a good breeze and the tide we crossed the river in a sail boat; this cost us 10 shillings. It is quite dear, but at least those who are responsible for your embarkation and disembarkation and who have taken no little trouble with our carriage and baggage did not ask for a tip as in Europe and particularly in Italy. The *bonna manzia* and the *Trinkgeld* are almost unknown in America. We disembarked above the New Jail [28] and avoided in that way the trouble of passing through the town.

After travelling for two miles along a road bordered with country houses and gardens we were shown a gate which led us to the house of Gl. Gates, and soon we found ourselves before a very beautiful facade of Corinthian columns which formed the peristyle of the General's house. We found on the threshold [12] the conqueror of Saratoga. He is a 75 year-old man, but still quite vigorous, urbane and remarkably high spirited for his age. Except for the battle of Cambden, Fortune has smiled on him throughout his whole life. He was born in England and was for a long time in the British service. In the Revolution he warmly embraced the American side and was appointed a General at the very beginning. When peace came, besides the emoluments and land which were [awarded?] him by Congress, he also received from the State of Virginia a really immense stretch of land. The sale of all this brought him a rather large capital. It was further increased by his marriage to M. [blank] [29] who brought him quite a decent fortune.

In Mrs. Gates this old man possesses a real treasure. She is a woman of 50 with a still attractive figure and with the most happy disposition that one could hope to see. She alone could bring cheer to the sadness and the frailties of one so late in life. From the way which this couple live together, the little quarrels, jokes, and jealousies which prevail between them, one would say that this is the first year of a marriage of two people 20 years old. Gl. Gates is not less happy in his monetary affairs. The farm that he occupies, situated 3 miles from New York, contains nearly 200 acres, a magnificent house, orchards, vegetable gardens, fields, etc. Everything is there. The land belongs to a Mr. Kruger,[30] an extremely rich merchant and one who believes he can never be rich enough. His speculative greed has led him to make the worst bargain that ever was made. Counting on the advanced age of Gl. Gates and believing Madame equally close to the grave he leased the land for the lifetime of one or the other in consideration of 5,000 dollars. What was his astonishment when he later saw Mrs. Gates, then only 40 years old and enjoying the best possible health.

It is 7 years since Mr. and Mrs. Gates began to enjoy the house and land.[31] They have retained for themselves only the orchard, the kitchen garden, and enough pasture for 6 cows and 3 horses. They rent out the rest for about 300 pounds in such a way that, some time ago they had already regained their capital. They have a man in their service who takes care of all their business; they give him 200 dollars a year and all the provisions he needs. The rest of the household consists of a negro, a woman cook, and a negro woman servant, all free however; Gl. Gates having freed all his slaves.

[13] During the whole time that we stayed with Gl. Gates we had innumerable visits after dinner. It is impossible for me to remember all of them. I will mention only a few. We saw a dozen of the Livingstones male and female; among others Edward and John [32] whose wives, especially the latter, are extremely good-looking. It was at their house that I saw for the first time in America a European style of living, a magnificent carriage, superb horses, the servants in livery. Nothing could be less democratic than their whole style of living. That which the Potockis [33] are in Poland, the Livingstons are in the state of New York, that is to say a family excessively numerous and rich in landed property. I have been assured that between them they have as many as 600 tenants or farmers dependent on them. One can decide oneself whether they have the upper hand in the elections. They are sworn enemies of the present Governor of New York, Mr. Jay,[34] and, since he is in the good graces of the government, that is enough to throw the Livingstons into opposition. How many times frustrated ambition does make men vulgar and ranting.

We were visited also by the numerous family of the Staversons,[35] the Misses Brooms,[36] Miss Johson, niece of Mr. Smith of Baltimor,[37] Mrs. Winnings [38] of Dellavare, a very good-looking young woman, very interesting, who sings and sketches, etc., and who with all these qualities is much to be pitied on account of her husband who is a libertine, spending his life with negresses and neglecting her in every way; Miss Nickelson,[39] etc. We had for neighbors Mr. and Mrs. Wilette.[40] Mme. is a celebrated chess player having spirit and education, but for a Quaker a little too fond of the town. Mr. Willete, a good man, is extremely attached to country life and to his garden which he cultivates with his own hands; Mr. Brigide,[41] eternal braggart, a silly fool.

Mr. Krugers, of whom I have spoken and who leased his land to Gl. Gates, married for the second time, in a very extraordinary fashion, a young woman [42] from the West Indies. While returning from the West Indies he found himself by chance on the same boat [14] as this young girl. Mr. Krugers fell madly in love and asked for her hand. The young woman, either from lack of inclination or because she could not believe that a rich old man would seriously consider a penniless young girl, refused him continually. Krugers, seeing that all his entreaties were in vain, swore to himself that he would never return to port unless he obtained her consent. He ordered the Cpt. at the same time to tack about at the whim of the winds without ever approaching the shore. Fifteen days passed in this way until finally the beauty, tired of the sea, promised to marry him. Landing on shore she kept her word and became the most exemplary wife that there ever was. A terrible misfortune later poisoned her peace. She had two daughters one of whom, 7 years old, enjoyed all her love. One day she was slightly indisposed by a little headache and a cough. The mother made her lie down and brought her some medicine. The little one showed a great repugnance in taking it. She defended herself as well as she could until threatened and forced by her mother she swallowed it. Immediately she was seized by convulsions and the most acute pains. Her mother, astonished by her state, examined the vial. What was her pain and despair when she saw that the medicine that she had forced her beloved daughter to swallow was none other than corrosive sublimate. The little one lived only a few hours. The mother has remained since that time in the blackest melancholy which nothing can dispel.

There are many French who have sought refuge in New York and its environs. I have become acquainted with the Duke de Liancourt,[43] cousin of the Duke de Rochefoucault, son of the Duchess d'Anville, who was so shamefully assassinated at the beginning of the Revolution. M. de Liancourt is a very worthy man with a frank and open face, who inspires confidence. He has spent many years in the United States and traveled everywhere and appears to have observed well. He has written many volumes on this country and in them has gone into [15] the greatest detail. It is said to be a very meticulous and interesting work. He has left for Hamburg expecting to obtain permission to return to France, where probably he will publish his book.

I must not pass in silence over the young Duke d'Orleans and his brothers, Montpensier and Beaujolais.[44] The perverse and ambitious character of their father makes a striking contrast to the honesty and friendliness of the sons. Of all the works of Mme. Genlis [45] these young people are unquestionably the best. She has prepared them to support with courage the immense losses that they have undergone, the exile and the privations to which they are condemned. The eldest has been obliged to support himself in Switzerland in the profession of a teacher of mathematics. The younger ones, after having languished for two years in the prisons in Marseilles, have finally obtained permission to embark for America and rejoin their brother. They have since passed through all the states of the *West* and the North up to the Mississippi and the Ohio. They have with them M. de Montjoye,[46] brother to the Chanoinesse de Mironieuil, an educated and interesting young man. They all traveled on horseback followed by a cabriolet where they rested in turn. They conduct themselves well and express themselves with precision and modesty, and one could not wish for more interesting companions.

The town of New York is situated in the best possible place, both for commerce and for the healthiness of its climate. Facing it is Long Island, separated from the continent by an arm of the sea called the East river; this river brings to it all the products of Connecticut and of Vermont, while the North River, navigable as far as Albany where it takes the name of the Hudson, brings it all the riches of the north. Moreover, the city communicates, by means of a canal already in use between this river and the Mohawk, with Lake Ontario and all the others successively, as far as the most northern parts. Another canal is in use between the same river and Lake St. George and Champlain. Thus by the means of the St. John river which connects with that of the St. Lawrence [16] it opens to it the trade of all Canada, above all in furs. The inhabitants of New York have known how to avail themselves of all these advantages. Their trade is immense. In addition to Europe they send a large number of ships to the East Indies, to China, to New Orleans in the Gulf of Mexico, etc. It is said that New York imports more than Philadelphia but that the export from this latter town is much greater. About two or three years ago (that is to say at the time when the American trade was less restricted by the rapacity of the French pirates) a general spirit of speculation took hold of the inhabitants of New York. Many, in the wink of an eye, made immense fortunes; others in contrast were ruined and find themselves today locked up in prison.

Interest on money has gone up in proportion to the advantage that working capital offers to merchants. They pay 10-20-30 and more per cent. The effect of this capital put thus in circulation, as well as paper money which increases the amount, has led to excessively high prices for everything. A day laborer earns up to a dollar a day; provisions and other commodities are in the same proportion. Those who are in trade or in agriculture are not aware of these exorbitant prices; if they pay dearly, so they sell. But a foreigner who wants to live on his capital will find that even in England he could live with greater means at his disposal, with more pleasures, and many fewer expenses.

One can see the town growing; in the space of three years its population has increased by 10 thousand souls. It is less orderly than Philadelphia, but infinitely more gay. Broad Way is superb, with very beautiful houses on it. Perle Street runs almost across the whole town. Nothing is more cheerful than the part called the Battery. It is an esplanade surrounded by iron railings, which gives on to the canal and looks out on Long Island. One sees there boats passing continually. It is deliciously cool. This is the only promenade in the town. It is a pity that trees were not planted there [17] earlier. Those one sees there are small and too young to give any shade. The public buildings are spacious and rich. One must count amongst them the University, House of Correction, that for the insane, finally the Prison.[47] A new one has been built outside the town. All these institutions existed before the Revolution. The English [Americans] owe much to their old masters; they learnt from them the first rudiments of liberty, of the police and of social order. Liberty, when they fought for it and won it was not something new and strange to them. That is why they have not abused it.

I have seen a few detachments of their militia. The cavalry is very well mounted, very richly dressed, but one should not look at all there for military science. They mount their horses, they parade, they drill in a dilettante manner. The well-to-do citizenry who make up the companies of grenadiers all have uniforms. I have seen a hundred in their everyday clothes with carbines or rifles, each one of a different caliber. In the country many arrive with pistols and even with sticks. These men, in spite of their lack of organization, inspire a very lively interest. The less they possess, the more moving becomes their zeal to defend their homes. It is to be hoped that the legislatures of the different states concern themselves with having arsenals sufficiently well stocked with arms to arm the citizens in case of need. These militia lack a great deal; in times of peace this is an amusement for rich young men, for do they not have officers, flags, trumpets, drums, and fifes without number? In the interior of the country the musters and the drills are much neglected. The rich can get exemption by paying a certain sum.

The old debtor's prison [48] is still in the center of the town. It is filled with those who, having speculated wildly, have lost their fortune and what is worse that of others. Their whole punishment consists in not being able to leave the prison; for the rest, they receive their friends, live sumptuously, provide themselves the pleasures of music, gaming, etc. Surely some distinction should be made between [18] those who have been simply overwhelmed by misfortune and those who by fraud and dishonesty have involved in their misery innocent families. These latter, so it seems to me, should be confined a little more severely. Many times, while passing near the prison, I have [seen?] these gentlemen strolling on the roof, laughing and talking, while a band of musicians played for them airs gay and tender by turn.

It was my good fortune to find in New York Mr. H. Gahn, [49] a young Swede whose family I knew in Stockholm. He is almost settled on this continent, and having received an excellent training, bought a business, and having made good connections in Spain where he has lived, he engages in very lucrative commerce. I found in him that politeness and that wish to be helpful which is characteristic of his countrymen. We went together to the Greenwich Street Theatre. [50] The hall, built hastily of boards, absorbs the voices of the actors. One hears almost nothing. One is being built in stone which should be magnificent; [51] besides, there is another theatre in John Street [52] and a third called the Circus [53] where they have equestrian displays and pantomime. It is there that poor Libiszewski [54] has found a place in the orchestra. He gets ten dollars a week. There are sixteen boxes in the theatre I visited; each one of them bore the name of one of the states of the United States. One is seated in the orchestra pit. The ladies are dressed for the most part in white. I did not notice any differences in their adornment; all appeared to me to be attired without luxury or splendor but with an elegant simplicity. One sees neither rouge, nor gold, nor diamonds. The men are all dressed alike; one sees there a truly democratic equality. Some little urchins in tunics and bare feet ran about the pit bestriding the benches, sitting themselves higgledy-piggledy amongst the elegant of New York. They were playing *the two Rivals* and the farce *the Critic,* both of them by Sheridan. [55] The company was quite good and may be compared to that of Bristol in England.

I was less occupied with the play than with the reflections that the scene excited in me. It was only 150 years ago in this place where today one sees an opulent city, a rich and orderly people [19] and finally an entertainment which could be only to the taste of civilized man; it was only a century and a half ago, I tell myself, that in this place where today there is this hall, one saw only raw nature and savages armed with bows pursuing game. Such is the strength of enlightened and industrious man, aided by a wise liberty, free from the chains of despotism and from the equally annihilating disorder of license and anarchy. In the wink of an eye he changes the deserts into fertile fields and impresses on everything he touches the seal of industry and of civilization.

The environs of New York are filled with the country homes of rich merchants. They have many clubs and once a week they gather for dinner and to spend the day together. Gl. Gates, a member of the Whig Club, took me one Saturday to Hales Gates [Hell's Gate]. We were 24 in number. The rules of the society are to have for dinner only fish and *beefs steaks*, but in compensation much Madeira. This society appears to have as its object only relaxation from the work of the week and spending the day agreeably. They do not discuss anything of substance; they do not even talk about politics or literature. There is reason for keeping silent on the first; it banishes the bitterness of altercations and fosters unity amongst the members. They divide into foursomes; some make parties of whist; the others play a game called [quoits?]. They drive a little stake of iron into the ground; each one of the players has two rings of the same metal. They throw them in turn. In order to win, the ring which is thrown must hook onto the pin. As this happens only rarely, those whose rings are thrown nearest to the pin fifteen times in a row win the money. Not being a player I passed my time gazing upon the awful beauty of the situation of this place.

Hale Gates lies facing Long Island in a place where the arm of the sea called the East river makes many turns filled with reefs which because [20] of their threatening aspect and because of the danger and difficulty of getting past them, has given this place the name, the Gates of Hell. When the tide is high, one sees the current of the river break foaming against them with a horrible crash. It is a very interesting sight—seeing the boats without number and of different sizes rounding these capes and passing through these reefs with astounding caution and dexterity. A single false move could break them into a thousand pieces. The ships which come down the river are, for the most part, from Connecticut and even from Vermont. They are loaded with wood, with cattle, and in general with all sorts of provisions for the city of New York. We returned towards evening. I noticed many places of uncultivated and barren rock. It is on such land that towns should be built and not on fields suitable for cultivation. Hale Gates Club is not the only place to which Gl. Gates took me. Our visits to town were not made solely for the purpose of social calls or to get the latest news. We went to market to buy meat, fish, vegetables, etc. I regarded this venerable old man buying his provisions himself with more respect than I would look on a Russian *Feld marshall* bedecked with his ribbons, giving audience to a pack of his servants in livery.

29 7br. We left the house of Gl. Gates and his kind wife with much regret. After embarking Gl. Kośc[iuszko] with much difficulty we once again embraced Gl. Gates, who had come to escort us to the bank of the North river, and crossed successfully to the other side. Soon we crossed a causeway a Polish mile long built by a company across the salt marshes. Besides two trenches along the side of the embankment they have built many drainage ditches. The hay that these fields produce is very coarse; the cattle feed on it for want of any other; it is also used to fatten them. These marshes [21] stretch out over a great distance. One sees them near Elizabeth Town, as well as on the road from Brunswick alongside the Raritan. Between Newark and New York in the space of 10 miles one crosses two rivers, of which one is the [Hackensack?] and the other the Passaik. They are both navigable for small boats, with waters of extraordinary clarity. They are crossed by two remarkably beautiful bridges. Newark is a very gay little market town and has many beautiful houses. The closeness to New York will make it very flourishing in a short time. From there it is only 6 miles to Elizabeth, where we arrived at noon.[56]

Elizabeth is a charming little town; there is, one might say, only a single street in the middle. Elsewhere one sees houses scattered about here and there, surrounded by weeping willows, gardens, etc. The Presbyterian church has a very tall and slender spire [57] covered with tin plate and is therefore very shiny. Because good architecture and magnificence in buildings, even public buildings, are very little known in this new hemisphere, all the pride of the inhabitants of towns and large villages consists in having high *steepels* on their churches. Who now will have a higher one! The Romans were never more jealous of their Capitol, nor the Athenians of their temple of Minerva than the inhabitants of Elizabeth Town are of their spire. The town is situated two short miles from the river of the same name, by means of which with a favorable wind one can get to New York in an hour and a half. I do not know why the town itself was not located there but that, in the place where it is settled today, there is a *Creek* well suited for running a mill; this was certainly a very important consideration at the time of its foundation and impelled the inhabitants to settle there. The town and the surrounding regions carry on a small export trade with New York. The place itself is inhabited by well-to-do people.

The most numerous family and one connected by marriage with nearly the whole town is the Dayton family.[58] The old general of this name has five sons, of whom four are married [22] and each in turn has his own family. The oldest, who is today the *Speeker* of the House of Representatives in Congress, is the most important personage in the family. More than 6 feet tall, with a Roman nose and features, he has an imposing gravity in his carriage. Successful in his speculations he has made a very large fortune. He is in trade. He owns a big store in New York. The other brothers, Elias and William, have shops in Elizabeth Town, as does their father. I have often seen the General in his store serving in his capacity of shopkeeper; here nothing is derogatory except idleness and bad character. The principal inclination of the old general appears to be towards agriculture; his farm is very near-by and there he spends a great part of the day. He manures and works his field so well that this year an acre has brought in up to 60 bushels of Indian corn.

This corn is selling today at 6 shillings a bushel (which is a very low price for this country). Ordinarily an acre gives only 25 to 30 *boushels*. In this country Indian corn is sown by preference because of its innumerable uses. Cattle prefer its leaves and stalks to the best possible hay; the grain serves to make bread for the servants. This bread is sweet and very good to eat. A mixture is also made of a third of corn to two thirds wheat flour for the bread made for their masters. They make a sort of gruel of it and excellent *cacks* [cakes] for tea. In summer when it is tender, they cook the cobs which, with fresh butter and some salt, are excellent to eat. But the most common use of this grain is to fatten poultry and livestock. Both are very fond of it and fatten up very fast. The cattle, the horses, and especially the pigs, are fed on it; for in this truly happy country of equality, the animals are better treated and better fed than human kind often are in other countries.

But this is too long to speak of grain in a place where there are much more attractive things. I mean to say the charming young ladies. Elizabeth Town is famous in this regard. [23] The Dayton family

alone provides many of them. It must be understood that I speak only
of unmarried women, for in this country of the most immaculate
morals and chastity who would dare speak only of married women?
The old general has two yet-unmarried daughters, Miss Pauli [Polly]
and Miss Salé [Sally].[59] The former especially can be counted among
those personalities who, in a circle of twenty women, would not fail
to strike a stranger who might be there among them for the first time.
That at least is the effect that she had on me when, on the day of
my arrival in Eliz. Town, I was invited to take tea at the home of
the *Spaeker*. In the midst of a large circle of ladies I was struck by
the elegance of her figure, the vivacity reflected in her whole person,
the beauty of her smile and the brilliant whiteness of her teeth. It
appeared to me later that her gaiety is perhaps at the expense of that
sweetness and sensibility which are the most attractive features of a
woman. Miss Suzon Dayton, the elder daughter of the *Speaker,* wins
the advantage on investigation; her head is that of a young madonna
in all its beauty, her eyes full of fire, and her smile is charming. She
has artless simplicity, grace, and sweetness; her young sister, Miss
Pauli; Miss Chandler; Elton, Dehart, Williamson, Jouete, etc.,[60] are
certainly to be esteemed for their charms and happy dispositions.

The society of these young ladies must be infinitely agreeable to
the young men who, as they, love gaiety. In the homes of their parents they enjoy a liberty unknown elsewhere. They go out, pay calls,
give tea parties, inviting to them whomsoever they wish; go to New
York accompanied by a friend or by a relative, etc. In the evening
when they gather together with the young men, there are games,
laughter, jokes, and pranks, which elsewhere might perhaps give of-
fense, but such is the innocence and simplicity of the manners here,
these are in no way immodest. There is hardly ever an occasion when
a young woman carries these familiarities a little too far; or indeed if
such an extremely rare case does occur, it is put right by marriage
before it becomes evident.

Liberty, gaiety, and the happy days of a woman come to end here
with her maiden state. [24] Once married she lives only for her husband and occupies herself with housekeeping and the cares of feeding
and raising her children. Infidelities on the part of the women are
almost unknown and those of the men extremely rare. The room where
the nuptial couch is found is a *Sancta Sanctorum* where no man approaches. There is a *Parlor* where the affairs of the day are conducted
and a *drawing room* for dining and in the evening for receiving guests.
Both are on the ground floor. The married couple, the family live on
the first floor. Business men, lawyers, merchants have also a room

which they call *the office;* it is there that they attend to their own particular affairs. There is nothing more unsullied than the conduct of their family life. They perhaps do not enjoy as much pleasure and amusement as Europeans do, but calm and moderate in their emotions, they pass their life in sweet tranquility. The families are close knit; every Sunday they entertain each other in turn. At that time one sees arriving the husband, the wife ordinarily carrying a child which she is nursing, three or four boys, as many girls (they marry very young and the wife never remains idle: either she is carrying a child in her womb or she is suckling one at her breast). The relatives greet each other with as much cordiality as one can reasonably expect of a people by nature cold. The children join together according to their age. They even put the *bebys* side by side. It is thus that they spend the day; and this picture of domestic bliss could not but affect every sensitive spirit. For the rest, already there is here, as in all seaboard states, as in all mercantile countries, a spirit of speculation and trading which little by little banishes hospitality. They live very economically. Their first concern is to amass as quickly as they can the most money possible. When they were only well-to-do, they gave dinners; today when they are rich, they offer you only tea.

Towards the middle of October [61] I attended the state elections for the members of the Legislature of the State of New Jersey. Two or three days before that appointed by law, the principal inhabitants of the County of Essex, where Eliz. Town is, had their *meetings* in order to agree among themselves whom they wished to nominate. As this state is very federalist and united, they were not a long time agreeing on a choice. Another circumstance contributed greatly [25] to excite the zeal of the leaders of the people. They had received notice that a Mr. Penni[n]gton [62] of a rival town to Eliz. Town and suspected of anti-federalism, was running for the office. This was enough to excite opposition to him. I came to the *Court House* at the appointed time. The whole ceremony consisted of the Mayor reading the law of elections, then swearing in the *Cheriff* and the *Clerks* that they would not allow the same person to vote twice, that they would permit to vote only those persons who had the necessary qualifications, that is to say those who possessed a fortune of 50 pounds. This last requirement is much overlooked. They examine hardly anyone who votes on the state of his fortune. It suffices that a well-known citizen testifies for the one about whom they have some doubt. Every man who has resided in the country a year has the right to vote [63] and I have seen many a French refugee exercise this privilege.

The first day one saw scarcely any one but the citizens of the town, who all came with their ballots already filled out. The leaders stood at the door with bundles of these ballots and offered them to the arrivals, who accepted them and placed them in the urn with an unparalleled indifference. The next day, which was the day the election was to be concluded, the leaders of the party seeing that the number of voters was very small and that consequently New Ark was leading, became alarmed. They sent carriages into the country to bring out the farmers. They were obliged to beg them, even to treat them, so indifferent are the people to their privileges. As long as their purse is respected, as long as one does not overwhelm them neither with taxes nor with onerous duties, it worries them little by whom and how they are governed. If, on the other hand, they abandon their indifference, it is only when people more enlightened and more vigilant show them the real dangers, or when schemers, in order to attain their own ends, show them the imaginary ones. In spite of all their efforts to acquire the most votes possible, they received the news that the opposing party in Newark was prevailing. In this extremity they had recourse to the last expedient; it was to have the women vote. All widows of property, all unmarried women who had passed the age of 21 had the right to vote. They scurried around collecting them. I need not say that the number of the latter was very small. What is the pleasure of voting in comparison to the pain of swearing that one is 21 years old! At the end of two days, after which [26] the votes of the *Townsheep* were counted, it turned out that New Ark had prevailed. They even printed in the newspaper of that town an ode on the power of the *Peticoat* of Elizabeth Town.[64] Colonel Craan, an old and wounded soldier nominated for councilor for the Legislature of Jersey, was rejected.[65] A few days afterwards I met him in his field filling a great wagon with his crop of maize. This sight increased my regrets on his loss in the election.

The only public building that they have in Elizabeth Town is the *Court House* with the prison underneath.[66] A prisoner myself for two years I have kept up a sincere interest for this unfortunate class. On making inquiries what kind of people were kept there, they told me that they have only negro slaves who have deserted their masters and have been captured by them. Their sentence and their punishment are uniquely determined by their masters; and this in a free and democratic Republic.

20 Oct. After having passed three weeks in Eliz. Town which I spent in hunting, reading and seeing a little of society, we left on the 20th October, to return to Brunswick. I left Eliz with regret. It is the place I would choose very willingly for my retirement. Its situation

is charming and healthy, a close-knit society without ill-natured med-
dling and gossip. The houses of the Broker Livingston and Dayton, the
Speaker, are interesting.[67] Furthermore one can agreeably spend the
evening in the homes of the French. I knew only the family of
Masson, but one can count nearly 120 French men and women [68] in
Eliz all refugees from the colonies. Some families have had the good
sense to buy land and to live there quietly. Finally an advantage of
Eliz is that it is very near to New York. One can get there by water
in an hour and a half.

I found once again in Brunswick the White family where we stayed,
as always, good, honest, and attentive, the family of Bayard and Paterson always friendly and the town always gloomy. I resorted to hunting more than ever. I have not attained perfection in shooting on the
wing but I rarely miss a *Robin* or any other bird perched on a tree.
There is a great quantity of partridge, which they call quail here, and
in the woods the big gray pheasant. I have seen very pretty birds,
called *black reed bird*.[69] They are black with wings edged with purple. There is a large species of woodpecker,[70] gray, red and blue.
There are many squirrels [27] of many species. They make an excellent soup.

In our first visit to Brunswick in the summer a female *humming
bird* was caught. It has nowhere near the pretty plumage of the male.
It was green mixed with gold on the back and with a little gray
speckled on the breast, the head flat, the beak long as a needle. It
had been put in a cage with many flowers and with sugar dissolved in
water for nourishment. It had touched nothing, appeared inconsolable
over the loss of its liberty. It sought incessantly to escape, flying about
with a hum that made the air quiver. The next day I opened the doors
of her prison and was in respect to this bird as Paul I was towards
me; I too was a poor hummingbird who had done no wrong but to
love independence. There is nothing more meticulous and more artistic than the nest of the hummingbird. It is no bigger than the half
of a peach. Mrs. White had told me that she had tried to keep one in
a cage for several months and that it had died from excess of weight,
or rather from the lack of exercise.

I was disconsolate that I had not profited by the nearness of Elizabeth to see the famous falls of Passaik.[71] My friends Gahn and Fasch [72]
coming to see me in Brunswick urged me to accompany them to Eliz
and to go from there and visit the falls. We left. I saw again with
pleasure all my acquaintances in Eliz Town. The next day after Mr.
Fasch and I had taken a cabriolet and a horse, we set out. We stopped
in the gay and pleasant village of New Ark and we had breakfast at

the home of Cl. Ogden.⁷³ The house, situated near the main road and on a height, is beautiful and spacious. We entered into a large *parlor* where we found five or six young women, three boys, a young man, with an agreeable face, with a huge woman—his wife; all children of the house. The father of the family and his wife appeared soon. One would have said that there was a large group of guests; however, it was only we two who were strangers. But alas is there any society, any company more interesting than that of a numerous family joined together and living with independent means and happy comfort. The good patriarch talked to us the whole time about the roads that one should take. He did not permit anyone to know better than he. He had a bee in his bonnet about this. We skirted then [28] for many miles the second or Passaik River through a smiling and open country, well inhabited and well cultivated. We saw to the right the house of Mr. Mark, German in origin. He worked a copper mine. The mine, it is said, is rich and the quality of the copper the best. The floods and the costliness of labor make the enterprise lag.⁷³ᵃ The whole country-side is inhabited by old Dutch colonists. I recognized them by their favorite bent for navigation. They were all busy constructing or refit-ting boats. They are said to be ignorant, avaricious and inhospitable. They love to work and to hoard. They have kept until now their mother tongue; however, nearly all speak and understand English.

Towards noon we arrived in Paterson, a little town situated in the neighborhood of the falls. We ran at once to see them. It is a beauti-ful sight, but it did not come up to my expectations. One sees the pre-cipitous descent of the river only in profile. The crevice of rocks through which it escapes is too narrow, hiding the whole width of the surface of water and, as I have said, can be seen only from the side. The height of the fall is 75 feet, which is just half of the falls of Niagara. The falls of Terni and of Tivoli ⁷⁴ are infinitely more beauti-ful, as much for the magnificence of the view as for the picturesque surroundings. The accompaniment here is the same as everywhere; the roar of the river escaping its prison and falling boiling and bub-bling into the abyss, a cloud of spray on which is painted a rainbow with all its colors; everywhere wild and rude nature. One must climb up and clamber over frightful crags to enjoy this spectacle from all sides. With a few boards they could have made the access less dan-gerous, especially from the side where a branch of the river continues its course on a bed of rocks. They have diverted a part in order to run some cotton machines and mills. Below, opposite these so noisy falls, there is a reservoir of quiet waters, a few trees here and there, in a word, a calm which contrasts in a striking manner with the roar in the background of this scene.

Afterwards we went to see the cotton factory. It is enormous and fitted out to perfection. There are four floors filled with spinning machines and looms, all the machines driven by water. One can never see this astounding mechanism, by means of which a child can do more work than could two hundred hands, without paying tribute to the genius of the man who invented it. Three-quarters of these machines still remain idle because of the lack of hands. They employ only children from the age of 7 to 14. They pay them from [29] two shillings up to 4 per day according to their skill. Nevertheless the fabric supplied by English mills is, in spite of commission and transport costs, cheaper. Moreover they furnish up to 6 months credit. These are the obstacles which will always oppose the growth of American manufactures. They use only cotton from Georgia and from Carolina, which is of very good quality. The fabric which is made from it is not fine but strong and very good for the lower classes.

We went to see the innkeeper Godvin [75] who keeps the book in which all the travellers who come to see the Paterson falls put down their names. The number of them is already rather large, that of verses, jokes, anecdotes even greater. I saw there with surprise a Russian name. It is that of Lissiansky [76] and another of a family established here for an extremely long time. He wrote his name as Zabryskie. It is certainly the Polish family of Zabrzyski.[77] Here, however, they are called *Dutsch family*. I was told that there was in the same state a citizen called Sobieski. He was a rather large landowner and enjoyed a distinguished reputation. He was a judge of the State. They said he had become a great drunkard. I am quite convinced that they confuse the names of Zabryskie and Sobieski and that they both are perhaps of the same family. The innkeeper Godvin is also an artist. He showed me a portrait of Bonaparte which he himself had engraved in *mezzo tinta*. It is quite good but as everything must be beyond price in this country, he asked two and half gourdes [78] for it. Who would ever have expected to meet an engraver amongst the rocks of Paterson?

There was in Paterson 8 years ago a man worthy of the attention of naturalists. He had a head so monstrously large that, as he could not support it by his neck, he was obliged to lie in a sort of a cradle. He survived in this complete inaction until he was 30 years old. If I am not mistaken, he had a prodigious memory and knew the whole Bible by heart. The celebrated Dr. Midnight [79] of New York had

found a way of obtaining his head after he had died and dissected it—
wanted further information.

[30] We left Paterson in order to go to Bo[o]nton, land belonging
to the father of my companion Mr. Fash. It is 26 miles from the falls.
On leaving the town we went off the road in order to see the summit
of the falls. There one is level with the river. Under one's feet the awesome crevice of the rocks and the sight of the whole extent of the
sheet of water is exposed in a bird's-eye view. The torrential current
of the river is such that one feels the banks of fissured rocks tremble
under one's feet. After having gazed on this terrible sight we went on
our way.

We plunged immediately into the mountains. The roads became
steep and horrible. The soil less fertile and often arid; and for the
first time in America I saw hamlets as miserable as ours. We rested
our horse every two hours; that is to say we gave it water and a measure of oats. They are not afraid of watering their horses even when
they are tired. We stopped among other places at a poor tavern of
which the innkeeper was a Major called Dods. In the time of the
Revolution the government gave this class of men much consideration
and gave them military patents. Finally in very cold weather and by a
beautiful clear moon we approached Bontown. Its presence announced
itself in advance by a muffled sound of a river which runs across rocks
and big blocks of stone and serves to turn the mills of the iron foundry.

We caught sight through the woods of the lights in the windows of
a large and beautiful house. We approached on foot in order to surprise the good parents of Fash. He called softly to the stable boy.
"My father, is he at home," asked the young man. "No," was the reply.
"He is at Mounthope." Our joy was diminished by half. We entered
the apartment and found Mrs. Faesch,[80] the stepmother of the young
man, with an old aunt of 86 years. Soon the young lady of the
house appeared. My companion was embraced and I was received
cordially. Although Mrs. Fasch was young and beautiful, the bloom
had already faded from her looks. Her husband, although one of the
most respectable people in the world, was a sexagenarian, which could
have contributed to withering Madame. The young lady played the
harpsichord and sang after a fashion. I recall an air of which the
words and music were equally touching. The theme was the complaint
of an African [31] and the refrain, *Spare have [half] pen[n]y for a
poor negro.*[80a] We had a good supper. I was then given a very attractive room with a good fire and excellent bed. I was in great need of it
after all the weariness of the day. This day we made nearly 50 miles
across the worst roads in the world.

The next morning I was awakened by the noise of the torrents, the hammers and anvils of the forges. I went with my companion to take a look at the mills.[81] The main one consisted in a big hall with six furnaces and as many anvils. The hammers and the cylindrically shaped bellows are driven by water. The raw material comes from Mounthope 10 miles away. They shape it into bars—*Pigs*, and in another hall into nails, long, thin, twisted rods, etc. It is a pity that they do not have coal in this place; the consumption of wood is great. There are, I believe, thirty workers there, for the most part Germans. Mr. Fasch himself is a Swiss from Basle. It was nearly 30 years ago when, under the English government, an American company was established with the view of exploiting the iron mines. Mr. Fash was called over from Switzerland. He brought the workers with him. They offered a considerable sum as an inducement. The enterprise prospered; today it still prospers, though less so. All the manufactured iron is immediately sold. They transport it by land as far as Eliz Town; from there it is carried by boat to New York. The workers are lodged in separate buildings; they are paid by the week. The contractor himself undertakes to provide their supplies. Mr. Fash came to America with very little; today he is the owner of large iron mines in Mounthope, of large forges, of a beautiful and comfortable house. However, such is the unrest and fickleness of man, he is weary of the noise of the torrents and the mills and the din of these hammers. He is trying to sell all his manufactures, to leave his forests to draw closer to the benefits of society. The situation of his house could not be more romantic. Torrents of water, towering rocks covered with firs and cedars, the whole aspect is wild but sublime. The host is very hospitable; in summer his house is full of company who come to spend whole months there.

After lunch we left these hospitable ladies [32] and we took a route through a country much more fertile and better cultivated than the one before. We followed the highway leaving Maurice Town [Morristown] to the right. We saw a large farm belonging to Mr. Blanchard, apparently French in origin. He himself was in the fields, dressed in an excellent suit of gray cloth. Mr. Faech told me that it was of his own manufacture *house spoon* [home-spun]. They raise much cattle in this district. We passed by the pretty village of Springfield and returned towards 3 o'clock to Eliz Town; after having made a circuit of 70 miles and passing through the counties of Essex, Sussex, Bergen and Mor[r]is. The foodstuffs there had fallen a little in price: wheat sold at 9 shill., oats 3 sh., ordinary beef 50 doll. I took advantage of the carriage of Mr. Paterson which was returning empty from New York in order to go back in it to Brunswick.

8 Nov. I found all the inhabitants of the town busy in preparing the reception and dinner for Mr. John Adams, President of the United States.[82] The cool heads, and the methodical manners of these solemn Americans lead them to go about the business of a dinner with the same rules that they use in discussing affairs of State. A committee was appointed to arrange the dinner and a President and a Vice-President to maintain good order at the table and to receive the chief magistrate. Many evenings were spent on arranging this important affair. Finally Mr. Adams arrived, but two hours before the appointed time. Nothing was ready. Immediately the militia, both mounted and on foot, ran about the streets; the authorities put their wigs on askew; the elegants arrived with their shoes half buckled. The cannon fired a half [hour] after Mr. Adams was already well warmed at the fireplace. Little by little everyone settled down and took breath. At one o'clock I was presented to Mr. Adams. He was sitting, reading a newspaper, facing the fireplace with Mr. [Samuel B.] Malcolm, a young man 20 years old, his private secretary. I saw a dumpy little man dressed wholly in gray, well-powdered hair and a long pigtail. His face appeared to me that of a good and honest man, touched nevertheless with a grain of malice. He received me civilly, asked me news of Gl. Kośc[iuszko] and then Mar. La Fayette. I passed then into a room opposite and I found there the true counterpart of Mr. Adams. It was [33] his wife. Small, short and squat, she is accused of a horrible crime. It is said she puts on rouge. What is certain is that if her manner is not the most affable, her mind is well balanced and cultivated. She was accompanied only by a niece and a maidservant.

At two o'clock Cl. Ne[i]lson,[83] elected President of the whole ceremony, accompanied by Gl. White and all the citizens entered into the President's room. Mr. Ne[i]lson in the name of all the inhabitants read an address conceived in a style filled with expressions of attachment for the Constitution and the leading public officials. Mr. Adams read his response; he spoke to some, shook the hand of all, and then he departed. At three o'clock the same ceremony to invite him to go into the dining hall. He made his way there through the ranks of citizens and thirty of the militia in uniform who lined his path. They saluted him by lowering flags. The table was set for 60 people. *Rostbeef*, turkeys, *Pays* [pies?], etc., were served in profusion.

In the middle of the dinner Mr. Goss, a man 6 feet tall, over 70 years old, tanner by trade and prattler by habit, got up from the other end of the table, came to the side where the President was, displaced Gl. White, who was seated beside him, sat down there himself and occupied his attention with the most coarse and silly tales possible.

The good President laughed, then considering his enormous height said to him, "You should have been born in the states of the King of Prussia. You would have been the ornament of his guards." "Would I have been the second in his kingdom, I would not wish to have been born there," the tanner said to him. "Nor I," answered the President, "would I have been the first."

The meal over, the toasts, prepared in advance by a committee, began. They gave as many of them as there are states, that is to say 16. Most of them contained sentiments and vows to uphold the laws, the Constitution, liberty, peace, agriculture, trade, etc. Toasts which seem boring in other countries are not without their use here. Honorable and patriotic maxims pronounced glass in hand, in contemplation of joys to come, engrave themselves on the heart in a more agreeable manner and perhaps more deeply than do maxims recited in high places. The President having retired, his health was drunk in more light-hearted toasts and the noisy gaiety of the guests [34] continued until ten o'clock. Nothing unseemly, however, took place. The President and *Mistress* Adams went to the home of Mr. White to take tea with them.[84]

The next day Mr. Adams and Madame set out at an early hour. Their whole entourage consisted of two carriages, comfortable but simple; a single servant followed them on horseback. He was escorted by thirty of the mounted militia and accompanied by all the well-to-do citizens in their carriages as far as halfway to Kingstown. There they again fell into line and the President bade a *tender farywell* [fare-thee-well] to everyone.

Gl. White and I went on as far as Kingstown. I was in the carriage of Cpt. Tingey,[85] settled in this village and enjoying (after 30 years of a stormy life on the sea) ease and peace. He was principally engaged in trade with the East Indies. He told me that except for iron, wine, and *mahogany* wood only payments in ready money are sent there. Mr. Tingey's house is neat and attractive. His farm is just beyond with 4 men on it, to whom he pays, I think, 50 or 60 pounds a year. His fare consists only of poultry and preserves. Butcher's meat is difficult to get in a village. We returned with Gl. White on foot almost half the way. I saw for the first time a farm run entirely by a negro family.

A few days before leaving Brunswick I accompanied Gl. White one evening to the inn where the coaches or *Stages* stop. Gl. White went there every day. It provided company for him. We found there a very extraordinary [group?] made up of six young Indian girls from Lake Seneca and the Mohawk River. Two Quakers, impelled only by a zeal

for humanity, went into that country in order to persuade some heads
of Indian families to entrust to them the education of their daughters.
The object of the Quakers was to teach them all the care and running
of a household so as to make them good housekeepers, good wives,
good mothers. They were to be distributed among many families living in the country. The idea of civilizing the savages, beginning by
enlightening their wives, appears to me to be very sensible; knowing
however the state of submission and near contempt in which this sex
is held among the Indians, it is to be feared that the result will not
correspond, perhaps, to the expectations of these good Quakers. All
these young women wear trousers [35] and a sort of blanket for a
mantle. They have laced boots. Most of them were pretty; none were
ugly. Their color appeared to me exactly that of our Gypsies; straight
black hair, hanging down, beautiful teeth, thoughtful countenance.
The Quakers told me that two of the fathers of these girls had accompanied them a very long way, that they had given their horses to the
Quakers and followed themselves on foot. The parting was sorrowful;
for two days the young girls had their faces covered with the edge
of their garments and wept bitterly.

The next day, which was, I believe, the 20th of Nov., I took the *Stage*
in order to go to Philadelphia to look for lodgings for Gl. Kośc[iuszko].
The *Stage* is a large covered carriage with leather curtains at the side
which can be raised or lowered at will. Three or four benches serve
as seats for the travelers. They change the horses and the carriage
every 10, 15 and 20 miles. There is no jump seat; they bring you some
steps for getting down. They take 14 pounds of baggage free; for the
excess one pays 3 cents per pound. It is the only way to travel by post
in America; a very convenient way in a country where everybody
spends nearly the same amount of money, where one finds neither
large amounts of baggage nor travellers with many servants. It has
nonetheless some drawbacks. One is often dependent on the coachmen who drive you and who, if it ever rains, contrive with the innkeeper that you should sleep there where they choose, and make you
lose much time. One pays in the inns twice as much as in the times
of M. Brissot; [86] breakfast consisting of coffee, tea and *Beefsteek,* 4
shil., dinner 5 and 6, and supper one dollar. You have to sleep in a
room where there are 5 or 6 beds. You pay often the women's share.
You retire [late?] after supper, but the topers remain. Hardly do you
begin to fall asleep when one of them enters into the room and thrusts
the candle into your eyes. You again fall asleep; an hour afterwards
a second drinker comes in and awakens you. This ceremony continues

until two or three o'clock in the morning and deprives you of sleep for the rest of the night.

I arrived in Phil[adelphia] Sunday morning and found lodging *at Eagle and Harpe,* 2nd Street North, in a dirty and wretched inn. Not knowing a soul I roamed the streets, a little like Benjamin Franklin when, coming from Boston and being nearly as rich as I, he walked the streets with his loaf of bread under his arm. With the help of Dr. Rush I found a lodging as small, [36] as remote, and as cheap as my instructions directed.

I was present at the opening of Congress. I will speak of it below. It was the 23rd of No. At first the Senate gathered in a body and took their places in the armchairs at the right of the speaker's stand. At noon the President, followed by three Secretaries of State and escorted by *constables,* entered into the House of Representatives. Everybody got up. The President made his speech standing and delivered two copies of it, one to the President of the Senate, the other to the *Speaker* of the House of Representatives. He was dressed wholly in gray with a sword at his side and a purse. Instead of pomp and luxury, one sees in the ceremony of this session only much propriety and dignity. I returned the next day to Brunswick.

My last visit from Brunswick was to Amboy. I made it on horseback with Mr. Butt.[87] One crosses the magnificent bridge of the town and, at 5 or 6 miles distance, one discovers at the right the most extensive and the most picturesque [views?], the whole course of the Raritan, its outlet into the bay, the immense crystal of it with sails carried by puffs of wind. Amboy contains 60 houses at present; the ruins of the barracks, government house, etc., bear witness that before the Revolution it was the capital of Jersey and the seat of the government. Consequently the inhabitants recall this with bitter pride. They were always attached to the English side, and even today it is not there that one should look for true American patriots. The greatest advantage of Amboy lies in its situation. It is one of the most beautiful. Its harbor could contain the whole English fleet. It is as safe as it is large and beautiful. The closeness to New York will never allow this place to prosper. The inhabitants are famous for their indolence, and thus you see them everywhere. For a few years now many people in easy circumstances have retired there and built some beautiful houses; all are on the bay and in the most enchanting situation possible.

Chapter II

PHILADELPHIA.
DEPARTURE OF KOŚCIUSZKO

28 Nov. We left with many regrets the quiet and hospitable house of Mrs. White and arrived the next day in Philadelphia. We lodged at no. 172 [37] South 3 Street at Mrs. Relf's in a very small house where medical students and a few other young apprentices shared common lodging. Its cheapness had made the choice for us. The Gl. had a small room where he could receive only 4 people at a time. I had one even smaller; [1] since no fire was made there, I could use it only for sleeping; this was extremely inconvenient to me. There is nothing more dreary than not having a place of your own, to be obliged to roam the streets or to watch for a moment when there would be a little table vacant in the *parlor* where you can read and write. I have scarcely had the time to jot down a few notes in disorder on what I have seen.

Prisons. 22 Jan. I went with Gl. Mason and Mr. Flamand to see the prisons of Philadelphia.[2] Those who have seen and described them have given them only well-merited praise. I do not believe that there is in the world an establishment conceived with better judgment and more humanity. Punishment and torture are not, as elsewhere, the sole object of this sad sojourn. Here they want only to correct and to turn the punishment itself to the advantage of the criminals and of society. The building is of stone; the great halls with separate beds and mattresses are occupied by the prisoners only at night. During the day they are all away and busy at different tasks. At the rear of the court one sees the rooms with the workshops, most of them for making nails, for the trades of woodworking, weaving, shoemaking, and turning. Below, the worst offenders are employed at cutting marble. The laws of Pennsylvania have abolished capital punishment except for murder. All other offenses are punished by imprisonment for a term corresponding to the crime. As soon as a prisoner is sent there, they arrange a job for him. If he knows a trade, he works at it; if not, he learns one. All that he earns is written down in a book. He pays from it his legal fees, for his food, his clothes; the surplus remains in safekeeping. In this way, a wastrel, who comes without a cent and knowing nothing, finds himself at the end of a few years with a knowledge of a trade and a small fund with which to begin a way of life useful to himself and to society. The greatest [38] punishment is that which is called *Solitary Confinement*. These are very small cells with double-barred doors, a pallet and a commode. Daylight comes from above. I, who have had the misfortune to spend two years in a similar prison, I can do justice to those who invented this, that they know human nature well, when they declare that boredom, the want of something to do, and the total deprivation not only of the society but the sight of their fellow men, is the most cruel punishment that one can devise.

When one of the worker-prisoners behaves himself badly, the director puts him in such a cell. Not eight days go by before he begs on his knees to be sent back to his work. The number of prisoners was about 200, of whom 50 are women. These latter are completely separated. They are mostly occupied in spinning and laundering, etc. Among them was a huge woman who was a sort of a housekeeper and spent her life in prison. I do not know if it was an inclination for this life or rather because of an irresistible bent towards larceny. For, hardly had her term of two or three years expired and she was freed, she immediately stole something, was judged and sent back from whence she had come. Mr. Thomas,³ the Quaker who guided us throughout, praised her to us most highly. Her industry and her energy are unequaled. I was distressed to see, in one cell, a poor unfortunate condemned to be hanged. He is an Irish shoemaker who had killed a man, as he had said, under the first impulse of anger. The *Jurys* had not wanted to see it in this way. There was no trace of villainy in his face.

This whole establishment is under the inspection of the Quakers and it could not be intrusted to better hands. The warder who conducted us, addressed a word to the prisoners, spoke to them softly and comforted them. They carry in their faces and dress more the air of workmen than of condemned criminals. There was no rattle of chains, no gaunt faces; the silence was interrupted only by the sound of sawing of marble, the hammer, or the wheels of the weavers. The greatest number of the convicts were there for larceny, [39] some for forgery of bank notes. They all eat together. They have soup, a little meat and some potatoes. I left this prison edified by the order which prevails there; the humanity practised there; and almost free of the

feeling of sorrow which the condition of these unfortunates would inspire in me in Europe.

City Assembly.[4] One should see everything, even balls; one can
catch there those features which portray the character of a nation.
The 25th of Jan. Mr. Montgomery got for me a ticket for the City
Assembly. As a foreigner they could have invited me gratis, but no,
I paid two piasters. The scene takes place in a hotel in a rather spacious hall lighted with 5 chandeliers of lamps. A full-length portrait
of the founder of the dancing Society is the principal ornament of it.
The hero is represented in a yellow suit with a black design, feet in
the third position, with hat off and holding his sword in his hand.
His memory is revered by the dancing tribe as is that of William Penn
by the Quakers. On entering one sees the rules prescribed for the Society by the *Managers*. They are covered by a glass and encased in a
gilded frame. The table of the twelve laws of Moses has not been
more religiously observed. This love of order is met everywhere in
this nation. They can neither eat, drink, nor dance without prescrib-
ing rules, without choosing officers who watch over the good order of
the society. Is it possible that with this calm and systematic mind, this
people could ever be seduced into disorder and anarchy? The Assembly was very splendid; one saw there more than 60 women. I saw
some pretty ones, but none of striking beauty. This lack of brilliancy
may perhaps be attributed to the absence of rouge, which the women
in this country never use, unless in stealth, and then so little that one
can not notice it.

Two things struck me in these beauties: their big feet and their
bosoms, so lean that one could scarcely consider them as such. All the
women [40] were dressed in white with silver ruffles. They appeared
to like to dance; perhaps it gave them pleasure, but they took care
not to show it to the onlookers. Men and women both are very far
from having that playfulness, that vivacity that one sees at our balls
in Warsaw. They dance the quadrille of the English and French. The
newly-married ladies are at the head of the lines; at the least difficulty
they hasten to the table of laws and the *Managers* decide. After ten
o'clock they play Washington's March;[5] everybody goes to supper,
or rather the ladies, and the gentlemen eat the remains. The table is
set with chocolate, coffee, tea, cold meats, *custards*, etc. The ball continues afterwards up to one o'clock in the morning.

The City. Philadelphia can be considered at the present time as the
capital of the United States. Its commerce, nourished by a countryside most fertile in grain and by its population consisting in large part
of German farmers, celebrated for their industry and their love of

work, will make it for a long time one of the principal outlets of the continent. It was founded in 1681, and when William Penn landed there, the countryside and the shores were so covered with trees that their branches often caught on to the sails of the ship and impeded its landing. Penn conceived the plan for it on an immense scale. If ever the town should occupy the space between the Dellavare and Skulkill that its founder assigned to it, it will equal Paris and London. Today it is already a city which would be considered large in Europe itself. The streets run parallel from East to *West*, and in this direction they carry the names of different trees, such as *Chesnut, Walnut, Spruce,* etc. Those that cross them from North to South carry the names of numbers, First, Second, etc. Market Street divides the North from the South. It is the most beautiful. Its width, however, has been exaggerated. It is not nearly as wide as Oxford Street.[6] All the other streets are straight and in regular array, such in fact that one sees in all cities built in modern times to a set plan; regularity [which can not be found] [41] in most of the ancient cities of Europe, which were begun in barbaric times, which grew by chance without any taste or symmetry, according to the whim of each private individual, and not under the surveillance of a commission who watch over their beauty and their usefulness.

As in London, the houses are all of brick, not plastered over; their lightness, the thin walls having only the thickness of one brick, the clean windows, the care with which the pediments of the doors are carved, their extreme cleanliness even on the outside (for they are not here as in London blackened by smoke), all that, I say, gives to these houses more the air of nice furniture than of buildings. At each of the doors of these houses there is a knocker and a bell; one knocks and a negro usually comes to open the door for you. You enter into a corridor and you walk on a narrow carpet. There is a *parlor* below for receiving, another for dining. In the houses of opulence you find *drawing rooms.* In all these apartments there is the greatest cleanliness, all the furniture in mahogany, a large sideboard with a case on top filled with knives, forks, spoons, etc. Some beautiful English engravings, and often some very beautiful porcelains, decorate the mantelpieces and little tables. Luxury already extends to mirrors. I have seen some very large ones. In general, it appears to me that the greatest luxury here is in the furniture; that of the carriages and horses is small in proportion. Ordinarily only women use them. There are a few very elegant carriages, elegant livery, arms and escutcheons as old as the carriages! Often they are displayed on an unfurled ducal mantling.

The most opulent and the most ostentatious of the inhabitants of Philadelphia is Mr. Bingham.[7] He enjoys, so it is believed, some 80,000 piasters a year coming from rents from immense lands and from interest on capital invested in various public funds. He owes his fortune to speculations during the last war as well as to his office of Commissioner and Director of privateers in the Indies. His house and garden, situated in the middle of the town, occupy a large area of ground. Their pompous appearance wounds a little the spirit of equality and excites envy. He is the Pisistratus of these parts with the difference that he has neither his talent nor his finesse, [42] keeping his gardens closed while the Athenian had them opened, entertaining at table persons of quality instead of treating the people; he could never become the Tyrant of this city. I was invited one time to his house. One mounts a staircase of white native marble. One enters an immense room with a sculptured fireplace, painted ceiling, magnificent rug, curtains, armchairs, sofas in Gobelins of France. The dinner is brought on by a French cook; the servants are in livery, the food served in silver dishes, the dessert on Sevres porcelain. The mistress of the house is tall, beautiful, perfectly dressed and has copied, one could not want for better, the tone and carriage of a European lady. She has traveled in France and Italy. The daughters are brought up more to be ladies than American citizens. In a word, I thought myself in Europe. This house, as opulent as it is, would never be pointed out in the big cities in Europe, but here it attracts attention, criticism and envy; and woe for the country if it ceases to astonish, if it ceases to be pointed out.[8]

Among the public buildings must be included the Bank of the United States. It was finished during my stay in Philadelphia and cost [blank].[9] It is in the Greek style, but it falls a little short. Corinthian columns of white marble support a richly sculptured pediment. The interior has no noteworthy features. The building would have a greater effect if it were situated in a great square, but being in the middle of a block, it overwhelms and appears overwhelmed. The Presbyterian church in Marquette Street is beautiful and built according to the rules of good architecture.[10] The Co[u]rt House, the house of the Assembly of Pennsylvania, the hall of Congress are devoid of all artistic ornaments and are distinguished only because of their simplicity.[11] I will speak of the hospital further down.

President's House, all but monstrous without any kind of architecture.[12] The house of Robert Morris, recently sold, is a monument to the folly of this man who, in spite of all his genius for commerce, has finished by becoming bankrupt. He undertook it in a spirit of rivalry with Bingham. He took as his architect another fool, Major Enfant. He built for him a real confection which was to be all covered with white marble. The undertaking was abandoned in that state most suitable to [43] show all its extravagances.[13] I shall not cite a large number of the private houses, very spacious, all built in the English style with large casements in the middle accompanied by two adjoining windows at the sides and semi-circular salons.

Except for Market Street, always crowded by a quantity of horses and wagons of German farmers who bring their flour there, the other streets have not that congestion of carriages, and that crowd of pass-ers-by as in Europe. Americans do not stroll; moreover everybody works. There is little difference in the way men are dressed: a rich man and an artisan are equally well but simply dressed. This is not so for the women. One can easily distinguish a rich woman from one of the common people; these latter, as in England, still wear their cloak of red cloth. No hubbub in the streets, a few carriages. The silence is interrupted only by the cries of the little negro chimney sweeps who with their heads thrown back cry at the top of their voices announc-ing that they are ready to offer their services to whomever wants them. In the evening these cries are replaced by those of the oyster vendors and finally, at night, by a sort of a dolefull and regular chant of the Wat[c]hman who chants the hour and the weather.

These Wat[c]hmens are the only patrol, the sole public force which watches over the security of the inhabitants. At the corner of each street they have their shelters. Equipped with sticks, they arrest the disturbers of the public peace; sometimes they themselves are worsted there. During my stay there have been many robberies and even mur-ders committed in the deserted streets, where one of these Wat[c]h-mans was killed. Otherwise there is almost no police. If the sidewalks are serviceable and quite clean, it is the result of a feeling for order and cleanliness on the part of the inhabitants and not on that of the officials who attend to these things. Often the cellars giving onto the sidewalks are left open. The snow is removed only by those who are willing to do it. To be given an order to this effect would be regarded as a *breech of Privileges and Liberty*, so ill do these people under-stand of what this good liberty consists.

[44] Mackenzi[e] [14] The 15th of Feb. Dr. Scandella [15] living at the home of the kind Macluer [16] has secured for me the pleasure of meet-ing the celebrated traveler Mackenzi. I scribble on paper what I was able to catch from his conversation which, on the subject of his trav-els, did not last a long time. Mr. Mackenzi is a man of about 35 years, blond, strong and well built. He is one of the associates of the com-

Fig. 21. A View of Paterson, New Jersey near the bridge. One of the buildings is supposed to be the Godwin Inn. "Drawn on the spot by Al[exander] Robertson October, 1795." Courtesy of The Historical Society of Pennsylvania.

Fig. 22. Passaic Falls in the State of New Jersey. Robertson-Jukes view, 1795-1800. The New Jersey Historical Society.

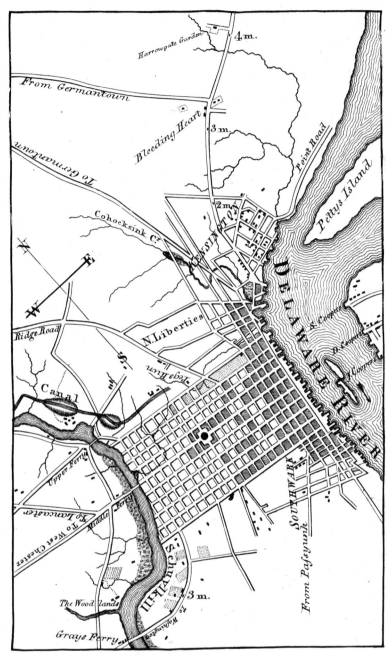

Fig. 23. Philadelphia. From S. S. Moore and T. W. Jones, *The Traveller's Directory* . . . , 1802. The New Jersey Historical Society.

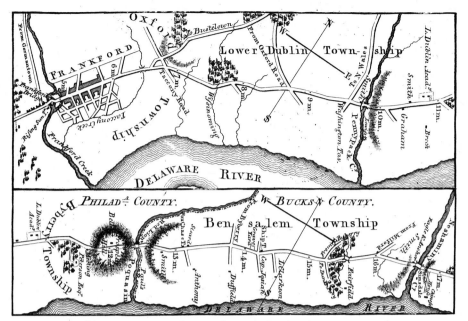

Fig. 24. Chinese House on the Road from Philadelphia to New York. Home of van Braam. From Moore and Jones, *The Traveller's Directory* . . . . The New Jersey Historical Society.

Fig. 25. "China Retreat." From William Birch, *The Country Seats* . . . , 1808. Courtesy of The New-York Historical Society, New York City.

Fig. 26. Above, Bank of the United States; center, The Bingham House; below, The Town House of Robert Morris. From William Birch, *The City of Philadelphia . . .* , 1800. Courtesy of The New-York Historical Society, New York City.

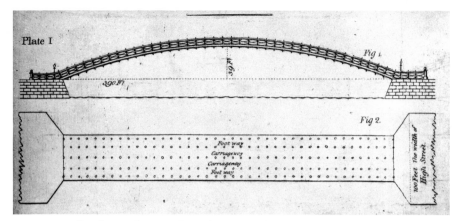

Fig. 27. "Bridge with a single arch . . . to be thrown across the Skulkhill."
Plate from Charles W. Peale, *An Essay on Building Wooden Bridges,* 1797.

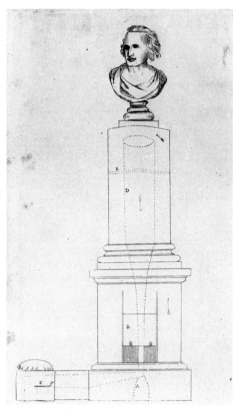

Fig. 28. Illustration from, "Description of the Stove lately built by Mr. Charles Willson Peale, in his Museum, and which burns the Smoke of its Fuel," *The Weekly Magazine,* 21 July 1798.

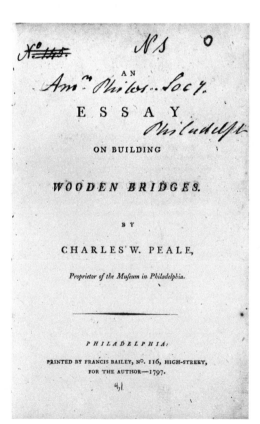

Fig. 29. Title page of the booklet in which Peale describes his bridge. The three figures courtesy of the American Philosophical Society.

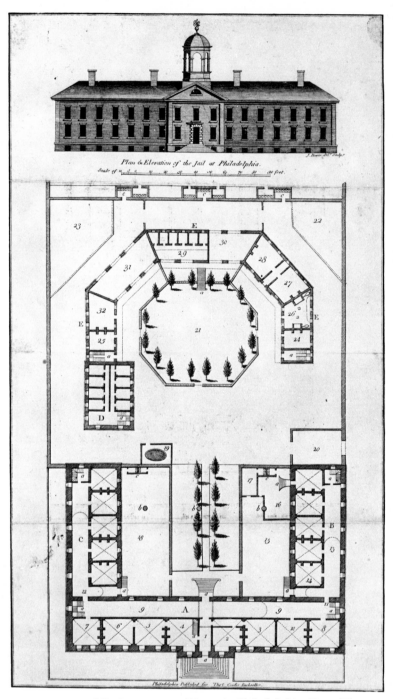

Fig. 30. View of the Penitentiary House in Philadelphia. From Thomas
Condie, *Philadelphia Monthly Magazine*, February, 1798. Courtesy
of The Historical Society of Pennsylvania.

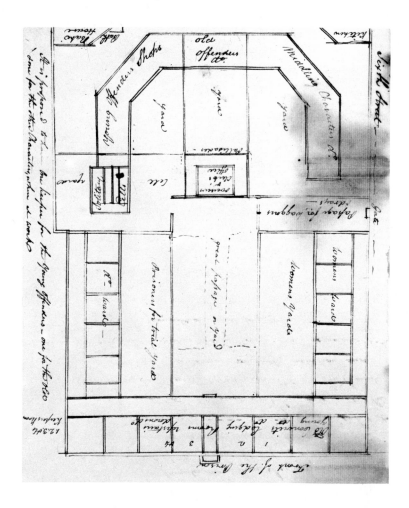

Fig. 31. Caleb Lownes' sketch and notes on the prison in Philadelphia. From *Schuyler Papers*. Courtesy of Manuscript Division, New York Public Library.

Fig. 32. An East View of Gray's Ferry, on the River Schuylkill. From the drawing of C. W. Peale. Courtesy of Manuscript Division, New York Public Library. Emmet, 3158.

Fig. 33. View of the City of Philadelphia, 1797. From the Holland-Fox view. Courtesy of Prints Division, New York Public Library.

pany formed in Canada for the trade in furs. He has made a journey
which is the most astonishing that has ever been undertaken, having
crossed the whole breadth of the immense continent of North America. At first from the Atlantic to the Arctic Sea at 70 degrees latitude,
then in a second voyage he took a route more to the South *West* and
came out at 52 degrees and 26 minutes latitude and 128 longitude
Greenwich, a little above Nutka Sund [Nootka Sound]. He found that
Nutka Sund was an Island and that all this coast is studded with an
Archipelago of tremendous islands. He went on a further 20 leagues
but was still not able to discover the open sea. This whole coast is
badly delineated on the maps, even on that of Arrowsmith,[17] but there
is a certain Van Couver [18] in the service of England who has made a
survey with great accuracy. It will probably be reserved for the use of
the *Cabinet* only. The most important discovery of his voyage is that
from Hudson Bay up to the Arctic Sea and even as far as the South
Sea, there is a chain of lakes, rivers and *Creeks* such that there is only
50 English miles of portage. All the rest of this huge continent can be
crossed by water. The *Stony* [Rocky] *Mountains* is a chain of mountains running from South to North. It is the continuation of that immense *spina-dorsi* of America, the Cordilleras or the Andes of Peru.
The country to the North East of these mountains is almost a continuous plain; a poor land producing only some stunted firs and in a few
places immense cedars. The savages do not resemble those of the rest
of America. They are agile and live on game, and their dwellings are
comfortable. However, they do not know the use of iron or, at best,
very little; they split, with the aid of wedges and hatchets of stone or
of hard wood, cedars 40 feet in height.

The country on the other side of the *Stony Mountains* towards the
sea is entirely mountainous. The savages on the shore of the sea live
only on fish. They are more indolent and fatter than the savages who
are hunters. All the rivers of this continent are filled with salmon. The
inhabitants eat them with a cake made from the bark of a tree called
the *Hemlock*, a species of yew. They [45] soak these cakes in the oil
of the salmon. Their clothing, Mr. Mackenzi said, is a kind of a mis-
cellany made of a fabric of the skin of otters cut into long and narrow
pieces like ribbons and interlaced with the bark of a tree. It is comfortable and pretty to look at. The inhabitants at the first sight of
white men seemed suspicious and ill disposed towards them, but when
they recognized that their intentions were peaceable, and when some
presents were distributed, they were found to be altogether well disposed and hospitable. Mr. Mackenzi found far in the interior of these
lands, in the ear of a savage, an American *half penny;* which proves that

the *Jankis,* or the inhabitants of New England, the most enterprising people in the universe, have already visited these far distant countries. One could say of them with Horace that they would climb up to heaven itself: *Coelium ipsum petet . . . Audax Japeti genus.*[19]

In general, Mackenzi's voyage has enriched geography by valuable discoveries. If the passage from the Atlantic to the South Sea by ocean appears to be proved impossible, one sees at least that with barks and boats one can cross this immense continent and get from the Atlantic to the South Sea without doubling the Cape of Good Hope. From day to day we know better our little house called the globe. Perhaps but a half century will slip away, and except for the burning interior of Africa all the rest of the earth will be as well known as Europe perhaps; and who [knows] whether in a century or two there will still be people on the earth whom we will call savages. In actual fact will the happiness of mankind gain by it or not?

I saw Mr. Mackenzi again. I must add that it appears that in his journey to the South Sea, he must have left from Hudson Bay. He arrived at the place called Arathapeskow or Carabesca [Athabasca] above Slave lake, and it is from there that he continued his way towards the South Sea and arrived there, as I have said, at 52 degrees, 26 minutes latitude and 128 longitude. But he avoided informing us by what direction. It is definite that he discovered a river there, but he said he abandoned it as well as his boat; one does not know for what reason. This river is other than the Columbia marked on Arrowsmith. During his first voyage to the Arctic Sea he followed a nameless river which went at first towards the North but turned rapidly to the *West*. He arrived at the sea, the 22nd of July at 70 degrees latitude. The inhabitants and their huts on this coast completely resembled the Greenlanders. Mackenzi had with him six Canadians and a young Englishman.

[46] Congress. As free America is a federal country, each state having its own independent government, enjoying the rights of sovereignty as far as internal affairs are concerned, there remains very little for the Congress of the United States to do. Foreign affairs, commerce, customs, finance, claims of individuals on the United States as a whole, the public debt—these are the things that take up their time; and as the United States, happily for them, is not yet a military nor a naval power, they influence the political system of Europe only as a mercantile nation. Since laws, the police and all that concerns the good order, the progress, and the internal prosperity depends on each individual state, the functions of Congress, as I have said, are not very extensive. This body, however, is very necessary; it joins all the states together

and makes of them a formidable whole. It is the keystone of an immense arch which holds all the parts together and prevents them from breaking up and falling to pieces. It is the safeguard of peace and concord between the different states which, otherwise, excited by ambition, rivalry, and other passions, would make continual war amongst themselves, as one has seen for example in Greece. There is an outcry against the immense sums that Congress receives from the Treasury for its salaries. Certainly the work that it does is not worth the money that they receive, but if one considers the harm that they prevent by their presence, by their existence alone, one agrees that the money it costs is well spent. What quarrels and wars perhaps there would be between the individual states if all were separate countries, if all did not have a single central point as the focus of their converging rays.

If the federal government maintains the peace and union between the individual states, if representing them all it presents to the world a single powerful nation worthy of respect; it must equally be acknowledged that the separate governments of the states are so many obstacles to the appropriation by the President and even the Congress of a power threatening to the general liberty of the nation. They are indeed so many salutary expedients against complete upheaval which could shake or even shatter the federal government. Let us suppose that by an unforeseen misfortune, by some access of frenzy or of disorder the Congress should be dissolved and destroyed. If the principal mainspring of government was broken, the separate governments of the different states, the secondary gears, as I will call them, would always continue to function. Order would be preserved. [47] There would be no anarchy. On the other hand, if the different states did not govern themselves, if the internal police depended on Congress, if, in a word, there were for this whole immense continent only a single constitution, a single legislative body, a single executive power; what latitude would one be obliged to give to it in order to maintain order and to keep the machine running. And in giving to it this power would one not expose the public liberty to the risk of becoming in time the prey of one man. It appears to me to be established that a country need not fear the loss of its liberty while there does not exist within it a permanent army. It is only by this means that Marius Scylla, Cesar, and Augustus robbed their fellow citizens of their liberty. It is finally only by the force of arms that liberty has so many times been violated in our days in France. And on the other hand, if one gives only a small share of power to the executive, could one delude oneself that he would govern well, that he would prevent disorder and even anarchy. These are the ideas which must be better assimilated and better expressed. I want to speak only of the external aspect and of the order that reigns in Congress.

After this body was transferred from New York, where at first after its establishment it had sat and where they had built a building expressly for it,[20] it has held its meetings in Philadelphia until the buildings that they prepare for it in the Federal City should be finished. They must be finished, according to the law, in the year 1800. Philadelphia has put up for it in the interim a suitable and commodious building. The hall for the Representatives is spacious. The galleries above and below could hold perhaps 400 spectators each. They are nearly always filled, which proves that there are idlers here as elsewhere. Or rather this shows that work is so well paid that a man, in working two days, can acquire enough to subsist on for the remainder of the week without doing anything more. The members have the privilege of introducing into the chamber itself all those whom they wish; these persons must then remain outside the bar. Four rows of chairs placed in a semi-circle and protected by a semi-circular enclosure are made ready for the members. Before these 4 rows of chairs one sees as many benches, or desks, in a semi-circle in such a way that each member has an inkstand, a sandbox, some pens, a wafer, and some paper to make notes and comments, and even for writing letters. Before the center of this circle there is a raised platform on which is the *Speaker's* chair, in front of him two tables on which are placed the volumes of law. Two *Clerks* remain there to keep the minutes or the records of the sessions and deliver aloud what is given to them by the *Speaker*. Four great stoves warm the chamber. [48] The members usually keep within the enclosure of the bar. They do not sit according to states but pell-mell.

During the debates of little importance some indulge themselves by leaving the enclosure and warming themselves near the stoves. It was at such a moment that the unseemly row occurred between Mr. Griswold of Connecticut and Lyon of Vermont when the latter spat in the face of the other and where Griswold, after ten days of deliberation, thrashed his antagonist with blows of a stick. This unhappy affair was the first blemish on the reputation for propriety and order which Congress had enjoyed.[21] With the exception of this single instance, it is impossible to see a more proper and imposing assembly. The sessions usually begin at eleven o'clock with the prayer of the Chaplain. It is fervent and pronounced with verve. The members listen to it, hat in hand; this is not done during the debates when everybody has his hat on except him who speaks. After the prayer the *Speaker calls to order;* everybody takes his place. They read the minutes of yesterday's session and the order of the day, and then they proceed to business. The order, the propriety, the tranquility that one notices in this assembly show that this people has for a long time been accustomed to deliberations and to a form of representative government descendent of the English. It seems that love of order, and sangfroid are qualities innate in them; as disorder and violence appear to be the attributes of other peoples.

The duties prescribed for the *Speaker* and the rules for the conduct of the Chamber are observed with the greatest fidelity and it is uniquely to this strict adherence that one must attribute the order that reigns. The *Speaker* gives the floor to the members, calls them to order when they digress from the subject or use some improper expressions. Each member may speak only twice on the same subject, but when the chamber meets as a committee of the whole, each speaks in his turn as many times as he wants, those who have not spoken having always the preference. During the committee of the whole they remove the fasces surmounted by an eagle which is fixed at the barrier opposite the *Chairman.* The *Speaker* then leaves. The messages of the President and the Senate are received only when the House is in full representation. The President sends his message by his secretary; the Senate by the Clerk. They bow, read it, and deliver the contents to the usher who, carrying the fasces, gives it to the *Speaker.* The galleries observe [49] the greatest silence. Members speak only one at a time; there is not ever any urgency to be the first to speak; each is sure his turn will come. They speak from memory; the members have only notes on which they cast their eyes from time to time. They discuss the business thoroughly, sometimes for many days, and it is only when no one has anything further to say that they ask, *Question, question.* They respond by rising or remaining seated. The *Speaker* counts and declares the majority. In matters of importance they vote by *Ayes* and *nos.*

What a difference from the way that we deliberated; but there is much to say in our defense. We built without square or line, without foundations, and above all without rules. During centuries the nation came together only formally and for six weeks. The Diet from 1788 to 1792 was confederated.[22] It was the first time that it deliberated and made laws. What a tremendous task it was that it had to fulfill. The hideous colossus of anarchy had to be overthrown and there had to be substituted for it the ordered fabric of a sound government; it was necessary to create an army, establish taxes, etc., etc., and that in the middle of a foreign faction, in the middle of prejudices rooted in centuries; always in haste, seizing the favorable moment which seemed so precarious and which lasted only as long as the troubles of our neighbors; without rules, without being used to order, holding forth in speeches written many days ahead and often having nothing to do with the matter that was being discussed; not possessing finally any of those advantages which facilitate and accelerate the deliberations of a people who for a long time have lived under a stable and free Constitution.

The chamber where the Senate assembled is above. It resembles more the rooms of a society than a sanctuary of laws. Thirty-two senators are likewise seated in a semi-circle. The President of the Senate, or Vice-President of the United States, performs the functions of the *Speaker*. A small gallery above can hold 50 spectators; they withdraw when the Senate is concerned with executive *business*. In both houses the speeches are delivered apparently with ease. It is necessary to assert that a large number are members of the bar; the others have sat in the State assemblies and have had the occasion to acquire experience. Gallatin, Giles, Nicholas, Brent, etc., are cited as members of the opposition party; Otis, Suvel [Sewall], Dena [Dana], Harper, etc., [50] are of the party of the executive.[23] They debate with clarity, simplicity, and brevity. However, on matters of importance, I have heard the members speak for nearly two hours and always from memory assisted only by notes. To speak from memory is a big advantage; one always makes more of an impression. One speaks to the point and as much as is necessary. With us what foolishness and discussions must be endured; with the business, for all of that, not advanced a step. The party spirit which today divides the nation and Congress merits detailed consideration: more about this later.

The 22nd Feb. Washington Ball. This morning all the ships were decked out with flags and there was a general salute from their guns. It was the celebration of Washington's birthday. Mr. Adams, now President, was invited to it. Piqued by the fact that his predecessor, no longer in office, should be fêted and more thought of than he who was now actually filling the role of President, Mr. Adams answered the *Managers* on the spot in an ill-tempered note, that he would not come. This incident shows well a little man, envious, and quick tempered. The celebration was held in the *Circus*.[24] It is a rotunda painted horribly from top to bottom. The gray and black colors absorb completely the light from the hundreds of candles suspended in iron rings. The dress of the women in white and plumes, very elegant though it might be, did not appear in this gray light to an advantage. The musicians were on a little platform in the middle. Ropes radiating from the center partitioned the whole circumference into eight segments. It was within these partitions where one danced. No one was ill at ease but neither were they gay. Only the Ambassadress of Portugal wore diamonds. The eyes of Mrs. Law [25] née Custis, granddaughter of Mrs. Washington, shone far more brightly.

Indian. *The Little Tortel* [Turtle],[26] Indian chief, was seated in a loge. They had dressed him in an American uniform with enormous epaulets. He appeared very content with the entertainment. He is an extremely sensible man. All his ideas are sound and correct, not at all perverted by misconceptions and wrong arguments. He has come here in order to negotiate with the government on the boundary line which must be drawn and on other problems relative to his nation, which is the Miamis. The point on which he insists the most is to urge [51] the American government to forbid under the pain of the most severe punishment the importation of spirituous liquors among the Indians. He feels this is their bane. He is equally aware of all the perfidy in the politics of the Whites who foment divisions among them, involve them in all their quarrels, brutalize them with drink, finally, using every means to keep them in ignorance and to exterminate them in turn. He recognizes extremely well the superiority of the civilized state to that of the savage. This discussion itself saddened him. "Do not speak to me," he said, "of your superiority if you do not want to furnish me the means by which my nation may attain the same advantages." He came to see Gl. Kośc[iuszko] and brought him a *Tomhawk,* a kind of small hatchet made by the English. Kośc[iuszko] gave him in return his *bourka.*[27] He noticed a pair of spectacles and appeared to be very taken by them. Nothing could equal his joy when Kośc[iuszko] made him a present of them. He could not conceive how it was done, nor tire of the pleasure of looking at objects grown larger by means of these glasses. "You have given me new eyes," he cried. It is the only moment when I saw a little of the savage in him. Other Indians, the Chicksaks and the Six Nations, have come to Philadelphia, but they were in all respects far different from the Little Turtle. The government provided for all their needs during their stay.

Elections. The 22nd Feb. was the day of the elections for a Senator of Pennsylvania; Israël Israël, Jewish in origin, having been excluded from the Senate for not having been duly elected. He is what one calls here a rabid Democrat. He is said to be an honest man. He did much good for the poor during the time of the yellow fever, and although a publican by trade, his mind and his manners are quite cultivated. His opponent was [Benjamin R.] Morgan, a lawyer of a Quaker family. In the great struggles between the two parties, Democrats and Aristocrats, each heaps calumny on the opposite party and praises his own.

Eight days before the election each party held special meetings at which they undertook in the most sacred manner to support their man. The great landowners went around to their tenants with ballots and urged them to come to vote for their friend. I do not have enough information to say whether corruption has entered here already. I happily do not know anything for certain.

The 22nd from 10 in the morning until 10 in the evening all the windows of the Co[u]rt House were opened; [52] at each of these windows there was a table with an urn on top. The voter came up; a judge examined him on whether he had the right to vote. In order to have this right one must have been a citizen of the State for two years, take an oath of loyalty, renounce all allegiance to a foreign power, and pay the tax. The streets were filled with people. The apostles of the parties were presenting ballots to the arrivals with the names of Morgan or Israël already written in. After dinner a swarm of Quakers appeared. This behatted phalanx advanced slowly and in silence; they all voted for Morgan. Everywhere this sect is for the government, enemy of innovations, friends of obedience and peace they would willingly sacrifice some part of their liberty rather than expose themselves to the smallest difficulty. As they are very numerous in Pennsylvania, they are able to tip the balance in the direction that pleases them. The election, except for some fisticuffs, went peaceably. It is not always thus. In New Castel in Dellavare, a man was killed. In Maryllande, seven men lost their lives. In Virginia, corruption, they say, is the order of the day and those who give the most *grog* are sure to be elected. Morgan won by nearly 400 votes.[28]

Prudery. The 28 Feb. I was at a ball of Cl. Yruxo [Don Carlos de Irujo], the Spanish Minister. The women were dressed in everything of the very finest, in gauze, fine muslin, flowers, ribbons, and above all hoops and fringes of silver and ostrich plumes. This is indeed the height of luxury and the ruin of a good many husbands. How many barrels of flour and salt meat are necessary to clothe one of these ladies. What was most noteworthy at the fête were two busts of Venus de Medici and of Antinoüs, copies of ancient sculpture placed in two niches in the ballroom. On entering the hall we found them already covered with two cloaks of Indian muslin. The chaste eyes of our ladies were still offended. They were satisfied only when on top of the muslin the poor divinities were decked out with two blankets. I do not know whether covering them with such care is proof of much innocence.

Wild Rize 1 March. I had dinner at Mr. Mackluer's with Dr. Scandella, [53] Mr. Volney [29] and Vice-President Jefferson. The instructive and interesting conversation of these persons made the time fly by quickly. The Dr. showed us a bag of *Wild Rize* and wild oats, *Zizania Aquatica,* grains which grow wild in marshy places in all of America up to Hudson Bay. Cattle are extremely fond of it. It even provides good nourishment for people. By cultivating this grain one could improve it.

Wild Horses. Mr. Jefferson spoke to us of wild horses on the other side of the Mississippi. The inhabitants of Kentucky go into this country expressly in order to catch them. These horses are Spanish runaways, agile, excellent in all respects, and very long lived. There was one of these horses in Virginia which lived for 47 years.

Peals Muzeume.³⁰ Nothing can be simpler than for governments or rich people to make collections, but for a single individual without a fortune and without any help on the part of the public to gather together already quite an extensive museum, this is remarkable in any country, but above all in one where the taste for sciences is still in the cradle. The museum comprises three large rooms. The metal section, the collection of medals is not much; that of birds is rich; many quadrupeds. I have seen the *mousse* [moose], indigenous to North America, which resembles the elk; many reptiles, and especially rattlesnakes. One was taken alive; it survived in a box for many months. It was found dead the day we were there. I do not know whether it was the cold that had killed it. I know still less if the tale that they tell about it is true. It is said that it has the peculiar ability to charm birds solely by fixing them with its eyes. It attracts them from the tops of the trees down to its jaws and devours them. Mr. Dayton, the *Speaker,* has assured me he has seen this himself. Mr. Peales is also a painter; there can be seen in his museum more than a hundred portraits of the more noteworthy personages of this country as well as foreigners who distinguished themselves during the Revolution. There is also to be seen a collection of figures in wax representing the savage natives of the most distant regions. They are life-size, covered with real skins, costumes, and with arms. The illusion is perfect. There are also some wooden sculptures done by the savages, and done rather well. It is thus true that man in the most uncultivated state senses the urge for and is responsive to the imitation of nature. All these are only curiosities.

Mr. Peal busies himself also with useful things. He has just constructed a model [54] in wood of a bridge with a single arch, which is to be thrown across the Skulkhil. It combines strength with lightness and elegance. He gave us a brochure which explains its construction. He has offered it to the Legislature of Pennsylvania, but the thing has been passed over in silence. In such a manner ignorance or false economy takes hold, alas, among this free people. Another of Peale's inventions is a chimney with a metal plate in it which increases or decreases the smoke duct, and with pipes to increase the heat and prevent it from escaping from the top. The description of this chimney is also to be published. Peale is an old man of 60; he has had two wives and ten children. A charming *baby* of five months is his last work. He can always be seen in the museum in the midst of the serpents, birds, etc. A boy of 16, his son, is the demonstrator of all these curiosities. He is a very intelligent child and follows in his father's footsteps. A few years ago he had made a present to the Philosophical Society of another son, a few months old; the Society adopted him and gave to him the name of Franklin.[31] One can see in the same building the room where the meetings of the Philosophical Society are held. Jefferson is at this time its President. They publish their proceedings from time to time. About fifty unbound volumes comprise the whole library. I have seen there the tremendous bones of an animal which must have been at least twice as big as a horse. It was found in Virginia; they believe it to be a carnivore. How many species have become extinct in nature; why have not combinations of matter produced some new ones?

Captures. The 7th of March. The city, or rather the merchant class, are in a state of general consternation. They have received the news of the taking of the vessel New Jersey, coming from China, by a French corsair.[32] This ship is valued at 600 thousand gourdes. The insurance company alone has lost 250 thousand, and more than 50 private individuals will feel the loss, and many experience their total ruin. By what right does a generous, victorious, and powerful nation commit such flagrant injustices. The Americans, they say, have made a treaty with the English admitting that they have not the right to act as an independent nation. Have they not sent Commissioners in order to give complete satisfaction to the French government? Why were they not admitted? Is it not to add insult to injury; and for what? Because the [55] Americans are feeble. Those for whom they have sworn an immortal hate have been treated otherwise. Why? Because they are strong. How is it that it is the free countries such as Poland, Venice, the independent cities of the Empire, and America; in a word all who are free, that have been destroyed or maltreated by a nation which professes to make war only for liberty? How has this nation in solemnly swearing for years an immortal hate against kings augmented, by its treaties, their domains, the force and power of each one of them?

The arrival of the vessel Dellavare from the East Indies.[33] The same day in the afternoon I went to the wharf and was witness to a moving spectacle. It was the arrival of a great American vessel returning from the East Indies. The day was beautiful and the wind favorable. One discerns first only the top of the masts. The ship then grows visibly larger; soon she can be seen with all her sails filled. She salutes the shore and her native land with 16 cannon salvos. Coming on then with the swiftness of a bird she comes about, drops anchor and comes to a standstill. No horseman ever knew better how to handle his horse than these navigators their winged castles. Immediately all the sailors in their red vests mount the yardarms; they give three glad shouts or *Houza,* and then in an excess of their gladness throw their hats into the river. How sweet was this moment for them, absent for a year, confined in a frail vessel in the middle of the stormy immensity of the seas. After so many perils and anxieties, they see themselves finally in port and look upon the cherished shore, and will in a moment take into their arms their wives, their parents, their friends. This reflection touched me especially when I considered myself. Alas did I not say; how different is my fate! I no longer have a country to see again. Alone, abandoned, harassed by misfortune and suffering, God knows when I shall see again those whose very presence would be a consolation for me.

In the middle of these feelings I was interrupted by the quarrel of two citizens apostrophizing each other with the names Aristocrat and Democrat. The Democrat rejoiced in that the boat taken belonged to the Aristocrats; the other reproached him for the hardness of his heart. The dispute was lively but happily without consequence. To what height the party spirit rises.

[56] 13 March. I passed the evening at the home of Paterson, professor of mathematics. He has a numerous family, of which three are of marriageable age.[34] One was to be married the following day. Her husband-to-be was sitting at the opposite end of the room, not saying a word, not even looking at her. Nonetheless he loves her and will make her happy after the fashion of the country. Their blood is cold like that of fish. They regard marriage as a social duty which all men must fulfill; and the intended espouses his beautiful one as a young *Juris consultes* [consultus] receives his doctoral cap. It is a degree which he acquires in civil life. They passed the evening in a game of questions. They begin playfully; they finish on an instructive note, on agriculture, natural philosophy, domestic management, etc. For example, they ask what is the best way to cook fish, *patetos,* etc. The young maidens listen, educating themselves as they amuse themselves.

I was not present at the marriage ceremony but the next day at that of *Drinking Punch*. 15 March. There is a table in the room, covered with cold meats, hams, wines, liqueurs, *Punch,* etc. The two *brinding grooms* [bridesmen: groomsmen] or young friends of the new husband do the honors to those who come to compliment the married couple. There are only men there. The new bride, who has also her maids of honor, receives in the evening at tea. Among those who had come to the home of the new husband I noticed a short, thick-set figure, with a red face and a puffed out wig. He came there without saying a word, shook the hand of the host, sat down to eat a big slice of beef, drank some wine; as soon as he had eaten his fill, he got up, put his hat on his head and said solemnly *I have done my duty,* and left. He was a priest.

The Prison in the evening. We went to see the prisons in the evening with Dr. Scandella. Mr. Launs, Inspector Gl., gave us some new information.[35] There are in all 260 prisoners, male and female, of whom 120 are *convicts;* the rest are sent by their masters, some sailors, [57] deserters, etc. The 120 are fed in the morning with a soup made of 33 pounds of meat and many vegetables; in the evening maize. The women never have meat but only a soup at dinner and a kind of gruel of maize for supper with *molasses.* The guards cannot praise this regime too highly. The most infirm and feeble women after having been on this regime for some time acquire a plumpness, and a clear and fresh complexion. We then visited the prisoners in their rooms. There are 15 in each. All are occupied in learning to read and write; it is astonishing the progress they have made. I have seen some who in three weeks time have learned to read, and to write passably. Besides the advantage of acquiring a skill which will lead them as a consequence to so much knowledge; what prudence in these institutions to occupy these people continually and not to allow them a free moment to talk of their misfortune and thereby increasing their affliction. They would pass their time in conversation of a sort which certainly would not be edifying. The greatest silence reigns throughout. The guard has shoes with cork soles so that he may not be heard as he goes about; he may catch the prisoners unaware at any moment. He can see, through a glass set into each door, everything that goes on there. The supervisors speak to the prisoners very gently; they praise their progress and encourage them. Finally, in everything and throughout, one sees the principal goal of the institution, that of reforming the man, of making him gentle and good. While in Europe it appears from the treatment to which he is subject that the intended goal is to torment him, to make him bad, and even to infuriate him.

Kaleb Launs, the man who in the whole world deserves well of mankind, maintains with reason that nourishment influences in the strongest possible way the temperament, honor, and spirit of a man. The most violent of men who have committed the greatest crimes, by abstaining from meat or strong liquor have become in prison calm, good, and resigned to all. So is man a machine; so are his passions and above all his mood dependent on the measure and kind of food that he carries in his stomach.[36]

[58] The next day we went to dinner at the home of James Pemberton,[37] one of the leading lights of the society of Quakers, a good man, 75 years old. His wife, rather talkative, made up for the deafness of her husband; the house is spacious and comfortable, simple furniture, excellent dinner, one or two glasses of wine. Maria Prayers, aged 70, was at dinner. Moved by the spirit she had embarked from London to preach in Philadelphia. The seams of the vessel opened and it was about to be swallowed up; in that very moment a *schooner* appeared and took all the passengers on board while the vessel disappeared under the water. "It was a terrible situation," I said to the old woman; "Not at all," she answered me, "my soul was at peace." And in that moment I believe she told the truth; the conviction of the immortality of the soul and the purity of her life could, in this contemplative spirit, have conquered the horror of death that nature inspires in us.

After dinner about ten of the old *Quackeress* came to see their sister. All, dressed in cloaks of gray cloth and cowls, carrying their canes, entered in the very attitude of our *dewotki*.[38] They took each other in their arms and embraced with religious tenderness. The rules of the Quakers are well known. They are contemplative as to their religion, industrious in work, sober in drink, simple in dress, but seeking in simplicity that which is best and most convenient. They are enemies not only of war, but even of all disputes. They are content to enjoy the protection of the laws and of the government without themselves taking any part, except when they believe that, by their votes, they may prevent some step tending to trouble the peace and quiet. They mistake meditation for inspiration; for it is impossible for a man who directs all his thoughts towards one single point, aided by silence, without any distraction, to avoid working himself up to a point of giving birth to some rambling maxims and phrases. They are very strict about their rules and excommunicate for the slightest deviation from them. Ordinarily they acquire rigidity towards these principles only when they are advanced in age. The young people carried away by high spirits and enthusiasm emancipate themselves as much as they can, attending in secret theatres and balls; the young women even lay themselves open to excommunication for the pleasure of powdering their hair and wearing gay colors.[39] I made the acquaintance there of Dr. Marssillac, one-time Captain of the Liancourt regiment, who left France during the Revolution and came to be a Quaker and professor of medicine.[40]

No. 3

[1] Bartram. I was acquainted with Bartram through his voyage into the Floridas.[41] Having learned that he was settled with his brother 5 miles from Phil, I went to see him. It was the 24th of March. The season was very late for this country; not a leaf had opened, but in spite of the winds, or rather the hurricanes, which were blowing for many days the roads were terribly muddy and our horses were sunk to their girths. We crossed at Grays ferry, which is skirted on the other side of the Skulkill by a picturesque and wild cliff. We arrived at the farmhouse. It is built of great stones with a few rustic columns of the same material. The garden extends as far as the Skulkill. It was not the moment to see it. There was not yet a green leaf. Straightway I came upon Bartram, the traveler and poet. He is a man between 50 and 60, small, spare, with a quick-tempered air. In a red vest and leather breeches, he was digging up the ground. Is this the giant, I said to myself, who engaged in such frightful battles with alligators and bears? He seemed to me gentle and upright. A little further on his brother [42] was squatting on the bank of a sort of a stream, his hands completely buried in the mud; he was planting something. His manner was not affable; he improved later; he showed us a few trees and bushes, brought for the most part from Georgia and the Carolinas, and the remainder from the Continent. His interest in botany, added to the profits that he has made from it, has led him to undertake, at times, journeys of 100 miles solely to go into a forest to collect there a plant or a bush. *Franklinia* [43] is a tree from Georgia, with a superb flower; *Gotheria procumbens* [44] from Jersey with its little leaves of deep green speckled with red; they taste like honey; during the wars it was served instead of tea. The hothouse is neither big nor luxuriant. I have seen there green tea from China and Boh[e]a. Its leaves are a deep green, an inch and a half in length when they are allowed to grow; but for drinking they are picked very young, especially those of Imperial Tea.[45] Bartram deals in plants, flowers, bushes, etc.; he sells much to Europe. He is the best botanist in this country.

[2] On returning we saw the house of Hamilton. It is the Villa Borghese of Philad.[46] Its situation is one of the most beautiful that one could see. Placed at a bend in the Skulkill, it overlooks the whole

breadth of its limpid waters, while from the other side one sees clearly all the city of Philadelphia. The house is spacious, arranged and decorated in a style rare in America: there are pictures, medallions, bronzes, etc. All this would be nothing elsewhere; but here the eye, deprived for a long time of all that resembles art, dwells with pleasure on all which reminds one of it. With what satisfaction did I not contemplate a good copy of the Venus by Titian of Florence. Hamilton was not there. He is a man of 50 who in the time of the Revolution took the side of the English. He narrowly missed being hung for this fine loyalty. His farm contains 200 to 300 acres of very mediocre land as is all that in the environs of Philad, but which cultivated could produce something. He leaves it fallow; he is interested only in his house, his hothouse and his Madeira. He carries his fastidiousness about the countryside to such a point that he is in a dreadful humor when one comes to visit it during low tide.

We passed briefly through this lovely place, returning by the Upper ferry. I saw the construction of a canal which is to join the waters of the Skulkill to those of the Dellavare and carry boats from Riding [Reading] etc. as far as Phil. The work appears to me mediocre; the earth is already subsiding; they have stopped it for lack of funds.

26 [March] I spent the evening at the house of Mr. Launs [Lownes], Quaker and Director of the Prison. Latrobe,[47] architect from Virginia, was there. They discussed only the prison: there are 100 male *convicts* and only 17 women. Sometimes the directors themselves avoid the enforcement of sentences imposed by law. They never keep in *Solitary Confinement* those who have been condemned to it, being persuaded that to torment is not to reform; that a man left by himself, deprived of the sight of his own kind [3] becomes embittered, instead of improving, becomes evil. They put them to work at a trade with the others. Thus it was with an Irishman [blank] condemned to be hanged. They have obtained for him a reprieve of six months. On the day of his execution the people assembled before the prison; when the *sheriff* announced that the punishment of the condemned was remitted, what *Houzas*, what cries of joy were there not heard! It would not be thus in all countries. The American people are not bloodthirsty. Never, I believe could they savor the tyrannic executions of Robespierre; never could even the leaders of the parties make them love the upheavals of revolution. Furthermore, everyone is content with his lot; each one has something to lose. Not having as yet what is called a rabble, one need not fear here, at least for the present, that which we have witnessed in France; no one can answer for the future.

N.B. I must buy *a* view *of the Penitentiary house in Philadelphia* [48] at Thomas Condie's, No. 20 Carter's Alley, *and a visit to the Jail and Penitentiary house* by Turnbull.[49]

The 30th of March I went to see the frigate of the United States. It cost [blank]. The reasons for this are first, I believe, little regard for public funds, then the lack of established shipyards, stores of wood for construction, and cordage. Each article is brought from a different place, the keel from Jersey, the *leive* [live] *oake* and cedars from Georgia, etc. Labor is perhaps four times dearer than elsewhere; a carpenter is paid up to two dollars a day. This frigate could carry up to 54 cannon. It is superlatively well built, with the finish and luxury that the Americans, true sons of the English, do not spare in any public work.

I dined yesterday at the home of Dr. Collins, a Swedish minister, an honest old man, a talker and having his *hoby horse* as everybody. He is engaged on a work on languages; he finds that they all resemble each other; [4] that even in Polish there were many Greek, Latin, and Swedish words. I saw with surprise at his house the dictionary of Trotz and a Polish Telemaque.[50] I spoke of Sweden and Gotheburg. I mentioned the Mitchell family when a spare old man with a frank face said: *"he is my owner."* It was Captain Daungman *of the ship* Apparences belonging to Erskin and Comp. How he interested me! How many memories of the happy days that I passed in Gotheborg came crowding into my heart and into my mind. It was there for the last time that sentiment touched me; since then my heart, closed to all tender emotions, has known only indifference or pain. I went on board the ship which belonged to my friend and wrote my name there. If they should see it, they will know that I carry them always in my heart, that all that belongs to them is dear to me.[51]

2 April. Climate. What a climate! What a climate this country has. In the last days of March it was as hot as with us in July. The thermometer stood at 71° Fahrenheit, the next morning a wind from the North and rain. This is what our winter was: December cold, winds, rains, little snow; January much more moderate, from time to time some warm days; February the same; in March winds, or rather terrible hurricanes.[52]

In the last beautiful days of March the visits of the young ladies to Gl. [Kościuszko] increased. They were truly flowers appearing at the first puff of the zephyr. All came in order to have him paint them.[53] It is impossible to see a greater number of beautiful women than those one meets in Philadelphia, superb complexion, beautiful eyes, beautiful hair, beautiful teeth. They are not figuratively but literally flowers;

they have their brilliance and life span. A woman of 26 is already faded, but [5] on the other hand at 14 she is formed.⁵⁴ The young unmarried women enjoy a great independence and do not abuse it. Their respect for their parents is not at all slavish; they even overdo this a little. In general parents love their children tenderly, but these do not always in return show a like affection. The scant respect that children here have for the authors of their being is in keeping perhaps with the general ideas of Liberty and Equality engraved on all their hearts. Respect and obedience, these one learns first under an arbitrary government, and the same relationship of submission which one finds between the ruler and the ruled extends into the family between parents and children. In the inverse sense one sees the same relationship in America.

N.B. Newspaper. The Barbary treaty cost the United States nearly 9 million doll. The advantages gained from the Mediterranean trade must be immense in order to counterbalance this onerous tribute. It is the journalist Beach [Bache] ⁵⁵ who has made public disclosure of this. This is one of the advantages of the freedom of the press: the government does not commit a fault but it is immediately criticised and denounced in the terrible tribunal of public opinion. Of all the means of enlightening a nation that of public newspapers seems to me the best and the most easily accomplished. A tome scares off the indolent, but a page by exciting curiosity instructs without tiring. Diffusing everywhere, it carries enlightenment into the most remote corners. Directed by the right-minded, the impartial, without hatred, party spirit, and passions; its effects resemble those of a brook which fertilizes and invigorates the fields through which it flows; but in the hands of a violent man, one imbued with prejudice, blinded by passions, it is a torrent which carries everywhere havoc and destruction. The public sheets or newspapers are of such importance in a free country that it appears to me indispensable that the authors should be elected by the people.⁵⁶ The writer should be rather a magistrate than a merchant.

[6] Commerce. This is the state of importation and exportation of the United States of America that I have received on good authority. Merchandise is imported to the extent of 81 million dollars; they export 51 million, of which 25 comes from products of the United States alone; the remaining 26 million are products of the Isles (*West Indies*). Thus the balance is unfavorable to this country by 30 million. England extends to them a credit of 22 million a year and more. They pay them back from their 25 million income at the year end and re-

ceive new credit. How they make up the remainder is an enigma. The amount of general export of the United States is some 600,000 tons.

Revenue. The revenue of the Treasury is provided by customs. It amounts to 7 million and more doll. per year. That which is collected from liquor does not reach 500,000 doll. There is thus an indirect tax; that is to say the worst of all. The final consumer without perceiving it carries the whole burden. The merchant loses nothing on this.

Taxes. The inhabitants also pay taxes to the Treasury of their respective states. In New England, especially in cities such as Boston, etc., and in Pennsylvania these taxes are rather large. But, if the federal government has shown unfairness in establishing indirect taxes, the individual governments of the states have had the wisdom never to permit any but the direct.[57]

The 10th of April we left with Dr. Scandella in a cabriolet to see Dr. Logan, the celebrated farmer and celebrated fanatic, living near Germantown. (The farmer, Mr. Logan, is the grandson of James Logan,[58] secretary of William Penn. He gave to each of us a letter in the hand of that great man [William Penn], and a newspaper published by Benj[amin] Franklin when he was a printer.) [59] The road was horrible. The large numbers of wagons which go [7] to town had made ruts in this clayey soil to the depth of two feet. The Assembly of Pennsylvania had directed at its last meeting that a public highway should be built as far as Germantown. If it had been done sooner, not only here, but everywhere, then what saving in broken axles, in wheels; what profit from the speed of transport and the comfort and convenience of travelers would accrue to the state. But the high cost of labor, the parsimony of the farmer legislators, and finally the slowness of popular government have been against it. They feel however the need of good roads and with time these will be made.

Although yesterday it was warm as in summer, today we had a very penetrating wind; and although it was the 10th of April and at 39 degrees latitude, except for a few weeping willows one did not see a tree in leaf. This bad road, to the shame of the farmer, continued up to the door of his house. It is of brick, large, and well kept. A smooth lawn like a green carpet, sown with groups of cedars and *Hamlocks* extended before one's eye.

Doctor Logan received us civilly, but with an air of preoccupation and pain. We did not wait long to discover the source of his ills. It was a preoccupation, a fixation, indeed a madness. He was convinced that his country was the most unhappy on earth, that it was menaced by the greatest dangers, that is to say, by total destruction. The authors of all these imaginary calamities were the English: they had bought and corrupted the government. They have ruined agriculture, opposed all types of industry, and aim for nothing less than to corrupt the country, to impoverish it, and finally to devour it. This was the subject of the conversation before dinner. Mrs. Logan, pale, with a rather good figure, has caught the same disease [8] and as the sensibilities of women are always more lively and more highly strung, so it happened that her discourses carried indeed infinitely more vehemence than those of her husband. The dinner was frugal but good. One drank only one or two glasses of wine but nevertheless the irascibility, the imagination of our hosts acquired a degree of intoxication which went as far as mania. It was no longer a simple and sober meal but rather an infernal banquet of evil-doing sorcerers. They consecrated there to public execration, to destruction, to eternal suffering this mercenary nation, corruptive, tyrranical, adulterator of gold and of blood, this infamous England, author of all the ills of humanity.

After having taken care of the guilty and the tyrants in this way, they began to sing the praises of, to render homage to the virtues of the nation which has revenged humanity so long oppressed, which has allowed men to taste happiness and true bliss. They began to praise the French up to the skies. Madame took out of a sort of sanctuary, a sheet of paper on which was an ode addressed to the French. "My dear," said the Doctor to his wife, "I beg you, when you read these verses, moderate your rapture. You read it with too much vehemence, with too much feeling." Madame began to read, and in spite of the advice of the Doctor her voice trembled, her cheeks flushed a livid red, and *afflata* [*adflata est*] *numine* [60] she declaimed these verses with all the fury of a Sibyl. Her enthusiasm was such that she even electrified and inflamed a Quaker. This was Dr. Marsillac, a Frenchman, one time Captain of the dragoons, today a Quaker, whether by vocation or calculation I do not know. He took fire and, whether to court the favor of his hosts or actually carried away by the sacred fires of fanaticism, he consigned all the English to perdition; and, in spite [9] of the principles of gentleness, humanity, and peace of the Society of which he is a member, wished them as much harm as he wished good and success for his dear compatriots.

Tired out by the cursing and the need to show enthusiasm we finally left the table and the Dr. took us to see his farm. It consists of 450 acres, the most part in pasture which he irrigates by the means of a creek which crosses the fields. He told us that two men are necessary for the cultivation of each hundred acres of meadow and three for those under the plough. He pays these men eight and ten dollars per month and feeds them; but they are obliged to provide themselves with lodging. He cuts the hay twice. Each acre gives him two tons, which is sold for 20 dollars per ton. Every spring he buys 20 cows at 25 and 30 doll. each. The milk, cream and butter which he sends to Philad., reimburses him for the money that he used for the purchase of these cows. Towards winter in order to reduce the expense of feed he resells them. In this way, apart from the milk for the needs of the household and the farmer, 20 cows bring him each year between 5 and 600 doll. clear. He seeds his fields in lucerne and fertilizes them with plaster of Paris. This same plaster does nothing for land with clayey soil. Dr. Logan has 40 acres of poor land to sell; he is asking 100 dol. per acre for it. Except for this it was not easy to draw information from him. If you put a question to him about the fields, occupied by his fixation, he answers you by a sally against the aristocrats; should you want to know something about the irrigation of the meadows, he would launch at you a malediction against the English. [10] He showed us his horses. He has a very beautiful one, full of fire, but although hardly 4 years old it is already at stud. Note how he shows a little greed in everything. He asked 1,000 dollars for this horse. At home one could get it for 60 ducats at the most.

We returned finally to the house and were shown into a new *parlor*. The curtains, the covers for the sofas and the chairs were made of cotton cloth in blue and white squares; and all was homemade. The clothes of Dr. Logan as well as those of the children were equally so. They did not fail to point this out to us while adding that if all American families did as much, the country would be free of the tribute that it pays annually to English industry. This observation, in fact absolutely true, was followed by a volley of invectives against England, and there began again more than ever the most bitter complaints on the subjection of America to this power, on the growth of the aristocracy, and on its sinister projects for the total ruin of the country. "We must have a revolution," said Mr. Logan, "That alone can save us; but would you believe it, our people do not want to hear talk of it. They are already corrupted. Ah! If I were now in France, if I might see all that goes on there, how I would rejoice." Madman, I said to myself, You do not know what you want; you have a large and comfortable house, fields which give you four times your need. You live under wise and free laws, and you pine after upheaval and blood. You are a fanatic, my friend, your brain is sick. The tranquility, the abundance with which you live weighs you down, bores you; you need to be [11] roused; you need to be shaken up, whether by the ruin of your house or your country. But go to France; go to Europe; see what goes on there and you will return cured of your madness.

Hospital.[61] This is a very large building which is not yet completely finished and which is only partly occupied. It is maintained by an old legacy. The State of Pennsylvania contributes to it only by the way; as for example last summer it gave 10,000 dol. in order to maintain the poor there, sick with the yellow fever. All the sick who come there are obliged to pay for their upkeep. If they are not in the position to do so, someone answers for them. However, those who have no resources whatever are admitted gratis. I have seen about forty of the sick; the others, in number more than 50, are idiots or the insane. They are kept in separate cells. Sitting or lying down they usually keep quiet as long as no one comes to speak to them. Most of them, even when spoken to, answer very sensibly, but the broken windows, their torn clothes, wild eyes and their chained feet show that they have attacks which make necessary the cruel state in which they are detained. A young Irish girl, with the most beautiful face that one could see, affected me the most. Hers was a folly of love. She spoke to us of her lover who was a sailor named Williams, and with whom she fell in love during the crossing. We asked her if he were handsome. "To me he was very handsome," she answered me. Poor unfortunate one, so young, so beautiful! The peaceful insane or the imbeciles walk about freely. They are even employed at work and in the upkeep of the house. They cut wood, work in the garden, etc.

[12] The doctors of the Faculty of Philadelphia care for the sick in turn and free of charge. All those who come to visit the sick pay a shilling entrance. If this tax is used for the care of the sick, it is fair. Curiosity owes this tribute to suffering humanity. Very near is a little building for those infected with venereal disease. It is too small for the number of persons who, they say, are infected with this cruel sickness. The Quakers are accused of opposing the enlargement of this building. Led by a false zeal they believe that preventing the unfortunates from curing themselves of this disease will deter young people from frequenting the source where they can get it.

Bettering house.[62] I will not say much of this house. I was there with ladies who, on entering the first hall, were so shocked at the bad odor that they left everything, fled and went to walk in the garden surrounding the house. It is very well cultivated, even adorned with flowers, plants, trees, bushes, etc. There is a little hothouse. But it was not the garden that I wished to see and to examine. It was the establishment itself and the work of those held there. I had no more than a glimpse of them. The house is immense and occupied by people of all ages. The sexes are separated. The courtyard was filled with pigs, poultry, etc. The admission fee for the two houses that I paid for the company cost me two dollars. I bought with it a lesson which is that when one goes somewhere in order to observe or be instructed, one must go alone, or with a like-minded friend; and not to play the gallant with the ladies, which especially at our age and with our means is very much out of place.

15 Apr. I was with Scandella at Gallatin's house. He is originally from Geneva [13] but has been established for 20 years in America. He is an educated man, what is more, is as clear headed and as logical as one could wish to meet. The role he plays in Congress though without any affectation of pre-eminence is well known. He is the leader of the opposition. The preciseness of his mind, his moderation, and his integrity prevent him, I would venture to say, from carrying his opposition to a point dangerous to the maintenance of order and the Constitution. He has published several pamphlets on the finances of the United States. Thomas Cooper has also written on the same subject but in a very diffuse manner.[63] He showed us the accounts for this year. The report of the Treasury is made with exactness and in adequate detail. Mr. Wolcot, secretary of the Treasury Department, is a very proper officer for this position.[64] The same can not be said of Mr. M'k Henri [McHenry], secretary of the War Department. Perhaps he lacks neither good will nor integrity, but he does lack the necessary knowledge for his position. The erection of forts, the building of the navy, the distribution of military forces, the maintenance of discipline among the soldiers, all are in his province; however he is not, as it is said, either a geographer or a soldier, or sailor. His reports are inexact. He puts for example "given to such a contractor such and such a sum," and then without specifying for what object, such and such, and these vague accounts are repeated endlessly. I do not believe there is any pilfering of the smallest sum of the public monies, but why give grounds for suspicion? Gallatin has insisted that the purpose for each expense should be specified, but up to the present without success.[65] He showed us that during two or three years the tonnage, that is to say the commerce of the United States has grown considerably. In 1791 it was 600,000 tons; today it is 800,000 and more, of which about 500,000 is in foreign trade, 200,000 in coasting vessels, that is to say of the United States; the rest in fisheries.

[14] Van Bra[a]m. The 19th of April I embarked with Dr. Bache [66] on a boat which performed the office of a carriage and leaves at each flood tide for Burlingtown. Barrels, casks, baggage, passengers, half-French, half-American, made up our group. The weather was rather fine, but the wind very weak. We enjoyed the beauty of both banks of Jersey and Pennsylvania completely at our ease. The former very

sandy and of sterile soil presented neither numerous nor rich farms; but the Pennsylvania bank was covered with houses not only well kept but elegant. I regretted that many were without trees, but the others of light wooden construction, all white with shutters and blinds painted in green, with a pretty bowling green in front, having in all the air of simplicity, of neatness and happy mediocrity, led me often to say with a sigh: It is not a mansion but a house such as that, a garden, a wife dear to me, indeed that would be my happiness. But, alas, as modest as are these wishes perhaps they will never be achieved.

After three and a half hours of sailing we arrived at the farm of Mr. Bache, the father. He is the husband of the daughter of Franklin, celebrated American philosopher and patriot. Mr. Bache has completely the air of a *Country Esquaire,* frank countenance and with a rather jovial humor. Madame by her natural wit and her conversation does not belie the origin from which she descends. We found there the whole family assembled with the exception of a little boy who was at school in Bourlingtown. It consisted of three [15] sons, of whom the first, Benjamin, is the printer known for his opposition newspaper. He has been to Europe with his grandfather and received a very good education in Switzerland. The refusal of the office of postmaster general to Father Bache has made the whole family since then very embittered against Gl. Washington and in general against the power of the executive. The second son was the doctor with whom I came, an interesting young man. The third, Louis, was destined to be a farmer; [67] three girls, one of ten, and two of marriageable age. They were very pretty and were neatly dressed, and nothing was more natural nor more touching than their behavior towards their parents. While one was holding his hand and leaning on her father (seated in an armchair at one time belonging to Doctor Franklin), she was caressing him; the other was singing very well, accompanying herself on the harpsichord. The good old man joined at times his bass voice to the piping voice of his daughter.

This whole family appeared to know good fortune, that is to say enjoying easy circumstances, independence, and tranquility. With these people domestic harmony is as much a virtue as a custom. Mr. Bache has a farm of 270 acres divided into meadows, cultivated ground and woodland. He has five men to work it and a gardener; a Negro and one girl do the domestic service. With these as much work gets done, and with more cleanness, than at a district magistrate's house with 30 peasants; at home we need a steward with a whip, lackeys, footmen, boys, wagoneers, jockeys, four or six girls, and with this, incessant laments, complaints and grievances. Here a few well-paid people, work willingly and well and the forehead of the landowner is unfurrowed from morning to night.[68] Fish, salt beef with all sorts of vegetables made up the dinner. *The mush,* a kind of gruel from Indian Corn [69] with milk added made a healthy and frugal supper.

The next day we had [16] a thunder storm, lightning, and a deluge of rain. The thunder is much more terrible here than in Europe. Its rolls spread out through the whole heaven with a din which at times imitates cannon fire, at times the rolling fire which passes from one flank to another of a large army. The whole firmament was covered with streaks of lightning; it all finished with a deluge of rain and hail.

As soon as the tempest had ceased, we took a small boat to go to the house of Mr. Vanbraam. The river was covered with wild ducks of different kinds and sizes. The females, very careless of their progeny, without troubling themselves at all, lay their eggs in the water. There were thousands of them there, some floating, others abandoned in the gravel of the banks. More than one traveler ready to give an account of everything and to find something marvelous where there is only simplicity and naturalness said, "In America there is a species of duck which lays its eggs in the gravel, and such is the property of this river mixed with the tidal waters that, by covering these eggs for six days and then leaving them exposed to the sun for the same length of time, it hatches young ducks there of the greatest beauty!"

We arrived finally at the house of Mr. Vanbraam.[70] He is a Dutchman who made an immense fortune in China and the Indies and has come to establish himself in this country. If he brought us great riches and great curiosities from that country, it seems that in return he has left there all his good sense and all his prudence. Instead of conforming to the simplicity of the country he has sought in his buildings and all his enterprises to flaunt an Asiatic luxury. Accustomed in China to making money easily, he thought that that which he brought with him would never be exhausted. Therefore, without consulting people of the country worthy of trust, on [17] one hand he placed his capital into the hands of a man who has not paid him on time, and on the other he has arranged to buy a piece of land at double its value; to hire a crowd of workers to whom he was paying or promised to pay double for their work; in this way besides that which the land cost him he has spent 80,000 dollars for the house alone. His creditor [debtor?] having failed him, he was not able to pay his own [creditors] and was put into prison. At once a Dutch Baron and a Chinese Mandarin he acutely resented this injury. He spoke of it with a heart wounded by grief, and his complaints would never have finished if I had not put him on the subject of the Emperor of China. Immediately his face became radiant. He began to tell us of the lunch to which he was invited by this prince; of the glass of wine and the preserves that the Emperor himself had sent to him, etc. He then showed us his house.

It is immense, surmounted with a cupola and decorated with golden serpents in the Chinese manner. Six tabourets of porcelain were arranged in a circle in the peristyle. The cellars are immense and the floor alone, made with great flags of stone, cost him 3,000 doll. In the dairy there are twenty porcelain bowls a foot and a half in diameter; they were filled with milk and cream. In the larder there were tubs, also in porcelain, for keeping fresh and salt meat. In truth everything was so much in porcelain that I thought for a moment that his wife was made of the same material, she was so pale and still. This is his own niece, aged 18, that Mr. Van Braam has just married.

We entered a hall filled with different objects from China, more curious than useful: two pictures made of ivory in relief representing birds, painted in lacquer, decorated with branches, flowers and arabesques in crystal, chalcedony; I believe even some garnets and rubies; [18] many chests in sandalwood containing dessert services; they portrayed rocks amidst waterfalls, houses, horses, men, etc.; figures in silver gilt and vermeil; a vase of a piece of rock crystal cut very artistically; a cup from the horn of a rhinoceros which, according to Mr. Van Braam, warns a man when poisoned liquor is poured into it; many landscapes and views of China in oil, well painted, especially of the clouds; other pictures painted on glass; finally what surprised me most, a copy of the celebrated Venus of Titian of Florence, made in China by a Chinese with an exactness of which they themselves alone are capable; many small oval pictures on ivory and in oil, as many on Chinese subjects as copies after the European engravings of Angelica Kaufmann and others.[71] All this, very precious here, very pretty, was made in China at a very low price; labor is considered as nothing there. But what is the most interesting in all this collection is about 60 notebooks of Chinese paintings representing with the greatest accuracy their techniques in arts and crafts, their sciences, their agriculture, ceremonies, criminal code, natural history, botany, geographical maps, etc., etc. This illustrated collection with a text by a man who has been there could give us precise information on these people, so ancient and so interesting. Mr. Vanbraam is publishing a work on China.[72] I doubt that it is complete. Moreover engravings made in America do not promise much.

Mr. Van[braam], thoroughly discontented with this country, is selling everything and is embarking for Europe.[73] They have acted badly towards him in this country, but much of it is his own fault. And thus what are great riches: one believes them to be inexhaustible and spends them without order and discernment; [19] one expands his desires in proportion to them, or one torments himself with difficulties to attain them, or if one attains them, one suffers a torment, perhaps even greater yet, that of satiety. I do not speak, moreover, of the envy that these riches excite in others, of the thousand snares that rogues set to plunder you. One does not experience these misadventures with a small fortune which does not go beyond the state of ease. Men will forgive this and let you enjoy it in peace.

We returned as we had gone, by water. We had a gust of wind which nearly broke our mast. This frightened our beautiful American ladies and still more the *babys* who were all *see [sea] sick*. How beautiful are the women of this country, as their children are robust and healthy! It is not to be wondered at: first of all this nation is for the most part descendent from the Irish and the English who are recognized as being in general both beautiful and healthy; then they marry in the flower of youth, not drained by debauchery and excess and not yet overtaken by destructive afflictions and the blight of worry: it is only afterwards that an abundance of succulent meats and hot drinks enflame their blood and make them old at forty.

At noon we arrived at Philadelphia and we went, each one, straight home. In Europe it would have been necessary to pass through a thousand formalities and indignities: they would ask you where are you going, what are you planning to do. They would open your portmanteaus, fumble through your pockets, etc. Happy is the country which does not know all these abominable ceremonies.

On my return I heard from Dr. Scandella that I had been elected a member of the Philosophical Society of Philadelphia.[74] This news brought me greater surprise than delight. By provoking serious reflection [20] on myself it humiliated more than praised me. I recalled with sadness both the superficial education that I received and the little effort I have taken since in order to acquire truly useful knowledge. What do I know? I ask myself. A little about history, travels, belles-lettres, a little acquaintance with the arts. Enough certainly to be elected a member of a small supper club of elegants, but a member of a Philosophical Society, of a Society where one concerns himself only with the exact and useful Sciences; I have no right there whatsoever. I am perhaps a philosopher only because I am poor and during 20 years that I have been in the world I have struggled against adversities of all kinds and have not yet succumbed.

N.B. 4 May. I was at a meeting this evening of the Philosophical Society. Its President, Mr. Jefferson, communicated to us several letters received from different parts of the Union concerning the discovery of bones of mammoths or other unknown animals. These letters were sent to the committees for investigation. They then discussed the different subjects of Science.[75] The Society was founded before 1750; it has at least 200 American and foreign members. I shall speak at length of it at another time; an extraordinary matter besets me.

On my return from this meeting at half past ten in the evening Stanislas Dombrowski, the General's servant, told me that his master asked to speak to me. Here is the extraordinary confidence that I received when we were alone. "Mr. Niem[cewicz] you must give me your word of honor that you will tell no one what I am about to confide in you. And that you will do what I ask of you." [21] "You ask nothing dishonorable?" "No, I give you my word." "Then, tell me." "I leave this night for Europe. I leave alone; I leave 100 doll. for my servant. You will dismiss him tomorrow. I leave 200 doll. for you. You may also dispose of my clothes that I leave here, as well as some plate that is at the house of Dr. Rush." Stupefied, petrified at this confidence which came as a bolt from the blue, I wanted, being recovered from my astonishment, to know the reasons for this journey and the place to which he was going. I was told that he did not know himself, neither where he was going nor why. I remonstrated with him, pointing out the dangers one would encounter venturing all alone on a journey of this nature. I urged him to reflect on it—I was silenced—"If nothing can deter you from your plan; rather than to see you chance it yourself in the state of your health, I shall turn a blind eye to all and offer to accompany you." "That is impossible." "Then it was to leave me all alone in this strange land separated everywhere by seas that you proposed to me, asked me to come here? Is it such a token of confidence and friendship that you give me that no more than a few hours before your departure you disclose to me an idea, a plan that you have had perhaps since Europe? Did you think that I would betray you?" "No, but, but—" "What will they think here of this strange flight?" "I beseech you to tell everyone that I have gone to take the waters in Virginia. You will leave Philadelphia in three days and you will go in that direction saying that it is to rejoin me." "You give me [22] then a fine commission. I must tell lies here; I must run about the country in order to tell more lies. Ah! in what embarrassment you have placed me! Alone, without friends, and without means. No, I will not touch anything that you leave me."

Thereupon a scene was on the point of arising; it was not the moment for it. I held my tongue. The servant was called (nothing was said to him, neither what was being done nor what was being left for him. All this embarrassment was reserved for me.) He had a portmanteau brought to him and put there a few effects, and said that he wanted to rest. I withdrew. Too moved, too agitated by all that I had just heard, I could not close an eye. At one o'clock in the morning I left and roamed the streets, weighed down by grief and by most sad thoughts. At 4 o'clock a covered carriage arrived with Mr. J[efferson] inside. K[ościuszko] got in without embracing me. In spite of all these goings on the idea of a separation, perhaps forever, the idea of the dangers to which he exposed himself in his condition and without any help, reduced me to tears. With my eyes I followed the carriage as far as I could. They took a route completely opposite from that to the harbor. I do not know for whom this precaution was taken for all the world still slept. I learned later that they had gone by land up to New Castel, where a boat awaited him.

Here I am then, abandoned in this foreign land without means, forgotten by my people, not being able to return to my home without running the risk of being persecuted and imprisoned again, not being able to settle here, nor even [23] to have the means of existence! There in Peters[burg] when he begged me to follow him, could I have ever expected such an end. According to my instructions I told the servant that he was dismissed; I told him what was left for him. He was outraged and cried treachery. "It is then for this that he made me come so far. He owes me two months pay. I have no more than 80 dollars to leave with, to recompense me for the unpleasantness and hard service to which I was subjected." "No, my friend, a 100 doll. are set aside for you. Two hundred was left for me. I give it all to you. Here then is 300 doll. I do not wish to keep a penny for myself." He raised some objections, not wishing to leave me without any resources; he was quite sincere. I insisted, gave him the money and took a receipt. I wrote a note to K[ościuszko] in these words: "I have remitted all the money you left with me to your servant; I enclose here his receipt. I have had your effects, clothes, etc. packed and had them sent to Mr. J[efferson]. I will not touch anything, not even the silver. Friendship is not paid for with money; it asks reciprocity, confidence; I have not received this from your side. Farewell, may your fate be as happy as mine is pitiable."

This departure, so precipitous, so concealed, so stealthy, caused general astonishment. I was assailed by questions; I lied a thousand times a day. What will they think of me when in the course of time all is divulged? Why this mystery? How in this time of mistrust and suspicion is one to explain this clandestine voyage, our separation, and my remaining here. I spent the following days packing, transporting his things and preparing myself for my departure.

[24] Before leaving Philad., on which I took so few notes, I restrict myself to say that at the moment of my departure men's minds there had reached a high degree of enthusiasm, or rather a high state of ferment. The government has taken advantage of the indignation that the publication of the dispatches has excited everywhere.[76] It has, I say, profited by it as much for actually building up its defenses as for providing itself greater resources and means, in a word to extend and increase its power. Speeches approving the conduct of the government and promising it all possible support arrived from all sides, even from Virginia, the State most opposed to the administration. The city of Philad, which could be regarded as the capital of the Union, showed this zeal more than all the rest. The merchants, the different groups in the city went en masse to the house of the President and to Congress to show this same zeal.

Today, the 6th of May, I saw a very moving spectacle; more than a thousand young people between 17 and 23, drawn up in ranks, preceded by a flag, music and drum beats, going to present their address to the President. I saw them march. Considering their zeal only from the most innocent point of view, the sight of this company moved me to tears. In truth, is there anything more touching than to see a thousand young men in the bloom of youth, hardly at the beginning of life, offering, at the first danger to their country, to die in her defense? Would that she, enjoying the benefits of peace never have the need for their help; but if heaven should strike her with the scourge of war, may they keep their word; may they fight and die as free men, and above all never stain their swords with the blood of their fellow citizens. Why must enthusiasm, such noble sentiments, be accompanied by faults of conduct that perhaps can be pardoned because of their age, but would be inexcusable if they were deliberately encouraged. Since these youths have begun to gather, [25] the peace of the night is disturbed by their cries and chants. Drunk with wine they go to serenade at the windows of the President; they then go to break those of the printer Bache; they have hoisted the black cockade. Why these outward signs? From whom do they want to distinguish themselves? Why affect by these distinctions to show or to raise suspicion that there are some Americans who, unlike them, would not go to defend their country? It is these same means that provoke divisions. Alas, how many times have we not seen pools of blood spilled for a half a yard of ribbon?

The members of the opposition are leaving Congress; Gails [Giles] and Nicholas have left.[77] The administration is strong and pushes with vigor measures of defense. A new department has been created for the Navy and great sums have been appropriated to increase it. They have ordered the purchase of 12 ships carrying between 16 and 22 cannon. They are raising 2 million dolls. from territorial taxes, a new regiment of artillery. They have given the President great sums to fortify the forts. The *bil* to raise an army of 20,000 men is to be discussed. Gallatin, the sole speaker in opposition, fights resolutely, not that he is against all the measures of defense; no one certainly has more at heart than he the safety, liberty and independence of America; but he fears that so much power, so many offices and so much money to distribute given to the President can only upset the equilibrium, sow corruption and become dangerous for American liberty. Already the *Alien bill*,[78] conceived in a truly Turkish spirit, shows to what point the administration attempts to adopt and imitate the arbitrary means of despots. There is nothing more proper than to be on guard against troublesome and dangerous foreigners, but indiscriminately to place under suspicion all foreigners comes from a desire [26] more to reign than to protect.

7 May. I had the effects of Gl. [Kościuszko] carried to Mr. Jeff[erson], the books to Sutcliffe, my things to Dr. Bache.

Chapter III

DEPARTURE FOR BALTIMORE AND WASH-
INGTON. FIRST MEETING WITH GEORGE
WASHINGTON. ALEXANDRIA. GEORGETOWN

Departure for Baltimore. N.B. I paid 5 doll. for a place in the *stage*.
8 May. The day ordained by the President for prayer and fasting was
that of my departure.[1] At 9 o'clock I got up on the *Stage;* I was the
ninth. We stopped before the prison. A Negro, in breeches, vest, a torn
shirt, and his hands tied with a handkerchief came out. One of our
company, whom I discovered later to be his master, placed him among
us. We were then, with the coachmen, eleven people tightly packed
and very uncomfortable. In France and elsewhere a company as numerous would be rather talkative, rather gay; here we were as so many
mutes. Three young women, very pretty but not having between the
three of them enough to make a single bosom; three young gentlemen,
an old woman, the man with his negro and I made up the complement
of this terrestrial vessel.

We crossed at Greys ferry and took the road to Wilmingtown. There
is nothing more fertile and better cultivated than all this countryside.
Some farms, or rather country houses, very neat, well-kept, proclaimed
that the owners are people from a rich mercantile city. In general one
can judge the wealth of a city by its environs. Man, confined in cities,
tormented by the thirst for gold, oppressed by anxiety and fear, tied
to work during the day, breathing only the dust of day and the infected air of night, pines in his fetters for the only true joy granted to
man, I mean a retreat in the country and the sight of nature. It is thus
on these retreats that the rich of the cities pour with full hands the
gain that they acquired with such risks and hard work; going so to
say to visit it just as one goes to see a mistress in secret [27] and for a
few minutes only. They love it ardently and take as much pleasure as
pride in ornamenting it and cultivating it.

We stopped at Chester, a small town built in stone. The road from there to Wilmington offers the most beautiful views that one could behold. To the left is the Dellavare where one sees boats, some departing under full sail, others struggling while tacking against the winds which drive them away from a long awaited shore. There are on this side numerous hills surrounded with groves of trees. Those who will build here will look out on the most varied scene, and the most picturesque and most magnificent prospect that one could ever hope for. To the right you see The Iron Mountains; [2] one arrives then at Brandywine Creek. Its waters flow between rocks forming a thousand cascades both natural and artificial which all serve to turn the immense mills which have been constructed there. Most of them remain motionless. It is thus that the depredations on American commerce paralyze everywhere industry and work.

We dined at Wilmington which appears as sad when one is there, as it appeared gay and animated when seen from the river. The society at table was as taciturn as it had been during the journey. I realized that they took me for a Frenchman and in this guise, by the coldness and extortions in the inns, they revenged themselves on me for all the depredations and injuries that America has received from France. On leaving Wilmington, I noticed that the poor Negro had manacles of iron on his hands. His master confided in me that he had fled two years before, that he was caught on the quayside in Philad and he was taking him back home. He told me that there were more than 500 negroes who had escaped from the Southern States and sought refuge in Philad, where they found themselves under the protection of the law and even more under that of the Quakers, who by the principles of their sect, and, perhaps, as their enemies accuse them, a little for self-interest, give them asylum and work for their emancipation.

We were in the state of Dellavare. It is wooded and cut up by *Creeks;* dwellings are more rare. [28] The houses are built not in brick but in undressed fieldstone that gives them a bizarre but not unpleasing appearance. The woods were in all the verdant freshness of spring. The most common trees are eight to ten species of oak, such as *White and black oak, live, water oak, etc. hicory, chesnut, walnut, mapple Tree.* I can not give their description having seen them only as we drove by. The wild vine is very common; its trunk curved and twisted, growing very high, but always supporting itself and twisting around another tree. It is a parasite which kills and chokes its support. I am astonished that they have not, up to now, tried to transplant and cultivate these vines. Perhaps they might succeed in making good wines. The roads are often bordered by cherries, trees indigenous to the coun-

Fig. 34. St. Peter's pro-Cathedral in Baltimore. Copied by Reverend J. A. Frederick from a painting by Thomas Ruckles of 1801. From *The Catholic Mirror*, 17 March 1906. Courtesy of Newspaper Division, New York Public Library.

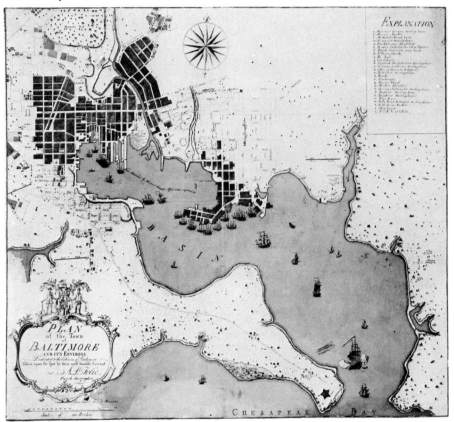

Fig. 35. Folie Plan of the Town of Baltimore. Courtesy of Prints Division, New York Public Library.

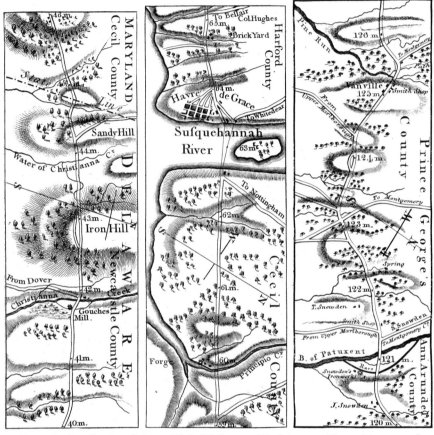

Fig. 36. On the Road from Philadelphia to Washington. From Moore and
Jones, *The Traveller's Directory* . . . . The New Jersey Historical Society.

Fig. 37. The President's House (1799) after a sketch by N. King. Courtesy of the Library of Congress.

Fig. 38. Winning project for the United States Capitol. East Elevation of the Capitol. From the drawing by William Thornton, rev. c. 1795-1796. Courtesy of the Library of Congress.

Fig. 39. Plan of the City of Washington. From the engraving of Thackara and Vallance, 1792. Courtesy of the Library of Congress.

Fig. 40. The City of Washington in 1800. From the drawing of G. I. Parkyns. Courtesy of the Library of Congress.

Fig. 41. Great Falls of the Potomac, 1800. From the drawing by G. Beck. Courtesy of Prints Division,

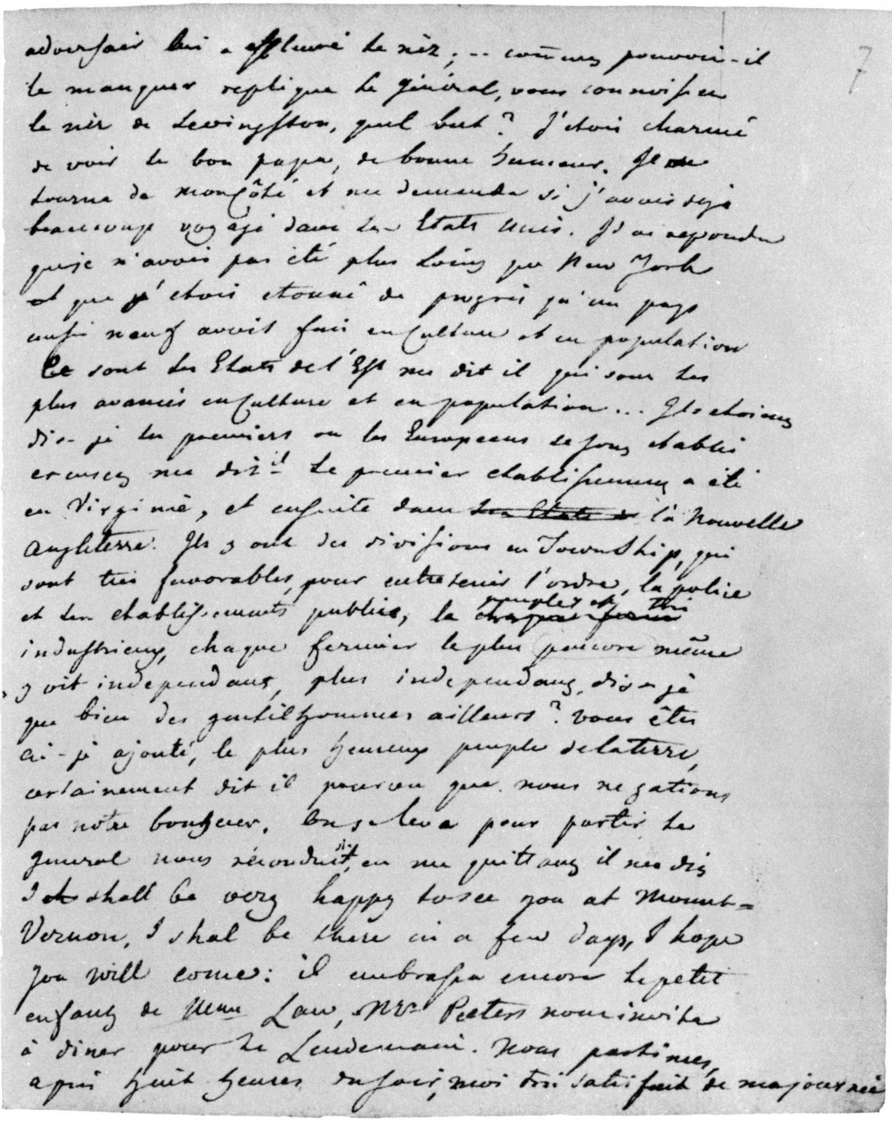

adversaire lui a effluvé le nez ; ... comment pouvoir-il
le manquer replique le général, vous connoissez
le nez de Levingston, quel bec ? J'étois charmé
de voir le bon papa, de bonne humeur. Il se
tourna de mon côté et me demanda si j'avois déja
beaucoup voyagé dans les États Unis. Il me repondis
que je n'avois pas été plus loing que New York
et que j'étois étonné de progrès qu'un pays
aussi neuf avoit fait en culture et en population
Ce sont les États de l'Est me dit il qui sont les
plus avancés en culture et en population ... Ils étoient
dis-je les premiers où les Européens se sont établi
et ceci me dit-il le premier établissement a été
en Virginie, et ensuite dans ~~son État~~ la Nouvelle
Angleterre. Ils y ont des divisions en Township qui
sont très favorables pour entretenir l'ordre, la police
et les établissements publics, la ~~~~ le
industrieux, chaque fermier le plus pauvre même
, y est independant, plus independant, dis-je
que bien des gentilhommes ailleurs ? Vous êtes
ai-je ajouté, le plus heureux peuple de la terre,
certainement dit il pourvu que nous ne gâtions
pas notre bonheur. En se leva pour partir le
général nous réconduit en me quittant il me dis
I shall be very happy to see you at Mount=
Vernon, I shal be there in a few days, I hope
you will come : il embrassa encore le petit
enfant de Mme Law, Mrs Peters nous invita
à diner pour le lendemain. Nous partimes,
après huit heures, en faisant moi très satisfait de ma journée

Fig. 42. A page of French text [IV, 7] from the Niemcewicz manuscript.
This includes Washington's invitation to Niemcewicz to visit Mount Vernon.

Fig. 43. The Old South Building. The first building
of the College of George-Town (1787-1788). Courtesy of the Archives of Georgetown University.

College of George-Town, (Potomack) in the State of Maryland, United States of America.

I. THIS College was firſt opened for literary inſtruction, not quite ſix years ago; and though many difficulties have oppoſed its progreſs, ever ſince the day of its eſtabliſhment, yet the public mind begins to be ſatisfied, that it is not far diſtant from that point of perfection to which its exertions have been invariably directed.

VI. THE ſtudy of the dead languages, that foundation of univerſal knowledge, which, in every Academy calculated for the purpoſes of extenſive utility, ought to engage a large pro-portion of the attention of the profeſſors, muſt have been indeed cultivated in *this* with un-common application, of which the extraordinary proficiency of many of its pupils, in ſo ſhort a period, is an unequivocal proof.

XVIII. VOCAL and inſtrumental muſic, drawing and dancing are taught in the College by well-qualified maſters, but form a ſeparate article—to be paid as follows:

        Muſic,   One guinea a month,
        Drawing, Nine dollars for three months,
        Dancing, Eight ditto   ditto.

INSTRUMENTS or books belonging to theſe accompliſhments will, of courſe, form alſo a ſe-

N. B. WHENEVER a ſtudent is withdrawn from the College, after entering on a new quarter, no deduction will be made for the remaining part of it.

GEORGE-TOWN, *January 1ſt*, 1798.

                      WM. DU BOURG, *Preſident*
                              of the College.

           ROBERT PLUNKETT,   JOHN ASHTON,
(Signed)   FRANCIS BEESTON,   CHARLES SEWALL, } *Directors.*
           FRANCIS NEALE,

Fig. 44. Excerpts from the Prospectus of the College of George-Town, 1798.
Courtesy of the Archives of Georgetown University.

try, infinitely bigger and bushier than ours of the same name. The fruit is said not to be as good as that of Europe.

Although there were meadows and the grazing in the woods is excellent, I found the cattle everywhere small and puny. They gave as a reason that throughout the winter, the cattle was rarely sheltered; it was left exposed to all the inclemency of the weather. It finds almost no forage; it finds no shelter and wastes away before reaching full size. That which makes the countrysides here less gay than elsewhere, in spite of all the richness of the vegetation, is that one sees no great herds: here five or six cows, there a dozen sheep. That is all you meet scattered over an immense expanse of country. You never find those many herds made up of hundreds of cows, sheep, and goats, completely covering the plain or returning in the evening to the village; no shepherds, no songs, nor the sound of pipes. Here all is bleak and gloomy. Yet all this is in keeping with the character of the countryside or rather the population, which is sparse; there are no villages. The farms are scattered, no *Commons*. Each keeps within the boundaries of his own property and confines his herd there. Every man, every child is more [29] gainfully employed than at the occupation of a shepherd, and the fields surrounded everywhere by hedges seem even to remove the need.

We crossed near Christiana, the line which separates the State of Dellavare from that of Maryland. We arrived late at an inn situated on the Elk river; it is here in this neighborhood that they propose to start a canal which will go as far as New Castel; and in cutting the peninsula at the place where it is the narrowest, they will open a communication between the Chesapeak and the Dellavare. Here our three young ladies and their escorts left us and got off at the house of their relatives or the friends whom they had come to visit. These journeys and these visits are very common in America; the inhabitants of cities go to spend a part of the summer months with their friends in the country, and these latter having business in the city stay with them every time they go there.

Descending at the inn I found there a gentleman walking the length and breadth of the room, a hat pulled down, looking from time to time at a big trunk which belonged to him—"*What news in Philad[elphia]?*" he asked me suddenly—"*Nothing material,*" I answered. Seeing by my accent that I was a foreigner and consequently in his opinion French, he frowned. "*I had, I believe, the pleasure to see you, Sir, somewhere,*" I said to him;—he looked at me, "*I never saw you, Sir,*" he answered me curtly and left the room to walk in the vestibule and then seeing me enter, he fled to walk in the courtyard. I left my misanthrope there. I ate two eggs for my supper, for which the innkeeper made me pay ¾ of a dollar, apparently in my role as a Frenchman. His extortions profit him: he was as big and fat as a pig; the better to fatten himself up he ate poached eggs with big pieces of butter all around, and with slices of ham instead of bread. I was conducted then into a room where there were neither more nor less than eleven beds; [3] they gave me the choice. I was not able to close my eyes [30] until midnight, every single minute someone came to interrupt me; there were shouts and the light was thrust in my eyes every time that a travelling companion came to take his berth.

At three o'clock in the morning I was awakened in order to leave. The night was very cold. Towards 5 o'clock when it was day, I looked out on the same countryside as yesterday, that is to say covered with woods, very infrequent settlements and these often as miserable as the huts of our peasants. Poor negroes in rags were working in the fields; horrible roads in a sharply undulating countryside, broken by a thousand *creeks*, ravines, falls, ironworks, etc. Before arriving at Charlestown, one sights Chesapeak bay, vast and magnificent. We breakfasted in an inn situated on the Susquahanak. The master of the negro told me that his slave narrowly missed escaping. During the night someone had come to file off his manacles. The noise had awakened this Argus who ran up in time; he could not discover who was the sympathetic man who wanted to release the poor victim. We crossed the Susquehana in a boat. No, there is no more beautiful sight anywhere than that one finds from the middle of this river. It flows majestically between two lines of crags covered with trees; to the right bluish mountains complete the distant background of the picture, while to the left the river opening up more and more forms an immense sheet of clear and limpid water. It is not deep enough for big ships; one sees only small boats which, coming and going, greatly enliven the landscape. On the other side they have begun to build a little town to which has been given the name of Havre de Grace. Up to now there are only 20 houses scattered here and there.

Two miles from there my fine gentleman got off with his negro. He had a saddle that he placed on his shoulders; I thought that he was going to get on his back, but he was content to attach a bridle to his collar and to lead him behind as a horse. Wretched humanity! He had his farm a half an hour away from there. God knows the fate that awaits the poor negro.

[31] It is 37 miles from Havre de Grace to Baltimore. The roads are a little bit better, not because of the care that is given them, but from the nature of the country which is less cut up. Yesterday and today

I have seen a lot of birds unknown at home, above all *blackbirds*, great destroyers of grain. Therefore one sees scarecrows everywhere to frighten them, and boys running in the fields in order to scare them off: this same *blackbird* has a big crimson mark at the very end of its wing. [One sees also] a bird half the golden color of topaze and half black, *the bleubird*, turtle doves, woodpigeons and a large number of woodpeckers; their head is the most beautiful crimson, the top part of the body white, the rest black. I called it *Il Cardinal frate*.

There remained of all my travelling companions only two old women, and a young boy ten years old, who was going to the college in George Town. He was a child of very rich parents. In what country would one allow a ten-year-old child to make a long journey all alone; but here indeed they are born so sensible, so well behaved, such good managers, that one can say that they are never children. At half past four we sighted from a high hill the harbor and city of Baltimore. The *Stage* stopped at the Indianne Queen.[4] I hurried to the house of Mr. James Barry [5] where I found my friend Gahn. All travel-stained as I was, I had to stay for dinner. I then went to find lodgings and to dress.

Baltimore. Eyes accustomed for a long time to seeing the beauty and regularity of Philadelphia are astonished not to find the same aspect in Baltimore. The town is situated on one of the basins of the Chesapeak. Market Street is a rather wide and well-built street, as are two or three others, but the rest are often unpaved and even without sidewalks. Many of the houses which are still part of the city are dispersed all about. It will take time to fill the gaps, to raze the shanties, and make a single whole; in the meantime one walks in the sand [32] and one is always covered with dust. The place where the city is situated is not the most advantageous; the peninsula, where there is a kind of a telegraph [6] for announcing the arrival of vessels, would be preferable. Another part of the city called False [Fells'] Point would be still better. The basin there is very deep; it is there that all the big ships anchor. This part is inhabited only by workers and the poorer class of citizens; the merchants find it sufficient to have stores there; they do not live there because, or so they say, of the bad air and the sicknesses that are prevalent there. The view from all sides is superb. The bay is enclosed by hills which rise into mountains and are covered with the most beautiful trees. Moreover the construction, the loading and unloading of vessels, the continual activity that one sees makes this section very animated and very lively.

I made a tour of the city by myself. I saw there neither big shops and stores as in Philadelphia, nor the appearance of luxury and wealth in the houses, with, however, the exception of those of Gl. Smith,[7] of another Smith,[8] and of James Barry. In the little streets the houses are poor and the interiors dirty. It was a rather sad walk. In Europe, a foreigner arriving in a big city, even if he knows no one, always finds something on his walk to satisfy his curiosity. Here, it is a large gothic building, there, an old cathedral, which attracts you; or a church in which the paintings, the tombs, the epitaphs, make you dream and nourish your melancholy. Do you seek distractions? You enter a public café. You find there newspapers and prattlers, who tell you everything you want to know and more. In America there are no cafés, for there are no people to visit them; their churches offer you a lot of benches, a pulpit and bare porches. All that is perhaps more philosophic, more reasonable; but [33] the imagination of an European needs to be held.

The commerce of Baltimore is, after that of Philad and New York, the most considerable of the United States; the exports are for the most part in flour and tobacco. I have been to the fort; it is situated three miles away, at the end of the town. It is built up of earth in a pentagon, entirely fallen in and ruined; there is, in addition, a battery for ten guns and a breastwork which conceals the magazine for the gun carriages and cannons and a building, destined, I think, to be used for barracks. I saw two sentinels there. The situation is suitable for the defense of the entrance to the harbor, but it needs to be fortified all anew. The view from this peninsula formed by the Chesapeak and the Patapsco river is magnificent. One sees there all the vessels entering and leaving, and if the peninsula itself is on sandy terrain, sterile, and cut up by ravines and crevasses which to the shame of the inhabitants are not at all leveled, the hills on the other bank of the Patapsco offer magnificent and cheerful woods. I was astonished to see so few country houses there. That of Colonel Howard [9] to the North *West* of the city situated in the middle of a park is the most conspicuous.

In New York and Philad, where the rich have their own carriages and the pedestrians good sidewalks, there is not a single hackney carriage. One counts about 40 of them in Baltimore; for the reason that the city is scattered here and there, many of the streets are unpaved and there are few carriages among the rich.

Lord Baltimore,[10] the principal founder of the State of Maryland, himself a Catholic, was followed by a great number of colonists of this religion. It must become the most widespread in this state; however, they tell me that it represents scarcely a sixth of the population. Sunday I went to the chapel; it is neither bigger nor more beautiful than the ordinary *Meeting houses*. I saw there with surprise a very

beautiful painting in the high altar; it represents Jesus Christ and the
Apostles; the composition and the coloring is after the style of Rafaël.
Bishop [34] Caroll had it done in Italy and paid for it only 100 doll.
It is without contradiction the best painting that there is in America.[11]
I was presented to the Bishop. He is an educated and enlightened
prelate, highly esteemed and respected in the whole country. He is
the sole Catholic bishop in the United States. He is of an old and
wealthy family; his bishopric does not bring him a cent. He was consecrated in London; he has traveled in Italy and in France. A chair
of wood standing under a canopy which is covered with coffee colored serge; a small mitre cut from silvered pasteboard glued on the
same material, is all that denotes his episcopal pomp and dignity. The
same priest who said the mass also preached. After the Credo he took
off his cape and mounted the pulpit and preached. The sermon finished, he descended, put on his cape and finished the mass. Before the
altar there was a tall spare figure with a biretta. It was the curé of
St. Sulpice of Paris. He came here to seek refuge after the Revolution,
accompanied by two other priests and with a complete *apparatus* to
form a seminary. He bought a house and has effectively established
one, but they say that only a single young American studies under
him.[12]

There is one thing very disagreeable about American inns. One
lodges there at great expense and without the slightest comfort. The
room where I am is without a lock and always open. There is neither
water nor a towel; one must go down to the pump to wash. If I must
leave at 3 o'clock in the morning, I must pack my own bag, etc. Nothing makes me more impatient than having to take care of shirts, stockings, etc., to pack and unpack. Have I the need of all this; must I run
about America; could I have ever foreseen being abandoned as I am!
Oh, Mr. Kościuszko, what you have done is most unfeeling!

All the way through Maryland one sees in the inns the doors covered with two kinds of placards or notices. The first announce that
such and such a stallion offers its services to mares at such and such
a price. The others all begin [35] with these words, *Run away*. Such
and such negro has fled, and the reward. What anxiety and trouble
is the price of this terrible custom of keeping slaves.

I paid 7 doll. in the inn for 5 days and four nights without dinner
or supper, only breakfast. It is dearer than in any other country in the
world. This day, 14 May, they came to awaken me at half past two.
There were 13 persons in the *Stage* (N.B. paid for a place in the *Stage*
as far as the City of Washington 4 doll.) [13] After a long dispute the
one who booked his place the last was obliged to remain behind. It

was, however, the fault of the clerk in the office, but here no one is in command nor supervises. I took the place beside the citizen coachman. It is perhaps the best place, as it is the most modest.

The night was very cold. The preceding days in Baltimore were equally so; at 38° lat[itude] and towards the middle of May one had to make a fire in many of the houses. This fashion of travelling by night is good in the summer in order to avoid the heat, but it deprives the traveler of the pleasure of viewing and surveying the countryside. When it was day, that is to say at 5 o'clock, I found myself still in the middle of oak woods, and on roads for most of the time horrible. Often the bridges, even though built in stone, were broken and collapsed. Why is it necessary that in a free country the primary public amenities, which are the roads and bridges, should be in such a bad state and so badly kept up? Is force the only way in which man may be constrained to maintain those works which he neglects because they do not belong solely to him (reminds one of the proverb, *property of everybody property of nobody*).[14]

The respective legislatures of the States concern themselves with the public ways but in a manner which in effect proves to be very faulty. Instead of establishing a tax in money for their upkeep, the law obliges each landowner to furnish so much labor per year. What comes of it? The *surveyors,* as much by negligence as to spare their friends and not to displease anyone, supervise this work and direct it in the worst possible way. If instead of workmen, each paid his share in money, this sum, used to hire workers, [36] would produce a job better done, a job by paid workmen, and not by people who appear to busy themselves on it without pay and as amateurs.

Up to the present in this long chain of woods, I have not seen trees of that monstrous size about which travelers have spoken so much to us. They say that they have seen them only to the south of Virginia. We crossed the Patapsco in a ferry. This part of Maryland appears to me to be more highly populated. One sees large cultivated fields, others newly cleared. All this work is done by negroes. Farms of medium size are rare; they are either great plantations with large houses of the landowners, or miserable huts having only little gardens and a few tilled fields. There is a big forge belonging to Mr. Snowden whom we met, he and his family in a big berlin with four superb horses.[15] It appears that the *gentilmen* of Virginia in the middle of his negroes resembles pretty closely a district magistrate in Poland.

We dined for a doll. a head at Bladenbourg [Bladensburg], small town or village, and at two o'clock arrived at the foot of an immense edifice situated in the middle of superb woods. 14 May. I left the

Stage. I had been advised that I was in sight of the Capitol and that here was the federal *City*, capital of the United States.

City of Washingtown. As soon as the present Constitution was established and, pursuant to it Congress assembled, a need was felt for a metropolis for the whole union and a seat for the legislature and all the branches of the government. The mutual jealousy of the different states did not permit that any of the cities already capitals of some State be chosen for this place. Moreover, it was desired that the capital of the United States be as far as possible in the center of the country. General [37] Washingtown, then President, and other most worthy citizens proposed that a separate city be built in a territory independent of the individual States. The state of Maryland and of Virginia then ceded 10 miles [16] between the Potomak and one of its branches called E[a]stern branch,[17] land which combines all the advantages that one could wish. See below the description given by Dr. Morse, a little manuscript of Mr. Law, as well as the map of the city.[18]

The plan of this city has been conceived and laid out on a vast and most magnificent scale. The enthusiasm and the pride of a people who have come freshly from winning their Independence, the immense stretch of land which from Nova Scotia up to the Mississippi belongs to them, the inner feeling of future greatness, these alone could inspire it. The city is to be [blank] miles in length and [blank] in width. The Capitol is situated right in the center. It is an edifice 352 feet long. All the exterior is in freestone, stone which has been brought from 50 miles away. Its architecture appears to me to be too heavy and too massive. When the whole building is finished it will make an impression; it will be imposing because of its size alone. (Mr. Thornton,[19] a doctor and the architect of the Capitol, told me himself that it was not long since he had begun to study architecture and that it is while he was taking lessons that he made the plan of the Capitol. Should one be surprised that it is bad? In building an edifice so costly and so important could they not have brought over one of the more celebrated architects of Europe, or at least ask them for plans?) [20] This today is the state and appearance of this budding city, which one day will astonish the traveler. One comes in by avenues [blank] feet wide, cut through the forests of oak wood. This wild site, the present state of the city recalls to me many verses of the 8th book of the Aeneid when Aeneas arrives at the domains of King Evander.

"Sol medium coeli conscenderat igneus Orbem
Cum muros, arcemque procul et rara domoroum
Tecta vident." [21]

The roofs, that is to say the houses, were truly sparse and scattered on this vast terrain, at a great distance from one another. Arriving at the foot of a hill I found a wing of the Capitol.

[38]   ". . . *Silvestris horrida dumis*" [22]

It was [blank] feet square, already built up to the roof and all in freestone. A huge scaffolding surrounded it and all around for a considerable distance the ground was covered with huge blocks of this same stone, some already cut and polished, others yet undressed. The lower part of this picture was composed of some sheds for cutting the stone and for working on the roof and the framework, some cabins scattered here and there, a shelter for the workers, two or three small shops for liquor and other articles of prime necessity. The top of the edifice was covered with 200 workers, raising the stones by means of machines and placing the first framework of the roof. All were working in silence.

> ". . . *pars ducere muros,*
> *molirique arcem et manibus subvolere Saxa*
> *Pars optare locum tecto etc. . . ."*

> "*O fortunati quorum jam moenia surgunt.*" [23]

I asked for the architect Mr. Hatfield, brother of Mrs. Cosway.[24] He was on the summit of the building and I went there to look for him. What a view, what a sight meets the eye from this elevated place! The great avenues cut into the forest of verdant oak, indicated the spaces destined for the streets, but today:

> "*Haec nemora indigenae Fauni Nymphaeque tenebant.*" [25]

One sees nothing and hears there only the silence of the trees, where one day some great houses will be built; one sees there only robins, red or blue birds flitting from branch to branch or flying through the air where thousands and thousands of inhabitants will come one day to live. What a contrast between the stillness of these silent forests and the uproar and all the tumult of passions which will come one day to agitate the poor mortals. (The avenues or principal streets are 120 feet wide, the others 60 and more. Mors claims up to 160 and 140, and the little streets 100. See Geography of Morse.) [26]

[39] The city is to be placed on a peninsula formed by the Potomak and the Estern branch. From one side the view is of the city of Alexandria, and from the other that of Georges Town and the majestic course of the Potomak; [27] a group of houses on the George Town

side where the President's house has been built, another group on the bank of the Estern branch and then farms and houses of the established landowners scattered haphazardly here and there. After having enjoyed this view, as much as my head, subject to vertigo, would permit, I descended from the Capitol and went on foot along the path towards the Estern branch where the house of Mr. Law [28] was situated. I was received and welcomed by him and his amiable wife with cordiality and friendship.

The next day we made a tour by carriage of the ground that one day is to be occupied by the city. We crossed Tyber Creek and passed the house of the President. It is nearly finished; the architecture by the same man and in the same style as that of the Capitol. The building is vast and imposing; made more to lodge a sovereign who can tax his subjects at will than to be the residence of a magistrate who receives from his fellow citizens only the modest salary of 25,000 doll. This house of the President and one part of the Capitol are the only public buildings to be seen. There is also a large hotel on which they ran a lottery: it has been won by a citizen of Philadelphia. They are soon going to lay the foundations of *offices* or public buildings for the different departments.

The funds assigned for the building of all these edifices are: 1st) The money coming from the sale of lots which are sold for 3 pounds, more or less, per foot frontage; thus the land to build a house 30 feet long cost 100 Maryland pounds or about 250 doll. The money received from these sales must amount to a considerable sum, but they could not tell me how much. The secret is very convenient for those who manage the funds. They say, however, [40] that the sum amounts to between two and three hundred thousand dolls. 2nd) The Congress has permitted them to raise a loan of 300 thousand doll. offering itself as security. This year they have drawn on the public Treasury for 100 thousand dol. which are part of the authorization of the 300 thousand mentioned above. 3rd) The State of Virginia has made a gift of 120,000 doll. to the City, and that of Maryland 70,000 doll. Thus the total sum can amount to 790,000 doll. (*and half of all the private estates within the city for the public benefit. These are in lots and amount to about two millions of Dollars and many of them have been sold by the commissioners.*) They say that the commissioners have already spent for the President's house, part of the Capitol and an office building 500,000 doll. In all other countries one would be able, with the same sum, to build four times more and four times better.

What then are the reasons for the slow progress of these buildings and their high cost, and the lack of haste that is shown in establishing them? This is more or less what I was able to gather together. The first fault of the government was to have chosen for commissioners or administrators of the public buildings and the sale of the lots, persons who had at heart more their own plans, their own interests than the general progress and growth of the City. All these gentlemen, White, Thornton, Scott,[29] inhabitants of Georgetown who have their farms close by, have found it much more convenient to establish themselves beside the house of the President and to promote particularly this end of the city because it was contiguous to their residences in Georgetown instead of establishing their office and their houses in the center of the city, that is to say near the Capitol (and encourage in this way others to establish there and form the first nucleus of the city.) They even neglected the building of the Capitol and wished to make Congress sit in the President's house. All this to make it easier for themselves and for their fellow citizens of Georgetown to force both the [41] members of Congress and the other officers to lodge in this town, being unable to find the least shelter elsewhere. Furthermore they stay on their farms much more than at their offices; from this arises the general delay and negligence in everything.

If the old President had chosen as Commissioners people from the states of the North or of the South, people who in fact would not have any private and local interest, who, instead of favoring by preference one section of the City, had at heart only its general growth; who, foreign to all speculation and biased interest, would set all their zeal, sacrifice all their time to their duty, the progress of the city would be other than it is. The enormous sums spent up to now for so little work are as much the consequence of the high cost of labor as of the poor management and useless expenditures of the administration. This same administration cost 20,000 dol. per year. Each of the Commissioners gets 1,600 doll; two architects each 500 guineas per year, the other officers in proportion.

The masons and workers are paid from a dollar up to two per day. They work from 6 in the morning to 8 o'clock; they then breakfast up to 9, work then up to one o'clock, eat dinner up to two, returning to work until six o'clock in the evening. Besides these times of rest I have seen them often quit their work, come into the little dramshop in order to talk while drinking a glass of *grog*. Once I went into the hut of one of these workers. I found his wife there dressed very neatly, good utensils for cooking, and all the service for tea in porcelain from China. Far from being scandalized by this small luxury, I rejoiced in it. Why should not a man who works by the sweat of his brow enjoy the comforts and the ease of life. Should it be only idlers who have these privileges? It is well to ask by what right they acquire them.

Nearly all these workers are Irish or Scottish immigrants from Europe. [42] If these people stayed at home, they would always be poor; here at the end of two or three years of work they amass enough money to buy lands in the interior of the country; they will end their days in ease, having assured it to their children. In a word it is a country for the poor and hardy. A European brought up, as they say, as a gentleman could certainly, by coming here and devoting himself to trade and to speculation, amass wealth; but if he wants to enjoy it according to his old habits and tastes, it is necessary that he return to Europe.

One further obstacle to the growth of the city is that at the beginning of its foundation some famous speculators, today bankrupt, Robert Moris, Nichelson and Greenlief, have tied up the best lots.[30] They have not paid for them and have prevented others from establishing themselves there. It is said that they are to sell them at public auction. The daringly extravagant mood of these speculators has, however, done some good for this city. They have built between 50 and 60 large houses of brick that sensible men with ordinary means would perhaps not have chosen to do.

The commissioners give account neither of the progress of the buildings nor the receipts and expenses, except to the President alone; they are responsible only to him. The result proves that the supervision of the chief magistrate (occupied moreover by so many other things, and who never comes here in order to see for himself) is insufficient. Without impairing the executive power, it would be more useful for the city that the Congress should nominate each year a committee composed of its members, whose duty it would be to go to the site themselves, examine the accounts, see the progress of the buildings, receive complaints, etc., etc. Above all, this committee should be made up of capable men of integrity, and above all of those who do not fear to displease, for therein lie the misfortunes of republican government; they each have need one of the other; they make mutual adjustments; they avoid making enemies, and the public good suffers from it. We have seen it at home, in Venice, and elsewhere. In arbitrary government one has only to command and punish; here one fears even to find fault.

No. 4

[1] Continuing our route, we crossed over Rocky Creek, the limits of the City of Washington, and leaving George Town at the right we

followed the Potomak. The course of this river, its steep banks covered with black oaks, indeed the view from all sides was as beautiful
as the road was horrible. We killed a snake called *Copper Snake;* it is
not the biggest, but, or so it is claimed, the most venomous of all. Its
belly is dirty yellow, its back covered with big black splotches. Soon
we were recompensed for our bad roads by the sight of a work as
beautiful as it was useful. It is a canal having a width of [blank] and
[blank] miles long. It has [blank] locks. Its banks are timbered in
planks of oak and the embankment on the two sides has the solidity
and a finish which pleases the eye. (See Morse's Geography, p. 480.) [31]
It has been made to avoid *the little falls* of the Potomak.

We arrived finally at a bridge thrown across the Potomak and finished recently. It has a single arch with a triangular frame construction
and supported from the sides by two abutments,[32] massive and immense
bases, constructed of chips of rock and large stones, held together at
the base by iron braces. The river there flows with tremendous speed;
towards springtime it overflows over a great distance; the aspect from
both sides is wild and romantic; there is not a single habitation. The
noise of the water roaring between the rocks, the cries of the blackbirds and the leaps of sturgeons and *Jawfish* [33] which from time to
time spring into the air and fall back, these alone interrupted the
reveries of the spectator.

"It has a single arch . . . supported from the sides by two
abutments."

This bridge, as well as the canal, was constructed by private companies. The tolls there are very high. One pays on the canal for a
bark of [blank] barrels [blank]; on the bridge, for a pedestrian
[blank], for a horse [blank], [blank] for a wagon. The man who takes
the money at the bridge gets 20 doll. a month.

[2] The 20th of May I went to the chapel, situated beside the Capitol, in the top of a shed where they saw marble. The congregation was
composed of 200 people, as many men as women, all very decently
dressed although for the most part they were only laborers working
on the Capitol. The women, mostly farmer's wives or wives of the inhabitants and officers of the town, were very healthy, very white-
skinned, very pretty. The sermon was given by a promising young
priest. On our return to the house we were agreeably surprised to find

there the Chevalier Freire, Minister of Portugal, whom I have often seen in Philadelphia.[34] He is very well educated, amiable, and what is more, an honorable man. As for amiable, who is not when he is happy? But when one is abandoned, fighting cruel necessity, the heart torn with grief, worry and afflictions, one's spirit is heavy, one's manner awkward, ill at ease and distracted.

Toward evening we went out for three miles on the Baltimore road. The carriages stopped. We climbed a rather steep hill called Camil's Hill; [35] it is all covered with reddish stone, porous and light, having the appearance of iron slag; perhaps these are volcanic products. From the top of this hill one finds one of the most extensive and picturesque views: the whole course of the Estern branch, the hills, a part covered with oak woods, a part bare with white or reddish earth whose colors contrast so well with the somber green of the forests. To the south one sees at his feet the whole vast plain destined to be the metropolis of the United States, the Capitol with its scaffolding, the house of the President and other houses dispersed here and there, the budding harbor of the Estern branch with its vessels and refinery, finally Tiber Creek about which Mr. Law recounted to us a rather [3] interesting anecdote.

Anecdote of Tiber Creek.[36] A short time after Europeans had settled in this country an inhabitant named [blank], first owner of the hill where today stands the Capitol and of some adjacent lands, being either taken by the similarity in the setting or inspired by a spirit of prophecy, gave to the *Creek* which flows there the name of Tyber; and announced that on his hill, covered then with brambles and trees, there one day would be built a city which would be, as Rome had been, one of the largest and most powerful in the Universe. I wish for the Americans neither the grandeur nor power of the Romans; the one and the other both bring in their wake ambition, the thirst for conquest, injustice, oppression towards neighbors, disorders, factions, and finally tyranny at home. I wish for them only that power and force necessary to resist and repulse all attacks from the outside and as many riches as necessary to make the people happy and comfortable. Luxury is as fatal to a nation as poverty is cruel to the individual. One takes an interest in this newborn nation as one interests himself in a handsome young man full of vigor and health who appears to give promise of becoming one day an ornament to society.

Monday 21 May. We enjoy the details, the anecdotes, the smallest incidents even, that Plutarch gives us in his lives of famous men. All that interests us so much; the reason for it is perhaps that man relates all to himself, that on reading he readily puts himself in the place of the hero whose history he reads and then, not being able in spite of all his self-esteem to compare himself always to the hero in his great deeds, he likes to resemble him in his private life. He likes to find common ground with him and if the hero's extraordinary talents, if the hero's superiority [4] often humiliates him; he consoles himself, he finds so much pleasure in seeing that the hero was often a man such as he. It is as much to justify this point of view as to give myself the very sweet pleasure that not being able, unlike Plutarch, to sketch with a master's hand the character and deeds of one of the greatest men of this century, I am happy to preserve in writing a few details on his person.

It was Monday the 21st of May 1798 that my respected host, Mr. Law, on returning from George Town where he had gone in order to settle some business with a few rascally speculators who had cheated him, announced to us that General Washington had arrived at Mr. Peeters' house.[37] This Mr. Peeters had married Miss Custis,[38] granddaughter of Mrs. Washington by her first husband. It was immediately decided that we should all go to present our respects to him that same evening. Consequently we set out, Mrs. Law with the Ch[evalie]r Freire in a cabriolet and I with Mr. Law in the wagon.

Mr. Peeters' house is at the far end of the city, very near Georges Town. We arrived there between six and seven o'clock. (I saw him through the window and I recognized him immediately.) One can guess how my heart was beating; I was going to see the man for whom, since my youth, I had had such a great respect, such a man as my unhappy fatherland lacked for its own salvation. There were about ten people coming out toward us. I saw only him. I was presented to him by Mr. Law. He held out his hand to me and shook mine. We went into the parlor; I sat down beside him; I was moved, speechless. I had not eyes enough to look on him. His is a majestic figure in which dignity and gentleness are united. [5] The portraits that we have of him in Europe do not resemble him much. He is nearly six feet tall, square set, and very strongly built; aquiline nose, blue eyes, the mouth and especially the lower jaw sunken, a good head of hair. In a word

"Iam senior, sed cruda Deo viridisque Senectus." [39]

He wore a coat of deep nut brown, black stockings, a waistcoat and breeches of satin of the same color. He began by questioning me about Gl. Kośc[iuszko]; my embarrassment and confusion were extreme. The first word that I said to this great man was a lie. This then is what I have been driven to by this needlessly mysterious flight. He continued then—*"How long are you in this country?"*—*"Eight month"*

—*"How do you like it?" "I am happy, Sir, to see in America those bless-*
ings which I was so ardently wishing for in my own country. To you,
Sir, are the Americans indepted for them—" He bowed his head with
a modest air and said to me, *"I wished always to your country well*
and that with all my heart." He uttered these last words with feeling.
The questions on Kośc[iuszko]'s journey to the waters, on his health,
etc., returned anew and again put me in torture. Happily the daughter
of Mrs. Law, aged 16 months, came in.[40] Gl. Washington called to her;
he took from his pocket a roll of peach cheese, *"here is something for*
you" he said and gave her a piece and embraced her. He then gave
the whole roll to her mother, *"take it, Mme for your little Law."* The
conversation turned then to agriculture, a favorite subject of the Gl.
They spoke of the long drought that prevailed then, the harm that
it was doing to the tobacco, to the maize, to the wheat, etc.

[6] I then went up to Mrs. Washington. She is the same age as the
Gl. (both were born in 1732), small, with lively eyes, a gay air and
extremely kind. She had on a gown, with an even hem, of stiff white
cotton,[41] fitting very tightly, or rather attached from all sides with pins.
A bonnet of white gauze, ribbons of the same color, encircling her
head tightly, leaving the forehead completely uncovered and hiding
only half of her white hair which in back was done up in a little pigtail. She was at one time one of the most beautiful women in America
and today there remains something extremely agreeable and attractive
about her. She has never had any children by Gl. Washington. She
had four by her first husband, Mr. Custis, of whom a single son lived,
married [blank] and left three daughters: Mrs. Law, Mrs. Peeters and
a third, still unmarried, all three the most beautiful women that one
could see, and a son, a young boy who remains with Gl. Washington
and his grandmother.[42] Mrs. Custis, widow, married Dr. Stuart, by
whom she has six children.[43] We spoke with Mrs. Washington of the
little likeness there is between the General and his portraits. She then
asked Mrs. Peeters to play the harpsichord, which she did, and played
very well for us the eternal Battle of Prague,[44] a favorite piece in
America. Tea was served. I found again the opportunity to be beside
the General. He spoke with praise of an address of the town of Norfolk to the President.

"Did you know," Mr. Law asked him, "Mr. Jones,[45] who was recently killed in a duel by Mr. Livingston?" "I believe that I have seen
him, but I was never on intimate terms with him." "They say that the
shot that he fired at his [7] opponent had grazed his nose." "How
could he miss it," replied the General. "You know Livingston's nose;
what a target!"

I was charmed to see the good papa in such good humor. He turned to me and asked if I had already traveled much in the United States. I answered that I had been no further than New York and that I was astonished by the progress that a country so new had made in agriculture and population. "These are the Eastern states," he said to me, "which are the most advanced in agriculture and in population." "They were," said I, "the first where Europeans settled." "Forgive me," said he, "but the first settlement was in Virginia, and then in New England. It is the divisions into *Township* which is so favorable for maintaining order, police and public institutions. The people are very industrious; every farmer, even the poorest, lives in independence." "More independent," said I, "than many gentlemen elsewhere. You are," I added, "the happiest people on earth." "Certainly," he said, "provided that we do not spoil our good fortune."

We got up to leave. The General took us to the door. Taking leave of me, he said, "*I shall be very happy to see you at Mount Vernon. I shal be there in a few days. I hope you will come.*" He again embraced Mrs. Law's little daughter. Mr. Peeters invited us to dinner for the next day. We left at about 8 o'clock in the evening. I was well content with my day.

[8] The next day I dined at the house of Mr. Peeters. They spoke of the offices that were going to be built for the departments; the expense of it is estimated at 96,000 doll. They discussed at length the difficulty that there would be to finish enough houses to lodge the members. Gl. Washington said jokingly, "Oh well, they can camp out. The Representatives in the first line, the Senate in the second, the President with all his suite in the middle."

The 23rd. Wednesday. He came with Mrs. Washington to spend two days in Mr. Law's house, where I was staying. The whole time he was courteous, polite, even attentive; he talked very little, now and then on agriculture, on natural history, on all that one would wish, except politics, on which he maintains an absolute silence and reserve; to the extent that he never asked the slightest question either on our unfortunate Revolution, or on the least thing that could be connected with it.

One time at dinner, the question arose concerning the travels that the Duke of Liancourt just published.[46] He said, "M. de Liancourt will be angry with me. When he came to this country, he brought letters of introduction from the most distinguished persons in England; he had no need of them. In the light of what M. de Lafayette had told me of him, as well as his reputation and conduct, I knew the respect that I owed him. I could not, however, receive him at my house; I was then in the administration—(it is thus that he always expresses him-self when he speaks of his office as President)—and I had made a rule not to admit to my house any Frenchman who was regarded as an emigree and who could not be presented by his Minister. I informed M. de Liancourt through my friends of the motives that obliged me to deprive myself of the advantage of seeing him, an advantage which otherwise [9] I would have so much wished, and as soon as I should be out of the administration, I would hope to see him. But it appears that he has taken it ill, and after all that," he added, "I read in Mr. Munro's book [47] that the French government reproached me for re-ceiving emigrees."

On the 24th I went with him to see the sugar refinery, an immense building situated near the *Warf* of Mr. Barry, where there was a three-masted vessel which was being loaded with tobacco. It is ex-traordinary how much movement and life this single vessel and this single sugar refinery were giving to this newly born place.[48] There are always 4, 5, up to six small *Schooners* loading one or the other. It is here that one can see how the least little trade gives life to a place and contributes to populating it and increasing the industry there.

The Gl.'s pastime was billiards; he plays with a mace and although it is 25 years since he has played, his attention and skill made up for the lack of practice; he played each game better.

He left us on the 25th between seven and eight o'clock in the morn-ing in a great hurry to see the effect that the last rains had had on his fields. He and Mrs. Washington pressed me very much to come to see them in Mount Vernon; I shall certainly keep my word to him.

Great Falls. In the morning the 26th of May I left on horseback with Messrs. Deforges and Debassins to see the Great Falls and the canal of the Potomwak. We stopped at the little falls to see a boat go down. This sort of a boat [10] is made expressly for the navigation of shallow rivers, canals and waters; the boat is [blank] long and very narrow; it carries from 100 to 150 barrels, but the most common loads are of 110 and 120 barrels. We crossed the bridge and each paid a

"This sort of boat . . . is long and very narrow."

shilling toll. Arriving on the other side we found ourselves in Virginia. We left the Potowmak on our right and we plunged into the depths of the woods composed, as in Maryland, of different species of oak, chestnut, and laurel whose flower, in pale rose clusters, is extremely

pretty. I searched in vain for the *Tulip tree* (*magnolia grandiflora.*) [49]
I found in its place only a poplar which has a flower of pale yellow,
very like a *Tulip*, different species of acacia called here *Locust*, some
cedars, a thousand other types of trees of a superb foliage and greenness. The fresh greenness and beauty of the forests contrast unpleas-
antly with the poverty and sterility of the fields. The soil nearly everywhere is sandy and reddish. I have seen fields planted with rye that
were bare, showing ears every three feet, such as one sees at home
only in the poorest and the most miserable soil covered with pines.
Here it is not the fault of the land for the beauty of its oaks proves
that it is not sterile; it is the lack of care and cultivation. They never
leave the fields fallow; they sow them continually and fertilize them
little or not at all.

Six miles from the bridge we passed along a field where ten negroes, men and women, were scratching at the soil and driving in
little sticks. Curious to see the planting of tobacco, we thought that
they were busy at this work, we tied our horses to a hedge, jumped it
and went to find our Blacks. Their emaciated and black skeletons were
covered with shreds of rags, bare legs, etc., etc.

[11] It was not tobacco but maize that they were planting; they
scratched the soil to a depth of an inch and threw there three grains
of maize and covered them. In this consists all the cultivation. After
asking them a few questions we were leaving when we heard a furi-
ous voice cry out: "*Stop, stop.*" We returned and saw two men armed
with guns, running all out of breath and very anxiously towards the
negro with whom we had just spoken and asking him what we had
wanted and what we had said to him. Right in the middle of these
interrogations we approached. "What were you looking for here? What
did you want with my negroes?" he asked us in an agitated and frightened voice. We told him we were foreigners, that we were curious to
see a tobacco plantation and we thought that his field offered us an
opportunity. "I beg of you a thousand pardons," he said to us. "I
thought that you had come to corrupt and seduce my negroes." What
more wretched existence is there than that of a man who lives in continual anxiety of seeing his unfortunates carried away; whom he knows
to be discontented with him and whom he does not cease, however,
to torment. We left. We saw at the side of the road a few miserable
cabins, dwellings of the Blacks. We would have been interested to
see their exterior [interior?], but after what had happened to us
we kept well away. The suspicions of these people have increased
since the disagreements between this country and France; they see
everywhere only emissaries and spies. They are suspicious because

they are tyrants and as such they are tormented by all the furies of remorse and a continual unease.

The *gentilmens* who, with a gun on his shoulder, was the sentinel over his negroes, was called Hampton or Hamilton Trifft [12] and this is a Virginian: this is a citizen of a state, more jealous than all the others of liberty, of equality, etc. Every day he himself tramples them under foot and never stops crying that he is their only defender. From childhood, accustomed to command and not to recognize anyone above him, the alarm sounds always for him; he does not like the magistrates whom he chooses himself because often in the name of the law they can give him orders.

Great Falls.[50] About two o'clock we arrived at the Great Falls. They are at a distance of 18 to 20 miles from the Eastern branch. There is one wretched tavern there and three or four houses. A few hundred paces from there we clambered up a rock to look across the face of the falls. Between two steep and forest-covered banks one discovers a valley a mile long and half a mile wide, throughout its whole length bristling with grayish rocks scattered in disorderly confusion; nothing can convey more the appearance of desolation and horror. The water of the river divided into a thousand threads was completely hidden by these blocks of rocks, sometimes forming rough and shapeless piles, sometimes hewn by nature into stony sepulchres, until arriving at the precipice it is divided by three segments of these same rocks; it escapes to the right and to the left in great masses of foam, and in the middle in little cascades of clear and limpid water. All these waters, reunited then in a single stream, flow majestically down a slope a hundred fathoms long, coming to yet another shelf of stone, falling there, and continuing to flow in the depths of a bed formed by sections of rocks of tremendous height. It is scarcely possible to see a situation more [13] wild, more picturesque, and more secluded or isolated. Except for three little houses, of which I have spoken, one sees no habitation there. One or two negroes stationed at the bottom of the precipice on a point of a reef, fished for *shad,* with nets attached as a sack at the end of a pole. I watched them for a half hour dipping and retrieving their nets but always without success.

The falls are 66 feet in height. It is in order to avoid them that a company has undertaken to cut through a canal; it is greatly advanced, made in part of freestone, in part of stones taken from these same rocks. Boats carrying more than 120 barrels already go down it. For only 200 feet they transport the barrels on a two-wheeled cart drawn by two horses. There they make the descent down a slope where other boats take them on and carry them by the little *Falls* as far as Georges

Town, Washington or Alexandria. It costs for the two canals one Virginia shiling, a sixth of a dollar, per barrel (the company will receive up to 30 and 40 thousand doll. revenue per year.) They claim that 50,000 doll. are necessary to finish the work. The company has appealed to the states of Virginia and Maryland for the money as a loan. Three separate opposing interests are found among the members of these Legislatures. There are those who want to promote a canal which by Squatara [Swatara] Creek would join the Susquehanna to the Skulkil; others were for a canal which would join the Chesepek with the Dellavare; others finally for that of the Potowmak. The force being equal on three sides, the body, according to the laws of physics, remains stationary. In the course of time when the population will increase, all these three canals will certainly be built. They are all of the greatest importance; that of the Potowmak will open a communication with the Ohio and the Atlantic (by means of the Mononagahella which falls into the Ohio and can be joined with the Potowmak. See Morse's Geography pg. 480) [51] and gain an outlet for an immense extent of country far reaching in all directions.

[14] We returned to the inn and found that our host was a French Alsatian who had come here to settle two years before. Perhaps he did not have a cent when he arrived; he is already comfortable and soon he will be rich. He can not fail to be from the way he fleeces everybody! We had for our dinner a salted *Shade* with a salad and some eggs; for our horses a little fodder. For that he made us pay a dollar per person.

I have forgotten to speak of the forge which is very near the falls. The iron is brought down from Barckley County 60 miles away; they use charcoal; they hammer the iron into *Pigs* and *bars*.[52]

We had as a companion at dinner a heavy-set farmer from the valley of the Shenondoach in Barckley County. According to his description and even more according to public opinion this valley is a paradise. The land there has prodigous fertility; it sells ordinarily for 40 doll. for an acre, but some of it has been sold for 100 dol. This is the price of land near Philad; those of Shanandonach bring in 40 *bouchels* [bushels] of maize and from 15 to 20 *bouchels* of wheat. There have been examples of an acre yielding up to 80 *bouchels* per year. This valley is populated by Germans and Quakers. They keep slaves. Our fat farmer, who was of the latter sect, declaimed a great deal against the custom of having slaves; however, although a Quaker, he had a few of them himself. He was apparently of the sect of the gay Quakers for he had buttons on his coat and spoke to us with the plural "you." [53] The condition of the slaves in Virginia, according to

his [15] account, is very miserable. They feed them only on bread and
water, sometimes milk. The masters usually sleep with the negresses,
and the children they have by them are slaves and are handed down
as such to their children; in a way that one brother is a slave of another brother.

We returned from there by the same road. In the evening by the
light of the moon all this country, the wide expanse of river between
the bridge and Georges Town, its banks covered with the most beautiful trees and reaching almost to the sky, the fishermen taking in their
nets and appearing in the background of the picture at the foot of
these enormous mountains as figures in miniature; the fragrance of
the plants and trees, the silence of the night, all this awakens a sweet
and sad melancholy. How events drive men from one corner of the
globe to another and bring them together where they would never
expect to see each other! Messrs. Deforges and Debassins, natives of
the island of Bourbon at the end of Africa, and a Pole from the end
of Europe traveled at night on the banks of the Potowmak and talked
about their past misfortunes and their apprehensions for the future.
The Ile de France and Bourbon [54] never wanted to receive the agents
of the Republic; they had expelled those that the Republic had sent.
Their distance and other preoccupations have caused this violation
to be passed over in silence; however one does not fear less the final
outcome. We returned to the house of Mr. Law at nine o'clock in the
evening.

[16] 29 May. Alexandria. We took a boat to go to Alexandria. It is
only 4 miles by water from the Estern branch, while it is ten to twelve
by land. We made an agreement at 4 and ½ sch[illing] per man. The
two sloping banks covered in trees are well cultivated, especially
those of the Maryland side; and seen from the middle of this great
stream they offer pleasant and picturesque views. We arrived at Alexandria about 9 o'clock after an hour and a half of sailing. There were
about fifty vessels in the harbor, some of 300 tons and more; there
were storehouses in brick, some very big; some streets the width of
those in Philadelphia were well laid out, some very well paved with
excellent sidewalks; 4 or 500 houses, half in brick, half in wood but
generally well built; a little market, some churches, and indeed a
theatre which is nearly finished. The odor of coal, many negroes, the
white women anything but pretty, little movement and activity in the
streets and in the harbor, such is the modern Alexandria. You would
search in vain for the column of Pompey and the remains of the magnificence of the Ptolemies. Who knows, however, if the inhabitants of
modern Alexandria are not a thousand times happier than those of

the Alex[andria] of Egypt under the Ptolemies, and especially under the Turks. This little town prospers and grows as all the others. It is within the boundaries of the territory ceded to the Union to build *the City of Washington.* As for the great name it carries and to which it will have less right in measure as the Capitol grows, one should attribute it only to the exalted spirit of the Americans; their arms are an eagle, a rising sun, a constellation; the three frigates are called the fleet; the seat of government the Capitol; [17] a little *creek* the Tiber, etc., etc. Is there not in the very depths and amidst the firs of Vermont a little town of ten houses which is called Carthage? [55] Perhaps the men who came here first to lay the foundations of a city tried to sweeten their present labors with the hope for grandeur and for the future prosperity of their settlement. What would man be if he did not console himself in his present difficulties by remembrance of the past and dreams of the future?

I learned that there was in the town a man who had once lived in Warsaw. I hastened to go to his house. I found him in a shop in the middle of casks of gin and spirits. His face startled me; it was Jean Richter, one time commissioner for Tepper, who saw me often in his house as well as at Falenti.[56] It would be impossible to describe the keen and sincere joy of this man; mine was not less so. He spoke of Poland with an outburst of feeling and tears in his eyes, and who would not speak of it in the same way! We spoke of times past; he showed me a portrait of Gołkowski.[57] I was vexed to be obliged to leave him so soon.

After having gone about the town in all directions we returned to our little boat. Our sailors were very angry to learn that we wanted to go to Georges Town; that lengthened their trip a great deal. We won over the Black who rowed where we wished, but the young white boy rowed in a contrary direction so as to return to the Estern Branch. With Mr. Debassin at the rudder our boat, steered in a contrary direction, went as if drunk. We got off on the shore beside the President's house and continued our way on foot up to Georges Town. We ate dinner table d'hôte and paid [18] in our capacity as foreigners double the normal price.

George Town College.[58] We went to see the College. It was founded by Roman Catholic clergy. The funds of some Jesuits who, without having an established convent, had, however, some property in land, were appropriated to this use. The new College, although occupied, is not yet completely finished. The old one serves as living quarters for the teachers and contains the chapel and refectory. Both are situated on an elevated site, which is healthy and enjoys the most beautiful view possible. One discovers at one's feet the whole course of the Potowmak and Mason's Island which is separated only by an arm of the river. This island offers a most enchanting view. It is 70 acres in all. It is a floating garden with two small pavilions, some trees, some fields and orchards. What a delightful retreat for a sage!

The students in the college number 70, of whom six only are Protestants living in a separate house. The Catholics occupy the new building; nearly half of these young people are French from the colonies; imbued from their childhood with principles of liberty and independence, they will carry them back home and contribute not a little one day to the liberation of these colonies. The fee including all expenses is 250 dollars per year. It is less when the parents provide the clothes, etc. They teach them chiefly languages, that is to say, English, French, Spanish, Latin, and Greek; then arithmetic, geometry, geography, etc.; music, drawing, dance, fencing are paid for separately. The institution is under the supervision of a President, Mr. Dubourg,[59] a refugee French priest, and of five directors. Mr. Dubourg, whom we found [19] at table with his colleagues, is polite and appears well educated and zealous. These gentlemen told us of the marvelous progress of their pupils. It would be necessary to investigate the whole thing more closely in order to know the truth. The children have nine hours of study a day, but these are interspersed with moments of rest and instruction. They go to mass every day; they keep the fast, etc. They all sleep in a big hall, each bed separated by a small partition. I saw beside each bed a crucifix and statues. Mr. Herman de Monte, music master, is quite a character: he claims that these pupils at the end of five months play the most difficult pieces without practice. He composes, that is to say, he filches little pieces of music known everywhere except in Georges Town. He is always using exaggeration and hyperbole; a genius here, perhaps no more than a fool elsewhere. N.B. See a prospectus that Mr. Dubourg gave to me.

31 May. We went this morning to roam about the Capitol. It was eleven o'clock. No one was at work; they had gone to drink *grog*. This is what they do twice a day, as well as dinner and breakfast. All that makes four or five hours of relaxation. One could not work more comfortably. The negroes alone work. I have seen them in large numbers, and I was very glad that these poor unfortunates earned eight to ten dollars per week. My joy was not long lived: I am told that they were not working for themselves; their masters hire them out and retain all the money for themselves. What humanity! What a country of liberty. If at least they shared the earnings! We went into all the neighboring

houses, not for any reason but from boredom; in order to leave behind everywhere some small part of the terrible burden of 24 hours.

My estimable host, Mr. Law, is an example of the fate that awaits a large number of our Europeans here. He was one of the Councilors in the administration of the Great Indies. He spent 16 years there. It is he who destroyed all the abuses, the whole system of feudal government [20] and introduced in its place the most salutary reforms. Accustomed to an active life, experiencing only a few vexations, feeling the sweet satisfaction of seeing that the happiness of thousands of its inhabitants, long time oppressed, was the result of his attentive care and of his labors; living under the best possible auspices in the world, increasing his fortune without self-reproach and without harm to his neighbors, tasting the charm of the society of his compatriots as educated and enlightened as he, he has grown too much into the habit of success ever to be happy in any place where he does not find the same advantages and pursuits. After experiencing some unpleasantness in London he betook himself to America.

From being a magistrate, commanding as the supreme authority, to become a simple American citizen, the fall is great. But that is not the greatest of the ills. It is not even the rogueries and continual losses that he has suffered at the hands of Robert Moris, Greenlief, Dikesson, Pircy,[60] etc., which afflict him the most. It is want of society, want of something to do, the idleness; for here he has no other occupation but the chicanery of and quarrels with just those whom he has served. A most beautiful and accomplished wife, a child, an immense fortune, all that, although he knows the worth of them, does not make him happy. Why? Because nothing really occupies him intensely, because time lies heavily on him, because he has not the resources to which he was accustomed. One could say that he is unhappy now because formerly he was too happy. If he had experienced great reverses in life, he would love repose the better. If he had been betrayed by friends, he would suffer less from being far from human intercourse. It remains only to add that, as I, he has a certain unrest in his soul and does not attach himself strongly to anything. If I am thus, it is not my fault. To what would I attach myself when I am alone, possessing nothing and condemned to the life of a vagabond. Oh. If I had a corner of ground to myself, all my hours would be employed and if I had the misfortune not to have a serious pursuit, [21] then as Uncle Toby I would have a *hoby horse:* I would need to keep myself very busy with something if it were only a folly.

Chapter IV

MOUNT VERNON

2 June. Mount Vernon. After many distractions and delays, at about eleven o'clock we set out for Mount Vernon. We crossed the river by ferry and followed the Maryland bank. From there Federal City or rather the land destined for the city rises in an amphitheatre. After having made 4 to 5 miles we arrived at the point opposite Alexandria; I saw there an immense field covered with the most beautiful wheat that one could wish for. I asked the reason for this fertility almost unknown in America and very rare in any country. I was told that the ground was fertilized with herrings; that is to say, with the heads and the entrails of this fish. We took 25 minutes to cross the Potowmak once again. I stopped in Alexandria at the merchant's Atkins to buy a pound of cut tobacco. It sells at a dollar a pound, which is excessive for a country which is the fatherland of all tobaccos. While paying I muttered against this costly habit, unclean and unhealthy, but it is not at such a time, bereft of all pleasures, that I could bring myself to renounce it.

We continued through a country scored with ravines and well wooded. After 7 miles of road we arrived at the foot of a hill where the properties of Gl. Washington begin. We took a road newly cut through a forest of oaks. Soon we discovered still another hill at the top of which stood a rather spacious house, surmounted by a small cupola, with mezzanines and with blinds painted in green. It is surrounded by a ditch in brick with very pretty little turrets at the corners; these are nothing but outhouses. Two bowling greens, a circular one very near the house, the other very large and irregular, form the courtyard in front of the house. All kinds of trees, bushes, flowering plants, ornament the two sides of the court.[1] Near the two ends of the house [22] are planted two groves of acacia, called here *locust*, a charming tree, with a smooth trunk and without branches leaving a clear and open space for the movement of its small and trembling leaves. The ground where they are planted is a green carpet of the most beautiful velvet. This tree keeps off all kinds of insects. There were also a few catalpa and tulip trees there etc.

95

We entered into the house. Gl. Washington was at his farm. Madame appeared after a few minutes, welcomed us most graciously and had *punch* served. At two o'clock the Gl. arrived mounted on a gray horse. He shook our hand, dismounted, gave a cut of the whip to his horse which went off by itself to the stable. We chatted a little; then he went off to dress and we to see the interior of the house.

One enters into a hall which divides the house into two and leads to the *piazza*. It is decorated with a few engravings of Claude Lorraine.[2] A kind of small crystal lantern contains the actual key of the Bastille. This relic of despotism was sent to the Gl. by the Marquis de La Fayette. Underneath is a drawing representing the demolition of this formidable castle.[3] Furthermore on the *piazza* one sees a model of it, wholly of a stone which was part of the Bastille; it is a foot and a half high, made with the greatest detail and exactness. It is a pity that the children have already damaged it a little. At the right, on entering, is a *parlor*. One sees there the portrait of Gl. Washington when he was still in the English service, in a blue uniform, red vest and breeches, the whole trimmed with narrow silver braid, and a small hat in the shape of a mushroom. He is represented in the attitude of an officer on the march; lest there should be any doubt he takes out of the pocket of his vest a paper on which is written *March order*. He has a gun slung across his back and a violet sash over his shoulders.[4] Mrs. Washington (née Dandridge), which makes the pair, has a blue gown with her hair dressed a half an inch high and her ears uncovered. In her right hand she carries a flower. This portrait, which was never good, is in addition badly damaged.[5] [There is] a picture representing the family of the Mar[quis] de La Fayette: The Mar[quis] in an American uniform is presenting to his wife, who is seated, his son aged 4 also in an American uniform; [23] his two daughters nearly the same age complete the group. The picture is well painted and well composed but the paint has fallen off in many places. The marquise has a broad slash the whole length of the left side of her face, a slash which has deprived her of an eye; the older of the girls is also one-eyed, and the younger has lost the end of her nose.[6] There is a portrait of the son and daughter of Mrs. Washington by her first marriage: the child is only 5 years old. He is dressed in a suit with a purse, carrying on his fist a red bird. There are portraits in pastel of the Gl., of Madame, of the young Custis, of young La Fayette, and the divine Miss Custis with her hair blown by a storm.[7] An allegorical picture in enamel in honor of the Gl.[8] Two pictures embroidered in faultless needlework, etc., etc.

From this room one goes into a large salon that the Gl. has recently added. It is the most magnificent room in the house. The chimney-piece is in white marble, with beautiful bas-reliefs. A few pictures, engravings after Thrumbull, representing the death of Gl. Warren and of Gl. Montgomery.[9] At the side of the first room is yet another *parlor,* decorated with beautiful engravings representing storms and sea-scapes. One sees there a superb harpsichord of Miss Custis.[10] On the other side of the hall are the dining room, a bedroom and the library of the Gl; above, several apartments for Madame, Miss Custis and guests. They are all very neatly and prettily furnished.

On the side opposite the front is an immense open portico supported by eight pillars. It is from there that one looks out on perhaps the most beautiful view in the world. One sees there the waters of the Potowmak rolling majestically over a distance of 4 to 5 miles. Boats which go to and fro make a picture of unceasing motion. A lawn of the most beautiful green leads to a steep slope, covered as far as the bank by a very thick wood where formerly there were deer and roebuck, but a short time ago they broke the enclosure and escaped. [There are] robins, blue titmice, Baltimore bird, *the black, red and gold bird.* [24] It is there that in the afternoon and evening the Gl., his family and the *gustes* [guests] go to sit and enjoy the fine weather and the beautiful view. I enjoyed it more than anyone. I found the situation of Mount Vernon from this side very similar to that of Puławy.[11] The opposite bank, the course of the river, the dense woods all combined to enhance this sweet illusion. What a remembrance!

About three o'clock a carriage drawn by two horses, a young man on horseback alongside, pulled up. A young woman of the greatest beauty accompanied by another who was not beautiful at all. This was one of those celestial figures that nature produces only rarely, that the inspiration of painters has sometimes divined and that one cannot see without ecstasy. Her sweetness is equal to her beauty, and this being, so perfect of form, possesses all the talents: she plays the harpsichord, sings, draws better than any woman in America or even in Europe.[12]

After dinner one goes out onto the portico to read the newspaper. In the evening Gl. Wash[ington] showed us his garden. It is well cultivated and neatly kept; the gardener is an Englishman. One sees there all the vegetables for the kitchen, *Corrents, Rasberys, Strawberys, Gusberys,* quantities of peaches and cherries, much inferior to ours, which the *robins, blackbirds* and Negroes devour before they are ripe.

Opium, some poppies. Mr. Law, who lived for such a long time in the Great Indies, assures me that opium is made from ordinary poppies. When the heads are formed and before they begin to yellow, in the evening, a small incision is made the length of the head with a dull knife, taking care not to touch the seeds which are inside. In the morning one comes and finds there a whitish liquor. It is removed with a knife and put into a jar. The incision is repeated on the opposite side. This is done continually until the head dries and produces no more. When the pot is filled, it is exposed to the sun so that the liquid shall lose its serosity and be reduced to a solid mass. It is then cut into square pieces, wrapped in leaves, packed in boxes for China, Japan, Turkey, etc.

One sees also in the garden lilies, roses, pinks, etc. The path which runs all around [25] the bowling green is planted with a thousand kinds of trees, plants and bushes; crowning them are two immense Spanish chestnuts that Gl. Wash[ington] planted himself; they are very bushy and of the greatest beauty. The tree of the *tulip,* called here *Poplar,* or *Tulip Tree,* is very high with a beautiful leaf and the flower in a bell resembling a *Tulip,* white with a touch of orange at the base. The magnolia [is] a charming tree (this tree in South Carolina grows as high as 70 feet and perfumes the forests) with a whitish and smooth trunk; the leaf resembles that of the orange; in bud the flower is like a white acorn which opens out and gives off an odor less strong than the orange but just as agreeable; the fruit is a little cone with crimson seeds; these seeds are held to the cone by small threads.[13] The *Sweet Scented Shroub,* a shrub which grows in a thicket, with a very deep purple, nearly black flower, has a fragrance which from my point of view surpasses all the others: it is an essence of strawberries and pineapple mixed together.[14] The superb catalpa was not yet in flower. The fir of Nova Scotia, *Spruce Tree,* is of a beautiful deep green; it is from their cones that the essence of *Spruce* is extracted to mix it with the beer. [There was] a tree [blank] bearing thousands and thousands of pods like little pea pods. A thousand other bushes, for the most part species of laurel and thorn, all covered with flowers of different colors, all planted in a manner to produce the most beautiful hues. The weeping willows were deprived of their greatest beauty. Last winter there was such a great amount of snow that their branches, not being able to support it, broke. Instead of their floating crown these trees appeared like close-cropped whiskbrooms, which did not become them at all. In a word the garden, the plantations, the house, the whole upkeep, proves that a man born with natural taste can divine the beautiful without having seen the model. The Gl. has never left America. After seeing his house and his gardens one would say that he had seen the most beautiful examples in England of this style.

As the sun was setting, we saw the herd returning home. On the lead was a superb bull of English breeding, for which the Gl. paid 200 doll. We then went to see the asses. Mar[quis] de La Fayette sent to him a stallion from Malta and one from Spain with their females.[15] They are large and handsome of their kind. The Gl. keeps up to 50 mules; these cross-bred animals are excellent for work and burdens. [26] The asses service the mares and the jennies of the neighbors at a charge of ten dollars per season; for each female, as she is then on board, a half doll. per week is paid for her feed, which is a little dear, and besides this a ½ doll. for the boy.

3 June. The next day, which was Sunday, the Gl. retired to write letters, this day being set aside for this activity. I went out for a walk with Mr. Law. He showed me a hill covered with old chestnuts, oaks, weeping willows, cedars, etc. It was a burial ground. It is there that the inhabitants of Mount Vernon, their eyelids once closed, sleep a peaceful and eternal sleep. Mr. Law was present at the interment of Mrs. Liard who brought up the granddaughters of Mrs. Washington.[16] The ceremony took place in the evening of a beautiful day in Autumn. The sun was setting behind the bluish hills and thick forests of oaks and laurel, its rays falling obliquely on the smooth waters of the Potowmak. A light wind ruffled the leaves of the trees, already half-green and half-yellow. A pastor, a venerable figure with white hair, read the prayer for the dead while the assembled family, the young women with bowed heads, eyes in tears, observed a heavy silence. "I have never seen," he told me, "a more affecting and more august sight."

About one o'clock we had the pleasure of seeing Mrs. Law arrive with her little daughter and then a *gentilman* farmer of the neighborhood with his stout and red-haired wife who had a belt with a buckle of Bohemian Glass. In the evening no music, not even a game of chess; it was Sunday; everyone retired at nine o'clock.

4 June. His Fortune. We left on horseback with Mr. Law to see the Gl.'s farm. Mount Vernon was already a large property when Gl. Washington inherited it from his half brother of the first marriage. When he married Mrs. Custis, he took with her as dowry 20,000 pounds of the money of Virginia, about 70,000 doll.[17] He bought, with a large part of this money, lands at 20 and 30 shlings per acre, between 4 and 5 pounds (today he would not give them up for ten times as much). His lands in Mount Vernon today enclose 10,000 acres in a single unit. [27] He has just sold 23 thousand acres of land on the Kanhowa [Kanawha] at 8 doll. an acre, which amounts to 184 thousand at 6 p. cent. These lands were given to him by the Crown for his services in the defeat of Gl. Brad[d]ock.[18] Besides these he has prop-

erties in the Shenandonah valley, in Barkley County which he has just leased at 40 pounds per hundred acres, and also in Fridericks County.

This morning we saw vast fields covered with different kinds of grain. One hundred acres in peas alone, much rye which is distilled into *whiski,* maize, wheat, flax, large meadows sown to lucerne; the soil although for the most part clayey produces, as a result of good cultivation, abundant harvests. All these lands are divided into four farms with a number of Blacks attached to each and a Black overseer over them. The whole is under the supervision of Mr. Anderson, a Scottish farmer.[19]

We saw a very large mill built in stone. An American machine invented by Evens (who has published a work on mills) for the aeration of the flour is very ingenious.[20] Beside the different kinds of grain that that are ground for the use of the house, and for the nourishment of the Blacks, each year a thousand kegs of wheat flour are ground for export. A *boushel* of grain makes a *boushel* of flour; 5 *boushels* are necessary for a barrel. The lowest price being 5 doll. that makes 5,000 doll. per year. Outsiders who come to grind at the mill pay an eighth in kind.

Just near by is a *whiski* distillery. Under the supervision of the son of Mr. Anderson, they distill up to 12 thousand gallons a year (they can distill 50 gallons per day if the weather is not too hot); each gallon at 4 Virginia shilings; that alone should bring in up to 16 thousand doll. I do not know how Mr. Anderson maintains that the distillery produces only 600 pounds. If this distillery produces poison for men, it offers in return the most delicate and the most succulent feed for pigs. They keep 150 of them of the Guinea type, short feet, hollow backs [28] and so excessively bulky that they can hardly drag their big bellies on the ground. Their venerable and corpulent appearance recalled to me our Dominican convents, like so many priors. We saw here and there flocks of sheep. The Gl. has between six and seven hundred. They are not anywhere near as big as those of England. The rose laurel with which the forests abound here is a poison for them and many die of it.[21]

Blacks. We entered one of the huts of the Blacks, for one can not call them by the name of houses. They are more miserable than the most miserable of the cottages of our peasants.[22] The husband and wife sleep on a mean pallet, the children on the ground; a very bad fireplace, some utensils for cooking, but in the middle of this poverty some cups and a teapot. A boy of 15 was lying on the ground, sick, and in terrible convulsions. The Gl. had sent to Alexandria to fetch a doctor. A very small garden planted with vegetables was close by, with 5 or 6 hens, each one leading ten to fifteen chickens. It is the only comfort that is permitted them; for they may not keep either ducks, geese, or pigs. They sell the poultry in Alexandria and procure for themselves a few amenities. They allot them each *one pack* [peck], one gallon [sic] of maize per week; this makes one quart a day, and half as much for the children, with 20 herrings each per month. At harvest time those who work in the fields have salt meat; in addition, a jacket and a pair of homespun breeches per year. Not counting women and children the Gl. has 300 Negroes of whom a large number belong to Mrs. Washington. Mr. Anderson told me that there are only a hundred who work in the fields. They work all week, not having a single day for themselves except for holidays. One sees by that that the condition of our peasants is infinitely happier. The mulattoes are ordinarily chosen for servants. According to the laws of Virginia the child follows the condition [29] of the mother; the son or daughter of a mulatto woman and a white is a slave and the issue through the daughter, although white, are still slaves.[23] Gl. Washington treats his slaves far more humanely than do his fellow citizens of Virginia. Most of these gentlemen give to their Blacks only bread, water and blows.

Either from habit, or from natural humor disposed to gaiety, I have never seen the Blacks sad. Last Sunday there were about thirty divided into two groups and playing at prisoner's base. There were jumps and gambols as if they had rested all week. I noticed that all spoke very good English. Why then do the Blacks of the French colonies never speak a good French; rather make a jargon of their own? The reason for it is perhaps that the American masters speak and communicate with them more often than the French who depend entirely for the management of their farms on their overseers who are also black.

5 June. This morning the Gl. had the kindness to go with us on horseback to show us another of his farms. The soil of it was black, much better looking and more fertile than that of the others. We saw two young bulls only one year old of a prodigious size. If the Americans, instead of leaving their herds out to pasture all winter, kept them in the stables, they would be superb, but the opposite prevails, consequently their cows are thin. They prefer to use horses at the plow. The Gl. showed us a plow of his own invention: in the middle on the axle itself is a hollow cylinder filled with grain; this cylinder is pierced with different holes, according to the size of the grain. As the plow moves ahead, the cylinder turns and the grain falls, the ploughshare having prepared the furrow for it, and a little blade be-

hind then covers it with earth. He then took us to see a barn for threshing the grain. It is an octagonal building; on the first story the floor is made from planed poles three inches wide which do not touch, leaving an empty space between. Grain is placed on them and horses, driven at a trot, trample it; the kernels fall through to the bottom. All around the building there are windows for a draft.[24]

"The Gl. showed us a plow of his own invention."

[30] I have often heard the Gl. reproached for his reserve and his taciturnity. It is true that he is somewhat reserved in speech, but he does not avoid entering into conversation when one furnishes him with a subject. We spoke of the French Revolution, and these were his words, "The acts of the French, that which they do in Holland, in Italy, and in Switzerland, ought to warn all nations of their intentions; ought to teach them that it is not freedom nor the happiness of men, but an untrammelled ambition and a desire to spread their conquests and to rule everywhere which is the only goal of their measures!"

At the table after the departure of the ladies,[25] or else in the evening seated under the portico, he often talked with me for hours at a time. His favorite subject is agriculture, but he answered with kindness all questions that I put to him on the Revolution, the armies, etc. He has a prodigious memory. One time in the evening he listed all the rivers, lakes, *creeks* and the means to procure a communication between these waters from Portsmouth[26] in the province of Maine as far as the Mississippi. This man may have erred during his administration; he may not be exempt from a few faults connected more with his age than with his heart, but in all he is a great man whose virtues equal the services that he has rendered his Fatherland. He has shown courage and talent in combat, perseverance and steadfastness during reverses and difficulties, disinterestedness, having at all times served without reward, and in the time of general enthusiasm of a grateful nation he never wished to accept the slightest recompense. Finally he has shown that he was not eager for glory, for being able to remain all his life at the head of the government he resigned voluntarily from the office of President. The device that he has taken for his arms is very appropriate for him, *exitus acta probat.*[27]

Since his retirement he has led a quiet and regular life. He gets up at 5 o'clock in the morning, reads or writes until seven. He breakfasts on tea and *caks* made from maize; because of his teeth he makes slices spread with butter and honey. He then immediately goes on horseback [31] to see the work in the fields; sometimes in the middle of a field he holds a council of war with Mr. Anderson. He returns at two o'clock, dresses, goes to dinner. If there are guests, he loves to chat after dinner with a glass of Madeira in his hand. After dinner he diligently reads the newspapers, of which he receives about ten of different kinds. He answers letters, etc. Tea at 7 o'clock; he chats until nine, and then he goes to bed.

"The device that he has taken for his arms is very appropriate for him."

Mrs. Washington is one of the most estimable persons that one could know, good, sweet, and extremely polite. She loves to talk and talks very well about times past. She told me she remembered the time when there was only one single carriage in all of Virginia. Ladies invited to an entertainment arrived on horseback. All the trade consisted in the little tobacco that was exported. The correspondents in England did not fail to send to their friends one or two pounds of tea, which was a very great present.

I was not as a stranger but a member of the family in this estimable house. They took care of me, of my linen, of my clothes, etc. Mrs. Washington was born on the North river; her maiden name is Dandridge.

6 June. The 6th Mr. Law left for Baltimore. Mrs. Stuart, daughter-in-law of Mrs. Wash[ington], with four of her daughters by her second marriage and her husband arrived in a coach and four with two postillions, and two men on horseback, all black.

7 [June] I took a long walk on foot to the herring fisheries. They fish for them in April; they have caught as many as 100 thousand of them with a single draw of the net. It is the best nourishment for the Negroes. I have copied a few birds from the natural history of Catesby: it is an excellent book giving the birds, fish, plants, etc., of Florida,

the Bahama islands, Georgia, Carolina, etc.[28] The engravings are made with the most exact verisimilitude.

[32] 8 J[une] For three years the deer have almost disappeared from the Gl.'s park. When today we discovered three grazing on the grass a little distance from the house, the Gl. suggested to me to look at them close up. We left. He walked very quickly; I could hardly follow him. We maneuvered to force them to leave their retreat and go towards the field, but the maneuver, clever as it was, did not succeed; they plunged into the wood.

9 J[une] Mrs. Washington made me a gift of a china cup with her monogram and the names of the states of the United States.[29] Miss Custis gave me my monogram in flowers, which she herself has painted very well. This evening I received a letter from Bory[sławski] and another from Most[owski].[30] These were the first replies to all the letters that I have written from here. My emotion was such that I had a fever; I thought only of my friends, only of my poor country. I wanted to fly there with the speed of thought. At night I dreamt that I was in Poland and, a most extraordinary thing, I regretted being there. That too was only a dream.

10 [June] Sunday, cool weather, I caught a river turtle weighing at least 12 pounds. We retired at 9 o'clock.

Blacks. 11 [June] Monday I had a conversation with Dr. Stuart. He told me: no one knows better than the Virginians the cruelty, inconvenience and the little advantage of having Blacks. Their support costs a great deal; their work is worth little if they are not whipped; the *Surveyor* costs a great deal and steals into the bargain. We would all agree to free these people; but how to do it with such a great number? They have tried to rent them a piece of land; except for a small number they want neither to work nor to pay their rent. Moreover this unfortunate black color has made such a sharp distinction between the two races. It will always make them a separate caste, [33] which in spite of all the enlightenment of philosophy, will always be regarded as an inferior class which will never mix in the society of Whites. All these difficulties will increase from day to day, for the Blacks multiply. Only a great increase of the population of Whites, a great emigration from Europe, could render this less apparent.

N.B. The real cause, or so it appears to me, for the necessity and the existence of Negroes in the United States is the excessive extent of the individual properties, and the small number of Whites that there are in view of the size of the country. The owners, not being able either to cultivate their lands themselves or to find white cultivators to lease them, find it necessary to keep this large number of Negroes.

It is the greed of the Liverpool merchants who before the Revolution peopled this country with Blacks. This greed, in spite of all the remonstrances of the Legislatures then, served only to make this infamous traffic grow daily. The cultivation of tobacco and of cotton is again one of the reasons why the Southern States still have slaves; while those of the East, where properties are more divided and where they do not cultivate this sort of produce, do not have them.

12 [June] We spoke of the authors who have written the History of the Revolution. Gordon, who has the most details, came to visit the archives of the Gl. They consist of between 30 and 40 cases of papers, containing all the military expeditions, reports, journals, correspondence with Congress, with the Generals, etc. What a wealth of material! However, Gordon stayed only three weeks to read them and extract them.[31] The Gl. intends to build a separate house for the deposit of his archives since the collection has become so voluminous.

Mrs. Washington showed me a small collection of medals [34] struck during the Revolution. There is one of at least 100 ducats in gold, with the head closely resembling that of Gl. Washington, which was struck on the occasion of the evacuation of Boston; one for Gl. Gates for the defeat of Bourgoyne; others for Gl. Green, Gl. Morgan, Col. Howard and Col. Washington on the occasion of the battle of Cowpen; one for Franklin, for M. de Fleury, for Paul Jones; one with the head of Liberty on one side and on the reverse France defending America with her shield against Gr[eat] Britain. Further there is the order of Cincinnatus in diamonds presented by the French Navy;[32] a box in gold, very badly turned, presented by the city of New York with the freedom of the city.

In the evening the General went to the storehouse to look over things which had come from Europe, just as we do when goods come from Gdańsk during the spring floods.[33]

Every day I notice new birds arriving to nest in the peaceful garden of these parts: turtledoves, cardinals all crimson. The Baltimore, orange with black bands, these latter singing very well. They are beautiful; they are magnificent; I would prefer, however, a nightingale from Poland.

I have read the ode to the fatherland by Gresset. It moved me to tears. Here is a verse.[34]

> Heureux qui des Mers Atlantiques
> Au toit paternel revenu,
> Consacre à ses dieux domestiques
> Un repos enfin obtenu;

Plus heureux le mortel sensible,
Qui reste citoyen paisible
Où la nature l'a placé,
Jusqu'à ce que sa dernière heure
Ouvre la dernière demeure,
Où ses aïeux l'ont devancé.

[End of French text]

[35] June 13. Mr. Law returned from Baltimore where he had ridden to consult with lawyers in a matter instigated by litigious associates and false friends.

In the morning we went out with the steward Anderson and some negroes to catch fish. The manner of fishing is similar to ours but the fish are entirely different. When the nets were hauled in, they were reasonably well filled but only with small fish. The largest fish was the *garfish*, nearly two feet in length and rather similar to one that is called in the Mediterranean the *pescespada*.[35] Its skin is as tough as shagreen and mottled with leopard-like spots, a snout six inches long like the beak of a bird, with both lower and upper teeth as sharp as needles. This fish is skinned while still alive. The flesh is red and it is little esteemed, serving only as food for negroes. *Cat Fisch*, so called because it has a head somewhat resembling that of a cat and, when disturbed, it gives out a cat-like cry. It is about a foot long with a very large head in proportion to its length, "whiskers" in four rows, and fins which when touched inflict a painful wound. There are two kinds, white and black. The first is considered excellent, especially for broth; the second, which is black, is left for the blacks. We caught 30 of the latter kind; the hapless negroes got them all. *Tobac[c]o box*[36] is a flat fish five inches in length and practically circular. Its scales are dark green, pierced through with gold; around the head at both sides it has two circles like shilling pieces; half crimson, half black; it is difficult to find anything more lovely. These fish, which are abundant in practically all American rivers, are as good in taste as they are beautiful to behold. There are many perches and silver roaches. River turtles, one foot in length, have a black shell shot through with red. They provide both meat and eggs which are excellent. Finally we caught a crayfish. It was the first which I had seen in America; the inhabitants of these parts hold them in disdain and do not eat them.

On our return we found a notable and unexpected [36] company from Alexandria. The table in the great hall was set out with a Sèvres porcelain service with places for 20.[37] The General, in high spirits,

was gracious and full of attention to everybody. Amongst the guests
were the young Randolphs; I do not know whether both their ages
would add up to 38, and already they are the parents of three children. Mrs. Fetus [Fitzhugh],[38] who in corpulence and girth gives way
only to the late Semiramis,[39] was in a gay humour and had an enormous appetite. As she swept through one platter after another, her
husband laughingly encouraged her with these words: *"Betsy, a little
more, a little more."*

In the evening, after the departure of the company the General,
sitting with Mr. Law and me under the portico, read to us a letter
which he had just received from a friend in Paris. This letter written
with sense, dispassion, and with a sound knowledge of the situation
in France and the politics of those who rule her, gave us an opportunity for conversation about the wrongs suffered by America at
French hands, and about the bloody struggles which might shortly
break out between the two countries. This conversation aroused the
passionate wrath of the venerable citizen and commander. I have
never heard him speak with so much candor nor with such heat.

"Whether," he said, "we consider the injuries and plunder which
our commerce is suffering" (up to 50 million dollars) "or the affront
to our national independence and dignity in the rejection of our envoys, or whether we think on the oppression, ruin and final destruction of all free people through this military government, everywhere
we recognize the need to arm ourselves with a strength and zeal equal
to the dangers with which we are threatened. Continued patience and
submission will not deliver us, any more than submission delivered
Venice or others. Submission is vile. Yea, rather than allowing herself
to be insulted to this degree, rather than having her freedom and independence trodden under foot, America, every American, I, though old,
will pour out the last drop of blood which is yet in my veins."

"They censure Mr. Adams for haste in deeds and excessive boldness
in words; from the moment [37] that I left the administration, I have
not written a word to Mr. Adams, nor yet received a word from him
except the dispatches which we have seen in the papers; I do not
know what are those other sources of information on which he acts;
with all this I am certain, as a reasonable and honest person, as a good
American, that he cannot do other than he does. I, in his place, perhaps would be less vehement in expression but I would prepare myself steadily and boldly in the same fashion."

The strong and noble feelings of this man pierced my heart with
respect and emotion.

June 14. In the evening, for the last time, pretty Miss Custis sang

and played on the harpsichord. The next day, after having risen before dawn, I walked, now for the last time, about the green groves of
Mo[u]nt Vernon. For the last time I looked out on the open view, on
the clear and beautiful stream Potowmak. Then at six in the morning
with gratitude for the hospitable welcome, and with sorrow silent and
unexpressed, I took my leave of the honorable Washington, his worthy
wife and the beautiful, good and kind Miss Custis. In company of
both Mr. and Mrs. Law and their beautiful *baby* daughter I returned
through Alexandria to George Town. We spent the heat of the day at
Mr. and Mrs. Peters' (Mrs. Peters is a sister of Mrs. Law). I was welcomed there in what was for me the most gratifying way possible, that
is, I was treated as a member of the family.

Chapter V

ROAD TO FREDERICK TOWN. PENNSYL-
VANIA. NEW JERSEY. NEW YORK CITY.
DEPARTURE FOR CONNECTICUT

Road to Frideriks Town. Since a large part of my life has been spent in wandering, I should be accustomed to changes in places and in people; every farewell, however, costs my heart a great deal, how much more so leaving a family which for so long a time has treated me with the greatest goodness, graciousness and affection; I could not have known [38] greater care and attention with either friends or family than at the home of Mr. and Mrs. Law. Let Heaven rain down on them all happiness and remove from them all cares and sorrow.

At ten at night we started for George Town. Again I passed through all the land which has been set aside for the future Capital of the United States. After a hundred years, a traveler riding along this same road will find on both sides sumptuous buildings illuminated with lights enclosed in crystal, a crowd of pedestrians, the noise of carriages passing each other at full speed. Today I, in the darkness of night, heard only the rustle of oaks and immense poplars, the murmur of the running streams and felt only the jolting blows of the carriage hitting continually against the holes and tree stumps in the road, so recently cut out of the wilderness.

June 15. After dozing till four in the morning I set out the next day for Friderik Town. The companions of my journey were: a lady with the name of Mrs. Simmers going to her family, her high box, filled with hats and hoods, was a great hindrance to those sitting with her; Mr. [blank] [1] from Virginia, a doctor, a tall, handsome and pleasant person who, in his twenty-fifth year, actually just a few weeks ago, inoculated himself against smallpox; two boys perhaps 12 years old and finally two wagoners, extraordinarily cheerful and ribald. I took up my favorite place, that is, on the driver's seat next to the citizen driver. The reasons for my predilection for this place are, coolness, the fresh and open air, a view on all sides, and finally a pleasant, interesting and intimate conversation with the citizen coachman. Whosoever sits within the carriage has a more honorable place, maintains his dignity better, but does not taste all those morsels which the person sitting in this undervalued place, called the coach box, can enjoy. And so, in a diligence as in life, [39] every place high or low has its own rewards and pleasures.

My friend, the coachman was a third-generation German settled in America and, even now, pronouncing *p* as *b* and *b* as *p*, and therefore instead of *big pox*, which means "big pox," or rather more than that, he said *pig box*.[2]

Another phaeton gave to each of his horses a name. There were four, and they were called Pop[e], Princ[e], Roebock and Dżoli [Jolly]. Convinced that honor and good faith have more [influence] on creatures than do force and punishment, he encouraged his horses with words rather than threatened them with beating. The Pope was far better treated in harness than in Italy.

I remember, before I knew the advantage of sitting on the coach box and sat myself in better places with the others, often, to a curious question of mine a gloomy *gentelman* would coldly reply: "*I don't know, I am sur[e]*," or "*That's more than I can tell*." In contrast, the driver not only told me about everything I asked, but even things I did not ask; and we were yet 40 miles from Frideriks Town when I already knew the whole history of the town and its environs.

After leaving George Town the countryside is covered with forest as on the other side, but here it is better cultivated and with better soil. I saw great tracts covered with rye; for the last few years this grain has been sown extensively, not for bread, for practically everybody eats wheat bread, but, alas, for *whiski*. Rum, or French brandy, mixed with water are the common drinks in America for the well-to-do; the poorer people drink *whiski*, mixed half with water. Because of the expense and difficulty nowadays of bringing in rum and brandy by sea, the latter drink is more and more common.

I saw some fine looking flax, though not as much as is necessary to provide everyone with his own cloth. Wheat, formerly so profitable, and maize—enough for the requirements [40] of the farm—occupy the farmer's industry and effort. Tobacco is sown only on big plantations, every leaf watered by the sweat of the unhappy negroes.

Apart from poplars, sycamores [3] and *sas[s]afras*, etc., the forest is mostly filled with oaks. There are numberless kinds; all, however, have *un air de famille* which indicates that however much they differ, they are all related to each other.

The homes of the free white farmers are much less impressive in appearance and are ill-kept compared with those in Pennsylvania. Whenever a stone house appears, one sees immediately about a score of huts of negro slaves surrounding it. Nowhere are there great herds; there is a little poultry. Geese, plucked alive, drag themselves about pitiful and naked. The owners pluck their down two or three times a year. This terrible practice is the result of need, or rather greed. For a pound of down one pays 5 shillings.

Our *Stage* stopped on the road to pass out papers and letters. Once we stopped at a very poor hut and a spare and small figure emerged asking for the newspapers. The printer from George Town had forgotten to send them. The shoemaker, for it was a shoemaker, accepted this disappointment with the indifference of a true stoic, but all in all, I am certain this was a severe blow for him. After tea these people like nothing better than their newspapers.

After travelling 14 miles we stopped at Montgomeri Court House [4] for breakfast. This is a little town with 30 houses. The occupants are shopkeepers and artisans. Our breakfast was composed of yellow water which they call coffee, of tea, fried chicken, broiled ham, butter, etc. An American eats more for breakfast than for dinner. We paid $2\frac{1}{2}$ shillings per person. Fourteen miles further on, after riding through similar country and jolting along, always on poor roads, we stopped for dinner. Again boiled ham, chickens, and salad; the drink was water with peach brandy—3 shillings a person. We met there a few [41] travelers on horseback. A portmanteau filled with two shirts, a pair of shoes, trousers, and a stock composes the whole wardrobe of an American. With it he would set out for the end of the earth. Moreover, women make rather long journeys on horseback.

Four miles from the town we forded the river [blank: Monocacy]. On its banks one can see a row of wooden houses and one stone house with the upper storeys painted white. This is the residence of a Frenchman called Payant, who left San Domingo with a substantial sum and with it bought two or three thousand acres of land, and a few hundred negroes whom he treats with the greatest tyranny. One can see on the home farm instruments of torture, stocks, wooden horses, whips, etc. Two or three negroes crippled with torture have brought legal action against him, but the matter has not as yet been settled. This man is 60 years old, without children or relatives; he keeps an old French woman with two daughters; she, in sweetness of humour, even surpasses him. This charming group has caused about 50 legal actions to be brought.[5] They foam with rage, beat the negroes, complain and fight with each other. In these ways does this man use his wealth, and comforts his life in its descent toward the grave.

The closer we approach to the town, the better the land becomes and more abundant growth can be seen. The chain of high mountains, which we could see in the distance after leaving George Town, now appears beautiful and impressive. Blue vapor or fog always covers them, and that is why they are called the Blue Ridge. The tremendous heat, which had baked us all night [day?] began to let up with the advent of the cool evening breeze; the sun, a full crimson, etched across with the edges of a blue-colored cloud, was setting beyond the horizon.

After seven in the evening we stopped in Frideriks Town. This is one of the more important towns in the interior of America. It encompasses mainly the length of one street and of another which crosses it. The houses are in general of masonry and rather well kept. Sidewalks for pedestrians are laid out with stones but the streets are not paved.

The inhabitants are largely of German descent, with the exception of perhaps 20 families in town and in the environs. [42] They preserve to a large extent the customs and the language, especially among themselves. A few of the more well-to-do are beginning to be ashamed of this and prefer to speak English. With the years the German language would disappear, especially in town, if only the pastors in their own interest did not retain it as much as possible. Their employment would prove unnecessary were the people to go to the English church. Though even the oldest inhabitant was born in America, nevertheless by dress and way of life it is easy to recognize them as Germans and even to place them as Germans of the 16th century. Old women, with coifs tied under their chins, wear on top of them large white hats without crowns like huge flat plates. The men have long, wide linen trousers. They are hard working, industrious, neat and clean and extraordinarily diligent. It is perhaps, as much because of this, as from lack of understanding that they shrink from the smallest tax. For them, a government is good as long as it does not require payments of any kind. One shilling per hundred is called tyranny. In the last insurrection caused by a tax on whisky the citizens of this county showed themselves to be fiercely stubborn. They are fat and sluggish horses which rear at the slightest prick.[6]

There is nothing more fertile than this land. They rarely manure it; it never lies fallow, nonetheless it continually produces all sorts of grain. The fields groan under the weight of Indian corn, wheat, rye, etc. The meadows are covered with clover, the orchards filled with fruit, the forests all around are full of the most beautiful oak trees; in a word the land flows with milk and honey but, in the measure of its worth, it is expensive. One pays for an acre of land near the town 50 to 100 dollars. I myself saw a field of only 4 acres for which nearly 400 dollars was recently paid. An acre ordinarily yields up to 30 bushels —a bushel, 8 *gallons*.[7]

[V, 1] I had to wait a whole week in this remote town for a *Stage* or a post coach leaving for Lankastr. I was therefore gratified to learn that one of the most famous views in America is to be found only twenty miles away (i.e. where the two rivers, the Potowmak and the Szanandor [Shenandoah], break through the Blue Ridge). For three days my efforts to find a horse for hire proved fruitless, either because the German farmers wanted them for plowing, or being careful and untrusting, were afraid to accept the good faith of a stranger. Happily, an honest Frenchie, who for eighteen years has been teaching French conjugations in this new hemisphere, offered me his nag. After arranging that the horse be fed well for two days and having her shod so that she could walk, finally, June 20 at five in the morning I set out on my journey.

I rode through countryside both well-cultivated and bountiful. Except for forest regions which were not extensive but occurred more often, the eye everywhere sees tremendous tracts of all sorts of grain. Great farm wagons harnessed to six horses were carrying flour and goods to and fro, and filled the fields and woods with the sound of horse bells as they plodded slowly along. I, on my nag, went scarcely any faster. In spite of this, it seems to me that travel by horseback is much pleasanter, more advantageous, and perhaps even more economical. A person is not locked up in a tantalus, the whole horizon is open before him; he sees everything, sees better, and with greater pleasure. Whether it be a tree, a bush or a flower which particularly attracts him, he turns his horse, approaches close and satisfies his curiosity. He stops where and when he wishes, rests, completely immersed as it were in the free air and, without excessive exhaustion, takes exercise which is necessary to health and to continued vigour.

[2] Eight miles from Fryderyk I stopped at New Town.[8] Though it calls itself a town, today it has only 20 houses, but after ten years (considering the enormous rate at which everything in this country grows) this, indeed, will be a well-inhabited and imposing town. There are already four guest houses here. From these all settlements begin. The guest houses are established not only because of the large traffic

of wagoners and of individual travelers, but also because the trade of innkeeper is profitable without a great deal of work.

However, in small towns innkeepers do not forsake the plow completely for the inn, and thus the landlord with whom I stayed had 150 *acres*. In these parts for an acre one pays 6 *pound* 10 and 7 *p[oun]d* 10 shillings. A worker at harvest time gets half a dollar, while in the states near the ocean he would get, at this season, 10 shillings. Here the hire of workers has become cheaper and, it will become cheaper elsewhere. The falling price of grain, result of the ravages of the French, is responsible for this. My landlord had personally felt this and therefore he embarked on a political conversation with me, speaking judiciously, with an awareness of the facts, with great dislike for the Great Nation [France] and with zeal and warm attachment to his own.

Eight miles further on one rides out through chains of mountains covered with cedars, *Maple Tree[s]* producing sugar, and various types of nut trees, *Mar[r]on[n]iers*. The silence of this wilderness is broken by the murmur and clamor of streams falling from rocks. On a low cedar perched an inhabitant of heaven-reaching cliffs, a sad and rapacious vulture. His wings were so wet from the morning's downpour that I got as close as three feet to him before he was able to flap and unfold his wings. He finally started his [3] heavy flight and moved off towards the cliffs.

At last an opening in the branches disclosed a view of the clear waters of the Potowmak and the noise of crashing waters announced the nearby rapids. The road here is narrow, cut out of the rocks and very steep. One continues along it for more than a mile up to a point where a tremendous sheer cliff hangs poised over one's very head. It is difficult to gaze upwards without wonder; it is difficult, without some fear, to remain for long looking on this wild, gloomy, and terrible view.

I called for a ferry and crossed to the other side, where there is a promontory of land amidst the Potowmak and the Szanandor; there among the rocks and forests are only three little houses—one a storehouse for flour, a general store, and a house for the ferry. Going further up the mountain there is a guest house fastened, as it were, onto the rock. Its whole rear wall and cellar is cut out of rock. From the top of this house there is a glorious and beautiful view, of which I can give no better description than to provide a faithful translation of that written by Jefferson. It will be a picture by Salvator Rosa copied by Mr. Cybulski from Biała.[9]

"The passage of the Patowmac through the Blue ridge is perhaps one of the most stupendous scenes in nature. You stand on a very high point of land. On your right comes up the Shenandoah, having ranged along the foot of the mountain an hundred miles to seek a vent. On your left approaches the Patowmac, in quest of a passage also. In the moment of their junction they rush together against the mountain, rend it asunder, and pass off to the sea. The first glance of this scene hurries our senses into the opinion, that this earth has been created in time, that the mountains were formed first, that the rivers began to flow afterwards, that in this place particularly they have been dammed up by the Blue ridge of mountains, and have formed an ocean which filled the whole valley; that continuing to rise they have at length broken over at this spot, and have torn the mountain down from its summit to its base. The piles of rock on each hand, but particularly on the Shenandoah, the evident marks of their disrupture and avulsion from their beds by the most powerful agents of nature, corroborate the impression. But the distant finishing which nature has given to the picture is of a very different character. [It is a true contrast to the fore-ground.] It is as placid and delightful, as that is wild and tremendous. For the mountain being cloven asunder, she presents to your eye, through the cleft, a small catch of smooth blue horizon, at an infinite distance in the plain country, inviting you, as it were, from the riot and tumult roaring around, to pass through the breach and participate of the calm below. Here the eye ultimately composes itself; and that way too the road happens actually to lead. You cross the Patowmac above the junction, pass along its side through the base of the mountain for three miles, its terrible precipices hanging in fragments over you, and within about 20 miles reach Frederic town and the fine country around that. This scene is worth a voyage across the Atlantic. Yet here, as in the neighbourhood of the natural bridge, are people who have passed their lives within half a dozen miles, and have never been to survey these monuments of a war between rivers and mountains, which must have shaken the earth itself to its center." *Notes on the State of Virginia by Jefferson.*[10]

After having sated my eyes on this view, I stepped below. The landlord showed me a hill covered with cedars. It was a cliff in which was cut out a large cellar, and so nature itself has provided for these people shelter and even comforts. To the left on a steep slope of the mountain there was again a rock slide; the stones are thrown hither and yon. There at first hand, one can see the terrible violence of nature's upheavals. In outline the rocks, some with great rounded prominences and others hollowed out completely, corresponding to each other and, if it were possible to fit them together, they would form perfectly one whole rock.

A downpour of rain prevented my further perambulations and I returned soaked to the skin, but the good Germans, the landlords here, dressed me from head to foot in dry clothes. This and other kindnesses are due to the fact that I spoke German.

For the first time I happened to see a family with all their goods and chattels going out as settlers. Husband, wife with six children, everyone walking, and driving before them two cows with their calves, carrying pots and small bundles.

It cleared up towards evening and the night shadows closed in on this wild and vast region and imposed sad thoughts on the mind. Looking about I noticed on the other side, right at the very foot of a cliff, under a hanging rock a tiny hut lighted up with a small fire. On inquiry as to who might live there I was told it was a pretty young woman. She, though white, carried away by most unusual feelings, married a negro; they have lived together now for three years in this wild and silent place. There are already three small children who make up the family. True love needing a hiding place could not have found a more deep and gloomy hollow.

The next day I saw boats which were being towed up stream. In spite of frequent rapids, these boats come down from Cumberland and even further, going to the Great Falls, carrying up to 130 barrels. There they cross the falls by canal and the loaded boat is pushed on rollers over [6] a small incline of land as far as George Town. The boatmen are paid a dollar a day. One of them spent practically a whole day in the tavern drinking *whiski*. Why not? After all, three days work is enough for a week's drinking.

At seven in the morning I set out on my return journey along the same road. I noticed many bushes of wild indigo in the forests. Every few miles I met a different person on horseback, asking whether I had seen a horse which had been stolen from him the previous night. One time it was a bay, then a gray or a chestnut. There is nothing more frequent in America than this particular joke. I returned to Fryderyk at noon.

In the evening I saw a parade of 40 recruits enlisted for garrisons in the western provinces. These are a tall and sturdy people, handsome and elegant. A soldier gets 4 dollars per month besides bread, meat, whisky, and uniform, which amounts to a cost of 450 dollars a year for each soldier. It is difficult at such a price to have a large army, and all the better. It would always be better if the citizens themselves defended their fatherland and nowhere were there slaves as mercenaries. These soldiers are kept in rented quarters.

Beyond the town there are armories built during the time of the

Revolution for quartering the prisoners taken from Burgoine's and Lord Cornwallis's troops, but these buildings are completely ruined.[11] Many of these prisoners, especially the Hessians and those from Brunswick did not wish to return home after peace was signed. They settled here and contributed greatly to the task of peopling these parts. These people are now substantial farmers and have realized a destiny which they could never expect in Europe. There are evident signs to show that a large number of Germans from the auxiliaries of the English settled in America and made up the loss of the Americans killed in the same war.

[7] The people with whom I lived, as I mentioned above, were Germans:—simple, rudely ignorant, and to ignorance is joined her true sister, suspicion. Because I traveled to look at the passage of the Potowmak through the mountains, because I sat at the hearth and read and wrote, all these were to them infallible proofs that I was nothing less than a French spy. These faults were recompensed by many real virtues, honesty and uprightness to the highest degree. It is true that our fare consisted of smoked pork products and radishes, but the price did not exceed the value. What is more, the day and a half which I spent away from the house was credited to my bill, and this was the first example of such probity that I have seen in this country.

At last we moved out on June 23 by a stagecoach belonging to the driver himself. The country as before was wonderfully beautiful and most bountiful, covered with forests of different varieties of oaks and nut trees, *hi[c]kory, walnut, ches[t]nut* and *sassafras*. In the distance the line of Blue Mountains continued on our left; after 11 miles we stopped at Woodbery.[12] Proceeding further on our journey and descending the hump of a hill we came to the bottom and found there in an oak forest, a view felicitous for the painter's brush. Amongst the shade of the oaks and maples on a twisting and narrow road was a cavalcade of at least one hundred people, men, women and children, everyone on horseback proceeding at a solemn and deliberate pace. There were differences of habit and complexion, vari-colored dresses, brisk rosy-cheeked girls with straw hats and white bodices, and their elders with hair curled in snowy ringlets which fell down on their arms. The sun, breaking through the branching shade of the trees, here and there threw a dappled light on the group, [8] and created the most pleasant sight. At the head of the cavalcade was a wagon with four horses; on it sat two women and equally two men with heads lowered and eyes in tears. They had amidst them a coffin covered with green branches. This was the funeral of an honored and beloved countryman to whom the whole neighborhood paid their last respects. Just as this sight appeared to us at first gay, so at the end it seemed tenderly affecting. Affecting, I say, but not drear; there was no shroud nor gloomy bells; there were no candles nor bellowing monks who, it seems, needs must lower the dead into limbo with wailing and gnashing of teeth; these were friends who were accompanying a friend to his resting place, where, joined with family and friends, he will rest with them forever in an unbroken sleep.

After 24 miles we stopped for dinner in Tan[e]y Town, a so-called town, inhabited by Germans, with 30 houses. The inn was very good and the dinner tasty, after the smoked meat of Friderik. These citizens sporting their national cockades read the newspaper Porkupine.[13] Ten miles further on we crossed the boundary between Maryland and Pennsylvania. Here the land is much inferior in quality; it is sown mostly with rye as much for making *wiski* as because the wheat has been spoilt extensively here by a fly called the *Hessian fly* which eats the roots completely.[14] In many places the farmers work at haying in groups. My companion, Dr. Armstad from Virginia and I, after a stay of nearly two months both there and in Maryland [9] were equally impressed by the number of white people working on the farms in Pennsylvania; while in the other two states the burden of work is left to the negroes and the burden of idleness falls on the whites. It is for this reason that, though the land is somewhat poorer in quality, it is much better cultivated. Perhaps it was simply because the land was so poor that so many people worked it. Man's industry and labor are increased and strengthened by adversity. In fertile Sicily the peasant grows lazy scratching a little patch of earth, while in China a farmer labors to haul baskets of fertile earth to the jagged cliff top in order to reap a bit of grain.

Not only are the houses surrounded by cherry trees but the roads are lined with cherry trees, some as big as the tallest oak trees. They are wild black cherries rather than ordinary cherries; I have not seen those we call the morello [15] anywhere. Whatever kind they may be, they provide both the traveler and the local inhabitant with a good taste and with pleasant refreshment. For those riding by, it is enough to reach out in order to get a handful. Many birds, and almost as many boys and girls perch on the branches right up to the very top without picking the tree clean of this abundant and prolific fruit.

A few miles further on we rode through a small town called Petersburg.[16] At the very name my skin crawled, *"steteruntque comae et vox faucibus haesit."* [17]

Forty-one miles from Fryderik we stopped for the night in Hannower. It is a rather large town, well built, clean and cheerful. It ships to Baltimor, 45 miles away. The inhabitants are practically [10] all Germans; habits, speech, newspapers, cooking—all German. A platoon of very well-dressed volunteers with helmets and plumes was returning from a muster.

It is my habit to walk about each town where I stop and to wander through all of its streets, in the evening. It is at this time that practically all the inhabitants, whether returned home from the plow, from the workbench or from trade, sit on their porches in the company of their wives and children, breathing the cool evening air and having intimate and sweet conversation amongst themselves. There is no drunkenness, no loud shouting. Recreation and entertainment for these people is rest and quiet. All the conversation was in German. The open doors of the houses showed to the passer-by the German's worldly goods, that is, a featherbed almost reaching to the ceiling, a cupboard with pewter utensils, burnished until they shone. The decorations on the wall—usually seven copper engravings made in Augsburg and representing the story of the prodigal son. From this story the fathers give to their sons all their moral instruction. The one picture wherein the prodigal son feeds the swine makes the most dreadful impression. The old man points to this one, calling to his young, this is what awaits everyone *"wenn nur nicht sparsam ist."*

In Hannower two new companions joined us: a young lady and a youth. After 18 miles of poor roads we stopped for breakfast in Jork [York]. Jork is an old town and rather large; it has an academy for teaching young people, and also a few types of handcrafts; the houses are rather well kept. A few days ago a case of some [11] interest was tried here. A certain [blank], German by birth, taking advantage of the ignorance and gullibility of his fellow countrymen, began to go secretively about the district and to persuade the farmers that he was a supernatural being who had the gift for discovering buried treasure. He indicated a secluded place in the forest, where the spirit with power over the treasures would show himself. The people, gullible, went there; the charlatan dressed in rude attire in the fashion of St. John in the wilderness, appeared before them in the phosphorus flame of a magic lantern, then hiding it and turning the light aside he disappeared completely. In this way he deluded their senses and accustomed them to miracles. He then prescribed for them a place where, and a person (in league with himself) from whom, they could, for a definite amount get a powder which on dusting would ward off the evil spirits who were hiding the charmed treasure. In a few weeks time he collected nearly 2,000 dollars for these powders. Finally, an accident uncovered the fraud. The Court gave him two years in the House of Correction and a stiff fine.

Our company increased to eight people in York, and on the way two more joined us. We had amongst others a Quaker stocking weaver. He had come to America with the English army as a surgeon. He confessed that even then and when he had settled here, he had succumbed to every dissolute urge, except for one impurity, with which from his twentieth year he had not once befouled himself. Suddenly a spirit entered into him and ordered him to be a Quaker. He has been a novitiate for five years, or rather on probation, during which time according to all witnesses he has lived in the most strict [12] moderation. Opposite him was a small person speaking excellent English, so much so that everyone took him for a native, when suddenly he broke into song—it was Sunday. At once the curtain parted and to the scandalized and astonished eyes of all he appeared as he really was, a Frenchman. Except for this crime he was in all an excellent youth, one to stir up pity; he had lost both his father and mother under the revolutionary sword.

We stopped about 2 o'clock at the Suskwehana [Susquehanna]. It is nearly a mile wide; its banks are mountainous; to the right and left rapids completely halt navigation. In the distance there were islands with clumps of trees; further yet and still unseen were the extensive mountains which lift themselves up, as one says, stepwise and merge into the horizon in a gray and misty haze. The whole situation provides an inexhaustible source of the most beautiful landscapes. Happy is he who has the opportunity to paint them. Ferried across this wide and shallow river we struck a rock but were pushed off in a while.

On the other side rises a town, Columbia, great in name but small in size. It has only eight, rather well-kept houses of which two are taverns. Both were full with a huge crowd of people who ate, drank, and conversed with the greatest phlegm; there was no singing, no fiddles, no dancing. Our horses, having gone almost 80 miles since Fryderyk Town, had begun to slow up; therefore half walking, half in the wagon we dragged ourselves to Lankaster.

Lankaster. Amidst groves and gardens of trees scattered in clumps rise the steeples of the churches and the many roofs of houses. This town is prettily situated, and, though in a valley, it has a bountiful and attractive appearance from this side. It is the biggest non-coastal city [13] in America. It is practically all inhabited by Germans, though for the last few years Anglo-American families have begun to settle here. Few of the houses are pretty, not so much as they would be if the people had built them less cheaply. The principal streets are not even paved, though here and there the lighted signs of the inns, here as in Hannower and Jork, give the German souvenirs of his late and beloved *Faterland*. One can see here reminders of the old Prussian king, on his horse or dismounted (he is not adored here as a King, but rather as a holy patron of the Lutheran religion and as the defender of Protestantism), in the uniform of the guards, etc.; the Duke of Brunswick etc. The town is sad at the present moment because of the lessening of trade owing to the depradations of the French. The Germans today are terribly soured; two years ago the price of grain was insane and a barrel of flour sold for 16½ dollars, now it has fallen to six. They would rather have it rot in a granary than sell it at such a low price. Rapid and excessive profits, so it is said, have spoiled them to such an extent that they are reluctant to bring any provisions to town; they use them themselves or bring something to the market only on such occasions when they need to buy coffee, sugar or some other similar necessity. I saw a few people with beards like Polish Jews. These are Mennonites, usually called *Dunkars*.[18]

I was at Mr. Barton's.[19] I did not find him in. He was busy getting a reception ready for Mr. Marshall,[20] one of the commissioners dismissed from Paris. After dinner the volunteers, both mounted and on foot, gathered for a review in his honour. The cavalry was 20 strong, beautifully dressed in helmets, and mounted on excellent horses; in a word having the complete appearance of English troops. They choose their own officers; one must get two-thirds of the votes to be chosen. The infantry was equally well drawn up, well-dressed, and armed. How pleasant it is to look on a soldier when the soldier [14] is a citizen as well, when he arms himself and lifts his gun only for the defense of his country and her freedom.

Lankaster and its environs, especially Strasburg, supply most of the grain and flour to Philadelphia so that in good times the road between these cities is completely filled with wagons.

N.B. The course of the Suskwehana is usually broken by many rapids. However, from the 15th of April to the 15th of June and through a short period in the fall it floods extensively and overflows its banks. At Sunbury it divides into two streams, east and west. The first reaches the northern part of New York, the other goes through Pennsylvania and may be joined by a canal with French Creek and then with Lake Erie. At the time of the spring floods not only sizeable boats, but the largest masts float down from northern New York. The rapids near Midleton were not circumvented until recently, and formerly all the grain stopped near enough to this place to help its growth. But just now a small canal has been finished (it is only a mile long; it cost 40 thousand dollars to dig) by which the rapids are avoided and navigation has been opened up to Columbia.[21] From there, grain can be either sent down further to the Chesapeake, or on wheels to Lankaster and then carried to Philadelphia. To expedite this transport a highway which already exists between Philadelphia and Lankaster is to be lengthened ten miles up to Columbia. Because of this Columbia will, with the years, become an important and wealthy place. The Juniata [15] which runs through a substantial part of the country falls into the Susquehanna and is navigable all along its length. Further it could be joined as well by a canal first with Kiskimanetas Creek, then further with the Allegani [Allegheny] and through it to the Ohio. Today a substantial part of the grain, and more especially staves and shingles are sent down by it.

Curious to find out the history of the Germans now settled in a large part of Pennsylvania and Maryland, I received the following information from Mr. Barten. Wilhelm Penn, after bringing the first Quaker colony to the banks of the Dellaware, returned at the beginning of this century to Europe. The Mennonite sect, or *Dunkers,* began to spread at that time in the Palatinate, in Holland and in a few Cantons of Switzerland. The views of this sect on many points agreed with the canons of the Quakers; persecution increased the number of proselytes. Wilhelm Penn went to the Palatinate and persuaded a few hundred families there and sent them to America. The bounty and beauty of the country, the unusual cheapness of the open land, the freedom and safety from all persecution so acutely and favorably impressed the newcomers, that many of them returned in order to persuade relatives, friends, and finally fellow countrymen to settle themselves in this so happy country. Therefore during a long period of time boats full of German emigrants came to America, settling one next another. Absorbed only with agriculture, they have little in common with other settlers. They have preserved their language, habits and their former simplicity. Agriculture is their constant activity, the gathering of money their one passion and joy. They live with the greatest economy, sour cabbage [16] seasoned with salt pork, potatoes, a piece of smoked meat is the food of even the most well-to-do. Not capable nor eager to hold office nor to advance themselves, they reject the enlightenment and education which are given to them, and they bring up their children in this same ignorance. They like or dislike the government and the ruling class to the extent to which their pocketbooks are touched.

One of these rich farmers came to the inn where talk arose of preparation for defense against the attack of the French and the indis-

pensable need of imposing new taxes for preserving independence
and freedom of the people. The rich farmer sat on the bench and
wiping the sweat from his brow:

"I," he said in an important voice, "have always been for the republican government because under this government one pays less
taxes than under any other whatsoever. However, as soon as this
should cease and under this government they should begin to impose
taxes, I do not see any advantage in such a government and I am
ready to sell and resettle wheresoever one pays nothing or very little
in taxes."

This person in his simple talk gave up the secret of the peasant
class not only here but in the whole world. Dignity and splendor of
the land, even independence and liberty, are a side issue with them
and not of primary concern; to preserve their own well-being, its
growth or its decline, that is their first aim. Their joy is not to use,
but to have and to increase. They do not want to use credit; they
have no confidence in bank notes and whenever they are paid for
grain in such currency, they quickly change it into coins and lock it
up in [17] boxes or bury it in the ground. If therefore in this country
money does not circulate as one would expect, it can be ascribed in
large extent to the frugality of these ignorant people. Money leaves
them only on one occasion, when there is bountiful and fertile land
for sale near their own. Then they are willing to give the highest price
and even to pay beyond its worth should an Irishman, by chance, be
interested in it. There is the greatest antipathy between these people
and that is not to be wondered at, their attitudes are so contrasting.
The German works but does not enjoy. The Irishman loves to enjoy
and would never wish to work.[22]

In the evening with the sound of bells, amidst an escort of militia
on horseback and on foot and a crowd of people, Gen. Marshall, one
of the commissioners dismissed from Paris, arrived. The more trouble
he received in France and the less honor that he was accorded, the
more, on his return, the people with public show, with honor and
respect, have tried to sweeten the humiliations long undergone. Gen.
Marshall is a man of more than 40 years, quite handsome and one
could recognize in his bearing that he had breathed the air of Paris.
In talent, expression and humor he probably surpasses his colleagues
Pinkney and Gerry, and therefore the Directory did not care for him
and dismissed him.[23] I was presented to him. In the evening the town
gave him a splendid supper.

The next day, in the morning, when I was getting on the public
stage, the very same Mr. Marshall, ambassador extraordinary who,

here as everywhere he went, had been greeted with show and pomp was now leaving with bag [18] in hand, and seeing that every seat was occupied, he sat quietly on the seat next to the coachman.

There is no incident which better paints a picture of the government, the attitudes and habits of this country. The height of office, the applause of the populace, great favor with all, never erase from the American mind the idea of equality and simplicity. The people's representative to France negotiated and spoke with the strength and the dignity of a republican who does not recognize a sovereign. Returning to his fellow citizens he returned to their habits of simplicity and equality. Neither with the publication of the "Rights of Man," nor with a constitution, nor with the guillotine will they be able to bring this simplicity and true equality to a people once spoiled by luxury and prejudices. In America these qualities are natural, brought here by the first citizens who settled here. They grow and branch out with them. In France, where through so many centuries completely opposite views and attitudes have prevailed, neither by the sword, nor by fire nor by violence will they ever suddenly wipe out those views and attitudes of a people spoiled by luxury and voluptuousness. The initiators of the Revolution knew these truths; they knew the character of the people; they knew that the Frenchman must be influenced through external impressions, and therefore they surrounded themselves with guards, decorated their own dress with embroidery, strung themselves with all sorts of trinkets and brilliants. In a word, they have changed only the name; they have returned again to that they overthrew. I say they have returned to a royal rule with all its pomp and show, but with a stronger, more able and more dextrous organization of the power and rule in their hands.

Marshall is from Virginia and lives in Richmond. He is a lawyer, to which profession he has returned. I was told that after Washington [19] he is held in the highest regard and trust in that state. He was hurrying to his wife. Distressed by the danger to which her husband was exposed in Paris, unhappy one, her mind has been affected.[24]

The road from Lankaster to Philadelphia is a highway and does not take second place in any respect to the best even in Austria or England. The toll on it, as with everything in America, is extraordinarily high. One pays for a stage by the year 1,400 dollars—a man on horseback ¾ dollars and a wagoner with a loaded wagon pays, if I am not mistaken, 8 dollars.

The countryside everywhere is beautiful and cultivated, with well-kept houses. We were only four on leaving but as a ball of snow grows larger, our company increased along the road and it reached 15 by Philadelphia.

I stayed only one day in this city.

June 27. When I had left it the 8th of May there was not a single soldier there; today I saw a body of mounted militia at least 200 strong, and of infantry 300 or 400, every one not just dressed well but with splendor. Equally, in these four weeks Congress has passed more laws of importance than in the previous six months. The danger, the losses, the affront to dignity have awakened the sleeping energy in their minds. The power of the executive knows how to inflame skillfully that energy and knows how to use it skillfully. The President obtained power equal to that of the King of Great Britain. The fate of new-comers was left completely in his hands. The Treaty with France was declared as non-existent. *The Sedition Bill,* trammelling the freedom of the citizen, autocracy left in the hands of the President is justified only at a moment of danger and by the need to put down at that time the smallest disturbance or discord in the people.[25]

[20] The 28th, in order to escape all questions of where K[ościuszko] might be and to free myself from the sad necessity of constant lying, I left early so as to see as few people as possible. For the fifth time I rode along this road, that is that part of Pennsylvania up to Trenton and further into Jersey. The fields were covered with grain, for the most part maize and rye. I stopped in Brunswick toward evening; I was received by General and Mrs. White with the greatest welcome, and in the same way by the family of Bayard and Patersson. In my sad and abandoned situation every occasion of pleasantness and friend-ship is sweet comfort for me and awakens in me the most heartfelt thanks.

The 30th, in the morning I continued on to Elizabeth Town. The day was cool, the travelers only three, the horses and road excellent; this was not a journey but an excursion. This was the first time, as it happened, that I had seen a young woman plowing in a field while her husband went ahead leading the horse by the rein. This was a young marriage, the couple only recently beginning to farm. What a lovely view to catch the eye. What a lovely painting one could make from this, representing the young pair occupied with tilling the earth and adding above a cupid who is either prodding the young woman or goading the horses with his arrowhead.

I met my friend Mr. Gahn in Elizabeth. We visited some of our old acquaintances. The company here, as in Brunswick, increases as new families from England settle here. Amongst others settled in Elizabeth Town, the family Bielassas [Belasise]; [26] in Brunswick,—Garnet.[27] With

respect to the situation in England both now and in the future there
is a great likelihood that emigration from there will continually increase. They are fortunate that in this part of the world they have a
fraternal people, a people coming from the same stock. [21] Crossing
the Atlantic Ocean they find the same language, the same customs; in
a word, an excellent reproduction of their old fatherland. Alas, there is
no country, nor a reproduction [for me]!

The 2nd of July we crossed by water to New York on a river called
[blank]. We went at dinner time to the home of Riars, living on
Staten Island.[28] From there we caught a sailboat from Elizabeth and
with a following breeze we sailed across the bay to New York. On the
distant horizon rose the towers and buildings of the city of New York,
in the background Staten Island, to the left the Jersey shore, to the
right Long Island, the bay filled with ships and boats sailing here and
there, and nearer to the city Bedlo[e]'s and Governer's Islands. The
latter somewhat fortified; the first, not at all. New York, though ideally
located for trade, has the disadvantage of defenselessness as it is open
on all sides and could be easily attacked and razed by an enemy. In
this century this defect, the possibility of attack and sacking, is most
acute. Should Providence keep this country in peace, New York, in
beauty of its situation equal to Naples and Genoa, will equal and surpass them shortly in power, people, and wealth; and anyone, after a
century or even a half a century sailing this arm of the sea as I am
today, will see on all these shores, on all the islands, forts and new
cities rising up, occupied by thousands of people.

This day and the following, that is the 3rd of July, were marked by
extraordinary heat like an oven. [22] The Fahrenheit thermometer in
the sun stood at 105°, in the shade 96°. I do not remember comparable heat in Italy.

The 4th of July. This day is remembered in the annals of America
as the day of the declaration of its independence and over the whole
of the United States it is celebrated with solemn joy. Just as the sun
rose 16 cannon rounds were fired in honor of the 16 united states. The
people at this moment, dressed in holiday attire, spilled out onto the
streets; the militia began to gather in companies; the reverberations
of the bells from all the churches, the pistol shots, the noise of the ex-
ploding rockets and a joyful uproar filled the air. After ten a parade
began. At first citizens in civilian dress and without arms rode on
horseback, their guilds, companies and various organizations with
their banners and insignia, the shield of the United States, with liberty
caps held on high lances; officers leading this body had on their hats
the words, *Freedom and Commerce*—these are the two arteries by

which America lives. There was a company of artillery, a squadron of militia on horseback in dark blue uniforms with crimson facings and gold braid, and on their heads helmets with black feathers and crimson plumes; another squadron of mounted militia in green uniforms mixed with black, also with braid, helmets with green feathers, excellent and lively horses. This company in ostentation of dress, quality of horses, and in the elegance of its young men had the appearance of troops made up entirely of officers. Further, militia of infantry in helmets with black feathers and a crimson crest with blue uniforms and braid; a band made up entirely of negroes in crimson uniforms with gold braid, all this in ostentation and order did not take second place in any respect to the mounted group. There was the Tammany Society in memory of an Indian leader [23] who under this name lived in this section with his people.[29] This society is not for anyone from a European power; in a word, it is made up of true and pure Americans. Let it not happen that the rules and feeling of this society should be recognized throughout America. Again there was a troop of cavalry which closed the parade.

This procession marched through the principal streets of the town, stopped outside the town in a field where the Declaration of Independence was read. The *Governor* conducted a review, a military drill was executed and at two o'clock a *feu de joie*. At this time the organizations and guilds gathered in various churches. Amidst all these people the quiet, good order and respect were not maintained with bayonets, nor with soldiers; there were only a few constables with white billies in their hands stationed here and there just in case of untoward happening. The chosen orators had speeches appropriate to the celebration of the day. The hymns sung were as warm and lovely in rhyme as they were inharmonious; however they were tolerable.

At 4 there was a public dinner for 300 or more people, toasts of citizens; cannon fire, pistols and bells continued throughout the day. In the evening walking the streets one could hear a hundred times the shouting of *hura* from the citizens dining in public. At eight they left the tables.

I went to an evening party at the home of one of the leading families, a Mr. More.[30] When the son and the son-in-law, one serving in the cavalry, the other in the infantry of the militia, came in a little drunk, it was for the first time that I saw a little more warm feeling and affection than is usual among relatives; such that husband kissed his wife on the hand, and a brother embraced his sisters. At the same time the women took off their helmets, wiped their brows soiled from the gunpowder shot, and with the greatest attention listened to the tales of the difficulties encountered under arms, the dexterity in drill, firing, etc.

[24] So ended this holiday, Day of Independence, a day only Americans in the whole world have the right to celebrate. What people in Europe, what people in the world, can call themselves freemen. They are all crushed either by chains at home or by foreign bonds; from the Tiber to the Volga people groan in fetters.

The next day the greatest quiet succeeded the holiday and noisy entertainment. The laborer, the artisans returned to their work and the merchant to his usual tasks.

Though New York in the extent and regularity of its streets can not compare to Philadelphia, in the beauty of its situation it surpasses that town by far. The Promenade on the Battery cedes nothing to the famous promenade in Naples, La Chiaja.[31] It is unfortunate that, because of the necessity for fortification, trees planted after the last war have been cut down, just as the passers-by were beginning to enjoy their shade. So the mad implacability of the people would not let even the trees grow peaceably. Here the inhabitants of various professions, sex, and age are all accustomed to gather in the morning and evening hours. It is here that the weak with a slow and halting step breathe in the gentle and healthy air. It is here that they, after a serious and long sickness, return to health and with emotion and joy feast their eyes on the beautiful and extensive view stretching out on all sides. It is here that a young and loving pair under the flickering rays of the moon expose the feelings of their hearts in sweet whispers. [25] An anxious and greedy merchant gets a head start on the dawn as he searches with the aid of a spyglass for a long-awaited ship. If far away on the horizon under the vaulted sky there glistens a white sail, his heart beats with joy and fear. But when the billowing sails of the nearing ship show it up ever larger, when finally with an unfurled flag, carried by the force of the current it blows gracefully into port, then, when he recognizes his own property—what joy! The captain in a little boat first comes ashore; the news is spread through the town; everyone runs to the exchange, or, as they call it here, coffee house. There, in a book already opened for this purpose, the Captain writes whence the ship came, how long a voyage, what cargo it brings, and what is the mercantile and political news. These are matters for conversation of everyone until tomorrow, or for a few days, or for a few hours, until a new ship comes in. Amongst the important profits which a port town has over others, and these are not minor ones, are the interesting events and expectations which exist for a man in the in-

cessant coming and going. These do not permit him ever to know the
weight of boredom and monotony.

At the side of this same Battery is a *foxhall* [Vauxhall]; [32] it is illuminated at night in the summer and has music and cold refreshments. There is another one a mile from town with a much bigger
garden. They are both kept by French people who through the sale
of ice cream alone have gained a large fortune. Both these places are
very much frequented. The inhabitants here are much more lively,
much gayer, and enjoy their recreation much more than in Philadelphia.

The city, ruined during the last war—it was held by the English
[26] throughout—has in a few years sprung back wonderfully. Broad
Way, Broad Street, Pearl Street, Wall Street, etc., all have lovely houses
sometimes even splendid. Their interiors are always well kept and
often overfurnished. The public buildings are equally good (see
Morse's Geog.).[33] St. Paul's *church* [chapel], though in bad taste, reminds one in form of the shape of an ancient Greek temple.

9th of July at 3 in the afternoon my friend Mr. Gahn, Libiszewski,
and Mr. Le Juin escorted me to the boat in which I was to sail to
New Haven. Throughout all the time I have been in this country I
have found in Mr. Gahn a warm heart, friendship, and service which
I could expect only from a fellow countryman and relative. Parting
from him, perhaps forever (for he is sailing to Spain) at the moment
when I am completely abandoned in these strange parts was for me
acute sadness.

The boat on which we were sailing was 40 *Tons* burden with reasonably well-kept berths and amenities. Our company was composed
of Mrs. Farquar, Miss Sittons, four boys and two girls and Mr. [blank],
related to them.[34] He was born an Englishman but after settling in
America he trades with China.

We sailed that arm of the sea which separates the land of New York
from Long Island. This island was on our right hand, on the left were
the houses of the city, behind us New York itself and Governor's
Island. The feeble wind gave us the time to enjoy the most pleasant
and varied view. On both shores there were thickly placed houses,
gardens, fields, and groves; here and there small islands on which [27]
occasionally stood a solitary house. Such a house was clean and well
kept; living in it was a family whose principal property lies beyond
the boundaries of the island, but not often of more than two or three
acres in extent. We sailed happily without trouble through a dangerous place called Hell Gattes or Gates of Hell. The tide covers the
rapids and here the rocks are strewn thickly, and the tide hurling

against them with force creates whirlpools and a piercing roar. The two banks move further apart and the arm of the sea or Estern River becomes ever wider and more beautiful. Long Island is 140 miles long, 10 wide and has 40 thousand inhabitants. A huge ship sailed close by us en route to Boston. One of the company called it in jest a French corsair. At this moment the startled children ran to the cabin, such is the great fright and impression the words *French privateer* make on children, who hear nothing but the complaints and wailing of their parents ruined by French depredations.

The next day the wind though always light brought us opposite the shore of the state of Connecticut. The countryside is hilly and as far as one can tell from a distance cultivated and fertile. Villages and towns were spread out both on the tops and along the slopes of the hills. The houses were white with red roofs, light and steep. The towers of the churches and town halls rose amidst the green and densely packed roof tops. All provided a most cheerful appearance. We met a big ship coming from Halifax in New Scotland [Nova Scotia].

At five in the evening we sighted the city of New Haven. Except for Hartford it is the most important city in Connecticut. It lies at the head of a wide gulf; high hills surround it on all sides. Here the bay, except for a few places known only to the inhabitants, is shallow although at high tide rather good sized vessels may come up it. We found in the port up to fifteen, the largest of 150 or 200 tons burden, two of them were then being loaded. The most important trade of this town is in cattle which are sent alive to the West Indies. [28] The ships are deliberately altered for this. On the deck of the boat along its whole length there are partitions made of poles, with bales of hay closely packed on top of them. Both for the cattle and for the people the voyage cannot be too comfortable, but those seeking profit are not interested in this. I hear that the waves of the wild sea sweep the cattle off the boats. Nowadays French corsairs take the boats and eat the cattle.

Chapter VI

NEW ENGLAND JOURNEY. CONNECTICUT. RHODE ISLAND. MASSACHUSETTS. NEW HAMPSHIRE. MAINE

CONNECTICUT

About six in the evening we landed on shore. Though warehouses extend as far as the port, the city of New Haven itself is nearly a mile distant. New Haven is both a city and a village. The houses are practically all of wood, or rather made with light, smooth, closely fitting boards painted white. The houses rarely touch each other and each one of them has rather a large garden, and many of them even have a field planted with *mais*. All this is scattered on so huge a terrain that it is more a place where there is a collection of country houses near together than a true city. The streets are not paved. In the center there is a large *square* or a place with trees planted along a few streets. The *College* or boarding school for students consists of three buildings which take up one whole side. In the center is the *State House* and a church with a large cemetery; its vaults and gravestones thickly scattered in the middle of a public promenade gives a solemn and sad appearance and reminds one of the moving inscription *"Et in Arcadia ego."* [1]

Dr. Dwight,[2] to whom I had letters of introduction, was away. Rain, falling from early morning, did not permit further exploration of the town and its environs. The post stage leaves at eleven and then I leave for Harford [Hartford]. Mrs. Farquard with her four boys leaves for the country to place them in a parish school. This is one of the richest [29] and best-known families of New York. The boys, however, are often without stockings and run around barefooted. This is common here.

Yesterday evening we walked about the streets. Everywhere there was the greatest quiet and peace. We met two or three cabriolets of the two-wheel variety, with only ladies in them. There is no public entertainment except in winter when once every two weeks there is a ball. The innkeeper, Justus Butler, for his most gracious attention gouged me mercilessly.[3]

July 11. In generally rainy weather and a sudden downpour we rode out of New Haven. The *Stage* was filled to the roof; two ladies, a Frenchman from Martinique, three sailors who had been taken by a French privateer and were returning home denuded and in rags, two other personages, and between our legs trunk after trunk. The countryside alternates between valleys and hills; there are many meadows, some drained by ditches. Herds of domestic animals are seen more frequently than in other states, especially sheep. The fields, for the most part, are covered with *maïs*, rye, very little wheat, and are mostly bounded with stone walls. The houses and settlements are much more frequent than in any state I have seen so far. A few of them, which is rare, are old; that is they are 60 or 80 years old, which is considered here as ancient, as are gothic buildings by us. In all, these do indicate that the country here has been settled for some time. We rode through Norfolk [Northford], Durnham [Durham], where there were refreshments, and Midletown [Middletown], on the Connecticut river. Its situation is wonderfully beautiful; the river is wide and clear; the banks, which rise in the form of an amphitheatre, are cultivated and settled. The trees: oaks, various kinds of nut-bearing trees, mulberries and *Shumek* [sumac], its leaves like those of the mountain ash, its fruit is covered with a crimson-colored plume [hair], each one is like a small pea. From afar it looks like a beet. In Midletown there were several ships, for the Connecticut river is everywhere navigable.

[30] Further on, Weathersfield [Wethersfield]. Here we smelled air full of a strong odor. It came from the fields and the gardens, all planted with onions. All the agriculture and trade of the town is solely in onions, which are sent to the West Indies.[4] This little town, like Midletown, is spread out on an area two or three miles in extent. Gardens and even whole fields separate one street from another and one part of the town from another. The roads are much better than usual, partly because of the nature of the terrain, partly through the efforts of the inhabitants. The Frenchman who had fled Martinique early, before the return of his fellow countrymen, told me that the colony there was never in a more flourishing state. The causes of this were first the peaceful and benevolent rule of the English, second the importation of sugar cane from Tahiti. This variety, thick as one's fist and full of syrup, gives twice as much sugar as the cane formerly planted on these islands. Its only defect is that it rapidly exhausts the land.

Today at lunch we learned that the armed ship the U.S. Dellaware,

C[a]pt. Duterer [Decatur] took a French privateer of 70 men and twelve guns.[5] Let Heaven bless further the aggrieved and the insulted. After eight in the evening we stopped in Hartford.

Hartford: the city, on the Connecticut river, is in equally as happy, fertile, and beautiful a situation as Midletown, etc. The houses are closer together, as in Newhaven, which makes the place appear as a true town. Some [31] are built with taste and a knowledge of archi‚ tecture and have porticoes raised on light columns, which gives them the appearance of small Greek temples. The inside decorations do not yield ground to the outside. Americans, economical in domestic ex‚ penditure, do not economize on the outward decoration of their houses; a pure calculated vanity. No one sees their meals, however people do come into the house and one must show some ostentation.

The city lies on the Connecticut river, whose source is in Canada. It divides the state of Vermont from New Hampshire, cuts Massachusetts and flows across Connecticut to the sea. The river is navigable for barges from Hartford, and, more especially from Wethersfield, boats of 200 tons go down to the sea. The whole of Vermont has no other waterways excepting in the part touching on Lake George and Lake Champlain and on the North River. This river rises greatly in the spring, flooding all the lower streets. It is at this time that the bigger ships are loaded and sent out. At the time of low water they must go to Wethersfield, where there is a deeper channel. The principal trade here is in cattle, salt meat, horses, etc., all sent to the West Indies. For a horse costing 30 dollars here, one pays up to 100 and often 150 in the islands. Besides this, the bold spirit of the inhabitants in enter- prise ventures for gain to the ends of the earth.

Colonel Wathsford [Wadsworth][6] and his son have many times sent out vessels and have just now equipped one which will, at first, sail to the Falkland Islands and there stop, divide up the cargo and the gear in the boat completely, then cut down trees in these wild islands and build small boats. The sailors and officers then divide [32] up into groups and sail along the shores of Patagonia, etc., stopping here and there, going on land to trade iron tools and toys with the Indians for skins called *l'outre*, etc. Collecting all they can they then double Cape Horn and sail to the Sandwich Islands. There for similar tools and toys (*trinkets*) they take on fresh provisions, water, etc. They then sail to China where the trade in furs is the best; sell them, take on tea, porcelain, silk, etc., and return again around the Cape of Good Hope, achieving in this way a voyage around the whole world. The captain who makes this journey so boldly and successfully, is called Green.[7]

I went to dinner at Col. Wadsworth's. At four we rode out with his son to look over the neighborhood and the town. The public buildings are beautiful and well kept: *State House,*[8] *Court House, Gaol,* or prison, and *Bank.* This latter is found in every town of any importance in America, and if in one way it encourages industry, makes great enterprises easy through loans, and provides the possibility of starting trades or business for those without money; yet in another way by doubling the price of riches—money—it doubles the price of everything. We rode out of town to a rise called Rocky Hill.[9] From there the countryside is spread out over the wide horizon; the valleys, separated by hills, are covered with cultivated fields; here meadows and pastures through which wind small streams, there groves, everywhere well-kept houses with gardens, and finally on the edges of the horizon a continuous chain of high mountains hold back the searching eye. This country in general reminds me [33] in its situation and fertility of lovely Tuscany. The inhabitants, in their government, in the simplicity of their habits, in the freedoms which they enjoy, differ completely, however, from the men of Tuscany. In reading accounts of past deeds or in the observation of present events here, we find that nothing can give us a more just picture of a true Commonwealth than the state of Connecticut. True freedom, true equality, for which reasonable men sigh and which frenzied men pursue with phantom shadows, drenching the land with blood and covering it with ruins—and they cannot find it. True freedom and equality is found here, I say, discovered and fostered only through clear and simple judgments. The first inhabitants of Connacticut, as equally in all of New England, were poor, hard-working people, simple and honorable men. European luxuries and corruption were not brought across the Atlantic Ocean by them. Rather we should say that the inhabitants came here from Massachusetts to settle and that they brought with them the severe *principia* by which those Presbyterians ejected from England, differed from other men.

This equality, this simplicity in habits, the industry and hard work will continue on as long as the passage of the centuries, the wealth of the people, abundance, and changes in government do not bring corruption. Then, neither a revolution, nor the most intelligent constitution ever written on paper will succeed in returning the people to their original innocence and simplicity. Beer, made from fresh hops is tasty and clear, but let it once, through age and fermentation, sour and turn to vinegar, then all chemical operations will be useless; it will remain vinegar always. We see this in France, and Rousseau has well said, *"On n'a jamais vu de peuple une fois corrompu revenir à la vertu."* [10]

Fig. 45. View to the North from the Lawn at Mount Vernon, 17 July 1796. From B. H. Latrobe's views at Mount Vernon. Courtesy Maryland Historical Society.

Fig. 46. Robertson-Jukes view of Mount Vernon, 1800. Courtesy of The Metropolitan Museum of Art, Gift of William H. Huntington, 1883.

Fig. 47. The Washington Family (after J. Paul, Jr.). Courtesy of The Metropolitan Museum of Art. Fletcher Fund, 1929.

Fig. 48. Niemcewicz's sketches of women dressed in the old German style. From [IV, 42] and outside back cover leaf of notebook IV.

Fig. 49. A view on the Potomac at Harper's Ferry.

Fig. 50. A Ferry scene on the Susquehanna at Wright's Ferry. Both scenes from water colors c. 1812 by Pavel Petrovich Svinin. Courtesy of The Metropolitan Museum of Art, Rogers Fund, 1942.

Fig. 51. Lancaster, 1798. From Edouard-Charles-Victurnien Colbert, comte de Maulevrier, *Voyage dans L'Intérieur des Etats-Unis et au Canada,* 1935. Courtesy of Johns Hopkins Press.

Fig. 52. Drayton's view of the Battery, 1793 and the "two rows of elms . . . which in a short time will afford agreeable shade." From Iconophile Series V, 10. Courtesy of Prints Division, New York Public Library.

Fig. 53. A view of St. Paul's Chapel in 1799. From Iconophile Series XV, 5. Courtesy of Prints Division, New York Public Library.

Fig. 54. U.S. Ship of War Delaware capturing the French Privateer La Croyable off Egg Harbor, New Jersey, 7 July 1798. Detail from the Decatur Bowl. Courtesy of Mr. Storer G. Decatur.

Fig. 55. College in Providence, c. 1800. Courtesy Brown University Library.

Fig. 56. "Et in Arcadia Ego." A view of Yale College, New-Haven, 1813 by Baroness Hyde de Neuville. Courtesy of The New-York Historical Society, New York City.

Fig. 57. West Boston Bridge. From Robert Gilmor, *Memorandum* . . . .
By courtesy of the Trustees of the Boston Public Library.

Fig. 58. The Story view of Harvard College, 30 May 1795. Courtesy of
Fogg Art Museum, Harvard University.

They divided the land amongst themselves in equal portions. The smallest *farm* or holding had 50 acres, the largest (and the number of these is very small) does not exceed 400. It is from this that civil equality breeds moral equality. Every citizen, with his family, wishing to live honestly must work, therefore toil here is not only necessary but honorable. In Europe to say of someone that he rose from nothing is a disgrace and a reproach; it is the opposite here; to be the architect of your own fortune is honorable; it is the highest commendation. [36] Colonel Wadsworth, to whom I had been recommended, the best-known and richest citizen in the state, was proud of the fact that he had been a simple sailor, earning a dollar a week. Today though counting his wealth in thousands, he still works himself on the farm, more from force of habit than from need. And so everyone. The representatives of the state in the lower or upper house are taken from the plow. How can their discussions and laws be other than sensible and salutary for the whole? What is more, the first magistrate of the commonwealth, the *Governor* can be seen amidst his workers with a scythe and a rake in his hand. In spite of this, in the execution of his office nowhere is the officer held in higher esteem. The maintenance of this simplicity, equality and uniformity of habits owes a great deal to the fact that there are no immigrants among the inhabitants; there is no mixing of nations as there is elsewhere; everyone is from one stock, everyone a descendent of the English. The density of this population, the natural consequence of a hard-working and free life together, is greater in proportion here than in any other place in the U.S.

Connecticut is populating Vermont, earlier New Jersey, Kentucky, the Western Territory, and the Genesee. A farmer, settled on 50 acres of land and having, for example, four sons, sends all to school from childhood. (The law provides that each village have its own school; therefore education for all will be the same. Enlightenment for all, as I have said, contributes not a little to moral equality. [34] People do not lord it over others except through that natural superiority that light has over darkness.) A man with four sons sends them all to school and notices their abilities and inclinations, then according to these indications directs them. One of them, most able at school, is destined for a lawyer, doctor, priest or writer. Another goes to the sea as a sailor, with a great and very often a successful wish that he will become a captain. A third learns a trade or a business. The fourth remains with his father and, as his father, dies happy as a farmer. If there is a fifth son, this one takes 50 or 100 dollars, a pair of oxen, a wagon, axe, and scythe, and sets off into the depths of still unsettled regions. After about a score of years, of at first very hard and later somewhat easier labor, he builds up an important estate, even wealth and honor. In this way a state not only populates itself, but settles the wilderness with industrious people, and thus each one with work and industry builds for himself a free life.

Wealth is rare; poverty is still more rare. A good situation is common practically everywhere. Almost everyone, except for wine and comforts from abroad, eats, drinks and dresses in the same way, and one can see the most obvious inequality only in the dwellings. English law, or rather Roman, establishes the father as the sole power of an estate. He may bequeath [35] everything to one of his children, or even bequeath everything to a stranger. However, in general the common practice is that all the children, that is both sons and daughters, receive equal shares. The education of women is adapted to their sex and form of life. They learn to read, write, sew, spin and weave. On this they spend the whole day.

Tea time is the moment when work stops and rest and recreation begin. It is at this time that the father and sons return from the fields, from the shop and from the workbench. The table is set out and the preparations are begun for the "Offering." The presence of the urn of hot water, of many other utensils, the respect and quiet with which the tea is poured and drunk, has the appearance of some sort of solemn and holy sacrifice. At this time the principal personage of the village, the *School Master*, comes to tea. To the parents he talks farming and politics; to the daughters he talks about romances, for young ladies here too, love *The Novels*. In them characters and habits which appear ordinary and natural to us and which we see daily, awaken here the greatest wonder and even appear as fabrications. Men with an income of one hundred thousand, who have ten to twenty servants, who do nothing all day; a lady who wears diamonds and carries roses, who can make neither puddings nor cakes; these are to them unnatural creations, they are magic, one thousand and one nights. They read them for entertainment, but they cannot understand them and do not even want to believe them.

We returned through another part of the town. Every house is either a workshop or a store. On the signboards which [37] indicate their trade there is always an addition in big letters: *Cash in the hand,* i.e., "Don't come without money in your hand." Money and profit are the passions of this hard-working and industrious people. This leads sometimes to greed and extortion. It was only today that I myself was a victim. It happened that I wanted to ride from Hartford to Norwich. Public transportation goes there only in a week; I had to hire a *sulky* or a small carriage with one horse. The journey was no more than 40 miles, that is close to six of our miles. I had to pay 10 piasters or 5 ducats.

In the evening I took tea at Colonel Wadsworth's. Three old ladies sat before the offering. These three ladies and the sisters of the host did not utter a word. You cannot find a life *plus passive,* nor with the fullest renunciation of all of the world's happiness than that of these ladies. One half of the day they sit sewing shirts; the other half they read the Bible, and while reading sometimes doze, sometimes weep, but remain always true believers.

The next day at five o'clock I started off in my carriage bought with gold. The *Gentilman,* or its owner, in well-kept attire and in new silk stockings, was himself my coachman, and seeing that I could not forgive his extortion and that I was treating him coldly, tried to justify himself by relating the story of his life. His father left him barely 50 dollars. With this he began to learn the trade of harness maker, and later he bought and rented out horses. From this double activity he improved his position to such a degree that he now owns two homesteads, one near the town, [38] the other in the depths of the country.

"I let out to you, Your Honor," he said, "At a high rate, it is true, but everything is high here. For a horse you pay out 40 shillings, and now it is mowing time, I alone must do the driving. My work for two days is worth 14 shillings. Further there is the forage for the horse and my own board. I hired three people," he continued, "for cutting and gathering the hay. To each one of them I must give 7 shillings, or 10 Polish złotys, and a meal three times a day."

"What do you give them to eat?"

"In the morning they have chocolate and cold meat, dinner the best you can give, in the evening coffee and again meat. These are *gentilmen* as well off as I. They have their own farms in the back country. They have everything except a little ready cash. They come here for a few weeks so as to earn some." With this information and these excuses I gave up.

The countryside through which we were riding from Hardford to Norwich is not comparable in beauty, fertility, or extent of settlement to that stretching from Newhaven to Hartford. There is a great deal of forest; the land is poor and rocky with frequent hills. However, roads either have been or are being built everywhere. The traveler pays a toll. We often met women on horseback with a bag behind and children in their arms.

At one o'clock we arrived at the hamlet of Lebanon where Mr. Thrumball, the *governor* of the whole state of Connecticut, lives. His brother, whom I had known in London, had given me a letter of introduction.[11] His house does not differ in any respect from the others. He came out himself to greet us in simple attire and gray hose. His bearing was open, gracious and pleasant. He greeted me and my driver most cordially. The whole retinue of the chief magistrate of the state consisted of one girl servant. A stew of meat and eggs was prepared in haste. The talk was of the simplicity of manners [39] and the frugality of the inhabitants. The *Governor* sitting before me:—I had evidence of it before my eyes.

The population of this state grows remarkably and that in spite of large and constant emigrations. Last year there was an increase of nearly 2,000 taxpayers, that is those older than 16. Near Lebanon there is a foundry for casting cannon and near Norwich an iron forge where they make boat anchors.[12] Towards evening we stopped at Norwich.

July 13. Norwich. Norwich is more widely scattered than any other town in Connecticut. It is divided into three separate towns, at first Bean hill, a mile from there Norwich itself, another mile further on Chelse[a], or Landing Place. Its situation, in a hollow amidst high rocks and rather melancholy, is one of the prettiest which I have seen. Perhaps it may have seemed that way to me to conform to my sad spirits. I went to present my letters of introduction to General Huntington.[13] His home was well kept and attractive and in it only women. The hostess was pleasant and kind; there were three old ladies, silent with me but talking briskly with others, and some sort of a young dolt who is supposed to be mute. I did not find the General in as he was at his store at Landing Place. I had to wait two and a half hours for his arrival. During this time the old hens kept up their Homeric chant as if I were not there. This indifference and impoliteness to a guest one must attribute to the dislike which, because of the depredations and insults of the French, the Americans feel for all foreigners. For, to them every foreigner is a Frenchman. To them the world is divided into two peoples, the people who speak English, and those who do not, that is, the French.

After tea I went [40] with another letter to the house of Daniel Coit. The sun had set a long time ago and the evening dusk left only a half-light. I found the family surrounded by children, and a young well-dressed woman. This was an English woman who, escaping the storm in Europe with her husband was hiding amidst these hills. Mr. Coit's house stands on a raised hillock. Directly before the windows are two giant elms which sweep beautifully down in a towering semicircular vault.[14] Under their branches a most beautiful scene unfolds. The country falls away punctuated by hills and valleys, further on stark and gloomy rocks, and from a distant forge large billows of black smoke are clinging to the pines and the oaks. Below these, in an untilled and abandoned field, are many mounds and here and there fresh stones already somewhat tilted toward the earth of the graves. The moon with its weak shafts began to light up this place, both sad and lovely. Happy the man who can spend peaceful hours with wife, children and friends in this quiet hollow.

In times of war Norwich is one of the safest of places. During the time of the Revolution the English left it untouched. The town is advantageously placed for trade. A few years ago they started some factories, cotton, etc., but these had to be given up for the reason common everywhere here, that is expensive labor; only paper mills remain.

The next day Mr. Coit was so kind as to drive me in his carriage to the separate part of the town called Chelse[a] or Landing. This is on rocky ground on the very [41] bank of the river Thames. Another small river flows here too amidst the rocks and steep banks but it is not navigable because of its shallowness and rapids. This part here is rather lively and busy with commerce. Smaller ships dock at the banks; larger ones sail to New London, a few miles away and one of the best ports in the country. The trade, as in the rest of the state, is in cattle, salt meat, and lumber for building. The abundant hinterland provides everything. Land in town for the building of houses costs up to 180 and 200 dollars an acre. Beyond the town one pays usually 20 and 25 dollars an acre for tillable land for farming. Every house was a store or a warehouse; everyone was busy doing something. I was in General Huntington's store. The General himself stood behind the counter. The goods are what we call notions and are not of the first quality, like the things which in our country Jews sell in Brest. The profit from them cannot be very great, especially as the streets are filled with many similar stores. In spite of this the General spends the whole day in this shop, either because every American must be in trade, or perhaps also to avoid boredom and to be busy doing something.

The Huntington family is as numerous as Smith and Jones in Smithville and Jonesville; half the shopkeepers and artisans are called Huntington.

I saw a few Indian women. Their tribe consists of maybe 70 people who up to this time have remained on a reservation of 3,000 acres which has been set aside for them by the law of the state.[15] This reminds one of the Petersb[urg] court bestowing on Poles in Poland the country's estates. No one is allowed to acquire these lands [42] and what is more, there are overseers established by the government who keep them inviolate and have the people in their care. This people has lost its courage and all the honor of its forefathers; it has retained only their defects; laziness, inertia and an inclination to drunkenness.

They either do not cultivate their land at all or very little. The women bring baskets and berries to the market. Those whom I saw were of a bronze color with hair hanging straight. They speak in English but in spite of this, preserve their own language among themselves. This is the whole memorial of a people who were the first and lawful rulers of this country.

It is a strange change and turn of fate in human affairs; a handful of Europeans from the smallest part of the world have driven back and destroyed practically the whole trace of the true owners of a whole hemisphere of the world. If we consider our colonies in Asia, both those which exist and those which are likely to be founded by the French in Africa, who knows if in the following centuries the descendents of Europeans will not have settled the whole world.

Returning we went to see a waterfall. A mile from town a small river cuts through some sharp rocks and in a few cascades falls with a roar to the bottom. Americans seek usefulness everywhere. They have blown up a part of the rock with gunpowder and made an underground canal; the water pouring through this runs a few mills.

The 14th at eleven in the morning I set out on the road to Providence. The countryside through which I rode today is so rocky that only the region [43] of Łosie in Podlasie can be compared to it.[16] The citizen here is more hard working (for everyone works for himself) and knows how to surmount these obstacles. Gathering these stones from the fields he builds with them high walls around his land. Often for a stretch of a few miles from both sides these fences of rock arise like the walls of China. In this way two advantages are gained: the fields cleared of obstacles and they are protected. Besides fences one also sees stones piled up in the meadows and fields. Everywhere roads are still being built rather than now completed. This one does not see further south. It shows how far the citizens of this state surpass in organization those of the South. The rye harvest had begun. Since this grain and maize are the principal products of the state, the citizens mix the flour of both these grains together and make an excellent bread.

Twenty miles from Norwich is the boundary of Connecticut, a region which for good order, industry, hard work, and manners surpasses the others. The citizens are all Federalists, that is warmly devoted to the Constitution. The newspapers were filled with accounts of the celebration of the 4th of July, that is the memorial to the Declaration in 1776 of Independence. They read in detail about the toasts proposed in the various towns at the public banquets. In the wording of the toasts or expressions of good health may be found that measure of the degree of warmth or coolness in the zeal of the citizenry. With us in the tribunals or elsewhere wherever His Honor should appear, they [toasts] were drunk with an homage—the homage that flattery pays to pride. Here the toasts are sentiments or expressions of the attitude of mind of a citizen towards changing public events.

RHODE ISLANDS

[VI, 1] About 20 miles from Norwich one comes into the province or state of Rhodes Islands. It is the smallest of all of the United States of America, for it has a maximum length of only 47 English miles, or about 9 of ours, and has a width of but 37 English miles, or 7 of ours. It is a small and meager country indeed, but the commonwealth of Athens, once so important and still famous to this day, was not much larger, I did not notice any differences between this state and Connecticut in the character of the land, its cultivation or in the habitations.

Six miles before reaching Providence there suddenly appears a region which is open, fertile and cheerful, and in place of the stones we have seen hitherto there are green meadows and fertile fields. The *Stage*, in which for the first time I did not have any company, stopped for a rest near a public inn. Though it was the 15th of July, the morning felt cold, as it might have felt in the fall. A tall, big-bellied man with a wig and in slippers came out of the inn with a basket in his hand, in which there were grains of corn. At the same time a crowd of well-proportioned pigs, loudly demanding their breakfast, surrounded the impressive-looking innkeeper. At the time he was distributing the feed with a generous hand, the driver called to him.

"Colonel, have you got good gine?"

"An Excellent one!" answered the Colonel-innkeeper, and finishing his business with the pigs he returned to his drams and goblets. In a country where there are no hereditary titles, such as Prince, Count, etc., military rank replaces them. These (from the time of the Revolutionary War, when the militia, when every citizen went to war) are still jealously guarded. And since the innkeepers had their houses then full of people, they had a great influence on peoples' thoughts. General Washington, in order to keep their adherence, gave to almost all of them an army rank.[17]

[2] Providence. At the beginning of the 17th century the Puritan sect, persecuted in England, had to seek safety and peace in the empty wilderness—America at that time. It was they who first inhabited the state of Massachusetts. The suffering which they had undergone from fanaticism and intolerance did not make them any more gentle or more humane towards others. Scarcely had they ceased being persecuted, than they themselves at once began to persecute others. In 1631 Roger Williams, Protestant minister, differing in religious opinion from his fellow countrymen, was expelled by Massachusetts in the midst of a very hard winter. After long wanderings he, his wife and children finally found shelter amidst savage but humane Indians. He was the first to settle the place where the city now is. Because of gratitude to Providence, which had protected him, he named the place that sheltered him Providence.[18] His family on the female side still exists. Today there is a stable on the site where he lived. The only memorial of the first founder of the town is a well from which he drew water.

The very appearance of Providence arrests and gladdens the eye. It is in a valley on a wide and splendid river which divides the city into two parts. These are joined by a lightsome bridge, wide and illuminated by lamps raised on posts with huge gilt balls.[19] This bridge, the straight, paved streets, the houses, the churches with columns and raised steeples, the beautiful buildings on the hill, all give to the whole town [3] a gay and spanking new look, as they say in Polish "as if it were just taken off the needle." All the buildings are of wood, but they are graceful, even elegant, and painted white. It would be difficult to find a more spick-and-span town. The river which carries the same name as the town rises in the hills a few miles away, and what is more wonderful is that at the head of the town (*at the point*) it becomes at once so wide and deep that there, a ship of 950 *Tons* destined for the East Indies and fully loaded, was sailing safely.[20] This river joins itself immediately with a gulf of the sea which extends up to New Port.

Rhode Island, and the richest city in it, Providence, carried on in good times—that is, from the time of peace in 1783 up to the difficulties with the French in 1793—a tremendous trade. More than 600 ships both large and small had their home ports here. The whole trade is *de cabotage,* that is carrying, for the most part other than local products. Flax, flour, salt meat, fish, cattle, etc. are brought to Providence from Vermont from the boundaries of Massachusetts and Connecticut partly on wheels, partly in smaller boats by way of the Connectikut river or by coastal waters. They are loaded here onto big ships and sent to Europe and to both the Indies. Goods brought back from there are then shipped out again to Savannah, Charlestown [Charleston] and other American cities. Today, through the depredations of the French, this trade has been tremendously reduced and in the port one can see ships stripped of their lines and sails. Only here and there is there some slight activity and loading.

There is the utmost tolerance in this state. The Baptists are the most numerous. I was in their church. Their sermons do not differ noticeably from the Protestants'. Their church is splendid and elegant.

The *College* or boarding school for youth is a large building, situated on a hill with a beautiful view.[21] Up to a hundred young men are educated there; [4] they pay about 100 dollars a year. However, the general public in this state is less well-educated than in the rest of New England.

I was in the home of Mr. Clarke, one of the richest merchants here.[22] He was born in England. The sister of his wife, a sensible woman, told me that Brissot, who published a book about America, stayed only overnight in Providence. Volney and Liancourt, as did I, stayed in it only one day. The latter has already published his journey, the other will do so shortly. They will, assuredly, she said, write of the habits, trade, etc., of this town. Such is the complete information that Europeans have about America.[23]

In the evening I went once again to walk about the town and the port. The blackest depression enveloped my thoughts. My situation, the inhuman and thankless desertion of the one for whom I had done so much and for whom I undertook this journey, my separation from my homeland and friends, the difficulty and uncertainty of a return, not a soul either to cheer me or to give me help, all these thoughts acutely tormented me.

The next day, the 17th of July, I set out, on one of the packet boats which sail daily to New Port, for that town. The wind was completely against us and the gulf was stormy and bitterly cold. Besides a bit of bread and cheese there was no other food on the boat. Through 7 hours we had to wend our way, tacking from one side to another, when in a straight line our journey would have been only 30 miles. In spite of it all on this short voyage as equally in the long one from Europe, I saw that even with completely contrary winds one can with time and patience reach the destined shore. We sailed between the islands, Prudence and Patience. The first of these is 7 miles long and one mile wide. We continued between the islands, Rhode Island and Connenicut [Conanicut]; the latter a little bigger than Prudence. On these islands the land is fertile. The citizens, however, neglect farming for fishing and are inclined to drunkenness. The reason for this can, to a large extent, be assigned to the character of their work; continually at sea, in the drenching rain, and in the cold, they must restore themselves with hot drinks. [5] On none of these islands is there a town; the citizens are completely ignorant of everything. *"Ce sont des philosophes malgré eux."* Block Island, 30 miles from New Port in the open sea, has a town by the name of [blank].[24] They raise much cattle and make excellent butter and cheese there. Mrs. Green, the wife of the famous general and famous herself because of her coquetry, was born on this island.[25]

New Port. About six in the evening we sailed into the splendid harbor of New Port. Just opposite lies a small island called Fort Island, and one can see a little fort rising not very high above the ground.[26] The city is most famous for its harbor. In times of peace it enjoys all the advantages; it is large, protected from storms and tempests on all sides by extensive stretches of land. The harbor is everywhere at least 25 fathoms deep and even more. The largest fleet of warships can stay in it safely and its situation is such that a ship with any kind of wind can easily enter or leave. With the years, when the United States of America grows in naval power and strength, this port, I say, will be to America what Plymuth is to England and Brest and Toulon to France. Today with all these advantages and practically no defenses it could easily fall prey to an enemy.

Before the war the city was flourishing but with a trade of the most despicable kind, that is the slave trade, or the transportation of negroes from Africa. The merchants here took them from their homelands, transported them to the West Indies and sold them. Today the trade has stopped completely. America, especially the southern states, were engaged in this trade, as were all [6] the European maritime powers. Although this unfortunate class of people was needed on its southern plantations, America had the honor and strength to rise above selfish interests and to be the first to abolish this trade forever. Only Georgia reserved its rights until the end of this century. However, it too, not awaiting this epoch, abolished it last year with the others.

During the time of the last war New Port suffered cruelly from the English. Through three years they occupied the town, ruined and laid waste everything; a large number of the houses which were on the island, forests, plantings, even of fruit trees, were cut down for firewood. From this time, and with the abolition of the slave trade, the merchants left and the largest part of those remaining live in sloth and idleness. One can see them in groups standing in the street or gossiping about politics in a coffee house, or sitting at home, slovenly dressed and with attitudes more akin to the Italians than to their antecedents, the English.

The city is big and apart from a few houses is all built of wood. The houses are old, dark and dirty, and grass grows in the poorly paved streets. The inhabitants do not understand hospitality or even politeness. I carried to the chief merchant here, Gib[b]s, and to the merchant Hunter, letters of introduction.[27] I called on them; in return I was neither received with politeness nor even paid a return call. In a word, with a most beautiful situation, the most pleasant climate and most fertile island, this town is the saddest and gloomiest in the world. [7] There are 70 varieties of fish in this port besides *Homar[d]s* (*Lobsters*, oysters, etc.). One of the best fish is *Bass;* it can be two feet in length; however, it costs as little as 2 shillings; another, *thotog* [quahog]—an Indian name.

Even in this little state a small reminder of the Indians remains. There were 50 years ago 500; now less than a hundred remain. They live in the village of Charles Town. The states have protected their land, severely proscribing (as in Connecticut) the efforts of others to buy them. Strong drink at first reduced their number; a larger percentage went to the country where the *Six Nations* are settled near Lake [blank]. These people discovering from old traditions that the tribe of Indians in Rhodes Island was their blood relatives sent envoys to them asking them to return. As I have said, a large number went and easily accustomed themselves to the tradition of their forefathers.[28] Those who remained carry on a slothful and wretched life.

By chance I saw the famous pilgrim Stuart who has walked through a large part of the world.[29] He is an eccentric but of an innocent and honest type. His aim is to understand man and to uncover the means to make him happy. An imagination excited by this desire involves him in singularities, perhaps amusing to many but not harming anyone. He is a tall man, with an arresting and open face; ill-dressed, almost slovenly; bread, milk, butter and porter are his daily food. He rarely eats meat and then only for reasons of health. He does not ride in vehicles in order not to contribute to the torment and suffering of horses. Lord Bolingbroke [8] is his favorite author; he says that Pope in his *L'Essay sur l'homme* wrote only that which he had garnered in conversation with his lordship, and that the essay is often contradictory and unclear—this because Pope did not properly understand him. On my asking him in which country he had found man most happy he said, after long thought, that under the circumstances of the present situation, the customs, etc. of human society, it seemed to him that people are the happiest in England. He speaks with great exactness and with the best and most appropriate choice of phrase.

Rhode Island was the last state of the U.S. which accepted the present Constitution. The source of their objections was probably the abolition of the slave trade.[30]

After dinner I walked across the whole island. It is about three miles wide with fertile and well cultivated fields, sown most frequently with *maïs*, rye, barley, oats and flax. Wheat does not succeed very well near the sea. I sat on the seashore, on a high rock, before me was the expanse of the immense sea, here and there in the distance a white sail; the waves of the sea with a booming roar leapt one after the other, breaking against the sharp rocks or else washing the sandy and flat shores. *Le Guolin* [goéland], sea bird in the shape of a white pigeon, rent the air from time to time with its cries. For the rest, emptiness and silence. Between these shores and the shores of Europe, the shores even of a part of Poland, there is only the ocean. With what speed my thoughts flew over it and tarried with joy amidst relatives and friends. The delusion did not last long. The lovely dream disappeared and again I saw myself alone, sad and deserted.

In the afternoon a ship purportedly from Copenhagen went to Providence; from here [Newport] a *packe[t]-bo[a]t* sails to New York. I went on it. The passenger cabin has about 20 beds, clean, well-kept, and furnished in mahogany and brass.[31] [9] It costs 9 dollars for the journey and food. Such packets leave practically every day. There are so many means of communication and transportation from place to place in this inventive and commercial country.

The next day a miserable *Stage* with only one pair of horses arrived for me. As always in this country the rain came down in torrents. I was proceeding down the street when suddenly four gentlemen and a lady appeared to take the stage. They were relatives and friends of the impolite Mr. Gib[b]s. We had to stop at his house while the driver fetched a bigger carriage and another pair of horses. All this waiting was endured with the greatest phlegm.

We finally set off, driving through the whole length of the island called Rhode Island. It is wonderfully luxuriant, well populated and extensively cultivated. Land is sold at from 7 to 100 dollars per acre. As for climate, peace and beauty of surroundings it is difficult to find a more happy place on this earth than this island. Its whole length is 15 miles. I saw a flock of geese of a breed, wild and domestic mixed. Their necks are completely black and slender. Their meat has a much better taste than that of common geese. Citizens introduce this species either by slightly wounding the wild birds in flight or by gathering their eggs and setting them under the domestic geese. It is in this same fashion that in Virginia they mix the wild with the domestic turkeys and cross breed them, with infinite improvement.

Arriving at the tip of the island, Rhode Island, again a marvelous view appears; on one side the gulf of the sea washes it, on the other the Tau[n]ton River, and here and there are scattered green islets. After leaving our carriage and horses on this side, we crossed over to the other, called Tyberton [Tiverton]. This is an edge of land six miles across connected to Massachusetts. There at Howland's Ferry a bridge was built joining Rhode Island with Tyberton. In 1795 waves from the sea broke it down. [10] There according to the established schedule we should have found the stage from Providence waiting for us; but on the contrary there was not a living soul.[32] After leaving our trunks on the shore we had to go for some distance and by foot, to an inn. One hour, then two, and more went by; the carriage or post stage did not appear. All this did not create the least impatience nor even a grimace in my companions. They had cold lobsters with them, smoked meat and whisky. They ate and kept silent.

While they were eating I went off about a mile to a house in which lived a farmer with his wife and children. They had only 4 *acres* of land, completely devoted to a vegetable garden; because of the nearby commercial and shipping activities this man was able to support himself and his children honestly. Before the trade was ruined by the French, the onions alone, gathered from a half acre of land, brought him 100 dollars. The rest of the land provided him with vegetables and bread, and the sea with fresh fish daily. He repaired his own tools. His wife was cooking the meal, while the three children played about the house, and the fourth child, a small *baby*, sat before the fire tied to a chair. With such a small holding this family was, and acknowledged itself to be, happy.

At last I saw the long-awaited *stage*, full of travellers, with a pair of horses harnessed to it and plodding along, one leg dragging after the other. While we were all waiting, our trunks left out in the heaviest rain soaking on the shore, the coachman set off first, driving all over the countryside with the passengers he had brought. Finally he came for us. All this was borne with the greatest patience, and when the driver asked whether he should harness another pair of horses,

"*O, never mind*," called the company. "It is all the same whether we get to Providence by day or by night."

At three in the afternoon we came to Bristol.[33] [11] This is a small town but it is growing rapidly; it has its own harbor and its own ships. About a Polish mile from there we stopped at Warren. Not far from

Bristol there is a mountain on which lived the Indian kingling Philip. He was the terror of all Europeans until finally on this mountain he failed to survive one such encounter.[34] Even though it is scarcely a hundred years since all this happened, this occurrence, in this new country, belongs to fabled deeds, and in the villages they recount this tale as we do the one about King Krakus, the dragon and Queen Wanda.[35]

The town of Warren is also on a harbor and is equally engaged in commerce. A warship of 24 guns was being built there for the U.S.[36] The architect who could have been 80 years old with gray hair, danced about as if he were the youngest boy. Long life in Rhodes Island is not a rare thing. The coachman, who drove us from Newport was 60 years old, and his father, still living, nearly one hundred. The building of this ship and others gave to the small town of Warren unusual activity and liveliness. And so within a distance of six Polish miles, from Newport to Providence, there are four excellent harbors. With the passage of centuries and with peace what towns there will be; what population, what activity, trade and wealth, will a traveller see in this one small section.

The weather had cleared. The air was clear and the evening was warm but without excessive heat. Thus, this fertile and happy region was revealed in all its beauty. I do not know whether to assign it to the influence of the air, but I noticed a young married couple, Mr. and Mrs. Polock, riding with us, give an indication of a small sign of tenderness. I saw that Mrs. Polock had put her hand on the hands of her husband, and in this position they rode the whole way as two unmoving chameleons [12] or rather marionettes, not looking at each other nor saying a word. *Cette groupe inscience* [insciente] did not escape the attention of the rest of my companions who with malicious grimaces showed amongst themselves what terrible things were going on.

Further on a river and a bridge separated Rhodes Island from Massachusetts. We rode again into Providence over India Bridge. This part of the town is built on land dug out from a high hill, and it belongs to a rich merchant called Brown. Not far from the road one can see a foundry where cannon are cast for the U.S.[37]

MASSECHUSET[TS]

In the morning of the 19th of July I rode out of Providence. Three miles further on one goes through a small town, Pa[w]tucket, on a river of the same name. This river breaks through rocks and creates a wide and pretty cascade. Its beauty, however, has been spoiled for practical purposes. A large part of the water has been diverted for the use of mills, sawmills, etc.[38] In the town there are several factories. Because of its situation it could become a manufacturing center.

From Providence to Boston is 46 miles. The countryside is flat and fertile, with here and there fruitful valleys surrounded by hills. The trees [13] were bigger and their heads more widespread than any I have had the opportunity to see so far. Under the shade of their immense branches are guest houses placed in the most attractive settings. They are already gathering the rye. The Indian grain or *maïs* is abundant, as are all the other types of grain: the harvest this year is unusually prolific. There are many orchards, practically all apple orchards, and the trees are so covered with fruit that without exaggeration one may say that there are as many apples as there are leaves, and the owners will need to shake off a few so that the weight will not break the branches. Towns, or the beginnings of pretty towns occur often. Amongst others are Walpol[e] and Dodham [Dedham], the last only 10 miles from Boston. Some houses are built in the best taste, they are of wood as are practically all houses in Massachusetts. We met, in an inn, a large company of men and even more of women. These were well dressed, and had unusually fair complexions and blond hair, and a great likeness in their faces to their antecedents, the English. Nearing the city the houses became much more imposing and beautiful. There were many cabriolets and riders on horseback. We arrived at Roxbury, which is practically a suburb of Boston and is on the isthmus through which the *peninsula*, on which the city lies, is joined to the mainland.

At six in the evening we arrived in Boston.

Boston: I stopped at the inn of Cat:[herine] Gray.[39] Today was the second day of a famous annual celebration in this town called *Commencement*.[40] This is the occasion of the public examination of the students of Cambridge Col[l]ege, and the time when Doctoral and *Batchelor* degrees are conferred. A public dinner is given for 150 invited guests. [14] But besides these, curiosity brings people of all ages and both sexes to the scene; in a word the whole town.

I strolled in the evening on the bridge which crosses the Charles River to Cambridge. This bridge, together with the dam, is one and a half English miles in length; it is called the West Boston Bridge and is of graceful design, lightsome and elegant.[41] In the middle there is a lock with gates for the passage of boats. There are sidewalks with handrails for pedestrians, the whole is illuminated with splendid lanterns. Never before in any country have I seen a bridge so beautiful, and so long. There the crystal clarity of the water spreads out in wide sweeps beneath the overhanging bridge, to the left are distant fertile hills covered with houses, to the right Charlestown, behind, the old town of Boston and in the forefront gay meadows with the soaring pinnacles of Cambridge farther off. Every aspect of the view achieves an unsurpassed excellence. During this evening the bridge was crowded with more people than on any single day of the whole year. Whoever had carriage, buggy or horse or could find one for hire, rode in to the famous *Commencement.* Many hackney carriages, buggies, cabriolets and saddle horses wound ceaselessly by. Beside the hackney carriages of the prim and sedate there were others full of negroes, negresses and little black imps. Everyone free, everyone dressed in a similar fashion. There were hackney carriages and cabriolets full of gay young ladies with gentlemen escorts; other young ladies strolled by on foot with their escorts. How far away was the severe Puritan spirit [42] which once held sway in Boston. And thus have strict habits changed today.

This is the first city in America in which I have seen carriages bearing numbers; there were many of these. This indicates that conspicuous show is less evident here than elsewhere. It shows that individuals do not have their own carriages and that both the rich and the poor use public transportation when needed.

In the evening about nine o'clock, after finishing their daily work, youths gather in the former *State House,* [15] where in both the lower and upper halls they drill in the manual of arms and march about. I saw this same drill in Providence. Everywhere the spirit of war and at the same time of defense spreads among the citizenry.

The next day, the 20th, I gave letters of introduction to Messrs [John] Coffin Jones and Patrick Jeffery.[43] I was politely received and invited to dinner. In the afternoon I gave another letter to Dr. Ja[r]vis.[44] He is a famous and fiery democrat as doctors are everywhere. I do not know what is the reason for this, perhaps because war, revolution and medicine have the same object, that is the spilling of blood and death. The hapless doctor was a victim of his own fiery zeal. Both day and night, anxious for the success of the French and their party in this country, he grew thin; he began to turn yellow and then green and now can hardly draw breath.

Today I walked about the most important parts of the city. Boston was founded by the inhabitants of Charles Town in 1631. There is no other town in America that reminds one more of our European cities. The houses are old, covered with soot and, with a few exceptions, made of wood. The streets are narrow, crooked and often dirty. The newness, freshness and cleanliness which in Philadelphia and New

York are seen everywhere can rarely be noticed here. There are, however, houses which, though they are not equal in size to those in the above-mentioned cities, do surpass them in taste, in their settings and in their beautiful gardens.

The occupations here are similar to those in other ports and commercial cities. In the same way, by day they load and unload ships in the harbor; they roll barrels and hogsheads and there they load them onto wagons; here a ship unfurls her sails and departs; there another returning joyfully lowers her anchor. The merchants open their shops and *office* or *bureau*, which are always in a different place from their houses. Later auctions start up in the houses. Even the principal streets are filled with furniture, utensils, goods of all kinds which a man standing on a table and holding a hammer in his hand sells to the [16] highest bidder. A large group of people surround them. At noon in the coffee house, or the Exchange and *Insurance Office* is a crowd of merchants selling, buying and exchanging information. About two, everybody goes to dinner; all the activity stops and there is the greatest quiet. After dinner the activities continue with less liveliness until the time for tea. In the evening one takes a little walk; later the fishermen display *lobsters* or sea crayfish of tremendous size at the old State House. Surrounding them are a few glimmering lights and a crowd of buyers.

The next day, the 21st, I went to see friends of mine from Federal City. Messrs Desforges *et* Debassin. I went with the latter to the new *State House*. This is one of the biggest new buildings in America. It stands on a high hill; it is all of stone with a cupola and columns. The Legislature of the State of Boston [sic] has its debates there. Not far from there is Beacon Hill. The view from it shows up the whole city and the sea. On the top stands a column. It is not a monument *aere perennius*, it is made from brick, on it are marble tablets which have etched on them the events and the most famous deeds of the Revolution up to the time of the establishment of the Constitution.[45]

I went to dinner at Mr. Jeffry's, a gay *bon vivant*. There a good table was laid out in semicircular array with excellent food and a fantastic number of drinks. In the evening we stepped out into his garden, which mounts upwards in terraced steps and offers a most beautiful view; the whole city of Boston, the harbor scattered with islands, amongst them Castel Island defending the entrance. All this one can see at one's feet. Near Castle Island stood the frigate *The* Constitution, Capt. Nichelsson, and the armed corvette *The* Dellaware which had recently taken a French privateer.[46] Beyond the high peak of an island one could see the tips of the three masts of the frigate *The*

United States: Commodor[e] Barry.[47] On the left the city of Charles Town, burnt during the war and today risen from the ashes. Beyond them lie the hills memorable in American [17] history, Bre[e]ds' and Bunkers' Hills, to the right Dorchester Point, from which General Washington forced the English to pull out and to leave the city. In a word, the view is everywhere tempting; on all sides there is a wide expanse for the eye to see and points of vital historical interest to attract the attention.

The next day, the 22nd, in the morning I went to Charles Town, or rather to the eminence lying beyond it, Breds' Hill. There, and not as is mistakenly said on Bunkers' Hill (The order given to the Americans was to entrench themselves on Bunker Hill, on a place where the height dominated the whole neighborhood. It is not known for what reason the volunteers prepared themselves on Breds' Hill, rather than on Bunker Hill, and at night and in such silence that they were not heard by the English ships lying there, they dug shallow trenches to protect themselves); these farmers, untrained as soldiers, with poor arms, having in their favor only the love of freedom and that excellence in marksmanship gained from hunting, stood fast most valiantly and made heavy slaughter among the 3,000 regular English soldiers, backed by artillery and warships and led by Generals Gage, Howe, Buorgoyne, Clinton, Pigot and Lord Pearcy.[48]

The attack and the defense were equally lively and the whole scene was splendidly cruel. The whole of Charles Town with its steeples was in flames. Every high point, and the tops of all the houses in Boston and of every neighboring town were covered with a vast crowd of people, watching with apprehension and trembling heart the battle between those fighting for liberty and the others fighting for domination. Much on this day belongs to American courage and to the accuracy of American marksmanship. There is much to censure in the poor dispositions of the English commanders. Gordon and Ramsay write extensively of this in their works. The English lost 1,054 persons, counting both dead and wounded, the Americans 453.[49] Amongst these was General Warren, by profession a doctor, a man honored by all during his life and generally mourned after his death. On this hill in the very place where he fell they have raised a monument to him; that is, on a stone pedestal is a white wooden column [18] with a gilt urn on top.[50] The trenches dug by the Americans in haste are today plowed over and practically level with the ground. The hill itself is not very high and its approach is not at all steep. In a word the situation itself gives witness as much to the courage of the Americans as to the poor judgment and blind bungling of the English commanders.

Their negligence went so far that when the time came to shoot, the grape shot for the guns was discovered to be of larger caliber than the cannon. It was only after the third attack launched at them from three sides that the Americans retreated and then in good order taking a position on Prospect Hill while the English occupied the captured hill and Bunker Hill. Today on this American Thermopylae a quiet herd of cattle graze.

I went to dinner at Mr. du Ballet's, a native Frenchman who has been settled here for 20 years and carries on an extensive business.[51] Under the present circumstances a foreigner is looked at askance and with suspicion, and gets any information from the natives, only with great difficulty, who consider every question as treason or espionage. A European settled here can best and most truly enlighten such a man. He possesses the same information as the native and has none of his prejudices. One or two hours of conversation with M. du Ballet gave me the following information on the trade here. Fishing provides the first and the most important article of export of the state of Massachusetts and of its cities, especially Boston. Fishing is of two kinds and takes place in two seasons of the year. Whaling is practiced solely by the citizens of the island of Nantucket, inhabited by Quakers. The oil from the whales, known under the name of *sparmaceti,* is used to make the best candles; whalebone is used for corsets and petticoat hoops which, thank God, are worn less [19] than before. The other fishing, which takes place in April and August, is the only occupation of the inhabitants of Salem, Marblehead, Beverley and Cap[e] Cod. They catch herring, mackerel, salmon, but above all *cod* or *stokfish.*

Before setting out to fish the owners of the small fishing boats come to the towns named above, and especially into Boston to buy salt. These boats carry six or seven people. The owner, providing the boat and the salt, takes a quarter of the whole catch; the three other parts are distributed equally amongst the fishermen. After loading the salt they sail to the Newfoundland Banks and throw out their rods, each with two hooks. Half the company fish while the other half gut and scale the catch. Hardly is the codfish hauled in than immediately the cleaner with one stroke of the knife cuts off its head leaving only the tongue which, of the whole fish, is the choicest morsel. He opens its stomach, throws out its entrails, except the liver which is put in barrels and then rendered for oil for the lamps. The more offal that is thrown overboard, the more fish come near the ship to devour it; this in turn makes the catch the larger. The codfish is then split open, salted and packed. Fishing continues while the salt lasts and until the ship is loaded. Returning home they spread the fish out on the shore on shafts or slatted fences raised a few feet off the ground. The wind blowing through and the sun dry the fish.

They are packed in bundles and brought to Boston and other cities where wholesale merchants buy them by the hundredweight. These merchants divide them into two categories: the worst fish, called *Jamaica fish* [20] (because it was formerly to this colony that they were largely sent as food for the negroes), and the other class, the very best, called *marchand's fish*. These latter are sent to Europe, to the Catholic countries such as Spain, Portugal and Italy, and the profit here is the greatest, so that it is a habit of the merchants here to eat this fish for dinner on Saturday, and as a gesture of thankfulness and respect for this, their profit, they usually offer the toast, "to the health of *Codfish and Catholic religion.*" [52]

After receiving cash for the fish the fishermen with the greatest regularity buy domestic necessities, that is sugar, coffee, tea, rum and pork, etc., and celebrate the whole winter by increasing their progeny. They multiply in swarms. Whether this fecundity may be ascribed to the fact that they eat fish or to the separation from their wives throughout half the year, the men do return to them with renewed passion and strength. To the wealth that this type of industry and trade pours into the country one must add this advantage, that fishing provides the best school for navigators and sailors.

Another article of local trade is salt meat, carried by these sailors in their own ships to the West Indies. It is really very unfortunate that all the trade of these shores is in salted products, and must depend on salt imported from Europe. They have tried to prepare it here several times, but the result was not worth the effort. This may be perhaps because of the quality of the air, the wind direction with the shores facing eastwards. Finally lumber for building is an important item of export. Of grain they send only *maïs* in the kernel to Spain and Portugal. Wheat does not succeed here and all the white bread is baked with flour brought from Pennsylvania, Maryland, or Virginia.

[21] Boston is the first city in America which in [blank] sent a ship to China. [53] From that time this trade has increased and today ships out of this city are on the Indian Oceans; some of them carry on the newly opened trade in furs. They go as far as the shores of Kamchatka and trade there tools and cloth for skins which then are traded in China for tea, porcelain and silk. This trade does not always enjoy the same success. Sometimes those skins which wholesale would not bring half a Polish złoty sell in China for 60 piasters, and then too a skin which cost three times this amount may be sold for only 15 or 12 piasters, depending upon the quantity appearing in the market. Neverthe-

less, a ship returning successfully from this trade always yields 70 to 80 per cent profit. The Indians have so many utensils, tools and trinkets brought to them by the Europeans that they do not want to trade in them any more. They are eager only for cloth and are very discriminating as to colors. The Americans have it specially manufactured in English factories. Blue with white zigzags is in the highest fashion with the Patagonian elegants.[54]

In Massachusetts as elsewhere in the U.S. mills have been set up, but here as everywhere they necessarily failed because of the lack and expense of labor. Other types of manufacture, however, continue rather successfully, for example, nails, leather, writing paper, wallpaper, glass, etc. On these shores 1,500 boats are solely occupied in the fishing industry.

July 23. Officers from two frigates and the Chebek [55] Dellawar augmented the crowd in our inn. The uniforms, wigs, bearing are completely like the English with this one exception [22] that in their tone and conversation instead of the immemorial English haughtiness one can see the vanity and boastfulness of a new people. The officers from the fleet of Admirals Duncan or Jervis [56] do not talk more pompously of their victories, than these American lieutenants of their passage from Philadelphia to Boston. If the talk is about captains, then, *"To the most excellent officers and the best navigators in the world, they are ready to engage a man of war of 100 guns, they never will surrender their ship, etc."* If there is the question of a frigate, *"She is the most complete stand [57] and elegant vessel that ever was seen on the dominions of Neptune, she sails 15 nods* [knots] *by hour, etc."* The audience exaggerate even these praises. One time a tall and powdered lieutenant walked by on the street. The passers-by stopped, and looking at him with wonder: *"Look, look,"* said one to another, *"How he is like Alexander the Great."*

It is easy to forgive this natural vanity. It is like a child who, after receiving a watch for the first time, is beside himself with joy and presumes that his small ticker surpasses in construction and beauty the most famous clock by Harrison.[58] Their vanity is the result of youth, ignorance and sudden and unexpected success. Through luck, courage, and more still because of the incomprehensible blunders of the English, they brought about the shaking off of their yoke. That praise, which European writers vied with each other to accord them, was as acceptable as ready cash so that in their own esteem they were without peer. During the first three years a lucky increase in trade poured down on them unexpected and hitherto unknown riches. They have therefore adjudged themselves the most powerful and the richest of people. Ignorance, and finally the separation from ancient powerful civilizations, the lack of comparison between that which is elsewhere and that here, has strengthened this opinion. Hence, in spite of a natural coldness of character there is an unheard of exaggeration in expression. There is nothing more common than to hear a youngster talking [23] of a woman, "*She is monstrously beautiful; I am extravagantly fond of her, etc.*"

In spite of the heat I went to see that place famous in the history of Boston, Grifferson's [Griffin's] W[h]arf, where up to 400 boxes of tea of the English India Company were thrown into the ocean. The English had attempted to foist it on the Americans by force. These withered leaves were the initial cause both of the bloodshed spread wide over land and sea, and indeed of American independence itself. In the street near the house where I am now living C[a]pt. Preston, assaulted and reviled by the populace, gave the first order to his soldiers to fire.[59]

In spite of a thousand questions I have not up to now been able to find out where was that house where Doctor Franklin was born, where was the print shop—his brother's—where he learned the trade of a printer and read by stealth, and educated and developed his mind. Such indifference by the inhabitants to the memorials of a man, a part of whose glory has been shed on them, is not understandable. It is true that they have set up a monument, that is a stone urn without any inscription. It stands in the middle of a small greensward, fenced off with pickets and planted all around with Italian poplars. On both sides rise two fine stone buildings. Everything together creates the most beautiful square in Boston, but it would have been more interesting if the house in which he was born and the print shop where he worked were set apart, were carefully and piously kept and honored.[60]

I rode to Cambridge in the company of Desforges and Debassin in a hired hack which cost almost three piasters for four hours. Cambridge, which is three and a half miles distant from Boston, is the first and the oldest *Universitas* established in the whole of North America. In 1638 John Harvard, Puritan minister, bequeathed for its endowment £779 Sterling. Later other donations were added and the fund grew.

Standing apart on an open site are two large brick and stone buildings separated [24] by a courtyard. One of them serves as a residence for the students, who live together and eat at a common table. This is better both for learning and for manners than, as in Oxford and elsewhere, with the young people scattered through the town. In the second building are the lecture rooms, the library and natural history room and other points of interest: and finally physical apparatus and an anatomy collection. Students pay about 200 dollars for board and tuition. There are up to 150 students and those who cannot be accommodated in the academy live in the town. The library holds up to 12 thousand books, valuable and well-chosen works. The number increases daily by individual donation. The books are arranged in sections with the donor's names inscribed. Amongst others I saw the supposedly eight volumes *Unitarii seu Fratres Polonorum.*[61] These were Socinians, at one time a numerous sect in Poland. Members of this sect live in Boston and other American cities although so far I have been unable to discover whether any of the families here come from Poland. In the library there is a portrait of Cardinal Bentivoglio beautifully copied by Copley [62] from the original of Van Dyck. In the natural history collection there were pictographs of the Indian people who at one time lived in Massachusetts. These resemble hieroglyphics and show clumsy heads, whole human figures, zigzags, etc. There was also the skull of a *requin* through whose jaws a person could pass— snakes, reptiles, etc. In a separate hall there was a solar system in bronze made in Boston; portraits of famous Americans and of professors in the Academy, etc.[63]

The examinations had finished a few days before and it was vacation: vacations are too many and come too often, breaking the continuity in attention and learning for the young. Each season of the year has its vacation and they all add up to more than three months of wasted time.

On our return we visited the homestead or farm of Mr. Jarvis, the brother of the doctor.[64] The house was clean and well kept with a large family and up to 250 acres of land. The stock looked [25] well and much superior in appearance to the herds in Maryland and Virginia because they were much better cared for and watched over. The cows give up to four gallons of milk per day. There were many apple trees in the garden. In one of these trees we found a nest of the *colibris*, which was given to me. Who could have told that this delicate and tiny bird flies so far to the north. I spent the evening on the promenade called the Mall. This is an immense meadow rising to the river in hillocks. There is only one alley of trees planted on it. Along only half the road are old trees, branched out and giving shade; the rest have all been planted recently and grow poorly. In spite of this it is a public promenade of which there are very few in America. Strolling is not to the taste of the inhabitants who often, in the best and most pleasant weather sit at the windows, drinking one cup of tea throughout a whole half hour. On this same promenade gay young ladies walk about in pairs or alone, but they do so with a sad and withdrawn air.

Only an American can tell what kind they really are. A lower Vestal maiden of this class with a bolder and no uncertain mien runs about the streets and shores of the port where numberless arms of sailors reach out, waiting to embrace them. Every port city and other cities of any size at all have this type of women which proves that excess, here as in Europe, produces its own results. These ladies, if they were content with simple dress, could easily earn enough with their own hands, but having before them all the show and the luxury of the wealthy, womanly vanity and aversion to work pushes them into prostitution and forces them to cover their lost shame with fine muslin.

The inhabitants of Boston are celebrated amongst others in America for friendliness, hospitality and better education. A week was not enough to encounter and to experience these qualities. I truly found in the men and women much more awareness and entertainment and conversation. Bookstores, more in number and better stocked than elsewhere, certainly prove a more general taste for reading. [26] Mrs. Spooner, Misses Jarvis, etc. in their conversation show learning and wit.[65] The honors of the town, however, were paid me not by the citizens but rather by the foreigners, that is the French: M. du Ballet, Goutot staying here, and above all MM. Desforges and Debassin of whom I have just spoken. We had parties with them often where the table was set not in the American, but in the French way; champagne, and above all wit and gaiety which is inherent in these people reminded me of former happy moments in Europe. Desforges provokes interest in a more gentle and direct manner, with friendship and trust. Debassin has a more military and coarse manner. I asked them as inhabitants *de Isle de France et de Bourbon* whether the interesting and tender romance by St. Pierre, entitled *Paul et Virginie*, was based on fact.[66] They replied that there was some truth in it. It seems that a few score years ago a young man named Villarmois and Miss [blank], inhabitants of the islands, were returning together from France where their parents had gone for business reasons or some such. In fact the young pair were in love and were engaged. The ship S. Gizan, while entering the harbor during a hurricane, broke up and the young lady could have been saved if she had been willing to undress, but under no circumstances would she agree to this, and thus she fell victim of the waves.

The 27th of July I set off on the road to Portsm[o]uth in New Hamschire, 67 miles from Boston. The *Stage* leaves at 3 A.M. At two the coachman came to awaken me. We set out on the road through Charles Town and scarcely had we crossed one bridge than we saw another across the Mystic River, joining that town with Malden. Its length is

2,420 feet, width 32, with handrails and lamps along its length.[67] The night was warm, and after traveling through dark meadows we were covered with swarms of *moskitos*. Our hands hung weary from constantly brushing them away. This torment and sleeplessness throughout the whole night made the trip infinitely unpleasant. As soon as it grew light, I saw the shapes [27] of my companions. Sitting in the rear and taking up practically the whole carriage was a huge toad named Captain Seevesson, beside it a cricket, withered and old, as dried up and spare as his neighbor was fat and thick. This cricket, however, was already 60 years old; he was returning by land from South Carolina to Portsmuth, that is more than 800 miles. To batter oneself about for all this distance, to rise at two o'clock, to let oneself be bitten by mosquitoes and baked by the sun, all this for a wealthy man, and what is more a weak and aged one, could not possibly equal the profit that he hoped to get; *auri sacra fames.*[68] A third companion was a doctor, a person practically speechless; finally there were two youngsters going to their family.

The countryside about Boston is rocky and has more forests and meadows than fields; there are frequent lakes and creeks. We stopped for breakfast in Salem; the outskirts are extensive but miserable. This is one of the oldest cities in this country, big and rich. The trade to the East Indies is large and, what is more, it is carried on solely with American capital. The houses to a large extent are not painted white and look gloomy. Severe habits, gloom and quiet are observed here more than elsewhere. The breakfast was poor and it cost 3 shillings. Again there was a bridge of 1,500 feet joining Salem and Beverly.[69] Along this whole shore one sees only the sea or the arms of the sea, rivers and splendid bridges. Here in all the gardens, in the fields, and around each house there are fences placed on posts a foot and a half in height on which fish is dried.

In Salem another toad joined us, not ceding anything in girth to the first, with the difference that the lower part of his face was a deep crimson and blue veins came through thickly on his nose and cheeks. This toad was tremendously gay. The coachman considered for a long time how these two tubs could be placed so that a balance might be maintained throughout the journey. *Tandem* [at last] they were fitted in. The second toad was called Samuel Smith and like the first was once a captain of a ship. Hence sprang the most heartfelt exchange of greetings. The whole company kept silent; only these two talked and always of the sea, [28] of the winds, of how many times they had been taken by corsairs, etc., and with every word the addition of a thousand oaths. I noticed, not for the first time, that sailors are greater talkers than others, especially when, in old age, they give up the sea and settle on shore. Accustomed for a long time to an active life and one subject to a thousand changes, they cannot get used to the peace and quiet, and they sweeten their present inactivity remembering previous storms, dangers and fears.

In Ipswich we changed horses; they had gone 30 miles at a stretch. Here on the top of the above-mentioned fences were spread out thousands of codfish. I have even seen instead of grain, stocks of this dried fish in the barns. For it (as we for rye and wheat) these citizens get gold, silver, wine, coffee, sugar, etc.

In these places they improve the poor tillage. They sow buckwheat but do not harvest it and plough it in whole, letting it rot and mix with the earth. The ground is then improved for the planting of other grain.

Here Mr. Blanchard had his house; white, clean, surrounded with trees with a garden of flowers, and what is more, in this house a wife and beautiful children. Happy one! [Not] deserted, nor wandering aimlessly as I.

We traveled then through New bury and further through New bury Town. This city, as others near the sea, carries on an important trade. We stopped at a house where the first toad got out. He struck the knocker and the door opened and there appeared a true angel, a maiden of lilies and roses, the most beautiful and fresh in appearance and stature. Who would have believed that this was the daughter of the Toad. Thus from hairy and unpleasant caterpillar's larvae come rose and white butterflies. The second Toad, losing his companion, almost wept with sadness. The rum in the tavern where we came for dinner cheered him up a bit. A good dinner for 3½ shillings, which was cheap in comparison to the breakfast. In New bury they are building a ship of 26 guns for the U.S.[70]

The countryside is mostly level; the fields are covered with *maïs*, oats, barley, etc. This was just the time of the harvest. [29] I saw them cutting with the scythe and sickle. I did not, at any time, happen to see women doing this work.

A few miles from there are Salisbury and Am[e]sbury. The first does not have a cathedral as does the town of the same name in old England. The other carries on a business of building ships. Huge forests of oaks in the depths of the country provide the best wood.

Beyond New bury one rides on a bridge across the Merrimak [Merrimac]. The bridge is of special construction; all its support derives from a suspension from the top. Its arch is 160 ft. wide. The Merrimak river makes an island here and divides itself into two streams which join beyond the bridge.[71] And so through an extent of 10 Polish miles we rode over five costly and splendid bridges. On this point this young country need not yield to, and indeed often surpasses, the oldest and best-run European countries.

The toad, not finding anyone to talk to about the sea, picked out the doctor and began to tell this poor unfortunate about the bad state of his health. This red, enormously fat and short person had already once had apoplexy provoked by an unusual occurrence. The pigs had got into the grain and had been there some time when the Toad noticed them. This invasion had aroused so much anger in him that he was struck by apoplexy and was for a long time between life and death. Today in order to strengthen his health, he has dreamed up a medicine, that is raisins, which he eats incessantly. After riding 16 Polish miles in all, through level pretty, and well-settled country with six or seven seaports, we stopped in the evening in Portsmuth.

NEWHAMPSHIRE

A few miles beyond the Marimak river the boundary of New Hamschire begins. One has to inquire for it since there is nothing to point it out. There are no eagles, nor customs, nor sentries, nor do they stop [30] nor ask who one is, whence one came and for what purpose. They do not inspect nor put their seal on trunks. A traveler goes a thousand miles in America and nowhere will he be held up nor inspected nor tormented. In Europe one can not travel a score of miles without being exposed to all this unpleasantness. About a score of years ago New Hampshire and Vermont belonged to Massachusetts. As soon as they felt themselves sufficiently well populated, they broke away and are now separate states. The Province of Main[e] has submitted a petition to Congress requesting that it may become a separate state. Massachusetts did not offer any objection to the separation of these huge provinces. There was some controversy about the Province of Vermont with the State of New Hamshire. They will all be Americans, all members of the one body politic. The states here do not cherish any ambition to extend either their rule or their boundaries. Further, the taxes are not at the disposition of one man, but rather they are directed towards public need; they do not bring any profit to a single individual. In Europe, where every country possesses the vain pride of importance, and where the source of the treasury of its rulers is both the number—not of citizens but—of subjects, and the extent of its domain, where each one seeks to be bigger than his neighbor, there it is not strange that they wage war over a few miles of countryside or even over one town.

Portsmuth. This country was first discovered by the English in 1614 when Captain John Smith after having sighted the shores of Penobscot and Cape Cod discovered en route the Piscataqua river. He dedicated his description of these shores and a map to the son of James I, later the unfortunate Charles I. He called these parts New England.[72]

Portsmuth is one of the old cities in America. It has 5,000 inhabitants. It covers a rather extensive area. All the houses are of wood; the number of really showy ones is not great, but here none the less as in all American cities there are houses which in splendor substantially surpass others. Their owners, privileged by wealth, live on a higher plane. Though by the Constitution and at law there is neither nobility nor distinction of birth, though equality is well secured, wealth rejects it and creates differences between men.

Portsmuth extends along the Piscataqua river and has the most favorable situation for trade. The river is a mile in width. [31] Its depth everywhere is so great that the biggest warships can enter and leave, which advantage is as great in peace as it is dangerous in time of war. The waters run swift as an arrow's flight. This speed and the deep-flowing channel change and cool the air, making this town one of the healthiest in America. The river has its source 20 or 30 miles away in this same state.

More than two hundred ships may be seen in this port. The biggest trade is to the West Indies and Europe and is in fish, barrel staves, salt butter, meat, etc. If the voyage is successful, this produce brings a profit of 250 per cent. They are exchanged in the West Indies for coffee, sugar, cotton, or more often during wartime for English bills of exchange which later may be redeemed for *dry goods* or various English wares. The merchants, in spite of today's losses, are rich and closefisted. I brought letters of introduction to three of the best known. One was not at home; another, Mr. Rindge, allowed me a half hour of conversation. A third, Mr. Seafs,[73] did not invite me for dinner but did me a greater service since he sent his son in the afternoon with a cabriolet to show me the environs of the town and the famous bridge over the Piscataqua. We set out at five. The land hereabouts is not very fertile, planted mostly with potatoes and *Indian Corn.* Riding out of town one can see a huge rock which had been split into three parts by a stroke of lightning. Rising like an amphitheatre above the far-distant horizon is a blue-gray range of mountains. These, a hundred miles distant, are the Blue Ridge, or my old friends from Virginia.[74] I would not have recognized them at this distance.

Pines are the most common trees; they resemble but are not the same as ours. Practically all the produce of this part of the world at a distance and superficially appears to be like ours, but on close inspection large differences can be discovered. Thus, the pines are less rough and bent, their needles greener and softer. I saw a few grown so high with trunks so smooth that they had branches only at the very top. The birches are less attractive than ours, instead [32] of a compact head of drooping branches the limbs reach far out to the side and the leaves are larger and coarser. This is the first time I have seen this type of tree. They do not grow in the south.[75]

We came finally to the bridge. It is a mile long, but in beauty and excellence of construction it surpasses all the others that I have seen so far. Where the waters are less deep and swift it rests on pilings. Over the channel itself hangs an arch of 244 ft. The carpentry of the trusses is the most skilled and ingenious. It must be said that in this particular building talent Americans surpass all others and of these MM. Coxe and Thompson are the most famous. This bridge was built by a company to which, by legislative act, the tolls on it are forever reserved. An island of two acres divides the bridge. On the second span is a drawbridge which may be raised, when a ship would pass through, by two people, by means of a block and tackle. This bridge is seven miles from town. It is the fashion to ride there for tea. On the deck of the bridge there is a windowed opening which when lifted reveals a stairway to a hall or bower built directly under the arch of the bridge and over the stream. It is an interesting sight to see the crowd of Portsmouth elegants hung, as if in a cage, over the water near the bridge, with the cabriolets running over their heads.[76] This is a remarkably cool place. The bridge, though of wood and in a country where there are unusually severe winters, will never be broken up by ice. The speed of the current, the ebb and flow of the tide will never permit the river to freeze. They manure the garden on this little island with a seaweed called *Ill grass* or *Rock weeds*.[77] The tide brings it onto the beaches or hangs it on the rocks. The manure from it is excellent. It is commonly used on the coast of the Province *du* Main[e].

PROVINCE OF MAIN[E]

In the morning of the 29th I crossed the swift Piscataqua river by ferry. On the other side is an island where just now they are building 2 corvettes of 26 guns [33] for the U.S. As soon as these are launched, then immediately they are to build a new frigate of 46 guns.[78] One must give credit to the Government; proportionate to the availability and expense of labor it speeds the growth of the American fleet. It will continue to grow, but there will be the greatest difficulty in finding hands. The three existing frigates took four months before their complement was filled. At this moment the wages of seamen on merchant vessels have risen and they are paid 25 to 30 piasters, that is 15 ducats a month. How can the government, which pays only 14 piasters, expect to get them when, in the navy besides the dangers of the sea, there is the further danger of war. There is only one advantage, that the service and pay is steadier. On merchant vessels, for example, they pay only when the vessel reaches port; if it is taken at sea by a privateer, the sailor loses his pay. We stopped finally on the shore of the province of Main, the last of the United States.

This is the *Ultima Tuhl* [Thule] of America, huge in its extent. To the east and the north it is surrounded by Canada. On its broad expanse already live up to one hundred thousand inhabitants. After a hundred years there will be up to five to six million. The capital, Portland, has an excellent harbor on Casco bay. Its shore line extends for 240 miles. The produce is the same as that of New Hampshire, principally masts and here and there wheat. To Portland as to Portsmuth the produce comes mostly in the winter by sleigh from the depths of the country, from Vermont and even from Canada. The furs from there are paid for partly in cash, partly by exchange for European goods or those from the West Indies. Though there are hard winters here, I did not see stoves in any houses, these only begin to appear in Canada.

After making an excursion for a mile and a half into the countryside I stood on a rise [34] from which one could see the town of Kittery, divided as it is into two parishes, its splendid harbor and *Lig[h]thouse*. Here the birches appear more frequently and there is the *Locust* or acacia, a tree which though not large is very good for shipbuilding. In Rhodes Island and other places it is planted especially for this purpose. The scene *from the point* over the harbor, the winding river, the rocks covered with trees, and in the far distance the expanse of the sea, here is a scene, I say, both beautiful and melancholy. The river is unusually full of fish, especially excellent *makerel, lobster* or sea crayfish. On its shores are sea plants; the leaves of one of these are the size of a calf's skin and dark olive in color.

From the day of my departure from Boston and for three full days there was unusual heat. One breathed in flame rather than air. The citizens of Portsmuth have invented comfortable apparel for this heat.

> "In dressing gowns and nightcaps
> They walk about the streets."

They not only walk alone about the streets in this manner, but so dressed they escort ladies about the town and entertain guests at home, etc.[78a]

I went to tea at Mr. Sheafe's, who asked me if the ill-fated battle in which G[eneral] K[ościuszko] was taken prisoner took place in Germany and whether it was against the French. France formerly had its own consul here. The last one, Mr. Toscan, married an American, bought some land and is managing it very well. This is the second consul to have settled here. Toscan as Genet is a revolutionary, seeing divine deliverance in France; I do not know why they stay here and do not return.[79]

The 30th I rode out of Portsmuth on a road going [35] through Exeter. The stages in New England are much better than those in the middle states and in the south. One does not clamber over the coach shaft with the help of a set of steps; here there are doors and carriage steps. The carriage is large and the coachman has a separate seat. The road to Exeter was excellent. The town of Exeter, though the seat of the state government in New Hampshire, was rather sparse; the *State House*, two churches, an academy and a few score houses. In the academy there are about 80 youths; their tuition is free; they board for 2 dollars a week.[80]

Small boats go from here to Portsmuth. I saw an animal here called, in Indian, *muss* [moose]; it is like our elk. It was only seven months old. The Indians caught it in the upper reaches of the Patebscot river, not far from the Canadian border. A *Skwa*, or Indian woman, had suckled it with her own breast. In its conformation and bearing it appears part ass and part reindeer. Its head is hideously ugly; its shoulders form humps; its legs are long and it has no tail. It would be interesting to mate it either with a female ass or with a mare. One might crossbreed; how many new types of animal might not be discovered.

"I saw an animal here called, in Indian, *muss*."

We rode further through level country; the land was not the best and the houses were rather thinly scattered. After 30 miles New hampschire ends. Haverhill, where we stopped for dinner, is in Massachusetts. The town is well kept and quite lovely, lying in a valley between two hills just on the Merrimack river (the bridge does not take second place to any other in these parts).[81] Here too they are building *a revenu cutter to prevent smug[g]ling*. Each of the United States has such a boat, carrying 10 to 14 guns.[82] The inn in Haverhill was excellent and clean, the hostess affable and polite, more like a Frenchwoman in her comportment than an American. The dinner was excellent; we paid half a dollar for it and for the punch. [36] I had a conversation with my companion C[a]pt. M'Neel about service on the sea. Regulations for the navy here are just the same as in England. The Captain of a ship gets 3 dollars a day, a lieutenant 60 dollars a month.[83] There is drill three or four times a day. The sailors are trained in armed combat, to know their posts even at night, and finally in *abordage* or the storming of an enemy vessel. During this exercise *les marines,* or infantry, shoot continually, then, while some of the sailors ward off the enemy, approach with pikes, others with sabers, pistols and daggers, etc., jump onto the enemy ship, and within a quarter of an hour the battle is decided.

The road from Haverhill, practically all the way up to Boston, is exceedingly rocky. The countryside is flat and though not the most fertile, it is well settled. Every few miles there is a house, and sometimes even in the middle of a field is a schoolhouse swarming with boys and girls. Every parish is required by law to have a school. Any failure to comply calls for a heavy fine.

Medford. Four miles from Boston is a small and pretty town. Beyond it are the remains of the American and English trenches. From these trenches General Washington kept the enemy occupied while during the night, with the utmost quiet, his soldiers crossed to Dorchester Point and set up batteries. In the morning the English fleet, seeing with absolute surprise these batteries looming over their heads had to retreat, and thus the city was delivered.

After riding through the pretty city of Charles Town we stopped in Boston at eight in the evening.

[37] A few days before my departure from Boston, a disease of the type of the *yellow fever* broke out near the harbor region. In one day 12 persons died of it. The cause of this disease is commonly and with reason ascribed to the filth *des Quais,* or the wharves of the port. Refuse, manure, smelly and rotten fish with which the shores of a port are strewn poison the air of these places. The magistrate ordered all this foul mess to be cleared up, and it is to be hoped that these in-

dispensable precautions will eliminate the usual fatal outcome of this disease which every year ravages yet another of the principal cities here.[84]

Two frigates and as many corvettes have left here in the last three days. Capt. Nichelson of the frigate Constitution has named 20 sailors and *gardes marines* as deserters.[85] It is a sad fact that here under a free, and the best government the common man does not show any more zeal and attachment to his country, its defense, and its glory than anywhere else.

Chapter VII

JOURNEY FROM BOSTON TO ALBANY, IN-
CLUDING A VISIT TO THE SHAKER COM-
MUNITY OF NEW LEBANON. FROM TROY
TO NEW YORK ON THE HUDSON BY
BOAT. RETURN TO ELIZABETHTOWN

Road to Albany. The first of August I sat again on my stage waggon.[1] Passing through Charles Town, we took on a whole family from North Hampton. It was composed of a very fat gentleman, a very thin wife and a young woman supposedly their relative, two trunks, four bundles tied up, and a chair packaged and tied up, all of which took up as much room as the travelers. The other companions were less interesting. Up to Water Town, where we ate breakfast, the countryside, as is common near big cities, is full *des maisons de plaisance*—houses for the recreation of the most important citizens and the wealthy merchants from Boston. The houses are well kept and in good taste with large gardens full of fruit trees and everywhere fences or stone walls, and along them acacia—*locust,* and apple trees. Near Ma[r]lborough there was sand. We had an excellent dinner there for half a piaster, served by a lady 6 feet 5 inches tall.

It is difficult for people to ride in one carriage, to eat together and not to get to know each other. With the baked lamb and the jugs of cider began the acquaintanceship with Mr. Butler, owner of the various pieces mentioned above, and a companion of the journey.[2] He was a true American, a respectable man in all, but as most, excessively boastful as to his country, thoroughly convinced that the Americans [38] are the most enlightened and strongest people in the world, that all of France with its Bonoparte, that even the power of hell could not overcome her, that he himself would go against a hundred Europeans as if it were a game, etc. If this boastfulness is amusing, the internal conviction which is found in the heart and the mouth of practically every American that he is happy, is worthy of envy and rarely found elsewhere. *"We are a happy people, we laeve confortably";* these are their words, words of avowal which a traveler in Europe will hear in I know not what country.

To write in detail of the country extending from Boston to Albany, the towns, the local situation, the appearance, etc., would be to repeat oneself constantly. The whole extent of these 177 miles of nature's wild and beautiful domain can be framed in one picture. As far as the eye can see, the vast horizon is surrounded completely by high mountains covered without a gap by dark and thick forests. Hardly does the traveler scramble up these mountains than he sees a similar horizon and just at his feet an extensive and steep valley. In it, between jagged rocks winds a stream and near it a score of houses which they call a town. Further on a cultivated field with *maïs,* rye, flax, oats, an orchard with a few hundred apple trees, a house of pine boards, painted in red or white; this is a *farm* or homestead.

In the town practically every house is a shop and in it are every possible variety of goods of basic need. To the European it is all crazily mixed together, woolen and cotton goods, rum, whisky, mirrors, groceries, iron utensils, ribbons and, near a dried fish often may hang a watch, etc. These shops or storehouses are not only in towns, but are often in villages or alone in a field or on the top of a mountain. One must not conclude [39] that everyone of these shopkeepers is only a tradesman, with a prejudice against farming, and living a lazy life. Such a tradesman has, beside his shop a farm and garden, and besides this he is a wagoner, that is drives a public *diligence* or carries on some sort of trade. The desire for profit, the need for bringing up, feeding, and settling a large family requires that every means, all sorts of business and labor must be used to amass some property.

In separate farms spread out over a vast terrain where only farmers live, while the man works in the fields, the women are engaged in spinning and weaving. In every home the spinning wheel turns incessantly. *Home spoon,* or domestic spinning, covers the husband, the wife and children. Taverns occur practically as frequently as shops. A traveling American stops in front of nearly every one, if not for punch, at least for water with whisky. Every parish has a house set aside for a school. In the evening many children run in droves from the elementary schools. Boys and girls (this one does not see elsewhere in America) take off their caps or curtsy deeply before a passer-by. The inhabitants of New England are all from one race and are not intermixed with the Dutch, Germans and Jews. They keep the former habits of their ancestors.

When we consider the time period since Europeans came to these parts, the country appears well inhabited, but in proportion to its extent, the number is small and the region only sparsely populated. One of the principal reasons for this is the vast expanse westwards of the vacant but excellent land which tempts the restless spirit of the inhabitants to transport themselves there. To the American farmer, the Geneze [Genesee] near Lake Ontario, Kentucky, Ten[n]essee, in a word the whole Western Territory is the promised land, perhaps because of its actual value, or because it has been extolled by writers and travelers. Everyone yearns for this land, farmers send half of their sons so far away that here, parts of a family may live 600-800 even up to a thousand miles from each other, and the one may never hear anything of the other. This country is similar to chess at the end [40] of play, where on a vast chess board one can see here and there scattered pieces. And it is for this reason that in Massachusetts, the oldest of the states of the U.S., half the countryside is covered with forests.

In the midst of them are fertile valleys, cultivated and settled. In such a valley lies the city of Woorcester [Worcester], where we spent our first night. A street 300 feet in width has a greensward in the middle and along the sides trees called *booton tree*,[3] tall and many-branched; through its leaves one can see pretty, well-kept and attractive houses, everywhere signs of happiness and good fortune. In this city lives Isaiah Thomas, who has one of the most famous printing presses in the United States.[4] I was there. Five presses are constantly at work. It reminded me of past times when I was a part-time printer and worked a good part of the mornings in a print shop.[5]

The situation of Woorcester is one of the prettiest. Scarcely 4 miles away the hills open up and a vast, deep, and clear lake fills the expanse; overhanging it are rocks. The azure vault of the sky, the dark, thick pines, reflecting in its crystal, form the most splendid picture.

Not far from there on the very top of the hill Mr. Butler showed me a well-kept house with an excellent garden. In the window sat a figure with something foreign about it. This was a one-time officer, a Hessian, taken prisoner during the revolution. While even now his comrades, hired by one side or another, are shooting and beating each other up, he is settled here and is living in comfort. By the cut of his wig and the pout on his lips one could see he was a German.

The next day, the 2nd of August, amidst a dense fog which hung in streamers about the tops of the rocks surrounding Woorcester, the whole of our company got into the *Stage*. The first town which we noticed was Leicester. There was a factory for making wire brushes for combing wool.[6] In a country where the whole farming population makes its own clothes such manufacture is necessary. Two such brushes cost a dollar. Breakfast in Spencer. We rode by the house [41] of Mr. Swan, once not at all wealthy, today one of the richest merchants in Boston. Public opinion ascribes the sudden increase of riches by Mr. Swan to one of the most terrible periods of the French Revolution. It is known that at this time Robespierre was in complete control of everything. It is also known that when he was beheaded, he did not leave the smallest estate: but what is not known is that this cunning and circumspect tyrant, not forgetting the future, hid the diamonds, money, the most expensive furniture both of the king and of the executed nobility, and gave it to be hidden to Mr. Swan, who was in Paris at that time. Robespierre has gone, but the treasure secretly given remained with Mr. Swan.[7]

Further on there is the small and pretty town of Brookfield. The road to it was somewhat better. Two miles further on there was again a score of houses which they again call Brookfield. In America there are, often scattered on an expanse of ten or twelve miles, groups of houses all carrying one name as if they were children of one parent. Here the road goes only through rocks, cliffs and wild forests. Tired of sitting in the carriage we walked on foot gathering blackberries in the forest. We had dinner in Belshier Ton [Belchertown]. Here as along the whole road from Boston we saw women engaged in making cheese. Cheese, milk, butter, potatoes and boiled or baked corn is the principal food of the farmer. They eat very little meat; it is no wonder that they are strong and in good health.

After dinner we shook ourselves up again over the rocks and cliffs as far as the banks of the Conneticut river. After crossing this river by ferry we rode into the most fertile and the loveliest valley in all the world. There were hay meadows [8] and as far as the eye could see, fields, gardens, everything cultivated, everything pleasing to the eye; the earth is so fertile that weeds grow up like small trees. This fertility is the result of the flooding of the Connecticut river, which every spring overflows its banks and covers with floodwaters several miles of the countryside. During two or three weeks the waters seep into the ground and leave behind them a mud which enriches and fertilizes all these fields. On the marshes were immense piles of logs which had floated [42] down from Vermont and had arrived during the spring floods. The banks of the Connecticut river from the Canadian border down to the sea consist of the loveliest meadows and the best tillage. On them fatten numberless herds of cattle which feed all the islands of the Antilles and Madeira, etc., and are one of the richest sources of trade for the Americans. The whole river is navigable for rafts carrying up to 156 barrels. A canal has just been finished to avoid the rapids.⁹ In this abundant valley a mile from the river lies the town of North Hampton [Northampton], which in its situation and beauty exceeds even that of Worcester. The carriage stopped before the house of Mr. and Mrs. Butler, companions of my journey. They jumped out and went into the house together and at the same time the door closed behind them. Two days of acquaintanceship and conversation, sitting beside each other in the carriage, spending the nights together, dining together did not earn for me the words, "Come into the house." Such is the hospitality here, which is so much praised.

I stopped at the inn just as the dandies were returning with their ladies from an excursion in their cabriolets. According to custom as soon as they spotted the post chaise and the travelers, they began to gather in the hope of getting some news. My foreign appearance in itself raised not a little their inborn curiosity; they began to stroll about and to loiter near to me. One could see that they were teeming with a thousand questions but I, exhausted by the rocky journey and upset finally by the impoliteness of the Butlers, had such a ruffled mien that though they hovered about a great deal, none of them dared to engage me in conversation.

The next day I rode out of Northampton. Here begins the *Turnpike* or a highway that is somewhat leveled and cleaned of rocks. The countryside is, if possible, even more mountainous. In Chesterfield two ladies joined us, going on a fishing party. Their gentlemen friends in small *Sulky*[s] were going along by the side of the *Stage*, their eyes always turned to their beauties. On coming to the top of one of the highest mountains I, though used to similar situations, was struck by the beauty of the view which opened before my eyes. The high [43] cliff, on which we were, fell sharply, and in the abyss was a happy valley with a stream of lively water running loudly amongst the rocks. The road amidst the groves was, as though deliberately, strewn with golden sand, and was covered with many men and women riding on horseback and spreading out along the banks of the river. This was the youth of the nearby villages, to which party my ladies belonged.

There were wild, large and beautiful cliffs on all sides covered with ancient spruces, oaks and firs; here and there over the hills thick smoke poured out from the tree-burning of farmers clearing land. In a word all around gloomy and frightening views, while at the same time in the valley nature herself happy and lovely, men and women in vari-colored clothes, groups of horses hidden under the shade of spreading trees. All this, from the top of a towering cliff painted in diminished perspective, and finally the thought of how this innocent and pastoral pleasure may amuse the young people all day, presented a picture which both the eye and the spirit seized with joy.

Dinner was in Wort[h]ington, a little town of ten houses, the night in Pittsfield, a pretty town and laid in a fertile situation. Forty years ago the countryside from North hampton on was not settled and old-sters remember the time when sentries were posted in Northampton against Indian attacks.

In Pittsfield I met Mr. Coffin,[10] an Englishman and inhabitant of Canada who was traveling from Montreal to Boston. His appearance showed me at once that he was a foreigner, and this thought pre-vailed over my inborn shyness at accosting a stranger. I found him polite, kind and enlightened. The information which he gave me about Canada agreed with that I have received from others about this country. A benevolent government, better than the one that was there before and is now in France. Religion, language, customs are all strictly protected by the rulers. From the new Constitution given Can-ada in 1791 they have *habeas corpus;* they promulgate their own laws, in a word, they have the same privileges as the English. The people are good, polite, hospitable, with gaiety and all the other qualities of the former French without their new defects. Learning and education in the inhabitants is small and not general. In public debates the dep-uties speak in French. Mr. Coffin, [44] one of the legislators, speaks the language so well that he could easily be taken for a Frenchman. He warmly invited me to Canada, but lack of money, shattered health, and finally a curiosity blunted by these troubles and by other circum-stances do not permit me to undertake this new trip. I separated from this polite man with a great desire to meet him again somewhere. Why does fate sometime ordain that I shall live among foolish and suspi-cious people, while permitting me to meet the good and kind ones only in passing.

From Wortington to New Lebanon I had only one companion on my journey. He was a true *farmer,* or husbandman, who a score of years ago, according to the custom, left the family settlement and re-settled on vacant land at the source of the Dellawar in the state of New York. Uncultivated land there costs one and a half dollars an acre, cleared land 5 to 6. In Massachusetts on the contrary unculti-vated land costs 5 to 6 and cultivated 20 to 30, and in the valleys, as for example in North hampton, an *acre* of beautiful meadow is sold for a hundred or more dollars. This husbandman was returning home on horseback but because of his weight, as he was six feet tall, he stopped the horse and let it loose and sat himself in the *Stage.* He was therefore dressed completely in riding clothes, that is he had on jodpurs, shoes and spurs attached to his bare ankles. Very curious, he asked a thousand questions. He took me by the hand and examining it,

"It is evident," he said, "that you Sir have never worked at the plough."

He could not understand how a man could be unoccupied. Happy country, that they should wonder at this!

Saturday. In the morning we stopped at New Lebanon, 147 miles from Boston.

[VII, 1] New Lebanon. Over a region nine to ten miles wide houses lie in scattered groups. All this is called New Lebanon or as it is given in public decrees, Canon.[11] Baths or mineral waters are found on the slopes of the mountains; there are three large sanatoria, a general store and near it, or rather in it, a tub for bathing and a spring for drinking. There must be very little mineral in this water; it is soft, tepid and tasteless. I have not heard of any remarkable cures from the use of these waters. The response of one woman from Philadelphia describes it well. She was returning from these waters.

"How," I asked, "did the waters serve those who came to them this year?"

"Excellently," she answered. "Everybody returned well; since no one went there sick."

As a matter of fact, of course, in large part the people come here simply to enjoy the country air and to avoid the heat of the big cities. The effects of the baths (since it is only these in practice that are used) are laxative and often weakening. There were 15 or 16 persons in them at this time, amongst them two famous merchants from New York, Governis and Constable, Murfy from the island of Bermuda, and some very lovely ladies.[12] Here there is neither a *voxhal* [vauxhall] nor any public place where the company can gather. Everyone sits about in *bo[a]rding houses*. The men play checkers; the ladies both morning and evening either walk or drive out in carriages for little excursions.

I stopped at a distance from the waters at an inn, Mr. Cottel's, right beside the public road. In the afternoon there was a big public event, that is horse races. Mr. Constable had set 10 dollars as the winner's purse. Many of the farmers in the district had gathered for this show in various types of dress and equipage. The horses are of well-bred stock, but they are severely exhausted by farm work and constant running.

The races were not to start until five but already by nine in the morning races were being run over all the roads, not only with the horses picked for the races, but every single farmer's son took part, most often on a [2] pregnant mare with a colt running behind. Perhaps 50 horses were asthmatic today but it is not the local habit to show consideration for the horses. The wagoner, the farmer, everyone who uses horses tries to make, as quickly as possible, as much as he can with them, and cares less about how long they will last.

Finally at three the men and women of fashion came down in cabriolets and coaches from the spring in the hills into the valley where the small contest was to take place. Their dress and the airs they gave themselves stood out in sharp contrast to the dress and rude simplicity of the farmers about them. One could see here that silk, gold, ostentatious carriages and horses are associated with business enterprise, artfulness and often with cheating, while rude dress, coarse cloth and simple boots are the part of hard work and constant sweat.

The race course was a road between the mountains which, though twisting, was quite level. After two hours of getting ready and beating about the bush, two farm hands finally appeared on rather handsome though heavy horses; they were barefoot and dressed in white shirts and pants with red kerchiefs bound about their heads. They raced two times around at full gallop the distance of one eighth of a Polish mile; the horse of *Major* Stuart won the palm of victory both times, that is ten dollars.

I stopped in New Lebanon because of the very interesting sect of people there called *The Shakers*. It is not yet 20 years since the founders of this sect came to America and settled here. The most important group is two miles from New Lebanon. Another colony is near Pittsfield; in all they number up to 400 souls. The tenets of their religion are: wealth in common, chastity, that is celibacy, modesty, silence, obedience to their elders and work. Ceremonies: a service of meditation, wordless singing and dance.[18]

Sunday. In the morning I went to observe their settlement and service. One goes through a forest, mostly [3] of *maplle tree*[s], that is the tree from which sugar is made. The road on both sides is covered with a bush or a large weed called *silkweed*.[14] It is 4 or 5 feet tall, with a big, long oval leaf; its fruit is green and in the shape of a small oblong pear. On opening this up one finds a kind of thread in it which looks like silk. This thread when dried, or rather when ripe, serves instead of down to fill pillows and mattresses.

The Shaker settlement lies in a most abundant valley. It is made up of about 20 large, well-built houses and amidst them is the church, in the same form as the dwellings. On the first floor is a large hall where the service takes place, and on the second floor live the oldest man and the oldest woman. The community is divided into families; each one with a leader or elder, occupies one house, the men separate and the women separate. Some of the men farm; others work in various trades. The whole valley is covered with gardens in which are vegetables, orchards, fields—everything, in the best possible state of cultivation. The harvest from the fields and gardens, the things made by the workshops, everything, goes into a common warehouse from which the whole organization is supplied. These people are famous for their industry, hard work, and honesty; everything which comes from their hands is well made and of excellent quality.

A similar stretch of land with the same number of people on which everyone worked for himself would never yield as much produce nor so many manufactured goods. This is an obvious proof that people, in a common society, working together on a given extent of land will produce more goods than when the same fields are divided into parts and worked separately. But even here those at the top know how to turn to their own advantage the fanaticism, the ignorance [4] and blind obedience in which this flock is kept. Those in the highest rank do not work themselves; that which is the best in food, selected under the guise that it is for the sick, is in fact for them.

I do not know whether the situation of these people is a happy one. It is true they are not in need for any human want. But a life of perpetual silence and gloom, the renunciation of the sweetest relationships with husband, father, brother and sister deprive them of the singular joy that man may taste in this life. The Shakers consider normal people to be more like animals who alternately labor and mate, rather than creatures of reason born to share in common both hardships and happiness. Because this society is an unnatural one there are frequent desertions amongst the young, especially the girls who are wearied by the constant terror and constraint. They return where the promptings of nature urge them, to human society and become wives and mothers. However, fanaticism, necessity, the lure of the new and uncommon lead others to their places, and the society of Shakers maintains its numbers practically constant.

At eleven all these quiet houses opened simultaneously and there came out from one, men in pairs, and from the others similarly women in pairs, and they began in silence and with measured step to go to the house of worship. They entered the church through separate doors. The men were dressed in dark blue tunic coats and long cotton trousers; the women were in old-fashioned white German camisoles and black petticoats with big, flat hats on their heads, under which were fine white caps. Over the whole costume was a gray short coat. The hall of the meeting house is low, completely open in the center with benches on all sides, one half of them occupied by men, the other by women. Taking off [5] their hats, cloaks and outer dress the men and women sat down, remaining in the greatest silence for a good half hour. Suddenly they got up and arranged themselves opposite and facing each other, leaving a space of about four feet between the two *falanx* [phalanx] of men and women. They began to sing on a sad wordless note with their eyes closed, breathing heavily; their bodies shook and trembled. This cantata lasted a good quarter of an hour. After it was finished, the Elder started the lesson, but in such a low and breaking voice that it was hard to hear and understand him. The burden of the lesson was that they are one flock chosen by God, that the whole world is in blindness and error, but that there will come a time when the people will recognize the truth and will then press to join their society.

Amidst this very sermon a carriage drove up and there tumbled into the temple a herd of young blades with their ladies accompanied by the uproar common to this group the world over. The Pastor, scandalized, called out at once:

"Close your eyes, stop up your ears against the waywardness and wickedness of the world."

The diatribe continued for some time, after which the Elder called his little sheep to action. Immediately the two *falanx* arranged themselves in another way, that is each one in ten straight rows. The men were dressed only in waistcoats and shirts, their sleeves above the elbow tied with a black riband. Six men and an equal number of women standing out in front sang a note something like a Moscow dirge, after which the two *falanx* began to dance in the following manner: three steps forward, about turn, the same number of steps back, then ten or twelve in the style of the rigadoon. The sight they present, heads bent down, a sad and graceless appearance, their wild capers and finally the new, wondrous idea from human imagination to please the Almighty with a dance, a form of contre-danse; [6] the onlookers had to force themselves not to laugh.

These ceremonies, however, are much more seemly now in the last few years than they were at the beginning of the formation of the sect. In those times they undressed completely and there was no contre-danse, but they cut up the wildest jumps and capers. During these affairs should the view of the white and beautiful form of the maidens have an obvious effect on any of the men, the Elder with a rod in his hand would come and chastise that frolicsome member until he had humiliated him. This is a completely new chapter in the history of madness and folly in human imagination.[15]

After the dance is finished, there is a break, singing, and then again a little sermon. After twelve everybody put on their coats and left the church as they came, quietly and in order. Because a few settlements are some distance from the church, the women (who to a large extent are old) were brought in wagons. These, like the horses, are well-kept and in the best of condition. Between such a wagon loaded with

"Immediately the two *falanx* arranged themselves in another way, that is each one in ten straight rows."

Shaker females and a wagon loaded with sacks of flour an onlooker would find no difference. In each there is silence and no movement. A family of men, or a corporal's guard with ten or twelve in each group, walked off in two rows, one behind the other and most of them turned to the right amidst the mountains. In large part these belonged to a novitiate, which in this society is similar to a convent of our monks. Thus, a novice must be on trial for a few years before he is allowed to pass into the assembly. These small herds moved with the quiet of horses which, after being ridden hard for a long time to the stage, are unharnessed from the wagon, and worn out, with lowered heads, drag themselves one after another to the stable. Such horses, if flies should descend on them, at least flick them away with their tails so one can see that they are alive, but these Shakers beside whom I walked for nearly a mile, crawled along [7] feeling nothing, affected by nothing, the unbearable heat baked them, flies and mosquitoes together bit them; all in vain, not one of them gave a sign of life. I am sure that floods, downpours, thunder and lightening would not be sufficient to force their pace to increase a little.

Si totus fractus illabatur orbis
Immotos ferient Ruinae [16]

In the inn where I lived, there was a girl who had recently re-nounced this society. With sense and great honesty she related many details which were substantiated by others worthy of trust. The women work no less than the men. The men work in the fields or at the benches, at various trades; the women are occupied cooking food, making pancakes and cakes, weaving and above all with ceaseless laundry. Cleanliness is one of the tenets of this society. In the temple when they disrobe for the service, that is for dancing the contre-danse, one cannot look enough at the fineness and whiteness of their linen.

If in Europe, in spite of circumstances tending to change every-thing, orders of monks and nuns are destined to remain, would it not be a hundred times more useful if they had at least the arrangement that the society of Shakers have; that is, the nuns and monks accord-ing to their sex and strength would work together towards providing for both societies. It seems to me that it would even be a step towards improvement if they were permitted to have intercourse with each other and to have children. These, according to the writings of Plato, need not belong to the parents but to society in general, each one be-ing brought up according to his inclination. Thus the number of use-ful citizens of a nation could be substantially increased.

[8] Throughout the three days of my stay here my thoughts have been overwhelmingly heavy and sad. One could not ascribe it to ex-cessive food, for this has been sparse and light; nor to the air, for it is considered one of the healthiest in America. To what then? The need for society, my loneliness and abandonment. My situation, born of the most savage mistrust and ingratitude, unsweetened by friendship and confidence, not even alleviated either by companionship or by some interest which would actively engage the mind, weighed heavily and ceaselessly on my heart. On top of this, here is a place pressed in be-tween mountains, steep uphill and tiring excursions, without the sight of water, without gay meadows and fields. The people at home, though they are sensible and honest, are very simple. This convinced me that in this isolated country, cut off, without society which in some way

could recall Europe, in such a place I say, it would not be at all cheering to bury oneself and to live.

The 7th of August. In the morning I rode out on a *Stage* returning to Albany. The country is a little less mountainous and the road had a hard surface. In a few places the land was newly cultivated and what is more, one could see on it the most beautiful wood for construction, or for the most splendid masts, partly scorched, some half-burnt. The waste of such trees in such large numbers may be excused perhaps because of the lack of labor for removing, and transporting them by river.

The houses in this section are poorer than elsewhere, almost every one of them is a tavern. It was here, for the first time, that I saw a barn roofed with straw. The inhabitants for the most part are Dutch. Five miles from Albany we stopped to rest the horses at an inn. Under the portico sat a woman, a huge shapeless mass of flesh with a clay pipe in her mouth, putting out clouds of smoke. She was a Dutch woman melting from the heat and overflowing with good fortune. We finally stopped on the shore of the Hudson River where a ferry carried us to Albany on the other side.

Albany. The river here is clean, wide, and in a few [9] places shallow. The city of Albany is supposed to be one of the oldest in these parts. In 1620 the Dutch, bypassing the beautiful situation of New York, came to settle here. It remained *ni fallor* under their rule until 1664, at which time it passed under the English scepter and so remained up to the Revolution. The city is quite large, counting up to 8,000 inhabitants. It is all made from stone; the streets are regular, straight and paved. The houses in large part are in the old Dutch style, built high and with a stepped gable. The Dutch language and customs are more and more snuffed out and disappearing. The common people and the older inhabitants still speak Dutch, but the young people are brought up completely in the English tongue. What is more, even in the church, called the *Dutch Church*, the service and sermons are in English and the service is held in the old tongue scarcely twice a year.[17] It is in this way that peoples are transformed and are lost. This for Poland is a sad sign. Apart from the churches, the public buildings are: the City Hall, where the legislature meets, the Court House, Treasury and jail. Just before my arrival a public inn was completed; it also serves as an Exchange.[18]

This is one of the most excellent inns in America. Although expensive, a foreigner finds there not only comfort but also company. Downstairs the entrance hall where the merchants and travelers gather is big and there are five or six different newspapers and, on the table, the American edition of Dobson's Encyclopaedia.[19] This is a splendid idea and it should be copied in similar houses everywhere. It relieves the traveler from carrying a library with him, and whatever his class the visitor will find in this work interesting articles and can use his spare time to advantage. Because, just at this time, the legislature of the State of New York was meeting and many people were going to the waters in Lebanon and Bollstown [Ballston] [10] the house was tremendously full. I noticed that for one person reading the Encyclopaedia, two or three were playing checkers.

Albany is most favorably placed for trade. Sloops or small boats up to 80 *tons*–400 barrels, come and go from here safely in all seasons of the year. The hinterland is tremendous and fertile; it is rapidly being settled. The transport from the north, from Vermont and Canada, and from the west as far as Lake Ontario is by water, the former by the Hudson River, the latter by the Mohawk. This shipping is important today and soon, when the canals are finished, and with a greater population, it will increase immeasurably. To the north a canal has been begun which will join the Hudson River with the lakes S[aint] George and Champlain and further on will join the St. John's River. This canal has not yet been finished. The products from the west are brought by the Mohawk River. This river is much smaller than the Hudson and in many places is obstructed with rapids. To avoid these, three canals have been started. The first, from Fort Stanwix [20] joins this river [Mohawk] with Wood Creek, through it with Oswego [Oneida] Lake and then on to the huge Lake Ontario. Oswego [Oneida] Lake, Seneka [Seneca] Lake and Seneka River are also joined. This canal has been finished, as has the one at Little Falls; another canal to avoid the rapids called German Flats is in construction.[21]

Boats traveling along the Mohawk River carry only eight to ten barrels. They are brought to Schenechaty [Schenectady], whence they are carried the 16 miles by land to Albany. Not far from Lake Seneka is a lake called Salt, which provides an important amount of salt; this is prepared in kettles.[22] The abundant country called the Genese is becoming inhabited with immeasurable speed; the river of this name carries the region's produce to the Ontario and there through the Mohawk to Albany. Albany is the general center where all the streams carrying produce from the most distant parts come together. In the winter when the ice stops navigation, [11] sleighs take the place of ships; the movement never ceases.[23] 200 ships out of this town journey incessantly to and from New York. Today, however, here even as elsewhere one can hear the common complaint that trade is slack; that is that grain prices are dropping; everybody repeats one thing: *"The business is dull."*

The 10th of August the Assembly, or the Legislature of the State of New York, called in special session by the Governor, met.²⁴ The bearing of the representatives was imposing and appropriate; some of the young ones were dressed elegantly, most were dressed simply but neatly without powder; in some hands one could see evidence of farm work. The *Clerk* called the meeting to order to elect the officers, that is the *Speaker, Clerk, Serge[a]nt at arms* and *Door Keeper*. This was all done by secret ballot; these were placed in a hat. And here as elsewhere I saw gentlemen distributing ballots already filled out, and, what is more, I saw many who took them and voted them. After the election a *Message* was sent to *His Excellency* the Governor and the Senate with the information that the House was ready to proceed to business.

In half an hour an old carriage with a pair of horses arrived. In it was a spare figure with a wig. This was John Jay, the same John Jay who negotiated the last treaty with England. At first the Senate, then the *Governor, Leftnant Governor* and Secretary entered the House of Representatives. Everyone rose and the *governor* opened the session with a speech inspiring the members to the defense of the integrity and independence of the state, against the violence and iniquity of France. The defense of the port of New York, the need for an arsenal and for improvement in the state of the militia; these were enjoined the most. When he had finished, he gave one copy of his speech to the *Leftnant* Governor as the President of the Senate, another to the Speaker. In a word the whole ceremony was as in Congress.

After the departure of the Governor his speech was read once more and a *Comité* of three people was appointed to compose a reply. Amongst them was Mr. Provost,²⁵ past secretary to the famous Munroe [12] in Paris, a man between 25 and 30 years old, completely enraptured by the luxuries, fashions and the bliss of Parisian life; these charms have spread out his delusions over all so that he loves the government, the politics of the Directors, both the governmental councils equally as the opera, the *boul[e]vard* and the "misses" in the Palais Royal. He said to me these remarkable words: *"Le vice," dit-il, "est plus aimable en France, que la vertu ici."* Nevertheless, with such sentiments Prévost is counted as one of the most determined republicans, since today republicanism does not require honor or principles; it is enough blindly to love and to imitate the bad and the good in France. Considering the transports of Prévost and others who return from Paris, I am convinced that whenever peace returns and the young people from various countries in Europe and even from here begin to visit and to live in Paris, then the pleasing and gay character of the French, the charms of their women, the magic of the theaters and spectacles, the pomp and show, the magnanimity and sometimes even the touching aspect of a public national celebration, or finally, if not the essence, then at least the appearance of liberty; all these, more than all the dissertations of T[h]omas Paine and others, will join together the proselytes to, and the worshippers of, the French system.

I went to dinner at old General Schuyler's, father of Mrs. Church.[26] The house is half a mile beyond the town—large, handsome and comfortable. Evil tongues insist that this palace was built by General Bradstreet and given as a gift to Madame General Schuyler to cheer her during the long absence of her husband who, at that time, lived in England.[27] Schuyler is today more than 60 years old, spare, tall, with a physiognomy full of expression. When he is laid low by gout, and is carried in a chair, he reminds one extraordinarily of the portrait of the elder Lord Chatham.[28] Rich, with an extensive estate, he is one of the most important *matadors* not of the Federalists, but unfortunately of the true aristocrats.

[13] The 11th of August. I hired a horse and rode out 10 miles to the north of Albany to look at the cascades or waterfall at Cohox [Cohoes]. The road was one of the most pleasant that one can see. On the right hand the fertile fields and huge meadows, on the left a continuous natural hedge of powerful oaks and chestnuts around which wild green vines, hops, etc. wind and hang in festoons. Through openings in this hedge one can see the clear and beautiful Hudson River and its banks on the other side rising in hills covered with groves of trees and houses. In spite of the tremendous heat, the greenness of the trees and the meadows is everywhere of the freshest and liveliest. Nowhere can one see trees with seared and yellow leaves, as is frequent in Italy and in other European countries even less hot. The cause of this freshness is the frequent rain, almost downpours, and each morning a most abundant dew.

Six miles from Albany on the other side of the Hudson lies the new and pretty town of Troy.

> *Ce n'est pas cette Ville*
> *Si superbe en remparts, en héros si fertille* [29]

Instead of powerful walls, high towers and brass gates, one can see along the banks warehouses and granaries, and spruce houses surrounded by gardens. This city, only recently built, is quite commercial. In the spring, boats equal in size to those in Albany may enter and leave it. In the summer when the water is more shallow, the use of smaller boats is necessary. What the reason was for giving the little town the proud name of Troy is not known. In the state of Vermont there is a village of a few houses which is called Rome and there too amidst sandy and wild pine forests is another village called Carthage.[30] The Americans, convinced that in their country will be reincarnate all the powerful empires of antiquity, give to their villages now, ahead of time, the names of the famous capitals.

A mile [14] beyond Troy the Mohawk River falls into the Hudson. It is not very wide and the channel is quite shallow. The heat has not only dried up wells, springs and streams, but it has dried up the rivers in part. In many places the Mohawk trills in a thin thread on a black and rocky bottom.

Cohox. From a half a mile away one can hear the cascade; the road covered on all sides with forests hides it completely until suddenly from near by the whole view appears. The rock, in one straight line, is 100 ells long and in the shape of a mill dam it divides the water across from bank to bank. The water first breaks against the rocks scattered here and there on top, as it were, of the rampart; then it forms either in streams or around the rocks a glassy dome before it plunges from a height of 30 feet into the channel. This was not the moment to see the fall in all its beauty. The dry spell had lowered the body of water; the black rocks were stripped of all their growth; the channel itself was made up of sharp and protruding rocks, and only here and there trickled a thread of water: this gave the place a wild and terrible appearance. But in the spring when the river is brimming with melting snow and ice, it forces the current along in haste; then this cascade has a most beautiful appearance. At that time it carries a host of large blocks of ice, trunks with their roots, whole trees and throws them into the abyss with a resounding noise.

I would have arranged to stop here to rest and to feed myself and the horse but in vain; it has not occurred to anyone to build on this rare and beautiful place, not so much *une maison de plaisance* but not even a tavern. The last would be very profitable to anyone owning it, for not only travelers but even citizens of Albany would drive up for entertainment [15] and to feast their eyes on this beautiful view. What would our ladies in Poland not give for a place like this, and what is more, what miracles would not grow from their hands.

I returned baked and exhausted from this journey on horseback, and after having changed my clothes, had to set out on foot on another that is a good mile beyond the town to the house of the Vice-Governor of the State, Mr. Van Ranssellaer, where I was invited to dinner. Van Ranssellaer, *leftnant governor* or as they still say in Dutch a *Patroon,* is one of the richest citizens not only in the State of New York, but even in the whole U.S.[31] His family came with the earliest emigrants from Holland and took up a huge tract of land around Albany and further to the north beyond the Hudson.

With time, the increase in population and the number of immigrants from Europe the Ransselaers began to rent, or rather to lease, their land; from this their wealth and political influence, in elections, grew ever greater. The number of the leaseholders occupying their land is up to [blank]. The way the lease is arranged is in the following manner. The farmer takes land in contract for three generations, for himself, his son and grandson. Taking say, 100 acres of land he pays down once and for all 400 pounds or a hundred dollars, and then each year 25 *Bushel* of wheat. The leaseholder has the right to sell his leasehold to another, but he must pay 10 per cent of the selling price to the owner. Besides this, in some places there are rents of chickens, etc. At the conclusion of the tenancy through the third generation, the farm and land return to the owner and then is let out for the same length of time either with a new contract to the same family or to another. In this way there is a reciprocal gain. [16] The farmer is certain that the land will remain not only throughout his life, but his son's and grandson's; he builds a house, sets out an orchard, clears and cultivates his land as best he can. The owner, without toil, trouble and much ado, has a clear and certain, though not large, income and above this, after a few score years, he obtains from land once uncleared a farm with completed buildings, orchards and duly cultivated fields. Now for a much higher price he leases it again.

Nihil est ab omni parte beatum.[32] From these private mutual advantages stems a public ill: domination, the influence of the landlord and the dependence of the renters, or as they are called here, *Tenants.* The landlord, through a promise of the lengthening of the lease, by forgiving a few *Bushel* of wheat, and by other small favors, is the master of the will and actions of his tenants. Possessing thousands upon thousands of them he can tilt the scale of the elections in whichever direction he wishes. In the County of Albany and in a few others nearby no one can be a representative in Congress or in the State Assembly except him whom Mr. Van Ransselear chooses. Related to another wealthy family, that of General Schuyler, his influence in the state of New York is enormous. The word *Patroun* is pronounced by everyone with deference and a certain fear. He holds here the place held by the Radziwiłłs in Lithuania. The Czartoryski family, that is the Livingstons, is large, wealthy, and greatly honored. Today it is in

the opposition and can not always succeed in opposing the Ransselaers.

And so in spite of the best and most intelligent Constitution [17]
with principles of freedom and equality, here as elsewhere there is
established by the force of law, by habit and by public opinion the
dominating and the dominated, in a word the lords and the tenant
squirearchy. Everywhere there is one theme, everywhere wealth,
power and higher education rule over poverty, or rather over need
and ignorance, and will always have the ascendancy. I do not know
in what way to prevent this. Without perturbing the holy laws of property no law can prevent a citizen from having large holdings and
wealth or from doing with them what he will. Further, without removing from them every prerogative of citizenship, thousands upon thousands of the inhabitants cannot be denied the right to vote. There is
one circumstance which, it seems to me, promises that this unseemly
state of affairs will diminish rather than grow. There is here no primo-
geniture. The sons and daughters of a large family divide the estate
equally among themselves. With this division, and the smaller estates
resulting from it, their influence, both financial and political, will also
become smaller.

The house of the Patroon surpasses, as do his wealth and influence,
the concept of equality. It is rather a palace; apartments, servants and
equipages elsewhere may be excellent and well kept, here by comparison they seem princely. He for his part, though much richer in
silver and land than in wit, and she for her part, the sister of Mrs.
Church and the daughter of General Schuyler, is endowed by nature
with a good share of liveliness and wit. Her prejudice and rancor
against the French cannot be expressed. Everything evil and unjust,
which has happened, or now happens on this earth, she ascribes to
these people. [18] She is firmly convinced, even to this moment, that
the French divided Poland and not the Muscovites and the Germans.

We had a good dinner, plenty of wine and a well-chosen company,
but fire does not melt wax faster than the heat of these days dissolves
our flesh. It seems to me that the true story of the transformation of
the nymph Salmacis [33] into a spring of water is no more than an account of an occasion in ancient times when a young beauty, on such a
day of heat as we now have, by abundant perspiration and transpira-
tion ultimately dissolved into water.

In the evening we returned by carriage to General Schuyler's house
and from there went home.

The 12th of August. The morning was cooler. Ten Indians from the
Mohawk tribe came to the market with brooms, shovels and watering

cans for sale. In the summer, during the season of reaping, or when the fields are harvested, or whenever there is any hard work, it is left to the women, and the Indian men from beyond the shores of the Lakes Ontario, Oneida and Senaka come to the neighborhood of Albany. There they live in small and remote taverns, make brooms and other goods which I have mentioned, and sell them in the town. Towards the autumn, after buying woolen blankets, which are their only clothing, and guns, gun powder, etc., they return for the winter to their settlements. All these tribes through frequent intercourse and propinquity with the whites have become somewhat civilized. Arable land which is indolently and poorly farmed is common, while the pastures are divided into individual holdings on which each one grazes his own herd. [19] The houses are unusually poor and dirty.

I came near them. I could not look except with sadness at these, the lawful and true lords of this domain, brought low to the necessity of making brooms and providing their aggressors with them. The color of their face and skin was much darker than the complexion of *Little Turtel*, the Miami Chief whom I saw in Philadelphia; some of them were as black as mulattos. Their bodies are slender and long, their facial features are flat and square with little hair on the jaw. The hair is black, straight, and hangs straight down. In facial appearance there is a great likeness to the Tartars and Kalmucks; it would support the view that America was inhabited through the northern shores of Asia and Kamchatka. Their clothes: cloth leggings, no breeches only an apron over their genitals, on their back a woolen blanket with an old hat. The women are all wound up in a blanket like a mummy.

Two or three *Stages* go every day to Schenaktady from Albany. There is such a crowd of travelers on this road that I could not find a place in any carriage. I had to hire a horse and to make this 16 mile trip *solo*. This whole road is empty and gloomy—endless sand, endless pine forests without the least variety to gladden the eye. The total cultivation and settlement consisted of two or three fields of Indian corn with every five miles a tavern for travelers. Except for a few *Stage* filled with people I did not see any other travelers, nor carts, nor loaded wagons, which one would expect to meet on such a well-trodden highway, [20] on such a road along which are carried all the products from the distant western regions. A downpour forced me to seek shelter in a tavern kept by a Dutch family. The owner, spare and vigorous, entered into conversation with me and was vastly pleased that I had been in Holland, the fatherland of his ancestors. He took out a silver cup of old workmanship.

"This cup," he told me, "is already two hundred years old and it was more than a hundred years old when my grandfather brought it to this country. It occupies a place of honor; it reminds us of our fatherland and our ancestors." I took it in my hand and was moved to tears.

"O Fatherland," I reflected, "how sweet thy memory is to the heart of men; it passes in the blood from generation to generation; neither time nor change of place can efface it."

I was surprised when the old man told me he was 80. I would not have taken him for more than 50.

"You are going, Your Honor," he told me, "through a wild and unfertile country. This is wild Arabia, but if you go beyond Skenacktady, you will find fortunate Arabia.[34] Nothing can equal the fertility of that country."

He then began to talk about times past and the wars in which he himself took part, especially those with the Indians. For 30 years hordes of these Indians often attacked the neighborhood of Albany, spreading the characteristic terror of these wild people. Once they swooped down on this old man's house and after killing two grown-up children, they carried off a four-year-old girl. Seeing this, the father and two friends gave chase and caught up with them just at that moment when one of the Indians tore off the girl's scalp with his teeth and threw her half-dead on the ground. The unhappy father carried her to the house. There was no surgeon and they neither knew [21] nor understood how the exposed brain might be covered with a silver plate. The handiest and cheapest thing to do, appeared to be to take a piece of flannel and to cover the head of the girl. However difficult it is to believe, the child has grown up and still lives carrying a piece of flannel on her exposed brain.

Two or three miles from Schenactady I met young Mr. Jones, a nephew of Mrs. Montgomery, the widow of the famous General Montgomery who was lost fighting heroically at Quebeck.[35] After tying my horse to the shaft I sat with him in the cabriolet. We arrived at Schoenektady amidst the greatest flood and downpour.

Schoenektady. The city is situated in a flat valley, and in population and extent it is almost the equal of Albany. The Mohawk river is about 100 ells wide here and flows everywhere through extensive and green meadows. The banks are covered with *canoes* or large boats, each of which can carry 8 barrels of flour. With such boats flour and other products, from Fort Stanwix, Ontario, Genessee, Seneka and from a huge number of new settlements towards the west, go down to Schenektady, the terminus of navigation on the river. Then it is carried by cart for 16 miles to Albany. The Legislature of New York is consider-

ing building a highway along this stretch. This undertaking is very
necessary in such a difficult and sandy part, and certainly it will be
finished sooner than will the building of a canal to avoid the rapids
at Cohox.

There were two rather large boats standing in port, with coverings
like canopies, arranged especially for carrying travelers to Niagara and
to other far-western places. All I would have needed to do was to sit
in one, in order to get to Fort Schuyler or [22] Stanwix, and from
there to the plains of the Genessee, famous for their fertility, from
there to the Six Nations of the savage Indians, further still to Lake
Ontario and finally to one of the most beautiful wonders of the world,
that is the falls of Niagara. This journey together with its promise of
a wide and changing variety of always interesting views tempted me
strongly; however the apprehension of provoking in the present circumstances the suspicions of the government, the lack of a companion
for the trip, a lack of money, the temptations of curiosity suppressed
by so many cares, the constant waiting every day for letters from
Europe which might decide my fate;—all this kept me from the undertaking. For a long time I looked out over the peaceful currents of the
Mohawk and the gloomy and endless meadows through which it
passes, then I went away leaving it happy in its riches and position,
leaving behind the luxury of visiting these wonders and even more
the luxury, I say (for which almost all distant journeys are undertaken) of telling later that I had been so far and had seen things
which no one or only a few have ever seen.

I went through all the town with Mr. Jones. A few streets are paved
and supposedly illuminated. The stables, which will accommodate up
to a hundred horses, both for hauling wares to Albany and for the
harness on the *Stages*, which, as I have mentioned, go at least three
times a day through the town. The inns were filled with travelers. Of
these some were going for the waters at Bollston, near famous Saratoga, for reasons of health, others for entertainment, finally some were
pushing on to settlements in the Genese, Ontario, etc. After dinner,
Mr. Jones got into his splendid and comfortable cabriolet and I onto
my little roan, and we set off on the road, he to Bollston and I back
to Albany.

[23] All alone on my horse in the midst of the wild and unbroken
monotony of the forest my thoughts wandered with sad memories,
when the heavens covered with a black cloud, began to shudder with
tremendous thunder and to blaze forth ceaselessly with lightning.
This scene broke through my reverie. I had to ride, however, for five
miles through the storm before I found shelter in an isolated inn.

The thunder did not last very long; the evening was cool and pleasant.

A few miles from Albany I began to meet Indians returning from the town. The sale of brooms must have been good since the ladies and gentlemen were carrying on their backs packs of the blankets they had bought; they had gotten roundly drunk with rum and grog. Staggering to the right and to the left they were shouting gaily and also singing lively compliments to their wives and sweethearts in the most beautiful Indian couplets. Every half mile I met a lost group, asking one for the other. I understood that I was not far from our Praga—our peasants from Mazowsze returning from the market from Mother Warsenga staggered about and shouted so.[36]

On Sunday, the 12th of August, I booked a place on the *Sloop* Amelia from Troy, C[a]pt. Kunnenicut. This was a boat of 40 to 50 tons with a cabin and beds for travelers, though from top to bottom it was so loaded with boards that one could only squeeze through to and from the cabin. The companions of my journey were a tailor with his wife and child, one *gentelman* from the town of [Fort] Johnson on the Mohawk, another from Vermont not far from the Canadian border. *Item* three *fermiers*, [24] *item* a thousand boards. From the latter passengers the captain stood to gain more than from all of us, for he was to get a shilling per board in New York, which would bring 825 dollars. I have said before that at least 200 such boats sail constantly between Albany and New York. Let us suppose that each boat makes 20 such journeys back and forth. One can value each journey, or the cargo on the boat, at 800 dollars. Thus it will appear that each year between these two towns goods are bought and sold for 3,200,000 dollars. This valuation is probably too small.

The *Tide*, that is the flow of water, rather than the wind slowly raised us from the bank. Two or three miles out from the city we passed over shallows, where the captain employed the greatest caution in order to avoid running aground on the sand. This care was certainly justified there, as we saw two boats in just such a state that is, run aground on the sand and waiting for high tide to float them off. The captain said that if two old boats were to be sunk at the sides of the waterway or the channel of the river, the volume of the water would be raised here and ships could pass through with the greatest safety at all seasons of the year.

After a few hours *The Taide* had gone out; we weighed anchor. The tide comes in for about six hours and ebbs for six hours with a quarter to a half an hour advance in time. When the tide is rising, boats can sail even without a wind, and if the wind is favorable, they can sail even against the tide. We were not so fortunate; there was a complete calm; we were forced therefore to [25] cast anchor, for otherwise the rising water would have carried us back to Albany.

During this time of inaction we clambered back and forth about the boards. The *Gentelmen* began a conversation. One of them was in the army during the time of the Revolution; he, *qua* a veteran soldier, needs must be always a talker. Omitting some others of his stories, strange happenings, dangers, etc., I will recount only one of the incidents.

Two American officers from a division assigned to fight the Indians, who at that time had been aroused by the English to war; as I say, two of these officers, separated from their command, were surrounded in the forest by these savage people. After a strong and lively resistance the captain was killed and according to custom they tore off his scalp. The major too was wounded unto death and with his scalp half torn from his head was left for dead beside his dead comrade. The Indians departed. The major, still breathing, raised himself up and placed his bloody head on the body of his comrade and in this position awaited death. By chance this officer had with him his dog, he with plaintive whining and with whimpering appeared to understand and to feel the fate of his master. The dog licked at the steady stream of blood pouring over the face of the dying man. The effect of this licking and of a cool breeze which had begun to blow, so revived the unhappy officer that he, gathering up his last strength, began to speak to the dog and to signal with his hand that he should go for help. The dog would go away three feet, and then return three feet with plaintive whining, as if he were unable to leave his master in this state. The officer doubled his pleas and signs, and the dog finally disappeared and in an hour returned with four soldiers [26] dragging them along by their clothes, now one now the other, showing them the way. The soldiers came, took the officer with them and brought him to camp. There with the aid of the doctors, but even more because of his youth and innate strength, he recovered completely and still lives, a witness to the cruelty of people and to the feelings, initiative and attachment of animals.

At supper the favorite conversation among Americans started up among my companions, the government and politics. It is difficult to convey the good sense with which they talked on this matter, how enlightened they were, with what directness they reasoned concerning the constitutions of their states, their good points and their defects. The happy results of freedom. Its light penetrates into the poorest hut; its rays light up equally the rich and poor, while at the same time despotism with its depressing shadow overcasts, overwhelms, and depresses the mind and spirit of man.

The 13th of August. The day was fair and hot without any wind at all. The tide carried us slowly for six hours; the next six we again had to ride at anchor. The banks of the Hudson on both sides rise up into mountains covered with firs, *Spruce, hemlok* (all these trees of the pine family). Amidst these were well-kept homesteads and cultivated fields; along the flat banks of the river herds were grazing, or also seeking coolness were standing in the water up to their nostrils. On the river were boats with unfurled sails, either going to New York or returning to Albany; and every two or three minutes the sight of sturgeons two or three feet in length jumping out and again disappearing into the water with a plop, as if a large rock had been thrown in. The quantity of these sturgeons [27] is such that there is enough to feed half the population, but unfortunately this, the rarest and most delicate morsel for Europeans, here arouses distaste and disgust. The citizens of Albany are objects of derision because they eat this fish, and it is because of this that the sturgeon is called *Albany beef*.[37] Giants of 8 to 9 feet are sold for not more than 3 Polish złoty per monster.

Thirty miles beyond Albany on our right we passed the small town of Luneburg.[38] Here our tailor with his wife and child got out of their cabin and went ashore in a boat. This was his first appearance; he had sat throughout the whole time on his nest and did not let his eye leave his wife. This jealous supervision (so little necessary in this country where flirtation with a married woman is practically an unknown crime) astonished all the travelers not a little. While we were talking of this, the captain spoke up to say that jealousy is an inbred passion with tailors. Whence this arises, I do not know, he added, whether the constant sedentary life increases in them a quantity of bile and the bile breeds a gloomy and jealous humor, or whether it is owing to the kind of work he does, whereby sewing pantaloons for the most part, the sight of the flies reminds him how many instruments there are in the world conspiring against a maiden's honor. This humorous explanation of the jealousy of tailors appeared to everyone to be most convincing and satisfactory.

Hudson. After dinner we dropped anchor not far from the town of Hudson. The size, the warehouses and the shops of this place gave it a very showy appearance. The growth of this town is practically miraculous. In 1783, immediately after the Revolution, a few merchants from Rhode Island, wearied by the disorder, [28] controversy, and slothfulness which seemed at this time to vex the inhabitants, gathered together 1,200,000 dollars in capital, moved here and created the town of Hudson. Their inexhaustible activity, the enormous advantages and pledges given to newcomers, a period of time most advantageous for trade, the advantage (which Albany higher up on the river does not have) of sending boats of 300 tons to the sea; everything contributed to its rapid growth so that there were already 200 houses in it after the first two years. The growth continued for a few years, but today current opinion has it that the town is not growing but has started to decline. After shooting up like a mushroom it will last only as long. The principal reason for this is that Hudson does not, unlike Albany, have behind it an extensive hinterland both fertile and well-populated. The transportation of products to it is small and is dependent entirely on wheels. These reasons are important. All in all it seems to me that into this sudden denigration enters somewhat the jealousy of the citizens of Albany.[39] A city so well inhabited and built up and so favorably situated for seaborne trade cannot decline. The decline at the moment of business can be ascribed to general circumstances and to the darkening picture of trade everywhere. Once these conditions cease, industry with its former explosive development will break out again. The past year a ship, fitted out in Hudson for whaling, returned after a 19 month voyage with 1,800 barrels of *sparmaceti* or whale oil.

Not far on the western bank of the river is an even newer little town, Katskill [Catskill]. This, without any help [29] or inducements, settled itself and grows. It has, so they say, a hinterland more fertile and extensive than that of Hudson.

After terrible heat the evening cool was for us an unspeakable luxury. A few new travelers arrived in boats and boarded our ship. We sailed amidst flat islands of rushes and reeds, clouds of numberless birds rose up and hovered over them. The birds were the size and color of swallows.

While we were walking about the boards, dressed only in our shirts and waistcoats, the double-horned moon began to rise and gave my companion an opportunity for conversation about astronomy. They had heard somewhere of the new discoveries of Herschel.[40] One added that when he was in a museum in New York, he saw through the telescope mountains and valleys and that this planet was definitely inhabited. Another added: "*I dare say they rise there fine crops of whaete.*" So here too is proof that everyone sees, not the blemishes on the moon, but each his own favorite object: the priest, the belfry; the priest's housekeeper, pantaloons; Rzewuski,[41] the Marshal's baton and finally the American farmer, wheat.

Clermont.[42] The 14th in the morning on a hill amidst the tops of the rising trees we discovered the roofs of the palace of Chancelor Livingston. I had a letter of introduction to him. Bidding farewell to my companions, I got in a boat and came to the shore. A wild path meandering up the hill led me first to the garden and then to the attractive and well-kept homestead. It was seven in the morning, the whole family was still sleeping, the servants were busy cleaning and sweeping the house. [30] This house, as I have said, belongs to one of the richest and most substantial citizens of the U.S. Therefore, writing about him and about the way of life of his family shows that degree which wealth has attained in this country and how these citizens use this wealth.

The house, or rather a small chateau: one of its wings forms a dining room, another *the drawing room* or room for receiving guests, leading from it is another room for billiards: farther on a library in the *corps du logis*, downstairs three bedrooms for the family, upstairs five similar ones for guests. The floor below ground is for the kitchen and servants' quarters.

Near the house to the south is the English garden with only flowers and rare bushes. Amongst others jasmine, *du Cap de Bonne esperance*, high as an orange tree with dark green leaves and with big white flowers which give off the most agreeable odor.[43] It holds first place. This little garden adjoins and loses itself in the wild promenade which descends to the river. The other end of the house lies alongside a huge meadow. In the middle of it stands a weeping willow with hanging branches. On the right hand an alley of high locusts or acacias leads to a view of the whole course of the Hudson river and across it of the rocks covered with huge and everlasting forests; every morning before the sun begins to warm the clouds, they hang girdling the rocks on the far side, leaving only the highest points uncovered. The alley of acacia trees leads to the house of the Chancelor's mother, which is completely surrounded by the finest fruit trees. In the rear thick forests, meadows, leas and groves continue a long way and are then joined by cultivated fields rented out on lease.

The Livingston family, *origine* Scotland,[44] was one of the first to come to this country and has accumulated huge expanses of land. Later the family increased to such an extent that only the Potockis can be compared to them in the number of their members. [31] All in all because they marry among themselves, their estates are increased rather than broken up. The mother of the Chancelor, heiress to the rich Bigman [Beekman] family [45] brought more than one hundred thousand *Acres* of land to the Livingston estate; a large part of it is not yet settled but every day it increases in value.

In his youth Chancelor Livingston was one of the best and most eloquent lawyers; later because of severe sickness he lost his hearing and today occupies the position of Chancelor. This office, which is very important, is found in only a few states. He himself comprises, what is called here, a *Cort of Equity,* and on moot points, where the law is contrary to equity, he is appealed to. He himself decides not according to the law, but rather according to what is fair and right. From his judgment one can appeal to the Senate, which is the highest tribunal.

The Chancelor has an income of no more than 4 or 5 thousand piasters per year, that is about 45 thousand Polish złotys, mostly from leases. He does no farming apart from haying and fruitgrowing. For servants he has 4 negroes and 4 negresses. The table is excellent, the family well dressed, the library large and well chosen. He has none of the cares and troubles of farming. A well-kept and comfortable house placed in the most beautiful situation in the world, a wife, one would not wish for better, two daughters of whom one, by inclination of heart and the wishes of the family, married a Livingston, the other will do so soon.[46] In a word—an estate, honor, reputation, everything which a man could want, fate has showered down on him. Is he happy? It seems to me he is happy, although not completely so. The passion which torments a man when all [32] others are sated, that passion, I say, Ambition, disturbs his peace, that is the wish for a higher position than he possesses, to be governor of the state; for this he has tried twice, but because he was in the opposition, John Jay, a man of lesser reputation, prevailed.

Though this large and wealthy family are, for so they identify themselves, members of the Republican party, in truth they are simply dissatisfied with the government. The public blames the Chancelor for haughtiness and ambition. In the most zealous fanatics for freedom and amongst those who slandered the Government I often uncovered only ill will and jealousy that they themselves were not ruling. The most attractive conversation for these lovers of republican equality is about the ancient lineage of their family, about the arms of the Livingstons, about the ramifications of the family and the extent of their relationships, etc. They are called not by name but by title, even the women, just as in Poland, the first time I have remarked on this here. The wife of the Chancelor is called *Mrs. Chanceller,* the daughter, *Miss Chanceller,* the mother of the Chancelor, *Mistriss Judge,* exactly as with us.[47]

During the Revolution the English, with a barbarity similar to that of the Muscovites with fire and sword, laid waste this country and destroyed amongst others the houses of the Livingstons. On the place where had been a house burnt by the English, the Chancelor planted a beautiful weeping willow which I have mentioned above. Today the family regrets nothing more than the burnt portraits of their fathers and grandfathers. This weakness, everywhere inseparable from wealth and ancestry, is greater than laws; it is worthy of forgiveness when, to the passion for boasting of an ancient lineage, of an ancestry more distinguished than that of others, there is joined the praiseworthy ambition to surpass others in citizenship and honor. Such certainly is the Livingston family. In Clermont I saw all the domestic virtues, peace in marriage, love between parents and children, humanity and good will towards servants. These are treated more as acquaintances of a lower order than as subjects. They have the same food and practically the same comforts as do their masters. They serve, it seems, rather from enjoyment than from necessity. This humane and considerate treatment of servants is general throughout America, and I cannot see that the ruling class loses by it. With all the scolding, chiding, and even whipping, our lords are neither better served [33] nor are their houses cleaner and better cared for than these here. Under whatever circumstances kindness wins more from a man than force.

Amongst other servants here there was a quite black *Mulatress*. Having secretly had an affair with a white carpenter she had a daughter, not olive in color as one would expect according to nature, but completely white. This occurrence, though not unique, is definitely very rare. This girl and the other black imps, children of the servants, are treated and favored by their master as if they belonged to the family. With the two daughters of the family there is the same calm and kindness. The youngest daughter of the Chancelor is married, the oldest chirping on the nest. They were simply two pairs of lovebirds who will not be separated, and so blinded and deafened by love that they did not see nor hear anything that occurred near them. As far as society was concerned, they considered the house empty. It was necessary to remain alone; going downstairs one was certain that he would interrupt a whisper, or interfere with the fervent kissing of the doves. Busy occupying myself with an excellent library, promenades, the company of Mr. Amery from Boston (who by chance having broken his hand waited here for it to heal), I filled my hours very pleasantly and I would have remained here longer, but how could an abandoned foreigner, known to them only a little, remain long without importunity in a strange house.

Sunday, 19th of August, I rode out with the young Robert Livingston, the husband of the young Miss Chancelor, for 7 miles to visit General Armstrong, an old friend of Kośc[iuszko].[48] During this trip we rode largely through the land of tenants, or leaseholders of the Chancelor. The houses were rather well kept, the fields sown mostly with *mais* and buckwheat and not, so far as I could judge, cultivated to the greatest extent possible. I saw wild plums and cherries. The first, small, round, and dark crimson in color. The others were black like big peas; both fruits [34] were sweet and with a wonderful taste. I saw a curiosity, that is, in one trunk, two separate trees—an oak and growing from its side a chestnut. Probably the fruit of the latter fell into the hollowed-out trunk of the oak, and there rooted and grew and produced a large generation on the soil of another. It is a picture of two friends tightly joined together.

Three miles from General Armstrong's, at a turn in the road, we noticed another well-kept house. On the porch sat a fat object in a blue shirt and with pantaloons of the same color. This was a farmer who, from the position of overseer or manager, has today become the owner of an excellent homestead. Considered the best farmer in the whole neighborhood, he has now passed his cares on to his son, leaving for himself only supervision and rest. He sat, as I have said, on the porch, spread out on a comfortable chair with his eyes glued joyfully on the huge expanse of his corn. With like joy Frederick II looked out on the squadrons of his grenadiers and his cuirassiers gathered at Potsdam. We left him untroubled in this sweet contemplation.

I was glad to meet General Armstrong. His character was truly republican. Because of this intelligence, wit, grace and pleasantness, all combined, he is held in universal esteem. He is, because of the strength and beauty of his style, one of the best writers in this country.[49] His wife, née Livingston, is by her virtue and pleasantness, worthy of her husband.[50] They have four sons whom they themselves are educating with the greatest care. Pressed strongly to spend a few days with him I agreed to come back on the next day.

In the evening I returned with my companion to the home of the Chancelor. We saw again in the same place and in the same position the landlord on his porch always [35] with his eyes glued on his corn. Riding up to the house we met a hayrick; in it were three ladies and one gentleman. These, the sisters of Robert Livingston,[51] my companion, were going to one of their neighbors three miles away. Thus, the richest of families is not ashamed to ride in this way. How evil the day when they should become ashamed!

The next day, the 20th, I left this honorable and hospitable family.

My departure caused as much bustle and delay as is caused by an expedition of the whole homestead; the young people busy-with-love gave orders to amateur servants about the carriage and horse. They, systematically and with the usual phlegm which they show in house cleaning, finally went to the meadow for the horses, then for the cart, then with this cart for hay, and at last came for me. I sat on a chair set out in a hayrick as comfortably as in the best cabriolet. For the last time I rode by the extensive meadows and fields which surround the Chancelor's dwelling.

There is nothing at once more utilitarian and more beautiful than such use of land near the house; the green of these freshly-sown and sprucely-kept meadows gladdens and enlivens the eye; the groves at the side, the fruit trees, the large willows and acacias spread out in clumps interrupt pleasantly the monotony of these extensive meadows. One might say that all this serves only for beauty and decoration; but this very beauty and decoration brings a definite profit, for, as well as fruit, the best hay and clover comes from these meadows. At the same time horses and cattle find the most abundant pasture and give the whole picture a pleasant movement and liveliness. With the same small cost we could have this useful decoration in our country. Instead of a courtyard covered with weeds [36] and rubbish, instead of a woodyard covered with shavings and splinters, why are the houses not surrounded by the green and fertile fields; why are the prettiest parts of the farmlands hidden amidst trees and forest when the owner of the farm needs to hay? Would it not be better to have it all within view, looking out over his flocks grazing. In a word, we could make our farmland more cheerful without losing anything, indeed increasing rather the profits. I rode along the same road which I had ridden along yesterday and again at the turn of the road under the same portico as yesterday I saw the immobile fat-one with his face turned towards the corn. What the great attraction of this grain may be, I do not know, but it seems to me that this free proprietor had forgotten for its sake, rest, food, his whole world, and spends day and night in contemplation of this thing of such beauty.

At two I stopped at General Armstrong's house. The setting of his house, its beauty and the variety of the views surpass, I believe, that of the Chancelor. This place has been only recently occupied by the General. The house, though not showy, is comfortable. There are no crops growing, nor any decorative plantings, but nonetheless the kitchen garden is excellent. The General's time is taken up with household cares, with the education of his children and with study. In this way all the moments are pleasantly filled; they pass quickly by, while,

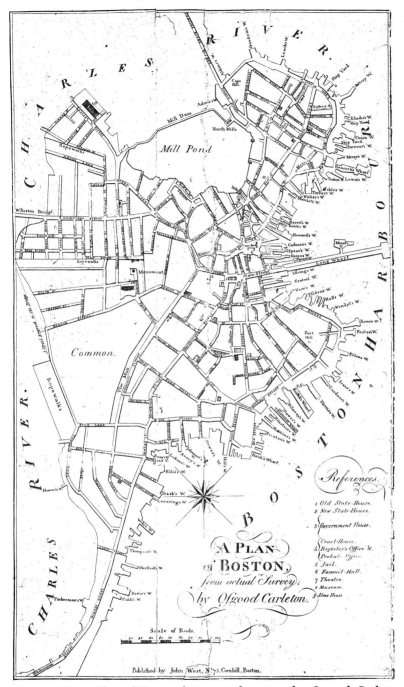

Fig. 59. A New Plan of Boston from actual surveys by Osgood Carleton, 1800. Courtesy of Massachusetts Historical Society.

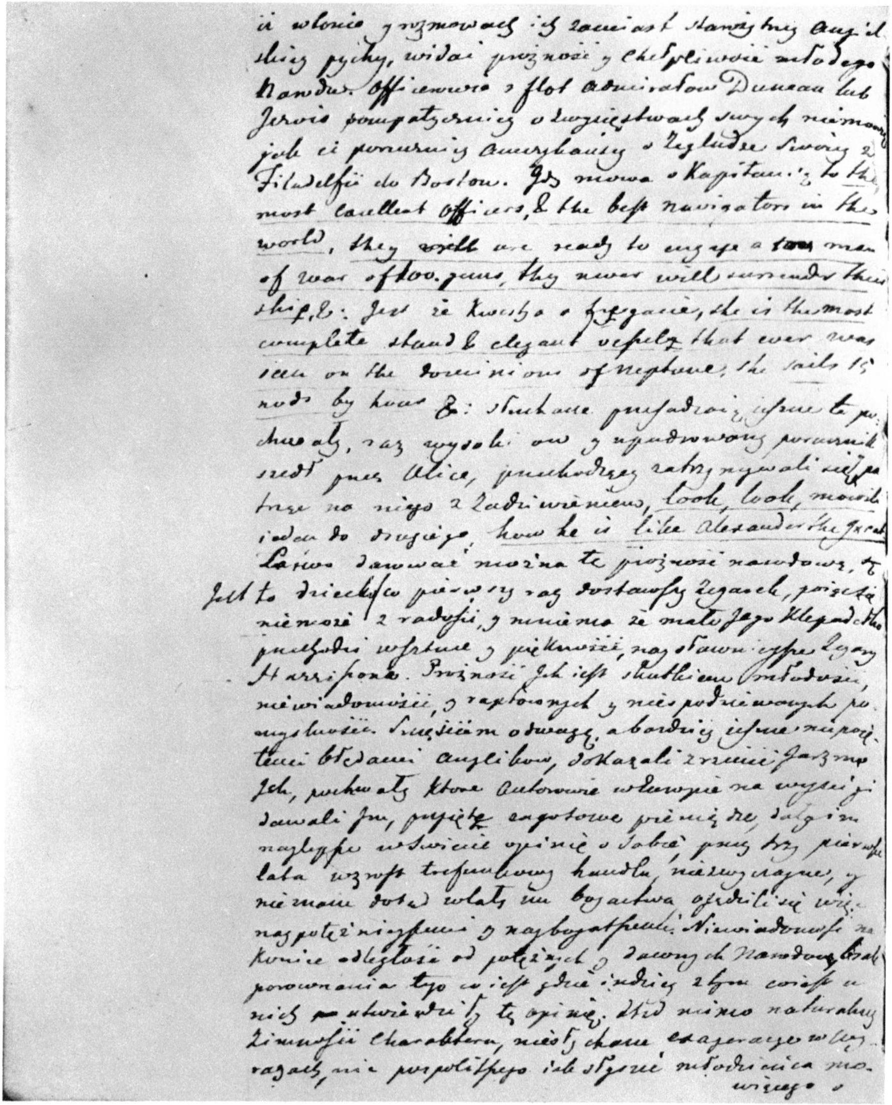

Fig. 60. A page of Polish text [VI, 22] from the Niemcewicz manuscript
with quotations in English.

Fig. 61. Beverly and Salem Bridge. From a painting on a wooden Fireboard, early 19th century. Courtesy of the Essex Institute, Salem, Mass.

Fig. 62. Newbury Bridge over Merrimack River. From *Massachusetts and New Universal Magazine*, May 1793. Courtesy of Massachusetts Historical Society.

Fig. 63. The Bridge over the Piscataqua near Portsmouth.

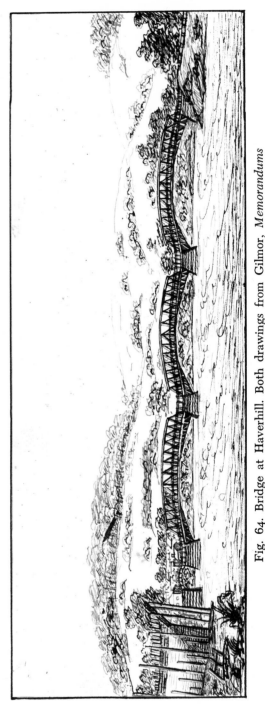

Fig. 64. Bridge at Haverhill. Both drawings from Gilmor, *Memorandums* . . . . By courtesy of the Trustees of the Boston Public Library.

Fig. 65. Niemcewicz sketch of a house in Albany in the Dutch style [VII, 9].

Fig. 66. Dutch houses, State Street Albany. From the water color by Baroness Hyde de Neuville. Courtesy of The New-York Historical Society, New York City.

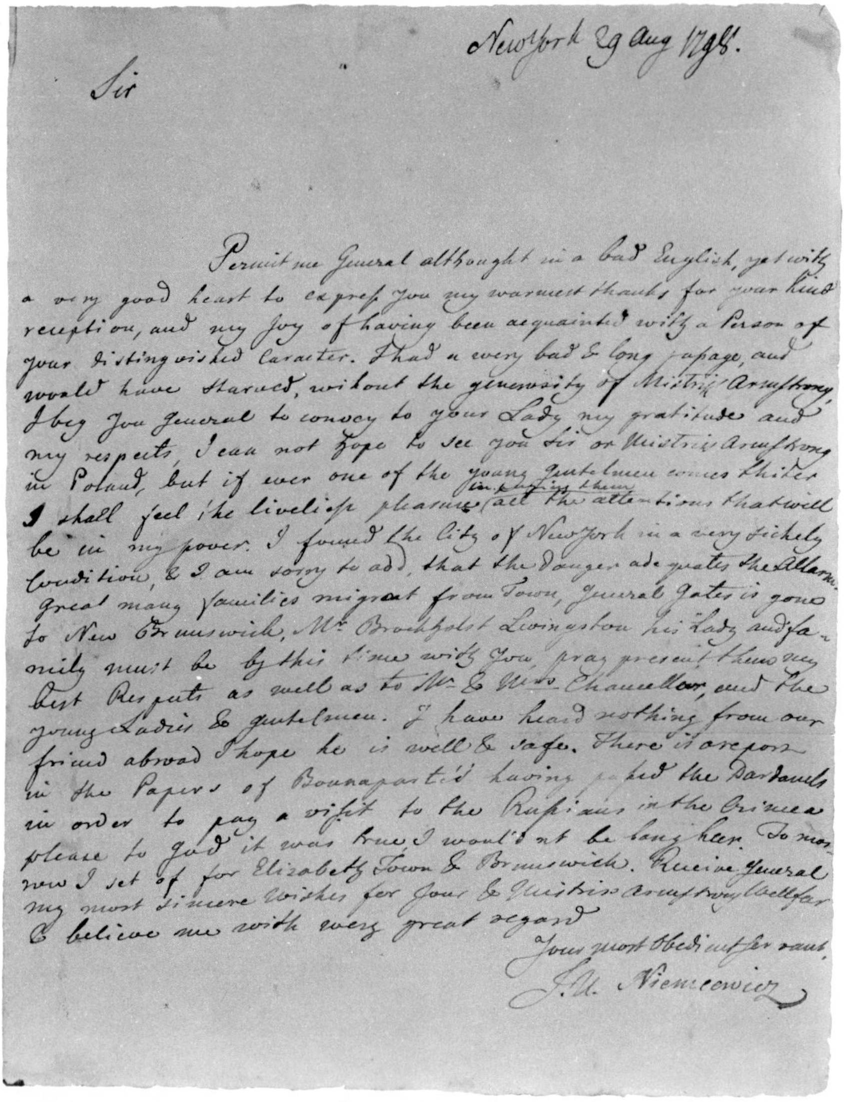

Fig. 67. Niemcewicz's letter to General and Mrs. John Armstrong, written after the occasion of his visit to their home on the Hudson. Courtesy of Mr. Richard Aldrich, Rokeby Collection, Barrytown, New York.

New York 29 Aug 1798

Sir

Permit me General althought in a bad English, yet with a very good heart to express you my warmest thanks for your kind reception, and my Joy of having been acquainted with a Person of your distinguished caracter. I had a wery bad & long passage, and would have starved, wihout the generosity of Mistriss Armstrong. I beg you General to convey to your Lady my gratitude and my respects, I can not hope to see you Sir or Mistriss Armstrong in Poland, but if ever one of the young gentelmen comes thiter I shall feel the liveliest pleasure in paying them all the attentions that will be in my power. I found the City of New York in a very sickely condition, & I am sorry to add, that the danger adequates the Allarm. Great many families migrat from Town, General Gates is gone to New Brunswick, Mr. Brockholst Livingston his Lady and family must be by this time with you, pray present them my best Respects as well as to M^r & Mrs Chancellor, and the young Ladies & gentelmen. I have heard nothing from our friend abroad I hope he is well & safe. There is a report in the Papers of Bounaparte's having passed the Dardanels in order to pay a visit to the Russians in the Crimea please to God it was true, I would not be long heer. Tomorrow I set of for Elizabeth Town & Brunswick. Receive General my most sincere Wishes for Your & Mistriss Armstrong Wellfar & believe me with wery great regard.

Your most obedient servant
J. U. Niemcewicz

Fig. 68. Albany from the Hudson, October, 1807. By Baroness Hyde de Neuville. Courtesy of The New-York Historical Society, New York City.

Fig. 69. Detail from the D. F. Sotzman Map of New Jersey (1797) showing the area Niemcewicz visited on his botanical tour. Courtesy of the Springfield Historical Society, New Jersey.

for a stupid man and an idler every hour in the country is like a generation. During the time of the Revolution here Armstrong was a friend of Kośc[iuszko]. There is probably no other officer or citizen in America who knows more, both about the most important affairs, or the least detail or anecdote of the war, the course of the government, or about the characters of the more important people. He knows everything [37] and he knows how to tell it eloquently with wit and charm. During the time of the Revolution, as now, he was the severest critic of those in command of the army and at the helm in public affairs. After the conclusion of the peace the discharged soldiers were paid by the Congress, at that time destitute of gold, in paper certificates for their seven years of service, for their wounds and sweat. Armstrong, impelled more by the flames of youth, and by the spirit of controversy than by thoughtful zeal, wrote a powerful, eloquent and stormy missive to the army, inciting the soldiers not to lay down their arms until they were paid to the last shilling. Happily cool heads, well aware of the consequences, used all possible means to restrict the circulation, and to mitigate the impression of these writings, otherwise the aroused soldiery could have made an uproar fatal to the country.[52] Though I admire Armstrong's talent, I could not personally but condemn, at the very least, the imprudence of this deed. I did not wish to remind Armstrong of this incident for I know that he considered this to have been a most honorable activity, and I do not know how to offer unremitting praise of that which I condemn in my heart.

The locale of his home is more splendid than the Chancelor's. Besides huge cliffs on the opposite bank one can see to the right, Redhook [Red Hook], a port, and near to it an island of 70 acres. Here Armstrong, in accord with Kościuszko's request and commission was undertaking the negotiations for a *farm* or a lot of a few hundred acres with an excellent house and the best possible locale in the world.[53] The island belonged to this estate. How peacefully, how happily we could have lived here, but he scorned it and left. If it were done for his country—praiseworthy, if for other reasons, then savage and wanton.

Armstrong, friend of Kośc[iuszko] during the war, described him thus: Shortly after entering the service he became a lieutenant colonel, then a colonel; at his discharge he was a *Brigade General*. He served actively the whole time in the corps of engineers, courageously and patiently undergoing all sweat and toil. He did not like Fayette—the cause, jealousy. Green[e], the greatest flatterer of his officers, he adored. Attached to the commanding officers Gates and Greene, he never had his own command, except towards the end of the war when he was given a battalion of light infantry.⁵⁴

[38] One of the greatest advantages of living here on this beautiful river is the pleasant neighbors who are in good accord. The trunk of the Livingston family is wide; it spreads its branches in all directions. All these people are well-to-do, polite, related, closely knit in friend-ships and sentiment. I could spend a week or a month visiting them in a *kulik*,⁵⁵ but as a foreigner anxious to avoid even the hint of im-portunity, I ended my visits here.

Further Journey on the North River. The 23rd of August, in spite of sincere invitations from my host to remain longer, I decided to leave. Madame General provided me with everything necessary for the journey, a mother could not have done more. I got into a rowboat and searched for a long time for a ship sailing to New York. However, I had to get on shore at Red Hook in order to wait. This is a small port with a few houses and stores; near the w[h]arf are small boats, and rising above all this in an amphitheatre, four or five splendid houses all spruce, white, with green blinds and surrounded with rows of acacias, poplars and other trees. All these dwellings belonged to the various members of the Livingston family.

While waiting for the afternoon *Tide* at 4 o'clock I had to wander about alone. We discovered finally a small *Sloop*, beating left and right into the wind. I hired a negro with a boat and got to it. My God, what a boat! It was no bigger than 10 *Ton*. One had to stand and enter backwards into the *Cabin* or hut, half of it was cluttered up by a chimney, the other half by two chests and two people. One was the captain and the other, the whole crew. What to do—either board her, or wait for a better boat and lose more time. I decided on the former. My small baggage and provisions were transferred from the rowboat. These last, gifts of the generous Mrs. Armstrong, consisted of roast lamb, [39] ham, butter, bread, melon, watermelon and a bottle of madeira. With this last I treated my new companions. Oh beneficial drink, how manifest your dispensations, lightening and touching the heart of mortals. At once the brow of the captain cleared; he went into the cabin, took out of it a chest, on the side of the upper deck he laid out a piece of old sail and in a word made for me as good a bed as he could. Arranging myself in this way I went out onto the deck.

The evening was pleasant. The wind was against us, but for those going up the river it was the best possible. A big three-masted ship going to Hudson passed us by with the wings of an eagle. We were weaving to the right and the left, and after the tide ran out, we cast anchor for the night, not far from the palace of Jones Levingston [56] that is, about two miles from G[enera]l Armstrong's house. My night on deck covered with a piece of sail would have been excellent but for the company of all kinds of insects: flies, fleas, the hum of beetles and many centipedes. All these promenaded all night through, over my face and hands until finally the centipedes retreated. The next day I saw that they had a much better position; they had made camp in my melon. This large and self-indulgent band of Cossacks had razed it to the ground; we were able to save only a part of the spoils.

The 24th: the wind was continually against us. While we condemned it, those who went upstream blessed it; what is bad fortune for one brings another prosperity. Our small boat must be the oldest of its generation of the whole American mercantile fleet and is breaking apart; it takes on water so abundantly that every two hours we had to pump it out in barrels. Every six hours at the change of the *Taide* we had to drop anchor. At that moment, whatever the hour happened to be, it was the time for dinner and breakfast combined. This consisted of black coffee, salmon, bread and butter. [40] At night we stopped not far from a small town, Cotling.[57]

The next day, the 25th, a slightly more favorable wind brought us in the morning to Pokipsy [Poughkeepsie], one of the important towns on the Hudson river. There were a few boats and houses in the harbor, the city itself is at a distance from the water. Here we bought a piece of meat and a flask of whisky. We went a few miles farther and while the *Taide* changed, we lowered anchor on the right side of the river amidst wild and rocky banks. Just as the eastern bank of the North River is largely inhabited by rich and substantial families, so the western bank which, in large part is under corporate Town ownership, is rocky. Up till now it is very little cultivated and is inhabited only by farmers. Here the river waters are somewhat mingled with those of the sea and we were obliged to seek a natural spring of fresh water. Taking a boat and a barrel we rowed with the captain to a small house at the very edge of the water. We found the owner in bed in the last stages of consumption, the lady of the house busy in the kitchen, and upstairs a woman spinning on a spinning wheel. One may hear the noise of this instrument in constant motion in every farmer's house. The petticoats, pantaloons, shirts in blue and white stripes, and indeed almost all country wear made by the women in America, remind one of the innocent simplicity and industry of ancient Greek and Roman maidens. After filling our barrel with spring water we returned to the boat.

During the afternoon sail the river opened up ever wider and presented us with new views. The shores on both sides are made up of limestone hills; these were covered with white kilns. The thick black billows of smoke coming from these chimneys, workers covered with soot and dirt halfway up their arms reminded one of the gloomy forges of Cyclops at the foot [41] of terrible Etna.[58] Towards the evening we came on eddies and the opposition of two *Tide*[s] one going up, the other down. A strong wind rose up suddenly and if we had not in one moment luffed the sails, it would have overturned our frail bark and sunk it. It was already late at night when we dropped anchor at New bury [Newburgh]. New Bury is an important town, active in trade. A large *Sloop* was moored at the shore. Its sailors, returning from New York, were the first to tell us about the pestilence that was current there. Two ships which had come from Philadelphia had a few sick, and had thrown their few dead into the sea; by order of the magistrate they were not allowed into the harbor because of the fear of increasing the pestilence. In vain they put out a flag of distress; no one dared to go near them or to help them. By now perhaps all their passengers and crew are dead.[59]

The 26th: in the night a favorable wind arose and at sunrise when I went out on deck, we could barely see the towns of Newbury and Windsor in the distance. Before us we discovered the narrow entrance into the Highlands and shortly after we found ourselves between two walls of steep cliffs, their tops piercing the clouds. Here the river turns suddenly to the west; farther still on the western bank and on the top of a sharp cliff, one can see the white shape of a mighty fortress appearing, and beneath it a large battery dug in all around. This is West Point, a fortress built during the Revolution and known forever in the annals of America, as much for its beauty and stout strength as for the treachery of Benedict Arnold.[60] This fortress is a defense against enemy access to Albany, whether by river or by land, and it cuts communication with the western states and Canada. It was an outpost of the greatest value for the U.S. [42] No expense or labor was spared in fortifying it. Not only was the fortress guarded by cannons and a numerous garrison but in addition, the tops of all the nearby hills, all approaches from both sides of the river were bristling with batteries. Tremendous iron chains cut across the river from shore to shore.[61] It was impossible to take this place by storm; there remained only treachery, and at this the English grasped. Dr. Ramsay relates this fatal treason in the following manner:

"A distinguished officer engaged for a stipulated sum of money, to betray into the hands of the British an important post committed to his care. General Arnold who committed this foul crime was a native of Connecticut. . . . He had been among the first to take up arms against Great-Britain . . . His distinguished military talents had procured him every honour a grateful country could bestow. . . . Though in his accounts against the Staates there was much room to suspect fraud and imposition, yet the recollection of his gallantry and good conduct, in a great measure served as a cloak to cover the whole. He who had been prodigal of life in his country's cause was indulged in extraordinary demands for his services. The generosity of the States did not keep pace with the extravagance of their favourite officer. A sumptuous table and expensive equipage, unsupported by the resources of private fortune, unguarded by the virtues of oeconomy and good management, soon increased his debts beyond a possibility of his discharging them. His love of pleasure produced the love of money, and that extinguished all sensibility to the obligations of honour and duty. The calls of luxury were various and pressing, and demanded gratification though at the expence of fame and country. Contracts were made, speculations entered into, and partnerships instituted, which could not bear investigation. Oppression, extortion, misapplication of public money and property, furnished him with the farther means of gratifying his favourite passions. In these circumstances, a change of sides afforded the only hope of evading a scrutiny, and at the same time, held out a prospect of replenishing his exhausted coffers. The disposition of the American forces in the year 1780, afforded an opportunity of accomplishing this so much to the advantage of the British, that they could well afford a liberal reward for the beneficial treachery. The American army was stationed in the strong holds of the highlands on both sides of the North-river. In this arrangement, Arnold solicited for the command of West-point. This has been called the Gibraltar of America. It was built after the loss of Fort Montgomery, for the defence of the North-river . . . Rocky ridges rising one behind another, rendered it incapable of being invested, by less than twenty thousand men. Though some even then entertained doubts of Arnold's fidelity, yet Gen. Washington in the unsuspecting spirit of a soldier, believing it to be impossible that honour should be wanting in a breast which he knew was the seat of valour, cheerfully granted his request, and intrusted him with the important post. Gen. Arnold thus invested with command, carried on a negociation with Sir Henry Clinton, by which it was agreed that the former should make a disposition of his forces, which would enable the latter to surprise West-point under such circumstances, that he would have the garrison so completely in his power, that the troops must either lay down their arms or be cut to pieces. . . .

The agent employed in this negociation on the part of Sir Henry Clinton, was Major André, adjutant-general of the British army, a young officer of great hopes, and of uncommon merit. Nature had bestowed on him an elegant taste for literature and the fine arts, which by industrious cultivation he had greatly improved. He possessed many amiable qualities, and very great accomplishments. His fidelity together with his place and character, eminently fitted him for this business; but his high ideas of candor, and his abhorrence of duplicity, made him inexpert in practising those arts of deception which it required. To favour the necessary communications, the Vulture sloop of war had been previously stationed in the North-river, as near to Arnold's posts as was practicable, without exciting suspicion. Before this a written correspondence between Arnold and André, had been for some time carried on, under the fictitious names of Gustavus and Anderson. A boat was sent at night from the shore to fetch Major André. On its return, Arnold met him at the beach, without the posts of either army. Their business was not finished till it was too near the dawn of day for André to return to the Vulture. Arnold told him he must be concealed till the next night. For that purpose, he was conducted within one of the American posts, against his previous stipulation and knowledge, and continued with Arnold the following day. The boatmen refused to carry him back the next night, as the Vulture, from being exposed to the fire of some cannon brought up to annoy her, had changed her position. André's return to New-York by land, was then the only practicable mode of escape. To favour this he quitted his uniform which he had hitherto worn under a surtout, for a common coat, and was furnished with a horse, and under the name of John Anderson, with a passport "to go to the lines of White Plains or lower if he thought proper, he being on public business." He advanced alone and undisturbed a great part of the way. When he thought himself almost out of danger, he was stopped by three of the New-York militia, who were with others scouting between the outposts of the two armies. Major André instead of producing his pass, asked the man who stopped him "where he belonged to" who answered "to below" meaning New-York. He [Niemcewicz wrote Arnold] replied "so do I" and declared himself a British officer, and pressed that he might not be detained. He soon discovered his mistake. His captors proceeded to search him: sundry papers were found in his possession. These were secreted in his boots, and were in Arnold's [Niemcewicz wrote his] handwriting. They contained exact returns of the state of the forces, ordnance and defences at West-Point, with the artillery orders, critical remarks on the works, &c.

André offered his captors a purse of gold and a new valuable watch, if they would let him pass, and permanent provision and future promotion, if they would convey and accompany him to New-York. They nobly disdained the proffered bribe, and delivered him a prisoner to Lieutenant Col. Jameson, who commanded the scouting parties. In testimony of the high sense entertained of the virtuous and patriotic conduct of John Paulding, David Williams, and Isaac Van Vert, the captors of André, Congress resolved "That each of them receive annually two hundred dollars in specie during life, and that the board of war be directed to procure for each of them a silver medal, on one side of which should be a shield with this inscription, *Fidelity;* and on the other, the following motto, *Vincit Amor Patriae:* and that the commander in chief be requested to present the same, with the thanks of Congress, for their fidelity and the eminent service they had rendered their country." André when delivered to Jameson continued to call himself by the name of Anderson, and asked leave to send a letter to Arnold, to acquaint him with Anderson's detention. This was inconsiderately granted. Arnold on the receipt of this letter abandoned every thing, and went on board the Vulture sloop of war. Lieut. Col. Jameson forwarded to Gen. Washington all the papers found on André, together with a letter giving an account of the whole affair, but the express, by taking a different route from the General, who was returning from a conference at Hartford with Count de Rochambeau, missed him. This caused such a delay as gave Arnold time to effect his escape. The same packet which detailed the particulars of André's capture, brought a letter from him, in which he avowed his name and character, and endeavoured to shew that he did not come under the description of a spy. The letter was expressed in terms of dignity without insolence, and of apology without meanness. He stated therein, that he held a correspondence with a person under the orders of his General. That his intention went no farther than meeting that person on neutral ground, for the purpose of intelligence, and that, against his stipulation, his intention, and without his knowledge beforehand, he was brought within the American posts, and had to concert his escape from them. Being taken on his return he was betrayed into the vile condition of an enemy in disguise. His principal request was that "whatever his fate might be, a decency of treatment might be observed, which would mark, that though unfortunate he was branded with nothing that was dishonourable, and that he was involuntarily an imposter."

General Washington referred the whole case of Major André to the examination and decision of a board, consisting of fourteen general officers. On his examination, he voluntarily confessed every thing that related to himself, and particularly that he did not come ashore under the protection of a flag. The board did not examine a single witness, but founded their report on his own confession. In this they stated the following facts: "That Major André came on shore on the night of the 21st of September in a private and secret manner, and that he changed his dress within the American lines, and under a feigned name and disguised habit passed their works, and was taken in a disguised habit when on his way to New-York, and when taken, several papers were found in his possession, which contained intelligence for the enemy." From these facts they farther reported it as their opinion "That Major André ought to be considered as a spy, and that agreeably to the laws and usages of nations he ought to suffer death.

Sir Henry Clinton, Lieutenant General Robertson, and the late American General Arnold, wrote pressing letters to General Washington, to prevent the decision of the board of general officers from being carried into effect. General Arnold in particular urged, that every thing done by Major André was done by his particular request, and at a time when he was the acknowledged commanding officer in the department. He contended "that he had a right to transact all these matters for which though wrong, Major André ought not to suffer." An interview also took place between General Robertson on the part of the British, and General Greene, on the part of the Americans. Every thing was urged by the former, that ingenuity or humanity could suggest for averting the proposed execution, Greene made a proposition for delivering up André for Arnold; but finding this could not be acceded to by the British, without offending against every principle of policy. . . . As Greene and Robertson differed so widely both in their statement of facts, and the inferences they drew from them, the latter proposed to the former, that the opinions of disinterested gentlemen might be taken on the subject, and proposed Kniphausen and Rochambeau. Robertson also urged that André possessed a great share of Sir Henry Clinton's esteem; and that he would be infinitely obliged if he should be spared. He offered that in case André was permitted to return with him to New-York, any person whatever, that might be named, should be set at liberty. All these arguments and entreaties having failed, Robertson presented a long letter from Arnold, in which he endeavoured to exculpate André, by acknowledging himself the author of every part of his conduct, "and particularly insisted on his coming from the Vulture, under a flag which he had sent for that purpose." He declared that if André suffered, he should think himself bound in honor to retaliate. He also observed "that forty of the principal inhabitants of South-Carolina had justly forfeited their lives, which had hitherto been spared only through the clemency of Sir Henry Clinton, but who could no longer extend his mercy if Major André suffered: an event which would probably open a scene of bloodshed, at which humanity must revolt." He intreated Washington by his own honor, and for that of humanity, not to suffer an unjust sentence to touch the life of André, but if that warning should be disregarded and André suffer, he called heaven and earth to witness, that he alone would be justly answerable for the torrents of blood that might be spilt in consequence."

Every exertion was made by the royal commanders to save André, but without effect. It was the general opinion of the American army that his life was forfeited, and that national dignity and sound policy required that the forfeiture should be exacted.

André though superior to the terrors of death, wished to die like a soldier. To obtain this favour, he wrote a letter to Gen. Washington, fraught with sentiments of military dignity. From an adherence to the usages of war, it was not thought proper to grant this request; but his delicacy was saved from the pain of receiving a negative answer. The guard which attended him in his confinement, marched with him to the place of execution. The way, over which he passed, was crouded on each side by anxious spectators. Their sensibility was strongly impressed by beholding a well dressed youth, in the bloom of life, of a peculiarly engaging person, mien and aspect, devoted to immediate execution. Major André walked with firmness, composure and dignity, between two officers of his guard . . . Upon seeing the preparations at the fatal spot, he asked with some degree of concern, "Must I die in this manner?"—He was told it was unavoidable—He replied, "I am reconciled to my fate, but not to the mode;" but soon subjoined, "It will be but a momentary pang." He ascended the cart with a pleasing countenance, and with a degree of composure, which excited the admiration and melted the hearts of all the spectators. He was asked when the fatal moment was at hand, if he had any thing to say; he answered nothing but to request "That you will witness to the world that I die like a brave man." The succeeding moments closed the affecting scene." [62]

[VIII, 5] By this death André became the object of everyone's most touching sympathy, while it increased the abomination in which Arnold, the instrument of this young man's ill fortune, was held by everyone. Pretty American girls remember André even now with wistful sighs, and the romance *Major André's Complaints* or Laments of André is one of their favorite songs.[63]

It is a circumstance truly to be wondered at, and one which military men in other countries would find hard to believe, that in time of war when the enemy were so close by, Arnold, the Commander of such an important fort, should have his quarters on the opposite side of the river, at least three English miles away from the fortress. We stopped not far from this house at the time of low *Taide*. It is a large house with a garden, fields, etc. Arnold lived there with his wife, one of the most beautiful women in America. Dr. Gordon in his history of the American Revolution maintains that Arnold's correspondence with the enemy started from a correspondence of his wife with the wife of Clinton.[64] These two ladies wrote about the materials of fashion, of coifs, hats, hairdressing, etc., and through them an opening was made for Arnold, and later, as we have seen, they almost led America into complete disaster. And so, in this instance, as with almost all women's plots, though at first innocent they represent the thin end of the wedge.

Arnold [6] scarcely had time to get away to the enemy. Later G[enera]l Washington permitted his wife to join her husband. This incident appears to me to raise an important question which should be resolved. It is this: if, for example, a husband should betray his country and go over to her enemy, do the duty and vows of a wife tie her to the condition of being a partner to this crime, that is to go over also to the enemy? I would boldly decide in the *negative*. Every young maiden is born a citizen and only becomes a wife later, her country first, husband later. There should be nothing more dear or holy in the world than one's own country. Neither vows nor oaths can free one from duty and fidelity to her. After going over to the English Arnold published manifestos urging the Americans to put down their arms. Nobody paid any attention to him. His terrible barbarity, the burning of New London, etc., is known. After the end of the war he sailed from Europe to the shores of America, though he never dared to leave the ship. At night his wife went on shore to make arrangements about their property left in this country. Up until now Arnold has been receiving a pension from England. This, no matter how large it may be, can not repay him for the loss of peace and honor, nor ever quiet the savage pangs of conscience in his heart. He lives despised even by those for whom he sold himself. I would advise him to settle at Biała Cerkiew or Tulczyn and there in like company finish out his dark days.[65]

About ten the *tide* threw us upon the eastern bank of the river where we tied our boat to a tree, and while the sailors were laying a fire and making coffee, I read, in the midst of the tremendous heat, the *Demofente* of Metastasio.[66] After first finding some sort of shade in the bushes I fed my eyes on the beautiful view, and the rocks and the fortress West Point [7] still showing itself in the distance. The sound of the drum and the gleam of bayonets of about 20 soldiers going on sentry duty awakened in the owner of my boat the old spirit and memories of camp life. At the time of the war he was a sergeant of artillery in this fort. He began to tell various anecdotes; he pointed out the house of Kośc[iuszko], who was a colonel of the engineers attached to this fortress. No more than a quarter of a mile from this shore he showed to me the house in which Arnold had his quarters and from whence he ran away to the English. After his departure there was found in a stable a fatted ox of tremendous size which Arnold, my old sergeant maintained, was getting ready for the banquet he intended to give for the English after the surrender of the fortress into their hands. Leaving this bank and pushing further into the Highlands:—here the scene is even more beautiful and its stark magnitude astonishes and often overawes the mind of the onlooker. Here a huge wall of stone extends from the clouds down to the river as if it were carved perpendicularly. It is either covered with firs and cedars or is completely bare and its outline gives an impression of walls and ancient castles. Amidst them on the eastern bank is the highest and most famous mountain, *Ant[h]on'ys Nos[e]*, covered completely with *hemlock* and *Spruce tree*. The river, somewhat confined in its channel and overcast by the lengthening shadow from the rocks, was melancholy and black; everywhere was a quiet awesome peace. On the eastern bank were the inconspicuous remains of Fort Montgomery, taken by storm by the English and leveled to the ground. The American Governor Clinton,[67] seeing the fort taken and the garrison captured, threw himself, weapon in hand, into the river and swam across.

Towards evening we found ourselves in a huge bay (*Bay*) called Pigskill [Peekskill]. This bay is practically round and is formed by the North River and small streams [8] (*creeks*) that come down from the mountains. It reminds one of a lake, clear and peaceful. On the right hand wild and savage cliffs, on the left the banks rise in an amphitheatre, with a town from which the bay takes its name. There is a church and steeple whose extended and sharp shaft reflects itself in the transparent crystal of the lake. The houses of the farmers are scattered over the hills with fields of *maïs* and buckwheat in alternating bands, and innumerable apple orchards whose fruit, already ripened, tempted the eye with its gold and dark purple. In the bay were a score of boats standing quietly at anchor and awaiting, as did we, the current (*Tide*). Many herds of cattle from the shore were standing in the water up to their backs, seeking a little cool during the heat of the day. The dying rays of the sun sinking behind the mountains amidst fiery red clouds illuminated this scene.

We went on shore with the owner of the bark to buy milk and to gather fruit, but the night fell before we could reach the first house. Thus we gathered only two kerchiefs of apples which is not considered here as even the smallest transgression. During this time our old sailor who was lieutenant, helmsman, and the whole crew, threw out his line with untold patience and kept his eyes glued on it for two hours. Finally he drew it in with an empty hook. It was not his fault but rather that of the river which except for sturgeon supports very few other fish. A piece of cold meat and two apples was the supper for everyone.

We went to bed, but the humidity and the insects chased me from the cabin onto the deck. I laid myself in the sail hung in the shape of a cradle. Shortly a view of the most splendid terror dispersed sleep from my eyelids. Towards the west, clouds like dark blue fleece covered the whole horizon; a sound like that of cannons a few miles away began a hollow reverberation against the cliffs. At the same time but at first only intermittently the lightning began to tear apart the curtain of night. This was to be repeated more often until finally the whole horizon was shown up in one continual fire. [9] One would say that all this side of the heaven burned with a white flame. This view, truly awe inspiring amidst these wild cliffs and the quiet night, pierced the soul with fear and wonder. After two hours, the storm, showing its awful appearance only far off, turned to the east. My thoughts flew constantly from these distant and wild places to my beloved corners of Europe; they finally disappeared and were erased in sleep.

At two in the morning the captain awakened me saying that for the first time during our sail a favorable wind had arisen and we were beside Stony point. I noticed we were a score of miles from the beautiful bay of Pigskill in which I had fallen asleep. The heavens, no longer a black curtain, gleamed a clear azure in the midst of which the moon with its spreading circle of light shone beautifully. With the help of its rays I saw the rather unremarkable remains of Stony point fort scattered over the sharp tops of the cliffs. Here the Americans had carried off one of their greatest victories of the war when, in a small number and in spite of an unassailable position, they took the fort by storm, armed only with bayonets and unloaded guns. General Wayne led on this occasion.⁶⁸ When the sun arose, a favorable wind hurried us always forward amidst the walled cliffs of the Highlands. These cliffs are called the Closter Mountains.⁶⁹ Further on the captain showed me those places where Fort Washington, Fort Lee and others had stood. All these forts are today in ruins, disappeared almost without trace, as though a thousand years had gone by since their existence.

The further we continued, the nearer we came to the eastern bank of the river, which took shape as pleasant hills, cultivated and settled. I saw amongst others a pretty house with a large and beautiful garden. [10] It belonged once to the Filips [Philipse] family, which at the time of the Revolution naturally took the side of the English and had all its estate completely confiscated.⁷⁰ Examples of this severity, this confiscation, are rare in America either because the national character is not revengeful or because in this civil war those who held with the government, which through two centuries had been considered lawful, were not treated with the severity that a citizen who had attached himself to a foreign enemy should justifiably suffer. Furthermore, a family divided between both sides would find ready defenders among its own relatives and friends. What a difference from the terrible proscriptions, confiscations, sequestrations, jailings, etc., perpretrated on the unfortunate Poles who had no other fault than that they were defending their Fatherland from violence, incursions, and finally from the gobbling-up of it by enemies conspiring against it. No one has more truly proved the words of Tacitus than they, *Proprium humani Ingenii est odisse quem laeseris.*⁷¹

Not far from this place is a *Creek* or small river which joins the E[a]st and the North River and forms a beautiful island, on which stands New York. At the beginning of the war the whole American army, driven out of Long Island, stopped on this island. The English ships surrounded it on two sides. If How[e], Gage and Clinton had placed themselves with their soldiers and artillery at Kingsbridge, near the *Creek* referred to above, the whole strength of the Americans would have been trapped as if in a net. They would have been forced to surrender either by force of arms or from hunger. The war would have ended and these states would, till this day, be under the rule of Great Britain. The English generals were not so dull that they did not see advantages as obvious as these, but a speedy ending of the war did not accord with their greed; it was necessary to prolong the war so that they would be needed longer, a longer time in which to give orders, and above all in which to grow rich.

A few [11] miles from the mouth of the North River there were no longer sturgeon but only *Purposses* [porpoises]; these monsters of the sea entertained us with their leaping and snorting like pigs. These fish go up a score of miles into the North and E[a]st Rivers seeking food.

Finally about 2 o'clock in the afternoon of the 28th of August, after five days journey from Red hook, we sailed into New York harbor. This river voyage, although on a boat of the worst kind, although always into a contrary wind, without any comforts, even without necessities, was not in the least disagreeable for me. The beauty and splendor of the river banks, the changes of scenery, the memories of wartime, entertain, inspire wonder, and make, in the mind of the traveler, an impression which will never be erased. If one can compare small things to large, Nature with the chisel of a Michelangelo carved the banks of this beautiful river, while at the same time she scattered the beauties of Poussin and the charm of Albani in the verdant country scenes.

After reaching the city the news we had had in Newbury about the pestilence, was proved by the appearance of the town. A large number of the inhabitants had left; many stores and houses were closed; everywhere there was gloom and sadness. I shall write later about the causes and the results of this terrible plague from heaven and about the pitiable state of the city so scourged by it. I stayed three days for some shopping in the city. The number of the dead increased daily.

The 30th I went by boat to Elizabeth Town, and there as everywhere I was pursued by contrary winds. Instead of one hour, I was on the water for eight hours. In the evening I stopped in Elizabeth Town in the ordinary [12] house of Mr. Rivers.[72] Here Faesch, *contubernalis* and my friend, first brought to me news of the whispers spread about concerning the mysterious nocturnal departure of Kośc[iuszko]. Colonel Touzard, a Frenchman in the service of the U.S., came here and spread the news that the government had definite knowledge, through letters from Virginia, that Kośc[iuszko] had left the country alone and mysteriously, as part of a secret and unfriendly design against this country; what is more, that all his wounds and his limp were also a pretense—in a word that he was seen walking.[73] What an affront and wonder this news created, what suspicions of me, what kinds of mischievous, tormenting and embarrassing questions—equally as painful to write about as to experience. After two weeks respite in Elizabeth I went to see my friends in Brunswick, Col. White, etc. 26 September I returned again to my small room.

The disease, *the Yellow fever*, continues to scourge terribly in Philadelphia and New York. In Philadelphia the comparison between the dead where the infection prevailed in 1793 with those in the year 1798 is, according to the papers, as follows:—[74]

	in 1793		in 1798
in August	325		623
in September	1442		1831
in October	1903		942
in November	118	from the 1st to the 3rd	50
Jews, Methodists			
Quakers and			
Catholics	164		
	3952		3446

This year the disease was perhaps much more infectious but the citizens in Philadelphia left the city so early, that on the 7th and 8th of November there were only 7,000 counted. [13] In New York, according to the papers, 1903 have died this year, but actually there were many more since the municipality and the officials, either through carelessness or more probably in order to maintain commercial confidence, have kept secret the number of dead.

Chapter VIII

A NATURAL HISTORY TOUR OF THE ENVIRONS OF PHILADELPHIA AND OF THE PINE BARRENS OF NEW JERSEY. VISIT TO THE IRON FURNACES AND IRON FORGE AT MOUNT HOPE

[15] The 30th of May [1799] with Maklure [William Maclure] and Thomas Smith; [1] we rode out to gather plants on a side road which was steep and far from any highways. The countryside, as is usual here, was covered with forests and alternated between mountains and valleys. At times on the wide horizon mountains seem to follow on mountains with their colors growing steadily weaker and disappearing into a bluish haze, then the horizon suddenly appears again and catches the eye. There are meadows, the most fertile in the world whether in their natural state or sown with clover. There are many streams and brooks; little rivers held back by dams form wide and translucent cascades, serving to turn mills, enhance the neighborhood and to tempt the painter's brush. Even the largest and practically inaccessible cliffs do not appear barren and are covered with trees and bushes, mostly *kalmia latifolia*—a type of laurel as pretty in leaf and flower as it is poisonous. A mineralogist has abundant treasures here, the cliffs, the rocks along the road are of granite often crystalline, *horn blend[e]*, *brescia* [breccia], *serpentine, mikacious* [micacious] *S[c]hist,* quartz, crystalline quartz, etc.[2]

Our object was to search for botanical specimens, and the poor road forced us to travel more on foot than by carriage. We did not find any plants unknown to us until we paused for refreshments 18 miles from Philadelphia. There we found a *Spirea trifolium* and the smaller yellow *Cypripedium*.[3] The meal consisted of broiled ham with eggs. This common dish has been brought by the Germans to America. The landlord had six strong and healthy children. The smallest, nine months old, stood up straight on the palms of her father's hand, who lifted her up and turned her around as one might a puppet. After dinner the countryside continued the same and the road was steep. We spent the night 24 miles from Philad[elphia]. Distance here is measured by the inns—so many miles from the King of Prussia, the patron and favorite of the Germans, so many from the Black Horse, Lion and Bull. The inn in which we stayed was called "Under the sign of the Bull" [16] and was a quarter of a mile from the Skulkill.

The river, full of gay and green islands, flows at first through meadows, then the stream is confined by the rocky walls. Here, the plants to be gathered were more abundant, *Tradescantium, Phlox,* the larger *Cypripedium, Agrostemum,*[4] and many others which we had neither time nor talent to recognize. The landlord told us much of the well-known value of the weed *Rattle Snake root* against the bite of the rattlesnake, *Serpent à Son[n]ette[s].* This is the third plant to which this virtue has been ascribed: *Hierascium, actea,* in the latter the leaf is rather large and in the form of a sharp pointed sting.[5] The uncertainty as to the plant, it seems to me, throws some suspicion on the certainty of its virtue. After breakfast we again cut across the countryside on the worst possible highway to Lancaster. During the whole of yesterday and today I saw many fields covered with rye but very little wheat; not because the farms are fertile and suitable only for rye but because of the fear of an insect called the *hessian fly* which for the last few years has devoured the wheat harvest. A farmer with whom we stayed had harvested only three bushels from 45 *acres* sown with wheat. The country is again most abundant in minerals, granite and other rocks most often mixed with mica; iron is found in many of them. The road from Lancaster is made up entirely of broken bits of granite, serpentine, quartz, etc. Often in the granite one can find garnets. Dinner in the inn "Under the Sign of Admiral Warren," on the highway to Lancaster. The landlord is German.[6] Again ham and eggs, fresh butter but smelling so of onions that it is most unpleasant to eat. The meadows in Pennsylvania are covered with chives introduced, so they say, by the Germans. It is the first plant which shows itself in the spring and they give it as feed for the cattle.

In the evening we returned to the house of Maclure, 6 miles from Philad[elphia]. The next day, June 1, the day was so cold that we had to stir up a fire in the fireplace. [17] On another plant-seeking pilgrimage we set out the 6th of June. In the morning we crossed the Dellaware at Gloster point [Gloucester Point]. The river is tremendously wide, the water crystal, the shores: on one side a splendid city, everywhere large trees and gay showy meadows forming the most splendid view. Stopping on the other side in the state of Jersey, the appearance of the landscape changes suddenly. The land is everywhere sandy and low-lying; fields and meadows are small in number and there are continual forests. *Euphorbia Ipecukana,* and *Cipropedium* grow here abundantly.[7]

We had dinner in little Timber Creek; an inn and two houses make up the place which carries this name.[8] The drinking water is excellent as it is everywhere where it seeps through sand and thus loses its foreign and unclean matter. T. Smith tested the water in Philadelphia by adding a drop of *Nitric of Quick Silver;*[9] the water took on the color of milk, the infallible sign of a great deal of salt in the water. Here the water mixed with the same solution did not change color nor lose any of its clarity. After dinner we traveled along a road through forest and swamp. The latter is covered with trees that would decorate the most splendid garden. The tree is *Magnolia Auricularis;* it is similar to the orange tree in leaf and smoothness of the bark, with a white flower, folded like a rose, with a most pleasant odor which fills the air.[10] Nature, placing this bush which is so pleasant in inaccessible and gloomy swamps, has attempted to show that there is no place that it can not favor with adornments and beauty. I saw dirty negresses wading about in the mud and picking bouquets of flowering branches for their mistresses. We spent the night in Great Timber Creek. It is a small town on a river swampy and only navigable for small boats.[11] The ravages of yellow fever are great here, either because of its humid situation, or of its nearness to Philadelphia.

[18] The 7th of June. It is raining and cold, the road goes through sand and forests for eight miles to Long-[a]-Coming,[12] breakfast near the fireplace. From there 9 miles again through a barren pine forest to the inn *Bluë Anker.*[13] Here our field trip through forests and bogs was unsuccessful. *Sisyrynthum Bermud:, Lisimachia, Galliya virgn:,* like *Lupinus* with a white and red flower.[14] Nothing new. In the evening two Quaker women rode up in a carriage like a gigantic tantalus, or rather like a Turkish carriage from Moldavia. After them in a cabriolet a very drunken young man. He threw himself immediately on the bed and throughout the whole night addressed himself to heaven in hymns and psalms composed *ex tempore,* at times in moral and philosophical maxims. The next day he began the day with the morning libations of rum and whisky. Seeing us with books and taking us for doctors, he asked us for *Opium, in order to rase the Spirits.* He knew his bad habit well, and he was more the object of

pity that he was aware of it; though the strength of this persistent habit destroys a moment's pause for judgement.

The 8th of June: He rode after us for 20 miles lurching from side to side in an open carriage along a road full of holes, in the heaviest downpour and through a thick forest. A friendly genii brought him without harm to a place inappropriately called Egg harbor.[15] We stopped at the inn of Colonel Westcot.[16] In spite of the great downpour *Hellonius Asphodeloides* [17] with its splendor and beauty struck our eyes.

The rain kept us in the house throughout the whole day. We spent it examining the plants which we had gathered along the way, and on the examination of the habits of a small group of the inhabitants scattered over these huge forests and swamps. Their whole pleasure is to spend all their free moments away from their occupation with saw mills and building (there is very little farming here), all free moments, I say, consecrated to attendance at the taverns and to drunkeness. A few ships carpenters spent the whole afternoon drinking *Rum de St: Croix* and whisky. In the evening, when the time came to leave, the master carpenter found his legs *en pleine insurrection contre la volonté*, for every step he took forward he took one backwards. His friends, [19] less drunk than he, supported him and dragged him along as well as they could. The landlord, Colonel Westcot, encouraging others by his example, was very drunk all day. Three-quarters of his face was already covered with carbuncles. This vice of drunkeness which is so common in these desolated places must be ascribed to the lack of society, wild loneliness, and the torpor of these people's work. Whereas the farmer works all day in the field, returns home exhausted in the evening, recovers himself eating in the bosom of his family or with neighbors, breathes for an hour the evening cool and then exhausted goes to rest. Here there are very few farmers. A man stands all day over a saw, the water and machine do the work; he only oversees. Bored, rather than exhausted after the long hours, the weight of inaction, he cheers himself up with a bottle. In the evening without neighbors, more often without a family, he goes to a tavern where again whisky takes the place of family, companionship and conversation.

June 9. On Sunday, taking advantage of the good weather we rode out again on the same road as yesterday to a place called Penypot,[18] recommended to us by Bartram as an excellent one for a botanical field trip. Again sand and pine forests, the more sad because it was all burnt over. This tremendous damage is caused by indigent inhabitants who, having no meadows in which to feed their cattle, burn

the woods. The fire, running along the ground, turns the lower bushes
to ashes; with this the earth is enriched and puts forth grass and other
plants—in a word excellent pasturage for cattle. This advantage does
not compensate for the harm done by the fires which rise from the
lower growth to the tops and burn the taller and more useful trees.
The largest part of these woods belongs to a company of people living
in England. With the owners so far distant the harm done their property is given little attention and is not investigated. There has not been
a single instance of one of the fire setters being prosecuted.

This land is sold, at most, for one and a half dollars an acre. All the
profit comes from the bogs which are covered with thickly growing
cedars. These cedars when brought to the saw mills make excellent
lumber. The water, seeping [20] through the bogs and the roots of
the cedars, takes on a dirty yellow color; all the *Creek* or little rivers
which turn the mills or saw mills, or which provide navigable waters
are of this color. Our guide led us through swamp and burnt woods
for 6 or 7 miles. I asked him why up to this time we have not met a
single *Rattle Snake*. He answered that in truth their number has de-
creased tremendously and that for the most part pigs dispose of them,
considering them the tastiest of morsels.[19] He added that in winter
and even now 200 or 300 snakes of this type are to be found buried in
the ground in a rigid condition. There are in the forests not only
birds, but also deer, wolves and bear. One of these latter, killed last
winter weighed 400 lbs. The Americans eat not only the paws but
the meat of every part of the bear.[20]

Among the number of plants we found, the most interesting, though
common enough in the bogs of Jersey, is the *Saracenia purpurea*. The
stigma is large and divided into three lobes which arch over and cover
all the stamens; the corolla is dark purple. The strangest thing of all
are the leaves which grow close to the soil. These are in the form of
large convex pitchers of the prettiest shape. These plants are unable
to live without moisture, thus with prudent and praiseworthy fore-
sight, the pitchers fill up with water during the rain and this is stored
against the heat.[21] I went up to an attractive-looking tree and, as I
lifted my hand to pick a flower, my startled guide pulled me away
by the arm, shouting,

"Poison, poison. Do not touch."
It was *Poisonous Ash, Rhus Vernax*.[22] Doctor Barton, who is far
from prejudiced, confirmed that for him as for many others, one touch
will result in poisoning.

Around two o'clock we went back to Wesscot; baked ham [21] and
eggs, the usual fare here, was served by a nymph, the result of a union

between an Indian woman and a negro. This lady resembled a kettle
well blackened by smoke. The Wesscot tavern lies on a gulf formed
by the Egg river. Although it is in a wood, because of the tremendous
expanse of water the situation is splendid and beautiful. After dinner
we went along the road to Egg Harbor itself. Once again the same
sand and pine forests. Five or six miles further on there are oak trees
and better land covered with a rather good-looking stand of rye. We
rode through a *Kryk* [creek] or rather a freshet of water, dark copper
in color. Out of it arose a forest of large trees, dried up and stripped
not only of its leaves and branches but also of its bark. This sight
of nature-in-death provokes melancholy.

After our arrival at eg[g] harbor proper the appearance of the
pretty landlady dispersed this melancholy. With the most regular features, complexion, the liveliness of color, she had all the charms of
beauty, goodness and modesty; she was deficient in one embellish-
ment which indeed is rarely found among American ladies; a corset
covered a board flat both from the front and the back. The house of
Mr. Summers, Collector for the U.S. and innkeeper, was comfortable
and well kept.[23] It lies a half a mile from the edge of the sea. The
island, Pecks Beach, extends for seven miles and cuts off a view of the
ocean. This town consists only of Summer's Inn and a house of an old
fermier half a mile nearer to the ocean. However, twenty *Co[a]sters*
or boats which sail along the shore belong to this town or rather
dock here. Here various *Creek* or small rivers flowing from various
parts of Gloster [Gloucester] County [24] bring cedar and other lumber
sawed by many mills in the local woods. From this port [22] *the
Co[a]sters* carrying up to 80 to 100 barrels, transport them to Philadelphia and New York, often even to the West Indies. According to
the calculations of the well-informed Captain each one of these 20
boats loaded with 35 thousand feet of boards makes 16 trips a year
to Philad[elphia] or New York: 1,000 feet of boards sell for 9 dollars.
The trade in boards alone is thus 100,800 dollars, or 50,400 ducats in
hand. What would it be if we were to add iron, tar, etc.? And so an
uncultivated, uninhabited country, covered in forests, has a more
profitable trade than many fertile and well-populated provinces in
Europe. In the evening we took a walk near the sea.

June 10: In the morning we set off in a boat for the island Pegs
[Pecks] beach. Its shores are completely sandy; in the middle it is
covered with a thick and impassable wood of cedars, laurel, various
thorns and laurel bushes, *Myrtica* [Myrica] *Cerifera*, commonly called
Bayberry. This bush carries light green berries which are full of fat.
The inhabitants boil these berries and, by adding a little tallow to the

wax, make excellent candles. The color of these candles is green; the fragrance of the smoke is most pleasant, but the light is not as clear and strong as that of wax candles. I saw on this island as on the seashore an Indian plant, *Cactus* or wild fig.[25] They have leaves half an inch thick like shoe soles, full of needles. As I remember, the plant grows in Sicily but is much bigger there. The thorny and impassable woods are shelter for sea birds which make their nests in them; pelicans, *Fish hawks, golets, pluwers* and others, pierce the wild emptiness with their cries.[26] In only one place amidst the cedars did we find a flat clearing. There, a great vine from one tree caught up on another 4 feet away creating a natural cradle, perhaps the hand of man helped nature. [23] We found, as well as the prickly and vexatious *Rubus,* a bush which carries black berries, *Convulvous, Oenotherus, Cistus* [27] and, here and there amidst thorns and needles a wild rose blushed.

"There, a great vine from one tree caught up on another 4 feet away creating a natural cradle."

This island, totally uncultivated, serves only for the grazing of cattle which even winter there. In all this expanse one finds only one house. To it, a few months ago, a poor family moved and supports itself on the garden and on milk. If one likes solitude one must surely be happy here; one could not find a wilder place. In the evening a million mosquitoes *arrivent pour passer la Soirée.* In vain one lights fires to drive off the intruders. They are at once uninvited physicians and musicians, passing through fire and smoke with their lancets and clarinets. The bare and sandy shores of this island are covered with a tremendous number of small crabs. They are no more than an inch long. As well as their usual claws and legs they have a claw in the form of a huge shovel which is carried folded on their back. This shovel is bigger than the whole body, and it seems to me to be the biggest hindrance for these small creatures, but it must serve them somehow, perhaps for defense instead of a saber, or for eating, instead of a hand or a spoon, or as a spade for digging themselves into the sand.[28]

We returned again to the land through a cloud of various sea birds which undisturbed find abundant food in the rushes of the island and on the seashore. Amongst them the *pluvers* were in the greatest number, feeding on little snails. These birds, so they say, are excellent to eat. They are a sort of duck, very beautiful in both shape and plumage. Getting out of the boat we walked for nearly a mile alongside the sea. The view of the tremendous ocean, the periodical roar of the booming waves, the cries of the birds and the quiet and solitude of nature all around evokes melancholy [24] which is not without sweetness. The shore was covered with seaweed, *algae marinae*, and with various types of mussels. Amongst these, the common mussel, in America called *Clam;* egg-shaped with a smooth shell, meat like an oyster but tougher. I ate a half dozen, fresh from the sea—they are quite tasty.

But above all our attention was drawn to the hideous and awkward creature, *Kings Crab*. They are a foot and a half in length. One can see

"The hideous and awkward creature, *Kings Crab*."

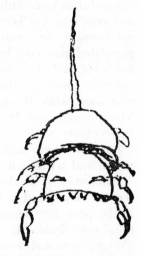

from head to foot only a shell in the shape of a helmet. I could not discover the head; the tail is of horn, hard and standing up like a Prussian pigtail. These hideous things came out on the shore in thousands—it was mating time. Who would say that these cold and hard shells know how to love. However, I, who have been at fifty of their weddings, can say they not only love passionately forgetting all else, but in spite of this are considerate and full of attention. I demonstrated this by a trick of which I should be ashamed. I turned one of these ladies on her back. It is known that a crab, left on the sand in this position, and being unable to right herself again and return to the sea, must die. Madame crab found herself in this situation as a result of my cruelty; her lover noticing the danger to the life of his mate ran up and in two or three minutes dragged her along six inches. Now with claws, now with his shell, he tried to turn her onto her feet, but in vain; the lady was fat and would have been lost had not I —softened by the concern of the two of them—placed her again on her legs. The waves of the sea grasped both of them and protected them from further dangers.

As I have said, all this seashore for three or four miles [25] does not show a single dwelling place and there is very little farming. Apart from the poor quality of the land a reason for the lack of habitation is the holding of large acreages in one hand. Summers had 500 acres near his inn, his brother 1,500 or 2,000, and the old man living by the shore a like amount. And thus scarcely a tenth part of the land is cultivated; the rest lies fallow, at first because the owner himself either can not or does not want to make a profit. The income from the inn and from trade satisfies, without a great deal of work, all his needs and comforts. Furthermore, hired hands are expensive and hard to get because the greatest number of the inhabitants of these thinly populated places are busy at the iron or saw mills. Finally, the owner holds his land at a high price. It is rare to find an American who is not fully convinced that the land must, with time, rise in value, that in a short while it will become ten times more valuable than now. These dreams may be barren, and then perhaps, with the upset and persecutions in Europe, they may come true. But these hopes contribute, as I have said, not a little to the postponement of the cultivation and settlement of many parts of America.

Exhausted by a whole day's walk, we returned in the evening to the inn. We found it filled with the captains of the ships standing in the port; Mr. Summers the landlord, a well-built young man, as usual very drunk. However, drink instead of arousing joy made him gloomy, stern and seemingly jealous. His wife was more of a servant than a wife. She did not sit at table; she waited on everyone, but had her eyes glued on her husband, anticipating all his thoughts. All these attentions were accepted with an icy indifference. This sort of a situation for a lady always arouses sympathy. Because of her beauty and goodness this sentiment is even more strongly felt.

[26] The wind, blowing almost always off the sea, makes this place cool and pleasant even in the greatest heat. The 11th day of June we left for Little Egg harbor. Halfway there we learned that on the river of this name there was no ferry large enough to carry our carriage across. Nothing demonstrates better the limited facilities for land communication existing in these parts. That is, in these eternal forests whose constant view is interrupted only by the sound of water turning the saw mills, by noise of furnaces and the hammers of an iron forge.

The most important of these is the iron foundry of Mr. Richards in Batstow.[29] There was no inn there but we were told that the owner willingly accepts travelers into his home. This hospitality so common in simpler times in America, so much praised by various writers, I found here for the first time. Unknown as we were, carrying no letters of introduction, Mr. Richards greeted us with frank openness but without any excess, without even any compliments. His son helped to bring our things into the house. There was no scurrying about the house; the host and his wife did not change their dress on our coming; they set out, as is their custom, tea and coffee.

At eight in the evening we went to the furnaces, or forges, where they melt and pour the iron. These furnaces burn with a ceaseless fire through months, in a word—as long as the crude ore remains. The ore is not dug out of the depths of the earth but from its surface; it is found near the swamps and bogs. The iron is called *Bog Iron*. Water seeping through bogs grown over with cedars, draining through ground made of *Silex* or flint sand forms this ore. What is more interesting is that the metal [ore] dug out, renews itself, and in such quantity, [27] that in the course of 28 years the ore has been dug out of the same place three times, and three times it has renewed itself. It is melted after adding to it a mixture of 15 parts of charcoal and one part of shells from oysters or *Clams* or of limestone. This addition they call *flux*. The largest number of workers were from Ireland. A few marry and settle in this country. Others come across the Atlantic Ocean only on formal hire. After 6 or 7 years of hard work and economical living they gather 700 or 800 ducats and return to their native land. Mr. Richards manufactures at least 500 *Ton* of iron a year. A *Ton* consists of 2,000 pounds and sells for 40 dollars—a sum of 80,000 dollars [sic]. It is true that carrying out the whole activity is costly; the workers are highly paid; there are horses and oxen for transport;

the ore and charcoal in large quantities; in spite of this the net profit must be large.

Every eight hours a furnace is opened and the iron is poured in the following manner. In front of the furnace a small trough has been dug, six inches in width and as deep as it is wide. From the sides of this trench there are shorter trenches communicating with it, on both sides. The molten iron is poured into the transverse trough and spreads out over all the side trenches filling them. When the metal cools, the masses are removed from the side trenches; these are called *Pig*. They are then carried to the forge where they are made into bars. While I was looking at this metal flowing in a fiery stream, and on the half-naked and baked cyclopes, dripping with sweat, busy over it; I thought, how useful how much more valuable than gold it is, if it is turned into ploughshares and farmers' tools, but how diabolic if swords or murderous cannons are cast from it.

"In front of the furnace a small trough has been dug. . . . From the sides of this trench there are shorter trenches . . . on both sides."

[28] The next day for eight miles we had to pass through the most difficult sands. We went more on foot than in the carriage. We saw the place whence they take the iron, the very place I mentioned above which in 28 years has renewed itself three times. This metal is on the surface of the earth near the bogs, in which there is a large number of the most strange plants, *Saracenia;* we found also *Limodorum Tuberosum* (*Ginandria*).[30] Farther on were the forges of

Mr. Richards and others, where the iron, melted into pigs, is turned into bars. Both cylindrical bellows and the huge hammers are turned by water.

We had our dinner amidst emptiness eight miles from there. There are no longer bogs, sand, gloomy cedar and pine forests, but an open and fertile country. My eyes wearied for a long time by the sunken emptiness were cheered by this sight. With the fertility of the land there is much more settlement and the mien of the inhabitants is more prosperous. An abundant tillage is the one bosom at which the inhabitants are fed their needs, their comforts and their affluence. With these gifts their lives are made more comfortable and this makes them both more willing and able for the state of marriage. And that is why the population of Mount Holy [Holly] is large. This is a well-built town in a fertile and pleasant situation. A river, not large but navigable, flows by its side with clear and healthy water, and there are canals dug out alongside the streets.

Beyond the town of Mount Holy, from whose top the eye discovers an extensive countryside, there are fields covered with sheaves, meadows, and dense belts of woods. On the very edge of the horizon glitters the Dellawar river and near it, seen as in miniature, the city of Philadelphia. While a crowd of young girls gathered strawberries, we gathered plants. As well as the common plants; *Silene, Prunella vulgaris,* [29] *Asclepias, Apussinum Canubinum,* which the Indians used instead of hemp,[31] we found *Itea Virginien,* a bush with flowers growing in a white raceme which is found more to the south, *Thalictrum Dioicum, Arbustus* with light leaves hanging near the base, this bush was *floro masculo* with many stamens, *Sysirynthium Bermudianum,*[32] etc.

The next day at nine we stopped for breakfast in Burlington on the banks of the Dellawar. The well-built town is in keeping with the beauty of the situation, the Dellawar, clear and wide, and across it Bristol. The banks were full of boats from Philadelphia covered by the shade from the hanging branches of weeping willows. The town is paved, with wide streets; the houses reflect the substance of the inhabitants, peace and quiet, a settlement of Quakers, for in these parts all Americans are Quakers. There is no noise of carriages. There is no fife and drum accompanying a guard of armed loafers, going on sentry duty. The law and good customs watch over all. In Burlington there is a *College* [33] for the young to which parents, even from as far away as Philadelphia, send their children to avoid distractions. Unhappily there are also rum and whisky distilleries. In this town, for the first time I had an occasion to see a dwarf. He was a Quaker, already elderly, a widower with three children. Through sand and forest we continued our journey to Cooper's *farry*[34] opposite Philadelphia where we stopped at two o'clock on the 14th of June 1799.

[1] Nov. 1 in company of Mr. G. G. Fasz [J. J. Faesch] my household-companion, I rode out on a visit to the furnaces of his iron forge at Mount Hope.[35] The countryside, cultivated and inhabited, is familiar to me as far as Springfield. In Springfield Mr. Lacase brought me to M. La Croix, a merchant or rather the captain of a ship, who has acquired a house and land here and settled here as have many of his fellow countrymen. The object of my visit was to see some pictures of which I had heard many times. I was attracted more by the civility with which the host showed me his cabinet than by the beauty of the pictures. There were a few copies in the Flemish style such as one finds everywhere in houses in Europe, even offered for sale on the streets. But in America the eye, grown unaccustomed to that which is beautiful in art, looks with joy on these indifferent reminders. The most beautiful of M. La Croix's pictures was his wife, a tawny, elegant, black-eyed creole.

Leaving Springfield one can see a big mill serving the sole purpose of cutting bark for a tannery. In the inhabited parts of the U.S. it is difficult to drive for 10 miles without seeing some outstanding building, examples of the public interest or of the industry of the inhabitants. During the last 50 years this country has come to fruition more than many of the ancient countries in Europe have progressed in, I can almost say, many centuries. Why?—The freedom, which for a long time has existed in America. Freedom, I say, is Real for people in the same way as the sun is to the elements and vegetation; it speeds their growth, increases their strength, warms and ripens the fruits of their labors. [2] Chat[h]am is beside rushing and lively waters, with scattered houses and tremendous sawmills.

Eight miles farther on Moris Town [Morristown], the seat of the County Court, has been in existence for 60 years.[36] A square of houses, closing off a huge open common; at the sides the houses are a furlong or more from each other. The most showy cities in Europe had such beginnings. The first inhabitants are farmers, drawn by the fertility of the soil and the good location. They have plenty of land; they occupy and fence as much as need requires, or greed tempts. The increase of population diminishes the size of these enclosures and with the centuries the huts, barns, fields and meadows change into continuous streets and proud buildings. Many are the denizens of New York, who have seen harvests where today stand the most important parts of the town. In Morys Tow[n] one can see proof of public intent, the sentiment through which a citizen (in the success, the advantages, the splendors of the city in which he was born) finds an internal joy and satisfaction. The water from the surrounding hills is brought by underground pipes. This activity is undertaken by a company, each share in which costs 50 dollars. For the same reason that three U.S. frigates are called a fleet, these oaken pipes carrying water are called here an aqueduct. For reasons of empty vanity the town is also beginning to build a stone bridge.

[3] In Moris Town we had dinner at C[a]pt. Ford.[37] The Ford family in Moris County is as great in number as, for example, the Paszkowskis in the Brześć County.[38] Mrs. Faesch, Dr. Darby, Miss Carny composed the company.[39] Miss Carny, a little lady of 86 years, lives New Jersey history. She remembers this country in the hands of the Indians, remembers the founding of a large number of the cities; in a word, she remembers the transformation of a wilderness into a cultivated land inhabited by industrious and enlightened people. And so the progression of human designs, the steps of civilization in society encompassing the span of a thousand years, actions filling *Volumina* of deeds in which perhaps twenty generations, one after the other, took part in their different ways: on all this, on all the deeds, I say, of so many centuries, one person looked on in one life span.

In the evening we stopped at Boun Ton [Boonton]. It has been just two years since I was for the first time in the residence of the Faesch family. The father, an upright and hospitable man, is no longer alive. He was born in Switzerland in the city of Basle. When he was 31, he was brought over in the company of Germans to mine and work iron ore. He, as every European in America who knows a craft or a trade useful here, earned himself an estate. For a very small sum he bought 10 thousand acres of rocky country of very little use for cultivation, covered with trees but beneath, offering an abundance of iron metal. This place he called Mount Hope. He set up the first forges, mills, etc. With several score of Germans who had come with him [4] he worked for many profitable years after which floods, fires, the acceptance as partners of people who knew more of how to cheat than of business, buried him in debts to which the heirs had to assign all the estate before it could free itself of them. In Bounton on lease, is a place where the iron converted from ore in Mount Hope is turned into bars and rods. Bounton, set amidst steep cliffs, with all about the noise of crashing streams, amidst dams, dikes, forges, mills, a general din, the noise of turning wheels and of hammers beating ceaselessly; Bounton, I say, is a singular place in its way. Wild and savage nature has enhanced this place with all its attraction; poets, painters and lovers will find here an abundant and inexhaustible feast for their eyes and senses.

I was present when the rods of iron, from which rails are made, were drawn out. The machine for cutting bars of iron into 5 or 6 rods at one time is interesting. The younger Fasch worked like an ordinary laborer.[40]

The next day with the older Faesch and two sisters we set off for Mount Hope. The road was rocky and steep. Before we got to Rokoway [Rockaway] I heard about a romance which one would not expect to find in this rocky, hollow and uninhabited place. [5] Capt. Hall, a man of some wealth, and what is more, married, fell in love with Mrs. Cooper, who had a weak and sickly husband.[41] After collecting all the ready money he could, Capt. Hall gave up his patrimony, family and ran away with his beloved one. And so blind love, and incontinent lust finds itself not only in populous cities spoiled by excesses, but equally amongst people living far from society, simply and in moderate circumstances.

Rokoway is a valley compassing a few miles of rather fertile land in the middle of unfertile and rocky country. The little town or village has several score of scattered houses, one or two forges and as many sawmills. After a 4-hour journey we came finally to Mount Hope. This place was deserted 30 years ago. The father of the young Faesch, finding the ground practically all iron ore, set up a furnace for smelting iron and built a house. The house is on a little hill, with before it a huge quagmire of a pasture. Here and there are scattered the houses of the workers; on the left hand is a large lake which provides the water for the mills. The horizon on all sides is lined with mountains covered with forests. Four shafts provide the main access to the iron ore, which is the raw material. The deepest are 30 to 40 feet; two or three people work in each one. From one hundred to two hundred souls, counting women and children, belong to this tremendous undertaking. There are four or five teams of oxen and horses, of these the greater [6] number haul charcoal. For a *Ton* of iron, which is two thousand pounds, 14 *Cordes* of wood burnt to charcoal are used.

The furnace, once started, burns day and night until the frost stops the water from running and therefore the wheels. Here they either melt the iron and pour it into *Pigs* which are then sent to the forge to be turned at once into bars and rods, or they pour it into forms for fireplaces, stoves called Franklin, kettles, fire pots, andirons for fireplaces, bombs, bullets, but mostly ballast for ships. They also make there *Shot Metal* or tempered iron. The iron is heated to melting and then they pour it with big ladles into cold water. By this operation it is turned into small balls, gravel or sand and has a yellowish color like brass. Iron tempered in this way, when mixed with the ordinary metal, gives first class iron of the best quality.

Of the large number of these people belonging to this factory, only about 40 are truly workers. Some of them are paid 10 and 12 pounds or ducats a month; others are paid by the *Ton* of finished metal. Though the pay is good, there are no instances of one of these workers having built up a fortune. Attached as they are to the place on which a large number of them were born, and above all subject to the force of habit, this strong lord of human nature, these people keep their place. Above all their trade, or life, which at first glance appears so heavy and so industrious, when looked at more closely is seen as only a constant alternation of heavy work with complete inactivity. During an 18 or 20 hour period there is a half [7] an hour of heavy devilishly hot work when they take the molten iron from the furnace and pour it into the forms. For the rest of the time, whether by day or by night, there is needed only the adding of charcoal and flux and light supervision. The largest part of the time is spent in talking, cards or sleeping. Furthermore, these people do not know the cares and troubles of domestic life. The owner keeps a store, from which he provides food, drink, and clothing, etc., taking the money from their pay and reserving 10 per cent for himself. It is not strange that in this situation, where the sum of inactivity so pleasant to man, exceeds work, and far distant from the sight of better conditions, they are content with their lot. They are born and die charcoal burners and iron workers. When the ice stops the mills, they spend the wintertime cutting wood and making charcoal.

I spent the time during my week in Mount Hope in the huge forests surrounding this place. With a gun in my hand and a book in my pocket, I chased after squirrels or sat exhausted on the stump of a tree or on a stone, and read Montaigne or the Comedies of Molière. From the creation of the world this was perhaps the first time that the rhymes of Misanthrope and Tartuffe echoed in these wild and uninhabited places.

These wilds, as I have said, rise up rocky and mountainous. Centuries were needed before fallen leaves, rotting and mouldering growth, formed on these rocks sufficient *terreau*, or soil which could produce from the rocks such tremendous trees. Oaks, elms and mostly various varieties of nut trees comprise the woods of these places.

A propos the nuts: [8] I saw in this free country, in this corner so close to the state of nature, I saw, I say, despotism as defined by Montesquieu demonstrated in action.[42] The sons of the iron workers, in order to save themselves the work of shaking or pulling off the nuts, find it simpler to cut the tree and gather the nuts from it, as it lies on the ground. This damage is as disastrous to the forest, as it bears witness to the stupid indifference of the delinquents.

The forested cliffs are often divided by valleys which are covered with an impenetrable thickness of juniper, thorns and bushes. Two miles to the north the Rokoway river flows amidst these rocks and woods, and here and there among rugged rocks forms noisy cascades. Apart from raccoons, skunks (a sort of polecat), and squirrels, of which there is a multitude, there are only a few large animals in these wilds. The squirrels are of various varieties, rather few flying squirrels, *ground Squarel* the size of a young rat, spotted like a suslik and easy to tame, they are entertaining and attractive to look at.[43] The most common squirrels are ash-colored, twice as big as ours, with a skin like our gray squirrel. The Americans do not use the fur (surely because it is common) but eat the meat. From the four I killed, we had a quite tasty soup. Apart from squirrels, four-legged animals are rare in these wilds. Pheasants it seems have made their settlement here. They are not like ours with gold and red feathers; they are unlike those from Bohemia, but of a type indigenous to this part of the world, somewhat similar to but a bit bigger than our partridge.[44]

The 8th of Nov. I returned to Elizabeth Town on horseback on a direct road through Moristown.

Fig. 70. George Richard, 3rd Viscount Bolingbroke and 4th Viscount St. John. From the portrait by John Hoppner. Courtesy of the Viscount Bolingbroke and St. John.

Fig. 71. Passaic Bridge at Acquackanonck. By Baroness Hyde de Neuville. Courtesy of The New-York Historical Society, New York City.

Fig. 72. View of Utica from Hotel. By Baroness Hyde de Neuville. Courtesy of Prints Division, New York Public Library.

Fig. 73. The Holland Land Company's Hotel, Utica. By Baroness Hyde de Neuville. Courtesy of The New-York Historical Society, New York City.

A Map of the STATE of NEW YORK

SIMEON DE WITT
Surveyor General

Contracted from his large Map of the State

1804

KEY TO PLACES

1. Elizabeth Tow[n]
2. Newark
3. Acquackanonc
4. Capt. Hopper's
5. Suffern
6. Chester
7. Goshen
8. Montgomery
9. Springtown [N
10. Mme. Delame
11. Kingston
12. Catskill
13. Coxsackie
14. Coeymans
15. Albany
16. Schenectady
17. Verder's
18. Pride's Tavern
19. Fonda
20. Canajoharie
21. Palatine
22. Little Falls

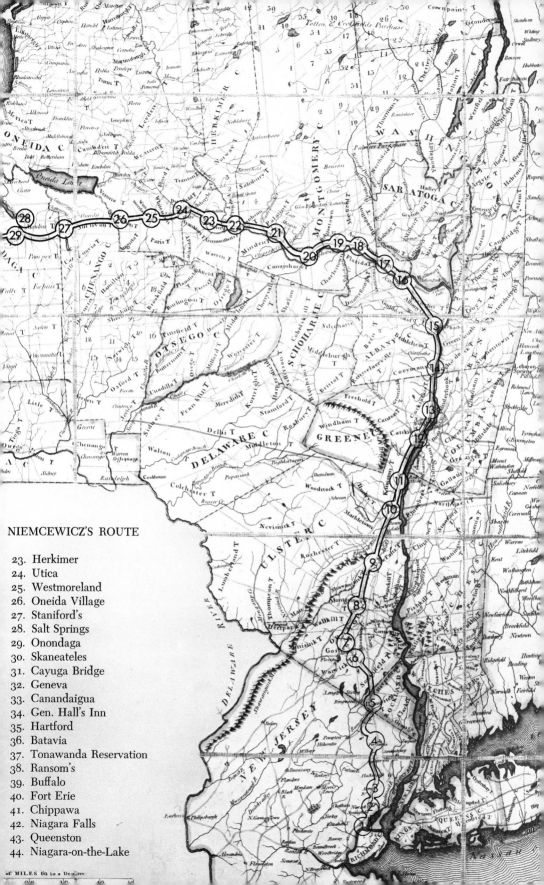

NIEMCEWICZ'S ROUTE

vue de geneva et du lac Seneca

7br 1807.

Fig. 75. View of Geneva and of Lake Seneca. By Baroness Hyde de Neuville. Courtesy of The New-York Historical Society, New York City.

Fig. 76. Niagara Falls, 1804. From the oil painting by Antoine Philippe d'Orléans. Courtesy of The New-York Historical Society, New York City.

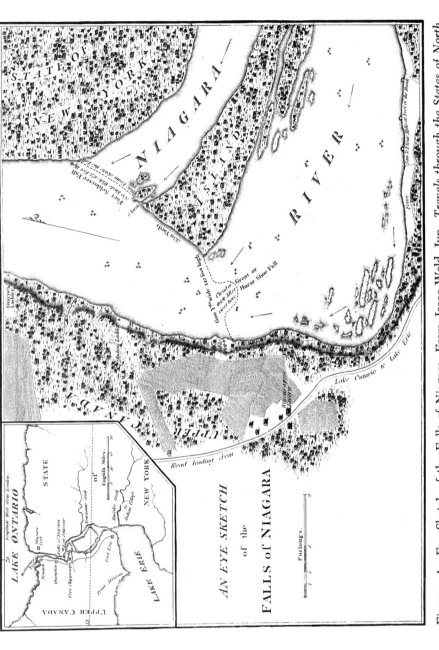

Fig. 77. An Eye Sketch of the Falls of Niagara. From Isaac Weld, Jun., *Travels through the States of North America* . . . *1795, 1796, and 1797, 1807.*

Part II

JOURNEY TO NIAGARA, 1805

JOURNEY TO NIAGARA, 1805

Ever since coming to America, I have wished most ardently to see the famous Niagara Falls. Eight years have passed by and various impediments have always thwarted my plan. At last I am compensated for this long delay by the splendid opportunity that now presents itself, this being a journey to the same region by my neighbors M. and Mme. B.[1] They suggested that I join them. Their company made me forget both the difficulties and the hardships and even the lateness of the season almost as far advanced as my age. I accepted. In half an hour my small portmanteau was packed and all the preparations for the journey were finished!

We left at half past four the fifth of October 1805, with a fine carriage, two good horses, a reliable servant, and a good hunting dog. We passed through Newark, a small town, where there is much activity and trade, which from day to day promises to be more flourishing. After that one skirts the Passaic River, bordered on both sides by houses which bespeak affluence. At Acquackanonck[2] one crosses the river by a wooden bridge and instead of a cheerful view one sees a dry, rocky, somber land, whole fields covered with Gnaphalium (mouse's ear) which gave off a strong odor.[3] This plant is always the sign of bad soil. We stopped at the house of a farmer of Dutch descent. The delapidated house of massive stones indicated an old settlement. Everything was neat and clean. While our horses ate their hay, we were served a dinner which would have tempted St. John in the Wilderness; we had honey in the comb and, instead of grasshoppers, bread and fresh butter. The Paterson [Passaic] Falls are not far from here. The farmer told us that the land was exhausted, as so must have been the lands of ancient Europe. We continued our route skirting always the Passaic River, its waters wide and clear, its banks lined with huge chestnuts, oaks, and *hemlocks* and the horizon cut off by a chain of mountains which blended their grayish peaks with the blue of the sky—all spreading out before our eyes picturesque landscapes and cheerful scenes. We arrived at Captain Hop[p]er's.[4] His inn, scorning a nearby hill from which there is a charming view with a waterfall, stands in a damp and gloomy hollow. The meal was, however, very satisfying and the bed very comfortable.

Sunday, the 6th. We continued our way by a rather bad road leading through mountainous country. The fields however were well cultivated, and seen from across the heaps of stones the rye appeared
quite good. We found ourselves stopped often by wagons filled with
men, women, and children going to church. All were well dressed.
We even met some women dressed in silks. There were commodious
farmhouses solidly built for the most part in the Dutch style. The
[Ramapo] ⁵ river winds across this country; to the right and to the
left there are jagged and fissured rocks. The rocks are of granite im-
pregnated with talc and mica. I saw two iron forges. One finds in
these mountains bears, deer, grouse, and pheasants and, what is worst
of all, rattlesnakes. They are beginning to disappear, however, for as
soon as the *Ash* drops its leaves these snakes disappear, either because the leaves are poisonous to them or because they cannot stand
the cold which caused this fall.⁶

Leaving a pass through these mountains, which are but a branch
of the large Allegheny chain, we came into the broad expanse of a
great valley. To the right were meadows, to the left fields of hemp.
This is as yet a new crop, but it is visibly flourishing and can only
become a source of wealth for this country. Already Orange County
alone grows 150 tons of it. A ton sells at times for over 300 dollars,
never less than 200.⁷

We had good lodging at Chester. The hostess was good-natured
and cheerful. On entering their parlor I found there six young men,
well-dressed and of fine stature. I supposed them to be a gathering of
all the young people of the village. The hostess disabused me, telling
me that all these men were her sons. Here is a woman who deserves
well of her country, furnishing it so abundantly with the commodity
most needed in a new land. It froze this night to the point of killing
the *potato* vines. The ice was the thickness of a silver dollar. Only fifteen days ago we were dying of the heat; this is a ridiculous climate.
The next morning we saw all the gentlemen of the town preparing to
go fox hunting—they had about ten hounds. It is not certain that they
will take the fox, but it is certain that they will get drunk.

7th of October. We continued our route through Goshen, situated in
a fertile plain. Montgomery and Springtown ⁸ are watered by the
Esopus ⁹ river which is lined by a special type of oak called river
oak.¹⁰ We rolled through woods of chestnuts, oaks, etc., along a smooth
and even road with the peaks of the same chain of mountains on both
sides. We met a procession of about thirty wagons filled with men
and women who were going six miles or more in them to an interment.
Thus a lot of time and labor is lost with the principal actor the least

of all aware of the proceedings. But, while partly a religious duty, it is much more an Event, a holiday even, if you prefer, which brings them together for gossip and drinking and thus breaks the uniform monotony of the ordinary day.

We slept in an inn completely isolated in the middle of a big forest. We certainly did not expect to find there one of the most attractive women one could hope to see. She was Mme. Delametre,[11] innkeeper in these parts: with youthful candor, perfect features, magnificent complexion, unconscious grace, enough animation to be lively, yet with a certain hesitation in response which adds a veil of mystery to her beauty and quickens one's interest. She and her husband, a polite and well-built young man, hurried to make our lodgings as pleasant as possible. Mme. Delametre, carrying a child whom she was weaning [12] on one arm, with the other opened the cabinet, drew out the linen, carried the cream, the preserves, etc. In Europe, when I was younger and more gallant, I could not have borne to see her take so much trouble; I would have perhaps asked her to marry me, but this is not the custom of the country!

October 8. We regretfully discovered that our baggage [13] and the carriage had quarreled, and the back of the carriage was all battered from this affair. This put us out of temper and made us lose much time. We tore ourselves away from Mme. Delametre.

Land, even though hardly cleared, sells at the rate of 15, 20 and 25 dollars. Without ever being manured it produces excellent rye and above all clover. Further on the boulders reappear with their enormous crevasses, blocks torn off and thrown here and there in frightful confusion, evidence of a violent upheaval. Sometimes they are carved in perpendicular walls and appear in the perfect likeness of the curtains and flanks of a bastion with their banquettes. At other times they border the highway like very regular, high ramparts. The firs, the yews, the larches become more common as we proceed towards the north.

Kingston is rather a large town, containing many fine houses and many ruins. One reads on the Town Hall, *"This town has been burnt by British cruelty."* [14] This inscription may have its merit as a political sentiment, but in the moral sense, to perpetuate so ostentatiously the animosity and hate between nations, is neither humane nor Christian.

At some distance from there we met a pretty, young girl on horseback. She was the rear guard of a caravan composed of five big covered wagons drawn by oxen and horses. Many cows walked at the side. The wagons were loaded with chests filled apparently with hatchets, saws, etc., and with a large quantity of featherbeds, and with an even greater number of children heaped topsy-turvy on the beds. It was a colony coming from New England [15] to settle in the open country along the shores of the lakes. It was a nursery of MEN who were going to plant themselves in regions which have never seen any kind of human habitation. To venture such a settlement, so fraught with hardship, one must have both strength of mind and youthful vigor. Such was, however, the origin of all these American States which today we see so well cultivated and flourishing. Such was formerly the origin of all empires. The family arrives in the midst of gloomy and silent forests. Immediately they cut some trees and construct a log house. They clear the land as soon as possible. They harrow or rather they scratch at the soil and they seed it with wheat or other grain. Provisions of salt meat, *spirits,* fish and game sustain the family until the first harvest, which is always very abundant. Men and women work without rest to clear their land and to improve their cabin. The swine and fowl visibly multiply. In about three years the land is already under cultivation. The forests give way to the axe and to the plow. The *log house* is transformed into a *frame house.* Neighbors arrive from all sides. It is at first a small village, then a town, then a city. Without oppressive laws, without hindrance by the government, without taxes, without compulsory military service, man left to his own devices prospers better than when so-called benevolent governments meddle with his affairs.

We arrived in Catskill by a good road; it is an important town situated at the confluence of the river of the same name and of the Hudson. We got out at the City Hotel, where we found much pretension, but the food and the service were wretched. Five or six bespectacled jades both white and black ran about like lunatics, without their galloping about and their clamor producing anything worthwhile. The innkeeper went out at nine o'clock in the evening to search for provisions in the market, and therefore these were all tough and bad. The windows which had been completely broken since the celebration of the Fourth of July were not yet repaired. Others with panes missing were stuffed with the dirty petticoats of the Negresses or with old hats. The bill was exorbitant. If the inn is bad, the small town, thanks to its situation, is full of commercial activity, with many *sloops* in the port, some saw mills, and a quantity of planks and *shingles* ready to be exported.

The 9th. We left Catskill in the morning. At Coxsackie we found the militia drawn up for drill just at the moment of loading rifles. Our carriage passed; immediately the whole battalion forgetting its commander and the maneuver turned to look at us. This idle curiosity would scandalize a Prusian officer. But let me tell the Herren Hautp-mann that this battalion is not composed of those torn by violence from their family and their plow, paid five cents a day, beaten twenty times a day with blows from a cane, but these are free men who are gathered together in accordance with the law that they have made for themselves. However inferior they may perhaps be to regular troops drawn up in battle, they lack in case of need neither courage nor perseverance to defend their homes to the last drop of their blood.

We arrived at Coeymans [16] at two o'clock in the afternoon and, as the countryside promised abundant game which M. B. ardently craved, we stopped there. The appearances were not misleading. In less than two hours M. B. brought down three pheasants, seven quails, and a woodcock, to the great astonishment of the inhabitants and perhaps even of the feathered tribe, neither the one nor the other having ever seen shooting on the wing and above all such good shooting.

There remained sixteen miles to Albany which we reached in the middle of a rainstorm and by the worst possible road. On our route from New Jersey we have seen only three or four *turnpikes* or high-ways. But here, instead of following the mail routes, as they so obviously do in Europe, they cut right into the interior of the provinces, towards the lands whence come the produce and the principal commodities. One must assert that the interests of private individuals are also involved. Those who have large acreage in the *back countries* try to obtain charters for these highways which give that much more value to their properties and thus attract a larger number of colonists.

October 10th. We arrived in Albany, a town already large and well populated, which is situated at the confluence of the Mohawk and the Hudson. Placed as it is 170 miles in the interior it does not have a maritime trade, but it is the commercial center for all the merchandise which comes there from an immense expanse of country, as much by the boats of the Mohawk as by wagons from the Genesee and other regions. We stayed at the Tontine Coffee House,[17] an inn setting a good table but with bad service and the house scarcely clean. We found there fourteen people eating at the common table, a great advantage for the traveler, who in a short time can thereby acquire information on the locale which he would not otherwise be able to obtain. These gentlemen were polite without affectation, communicative without garrulity. They had that appearance of ease that one finds in Europe only in the upper classes. Here, it is the fruit of a liberty which they enjoy from infancy and of that spirit of independence which produces hard work and industry; architects of their own fortune they owe nothing to anyone; they believe themselves equal to everybody. The advice that they gave us on our journey to Niagara was in some respects comforting, in others disquieting. From the manner in which we go, the greatest marvel will not be the falls themselves but that we arrive there at all. I have been to see Mme. Belle, a friend of my wife who spent some time in our house five years ago. A woman of such wit, fine judgment, and learning is most uncommon in this country. I bought a map of New York by de Witt.[18]

[October 11th]. I was awakened the 11th at daybreak by a violent storm and the roll of thunder. The sky cleared toward ten o'clock and we left in very hot weather for the season. The road from Albany to Schenectady, which on my first trip seven years ago was a sea of sand, is now a highway and furthermore a highway extending up to Geneva, 200 miles from Albany. The road is straight as an arrow, lined on both sides with woods of spruce. There are few farms but many inns and loaded wagons coming and going.

Schenectady, as old as Albany and built by the Dutch, is the end of the run for the boats coming down the Mohawk. The Cohoes Falls prevent further navigation. There is talk of a canal which is going to remove this obstacle. The shallowness of the river allows navigation only in the spring and then rarely for boats carrying more than 150 bushels. During the rest of the year everything goes on wheels. This river, as do almost all in this country, yields few fish. The eel is most common; there are a few perch and pike. We crossed the Mohawk River by ferry. The rain had washed out the highway which appeared to me to have been built in haste and poorly designed. The countryside on this bank took on a different aspect; instead of clayey and sandy soil with spruce, one sees black soil with oaks.

We made only seven miles and slept at the house of Verder [19] in the middle of woods. A gradual slope leads to the river. The opposite bank is crested by a ridge of high mountains covered with gloomy forests. Our hosts, the good Dutch, certainly do not recognize how romantic this situation is. Men and women here appear to be tall and strong. Our hostess, nearly sixty years old, came to sit by the fireplace and entertained us with tales of the good old times, when the huts of the Indians were only two steps away and Sir William Johnson, the English general, had his house [20] a few miles from here. She told how he used to entertain at dinner both whites and redskins; how he had taken as a wife or mistress a *Squaw* (Indian girl), dressed as a savage with large earrings and a ring in her nose; how by this marriage and by his perfect knowledge of the Indian language, his humanity and generosity, he had won for himself the love of all the tribes; how he had had educated the celebrated Brant,[21] chief of the Mohawk nation;

how his death had been mourned by all the Indians who believed they had lost their father. Indeed this tribe did not long survive him; the advancing whites swept them toward the Six Nations [22] who in turn began to scatter and disappear.

As evidence of the fertility of the countryside along all the length of the Mohawk and of the wealth of the farmers, I may say that a few miles from here a farmer sowed 210 bushels of wheat in a plot of 140 acres and harvested 3,000 bushels from it; this, at 13 shillings, 6 cents the bushel, the actual price in Albany, gives him 5,055 dollars or piasters.[23] Despite the fact that this land has been farmed for fifty years, it is still so good that it has never been manured. They fertilize only the hillside lands. The excellence of the products bespeaks the excellence of the soil; the bread, the potatoes, the beef, and the mutton are infinitely better than in Jersey and, while at home we pay 6 and 8 cents for beef, one can get it here for 4½. Butter is one shilling. The countryside does not produce any peaches, but there are plums in abundance.

October 12th. The surface of the *turnpikes* is now more and more broken up. Our horses are very tired; it is only with difficulty that we make thirty miles, travelling all day. We continually skirt the Mohawk. There is nothing more cheerful, more picturesque than this countryside, the clearness of the water, its beautiful meadows, its islands, its fields, the whole framed by mountains now retreating, now approaching, enchanting the eye and bringing to the spirit that pleasure which such beauty and abundance inspires. The countryside, though rather well populated for America, could easily hold fifty times more inhabitants.

Although most of the time we plod along a muddy road in the middle of thick woods, the monotony is broken by the variety and multiplicity of all the hues, shades, and colors with which Autumn has adorned the trees, and by the vistas on the river which in many places are as beautiful, perhaps even more beautiful, than the Thames at Twickenham, Strawberry Hill,[24] etc. Amongst a large variety of oaks one notices the unfamiliar *Turkish oak*,[25] yews, cedars, *hemlock*, and white spruce with its long and silky needles.

We passed by Stone Arabia, a small town in the mountains. For three to four miles one sees some dwellings, most of them inns. All these are perhaps necessary because of the great number of wagoners who cart the products of the country such as flour and potash and bring from Albany European merchandise. For, particularly in the season when the roads are good, this means of transportation is no more costly than going by boat. We breakfasted at Pride's Tavern [26] and slept at Shepherd's.[27] His house, not yet completed, stands on rising ground overlooking the river. A bridge [28] with a single arch of buoyant grace, the river flowing by, a smiling and well-cultivated country—all offer the most picturesque views.

October 13th. Because of the bad state of the roads, and the continual exhaustion our horses have suffered for the last eight days, we had to hire two horses. We continued our route across the eternal woods. I was glad to see some lindens, but as with all other trees in this country they surpass ours in girth and above all in height. Many of these trees appear to me to be 125 feet high—and I do not exaggerate. Their roots do not reach very deeply into the ground and so they are easily blown over by the winds. They grow very rapidly but the wood is not so durable as that of European trees. Everything in this hemisphere goes at a grand gallop, men as well as vegetation, but equally then all decays and perishes more swiftly. Nothing is more beautiful than the shades of the autumnal colors of these trees. The vivid scarlet of the *soft maple* [29] and the yellow of the poplars, blending with the deep green of the *hemlocks*, yews, and larches, spread out a most lively pageant of color.

Before one reaches the *small falls* [30] there is a place on the left bank of the Mohawk where steep walls of red granite come down almost to the river's edge and completely cut off the trail so that, to open a way for the road, they had to blow up a part with cannon powder. To the left one can see a tremendous block torn loose which by its size and shape reminds me of the block in St. Petersburg on which stands the statue of Peter the Great. On close inspection of this chain of mountains, which the road has followed since Schenectady, I found it to be of granite, but here and there along its margins are beds of laminated sandstone and even of schist—proof that in remote epochs the sea was here. The mountains we crossed while skirting the right bank of the Hudson were all of sandstone or slate, filled in many places with prodigious quantities of talc or mica.

In the place called the Palatinate (for the most part the establishments here carry the name of the innkeeper-proprietor) we stopped at the Zabriski Inn.[31] This name, with its Polish termination recalling that of Zabrzyski, had for a long time excited my curiosity but, though it was very common in Pennsylvania, in New York, and above all in Jersey, only now have I met someone who bears it. He gave, however, only vague answers to all of my questions. He said that he had lost his father at an early age, that his uncle had taken possession of the family papers, that he had been told that his great-grandfather had come from Poland 103 years ago, and as all ancestry must according to the rules be fabulous and illustrious, he added that this great-grandfather was brother to King John Sobieski,[32] that he had brought with him much money and bought an immense stretch of land. I do not speak of his other stories, of the letters that his uncle had recently received from Poland of the huge inheritance, of the strong trunks that he had been directed to bring in order to hold all the gold to be given him. All these trifles completely frustrated the kinship, the pleasure I had expected, in finding again in the wilderness of the New World a compatriot who would show me some writings, tell me some interesting anecdotes of my unhappy country. There is no doubt, however, that the ancestor of this young man did come from Poland. He was probably some young Socinian or Calvinist studying in Holland (as I have seen in my own time in Haarlem) who, stirred by some spirit of adventure, embarked with other Dutch colonists then emigrating to New York and New Jersey, and settled there. This group has increased enormously. This young man has a pleasant face. He is married to a Dutch girl who washes and cleans his home and keeps it very neat. He has built a fine house and has an excellent farm and is certainly much happier here than he would be in his village in Poland under the thumb of the prefect of the district.[33]

Let us return to the journal.

Having gone beyond the big block of red granite, one comes upon a bridge and view of a part of the Little Falls, then to a small town from whence one can see the whole descent of the falls. The falls are created by a sloping wall of rubble which blocks the river. To correct the situation there they have built a canal [34] whose locks for sound strength, beauty of the stone, and workmanship yield nothing to the quays of Paris, and all this in the middle of woods! Opposite the falls and this canal there is a fine-looking house. We were told that it belonged to a Mr. Alexander.[35] This interested me because of the identity of the name with that of the family I love so well, but it is impossible that it should be the family of Mme. Williams; [36] she would certainly have arranged an introduction.

A few miles further one finds the fertile plain called the German Flats. It stretches out very far lengthwise but it is narrow. All that is level presents a picture of the greatest fertility and of fine cultivation. It is divided into large regular squares covered with corn, wheat, all sorts of grain and meadows, through which the river winds. On both sides houses and villages occur more frequently than I have seen up to now. All these are inhabited by that hard-working race, the Germans. The town of Herkimer, which is in the center of this valley so favored by fortune, is entirely populated by families come from Connecticut. There are about fifty houses, so white, so new, so spick and span that one might say they were finished this very day. We stayed at Mr. Snow's [37] who came from New London with about ten male and female cousins. The men and women had a pleasing mien, and the speech and manners which characterize all the people from that part of America, the first settled and the most enlightened. I have however a complaint against the pretty innkeeper. She gave us coffee this morning made, I suspect, from corn or from the seeds of Palma Christi. They grow whole fields of this here under the name of Coffee Bean. [38]

October 14th. This happy valley continues further, but it ceases where the land rises and the trees take over their domain: and all for want of labor. It is true that in many places steel and fire have already waged mortal combat with these ancient forests. Without doubt the trees must go in order to have cultivated ground but, in getting rid of them one should recover some profit from them. But here it is a sorry sight, to see for mile after mile these enormous skeletons, these gigantic cadavers, shorn of their bark and half-burnt lying about wasted. I have seen railings made of enormous trees which could have served as the masts of the largest men-of-war.

Again today we met another caravan of emigrants from New Hampshire for the Black River 25 miles from Lake Ontario. It was made up of one family loaded with a lot of children. The women were in the wagon with their featherbeds on which in a confused heap, as is the custom, were the children, spinning wheels, chairs, and trunks. Two cows followed the wagon. These people travel economically. They feed their children with milk from the cows. They themselves have salted provisions and while stopping from time to time they make their own bread. I was astonished that they were going so far while the very country through which they traveled held soil so rich that it did not need to be fertilized. But the reason for this is that the speculative greed of the owners keeps the price of this land pretty high even though it is uncultivated. Land for land the colonist prefers an acre at a few shillings to an acre at 15 to 20 dollars. It is because of this that the population of the United States is so widely dispersed, but it is in this manner too that even in the most distant of her territories there form small nuclei of future populations. After reaching their goal these groups, in time, will spread backwards whence they came and fill those voids that they had left behind them. The Eastern and Middle States will doubtless populate that vast expanse of land bounded by the five lakes; while Pennsylvania, Virginia and much later Kentucky and Tennessee will send the excess of their population towards the immense plains of Louisiana. I do not believe that the two Carolinas and Georgia with their large estates under single ownership, their Negroes, and the scarcity of small landholders will ever need to send out colonists.

Towards noon we arrived at Utica. It is certain that the great Cato would never have suspected that two thousand years after his death his name would be given to a town in a hemisphere the very existence of which would at that time have seemed to him a myth. The inhabitants of this place themselves seem almost as little informed about Cato as Cato was about America. To the question I asked them as to why their town was called Utica one of them answered, *"It was christened in compliment to a gentleman of some note in the old countries."* The old Utica certainly did not grow so rapidly as the new one. Seventeen years ago Fort Schuyler was simply a wooden square called a fort which was adequate against the Indian Corps of Engineers. There was only a single house outside. Today one can count more than two hundred, with many workmen and shops even of luxury goods. I have seen jewelers' and wigmaker's shops. One of the principal streets was built up in only two years. We dined at a magnificent hotel built by the Holland Company,[39] which some time ago bought entire counties in this region.

We were visited by Mr. De Peyster,[40] a young man of 24 with the handsomest face I have ever seen. Whilst admiring its bloom and beauty I said to myself that in Paris and elsewhere with such a face he would be the delight of all the boudoirs. What, then, was my astonishment to learn that this American Paris was no other than a sea captain, that besides journeys to Europe and the West Indies he has been twice to Batavia and China, and that on the high seas he was the most fearless of all the sailors facing up to all the hardships. He has been on land for only a month with his kinsmen and all the comforts of life, and already he is bored and sighs for his beloved storms. One must not be very surprised to find the comforts of life so widespread among the inhabitants of the United States; they set about this in the only right way, beginning to work at an early age and fearing neither hardship nor danger.

In the evening we arrived in Westmoreland, passing through country more completely cleared and less sparsely populated. The roads here, being less often shaded by the high and everlasting forests, were both firmer and drier. Westmoreland is today a town of only three houses; in three years it will have three hundred. A few days ago an inhabitant there bought a lot of ¾ of an acre for which he paid 60 dollars. We found there a company of ladies and gentlemen who had come in a wagon from Lake Oneida, 30 miles, simply in order to take tea.

October 15th. The lodging and food were mediocre. Reed, the servant of M. B., poor fellow, has become sick; it is the first serious unpleasantness that we have had on our journey so far, although more than once we have been exasperated by stupidities. Mme. Belassis has given the sick man the most touching care. She has given up her place in the back of the carriage to him. She has given him drugs and cooling medicines. Whether things go well or ill, it is equally good to be with her. On this journey she is our main bulwark; she sustains us all and finds pleasure in everything.

We left early and came into completely new terrain. Here in the midst of forests, the enormous height and thickness of whose trees filled us with astonishment, we came from time to time upon clearings. In these one sees only the stumps of trees with a little cabin and, in the center of the clearing, on soil the surface of which was scarcely scratched, a few potatoes, some corn, a few chickens and pigs. It was quite surprising to see coming out of these huts good-looking and well-dressed women whose white hands draw water from a hole which serves as a well. When a traveler arrives in this place two or three years hence he will find a fine house, well-cultivated fields, and all the amenities of life.

We rose very early and arrived for breakfast at [blank], always through waste land or through country bristling with tree stumps and just beginning to be cleared. While breakfast was being prepared and while M. B. went to inspect the pheasants, I hurried to visit an Indian village of the Oneida tribe. The tribe has no more than 750 persons scattered on a terrain of 80,000 acres. That is all that remains of the indigenous inhabitants of this vast region. The legislature of New York has made a law by which individuals are forbidden to buy Indian lands. The State reserves this right to itself alone and in turn it resells them to individuals.

In spite of the evil of these savages as told by modern travelers, in spite of all the charges made against them which they fully deserve in many respects, one cannot help but feel an interest in the remnants of a people at one time so numerous, absolute masters of this rich hemisphere, who today, dispossessed and pursued, are disappearing and soon will be wiped out. Going toward the village, I met many of them, both men and women. Some were running with great speed, the others going hunting, and it astonished me that they were still carrying bows and arrows. Both men and women are slender and extremely tall and they are knock-kneed. Their faces and bodies are more or

less the color of copper; they have Tartar features with expressions
wild or witless. The men have leggings to below the knees, then a
clout to cover the genitals, the shoulders and the rest of the body
covered with a blanket. Their hair is black, long and straight; sometimes they wear a sort of kerchief on the head but more often nothing.
The women carry their babies lying on a small board swaddled in
rags, tied together with rope and hung from their necks. A piece of
cloth tied around their thighs serves them as petticoats and a blanket,
like that of the men, covers the shoulders.

When I got to the village I found an American who gave me some
interesting information about these savages. He told me that a marked
change for the better has been noticeable among them during the last
two years, due to a charlatan, or to a great man if you prefer, such as
were Moses, Mahomet, and all the great reformers of simple people.
This person—his name is Ga-ne-o-di-yo [41] [Handsome Lake]—who
lives in Buffalo Creek, pretends to be a prophet and has had direct
communication with Manitou [42] or the Great Spirit. He has been to
heaven where he has seen the souls of Indians who during their lives
had tilled the land and never got drunk. He has been to hell where he
has seen the souls of drunken Indians tormented by the most cruel
punishments. Beyond the principles of his doctrine and of his sermons,
that one should not drink, and that one should till the earth, he teaches
further that by not mixing with the whites, by teaching themselves
to be brave and hard-working, they would prevent the total extinction
of the Indian race: they would multiply and would even withstand
the white man. Although, unfortunately for these people, this prophet
has come a little late; nevertheless if his counsel were to be followed
by all the tribes and if he could succeed in impelling them to wipe out
the vice of drunkenness, to settle down as farmers on the land, his
prophecies could in part be realized.

Even now, I have been shown a building that is being put up to
serve as a school for the children. In a church already built a white pastor [43] who speaks Indian preaches to them Sunday after Sunday. Here
the squaws or female Indians sing psalms translated into their language
in a voice which I have been assured surpasses in sweetness any that
one hears among the white people.

My helpful American took me to the house of the chief of the tribe.
His house is quite well built and is painted red. In front of the door
we found two royal princesses who were washing down two sorry
little horses. There were some pigs and dogs; these made up the
palace guard. On entering the room we found wooden beds all around,
without any mattresses, only the same woolen blankets which serve

as clothing. His Majesty the King [44] had been sitting on one of these beds and was just getting up. He was an old man of 86, tattooed on his chest and hands, and with enormous ears. The queen, wearing leggings and a piece of cloth around her hips, was seated beside the fireplace before a big cauldron. A little girl of two ran around the room. I was presented and received warmly. My guide, who knew a few words of Indian, said that I had come from the Old World beyond the great lake. The king is a great friend of the white man and has thus incurred the animosity of the tribe. His power is limited to negotiations with the white man and to presiding in council; for the rest, he has not the least authority over his fellow tribesmen. Here indeed is realized that dream of perfect equality dreamt of by the French demagogues.

The law of talion exists alone: that of property was unknown until they began to build houses, or rather huts, and to till the ground a little. This cultivation still amounts to practically nothing. I have been through the village; I have seen the fenced plots but rarely anything inside—here and there a few potatoes, a little corn. It is already a great change from the life of a nomad. I have even been told that a little further on there are some Indians who are rather good husbandmen, who have all sorts of grain and stock, but that they are the envy of their compatriots. The king himself, who cultivates a considerable piece of ground, is exposed to continual pillage. It seems that instinct and the old customs of these people always attract them to a nomadic existence. I visited some of the huts of the ordinary tribesmen and returned there later with M. and Mme. B., but we found only women about. To them is left all the work of the fields and all the domestic chores. We saw very tall and beautiful girls digging potatoes and carrying them to their cabins. The men do nothing but rove about the woods fishing, hunting bears, deer, *raccoons,* squirrels, etc. They also make distant expeditions to the lakes. We have met them armed with excellent *rifles.* I observed in the village many old people, especially women. There are also many children.

Having traveled all day, either among the Indians or in the middle of the forests, having crossed one of the highest mountains [45] from where one can discern Lake Oneida, although the fog prevented our seeing it, what was our astonishment to find a large and beautiful house. It was the inn of Mr. Staniford.[46] The interior met the standards of the exterior. The neatness, the good meat, the service which was not provided by Negroes (they are barely known here) and therefore done the better, the industry and the attentiveness of our host, the certain hope that was given us that we would kill some bears tomorrow—all this put us in a rose-colored mood. The situation of the place is pleasant: all around, fertile country crowned in the distance by mountains which rise in a semicircle. It is here that Oneida County ends and Onondaga County begins.[47] It is a vast region holding the *military reservation* appropriated by the State of New York for the officers and soldiers who served during the War of Independence.[48] It extends over 1,500,000 acres divided into townships of 60,000 acres each. The names of these townships form a catalogue or rather an almanac of the great men of antiquity and of our day. They are, beginning from the north: [   ].[49]

The government held back 60,000 acres and Lake Onondaga. It is there that the salt springs are found.[50] It is given on lease to private individuals: today one can count 150 cauldrons which make five bushels a day. These sources are very rich; the water contains $\frac{1}{12}$ of its own weight in salt. It is of the most beautiful whiteness and of the best quality. If one had the workmen it could be taken out forever. It is a real source of wealth for this country which, lacking this commodity, a prime necessity in preparing the many salt provisions for its sea voyages, was paying immense sums for it to foreigners. However, the extraction of this salt by heat from fires causes a consumption of wood which will end by devouring all the forests in the vicinity. Up to 100 cords are burnt in a day. Already all the neighboring woods have been devastated. In order to spare themselves the hardship of carting the wood, they lead the water by canals into the depths of the forests. When all this finally fails, they will be forced to adopt the method used in other countries. That consists of making basins with little drain-ditches and raised ledges all around and letting the fresh water be evaporated by the sun's heat. The summer's heat here is powerful enough for this. The salt sells today at 4 shillings a bushel.

The roads grow worse as one goes on and, as our horses become more and more worn, we have been forced to hire another wagon here. This transaction detained us for more than a half a day. We spent the time wandering through the woods. I saw under the sugar maples a lot of hollowed-out wood blocks in which in the spring they collect the sap which produces sugar. The bears, in spite of all the promises, have failed to appear. I killed one of them in miniature, i.e., a black squirrel. It is the first of this color that we have seen. It provoked a great curiosity: it was completely castrated. The people here assure me, and credibly so, that of a hundred male squirrels killed ninety are found thus mutilated, the reason being that the papa squirrel, in calculated lechery and the hope of enjoying the female more, thus castrates his male young.[51]

Our inn was constantly filled with passers-by and idlers. The American works, but he likes also to enjoy himself. Horse racing, gaming, and drinking are their favorite pleasures and pastimes. The first part of the day is spent at the races. I have seen in an inn, a merry group playing at *petit palais* [52] and, amongst them, an old man with white hair: alas, why do not vice and bad habits lose their strength and become old as our bodies?

This land, new as it is, thanks to abundant pasturage in the woods, produces herds of cattle and horses of a size and quality far superior to anything I have yet seen in America. Our innkeeper Staniford deals in them. He sends them to Connecticut whence they are exported to the West Indies. We slept the 16th in Onondaga at the house of a very sensible Yankee.

The 17th: To the right of Lake Onondaga we saw a reservation 4 miles square for an Indian tribe of the same name, which has three hundred members. It is also one of the Confederation of Six Nations. The six nations or tribes are the Mohawks, Oneidas, Onondagas, Senecas, Tuscaroras, and Cayugas. Besides the land set apart for them, the government recompenses them for land-takings, pays them annual sums both in money and in blankets, munitions, and to a slight extent agricultural implements.

We passed near the charming Lake Skaneateles. One sees there a few pleasing houses, the embryo of a future town. A little further on, the road is frightful. It was in the middle of this mire that we met His Excellency Mr. Lewis,[53] Governor of the State of New York, who was returning from a revue of various militia. He was in a *sulky* with one horse, followed by a Negro; in this way travels the elected head of a country larger than many kingdoms. One day this will be dismissed as a fable.

In order to cool off our horses we stopped at the house of a good Yankee who, having just soaped his beard ready to shave, made the generous sacrifice of his soap to receive us, as he said himself while washing off the lather, *"Till the bustle was over."* He served us a dinner of brahmas or grouse,[54] with the most delicious white honey that I have tasted, and metheglin.[55] I recognized the famous *Lipiec* [56] of Lithuania. This whiteness, this exquisite taste, comes solely from the flowers of the linden, a very common tree here. The birch too is beginning to appear more often, but it is different from ours, the branches not being pendulous.[57] We slept by Lake Cayuga, which is abundant in fish and is filled with wild ducks and geese. A bridge, a mile and a quarter long, crosses the lake—a truly surprising thing in such a new and sparsely populated country. And, not the least remarkable is that

Crevit, our innkeeper and dear fellow countryman from New Jersey, tells me that in good weather not a single day goes by that he does not see crossing this bridge six wagons of families emigrating westwards.

The Cayuga Indian tribe which has a reservation here is not seen anymore. This retirement dates from an incident which will give an idea of their primitive character. One of these Indians killed a white man in cold blood. Taken and questioned, he answered that he had no rancor against the dead man but that he had felt a thirst, a pressing need to shed blood that he could not overcome, that he asked nothing better than that his own blood be spilt, that he had lived long enough. He was tried and condemned to be hanged. He certainly wanted to die but the means did not please him,[58] perhaps because of a superstitious belief the Indians hold that they will not be happy in the other world unless they shed the blood of their enemies and spill their own. My travelling companion, M. B., also feels from time to time this thirst and need to shed blood but, as he is kindhearted, that of partridge and quail satisfies him, though at present he longs to kill a bear. On our return we promise ourselves good and pleasant hunting in Cayuga. This night and morning there was a violent wind; the surface of the lake, however, was scarcely ruffled.

Oct. 18: The road leading to Geneva is sandy but good and smooth. We arrived there at noon. The situation of the town, which dominates an enormous lake, is very beautiful, but the thinly scattered houses and the nearness of great forests make it seem still a wilderness. The hotel is magnificent. Numbered among the new colonists is Mr. Nicholas, famous Jacobin of Virginia.[59] He has brought himself here, together with his principles of liberty, equality and independence, and with his 70 Negroes who are neither free, equal, nor independent. It is thus that this zealous friend of liberty would introduce the colored man, would sow the first seed of slavery in a new country that without him would never know it. Because of its extreme depth, fishing is difficult in Lake Seneca and the fish are very scarce, but in compensation the district abounds in fruit of all kinds.

Oct. 19th. We left our carriage and horses here and conforming to custom, or rather to the state of the roads, we hired some wagons to which are attached coopered arches covered with canvas. This vehicle is certainly not comfortable but is the most suitable for these roads.

Here is the famous land of the Genesee that Sir William Pulteney bought in the first instance and that his agent Col. [Charles] Williamson divided up and resold in lots and peopled with colonists.[60] He was a man without peer for such a task; he had all the qualities—probity, patience, talent, and goodness—appropriate both to attract the settlers and to minimize the obstacles and ease the burdens inseparable from a first settlement.

We stopped at Canandaigua, a small town situated on the lake of that name, 14 miles from Geneva. The inhabitants of this place instead of enjoying the view, moved some distance from it and have settled themselves on a very gloomy site. This small town, inhabited by men from New England, prospers rapidly. I saw a bookshop there. The innkeeper Taylor,[61] in whose house we stopped, charged us 9 shillings for 10 eggs.

We continued on our way through country which appeared to me more completely cleared and populated than on the other side of Geneva. We slept at General Hale's [Hall's] Inn.[62] If his regiment was as well organized as his inn, he deserves a medal. A farm of 600 acres, many animals, and many children make up his wealth.

Twenty-eight miles from Geneva.

Oct. 20. We breakfasted 12 miles further on at Hartford [63] and made today 36 miles and came to sleep in Batavia. The last 12 miles are execrable so far as the roads go. Batavia is the main center of a district of three and a half million acres which the Holland Company bought from the government.[64] The lands do not sell so fast since they do not have an agent such as Col. Williamson. Their price is from 12 shillings to 5 dollars. Only three years ago the first settlement was made in Batavia. There are about thirty houses, with an attractive courthouse. The town site is in the bleak lowlands. The day laborer is satisfied with 6 shillings and board. Their hearths or fireplaces are curious sights. They put 7-foot logs in them; our host assures me that in the depth of winter four fires consume three cords a day.

Oct. 21. Four miles further on we came to a place that one may call deserted. It is a stretch of country extending for 18 miles, covered with woods without any habitation, one could even say without any roads, for one could not give this name to a tortuous track full of tree trunks and rocks and holes filled with water. Whoever has not traveled these regions has no idea what a bad road is.

It was scarcely surprising then that all this wasteland constitutes the *Indian Reservation,* land still left to the poor savage. We met many of them, the men walking briskly, their guns on their shoulders while the poor *squaws* or women carry all the burdens. These were provisions, clothes, tomahawks or Indian weapons, and, besides all this, one or two *papooses* (that is how they call their children). All this load is attached by a band that they pass around the forehead. It is on this that all the weight rests. Many eat pumpkins raw or cooked, I do not know which. [cooked.] We saw the remains of their camp. Their shelters have roofs of linden bark attached to four poles, built usually on the banks of streams. One saw there, lying about, trees completely or half burnt, some fallen and obstructing the roads in such a way that they must be sawed in pieces in order to open up the roadway.

"Their shelters have roofs of linden bark attached to four poles."

We stopped on Tonawanda Creek to rest our horses and to eat a morsel ourselves. There is no more romantic spot than this, a clear stream running over rocks, the melancholy woods with a savannah or a natural meadow in the foreground, the breathless silence such as is found only in the wilds. This silence was interrupted by the report as M. B. shot at an eagle soaring in the sky.

We continued on, still passing through these savannahs and woods. It was just at sunset that we came upon any sign of habitation. It was the inn kept by a farmer, Vandiven.[65] We met there M. and Mme. Simon [66] of New York. They were returning whence we were going. Mr. Simon showed us some very beautiful sketches of Niagara he had made there. A scene no less picturesque was that of a group of Indians who had made their small camp and lighted a big fire in the forest not far from the inn. Men, women, and children had cast off their clothes to warm these and themselves. All these copper forms mingled there in the depth of the trees, illuminated only by the reflection from their fire, make a picture worthy of Girardon.[67] I envy neither their supper nor their shelter. Before nightfall a young Indian with a very pleasant face came to our room carrying a *papoose*, a rather pretty, smiling baby of six months. It was a girl with her ears already pierced and wearing long earrings, her little arms laden with beads.

The 23 [22d]: I got up before sunrise and saw the Indians around their fire. We went on our way forever through the everlasting woods and along very bad roads. These lands belong to the Holland Company; colonists, all of them from New England, were laboriously occupied in clearing them. We stopped at Ransom's.[68] He paid 3½ dollars for his land. He told us that, though the deforestation or *clearing* cost from 14 or 15 up to 18 dollars, there were frequent instances where one single harvest of wheat paid for the purchase of the land and all the expenses.

Eight miles more of woods and savannahs covered with wild strawberries led us to Buffalo Creek, which the Dutch have named New Amsterdam [now Buffalo]. It is a small town which in appearance already promises rather well, and which in time will become a center of business. There is already a rather large fur trade with the Indians. The waves of Lake Erie, that lies before us, simulate remarkably the roaring of the sea.

The streets are filled with many Indians, both male and female, much more lavishly decked out than all those whom we have seen so far, with earrings and with rings or disks hanging from their nostrils. I have seen some of them with one or two crosses of silver attached in the fashion of a pigtail and with all sorts of feathers in front. These Indians are of the Seneca tribe. They have a reservation a short distance from here and some of them farm there. They have put 100,000 dollars in the Bank of the United States, money provided from the sale of immense tracts that they sold heretofore. This action shows an awareness and forethought that is far from primitive. The interest from this sum provides them with blankets, arms, munitions, and other necessities. These are distributed among the families and there are never any quarrels; further, the English government gives them gifts. It is for this reason that we saw so many Indians assembled in Buffalo. Some were drunk and very disagreeable. One of the chiefs, the famous Farmer's Brother,[69] accompanied by a young man and a *squaw* came into the room and, to my great astonishment, the innkeeper forgetting the respect due his majesty prayed him to leave, which he did. Another, completely drunk, would leave the shop, where he made a great din, only after extorting a shilling. Nevertheless, they assure me that the Indians are in a progressive state of civilization, becoming less addicted to drink and beginning to devote themselves to agriculture. Very few know any English.

Besides the untoward incidents with the Indians, the inn offered a thousand others. I would have taken it for a Polish Jewish tavern, it was so dirty: with broken windows, no door that would close, and a mob of land speculators from all the corners of the United States. In town, the lots of half an acre sell at $60, further out at 5, 3 and 2 dollars. I have seen an old farmer from Massachusetts, who some years ago established his son in Cayuga and has come to buy land here for

his grandson. Thus one single man would provide farmers for regions
200 miles apart.

The brisk and bustling spirit of the Americans thrusts them always
forward: with virgin and low-priced land, already lost to them on
this side, they emigrate to Canada. Thus having struggled for nine
years to shake off the English yoke, and having shaken it off, they go
of their own free will to submit themselves again. I believe that, were
they to learn that even in Hell there were lands producing excellent
wheat and corn and at six cents an acre, despite all the flames and all
the torments, they would give up their *liberty and equality* to go
and settle there. On the other hand this adventurous spirit is perhaps
a boon, a means that Providence has chosen to populate the vast
deserts of this new continent.

The 23rd: We left as soon as possible the dirty, noisy, and uncomfortable inn of Mr. Crow.[70] It is 3½ miles to the ferry. We skirted the
sandy shores of Lake Erie, one wheel of our wagon often wetted by
its waters. This fresh-water sea (for, considering its extent, one must
call it thus) is as stormy and treacherous as its older sisters of salt
water. Only eight days ago two or three American boats were shipwrecked there. The waves have thrown up on land six bodies, barrels,
baggage,[13] and other goods. An American from Detroit, persuaded by
his son-in-law, sold his farm and, for the $4,000 he received, bought
some merchandise and he and his goods were swallowed up in the
abyss. This lake has rather a lot of fish; they fish here for white and
black bass, some pike and whitefish, which is the most delicious of all. I
noticed on the shore shellfish which, though very much bigger, resemble those of fresh-water rivers.

At the ferry the lake becomes narrower and is changed into a wide
river. It is the famous St. Lawrence [actually the Niagara River], having its source in Lake Superior, passing through Lake Michigan, Lake
Huron, and Lake Erie, then hurling itself from a height of 170 feet
at Niagara and falling into Lake Ontario. On leaving Lake Ontario
it takes shape as a majestic river [the St. Lawrence] and, crossing thus
the two Canadas, discharges itself at Quebec into the Atlantic Ocean.

At the ferry site the rapidity of the current manifests itself markedly.
We crossed the river, which here is more than a mile wide, in 12 minutes. The customs officer seeing that we were simply travelers without merchandise let us pass without asking our names, without going
through investigation, without the search and examination so religiously followed for the torment of all travelers in nearly all the countries of Europe. We skirted the river for 16 miles, leaving Fort Erie
behind us. The road would have been half as short if it had not fol-

lowed the windings of the river. All this side is rather well inhabited and cultivated. The countryside produces every possible grain and fruit. Even in the open air the peaches thrive better here.

We arrived at Chippawa towards evening. It is a village of 50 houses with barracks and a garrison. We saw there a large number of long boats, the largest of which carry seven tons. They serve the fur trade and go as far as Michigan. Navigation ceases here; the force of the current will not allow any boat to go further. The famous falls are three miles away. Full of impatience M. B. and I ran a mile to see the rapids; before getting there, we heard a muffled and dreadful roar and noticed in the depths a mist of white vapors. Night was advancing, happy with this introduction to a sublime creation that we were to see tomorrow, we returned to our inn.

October 24: Thus finally we were near the object of our desire at the foot of Niagara, at the end of an uninterrupted and tiring journey of 20 days. I have neither the time for, nor the intention of, describing the falls. Volney has given an account with the greatest veracity and detail,[71] and others before him have spoken as painters and poets,[72] but I must acknowledge that neither the spoken word nor the pen nor the brush can recall this scene faithfully. One must see it oneself to imagine a true idea of it—sublime and awe-inspiring. I do not describe it, I simply note the effects and impressions of this marvelous phenomenon.

We left our lodging at 10 accompanied by Mr. Street,[73] a gentleman living in these parts and an acquaintance of M. and Mme. B. Arriving at the place where we were yesterday, we saw the waters increasing in speed and violence, breaking against rocky, underwater ridges and forming three tiers of cataracts boiling with foam with a noise like that of a [illegible] in a rage. An island in the middle of the stream divides it; one part turns to the right towards flanking, precipitous rocks covered with yews and spruces; the other part, sweeping in a semicircle to the right, forms a broad and deep bay. A small island has been created there—use has been made of this land to set up many stone and saw mills. One climbs a steep hill and the woods to one's right hide everything. One hears only an awful, muffled roar. Soon the view of the rapids and of the river appears again spread out in broad expanse. Walking further, one comes to low ground—to a swamp covered with woods of cedar and *hemlock*, etc. After passing through, one finds oneself on a platform of rocks called Table Rock.[74] It is here that one sees the Niagara Falls in their full sweep; it is here that the river in forming a horseshoe hurls itself into an abyss 170 feet below. The breadth of this curve is about 1,200 feet.

To the right a perpendicular rock separates these falls from another of a totally different appearance. Those in the horseshoe are wild, huge, and sublime: their volume, their enormous weight, their edges arching backwards, boiling, snowy, all throwing over the surroundings a pale green shadow; the appalling sound of these waters falling into the black abyss; the waves of foam that the rapids throw back from below, these waves of foam rising in clouds of mist and losing themselves in the air in silvery dust; the rainbow in the brilliance and the liveliness of its colors encircling these mists like a glittering sash; the rocks, the black yews, the wild untrammeled view; all these overwhelm the spirit with astonishment, admiration, and dread.

It is not like this in the other half of the falls, separated, as I have said, by a perpendicular rock covered with soil and a thick black forest. There, over a sheer wall 300 feet wide it hurls its crystalline mass majestically and one might add with elegance. Rock slides to the right have cut down the height on this side. It has, by comparison with the other, a calm and sublime beauty. A jagged cleft of rock to the right has separated a part of it to form a cascade which, beside these enormous torrents, appears small, but in fact it is more beautiful and more abundant in water than the famous Cascade of Terni.[75]

Our eyes ranged in turn over these sublime sites; we could not be sated. Several times advancing to the edge of the embankment, we looked into the depth, bristling with rocks covered with trees, planks, all the other wreckage of everything torn from the sides of this frightful place, all that is brought or hurled down by the fury of the current. One cannot contemplate these horrors without fright and without turning dizzy.

If Niagara had been known to the Greek poets, they would have embodied it with an awesome divinity. Ovid himself would have woven a delightful tale. Perhaps he would have imagined that the god of the river had fallen in love with the beautiful naiad, Niagara, that with the violence and fury known to streams, he had pursued her across the breadth of Lake Superior, then Michigan, Huron, Erie, that there, the beautiful one, on the point of being seized and with her virtue in the gravest jeopardy, was carried away by despair and threw herself from the pinnacle of a rock. The gods, touched by her fate, send the beautiful Iris to end a cruel and sad death by cutting the cord of her life and transforming her into a cascade. The savages, who are not great poets, have not deified her, have invented no stories to make her origins sublime. I, living in their country (imitating their spirit and style), have sought to repair this omission.

Before leaving Table Rock M. B. killed a *woodcock* in honor of the

Goddess and I gathered some flowers which sprang up at her feet. They were, I believe, a very beautiful Betonica [76] and a Trachelium.[77]

After we had refreshed ourselves in a neighboring house, we continued on our way; and after jumping over some enclosures and some gullies and crossing one of the prettiest meadows that one could see, the continual sprinkling from the falls giving them a fertility without equal, we found ourselves facing the falls which, if it is possible, from this side appeared even more beautiful. Just here the approach is not difficult and we enjoyed it in reasonable comfort.

The most difficult and, I may say, the most dangerous part remained —that is, the approach to the bottom of the precipice. The descent is by means of an almost vertical 50-foot ladder. There is no danger other than from dizziness that the view of the precipice might occasion. We reached the bottom without any accident; there remained a very steep height which because of the damp was very slippery; a fall I had, made me lose my hat. We took the path to the right and climbed up the side of the precipice across the scrub and the jagged rocks. Under our feet was the foaming torrent of the river and above our heads overhanging rocks. On top of these were trees, some of them with part of their roots entwined in the rock, and the rest hanging in the air. The air was thick with fog, and gulls and eagles were gliding about. In spite of these horrors and difficulties we reached a point two-thirds of the way; there we were stopped short by a rock barring the way. This left above the precipice only a rocky ledge which was both very slippery and above all extremely narrow. Mme. B. wanted to risk this very hazardous ascent, and we had to employ all possible entreaties and add our earnest pleas to deter her from doing so. Reed, accustomed to the rocks of Scotland, went first and climbed the frightful gap. I followed him and in the most dangerous part took the hand he stretched to me and thus passed to the other side. Further on I did not find the passage so difficult but it was much more painful. At times we were walking but more often we were climbing on all fours, hanging onto the undergrowth, climbing rocks and then lying on one's back letting oneself slide below. Thus I came upon this dreadful sheet of water; I approached it, the gloomy air which hangs over this terrible cave, the heat, the sulphurous odor, the terrible noise of the water with all its weight falling from that great height in full force above our head—only a single step between us and death; all this, I may tell you, drives out all reason and leaves only an involuntary terror. One is well contented to have satisfied one's curiosity, but one does not want to prolong it for a long time. As I left this abode of horror and destruction, its image haunted me for a long time and I could not ever wipe it from my memory. Going toward the sheet of water I saw in the rocks of primitive sandstone some very distinct impressions of oysters and other shellfish. Others appeared in pieces of quartz. Under the great sheet of water and at the side were many stalactites. An odor and discharge of sulphur establishes it either as the source or the remains of a volcano. Absolutely exhausted by fatigue, streaming with sweat and damp from the spray of the falls which penetrated to my very bones, I had scarcely the strength to reascend the ladder. On returning, a good fire and a good dinner reestablished my strength but the next day and for many days after, I felt shattered.

Oct. 25. We left for Queenston, wanting to push forward as far as Lake Ontario in spite of the wind and the snow. To our right was the river, and to our left some farms and houses whose appearance did not suggest that degree of well-being that one notices along the seaboard regions of the United States. One may certainly attribute this inferiority to the great distance from the sea and centers of commerce and the consequent much greater difficulty in selling produce and in getting the necessary commodities and, even more, luxury goods. For indeed, the industrious inhabitants of Canada are not shackled any more than in the United States. They pay, if that is possible, less taxes and as for chatter, political quarrels, papers and elections, they are wholly as free as their republican neighbor. They have told me that it will not always be thus. Today the government leaves this country, so to speak, to itself as one leaves a little child to run in the yard without paying attention to what it does; but when it grows, the school, the rod, all the authority of the ruling class begins to make itself felt. And so, when this country becomes more inhabited, a greater coercion by laws, for the greater needs of the state, will become necessary with all the attendant disadvantages. It will enjoy, however, a boon more certain in a well-organized monarchy than in a republic—the boon of tranquility and surety.

Among these farms one house of very singular construction is remarkable; it is very long and narrow with a long porch, but it is rather attractive. It is that of Mr. Puisaye, leader of the unfortunate expedition to Quiberon; he and a few of his party, unhappy remnants of a foolishly conceived plan, have received some land in this part of Canada from the English government. Mr. Puisaye also enjoys a pension of 5 to 600 pounds sterling. He stayed here for a few years but, bored and lacking the opportunity for conversation, he went home to England.[78]

We arrived at Queenston in cold and snowy weather. The town will be rather attractive. It is the terminal of navigation on Lake Ontario and one of the storage depots for merchandise coming by water from Lower Canada, as well as for that which comes down as far as Lake Erie and, in order to avoid the falls, is carted here. The beautiful house of Mr. Hamilton,[79] which dominates the majestic course of the St. Lawrence [the Niagara], is the most noticeable feature. We had some letters of recommendation for him from Col. Williams.[36] He came to see us in the evening and invited us for dinner on the next day. We accepted, in the first place, because many hours of conversation with the principal inhabitant and the most notable personage in the region could not fail to be interesting and instructive for tourists and, further, because these same tourists were tired of the food of the inns and were not ill-pleased to refresh themselves with a good dinner.

[October 26:] Not wanting, however, to lose the entire day (the 26th of Oct.), we went in the morning to Newark, today called Niagara [Niagara-on-the-Lake], situated at the entrance to Lake Ontario opposite the American fort. The English have constructed one a little to the south under the name of Fort St. George. It consists of four bastions with curtains but without any outside walls. There was a garrison there, as also in Chippawa and at Fort Erie. The soldier is dressed with the elegance and magnificence which distinguishes English troops from all others. It seems to me that the government indulges in unjustifiable expense in keeping troops in a country which has nothing to fear either from within or without. The snow and the fog have pursued us so that even from the edge of Lake Ontario we could distinguish it only imperfectly. The American fort is advantageously placed, though on the English side it is circled only by a palisade. It was built by the French as were the other buildings which were there. Here was our Ultima Thule, the last terminal of our peregrinations.

On the journey I have gathered together my observations rather poorly; always on the road, having time only to eat a bite, tired in the evening; in the midst of the noise of the taverns, not finding a quiet corner, I scribbled without order and in haste. It remains for me to glean them well and that is what I plan to do on my return journey.

At two o'clock we returned to Queenston. Mr. Hamilton came to see us and told us that a vessel was setting sail tomorrow morning for Kingston, capital of Upper Canada, and that if we got on her we could go from there to Montreal, the whole journey in five days; that from Montreal we could easily reach Lake Champlain, Lake George, and Albany, and in this way we would see new country and avoid the bad roads that we have had. It was extremely tempting to follow this plan. M. and Mme. B., having made arrangements which for them would make it impracticable, urged me to follow it. I decided immediately. The pleasure of seeing a new country, a country whose people and government each one foreign to the other, recalled the actual state of my own poor unfortunate fatherland, provoked my interest. Mr. Hamilton kindly sent one of his sons to Niagara in order to reserve a place for me aboard the vessel *Sirucae*. My imagination sailed in anticipation on Lake Ontario and let itself flow down the length of the St. Lawrence, walking along the streets of Montreal, tasting a thousand pleasures; in the midst of these happy daydreams the messenger returned with news that the vessel had left. I was brusquely awakened from my dreams; this is not the first awakening of this kind that I have had from the dreams of my life. I consoled myself with the thought that I am not to be separated from my amiable companions of this journey.

From a very high mountain between Queenston and Niagara we saw the immense crystal—Lake Ontario. Like all the other lakes it is very stormy and many boats are lost there. Last year Judge Cochrane [80] with all his escort of lawyers and notaries lost their lives there. It would have been consoling if chicanery had been shipwrecked with them but alas it survives whole. It was market day in town and we saw about a hundred farmers on horseback riding at full speed and flaunting their heavy-handed dexterity. The breed of horses is strong but heavy. It is probably a breed degenerated from the Norman horses introduced by the first French colonists.

At three o'clock we went to Mr. Hamilton's house. He is an old man, very intelligent and hospitable, a most attentive host, father of ten sons and one daughter, master of a large and beautiful house where everything suggests ease and domestic security. He gave us a very good dinner, and as excellent as the dinner was the conversation of our fellow diners, Messrs. Macdonnell [81] and Clark,[82] well educated Scotsmen who know the country well. The first is Speaker of the Assembly of Upper Canada sitting at York [Toronto] and agent to Lord Selkirk.[83] The other is an inhabitant of Queenston who by his skill succeeded in diverting in a stream a part of the waters from the Falls of Niagara and employing them to drive many of his stonemills and sawmills.

The patron of Mr. Macdonnell, Lord Selkirk, conceived the idea of a vast settlement in Canada; for this purpose he persuaded many a family of Scottish farmers to follow him there. He established some of them in St. John [Prince Edward Island]. This settlement has been rather successful, but because of extraordinary stubbornness, based doubtless on good intentions and a knowledge of the country acquired from books, he led others of his colonists into the vast plains of the St. Clair River above Lake Huron. There,[84] the heat of the summer, often reaching to 96°, the vapors from the bogs, and the circumstances inseparable from a land not year cleared, cut down nine-tenths of these poor Highlanders.

LETTER ABOUT THE JOURNEY
TO NIAGARA
23 November 1805

This letter was written to Mrs. Katarzyna Potocki Kossakowski, wife of the Castellan of Kamieniec.

Lisabeth-Town (in America) 23 November 1805

The tremendous heat of last summer tired me so much that a journey was prescribed for me in order that I might refresh myself with the open air and activity. So in company with an English family from my neighborhood we started out the 5th of October to upper Canada, taking the right bank of the Hudson to Albany. From Schenectady, we pushed on then by the Mohawk river beyond the Genesee through new country which 10 years ago was a trackless forest and which to-day is quickly rising from the wilderness. From the Genesee up to Buffalo-Creek on Lake Erie is virgin forest; one notices first that it is sparsely populated and then that it is teeming only with animals. In general one can say, that the 300 miles of road is more or less through a continuous thick forest with tremendous trees. This mournful monotony is broken at times by the sight of streams rushing amidst the cliffs, of lakes spilling out their clear waters amidst beautiful hills and happy valleys. Such are the lakes Oneida, Onondaga, Skaneateles, Cayuga, Seneca and Canandarque. These lakes are joined with each other by rivers and their tributaries and draw a single chain of communication through a tremendous extent of land; they link it to both seas of fresh water, as the enormous lakes Erie and Ontario may be called.

Amidst these woods, new settlements are beginning. The sight of the farmers coming with their wives and children fighting with a thousand difficulties, bearing up under want and discomfort, cutting trees with tireless effort, changing untouched thickets into cultivated fields; everything is an interesting and new sight for a European. For whereas in the old world the most favored amusement is to sack towns and to kill people, here the object of all pursuits is to build and to increase human kind.

The settlement called the Genesee is quickly becoming inhabited; it is one of the most fertile in the world. The earth, scratched only with a harrow, is so fertile that, for a few years because of too luxuriant growth, wheat cannot be planted. The soil must be exhausted by a five-year planting of maize and hemp before wheat is sown and then there is no need of a plow, even less of manure. It is true that this very fertility is deadly to the health of the farmer; there is nothing more unhealthy than the first clearing and opening of the fields; it seems that the earth, jealous of her treasures, sentences to death the bold one who dares to be the first to tear open her breast.

Th lakes teem with fish, mostly trout; forests with bears, mountain cats (type of tiger), deer, martens, swarms of red and black squirrels, partridge and pheasants. The Indians still wage constant war with the animals. In the course of my journey I saw them in settlements; I saw roving about those who go under the name of the Six Nations: Mohawks, Oneidas, Onondagas, Senecas, Cayugas and Tuscaroras. Either Volney did not give them credit or, what is more likely, they have changed remarkably for the better since the time he visited them. This improvement must be ascribed to the unusual genius of one of the Indians named Canadia [Ganio'dai'o], brother [sic] of the famous chief Ket Gallet [Red Jacket?]. This extraordinary man, as do many lawgivers among unenlightened peoples, uses their very ignorance and superstition to improve his fellows and make them more happy.

Canadia proclaimed himself a prophet; visiting the scattered Indian tribes, he preaches, teaches, pretends that the all-powerful spirit Manitou carried him off and brought him to heaven and to hell; that in heaven he saw the souls of the Indians who never drank but worked on the soil and built houses; they were partaking of joy with the most beautiful squaws or women, hunting in thornless forests thronged with various kinds of animals. In contrast, in hell he saw Indians who had spent their lives in drink and idleness; they were tortured with various torments, hunting in deserts filled only with poisonous contagions and vipers. The moral of these sermons that one must plough, sow, and build; one must not idle, and become overcome with drink. The results of this pious deception are obvious. I found in a settlement of Indians in Oneida a few quite neat houses, grain, cattle, horses; they are even building a school and a church; drunkenness is coming to an end and the population is increasing.

It is too bad that this prophet has appeared too late. The Indians through drunkenness and venereal disease are nearing complete extinction; their lands are being sold to the Americans; the interest on the sums owed are distributed by family; it provides for their clothes

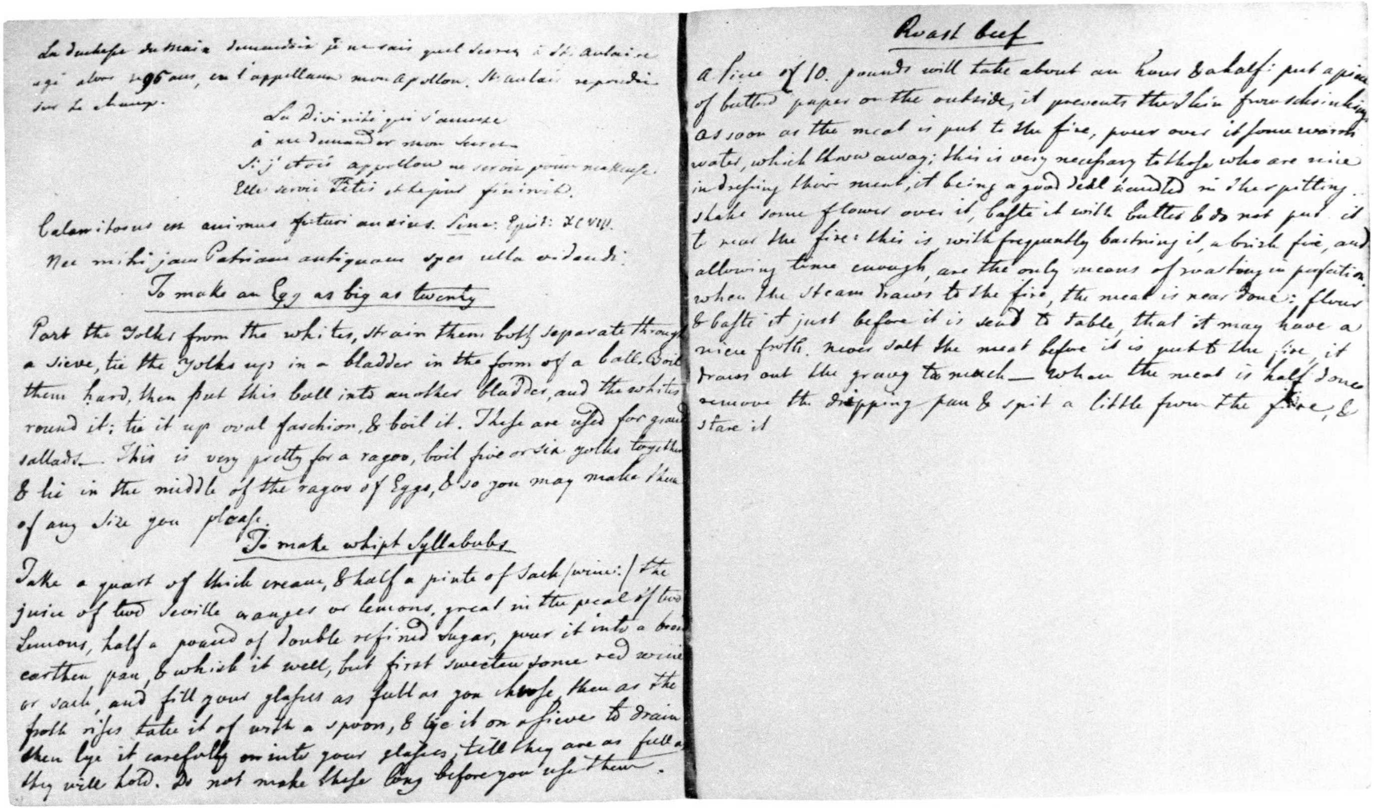

La duchesse du Maine demandoit je ne sais quel secret à St. Aulaire agé alors de 95 ans, en l'appellant mon Apollon. St. Aulaire repondit sur le champ.

La Divinité qui s'amuse
à me demander mon secret
Si j'etois appollon ne seroit point ma Muse.
Elle seroit Tétis et le jour finiroit.

Calamitosus est animus futuri anxius. Senec: Epist: XCVIII.

Nec mihi jam Patriam antiquam spes ulla videndi.

To make an Egg as big as twenty

Part the Yolks from the whites, strain them both separate through a sieve, tie the Yolks up in a bladder in the form of a ball. Boil them hard, then put this ball into another bladder, and the whites round it; tie it up oval faschion, & boil it. These are used for grand sallads. This is very pretty for a ragoo, boil five or six yolks together & lie in the middle of the ragoo of Eggs, & so you may make them of any size you please.

To make whipt Syllabubs

Take a quart of thick cream, & half a pinte of Sack (wine:) the juice of two Seville oranges or lemons, great in the peal of two Lemons, half a pound of double refined sugar, pour it into a broad earthen pan, & whisk it well, but first sweeten some red wine or sack, and fill your glasses as full as you choose, then as the froth rises take it of with a spoon, & lye it on a sieve to drain then lye it carefully on into your glasses, till they are as full as they will hold. Do not make these long before you use them.

Roast beef

A piece of 10. pounds will take about an hour & a half; put a piece of butted paper on the outside, it prevents the skin from shrinking. As soon as the meat is put to the fire, pour over it some warm water, which throw away; this is very necessary to those who are nice in dressing their meat, it being a good deal handled in the spitting. shake some flower over it, baste it with butter & do not put it to near the fire: this is, with frequently basting it, a brisk fire, and allowing time enough, are the only means of roasting in perfection. when the steam draws to the fire, the meat is near done; flour & baste it just before it is send to table, that it may have a nice froth. never salt the meat before it is put to the fire, it draws out the gravy to much— when the meat is half done remove the dripping pan & spit a little from the fire, & stare it

Fig. 78. A page of culinary notes [X, 36, 37] from the Niemcewicz manuscript.

Fig. 79. Enlargement of the Seal affixed to certificates of membership in The United States Military Philosophical Society. Courtesy of The United States Military Academy Archives.

Fig. 80. The Seat of Mr. John Stevens in Hoboken, N.J. From William Birch, *The Country Seats* . . . , 1808. Courtesy of The New-York Historical Society, New York City.

Fig. 81. The Certificate of Membership of Julian Ursyn Niemcewicz in The United States Military Philosophical Society. Courtesy of Mrs. John Kean.

Fig. 82. Portrait of Niemcewicz. Frontispiece from the copy of the collection of his works entitled *Pism różnych* . . . given by him to Princeton College Library. Courtesy of Prince-

Fig. 83. Sketch of unidentified head. From the back cover leaf of notebook No. II of the Niemcewicz manuscript. Note the letters, "Nie," written over the right ear.

JULIANA, Ursin

NIEMCEWICZA, 1757-1841

pism różnych

wierszem i prozą

TOM I.

~~~~~~~~~~~~~~~~~~~~~~

w WARSZAWIE,

w Drukarni N° 646. przy Nowolipiu.

1803.

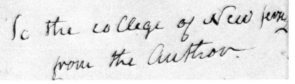

To the college of New Jersey from the Author.

Fig. 84. Title page of Niemcewicz's works given to Princeton College with the author's inscription. Courtesy of Princeton University Library.

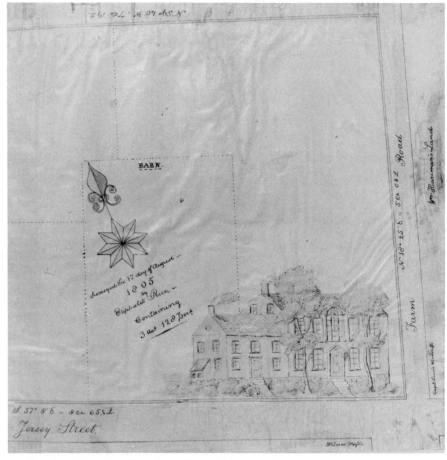

Fig. 85. The Hampton-Mayo-Scott House as it appeared when it was occupied by Julian Ursyn and Susan Niemcewicz in 1804-1805. The house
stood on the N.W. corner of East Jersey Street and the present Madison
Avenue. From a surveyor's drawing made in 1805. Courtesy of Mr. Edward
J. Grassmann.

Fig. 86. A section of the Map of Elizabeth Town at the time of the Revolutionary War by Ernest L. Meyer. The houses in which Niemcewicz lived
are represented in the appropriate locations. Courtesy of Mr. Edward J.
Grassmann.

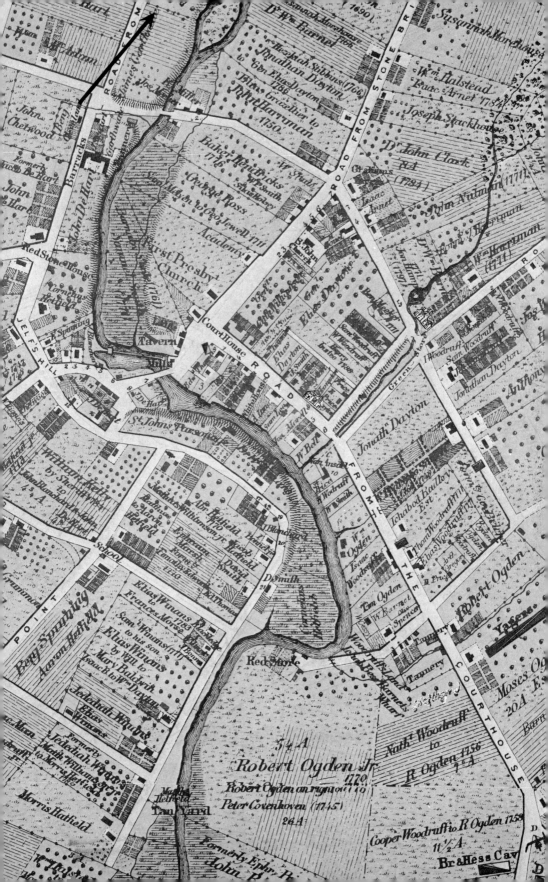

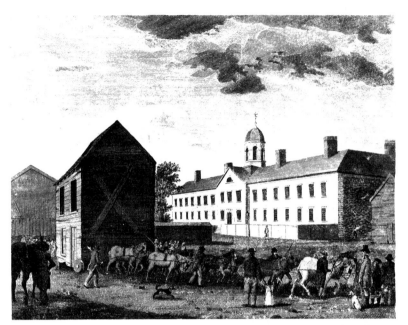

Fig. 87. Moving a building in Philadelphia. From William Birch, *The City of Philadelphia* . . . , 1800. Courtesy of The New-York Historical Society, New York City.

Fig. 88. The Pennsylvania Academy of Fine Arts, Philadelphia to which Niemcewicz bequeathed his art collection in America on his departure in 1807. From the water color of Pavel Petrovich Svinin. Courtesy of The Metropolitan Museum of Art, Rogers Fund, 1942.

and minor needs and makes work at farming not absolutely necessary. The larger proportion holds with the old nomadic traditions of hunting and wandering from place to place. We met them constantly, occasionally in family groups, or travelling alone. Their bearing is proud and well set, the color of the faces copper, with features resembling the tartars; for dress they have a woolen blanket thrown over them and an apron to cover their nakedness. The hair either falls straight down or is shorn in all sorts of zigzags decorated with feathers. As weapons they have bow and arrows, tomahawk and rifle. The women are rarely beautiful, perhaps because of their excessive toil; all the duties and tasks fall to their lot. While His Honor goes along with only a bow or rifle in his hands, the unhappy squaw is dropping under the weight of all the household goods and besides this there is an infant babe, in their language papoose, wound up in moss and tied to a board length-wise, and then tied to the back with a strap from the neck; a cow, pigs and dogs bring up the procession. The women have the lobe of the ear pierced through and filled with earrings. The men carry metal disks in their noses, paint their faces; a few, instead of pigtails, had attached silver crosses. The limits of a letter do not permit me to extend myself further over a people who have lost a great many of their primitive faults but none of their good qualities.

After breaking through the wilderness on the edge of Lake Erie we crossed the St. Laurence river to upper Canada. Advancing along its right bank for 10 miles we heard a tremendous roar. The river, constrained ever more by cliffs, courses with the speed of an arrow; there is nothing yet to see but a white cloud which towers up. The roar is ever more penetrating until, coming out from among the cliffs and cypress forests, the most tremendous and splendid sight strikes the eyes. The whole river hurls itself into an abyss of 174 feet, its waters striking the rocks below rebound into a snowy, foamy, boiling liquid mass rising up high, and breaking up into silver dust, losing itself in the azure of the clouds, while a rainbow embraces the humid mist with its broad sash, playing on the mist with the most lively colored brilliance. The falls are in the shape of a horseshoe; the right side is broken by an island; beyond a second part of the cascade falls in a straight line in the most splendid and beautiful flood. Add to this picture, Madame, a background of gloomy rocks dimmed by forests of cedars and pines, the loneliness and wildness of the site, the roar so powerful that the ground trembles under your feet, the horrible abyss, into which one cannot cast one's eyes for fear of becoming dizzy and you will agree that the emotions of this scene are not sweet and pleasant; everything fills one with wonder and appals one with holy terror. Still remaining was the view of the abyss and this was the most difficult and the most dangerous. One approaches it at first by a 50 foot perpendicular ladder and then along a steep cliff up to the edge of the frightful flood; here one has to climb branch by branch the bushes which grow in the cracks. Above there are torn cliffs and trees with half their roots jutting out in air and then below a deep flood carrying everything away. Eagles and birds of prey with their penetrating cries circle in this abyss to devour the fish and animals which the force of the current casts up, throws about and leaves lifeless. In a word all this did not make my expedition a happy one. Finally with enormous difficulty I got to the bottom of the whole flood of the cascade. I dared even to go underneath. At this time a wall of water divided me from the world and the whole weight of the river from its full height, with its huge roar poured over my head. This view, this roar, the slipperiness of the rocks on which I stood, the thought that one step separated me from death, shook me with a terror which I have never felt before. I was happy when I got back safely, soaked to the skin and so exhausted that the effects of this path made themselves felt for three days.

I have the journal of my whole journey which I keep *ad feliciora tempora*. The part of Canada which I saw is quite well populated and cultivated. Lakes Erie and Ontario are splendid and full of fish; there is much commerce and tremendously big trees nearby; I saw one near Cayuga which was 45 feet in circumference. We returned by land to [blank] thence by the Mohawk to Schenectady, from Albany by the Hudson River to New York. This town suffered much last summer from the yellow fever.

Just as I was finishing this letter I heard the knocker on the door and my porter Filipek announced that there were two wild figures standing there whom he could not understand. I went down and I nearly fell over backwards with surprise. Two Polish Jews with beards and curly locks of hair over their ears, one from Wysokie who has been swindling here for the last three years, learned in the rules of equality, threw himself on me and kissed me on both sides; the other Benjamin Efraimowicz, was born in Kazimierz. He came here as he said on a flat-bottomed boat to look for a man who owed him 4,000 ducats. This [blank] was never here; some one led the Jew astray.

I brought them to my house. I asked them to sit down and they drank some rum. Benjamin promised to drop in when he is on his way back.

I remain, etc.

Julian Ursyn Niemcewicz

Part III

UNDER OUR VINE AND FIG TREE

AMERICA REMEMBERED, 1799-1802

ELIZABETHTOWN, N.J.

This excerpt from the Memoirs of Niemcewicz written in his old age describes his life after he settled in Elizabeth following his travels, until he returned to Poland in 1802. It is the only account of this period written by him now extant, and includes his courtship and marriage. This translation was prepared from a microfilm of the Niemcewicz manuscript in the Bibliothèque Polonaise in Paris. See Julian Ursyn Niemcewicz, *Memoirs of My Times (Pamiętniki czasów moich)*, ed. Jan Dihm, 2 vols. (Warsaw, 1957), II, 229-241.

After having visited the eastern, middle and part of the southern States of the U.S. and having spent nearly all the money borrowed from Mr. Jeffersson, it was time to think of a corner where I could hide. I went therefore to Elizabeth Town where I had come to know the inhabitants earlier. This town was then a refuge for many French families from the islands of St. Domingo, Martinique and Guadaloupe, etc., fleeing from the cruelty of the Negroes. I remember only a few names—Carudeux, Kirkadeau, Musron, Jovin, Du Buc, Marolles.[1] Lord Bolingbroke under the name of Belassis can be added to this list. He had eloped with Miss Hompesch, niece of the last Grand Master of Malta. Lord Bolingbroke was a man of strong passion, he was, however, both polite and learned; all this reminded me of Europe, the memory of which it was difficult to lose. Among the local inhabitants the most prominent was the Ricketts family, Mrs. Ricketts née Livingston, was the sister of my future wife; there were also the many-branched families of the Daytons, Williamsons, Ogdens, etc.[2]

I rented a small room at a tailor's named Rivers, ate with him and his helpers, bought firewood and sawed it myself. I had only a few piasters left in my pocket when I received a letter from Warsaw from Mrs. Stanisław Potocki.[3] She informed me that as the audacious letter written to Paul by Kościuszko, after his return to Paris, sending back the sum of money given to him in Petersburg was ascribed to my advice, an announcement was issued by the government in Moscow to my brothers; that if they wrote a single word to me or sent one penny to me all their estates would be confiscated. She added that Prince

Adam Czartoryski, my old commander, hearing of this had sent to me, out of the generosity that he feels for everyone but has especially shown so many times to me, a bill of exchange for 250 ducats. Deeply touched by this gift, sent as if by Providence at the time of deepest need, I hurried to New York to get the money. The 100 piaster debt incurred with vice-President Jeffersson hung heavy on my heart and I immediately therefore returned it, living on the rest with my tailor as economically as possible.

Reading, writing, and hunting for birds, filled my hours. I was then in the prime of life, 40 years of age. Difficulties, straightened circumstances did not then burden me as much as my present deep unhappiness does now; at an age when both spirit and body are enfeebled with eyes on which the ray of hope that had deceived me so many times will not shine again. I did not then have a short future before me. There were great events in Europe that might perhaps change our fate—what is before our eyes today? A sorrowful grave.

From the year 1798 to the beginning of the present century, I remained in Elisabeth Town, New Jersey, rooming and boarding at my tailor's. I shall mention only the most important events that occurred. I made more and more acquaintances with the local inhabitants and my neighbors, among whom was Mrs. Kean, widow of a friend of Kościuszko, who showed a lively sympathy over my deserted state. Her interest made it possible to visit her more often. Once putting out her hand she said, "Do you wish it?" I accepted with feeling. I did not hasten the fulfillment of the promise, leaving time for further reflection. Our friendship continued for two years, before it changed into marriage. . . .

The next year [1799], more important to the lovers of virtue and freedom [Niemcewicz had just described the death of Stanisław August, the last king of Poland], the death of General Washington blanketed the United States with sorrow. The circumstances of his last moments are found in a letter written to me by Mr. Thomas Law, placed in the first volume of my works, *Polish Writers* in the edition of Mostowski.[4] All the important towns of America held mourning services. I was at such a service in New York. Governor [Gouverneur] Mor[r]is, one of the most eminent citizens of this city, gave a beautiful funeral oration. Free Masons carried his coffin in a pompous procession. All the militia of the city marched out and with a thrice-repeated salvo bade farewell to the shade of this great man. Everywhere true merit has its calumniators, perhaps more than elsewhere in Republics, where one is allowed to speak sensibly and therefore is equally free to rave and where such audacious envy goes unpunished. How many times have I heard it said that Washington was a coward and Franklin stupid. Their glory will be avenged by the shamefully oppressed Negroes. . . .

He [Jean Victor Marie Moreau] settled in a country home near Philadelphia and I visited him there. He used to come to New York and passing through Elizabethtown he visited at our home. Once he came to dinner with the son of Dupont de Nemours. I had brought with me to America two delicacies not known here: essence of truffles and old Hungarian wine. I treated him with them. He couldn't understand how I got such rarities. He said that it was the first time that he had tasted Hungarian wine since the Archduke Charles had sent him some at the time of the armistice.[5] . . .

I return to write about famous people whom I met in the time of my stay in America. The Negro uprising in the French Antilles forced the white settlers to flee before the danger of death with only the goods and chattels that they could carry with them. Many of them settled in the same town of Elisabeth Town where I was. From St. Domingo, Mrs. Caraday with her sister Kerludan, Mrs. Masson, Marolles, Jovin, d'Allemans, Budan, Cotineau, du Buc;[6] in Staten Island Dupont de Nemours, friend of Turgot, a man of wit, full of imagination but frivolous, author of the work *De la philosophie de la nature* in which he maintained that he was able to understand the languages of all animals. He returned to France under the Bourbons, but when Napoleon returned from the island of Elbe, he fled again to America to his son who had a gun-powder mill there and he wrote to France: *"Fuyant les dangers de la France, je me suis pour ma plus grand sûreté réfugié en Amérique, dans un moulin à poudre."* This Dupont de Nemours was for a short time the tutor of the present Prince Adam Czartoryski, but an innate instability drove him back to France.[7]

I had the good fortune to meet not only Washington but also his successor John Adams, and Thomas Jefferson and General Hamilton. Jefferson was more learned than the others, he published a little work, *Notes on Virginia;* being a zealous republican, he encouraged learning. It was he who during his presidency opened the first public library in Washington, and introduced the custom of not attending the opening of Congress himself but of sending an opening address. These three Presidents were those who, with a few others, signed the Declaration of Independence of the United States. It is worthy of notice that the Presidents Adams and Jefferson, after living a half century from the time of the Proclamation of Independence, both died in the same year, on the same day, at nearly the same hour [Fourth of July 1826].

I should not overlook General Hamilton, during the war an adjutant to Washington. He was without doubt the first genius in America not only as a lawyer but also as a *financier*. He was the first to invent the system of amortization of debts which later Pitt introduced so vigorously in England.

Having said so much about others, as far as I remember old times, let me now say a few words about myself.

I spent two years rooming and boarding with my tailor, Mr. Rivers. During this span of time my relationship with my future wife, Mrs. Kean née Livingston, grew closer. An abandoned exile, I did not dare to ask her for her hand lest she might consider, might feel, that it was not her own personal worth, but her considerable fortune that tempted a poor man. When once in conversation she put out her hand, saying, "If you want it, this hand is yours," I took it with gratitude and kissed it. I must sketch her portrait here. Mrs. Livingston Kean came from one of the first families in New York; of good height, blonde with blue eyes, light complexion, more vigorous and well-formed than beautiful; she was well read and remembered a great deal, was pleasing in her speech and witty in response. Nervous attacks made her at times irritable, but she was a woman of uncommon intellect and of an excellent heart. She had a ten-year-old son, Peter Kean, with whose education I concerned myself after our marriage.[8]

This marriage, however, took place only in 1800. I did not press it at all; she also hesitated at times, intimidated by the advice of her brother and of her sister, Mrs. Ricketts, not to unite with an unknown foreigner. Time passed; I contemplated going to the new city of Washington and opening a bookstore there, when my alarmed bride wrote me that she was ready to fulfill her promise and to set a day for the marriage. I answered that I did not wish to force her and released her from her promise, but that if she felt that she would be happy with me, I would not marry her unless it be stipulated in the marriage contract that I would renounce all rights to her estate. My distinterestedness surprised her brother and her other relatives. They did not now impede our marriage but urged it along. Our marriage took place in June 1800.[9]

While we were still chirping on the nest, my wife, until now boarding and rooming with Mr. and Mrs. William Dayton,[10] bought from Doctor Clarke a small house with a garden and in addition a meadow and 18 acres of land just beyond town, partly arable partly salt meadow, as those meadows which the incoming ocean periodically inundates are called in America.[11] This was all the landed property she owned in Elisabeth Town, New Jersey. In government bonds in banks, etc., she had, as it appeared after her death, a great deal; I still do not however know the total. The house consisted of two small rooms on the first floor, two on the upper with a tiny study, a kitchen and an attic; there was also a stable for a pair of horses and a cow. As for me because of the proscriptions of the Moscow government, I had perhaps a 100 Polish złotys [approximately eight to a dollar then] in my pocket.

On the day of the wedding and of the marriage contract in which I renounced all rights to my wife's estate I went before the ceremony to a nearby stream to bathe. I brought a bundle of my linen and clothes from my lodgings at the tailor's and went to dress in the stable. Only a few close friends were invited to this ceremony. An Anglican clergyman, Hobart, later a bishop, officiated at the marriage.[12] Tea and arrack punch concluded our modest wedding; at weddings here they have punch made only from arrack. It was in truth modest and quiet; the next day I went to bid farewell to my fat landlady, Mrs. Rivers the tailor's wife, and gave her a silver soup spoon as a souvenir. I took my small belongings and moved into my wife's house.

It will not be out of place here to sketch my way of life in this new state of matrimony. It was according to the customs of this country where everyone must have some occupation; farming, law, commerce, business, medicine, priesthood, or trade. My education in the corps of cadets, and furthermore my stay at the house of Prince Czartoryski, general-starosta of the Podolian lands and Commander of the Lithuanian troops, gave me but a slight knowledge of the military art, and a little more of literature towards which my innate inclination has never ceased to attract me. It was not expedient to go into military service in a country where there was a regular army of only 3 or 4 thousand although a militia of 800,000. I had unfortunately no other profession, but I could not remain idle. I decided to become a gardener and a farmer of sorts on the modest property of my wife.

The first year I dug my garden and manured it myself, seldom with any hired help; I had sweet potatoes brought in from Carolina. I took care to provide the best seed for sowing and the best grafts for budding and grafting fruit trees especially peaches, apricots and nectarines. Who gathers the fruit from my grafting? Not I, just as in my own Ursynów. Among the vegetables, there were, as well as the excellent common ones, *berangine* (*egg plant*) in the form of goose eggs and *poor man's beans*. This is a small bean; its seed planted in the morning of one day, has shot up by the next day, and in a week is ready for the table.

In the enclosed field beyond the town I raised *mais,* potatoes, tremendous *pum[p]kins,* and gathered salt hay. Along the road I planted trees in a row, *Liliodendrum Tulipferum* bearing a fragrant tulip-like flower. In my garden and also along the road I planted tremendous nut-bearing trees, *blacknut, hikory* and others. On my departure in 1807 all this was in a fine state.

Imported Persian melon seeds produced the most bountiful crop; watermelons weighed 40 pounds, pumpkins up to 70. After returning to Poland I brought these seeds to my Ursynów, also a tremendous cabbage called *drumhead.* Because of the lack of sun this seed gave somewhat smaller fruit, although much bigger than is usual with us. Dr. Malcz holds my confiscated property Ursynów, on a lease from the Moscow government.[13] That farm is no longer mine and I shall never see it again. I am happy that a good man has the care of it and makes use of the fruit sown and grafted by me.

I return to the matter in hand and will cursorily sketch the manner of my life in this secluded corner of the new world. After arising in the morning and giving God his due I took a basket and went to the market to buy meat or fish. Our table was frugal as everywhere in America. Plenty and show have their place in this country only when guests are invited. This begins after the New Year when all the prominent inhabitants of the town entertain each other in turn. Dessert consists of an enormous quantity of confections, local fruit or fruit imported from the Islands. At times there is fresh sugar cane. I remember how making jellies and *blanc mange* kept my wife and me busy for several evenings. Then an hour's work in the garden, breakfast of tea and a piece of baked sea fish, *schaad,* in French, *alos[e].* A supply of this fish is caught in April in large quantities almost in the same way as herring; it is salted and packed in barrels. A barrel costs only 8 Polish złotys. After breakfast I gave lessons to my stepson Peter Kean in Latin, French and geography, etc. He did not have a handsome face but he was an intelligent boy, with a very good heart. More work in the garden followed and in the field beyond the town if hired hands were available. This is expensive in America. A hired hand asks at least 8 Polish złotys for a day's work, breakfast, dinner, whiskey and tea. And then he says when he comes, *"I oblige you"*—Abraham Mann usually obliged me.[14]

I will now say a few words on the daily life of a little American town. One devotes all day to his calling. During the day there may appear a Negro child, a boy or a girl hardly able to talk, with a card pinned to its side; more important tasks prevent using a grown servant. The lady of the house unpins the card and reads it. This is usually an invitation for tea in the evening. For only in the evening does the work stop and friendly gatherings take place. When the ladies are assembled the men come, wash, tidy up; tea, bread, toast, smoked beef cut into slices are served. The men talk of farming, trade, politics. The ladies complain of the intractibility of their Negro servant girls, and so on. After tea homemade sweetmeats are served, fruit and Malaga wine. And so ends the day.

Our neighbor was Mr. Horace Dayton. He received his house and garden as a dowry when he married his cousin. The girl's relatives were against this marriage and, because the abduction of girls is a criminal offence according to the law of the land the lovers arranged that the young woman would abduct the young man. In fact she came for him with a horse at night. The lover sat behind her on the horse; he carried her to the first clergyman, married her and in this way he avoided the penalty, for she, not he, was the abductor.[15]

In the summer of 1802 I received an unexpected letter from my old friend Tadeusz Matuszewicz [16] informing me of the death of my father and saying that family business required my presence at home if only for a short time. Alexander I was now reigning and the interdicts and threats placed on me were without effect. Not without difficulty was I able to persuade my wife to let me go. I left in July and after a 50-day sail reached London.

JOURNEY TO AMERICA

DIARY OF SECOND VISIT, 1804-1807

This excerpt is taken from a published version of a copy purportedly made from the original diary found in Warsaw now lost. It was published as *Memoirs of Julian Ursyn Niemcewicz 1804-1807. Diary of his Journey to America* (*Pamiętniki Juliana Ursyna Niemcewicza 1804-1807. Dziennik drugiej podróży do Ameryki*), ed. anon. (Lwów, 1873), reprinted in *Lwow Review* (*Przegląd Lwowski*), V, VI (1873), and most recently in Wellman-Zalewska, ed. *Travels through America* (*Podróże po Ameryce*).

[17 Oct. 1804] A year ago Norfolk was destroyed by a great fire, today therefore it offers a strange combination of ships, new houses, shacks, unfinished houses, lakes, swamps, meadows, etc.[1] The streets are paved only at the sides for pedestrians; in the center there is mud. In the city there are tall, thin and pale figures, dirty and carelessly dressed; while those with a hale and ruddy complexion are not to be seen. The women are withered looking which no doubt is due to the hot unwholesome air and the exhalations from stagnant waters which the city, although rich and active in trade, tolerates rather than violate Liberty; as if it wished to demonstrate that the people must be forced to recognize their common good; for people are neither watchful nor careful except over that of *immediate* concern to each one individually; the public good, public advantage and comfort are considered as nothing.

After such a long sea voyage, oysters, at least a half a bushel of which were placed on the table, and above all fresh bread tasted wonderfully. A European is not a little surprised by the living arrangements in inns: instead of a separate room with a dresser, chairs and mirrors, he sees himself packed into a room with three beds, as many tables, without any other furniture, even the least bit; and what is worse, with persons whom perhaps he has never seen. This does not surprise Americans; they do not travel, they do not roam about except on business. To them, just for sleeping, only a bed is necessary; they do not need a room for they run about town all day, furthermore they have very little baggage, elegance in amenities is unknown to them; they wash themselves and comb their hair outdoors which, especially in the winter, is not at all pleasant.

Opposite Norfolk is the little town of Portsmouth. The surrounding land is infertile but the situation is most conducive for trade. At the customs I was treated in the most polite manner; only those nations which do not have a flourishing trade depend for their welfare on picayune and stupid inspections and impositions. I went to supper at the home of the French consul M. Otter [Oster].[2]

On Sunday the 21st of October, after a week's stay, I sailed on the packet boat "Eliza" of Captain Fergusson, to Baltimore.[3] This boat sailed with unprecedented speed down Chesapeake Bay. One could see the banks more or less on both sides. The company consisted of fourteen persons; the amenities and food were quite good. In spite of a 14-hour calm we reached Baltimore on Monday at 11 o'clock at night, a city 245 miles distant from Norfolk.

I stayed no more than about an hour in Baltimore. I went along a few streets. The beauty of the houses and thoroughfares, the luxury of the shops, the activity in mercantile trade, the large number of people everywhere, the appearance of prosperity—all would make one believe that this city counts many generations since its founding, when in truth twenty years ago it was a modest little settlement. Such are the results of freedom, an excellent site and the profits that America at peace gains from the bloody madness of Europe.

After asking the captain, who was sailing to Norfolk, to retrieve my watch or rather my signet, which I regretted losing the most, I transferred myself again with my baggage to a packet boat sailing to Frenchtown[4] and with a favorable wind we sailed along the middle of the inlet; on both sides there were green banks, houses and herds of cattle. We were many travelers, American, English and French; both male and female. There was a young English merchant of the most handsome appearance, witty and polite, perhaps only twenty years old; all these qualities he drowned in wine: it is quite inconceivable how much wine and whisky he drank and how many cigars he smoked. These two forms of intoxication made him talkative and gay almost to the point of giddiness. He had a most delightful voice and sang the gayest songs.

The boat made shore at 10 o'clock in rain and darkness. Two young Frenchmen, enticing a young and pretty American girl, repaired to a tavern in spite of the downpour—where, according to the discrete opinion of a third Frenchman, the faint-hearted virtue of the American girl was to expire on the laps of the Frenchmen. The rest of the company seduced by the pleasant singing of the Englishman treated themselves ceaselessly to French brandy, and caroused until midnight.

At dawn, we went on shore and here for the first time I got into an American diligence which carried us to Newcastle. There for the fourth time I transferred to a new packet, sailing the Delaware river, and after a four-hour sail we landed at Philadelphia the 24th of October.

I took a room in a French hotel on Fourth Street South.[5] At five in the evening I went down into the *parloir*. There was a fire in the stove and about fifteen handsomely-dressed young men sat around it, smoking cigars, neither moving nor saying a word. This lack of motion and silence continued for a half an hour. I left to see the Marquis Gouxe, the Spanish envoy.[6] In three hours I returned and again I came upon the same figures in the same places smoking and silent as before. What a sight for one returning from Europe and especially from France. There two Frenchmen can create more fuss, more talk, more laughter in a half an hour than a group of young Americans can here, perhaps throughout a whole year. There are indigenous reasons for this difference apart from enormous contrasts between the physical make-up of these people. In France loquacity is elemental for the French; the theatre and women, the subject of their conversation; here the theatre does not create such an impression; the plays are to be seen, not to be criticised; the actresses do not hold out any hope for sexual satisfaction. As for women in general, no one boasts of intercourse with those of ill repute; the virtuous are either married and do not recognize the gallantries or are unmarried and with them all the tribulations of love culminate in marriage. The day is spent on work; and a cigar and wine in the evening provide rest and relaxation.

The next day I went to see Mr. Peal[e], the owner of the museum (his two sons made the journey with me from America to London),[7] and Mr. Peterson [Paterson], professor of Mathematics, an old acquaintance of mine, an honest and enlightened man. Walking along the street I was surprised to meet unexpectedly Maria Ricketts, a niece of my wife, a comely and sensible girl. As acquaintances our greeting was pleasant enough, for relatives rather cool. The charm and freshness of Maria had begun to fade during the period of my absence. Maria was walking with the daughter of Mr. Dallas, the famous lawyer,[8] who invited me to her father's for dinner. The talk was of France and I heard with amazement that Dallas, friend and proponent of the French Revolution, defender of all its past violence in the hope that all tended to the establishment of freedom and equality not only in France but in the whole world, today, when freedom has been overthrown probably for centuries Dallas now worships the one who overthrew it, who cuts off heads to maintain his aristocratic rule as, at one time, he worshipped those who cut off heads in order to maintain the principles of their incomprehensible freedom. This aberration is all the more surprising to me since Dallas is one of the most enlightened people in the country; and whether it is excessive party spirit and prejudice or lack of knowledge and blindness—it comes out to the same thing.

I did not find that during my five-year absence from Philadelphia this city had increased remarkably in size. Although dull, it is symmetrical and handsome, and in its splendid buildings it leads all others. A steam pump which carries the waters of the Schuylkill all over town bears witness to the capability of the city and to the public will to apply itself to useful expenditures. The house of Mr. Bingham filled me with sadness. Five years ago it was the most resplendent and attractive house in Philadelphia: the host, rich and hospitable, his wife beautiful and flirtatious and the daughters full of charm. The younger was unhappily carried away by Mr. Tilly.[9] Today the parents have found a grave in a foreign land; the children are scattered; the house stands empty, offered for occupancy to whomsoever would wish to pay the taxes due. And so even in this new country there are awful examples of changes in fortune.

The 26th of October on a rainy and cold day I rode out of Philadelphia in a public carriage so filled with travelers that it was almost impossible to move. The road from Philadelphia to Frankfort [Frankford] is paved and they continue to pave it further. Nothing bespeaks the prosperity and industry of this country more than such undertakings. Paved highways and canals to a political body are as veins to an animate structure: the more there be and the better they are, the faster and more expeditiously they move about and exchange the products and wealth of the country. In all parts of America we see such roads more or less advanced; a private company with concessions granted by law builds them at their own expense and with time is rewarded with great profits; and so private profit is a source of public good and well-being.

We ate dinner in Trenton and spent the night in Brunswick. The next day only five Polish miles from my newly adopted home. How different were the feelings which touched my heart as I approached it from those when, after a long absence, after prolonged sorrows, after deep unhappiness, I set foot in my native land. There every place brought to mind my childhood, education, my youth, first thoughts, remembrances, first friendships, first loves, later public activity, wonderful and seductive hopes, terrible disasters, the final loss

of our Fatherland; the sight of it in an alien form, with an alien government, even an alien name; all this touched my spirit with sweet
sadness, with vivid emotion. But here, all is strange, all is calm and
of little concern.

Saturday, the 27th of October at 11 o'clock I reached home. I
found my wife living in the house of the deceased Mr. Stampton
[Hampton],[10] one of the finest persons in the whole town. She greeted
me with most eager friendliness. I was happy to find her in good
health and attached to me. I gave her some of my gifts. A fur-lined
coat of Turkish material in gold flowers—a gift from Prince Adam
Czartoryski, a Persian shawl from Mrs. A[leksandra] Potocki, Turkish
babouches embroidered in gold from Mrs. Czacki, a Persian wrap for
the shoulders from Mrs. Krasiński; and from me many trifles, mosaics,
earrings, necklaces, etc.[11] Her son Peter was getting ready for college
in Printstown. The boy had grown enormously.

> [*Memoirs*. I found that my wife, after having rented out her own
> small house had rented a larger one; I hurried there then all the
> faster, having my trunk brought after me. We greeted each other
> with feeling. I found her getting her son Peter Kean ready for the
> gymnasium at Printz Town. How many questions and how many
> embraces we exchanged! My baggage was brought. There were not
> many of my own things in the trunk; it was practically filled with
> gifts for my wife, stepson and friends and for the decoration of the
> house. I brought a beautiful furred coat of Turkish material with gold
> flowers scattered on a green background for my wife; a beautiful
> shawl, a necklace with mosaics, a clock and candlesticks of bronze.
> For my stepson I was given by my former commander a Turkish
> sword in a beautiful scabbard and a large hat, and my fine little
> stripling put it on and started to parade through the street with
> boys running after him. There were also portraits of my friends in
> miniature and in oils, views of Warsaw, Puławy, my home in Skoki
> and the like. All this left behind decorates the house of my stepson,
> bought after my departure and called Ursinów in my memory.] [12]

In the hour we rode out to our brother-in-law, Mr. and Mrs. Ricketts
and after being invited to dinner we called there on even closer
friends. Everywhere we were greeted joyfully, and with friendly courtesy. Neither in the town nor in the houses did I see any changes; it
seemed to me that I had just awakened and saw everything as before: everyone in the same place, doing the same things as before, in
the same clothes as before and these showing little wear.[13] The next

day I went to see *M. et Mme.* Belassis. Madame laid low by her yearly
sickness, that is pregnancy, but always pleasant and kind.

In a few days we received an invitation from my wife's brother,
Philip Livingston, severely invalided now for a few years. Afflicted
with the gout, the torments of this complaint forced him to look for
surcease in heavy drinking. Often when the pain was dulled with it
he lost all judgment; then his wife and servants were the object of
his irascibility. The first night at one o'clock he went down to the
kitchen in a wheel chair, threw out the cook, scolded the girl, etc.
Then he hoisted himself up again to the second floor and there in the
dead of night awakened with a tremendous voice those sunk in sleep;
first with a prayer to God followed immediately by terrible curses.
This was a terrible and horrifying scene provoking sorrowful reflections. This man, one of the wealthiest and most meritorious in this
country is brought in his old age by a pathetic illness to a state which
humiliates mankind.

After a two-week stay with the invalid we left his house because
of an indecent quarrel and returned to our own. This was rented for
only a year, and we tried to renew the lease for a few more years.
Young Stampton's [Hampton's] guardian, persuaded by relatives, in
contradiction to the will and to the truth, swore falsely that there was
not enough to bring up the child and obtained an order to sell the
house.[14] This news saddened us. As much as this house was large,
comfortable and pleasant, so our own to which we had again to move
was cramped and because of the rabble of neighbors very unpleasant.

The late fall ended work in the fields and in the garden; only petty
time-consuming problems and tasks remained, such as supplying the
house with foodstuffs and other needs, the bottling of the cider, etc.
To those who have many servants these things seem minor, but to
the one who must occupy himself with this it takes a great deal of
time. Howbeit there were hours left for reading and I even decided
to finish the *Poem of the Four Parts of Human Life* begun in Nantes.
This work went for me as from a stone. The monotony of home life
broken only by petty annoyances, the monotonous view of the surroundings, the complete lack of society which awakens and sharpens
the wit or quickens the heart; without an object to fire the imagination, except memories alone, and these blunted and interrupted by
the present; these rhymes would flow completely differently amongst
friends, in my own country, and in a gay and peaceful mood.

The 7th of December at 2 o'clock in the morning our negro servant
Betty [15] awakened us with the news that she felt birth pangs. I got
up therefore, sent for a midwife and lighting a candle I myself sat

through the whole night with a book. The childbirth was a success; we hired another negro girl to take care of her; there was no care nor attention which she did not receive. Towards evening, when her husband returned and I was the first to tell him that he had an addition to his family, I noticed mixed feeling in his face; there was more pain than joy. I understood that awareness of the fate and the state of this baby was the cause for these mixed feelings for although Negroes, even slaves, are treated better than are free servants in many places, it is a fact that the inborn desire for freedom in man does not permit him to be happy without it, in spite of all material advantages.

Winter was unusually heavy. Cutting wood for the fireplace in my room (often not being able to go out) brought me in part the exercise necessary for health. During my almost eight-year stay in this country I never saw such a heavy fall of snow. The northernmost countries in Europe can scarcely equal it. Often the road was impassable—it was the same even in the streets of our little town.

Towards the end of March the weather, as usual, suddenly warmed up, and luxuriant vegetation began to appear. The end of the month was the end of the year's lease on the Stampton [Hampton] house. Betty Gilman [Gilmore], cook of the deceased and the executrix of his will, persuaded by her relatives that the sum from the sale of the house would bring more interest than the sum from its rent, had the ruling, by force of which the house was protected (because of the minority of Stampton [Hampton]), annulled by dishonorable means. We were given notice to vacate; the sale was announced and the 26th of March was designated as the day of the auction. No one appeared and we were consoling ourselves with the hope that we need not return to our former hut, when in the morning of that day a very rich but even more a very stupid citizen from Virginia in the foolish clothes of that state flashed into the courtyard with a red collar and claret trousers. Because of the uncertainty in the title of the house, nobody rushed to acquire it and he bought it for 6,050 piasters.[16]

Scarcely therefore was I able to take advantage of a comfortable house before it was necessary to give it up. I deeply regretted my little room, the large porch which gave protection from the rain in winter, coolness in summer and at all times a spacious place for walking and meditation. To this, one must add the infinite bother of moving all the sticks of furniture, the contents of the larder, cellar, stable and woodyard and arranging everything in the most finical order in our former house. I hired two wagons; my negro Tom with one and I with the other went back and forth without stopping for three days.

With our return to this cramped house returned also in part our previous sad and vexing way of life—so strong an influence has the situation on one's feelings and thoughts. A continuously warm and fair spring (which in Petersburg would be called dog days) [17] rushed the work in the garden and the fields. In the garden in which earlier I had worked continuously for three years, the peach trees with my grafting were already giving fruit, the pasturage and flowers were bursting forth luxuriantly. I was happy to see that something useful had resulted from all my work. The Sandomierz wheat which I had imported myself and was planted last fall was completely lost, for no other reason than that the seeds held up for two years by the siege of Hamburg had aged and spoiled.[18] Where in the past year there had been *mais,* I planted, after ploughing and thorough manuring, flax, at first Livonian and if that did not succeed the flax of this country. On about three acres of newly-cleared land fenced in by hard work I planted *mais.* Except for the flax, however, all my farming was unsuccessful. I hired people to help; I sought the advice of my neighbor who, howbeit an excellent farmer for himself used different qualities with me: that is extortion, carelessness and cheating. The plowing was neither done on time nor as it should be; the bill for the job was enormous; the crows, hawks, ravens, pigeons, etc. ate up three sowings—in a word, bountiful payments for the most miserable harvest. In this country farming is as profitable for the one who works for himself and devotes himself wholly to it as it is a loss to the one who lives at a great distance from his fields and must use hired labor. Our Żmudzian [Samogitian] peasants say it well, "Farming is not for gain;" it certainly is not—for gentlemen!

The private life of a man, in a peaceful country in a small town without influence on public affairs or without any important personal [connections] with trade or a profession, without employment, does not offer anything of interest; year after year, day after day, all equally alike. Even our former circle grew ever smaller. My brother-in-law Ricketts with his wife and children received documents from England urging a journey there and, after selling his old furniture and arranging his affairs, he departed the 18th of July 1805. It was a loss for the whole town, especially for us. Their hospitality resting on an adequate income, the gaiety and the taste for enjoyment in both of them, the beauty of the elder daughter, the wit and friendly disposition of little Sarah Julia whom I had held for baptism,[19] made their home the most pleasant in the neighborhood. In it my wife found surcease from her spasms and nervous depressions.

After their departure, although the home of Lord and Lady Bolingbroke held those attractions found only in Europe, it was not to the taste of my wife, neither were the other houses of the French; because she did not understand the language she did not wish to go nor would she accept that I should visit them without her; therefore I dropped them almost entirely. A taste for recreation and entertainment (at my age) would have been a perverse and objectionable habit, and somehow noisy gatherings and entertainments had no lure for me; however after protracted loneliness shut fast in the house, talk with Europeans, the sounding of pleasant and once known notes, even the very change from gloomy thoughts brought recreation and surcease. However, I foreswore even these and I avow that I would not begrudge these sacrifices at all if I found peace and comfort at home. But alas! the spasms and nervous affectations of my wife deprived me of them; her disaffection and suffering distressed me; in addition to the male domestic chores even female ones fell to my lot. The intractability, disobedience and boldness of the Negroes, the very nature of the petty details with which I was constantly concerned and about which there was constant complaint filled my day continually with the unpleasantness of dissatisfaction. At times I concluded that the comfort or disagreeableness of human life does not depend on the great adventures that we meet from time to time, but on those common happenings which repeat themselves every day. The first occur rarely and are overcome by bravery and steadfastness, the second repeating themselves daily tire by their impatience and become unbearable. If the choice were given to me, whether to receive a deep cut from a saber or to be bitten constantly by mosquitoes and flies, I would much rather it be the first.

Howbeit the homage due truth, equity itself and sweet memories demand the acknowledgment that among the very large number of disagreeable days there were pleasant days, if not shining then at least without clouds. When my wife was well and gay, everything ran along in the most pleasant manner. With one's own home, independence, sufficiency in the primary requirements of life, comfort, peace, with the spirit undisturbed by sudden storms; in the summer the view of one's own fields, one's own fruit and produce in the garden; in the winter a fireplace and a book to speed the hours—sometimes the need for pleasant society receded from memory. After the loss of my fatherland, my home in America would be an agreeable, a reasonable refuge for me and not a shelter devoid of all pleasure, if it were not for the disastrous spasms and suffering of my wife, if it were less difficult to please her or if the running of the household depended on me alone; above all if I had but one Polish neighbor, one soul, in whom I could confide, with whom I could share my thoughts openly. At my time of life to seek out pleasure is pure madness; peace is the primary advantage, and friendship the one sweetness.

In the month of October 1805 Lord and Lady Bolingbroke setting out for Canada to see the famous Falls of Niagara urged most insistently that I join them on their journey. I also avidly desired to see this miracle of nature. The greatest difficulty was to get my wife's permission. Happily I write these notes for myself alone or perhaps for one other friend. If it were otherwise the reader could say, "This is a comical, truly a figurehead husband who like a little student of the primary grades can not leave his home without his mama's permission." However there is not one in my place that, born with a considerate heart, would wish to worry his wife who, in spite of irritability and sickness that made my days so sad, could soften her husband into submission with tears and gentle tenderness.

After long and difficult scenes I received permission for the journey. We set out the 5th of October. The diary of the journey to Niagara is written in a separate notebook and I will not repeat it here. One detail, however, which I forgot in my diary returns to my memory and I set it down here.

Crossing Lake Erie: the local inhabitants claimed as a fact without any doubt whatsoever that the squirrels (there are a great number of them there), when they wish to go from one side of the lake to the other, provide themselves with a piece of bark. They sit on this instead of a boat, and they raise their tails before the wind instead of a sail; they even wait for a favorable wind, then each one on its own bark sets out onto the lake and crosses it!

Shortly afterwards Lord and Lady Bolingbroke, the companions of my journey to Niagara, returned to England with their seven lovely children. They had been in America living in my neighborhood in hiding, for valid reasons, under the name of Belassis, and after the death of Bolingbroke's first wife they were freed from all restrictions. I accompanied them to the boat and the 6th of June 1806 they set out on their journey. Although I rarely went to their house I felt desolated by their absence especially the absence of Lady Bolingbroke who, although she was not beautiful, possessed not only all the virtues but also all the graces. She was calm and sweet with a lustful husband, the best possible mother, a good friend, with a heart in which trust follows respect once given, a heart which was not hardened and everlastingly closed with a lock as the hearts of the inhabitants of this country usually are.

To this loss in the society of our town we must add others, espe-

cially that of the Williams family, with whom my wife and I had
the closest ties. Williams is the nephew of the famous Franklin, and
he lived with him abroad primarily in France at the time of his mission. He took as his wife *Miss* Alexandre Hanke [20] from Scotland, a
kind, sensible, and well-educated lady with a quite considerable fortune. They moved to Elizabeth Town two years ago. A European education, a sojourn in France and in other countries, a sufficient income,
their personal qualities made their house pleasant and charming. One
could see there that an assured income from established capital, no
longer dependent on work or industry, or on chance decrease or increase, makes those who possess it more generous in its use and more
at ease in their mind. The Williams were in the minority of the inhabitants of a country in which, in general, everyone receives very
little from his father and must be the creator of his own fortune. On
many happy occasions we whiled away the hours in their house.

He is kind and an amusing character; she is compassionate and
sensible. The daughter, although not beautiful, is an agreeable singer
and a talented musician. Williams, whose mania was the military,
had given up the command of the engineers because he did not like
it. He has accepted it now that it has been offered again. Required
to have his quarters at West Point he had to transfer his whole family
there; [21] first he married his daughter Christine to Mr. Biddel of Philadelphia [22]—a very upright man. This was the Williams' first separation
from their beloved child. When I went to see her parents a few days
after her departure for Philadelphia, I found her father packing her
belongings and furniture. Amongst other things there was a large
clavicymbal. The moaning echo which the strings gave out on being
struck by the hammer made a melancholy impression on her father,
reminding him of his daughter's singing and of his regret that she was
no longer with him.

In the month of April 1806 they moved to our house for a week
until the wind was favorable to sail to West Point. The wind was unfavorable for longer than the leave of our beloved colonel permitted
him to be absent from his quarters. His zest and devotion to duty
were so violated by this irregularity that in his fervor and excitement
he said these words worthy *de l'oncle Tobie:* "The time of my leave
has expired, when I get to West Point, I will order out a *Kriegsrecht,*
and I will discipline myself for dereliction of duty."

This year on the Fourth of July, anniversary of the independence
of America, I visited him for three days at West Point at his post,
and saw him in all his glory commanding sixteen soldiers and eighteen cadets. Such is the garrison of the foremost fortress of the United

States. Nothing shows better than this that a republican government and a republican spirit does not base its strength on the military but on the civil courage of the whole mass of its people, and perhaps to a large extent on its remoteness from the conquests of the greedy European powers.

The Fortress of West Point built on the top of an enormous rock has the appearance of an abandoned Gothic castle. It was falling in ruins before it was finished. It is without cannon, without any means of defence. Lower down near the river there are trenches and a few brass cannon without gun carriages, captured from the English during the Revolutionary War. West Point is an important post and the key to the navigation of the North-River, so much so that in the last War the English, after bribing Arnold, tried to win it by treachery. When they did not succeed, they could not ever go beyond here to Albany and to the north country. An iron chain drawn across from the shore at West Point to Constitution Island cuts off and prevents all navigation. On all sides splendid and enchanting views spread out before the eye: to the north and to the south, the course of this splendid river, and the surrounding huge cliffs covered with dense spruces. The sail from West Point to New-York, in the midst of walls of gloomy rock along the banks where flourishing towns are rising speedily, is one of the most beautiful and interesting in nature.

This year in the month of June when the period of time required for obtaining citizenship of the United States of America had been fulfilled, I presented myself to the district of Newark where Colonel Ogden swore before the magistrate that I had conducted myself properly and had fulfilled all the conditions prescribed by law. After swearing away my nobility and taking the oath I was admitted to citizenship of the United States and shortly after received a certificate thereof.[23] In the instant when [blank] neighbors tore my Fatherland apart, I was no longer a citizen but a wanderer about the earth. This day created me a citizen of the first nation in the world. Although one cannot ascribe to her primacy in power or splendour, in freedom one must. Which nation is more intelligently free, which more generally happy than America? Although it is proper that I should pay homage to all the qualities of my new Fatherland, my heart never shall forget the old nor ever cease to pine for it.

In this month I had my first harvest from the meadow, which through my efforts had been continually cultivated and manured for two years. The hay called *timothé* was abundant and of the first quality; I had to sow it twice because the summer sowing after the harvesting of the flax was completely burnt out by the heat. The garden produced vegetables as abundantly as fruit, especially pumpkins some of which weighed up to 88½ pounds and were five feet in circumference; but in contrast our Polish radishes never succeeded and the cucumbers grew crooked and puny.

We moved the stable this year and added a new one to it. With the old deal I built a Lithuanian storehouse [lamusik].[24] This remodeling and moving would appear strange in another place but here one must recognize that everything is more flexible. Nothing is more common here than to see a house, even all the outbuildings, moved from place to place.

This summer we often visited Mrs. Rudekes [Rutgers],[25] a niece of my wife's who lives three Polish miles from us. She is a sweet, sensible and handsome woman, very happy in her domestic life. In the month of August while I was there I caught a fever and for more than three weeks it ravaged me horribly. Today English doctors cure it with a powder in which there is a very small amount of arsenic.

After my recovery at the end of September we set out for the improvement of my health to West-Chester beyond New-York to visit friends and relatives of my wife. In the environs of New-York both banks of the North-River are full of the houses and gardens of the merchants and rich citizens of the town. Everywhere one can see beauty, neatness, the comforts of life, even luxury, not so much in the number of servants, carriages and horses but in the furniture, which is all of the best quality. We visited the Wals, Lynks [Lynch]—an Irish-Catholic, [Thomas] Barclay—the English consul, Brock[holst] Livingston, general Stevens, Mrs. Gates—today the widow of my old friend, and finally on our return with Mr. Stevens again. He is wonderfully talented in mechanics and his house stands on a promontory in one of the most beautiful situations in the world, dominating the town, the river, the harbor and the sea.[26]

After our return in autumn my time was taken up by farming. A part of my land which I cultivated in partnership gave 300 *buszel* of *mais*, 3,000 pumpkins and 50 *buszel* of potatoes. This way of farming in partnership arose from the fact that in a country where hired help is so fantastically expensive it is not possible to cultivate one's farm alone. This way is probably also the most profitable. The owner gives the land, manure and half the seed for sowing. The tenant does all the cultivating; when the time comes for the harvest, they gather it together and divide it in two.

With my Negro, Tom, I went to husk the corn myself. In the evening when the wagon came, I measured the corn and placed it in the storehouse. A day spent in the fields on useful work strengthens the spirit, improves the health, disperses dark thoughts and cheers the soul with the knowledge that something useful is being done.

Winter was early and severe. Glued in the house like a snail in its shell, I did not go out for a week at a time and did not see a different face except that of my wife, suffering, wearying herself and wailing in ceaseless spasms. At times I did not come downstairs from my little room at all. I spent the morning near the fireplace in my room and the rest of the day beside my wife's bed in her room. In the morning if I were in the mood I worked over my *Poem Four Ages of Human Life,* but never have I been more convinced that being alone, separated completely from the world and society, blunts the imagination, weighs down the mind, and makes the writer incapable of literary work. I was rarely content with what I wrote and not at all with this particular work. If circumstances should change I must work it over completely. Meanwhile the time of life for poetic creation is practically gone by and even in the freshness of my strength, my work was never as good as that which I would have wished to leave to my fellow countrymen. This retired life was not particularly disagreeable for me when its peace was untroubled by domestic acrimony or the nervous illness of my wife; when from 5 o'clock, breakfasting, dining, we spent the whole day together in the same room, my wife over romances and I reading voyages or other books, forgetting the hours and hearing in surprise 12 or 1 strike when I would put out the candle.

In the small number of social gathering which we had this winter I must not forget the dinners at Mr. Robert's.[27] He was born in America, went to the island of Domingo and amassed there a considerable fortune in the profession of law. After losing his wife he settled with his three daughters in Elisabethtown, in the most beautiful house outside the town. This man as they say in English—*Ies a perfect gentleman.* This expression indicates a man courteous and pleasant in appearance, dress and bearing and with proper dignity. He liked foreigners and often gave dinners for men only, French and a few Americans. With the gay spirit of Europeans, with excellent wine and food, with a courteous host and much drinking, the dinners continued to the late hours with conversation and songs in the English manner. Even in recreation and social gatherings the difference in the characters of the two Nations strikes one forcefully. The French eat a great deal, drink little, their gaiety is boisterous and without order. With the English and the Americans the spirit of order is maintained even in celebrations; toasts are given in an orderly fashion; the telling of anecdotes, even songs go in a preordained manner. Mr. Robert joins in his person the good in both nations: he was a very good singer.

I had stayed at home from fall to spring, and had not visited New-York but for this one time, on business for my wife and to accompany Mrs. Arnold, the sister of Mrs. Armstrong.[28] After we reached town by boat, I received news of the tremendous advances of the French army after the battle of Jena [14 October 1806], and further, which was so joyful for me, news of the exciting promise for my Fatherland of the return of its existence. Napoleon was in Poznań, his soldiers in Warsaw and Toruń. He was greeted at the frontier by our best citizens—deputations from Warsaw made up of my friends and old colleagues in the Diet; they were welcomed and although not complete assurances, at least flattering promises were given to them. All this agitated my spirit. Only those whose long time oppressed fatherland is as dear to them as mine is to my heart can understand this.

I wanted to fly there like a bird. My feelings, my heart, even all my blood was in a storm of joy and uneasy excitement after so many disappointed hopes. I waited impatiently for letters from my friends in Poland, but from the time of my departure for America the last that I had received was on the 2nd of November. This silence increased my disquiet and my suffering, and this cruel situation not eased in any other way decided me to go to Europe once again. The decision was not reached without consideration and struggle with myself but this is how I analyzed it. Every citizen's first duty is to be useful to the society in which he was born. As long as Poland existed I tried to satisfy this obligation; when it was divided and I became an exile it was less important where I might drag out my sad existence. But today when such strong hopes shine, when the Polish eagles have risen from the ashes and have joined the fortunate and victorious flags of France, when fellow countrymen, known for their honor and good citizenship, have dedicated their work and fortunes to this bright hope, to remain here remote, indifferent, slack, even at an advanced age were, if not a crime, at least an ugly disgrace.

After preparing my wife by degrees I finally disclosed my intentions. It is not necessary for me to express her sadness and sorrow; I myself was strongly moved. Why was there not joined to this tenderness, to this touching affection for me an ease in manner without which there is no happiness in married life? There is nothing more unhappy than to be bound by unbreakable ties to some one person, who on one side has qualities which awaken respect while from the other has in her character a squeamishness and bitterness. These qualities by continuous repetition give rise to alienation; but should the unpleasantness suffered inhibit love, then a consideration of true values brings remorse and imputations of injustice. Perhaps it would be a hundred times better for one's peace of mind to have as a life companion one whose life was wholly reproachful. Then indifference and disrespect, being only a countermeasure of such vice would not be held up as unfair nor would one's heart be bruised by the opposing feelings of respect and dislike.

At the end of March my stepson Peter returned home before the vacation because of illness. This happenstance freed him from joining a rebellion which his fellow students raised in the Academy, in which he, because of his liveliness and high spirits, would certainly have been one of the prominent leaders and later like they would have received the punishment and the shame of being sent down with his colleagues. This young man has understanding, judgment, and ability uncommon for his years. He has basically a good heart; but his unbridled passion, arrogance and extravagance threaten him and his mother with a thousand tribulations. In eighteen months he will come of age and will take over his father's estate from the care and disposition of his mother. Since I have nothing in common with either of their estates it will be better for delicacy's sake that at the time of disposition I be not present.

Our friends, the Williams, and their daughter, Mrs. Biddel who lives in Philadelphia, wished to see me before my departure. Therefore with my wife and stepson I set out to see them. Our first stop was overnight in New Brunswick at the home of Mrs. White at the house where, when I came to America ten years ago, I stayed for a few weeks and received with Kościuszko evidences of the most sincere hospitality and friendship. After the death of Mr. White his wife and sister who survived him maintained these relationships. On the third day we dropped in on Mr. Izard.[29] Educated in military schools in France and Germany, he knows well all the important military arts but in America where there is no army, his science is in little demand and is ill rewarded. He married a rich widow who apart from other advantages brought him an estate and a large house where they live. The situation is most beautiful, the elegance, neatness and the decoration of the house indicates abundance. Such people with such an income would, at home, have about 40 servants and the same number of horses in the stable. Here there are hardly four in the house and the same number of horses in the stable. But from the owner and his wife down every one is employed from morning till night and with this small amount of help everything is in better order and state of cleanliness than with us. As for food and drink, everything is excellent and there is enough for all needs but no more. Supervision, good accounting and order are the sources of uninterrupted wealth.

Sunday the 16th of April in the evening we stopped in Philadelphia at our friends the Biddels. Their family was increased by an exceedingly lovable 5-month-old daughter. The more this creature makes for more tender relations in marriage the more this happiness adds to the daily work for the mother or father. From looking at and fondling the child they found joy and contentment. Alas they did not enjoy her long; a few days after our departure she died.[30]

I visited my old acquaintances. I spent Sunday with Mr. William Hamilton, owner of Wood-land, the famous residence near Philadelphia. The collection of foreign plants and bushes gathered from all three parts of the world, is the most numerous and beautiful which an individual may own. He has some fine pictures most of them signed by famous painters. The situation of the place amidst dark oaks and groves is strangely beautiful; before it lies Philadelphia and the Schuylkill river escaping in the distance in a wavy line. Philadelphia together with Pennsylvania has more factories and mills than any other place in America. Everything that is made from iron is made excellently here and is no longer brought from England; and there are also many other manufactures. The Academy of Fine Arts is just being created.[31]

Here the time of my departure drew near. The 24th of April my wife and her son in a coach and I going ahead in a public diligence went to New York in order to make the necessary preparations for the journey. While elsewhere there is too much attention to order here one can feel the lack of it. Although the number of people which the diligence can take is set by law, the owner through greed takes up to 12 instead of 6 to 8. It is from this that both the traveler's discomfort and frequent accidents arise. We broke an axle. In spite of this the next day at noon I got to New-York, where in one hour I looked over my ship, came to an agreement with the captain, and sold five shares of the Manhattan bank for 289 piasters. The next day in the morning I returned home. Because of the rain my wife did not return until the day after and without her I wrote once again to my friends the Ricketts. I made out my will at the request of my wife.[32] The three days remaining I spent on getting ready; I planted some more sweet peas and looked over my fields once again.

The 2nd of May: with my wife and Peter I went by water to New-York. It was difficult to leave the place which was our home without a heaviness in my heart, to leave the fields, the garden in which I worked myself, people with whom I lived, servants and their children. So many memories, vicissitudes strangely oppressed the heart.[33]

After getting to New-York we stayed with the Waats' [Watts]. The ship Acknomak was not to be ready until the 7th of May. The relatives and friends of my wife tried to make my last days pleasant; my gratitude demands that I record their names: [John] Rutherfurd, the cousin of my wife. He and his wife and children were educated, kind, pleasant, wealthy; I received much friendship from them. My brother-in-law Livingston, in an ever more sad state of health, Macomb, Fister, John Mur[r]ay, Church, Peter Cruger . . .[34]

My small trunk and things were brought to the ship. The whole of my money consisted of 50 louis d'or which I had brought from France and 75 ducats; the rest went to pay the captain and for food. The 7th of May between 11 and 12, not waiting for the sad parting with my wife, and after leaving a letter to her and my will, I went out. The ship was already leaving the shore. I could hardly get on deck. Twelve companions of the journey and as many friends who were seeing them off, all unfamiliar faces; the cries of the sailors, the unfurling of the sails and setting of lines and the yards, the dropping of the sails, the wind filling them, none of this could deaden nor suppress the sad feelings of departure.

NOTES

NOTES TO CHAPTER I

1. The account here of the time, place and circumstances of this meeting of the legislature is confirmed, completely and in detail by the archives. *Pennsylvania Archives,* ed. G. MacKinney, ninth series, II (part 1) (Philadelphia and Harrisburg, 1931), 1278-1280; see also fourth series, IV, ed. G. E. Reed (1900), pp. 380-394.

2. Thomas Mifflin (1744-1800), Major General (1777), resigned (1779); Governor of Pennsylvania (1790-1799).

3. Ignacy Wyssogota Zakrzewski (1745-1802), first Mayor (Prezydent) of Warsaw, 16 April 1792, in accordance with the new laws of the Constitution of 3rd of May 1791. Zakrzewski left the Mayoralty after the Confederation of Targowica (14 May 1792) and returned to the office 17 April 1794 by acclamation. After the failure of the Kościuszko Insurrection he was imprisoned in St. Petersburg until the death in 1796 of Catherine II. See Julian Ursyn Niemcewicz, *Pamiętniki czasów moich,* ed. Jan Dihm, 2 vols. (Warsaw, 1957), II, 330, n. 3, and passim—hereafter cited as Niemcewicz, *Pamiętniki* (Warsaw); Adam Skałkowski, Z *dziejów insurekcji, 1794 r.* (Warsaw, 1926), p. 157; W. F. Reddaway, J. H. Penson, O. Halecki, R. Dyboski, eds., *The Cambridge History of Poland from Augustus II to Pilsudski (1697-1935)* (Cambridge, Eng., 1951), p. 163.

4. *The Yellow Fever.* A contemporary account may be found in Richard Folwell, *A Short History of the Yellow Fever, that broke out in the City of Philadelphia, in July 1797,* 2nd ed. (Philadelphia, 1798), bound in *Select Pamphlets respecting the Yellow Fever* (Mathew Carey, Philadelphia, 1799).

5. Benjamin Rush (1745-1813), leading citizen, personal friend and physician to Kościuszko during his stay in America. See Rush to Gates, 25 August 1797, New-York Hist. Soc., *Gates Papers,* box 18, no. 171; see also correspondence (especially letter of British doctor to Rush about Kościuszko's wounds) cited by M. Haiman, *Kosciuszko, Leader and Exile* (New York, 1946), pp. 34, 50, 135-136.

6. Anthony Walton White (1750-1803), old friend of Kościuszko. For autobiography see *New Jersey Historical Society Proceedings,* 2nd series, VII (1882), 105-115.

7. Horatio Gates (1728?-1806), Major General (1776).

8. On the basis that a Polish mile equals 7 wiorstas and that a wiorsta is equal to 1064.5 meters, the Polish mile is approximately 4.6 times greater than the American mile.

9. Lawson. According to the newspaper account they stayed at Sarah Lawson's, 7 South Fourth Street, *The Aurora and General Advertiser* (Philadelphia), 19 August 1797.

10. Old spelling of Frankford; see Reading Howell, *A Map of the State of Pennsylvania* (Philadelphia, 1792).

11. A stone bridge built by Lewis Wernwag in 1796. A contemporary view may be seen in Robert Gilmor, "Memorandums made in a Tour to the Eastern States in 1797 with views from Pen-sketches by the Author," *Boston Public Library Bulletin,* new series, III (1892), 72-92; it is reproduced here.

12. Washington House erected in 1796 in what is now Holmesburg, known before 1801 as Washington or Washingtonsville; see S. F. Hotchkin, *The Bristol Pike* (Philadelphia, 1893), pp. 96, 122, 126.

13. This sentence was written in Polish. The phrase *las czarny*, translated as black woods, means in Polish woods of trees such as the oak, ash, maple, elm and birch.

14. The English oak Quercus robur, or more precisely Quercus sessiliflora.

15. Joshua Sutcliffe, companion of Kościuszko and Niemcewicz on their Atlantic crossing; see newspaper, *Claypoole's American Daily Advertiser* (Philadelphia), 19 August 1797.

15a. See "The soil is generally a light sand; and by digging, on an average, about fifty feet below the surface, . . . you come to salt marsh . . . 'I have seen an oyster shell that would hold a pint . . .' In the County of Monmouth . . . was discovered the skeleton of some huge carnivorous animal." Jedidiah Morse, *The American Geography, or A View of the Present Situation of the United States of America . . . and in the West Indies, and of Europe, Asia and Africa.* New ed. with 25 maps (London, 1794), p. 406.

16. John B. Bayard (1738-1807). John Bayard's third wife was Johannah White, sister of Anthony Walton White. *N.J. Hist. Soc. Proc.*, 2nd series, V (1879), 154.

17. William Paterson (1745-1806), Associate Justice of U.S. Supreme Court (1793-1806). Both Paterson and Bayard were married to sisters of Gen. White. William Paterson married Euphemia White. *N.J. Hist. Soc. Proc.*, 2nd series, VII (1882), 105-115.

18. David Ramsay, M.D. (1749-1815), *The History of the American Revolution*, 2 vols. (Philadelphia, 1789).

19. William Gordon, D.D. (1728-1807), *The History of the Rise and Progress and Establishment of the Independence of the United States*, 4 vols. (London, 1788).

20. Nathanael Greene (1742-1786), Brigadier General (1775), Major General (1776).

21. John Sullivan (1740-1795), Brigadier General (1775), Major General (1776).

22. Sir William Howe (1729-1815), Major General (1772), Lieutenant General (1775).

23. Cornwallis, Charles, 1st Marquis (1738-1805).

24. Accounts of these incidents as related by Niemcewicz are to be found in Gordon, II, 278-279, 314, 315, 354.

25. Rev. Abraham Beach (1740-1828); see Frederick Lewis Weis, "The Colonial Clergy of the Middle Colonies, New York, New Jersey and Pennsylvania. 1682-1776," *Proceedings of the American Antiquarian Society*, LXVI (1956), 176, and also William H. Benedict, *New Brunswick in History* (New Brunswick, N.J., 1925), p. 352.

26. Possibly William R. Boote, 2nd Lieutenant (1798). See Francis B. Heitman, *Historical Register and Dictionary of the United States Army from its Organization, Sept. 29, 1789 to March 2, 1903* (Washington, D.C., 1903), I, 230.

27. Old spelling of Hoboken.

28. New Jail: the state prison erected in 1796-97 at Greenwich Village north of Christopher Street between Washington Street and the Hudson River. A view is reproduced in John A. Kouwenhoven, *The Columbia Historical Portrait of*

New York (New York, 1953), p. 103, from the original in the Museum of the City of New York and reproduced here.

29. Née Mary Vallance, married in 1786, see *D.A.B.* s.v. "Gates, Horatio."

30. Nicholas Cruger (d. 1800), *The New York Genealogical and Biographical Record*, VI (April 1875), 78-80.

31. The details of this lease of Rose Hill, essentially as Niemcewicz stated them, are recorded, *Outline of the Title of Samuel B. Ruggles*, New-York Hist. Soc. (New York, 1934), pp. 12-13. See also William Kelby, Rose Hill Farm (Kelby MS. Notes), New-York Hist. Soc.

32. Edward Livingston (1764-1836), distinguished American statesman, holding many offices, U.S. Secretary of State (1831-1833), and John Livingston (1755-1851) married the daughters, Mary and Eliza, of Charles McEvers, merchant of New York City. See Edwin Brockholst Livingston, *The Livingstons of Livingston Manor* (New York, 1910), p. 398.

33. For an account of this family see *Cambridge History of Poland* . . . (1697-1935), pp. 21 ff. Niemcewicz was intimately connected with three members of this many-branched family, Stanisław Kostka Potocki (1755-1821) with whom he traveled to England and under whom he served in the Department of Education until 1821; Ignacy Potocki (1751-1809), his brother, one of the creators of the Constitution of the 3rd of May and one of the leaders of the Kościuszko Insurrection, and Stanisław Szczęsny Potocki (1752-1805), member of the Tulczyn branch and leader with Franciszek Ksawery Branicki (1730?-1819) and Seweryn Rzewuski of the traitorous Confederation of Targowica against which Niemcewicz directed much of his patriotic writings. See Niemcewicz, *Pamiętniki* (Warsaw), I, 242, passim; *Encyclopaedia Britannica*, 11th ed., s.v. "Potocki, Stanisław Felix"; Stanisław Kot, *Historja wychowania* (Lwów, 1934), II, 251.

34. John Jay (1745-1829). Governor of New York (1795-1801). In this comment Niemcewicz may be near the truth, see Henry Adams, *The United States in 1800* (Ithaca, New York, 1955), p. 78; cf. George Dangerfield, *Chancelor Robert R. Livingston of New York. 1746-1813* (New York, 1960), p. 241 ff. Kozłowski and later Wellman-Zalewska totally unaware of American politics cited this comment as typical of Niemcewicz's superficial observation of the American political scene which led to his estrangement with Kościuszko, Kozłowski, "Pobyt Kościuszki," p. 260, n. 1; Niemcewicz, *Podróże po Ameryce*, ed. A. Wellman-Zalewska, pp. xv, 48, n. 47.

35. Lt. Col. Ebenezer Stevens (1751-1823), later General of the N.Y. Militia, was head of this family (if this is the correct interpretation of Niemcewicz's spelling). A son by his first marriage, godson of General Gates, was named Horatio Gates. See Harriet P. Poor, *Stevens Family Notes*, n.d. pamphlet in New-York Hist. Soc.; Byram Kerby Stevens, *Genealogical and Biographical History of the Families of Stevens, Gallatin and Nicholson* (New York, 1911), p. 10.

36. There were six daughters of the well-known New York merchant John Broome (1734-1810), Mary, Sarah, Harriet, Julia, Caroline and Ann-Charlotte, some of whom were not married at this time. See *The Papers of the Lloyd Family of the Manor of Queens Village, Lloyds Neck, Long Island, New York* (1654-1826), Collections of the New-York Historical Society (1927), II, 890-891, 897-898.

37. No record of connection with two well-known Baltimore families of this name.

38. Probably the wife of John Vining (1758-1802), U.S. Senator (1793-1798 resigned).

39. Jehoiadden Nicholson (1783-1828), the then unmarried daughter of Captain James Nicholson (1736?-1804). See Stevens, p. 35.

40. Marinus and Susannah (née Nicoll) Willet. The marriage of the Willets was an unhappy one and ended in divorce in 1799; *D.A.B.* s.v. "Willet, Marinus." A letter of Mrs. Willet to Kościuszko was published in *Penna. Mag. of Hist.*, XXIII (1899), 122.

41. Thomas B. Bridgen, listed in David Longworth's *American Almanac, New York Register and City Directory*, 1797, as located at 214 Broadway. There are three letters of Bridgen to Gates in keeping with Niemcewicz's characterization. Thomas B. Bridgen to Gates, 14 March 1796, 2 Oct. 1797, *Gates Papers* (New-York Hist. Soc.) Box 18, no. 3, no. 200; see also Bridgen to Gates, 14 November, 1790, *Gates Papers,* Emmet Collection (New York Public Library).

42. Cruger's second wife was Anne Markoe of St. Croix and their two daughters were Sarah and Eliza. The latter died very young. See *The New York Genealogical and Biographical Record,* VI (April 1875), 77, 78-80.

43. François Alexandre, duc de La Rochefoucauld-Liancourt (1747-1827) refers, in his book, to meeting with Niemcewicz and Kościuszko and he reciprocates Niemcewicz's esteem. See *Travels through the United States of North America,* trans. H. Neuman, 2 vols. (London, 1799), II, 469. The book is dedicated to Citizeness La Rochefoucault D'Enville, "My dear and unfortunate Aunt."

44. Louis-Philippe (1773-1850), King of France (1830-1848), Antoine Philippe D'Orléans duc de Montpensier (1775-1807), Charles D'Orléans, comte de Beaujolais (1779-1831), sons of Louis-Philippe-Joseph, Philippe "Egalité."

45. Mme. Stephanie-Félicité du Crest de Saint-Aubin, Comtesse de Genlis (1746-1830), "gouverneur" of the sons of Philippe "Egalité," and writer of books on education see Madame de Sillery-Brulart, gouvernante de Mlle d'Orléans *Leçons d'une gouvernante à ses élèves,* 2 vols. (Paris, 1791). See also *Encyclopaedia Britannica,* 11th ed., s.v. "Genlis, Stéphanie-Félicité du Crest de Saint-Aubin."

46. A certain M. Montjoie was aide-de-camp to Louis-Philippe in Hamburg (1795-1796), see F. A. Gruyer, *La Jeunesse du roi Louis-Philippe* (Paris, 1909), p. 178; a M. Montjoie was also reported as accompanying Louis-Philippe and his brothers in Twickenham immediately after their return from America; see C. C. Dyson, *The Life of Marie Amélio* (New York, 1910), p. 100. An inadequately identified Montjoie accompanied Madame de Genlis to Switzerland in 1793; see *Memoires inédits de Madame La Comptesse de Genlis.* Memoires sur le dix-huitieme Siècle et la Révolution Française (Paris, 1825), IV, 178, 180, 182, 194, 195, 201. We have not found any evidence that Montjoye belonged to the many-branched family of that name although this appears possible; see De La Chenaye-Desbois et Badier, *Dictionnaire de la noblesse* (Paris, 1869) s.v. "Montjoye."

47. Columbia College, the Bridewell, Workhouse and Gaol; the relative position of these buildings is shown on a contemporary map of New York City; see Kouwenhoven, *The Columbia Historical Portrait of New York,* pp. 7, 104, 105.

48. The Gaol (see note 47) was called the Debtor's Prison and was so used at the time of Niemcewicz's visit. We have been unable to determine whether or not Niemcewicz referred to this building. It did not have a flat roof (plateforme); see Elizabeth Dike Lewis, "Old Prisons and Punishments," *Historic New*

York, eds. Maud Wilder Goodwin, Alice Carrington Royce, and Ruth Putnam (New York, 1899), II, 97-109.

49. Henry Gahn (d. 1834), a merchant well known in New York, appears in several Directories of this time, e.g. David Longworth, *American Almanac, New York Register and City Directory,* 1796-1804. Commercial Agent for Sweden in City Directory for 1804, p. 55. MSS. of this office in American Swedish Historical Museum in Philadelphia, Penna. For a rather unsatisfactory biographical sketch see Amandus Johnson, *The Journal and Biography of Nicholas Collin* (*1746-1831*) (Philadelphia, 1936), pp. 57 ff. See also Johnson, *The Swedish Element in America,* 2nd ed. (Chicago, 1934), IV, 23, 24. See also *Diary of William Dunlap* (*1766-1839*), ed. Dorothy C. Barck, Collections of the New-York Historical Society (New York, 1929-1931), III, 808. Henry Gahn was probably of the family of Dr. Henry Gahn (1747-1816), a practising physician, and Johann Gottleib Gahn (1745-1818), the famous chemist, his brother, both of Stockholm. See MSS. under dates 29-30August–6September 1800, *Mineralogical Journey in Europe of Thomas Peters Smith* [ca. 1777-1802] *in 1800-1801,* in American Philosophical Society. See also Niemcewicz, *Podróże po Ameryce,* p. 53, n. 55. For changed opinion of Niemcewicz on Gahn see Niemcewicz, *Pamiętniki* (Warsaw), II, 217.

50. This was John Bill Ricket's New Amphitheatre rented to the Thomas Wignell company of actors, *Diary of William Dunlap,* I, 111, 123, 130, 145.

51. Park Theatre or New Theatre, opened Jan. 29, 1798, on Park Row. A contemporary view in Kouwenhoven, p. 103.

52. A description of the John St. Theatre, which opened Dec. 1767, may be found in William Dunlap, *History of the American Theatre* (New York, 1832), p. 28.

53. This is Lailson's Circus. See *Diary of William Dunlap,* I, 144, 158, n. 16.

54. Libiszewski was a Polish officer from Great Poland who had been in jail with Kościuszko and Niemcewicz at St. Petersburg. He offered to accompany them to America; he was very strong and carried Kościuszko (crippled by his wounds) about in his arms. See Niemcewicz, *Pamiętniki* (Warsaw), II, 201-202, 224-225. See for employment *Diary of William Dunlap,* III, 268.

55. This performance is established as having taken place on Sept. 20, 1797, by Dunlap in his diary. See *Diary of William Dunlap,* I, 149.

56. In the *Centinel of Freedom* (Newark), 18 October 1797, under date line Elizabeth-Town 4 October 1797 there is the item, "On Friday last arrived in this town, that warm friend to liberty and mankind Kosciusko. He makes a stay of sometime in this place."

57. The 227 foot high steeple of the First Presbyterian Church which was founded in 1664 with the town. The steeple, built in 1792, was destroyed in 1899 but was rebuilt after the old model in 1901. *Historic Elizabeth* (*1664-1932*) (Elizabeth, N.J., 1932), pp. 29-30. (Note added in proof. Cf. here and elsewhere information on Elizabethtown in Theodore Thayer, *As We Were. The Story of Old Elizabethtown,* The Collections of The New Jersey Historical Society (Newark), XIII (Elizabeth, N.J., 1964).)

58. Elias Dayton (1737-1807), promoted to Brigadier General (1783) on direct recommendation of Washington; his eldest son Jonathan Dayton (1760-1824), Speaker of the House of Representatives (1795-1799); his other identifiable sons were Elias Bayley Dayton (1763-1846), William Dayton (1768-1843) and Horatio Dayton (1773-1813). They all remained in contact with Niemcewicz

when he later settled in Elizabeth. See *Webster's Biographical Dictionary* s.v. "Dayton"; see also *Biographical Index* in *New Jersey Historical Society* (Newark); see also Niemcewicz, *Pamiętniki*, II, 229, 238, 241, translated in part here.

59. A Miss Mary (Polly) Dayton and a Miss Sally Dayton are identified as marrying in 1804 and 1815 respectively, see *Biog. Index*.

60. Susan W. Dayton, who died in 1804 at childbirth in her 22nd year, married Rev. Frederick Beasley in 1803, see Rev. Edwin F. Hatfield, D.D., *History of Elizabeth, New Jersey* (New York, 1868), p. 618. Mary Goodin Chandler (c. 1774-1847), daughter of Rev. Thomas Bradbury Chandler (1725-1790), Loyalist pastor of St. John's Church in Elizabeth, married 6 May 1800 Rev. John Henry Hobart (1775-1830), later, from 1816, Episcopal Bishop of the Diocese of New York who performed the marriage of Niemcewicz with Susan Livingston Kean 2 July 1800. *Ibid.*, pp. 550-551; Niemcewicz, *Pamiętniki* (Warsaw), II, 238, translated in part here. The other young women were members of well-known families in Elizabeth, see Hatfield, *op. cit.*, passim.

61. October 10th and 11th, 1797. See *Centinel of Freedom* (Newark), 4 October 1797 where a public notice of an election to be held October 10 and 11 was given.

62. William S. Pennington, "a firm Republican was elected to the Assembly." *Centinel of Freedom* (Newark), 18 October 1797.

63. Article IV of New Jersey Constitution of 1776 stated "That all inhabitants of this Colony of full age, who are worth fifty pounds Proclamation money, clear estate in the same, and have resided within the county in which they claim a vote for twelve months immediately preceding the election, shall be entitled to vote for Representatives in Council and Assembly; and also for all other public officers that shall be elected by the people of the county at large." *Federal and State Constitutions, Colonial Charters . . . of the United States,* ed. B. P. Poore (Washington, D.C., 1878), II, 1311.

64. For a contemporary account of this event see *Centinel of Freedom* (Newark), 18 October 1797, with the Ode, "The Freedom of Elections" therein. See also Edward Raymond Turner, *Women's Suffrage in New Jersey: 1790-1807,* Smith College Studies in History, I, no. 4, July 1916, 165-187; reprints ode, pp. 170-171.

65. Colonel William Crane (1747-1814) fought at Quebec; see Ellery B. Crane, *Genealogy of Crane Family,* 2 vols. (Worcester, Mass., 1900), II, 473, 479; concerning wounds, Hatfield, pp. 660-661; Crane was defeated by John Condit (1755-1834) legislative councillor (1790-1798), see *Centinel of Freedom* (Newark), 18 October 1797.

66. Built 1797 and burned in 1808. *Historic Elizabeth (1664-1932),* p. 19.

67. This perhaps refers to Henry Brockholst Livingston (1757-1823) and his house "Liberty Hall" the former residence of his father William Livingston the Governor of New Jersey (1776-1790). It was this house sold (29 March 1798) to Lord Bolingbroke alias Belasise which eventually (23 March 1811) came into the possession of Niemcewicz's wife and stepson and was named Ursino in his honor. See Liber N95, L887, L889, O17 and S156, *Essex County Deeds* (Newark). The Dayton house is now called the Boudinot House (Boxwood Hall). See *New Jersey,* American Guide Series (New York, 1939), p. 246.

68. Niemcewicz lists other French names in his *Memoirs,* see Part III here. The Massons were probably the family which provided the first French and Drawing professors at the United States Military Academy at West Point through their common residence in Elizabeth with Jonathan Williams the first Commandant at

West Point. See "Francis Désiré Masson First Teacher in French and of Drawing 12 July 1803 . . . and Florimond Masson substitute for brother 15 April 1810," Bvt. Maj. Gen. George W. Cullum, *Biographical Register of the Officers . . . of the United States Military Academy . . .* , 3rd. edition (Boston, 1891), I, 36. F. D. Masson was also Recording Secretary of the United States Military Philosophical Society founded by Jonathan Williams, see MSS. of Society at the New-York Historical Society. For a limited account of the French in Elizabeth see Warren R. Dix, "Former French Residents of Elizabeth," *History of Union County, New Jersey,* ed. Frederick William Ricord (Newark, N.J., 1897), pp. 200-204.

69. Black reed bird—Red-wing (Agelaius phoeniceus).

70. This word was originally written in Polish with the archaic spelling *dzienciol.*

71. Paterson Falls on the Passaic River.

72. John Jacob Faesch, Jr. (1769?-1809), eldest son of John Jacob Faesch (1729-1799) who came to America from Basle, Switzerland in 1764 to work the iron mines in New Jersey. See Isaac S. Lyon, *Historical Discourse on Boonton* (Newark, N.J., 1873), pp. 14-15. *History of First Presbyterian Church (Morristown, N.J.),* Part II (1742-1885) (n.d.), p. 69.

73. Aaron Ogden (1756-1839) served throughout the Revolution; he was U.S. Senator (1801-1803), Governor of New Jersey (1812), old friend of Niemcewicz and sponsor of his U.S. citizenship. See "Pamiętniki Juliana Ursyna Niemcewicza (Dziennik Drugej Podróży do Ameryki) 1804-1807," *Przegląd Lwowski,* VI (1873), 486; also published separately in 1873; reprinted most recently in Niemcewicz, *Podróże po Ameryce,* p. 380, and translated here in Part III.

73a. Jacob Mark and the mine; see Herbert P. Woodward, "Copper Mines and Mining in New Jersey," Department of Conservation and Development in the State of New Jersey, *Geologic Series* Bulletin 57 (Trenton, 1944), p. 52.

74. Cascata delle marmore in Terni, cascatella delle Tivoli; Italy.

75. Abraham Godwin (1763-1835); see George C. Groce and David H. Wallace, *The New-York Historical Society's Dictionary of Artists in America (1564-1860)* (New Haven, 1957) s.v. "Godwin, Abraham"; see also *Diary of William Dunlap,* III, 757, 825.

76. Perhaps the name of Urey Lisiansky, *A Voyage Round the World in the Year 1803-1806 . . . in Ship Neva* (London, 1814). We have not seen this book.

77. For the origin and history of this name in America, see *New York Genealogical and Biographical Record,* XXIII (1892), 26; see also M. Haiman, *Poland and the American Revolutionary War* (Chicago, 1932), pp. 60-61, 111. For an appreciation of Haiman's work in general and an interesting sidelight on his research on this name, see Zygmunt Gross, "Mieczysław Haiman—historiograf polsko-amerykański," *Kultura i Społeczeństwo,* III, nr. 2 (1959), 163-175, esp. 169-170.

78. Gourde; money of Haiti corresponding to a piaster or an écu, therefore a dollar.

79. Chastellux had earlier reported seeing in New Jersey a young man with such a large head lying in a cradle; see *Voyages de M. le Marquis De Chastellux dans l'Amérique septentrionale dans les années 1780, 1781 et 1782* (Paris, 1788), I, 117-118. The doctor may well have been Dr. Charles McKnight (1750-1791). *The American Medical and Philosophical Register,* II (New York, 1814), 426.

80. Susan Kearney Lawrence Faesch. The elder Faesch had first married Eliza-

beth Brinckerhoff who had died in 1788. See note 72; see also *History of Morris County New Jersey* (New York, 1882), p. 54.

80a. "The Desponding Negro" [1793]. See for words and music *The Night-ingale. A Collection of the Most Popular Ancient and Modern Songs,* selected by Samuel Larkin (Portsmouth, 1804), pp. 122-124; for bibliography see Oscar George Theodore Sonneck, *A Bibliography of Early Secular American Music* [18th century], revised and enlarged by William Treat Upton (Washington, 1945), p. 106.

81. Niemcewicz visited the Mount Hope Forge again in 1799, a visit of which he writes in this diary. For another contemporary account of this and other forges see Samuel Gustaf Hermelin, *Report about the Mines in the United States of America, 1783,* ed. Amandus Johnson (Philadelphia, 1931), pp. 21-26, 69-70.

82. See *Centinel of Freedom* (Newark), 1 November 1797 and *New Brunswick Guardian,* 14 November 1797.

83. Colonel John Neilson (1745-1833). See Benedict, *New Brunswick in History,* pp. 283-287; *D.A.B.* s.v. "Neilson."

84. "The Presydent dining here today and as I write this the Canons give notice by their little noise of his approach near the town. I expect see him at Gen. White's where he will drink tea . . . ," undated letter of Tadeusz Kościuszko to Horatio Gates, *Gates Papers* (New-York Hist. Soc.), Box 21, no. 77.

85. Thomas Tingey (1750-1829). See *D.A.B.* s.v. "Tingey, Thomas" for account of his return to military service.

86. Jacques-Pierre Brissot de Warville (1754-1793), *New Travels in the United States of America Performed in 1788,* trans. anon. (London, 1792), p. 179.

87. Perhaps Lt. Boote; see note 26.

NOTES TO CHAPTER II

1. This description of Kościuszko's lodging tallies exactly with another contemporary account. See Moreau de Saint-Méry, *Voyage aux Etats-Unis de L' Amérique, 1793-1798,* ed. Stewart L. Mims, Yale Historical Publications, No. 2 (New Haven, 1913), pp. 256-257.

2. Probably Stevens Thomson Mason (1760-1803); although Mason was a Senator (1794-1803) he was a Brigadier General in the Virginia militia and was commonly referred to as General Mason; see *Biographical Directory of the American Congress, 1774-1949* (Washington, D.C., 1950) s.v. "Mason, Stevens Thomson"; see also *Aurora and General Advertiser* (Philadelphia), 1 December 1798. Niemcewicz was especially interested in prisons both because of his two year stay in prison in St. Petersburg and his concern with prison reform. See Julian Ursin Niemcewicz, *Notes sur ma captivité à Saint-Petersbourg en 1794, 1795 et 1796,* ed. Charles Sienkiewicz (Paris, 1843); Julian Ursyn Niemcewicz, "O więzieniach publicznych czyli domach pokuty, rzecz krótka," *Dzieła poetyczne, wierszem i prozą,* ed. Jan Nep Bobrowicz (Leipzig, 1839), XI, 115 ff.; published originally in Warsaw in 1818. Niemcewicz visited the Walnut Street Prison. See Thorsten Sellin, "Philadelphia Prisons of the Eighteenth Century," *Historic Philadelphia from the Founding until the Early Nineteenth Century,*

Trans. Amer. Phil. Soc., XLIII, Part 1 (1953), 326-330. For another contemporary account see Moreau de Saint-Méry, p. 381.

3. Daniel Thomas, member of the Board of Inspectors to Prisons. See J. Thomas Scharf and Thompson Westcott, *History of Philadelphia, 1609-1884* (Philadelphia, 1884), III, 1829.

4. For history of City Dancing Assembly see Scharf and Westcott, *History of Philadelphia*, II, 864, 878, 960-961. See Henry Wansey, *An Excursion to the United States of North America in the Summer of 1794*, 2nd ed. (Salisbury, 1798), pp. 119-121 for contemporary account of Assembly Room and Rules. Niemcewicz was a good dancer and interested in dancing. See Niemcewicz, *Pamiętniki* (Warsaw), I, 55, 230; Julian Ursin Niemcewicz, *Pamiętniki czasów moich*, ed. Karol Ursin Niemcewicz (Paris, 1848), pp. 33, 111.

5. Presidents' March. The words "Hail Columbia" were written to this music by Joseph Hopkinson. See John Bach McMaster, *A History of the People of the United States* (New York, 1885), II, 377-380; see also Arthur Hobson Quinn, "The Theatre and the Drama in Old Philadelphia," *Historic Philadelphia*, p. 316; for brilliant analysis of this piece see especially Sonneck, *Bibliography*, pp. 341-344.

6. During his stay in England in 1785 Niemcewicz lived on Oxford Street, London, at the home of the Parkers for whom he had a great fondness and a feeling of nostalgia; see Niemcewicz, *Pamiętniki* (Warsaw), I, 229, 233.

7. William Bingham (1752-1804); see *D.A.B.* s.v. "Bingham."

8. Map published as insert in *Historic Philadelphia*, q.v., shows the location on the corner of Spruce Street and South Fourth Street. See, for extensive account of house and family, Thompson Westcott, *The Historic Mansions and Buildings of Philadelphia* (Philadelphia, 1877), pp. 342-350.

9. First Bank of the U.S. built in 1795-1798, architect, S. Blodget, still standing on 120 South 3rd Street. See James O. Wettereau, "The Oldest Bank Building in the United States," *Historic Philadelphia*, pp. 70-79, on cost, contemporary view, etc.

10. The First Presbyterian Church. See Reverend Alexander Mackie, "The Presbyterian Churches of Old Philadelphia," *Historic Philadelphia*, pp. 217-220.

11. Niemcewicz is referring here to the "Independence Hall Group." The seat of the United States Supreme Court (City Hall), Independence Hall (State House) and Congress Hall (County Court House). See Edward M. Riley, "The Independence Hall Group," *Historic Philadelphia*, pp. 7-42, passim.

12. See Harold Donaldson Eberlein, "190, High Street (Market Street below Sixth), the Home of Washington and Adams, 1790-1800," *Historic Philadelphia*, pp. 161-178.

13. Robert Morris (1734-1806), American financier and statesman. "In 1794 Pierre Charles L'Enfant (1754-1825), later famous for his plans for Washington, designed and began construction of a town house for Robert Morris on Chestnut Street between Seventh and Eighth Streets. It was never completed. The house which is known from an engraving made by William Birch [see Birch, William and son, *The City of Philadelphia . . . as it Appeared in 1800* (Springland Cot, Pa., 1800)] had such characteristic late eighteenth century French details as marble reliefs over the long ground-story windows and a curb roof, which made it unique in the country." H. Paul Caemmerer, *Life of Pierre Charles L'Enfant* (Washington, D.C., 1950), pp. 256-263, cited in *Historic Philadelphia*, p. 296, n. 29.

14. Sir Alexander Mackenzie (c. 1755-1820), *Voyages from Montreal, on the River St. Laurence, through the Continent of North America, to the Frozen and Pacific Oceans: in the years 1789 and 1793. With a Preliminary Account of the Rise, Progress, and Present State of the Fur Trade* (London, 1801).

15. J. B. Scandella, M.D. (d. 1798), Venice. Italian traveler, member of American Philosophical Society. I. N. Phelps Stokes, *Iconography of Manhatten Island* (New York, 1895-1928), V, 1357; "Old Minutes of the Society from 1743-1838," *Proc. Amer. Phil. Soc.*, XXII, part 3 (July, 1885), 106.

16. William Maclure (1763-1840), a pioneer geologist.

17. Aaron Arrowsmith (1750-1823), the first of an English family of geographers, was famous for his maps, one of which was of North America (1796); see Mackenzie, *Voyages from Montreal* (London, 1801), for Arrowsmith's map as frontispiece.

18. George Vancouver (c. 1758-1798), whose *A Voyage of Discovery to the North Pacific Ocean and round the World . . . in 1790-95 . . . under Captain George Vancouver*, 3 vols. (London, 1798), with an atlas of maps and plates, was published posthumously; see Vancouver's map published by Charles Oscar Paullin, *Atlas of the Historical Geography of the United States* (Washington and New York, 1932), pl. 25 B.

19. "Heaven itself he seeks . . . Iapetus' daring son." Horace, *Odes*, I, 3, line 38; I, 3, line 27; see C. E. Bennett, trans. *Horace The Odes and Epodes*, The Loeb Classical Library (Cambridge, Mass., 1960); the translation here as elsewhere is adapted; for similar comment see Brissot, *New Travels*, p. 104.

20. City Hall, remodeled as Federal Hall, seat of Congress until 1790. See contemporary views, Kouwenhoven, *Columbia Historical Portrait of New York*, pp. 82-86.

21. The Matthew Lyon (1746-1822) and Roger Griswold (1762-1812) fracas which took place 30 January 1798 and 15 February 1798 with subsequent action taken is described in [Annals of Congress] *Debates and Proceedings in the Congress of the United States 1784-1924*, 42 vols. (Washington, 1834-1856), I, 955-1058, passim.

22. Niemcewicz refers here to the reforming Diet called "The Four Year Diet" which established the "Constitution of the 3rd of May," 1791. The Diet was set up as a confederation, a constitutional process which prevented the use of *liberum veto* and therefore the untimely dissolution of the Diet. For a brief account of the Constitution and the meaning of confederation under which the Poles operated, see *The Cambridge History of Poland . . . (1697-1935)* (Cambridge, 1951), pp. 49-71, especially pp. 56-60.

23. Albert Gallatin (1761-1849), member of Congress from Pennsylvania (1795-1801); William Branch Giles (1762-1830), member of Congress from Virginia (1790-1798), (1801-1803); John Nicholas (c. 1757-1819), member of Congress from Virginia (1793-1801); Richard Brent (1757-1814), member of Congress from Virginia (1795-1799), all Republicans. Harrison Gray Otis (1765-1848), member of Congress from Massachusetts (1797-1801); Samuel Sewall (1757-1814), member of Congress from Massachusetts (1796-1800); Samuel Whittlesey Dana (1760-1830), member of Congress from Connecticut (1797-1810); Robert Goodloe Harper (1765-1825), member of Congress from South Carolina (1795-1801), all Federalists. Fifth Congress, 2nd session, 13 November 1797-16 July 1798; see *Biographical Directory of the American Congress, 1774-1949*.

24. Probably the Circus at 6th and Chestnut, see Moreau de Saint-Méry, pp. 374, 416, n. 90.

25. Elizabeth Parke Custis, married Thomas Law, March 28, 1796. See Allen C. Clark, *Greenleaf and Law in the Federal City* (Washington, D.C., 1901), pp. 237, 242, passim.

26. See N. B. C. Love, "Me-She-Kun-Nogh-Quah or Little Turtle," *Ohio Archeological and Historical Publications* (Columbus, 1909), XVIII, 115-148, cited by Haiman, *Kosciuszko, Leader and Exile*, p. 167. For a contemporary account of a conversation with the Little Turtle see C. F. Volney, *View of the Climate and Soil of the United States of America*, trans. anon. (London, 1804), pp. 400 ff.

27. Burka: from the Persian berek, berk, a sleeveless, loose fitting cloak of felt or wool, probably first brought into Poland by the Tartars. See Zygmunt Gloger, *Encyklopedia staropolska*, photo-offset of 1903 ed. (Warsaw, 1958) s.v. "Burka."

28. Israel Israel (1743-1821); see *Universal Jewish Encyclopaedia* s.v. "Israel, Israel." Benjamin R. Morgan (1765-1840); see "Thomas Sully's Register of Portraits, 1801-1871," *The Pennsylvania Magazine of History and Biography* (Philadelphia, 1909), XXXIII, 151. For an account of this election see Harry Marlin Tinkcom, *The Republicans and Federalists in Pennsylvania* (*1790-1801*) (Harrisburg, 1950), pp. 176-179, passim, and *Claypoole's American Daily Advertiser* (Philadelphia), 24 February 1798 which gives Morgan's plurality as 357. See also Broadside 22 February 1798, "To the Friends of Israel Israel" at Pennsylvania Historical Society.

29. Volney, né Constantin François de Chasseboeuf, comte de (1757-1820). Volney wrote *Tableau du climat et du sol des Etats-Unis*, 2 vols. (Paris, 1803); see reference to the English edition in note 26. His earlier work, *Les Ruines ou méditations sur les révolutions des empires* (Paris, 1791), was reportedly much valued by Jefferson both for its anti-clerical tone and for its Ossian style. Volney came to America in 1795 and left in 1798 under attack by the Federalists. For a discussion of Volney's philosophy and his relationship with Jefferson see Gilbert Chinard, *Volney et l'Amérique d'après des documents inédits et sa correspondance avec Jefferson*. The Johns Hopkins Studies in Romance Literature and Languages, I (Baltimore, 1923); see also Howard Mumford Jones, *America and French Culture* (Chapel Hill, N.C., 1927), pp. 402-403.

30. See Charles Coleman Sellers, "Peale's Museum," *Historic Philadelphia*, pp. 253-259.

31. Charles Willson Peale (1741-1826); see C. C. Sellers, "Charles Willson Peale," 2 vols., *Mem. Amer. Phil. Soc.*, XXIII, 1947. For brief account of name Franklin given to his son see William E. Lingelbach, "Philosophical Hall," *Historic Philadelphia*, p. 58.

32. See *Naval Documents Related to Quasi-War between the United States and France, Naval Operations, February 1797-October 1798* (Washington, D.C., 1935), p. 190, and for further action to rescue boat, pp. 191, 199, 462, 464, 465, 483; *Claypoole's American Daily Advertiser* (Philadelphia), 8 March 1798.

33. *Claypoole's American Daily Advertiser* (Philadelphia), 8 March 1798 describes the arrival of the ship Delaware, 116 days from Canton with Captain Cooper.

34. Robert Patterson (1743-1824), professor of mathematics at the University of Pennsylvania from 1782; president of the American Philosophical Society

(1819-1824). Niemcewicz maintained his friendship with Patterson throughout his stay in America. See *Przegląd Lwowski,* VI (1873), 250 and translation in Part III here.

35.　Caleb Lownes, *An Account of the Alteration and Present State of the Penal Laws of Pennsylvania, Containing also an Account of the Gaol and Penitentiary House of Philadelphia and the Interim Management thereof,* published as an addition to Willliam Bradford, *An Enquiry how far the Punishment of Death is Necessary in Pennsylvania* (Philadelphia, 1793); for an exposition of Caleb Lownes' views on prisons see his letter to Thomas Eddy, 19 April 1796, *Schuyler Papers,* Box 37, New York Public Library; see also letter of Caleb Lownes to John Griscom, 13 August 1805, John Griscom Papers, New York Public Library; for contemporary appreciation of the work of Lownes see Duke de La Rochefoucault Liancourt, *Travels through the United States of North America,* trans. H. Neuman (London, 1799), II, 345, 346.

36. Niemcewicz subscribed to this same point of view in his later recommendations for prison reform in Poland; see his *Dzieła poetyczne,* XI, 148-151.

37. James Pemberton (1723-1809).

38. Dewotki: bigoted women. For an illustration of a "dewotka" see Aleksander Brückner, *Encyklopedia staropolska* (Warsaw, 1939), I, 607.

39. For contemporary accounts of the Quakers by other European travellers see Brissot, *New Travels,* pp. 375-412, passim; Moreau de Saint-Méry, passim; Liancourt, *Travels,* II, 670, 671, passim.

40. Jean de Marsillac. See Frank Monaghan, *French Travellers in the United States* (New York, 1961), p. 66, and Bernard Faÿ, *The Revolutionary Spirit in France and America,* trans. Ramon Guthrie (New York, 1927), pp. 244, 245, 294, 455, 456.

41. William Bartram (1739-1823); see *The Travels of William Bartram,* ed. Francis Harper, naturalists' edition (New Haven, 1958), pp. xvii-xxxv.

42. John Bartram, Jr. (d. 1812), see *D.A.B.* s.v. "Bartram, William"; see also *The Travels of William Bartram,* p. xxix.

43. Franklinia or Franklinia Alatamaha, Franklin tree; see *The Travels of William Bartram,* p. 511.

44. Gaultheria procumbens, Creeping Wintergreen, see Asa Gray, *Manual of the Botany of the Northern United States,* 6th ed. (New York, 1889), p. 315.

45. See *Encyclopaedia Britannica,* 11th ed. s.v. "Tea."

46. William Hamilton (1745-1813). See Thompson Westcott, *The Historic Mansions and Buildings of Philadelphia* (Philadelphia, 1877), pp. 421-426; S. Fiske Kimball, *The Domestic Architecture of the American Colonies and of the Early Republic* (New York, 1922), p. 192.

47. Benjamin Henry Latrobe (1764-1820).

48. Drawing published by Thomas Condie, *The Philadelphia Monthly Magazine,* I, Feb. 1798, cited by Sellin in *Historic Philadelphia,* with reproduction, pp. 329, 330, n. 8; for Caleb Lownes' manuscript drawing of prison with improvements, see Lownes letter to Thomas Eddy, 19 April 1796, *Schuyler Papers,* Box 37, New York Public Library; drawing reproduced here.

49. Robert James Turnbull (1775-1833). *A Visit to the Philadelphia Prison* (Philadelphia, Thomas Condie, 1796); see Charles Evans, ed. *American Bibliography* (Chicago, 1903-1934), XI s.v. "Turnbull, Robert James."

50. Nicholas Collin (1746-1831). See Rev. Nicholas Collin, D.D., "Philological View of some very Ancient Words in Several Languages," *Transactions of the*

American Philosophical Society, 2nd ed., 6 vols. (1789-1809), IV (1799), 476-509; "My aids in the Sclavonian have been . . . : The Polish-French-German Dictionary of Trotz, printed at Leipzig, 1764; another in German; The Polish Bible, Telemach," *ibid.,* p. 509; Abraham Michał Trotz, *Nouveau Dictionnaire Français-Allemand-Polonois et Polonois-Allemand-Français,* 3 vols. (Leipzig, 1764-1765); Fénelon, François de Salignac de La Mothe, *Przypadki Telemaka,* trans. Michał Abraham Trotz (Leipzig, 1750); see also Niemcewicz, *Podróże po Ameryce,* ed. Wellman-Zalewska, p. 95; Amandus Johnson, *The Journal and Biography of Nicholas Collin (1746-1831)* (Philadelphia, 1936), pp. 137-138, passim.

51. Mitchell in Gothenburg was the representative of Arrowsmith Kościuszko's banker in Stockholm. Erskine was also a merchant and banker in Gothenburg, see Niemcewicz, *Pamiętniki* (Warsaw), II, 207-208.

52. For contemporary account of climate see Volney, *View of the Climate,* pp. 122-142, passim.

53. See Haiman, *Kosciuszko, Leader and Exile,* plate facing p. 64 and note p. 168.

54. A viewpoint discussed by other contemporary writers, see e.g. Moreau de Saint-Méry, pp. 302, 303; Brissot, pp. 353-354.

55. Benjamin Franklin Bache (1769-1798), publisher, *Aurora and General Advertiser,* Philadelphia (1797-1798); in this newspaper for 31 March 1798 Bache wrote, "We shall now give a concise view of what it has cost us to obtain a peace with the Algerines, that our readers may be able to draw a comparison between the value of the Mediterranean trade to this country and its cost . . . here we have then the whole cost . . . $9,878,362.53." In his listing, Bache who was clearly critical of the government, included items which do not appear pertinent; cf. Ray Watkins Irwin, *Diplomatic Relations of the United States with the Barbary Powers 1776-1816* (Chapel Hill, N.C., 1931), pp. 78, 79, passim.

56. Niemcewicz had been an elected representative to the Four Year Diet (1788-1792) and published together with Tadeusz Mostowski and Józef Weyssenhoff *Gazeta Narodowa i Obca* (1791-1792). See Jan Dihm, *Niemcewicz jako polityk i publicysta w czasie sejmu czteroletniego* (Kraków, 1928), pp. 98-126; see also Anna Goriaczko, *Gazeta Narodowa i Obca* (Wrocław, 1953).

57. For extensive account of commerce, etc., see Liancourt, II, 549-619, 681-686, passim.

58. George Logan (1753-1821), grandson of James Logan (1674-1751).

59. *The Pennsylvania Gazette* (1729-1765); these two sentences brought in from margin. This material was placed on exhibition in Puławy the Czartoryski seat in Poland. See Adam Czartoryski, *Żywot J. U. Niemcewicza* (Poznań, 1860), p. 127.

60. "She feels the nearer breath of deity," Virgil, *Aeneid,* VI, line 50; see H. Rushton Fairclough, trans. *Virgil,* The Loeb Classical Library (Cambridge, Mass., 1960).

61. Hospital on 8th and 9th Streets between Spruce and Pine; see Edward B. Krumbhaar, "The Pennsylvania Hospital," *Historic Philadelphia,* pp. 237-246; Moreau de Saint-Méry, p. 382.

62. See Brissot, pp. 201-210.

63. Thomas Cooper (1759-1840), *Some Information respecting America* (London, 1794); *D.A.B.* s.v. "Cooper, Thomas."

64. Oliver Wolcott (1760-1833), Secretary of Treasury, 1795-1800.

65. James McHenry (1753-1816), Secretary of War, 1796-1800; McHenry spent the rest of his life, after his tenure of office, attempting to justify his stewardship. For an account of this and of his relationship to Gallatin, see Bernard C. Steiner, *The Life and Correspondence of James McHenry* (Cleveland, 1917), pp. 272-273, 500-504. See also two letters of McHenry dated 20 January 1798 and May 1800, *McHenry Papers Miscellaneous*, New York Public Library.

66. William Bache (1773-1814).

67. Richard Bache (1737-1811), married, 1767, Sarah Franklin; sons, Benjamin q.v., William q.v. and Louis Bache (1779-1819); daughters, Sarah (1775-1776), Eliza (1777-1820), Deborah (1781-?), and Sarah (1788-?); see "The Franklin Ancestry," *New England Historical and Genealogical Register*, VII (1854), 374; Richard Bache provided Niemcewicz with material concerning Franklin; see "I wish you to present the enclosed to Mr. Niemcewicz; it is the conclusion of your grandfather's instructions to me on his going to France in the year 1776, . . . Your affectionate father," letter of Richard Bache to Dr. William Bache, 7 May 1798, *Bache Papers*, American Philosophical Society, Philadelphia.

68. The fragment "than at a district . . . morning to night" was written in Polish.

69. The fragment "a kind . . . Indian corn" was written in Polish.

70. Andreas Everard van Braam Houckgeest (1739-1800); see Moreau de Saint-Méry, pp. 222, 226-227, 246, and passim; van Braam's house, China Retreat, is shown on map in S. S. Moore and T. W. Jones, *The Traveller's Directory or A Pocket Companion . . . from Philadelphia to New York and from Philadelphia to Washington* (Philadelphia, 1802), p. 19 and pl. 3.

71. Angelica Kauffmann (1741-1807).

72. *Voyage de L'Ambassade de la Compagnie des Indes Orientales vers L'Empereur de la Chine*, 2 vols. (Philadelphia, Moreau de Saint-Méry, 1797-1798). See Moreau de Saint-Méry, pp. 222, 247, 249, 255, 256, 403, 413, n. 64. Van Braam's collection of chinoiserie was offered to France and was finally sold in London, *ibid.*, p. 261; cf. Henry Watson Kent, "Van Braam Houckgeest. An Early American Collector," *Proceedings of the American Antiquarian Society*, XL n.s. Part 2 (1931), 159-174. For inventory of his Chinese drawings see *Voyage*, I, xvii-xliv.

73. See advertisement of sale in *Claypoole's American Daily Advertiser*, 25 April 1798 with description of house.

74. Elected 20 April 1798; see *Proc. Amer. Phil. Soc.*, XXII, July 1885, Part III, no. 119, "Old Minutes of the Society from 1743-1838."

75. *Ibid.*, p. 270, Niemcewicz listed as having attended on May 4th; communications "On Magnetism" from Rev. James Madison; "Natural Curiosities in Greenbriar City, Va., particularly of a tooth of a large non-descript animal"; "Description of a Mould Board of the least resistance, etc.," read by Mr. Jefferson.

76. The XYZ Affair. X, Y and Z were the letters used to designate the three agents of Talleyrand who demanded a bribe from the commissioners sent to Paris to negotiate a treaty. John Adams released, "The story of the envoys at intervals 5 May 1798-18 January 1799," Samuel Flagg Bemis, ed. *The American Secretaries of State and their Diplomacy*, (New York, 1958), II, 229.

77. A letter of Jefferson to Madison under date 26 April 1798 notes the Giles and Nicholas departure; see the *Writings of Thomas Jefferson*, Memorial Edition, X, 31, quoted in Gilbert Chinard, *Thomas Jefferson* (Ann Arbor Paperbooks, 1960), p. 339.

78. Niemcewicz may have referred to any or all of the Alien and Sedition Bills

which comprised four bills: 18 June 1798, Amendment to Naturalization Act of 1795; 25 June 1798, Alien Act; 6 July 1798, Alien Enemies Act; 14 July 1798, Sedition Act.

NOTES TO CHAPTER III

1. The two sentences "Départ pour . . . dans le *stage*," were brought in from the margin. 9 May 1798, date set by Proclamation; see James D. Richardson, *A Compilation of the Messages and Papers of the Presidents* (Washington, 1896), I, 269; see also J. B. McMaster, *A History of the People of the United States* (New York, 1883), II, 383.

2. The Great Iron Mountains form a part of the Alleghany chain, see Volney, *View of the Climate*, p. 15. Niemcewicz may have been referring to local hills laden with iron ore.

3. Comments of Europeans concerning the number of beds and travelers in one room in American inns were common, see, e.g., Liancourt, *Travels*, I, 110; Isaac Weld, Jun., *Travels through the States of North America and the Provinces of Upper and Lower Canada during the Years 1795, 1796, and 1797* (London, 1807), I, 28; by contrast see Brissot, *New Travels*, pp. 123, 448.

4. Inn in Baltimore, also known as Evans Tavern, see J. Thomas Scharf, *History of Baltimore City and County* (Philadelphia, 1881), p. 514.

5. See Allen Culling Clark, "James Barry (1755?-1808)," *Columbia Historical Society Records*, XLII-XLIII (1942), 11-16.

6. See Liancourt, *Travels*, II, 343*-344*. Niemcewicz gives a more extensive account of seeing a telegraph on his journey through Sweden on his way to America; see *Podróże po Ameryce*, p. 24; see also *Encyclopaedia Britannica*, 11th ed. s.v. "Chappe, Claude."

7. Samuel Smith (1752-1839). House built in 1796; see T. W. Griffiths, *Annals of Baltimore* (Baltimore, 1824), pp. 154, 155.

8. Probably Robert Smith (1757-1842).

9. John Eager Howard (1752-1827). See Latrobe Weston, "Belvidere," *Baltimore Evening Sun*, 9 April 1900. House begun in 1786 and finished in 1794; see also Liancourt, *Travels*, II, 131.

10. George Calvert, 1st Baron Baltimore (1580?-1632), with actual charter issued (1632) to his son Cecilius (1605-1675), 2nd Baron.

11. John Carroll (1735-1815); for an account of the circumstances of the founding of St. Peter's Church and of its use as the pro-cathedral see Peter Guilday, *Life and Times of John Carroll* (New York, 1922), pp. 324-325. The picture is now missing. Reverend J. A. Frederick wrote, without documentation, of a picture of Saint Peter in the main altar. See his "The Beginnings of Catholicity in Baltimore," *The Catholic Mirror*, LXIII, no. 12 (March 17, 1906), 5; for Niemcewicz as connoisseur see letter to Adam Czartoryski 7 December 1808 in Czartoryski, *Żywot J. U. Niemcewicza* (Poznań, 1860), p. 305; see also Alexander Kraushar, *Okruchy przeszłości* (Warsaw, 1913), p. 244; see also Wacław Borowy *Studia i rozprawy* (Wrocław, 1952), I, 124.

12. Francis Charles Nagot (1734-1816); see *Souvenirs D'Edouard de Mon-*

désir, ed. Gilbert Chinard (Baltimore, 1942). See also Guilday, *Life and Times of John Carroll,* pp. 467-470; for few students and first American student William Matthews, see *ibid.,* p. 470.

13. Brought in from margin.

14. Favorite sentiment of Niemcewicz's repeated in *Notes sur ma captivité,* p. 72.

15. Snowden's extensive properties are indicated in D. F. Sotzmann, *Maryland und Delaware entworfen von D. F. Sotzmann (zu Ebelings Erdbeschreibung von Amerika)* (Hamburg, 1797); see also Ralph H. Brown, "The Ebeling-Sotzmann Maps of the Northern Seaboard States," *The Geographical Review,* XXX (1940), 471-479.

16. Parallelogram drawn in body of text presumably showing square shape of area ceded. This shorthand in use in German geographical works of period, see Christoph Daniel Ebeling, *Erdbeschreibung und Geschichte von Amerika* (Hamburg, 1799), V, passim.

17. Eastern Branch: Anacostia River.

18. Jedidiah Morse, *The American Geography or a View of the Present Situation of the United States of America . . . and of Europe, Asia and Africa,* a new edition, illustrated with 25 maps, 4to (John Stockdale, London, 1794), pp. 468-470. Thomas Law (1756-1834). For bibliography of Law manuscripts see Allen Culling Clark, *Greenleaf and Law in the Federal City* (Washington, D.C., 1901), p. 326. See "Handkerchief Map," end papers in *Washington City and Capital, American Guide Series* (Washington, D.C., 1937), p. xiv.

19. William Thornton (1759-1828); see "Diary of Mrs. William Thornton," *Records of the Columbia Historical Society,* X (1907), 88-226, XIX (1916), 172-182.

20. Brought in from margin.

21. "The fiery sun had scaled the mid arch of heaven, when afar they see walls and a citadel, and scattered houseroofs." Virgil, *Aeneid,* VIII, lines 97-99; *op. cit.*

22. "Bristling with woodland thickets." *Ibid.,* line 348.

23. "Some to build walls, to rear the citadel, and roll up stones by hand; some to choose the site for a dwelling." . . . "Happy they whose walls already rise!" Virgil, *Aeneid,* I, lines 423-425; 437; *op. cit.*

24. George Hadfield (c. 1764-1826), *D.A.B.* s.v. "Hadfield, George"; Maria Cecilia Louisa Cosway, née Hadfield (1759-1838); see *D.N.B.* s.v. "Cosway, Richard."

25. "In these woodlands the native Fauns and Nymphs once dwelt." Virgil, *Aeneid,* VIII, line 314; *op. cit.*

26. Brought in from margin; see Morse, *Geography,* p. 469.

27. For other contemporary accounts of Washington, Georgetown and Alexandria see Liancourt, *Travels,* II, 312-339; Isaac Weld, Jun., *Travels through the States of North America,* 4th ed. (London, 1807), I, 49-90.

28. See *Washington City and Capital,* pp. 435, 707.

29. Alexander White (1738-1804), made Commissioner 18 May 1795; William Thornton, q.v., made Commissioner 12 September 1794; Gustavus Scott (1753-1800), made Commissioner 23 August 1794, see *Biographical Dictionary of the American Congress (1774-1949);* see also Wilhelmus Bogart Bryan, *A History of National Capital* (Washington, 1914), I, 237-238, 255.

30. Robert Morris (1734-1806); James Greenleaf (1765-1843); John Nicholson (d. 1800).

31. Brought in from margin. Morse has a general discussion of lock construction.

32. Parallelogram drawn in text between two and abutments.

33. Jawfish: opisthognathidae; or Jewfish: chiefly Serranidae.

34. Chevalier Cypriano Riberio Friere was a fellow member of the American Philosophical Society; see "Old Minutes of the Society from 1743-1838," *Proceedings of the American Philosophical Society*, XXII, part III, no. 119 (July, 1885), 238.

35. Camil's Hill: unidentified.

36. Tiber Creek: Anecdote repeated in Weld, *Travels*, I, 83.

37. The house of Mr. and Mrs. Thomas Peter at 2618 and 2620 K Street, frequently visited by Washington; see *Records of the Columbia Historical Society*, XLIV-XLV (Washington, D.C., 1944), 247; see also *Washington City and Capital*, p. 643.

38. Martha Parke Custis (1777-?), married (1795) Thomas Peter, son of Robert Peter, first mayor of Georgetown. See Charles Moore, *The Family Life of George Washington* (Boston, 1926), pp. 116-130.

39. "—Now aged, but a god's old age is hardy and green." Virgil, *Aeneid*, VI, line 304; *op. cit.*

40. Eliza Law, born 19 January 1797. Moore, *Family Life*, p. 106.

41. Niemcewicz wrote "une petite robe ronde de carton blanc." The two Polish words *robron* and *kartun* then current came originally from the French and Niemcewicz appears to have translated these two words back into the French robe ronde and carton. *Robron*—"a dress made of a material so stiff that it could stand alone;" *kartun*—fine stiff percale; see *Encyklopedia staropolska* s.v. "robron," "kartun." Compare Niemcewicz's own translation, J. U. Niemcewicz, *Dzieła poetyczne wierszem i prozą* (Leipzig, 1839), XI, 64.

42. Martha Dandridge married Daniel Parke Custis; they had four children, of whom one, John Parke Custis, survived. He married Eleanor Calvert, having three daughters—Elizabeth Parke Custis, who married Thomas Law; Martha Parke Custis, who married Thomas Peter; Eleanor Parke Custis (Nelly) and one son, George Washington Parke Custis. See Moore, *Family Life*, passim.

43. Eleanor Calvert Custis married (1783) Dr. David Stuart (1753-1811); Moore, *Family Life*, p. 102. They had eventually 17 children; see *Washington City and Capital*, p. 793.

44. "The Battle of Prague" by František Kočžwara (d. 1791), "extraordinary and musically quite valueless descriptive piece," *Grove's Dictionary of Music and Musicians*, 5th ed. s.v. "Kočžwara, František."

45. James Jones versus Brockholst Livingston in a duel in which Jones was killed 9 May 1798. See Dunlap, *Diary*, I, 254; see also McMaster, *History*, II, 381-382.

46. For publication of La Rochefoucauld-Liancourt's *Voyage dans les Etats-Unis D'Amérique, fait en 1795, 1796 et 1797*, 8 vols. (Paris, 1799), see Moreau de Saint-Méry, *Voyage*, p. 395.

47. James Monroe (1758-1831); *A View of the Conduct of the Executive in the Foreign Affairs of the United States Connected with the Mission to the French Republic, during the years 1794, 1795, 1796* (Philadelphia, 1797), p. 3 and esp. p. 317. A copy of Monroe's book from Washington's library, and heavily annotated by him, is now in the Houghton Library, Harvard University. The relevant passages are not annotated. The annotations were published in *The*

Writings of George Washington, ed. Worthington Chauncey Ford (New York, 1892), XIII, 452-493; see also *The Writings of George Washington 1745-1799,* ed. John C. Fitzpatrick (Washington, D.C., 1941), XXXVI, 194-237, and for the Liancourt-Washington correspondence, XXXV, 167-168.

48. See Clark, *Greenleaf and Law in the Federal City,* pp. 245-246.

49. In America the name tulip tree is given exclusively to Liriodendron tulipi- fera, also known as yellow poplar; it belongs to the magnolia family, see Asa Gray, *Manual of Botany,* pp. 49-50.

50. See *Washington City and Capital,* pp. 810-812.

51. Brought in from margin.

52. Berkeley County, West Virginia. This iron foundry was one of George Washington's enterprises and the remains may still be seen; see *Washington City and Capital,* p. 818.

53. The members of the Religious Society of Friends were enjoined to use plain language, "thou" and "thee" to one person and "you" to many; see *The Friends Library comprising Journals, Doctrinal Treatises and other Writings,* eds. William Evans and Thomas Evans (Philadelphia, 1837), I, 32, 64, 132. Vanity in fashion was to be avoided, *ibid.,* 132. Friends excluded the use of metal buttons; see John F. Watson, *Annals of Philadelphia and Pennsylvania* (Philadelphia, 1857), I, 510; for relaxation of principles; see Brissot, *New Travels,* pp. 380-382.

54. Mauritius and Réunion in the Indian Ocean.

55. Carthage, Vermont; township 1780, chartered to Governor Thomas Chit- tenden, 1792 under its present name Jay; see Zadock Thompson, *History of Ver- mont, Natural, Civil and Statistical in three Parts with an Appendix* (Burlington, 1853), part III, p. 97.

56. Piotr Ferguson Tepper (d. 1794), famous banker who went bankrupt in 1793, had several houses in Warsaw as well as in a suburb of Warsaw, Falenty. See Friedrich Schulz, *Podróże inflantczyka,* ed. Wacław Zawadzki (Warsaw, 1956), passim.

57. George Wenceslaus Gołkowski is identified as a surveyor for the Moravian Brethren in Pennsylvania; see Joseph Mortimer Levering, *A History of Bethlehem, Pennsylvania (1741-1892)* (Bethlehem, 1903), pp. 214 n., 275-276; see also *Cazenove Journal, 1794,* ed. Rayner Wickersham Kelsey (Haverford, 1922), p. 22. The Richter name appears in the lists of colonists of the Moravian Brethren; see Levering, pp. 234, 254.

58. See John Gilmary Shea, *Memorial of the First Century of Georgetown College D. C. Comprising a History of Georgetown University* (Washington, 1891).

59. Louis-Guillaume-Valentin Du Bourg (1766-1833), third President (1796- 1798).

60. James Piercy was associated with James Barry in a sugar refinery; see Clark, *Greenleaf and Law,* p. 246. Dikesson may be misspelling for Dickerson or Dickin- son; Mahlon Dickerson (1770-1853) was an official for bankruptcy, General Philemon Dickinson (1734-1809) and his brother John Dickinson (1732-1808) owned property in Washington; see Clark, *Greenleaf and Law,* pp. 76-77, 172.

NOTES TO CHAPTER IV,

1. See "Washington's Map of Mount Vernon" reproduced in Charles Oscar Paullin, *Atlas of the Historical Geography of the United States* (Washington and New York, 1932), Pls. 53A, 53B; see also Benson J. Lossing, *Mount Vernon and Its Associations* (New York, 1859), pp. 140-141; see also Ralph H. Brown, *Mirror for Americans Likeness of the Eastern Seaboard 1810* (New York, American Geographical Society, 1943), p. 295, n. 29.

2. Claude Lorrain, né Gelée (1600-1682).

3. See account and illustrations in Lossing, *Mount Vernon,* pp. 220-224.

4. Portrait painted by Charles Willson Peale at Mount Vernon, Virginia, May 1772 in the uniform of a Colonel of Virginia Militia; see John Hill Morgan and Mantle Fielding, *The Life Portraits of Washington and Their Replicas* (Philadelphia, 1931), p. 24; see also Lossing, pp. 80-82.

5. This portrait reproduced in Moore, *Family Life,* p. 51.

6. See *Inventory of the Contents of Mount Vernon 1810* with a prefatory note by Worthington Chauncey Ford (Cambridge, Mass., 1909), p. 3.

7. Portrait of John Parke Custis and Martha Parke Custis painted by John Wollaston, 1757, now at Washington and Lee University, reproduced in Douglas Southall Freeman, *George Washington. A Biography* (New York, 1948), II, 299; see also Moore, *Family Life,* p. 54. For the portraits in pastel see Katharine McCook Knox, *The Sharples* (New Haven, 1930), pp. 14, 67, 91-93, 95 and frontispiece for needlework.

8. This allegorical picture is described in some detail in Lossing, pp. 185-187.

9. John Trumbull (1756-1843). For account of the engravings (completed in 1786) see Dunlap, *Diary,* III, 729, 737-738.

10. For account of the harpsichord see Lossing, pp. 267-269.

11. The Czartoryski seat in Poland.

12. This description of Eleanor Parke Custis was quoted in translation by Moore, *Family Life,* p. 146. Moore presumably took it from W. M. Kozłowski, "A Visit to Mount Vernon a Century Ago," *Century Magazine,* LXIII (1902), 518.

13. This is a description of magnolia grandiflora; see *Encyclopaedia Britannica,* 11th ed. s.v. "Magnolia."

14. Calycanthus, L. Carolina Allspice. Sweet-scented shrub, Gray, *Manual,* p. 167.

15. See Lossing, p. 176.

16. The description of the funeral of Mrs. Liard which follows may be taken as an example of Niemcewicz's interest in interments reflecting literary pre-romantic influences. This is a recurring theme in his American Diaries.

17. "An aggregate in personalty of almost £20,000 sterling"; see Freeman, *George Washington,* III, 21.

18. For a discussion of these land grants see *ibid.,* III, 282, 300, 304. For documentation and discussion of this sale and/or lease, see John Alexander Carroll and Mary Wells Ashworth, *George Washington* (New York, 1957), VII, 485-486; see also, about grant to Washington (1774) on Great Kanawha River, Paullin, *Atlas,* Pl. 52B.

19. James Anderson: For an extensive account of the tenure of Anderson as Washington's farm manager and especially, in the light of Niemcewicz's later comments concerning production, Anderson's role in the whisky distillery, see Carroll and Ashworth, *George Washington*, VII, 399, 408, 478, 507-509.

20. Oliver Evans (1755-1819), *The Young Mill-Wright and Miller's Guide* (Philadelphia, 1795); "Oliver Evans fixed my mill," Washington in letter to Colonel Clement Biddle, 8 April 1798, quoted in *Pennsylvania Magazine of History and Biography*, XLIII (1919), 198-199. See also for letters between Evans and Washington, *The Northwestern Miller*, 22 December 1943, p. 6.

21. Kalmia angustifolia, popularly called lambkill, has flowers more crimson than those of Mountain Laurel, Kalmia latifolia. Gray, *Manual*, p. 319.

22. The comparison between negro slaves and Polish peasants was often made by Niemcewicz; see also Introduction n. 56.

23. In his Polish publication of this part of the diary Niemcewicz added the information, "The present President Mr. Jefferson has in his house a few such white slaves." See J. U. Niemcewicz, *Dzieła poetyczne wierszem i prozą* (Leipzig, 1839), XI, 85.

24. The fragment, "from planed poles . . . for a draft," was written in Polish.

25. The fragment, "We spoke . . . departure of the ladies," was written in Polish. In his published version this speech is much expanded; see Niemcewicz, *Dzieła*, XI, 87

26. Corrected by Niemcewicz to Portland in his Polish account; see *Dzieła*, XI, 88.

27. "The event proves well the wisdom of her course." Ovid, *Heroides*, II, line 85; see Grant Showerman, trans. *Ovid. Heroides and Amores*, The Loeb Classical Library (New York, 1914).

28. Mark Catesby (1682-1749), *The Natural History of Carolina, Florida and the Bahama Islands*, 2 vols. (London, c. 1730-1748).

29. Niemcewicz mentions this cup in a letter of thanks for his stay at Mount Vernon. It is printed from manuscript in Eugene Kusielewicz, "Niemcewicz in America," *The Polish Review*, V (1960), 71-72; see also *Pamiętniki* (Warsaw), II, 224; Adam Czartoryski, *Żywot. J. U. Niemcewicza* (Poznań, 1860), p. 127; and, for an interesting article on this china, see Samuel W. Woodhouse, Jr., M.D., "Martha Washington's China and Mr. Van Braam," *Antiques*, XXVII (May, 1935), 186.

30. Jan Borysławski, Niemcewicz's nephew by marriage and the member of his family who, at this time, was most concerned with Niemcewicz; see *Notes sur ma captivité*, p. 54; *Pamiętniki* (Warsaw), I, 140; II, 131. Tadeusz Mostowski (1766-1842), friend of long standing, fellow publisher of *Gazeta Narodowa i Obca* (1791-1792), publisher of some of Niemcewicz's works, especially of this visit to Washington, "Krótka wiadomość o życiu i sprawach generała Washington," *Pism różnych wierszem i prozą* (Warsaw, 1803), I, 209-328; see also Marjan Tyrowicz, "Działalność publiczna J. U. Niemcewicza w latach 1807-1813," *Ateneum Wileńskie*, VII (1930), 263, for Mostowski letter recalling him to Warsaw in 1807.

31. Two references are provided by Oscar Handlin, Arthur Meier Schlesinger, Samuel Eliot Morison, Frederick Merk, Arthur Meier Schlesinger, Jr., Paul Herman Buck, *Harvard Guide to American History* (Cambridge, Mass., 1955), p. 309, to accounts of Gordon as a historian; "William Gordon—Historian," *Massachusetts Historical Society, Proceedings*, LXIII (1930), 303; O. G. Libby, "Criti-

cal Examination of Gordon's History," *American Historical Association,* Report I (1899), 367.

32. A description of each medal may be found in James Ross Snowden, *The Medallic Memorials of Washington in the Mint of the United States* (Philadelphia, 1861). For a more extensive account of the history of these medals with correspondence and biographies of recipients see J. F. Loubat, *The Medallic History of the United States of America,* 2 vols. (New York, 1878). For illustration of Order of the Society of the Cincinnati see Lossing, p. 130.

33. The fragment, "In the evening . . . the spring floods," was written in Polish.

34. Louis Gresset (1709-1777); see "Sur L'Amour de la Patrie," *Oeuvres de Gresset* (Paris, 1811), I, 235-236.

35. The fresh-water gars are ganoids with elongate pike-like body with their flesh rank and tough. Pescespada—swordfish.

36. Tobacco box: any of the several fresh-water sunfishes. On the presence of gars and sunfishes in the Potomac waters see Waldo Lee McAtee, *A Sketch of the Natural History of the District of Columbia,* Bulletin of the Biological Society of Washington, no. 1 (Washington, 1918), p. 94.

37. For a description of the services see Lossing, pp. 239-240; see also *The Mount Vernon China,* The Mount Vernon Ladies Association of the Union (Mount Vernon, 1949), pp. 33-35.

38. Under the date 13 June 1798 we find, "Mr. Fitzhugh, Lady and daughter, Mrs. Beverly Randolph with her daughter and son-in-law Randolph and his sister, dined here," *The Diaries of George Washington (1748-1799),* ed. John C. Fitzpatrick (Boston, 1925), IV, 278. See also this page for notice of Niemcewicz's stay.

39. Catherine the Great.

NOTES TO CHAPTER V

1. Identified later in text by Niemcewicz as Armstad.

2. Big pox—syphilis.

3. In the text Niemcewicz transliterated sycamore adding the Polish genitive ending, thus sikomorów.

4. Montgomery Court House, now Rockville (since 1804); see *Maryland, a Guide to the Old Line State,* American Guide Series (New York, 1940), p. 512.

5. We have not been able to find records of the court cases in which Payant was said to have been involved. No record in Helen T. Catterall, *Judicial Cases concerning American Slavery and the Negro* (Washington, 1936).

6. Compare the description of Frederick and environs in Liancourt, *Travels,* II, 124-125.

7. We have translated the Polish word włóka, used here and elsewhere, as acre. Under the heading włóka in calculations at the end of manuscript notebook IV, Niemcewicz calculates the number of square feet in an American acre. He reaches a value of 42,849 sq. ft., whereas the true value is 43,560 sq. ft.

8. "Jefferson . . . known as 'Trap' and afterwards 'Newton Trap;'" J. Thomas Scharf, *History of Western Maryland* (Philadelphia, 1882), I, 626.

9. Salvator Rosa (1615-1673), painter. Cybulski is probably used here as a synonym for an unknown provincial dauber.

10. The excerpt translated by Niemcewicz is included in quotation marks. The English is taken from Thomas Jefferson, *Notes on the State of Virginia,* ed. William Peden (Chapel Hill, 1955), pp. 19-20. The translation occupies a part of manuscript page 3, the whole of manuscript page 4, and a part of manuscript page 5.

11. See Scharf, *History of Western Maryland,* I, 458.

12. Woodbery: Woodsborough; see map of D. F. Sotzmann, *Maryland und Delaware* (Hamburg, 1797).

13. William Cobbett (1763-1835), pseudonym Peter Porcupine, published *Porcupine's Gazette.*

14. Hessian fly: the larvae living between the base of the lower leaves and stalk suck the plant juices.

15. Niemcewicz used the word łutowa (łutówka) here which is a common cherry named after a word for weight; compare Russian and German, Lot. Lot is defined as one thirty-second of a pound or 12.8 grams, presumably the average weight of the cherry. English: "morello"; French: "griotte du Nord"; German: "lotkirsche." See also for gift of this type of cherry to the Emperor Joseph II, Niemcewicz, *Pamiętniki* (Warsaw), I, 163.

16. Littlestown was founded by Peter Klein in 1765 and was originally called either Peterburg or Kleine-staedtel and thus finally Littlestown. See A. Howry Espenshade, *Pennsylvania Place Names* (State College, Pennsylvania, 1925), p. 278.

17. "My hair stood up, and the voice clave to my throat." Virgil, *Aeneid,* II, line 774 and III, line 48; *op. cit.*

18. Dunkers: See William Allen Knittle, *The Early Eighteenth Century Palatine Emigration* (Philadelphia, 1936), p. 210, passim.

19. Benjamin Smith Barton (1766-1815), born in Lancaster, Pennsylvania. For an interesting sidelight on Barton see Jeannette E. Graustein, "The Eminent Benjamin Smith Barton," *The Pennsylvania Magazine of History and Biography,* LXXXV, no. 4 (1961), 423.

20. John Marshall (1755-1835), a Commissioner to France (1797, 1798).

21. For a description and discussion of this canal to avoid the Conewago Falls see Liancourt, *Travels,* I, 47, 48; see also Ralph H. Brown, *Mirror for Americans, Likeness of the Eastern Seaboard 1810* (New York, 1943), p. 60.

22. For discussion of the antipathy between the Irish and Germans see Knittle, *The Early . . . Palatine Emigration,* pp. 85-86.

23. Charles Cotesworth Pinckney (1746-1825); Elbridge Gerry (1744-1814), fellow Commissioners. For the relationship of the Directory to the Commissioners and the unique position of Gerry see Samuel Eliot Morison, "Elbridge Gerry, Gentleman Democrat," *New England Quarterly,* II (1929), 25-27; E. Wilson Lyon, "The Directory and the United States," *The American Historical Review,* XLIII, no. 3 (1938), 523-524.

24. See *D.A.B.* s.v. "Marshall, John" for nervous affliction of wife.

25. Sedition Bill, the last of the four Alien and Sedition Bills was passed 14 July 1798. Niemcewicz was always in favor of a strong executive, but here his attitude may well be compared to his opinion about the Alien Bill expressed earlier.

26. See, for affidavit concerning the use of this alias by Lord Bolingbroke, Liber L 889, *Essex County Deeds* (Newark).

27. John Garnett (1748-1820); see William Benedict, *New Brunswick in History* (New Brunswick, 1925), pp. 134-136. See also for extensive correspondence with the Gates family, *Gates Papers,* New-York Hist. Soc.

28. The river to which Niemcewicz refers is the Kill van Kull. For the Ryers family on Staten Island, see Ira K. Morris, *Memorial History of Staten Island* (New York, 1898), II, 112.

29. For a discussion of Chief Tammany of the Delawares, the early history of the Tammany Society, especially the restriction of its office of Sachem to native-born Americans, and its interest in promoting the 4th of July holiday, see Edwin Patrick Kilroe, *Saint Tammany and the Origin of the Society of Tammany or Columbia Order in the City of New York* (New York, 1913), pp. 129, 144, 149, 179-180, passim; for developing political character of this Society see Peter Paulsen, "The Tammany Society and the Jeffersonian Movement in New York City, 1795-1800," *New York History,* XXXIV (January, 1953), 72-84.

30. We have been unable to identify Mr. More. Even as Mr. Moore or M. Moré the description is inadequate for identification.

31. Riviera di Chiaja.

32. The Vauxhall Gardens in England were laid out in 1661, and known at first as the New Spring Gardens at Foxhall (Falkes Hall). Another Vauxhall Gardens in New York famous at the time of Washington's First Administration has been described; see *Historic New York,* eds. Maud Wilder Goodwin, Alice Carrington Royce, and Ruth Putnam (New York, 1899), I, 157, and map facing p. 226.

33. Morse, *The American Geography* (1794), pp. 382-383.

34. Probably the family of James Farquhar, president of the Marine Society and wine merchant; see David Longworth, *American Almanack, New York Register and City Directory* (New York, 1797), pp. 80, 176.

NOTES TO CHAPTER VI

1. Et in Arcadia ego. Inscription on a tomb found in the paintings of Guercino, Poussin, Reynolds, etc. Panofsky has brilliantly illuminated the history of the two readings of this phrase—the early and grammatically correct "Even in Arcady there am I (Death)" and the later "I, too, was born, or lived in Arcady"; see Erwin Panofsky, "Et in Arcadia Ego: Poussin and the Elegiac Tradition," *Meaning in the Visual Arts* (New York, 1955), esp. pp. 307-310, 318-319. In this context, the unexpected graveyard in the center of town, Niemcewicz's use of the phrase carries the implication of the first reading. His choice of adjective (tkliwy: moving) however implies the second "romantic" reading; see Apolonja Załuska, *Poezja opisowa Delille'a w Polsce* (Kraków, 1934), pp. 113-114.

2. Probably Dr. Timothy Dwight (1752-1817), President of Yale College (1795-1817).

3. Justus Butler (d. 1823) founded an inn in 1796; see Edward E. Atwater, *History of the City of New Haven to the Present Time* (New York, 1887), p. 390; see also *Vital Records of New Haven, 1649-1850* (Hartford, 1924), Part II, p. 602.

4. For comments on onion-growing in Wethersfield see Brissot, *New Travels*, p. 134.

5. Captain Stephen Decatur (Senior) (1752-1808). U.S. Ship of War Delaware captured the French Privateer La Croyable off Egg Harbor, N.J., 7 July 1798; see *Naval Documents Related to Quasi-War between United States and France, Naval Operations, February 1797-October 1798* (Washington, D.C., 1935), frontispiece and pp. 175-176.

6. Jeremiah Wadsworth (1743-1804). See discussion of Wadsworth and his shipping activities in Brissot, *New Travels*, pp. 130-131.

7. A log of a similar voyage has been published; see "John Boit's Log of the Second Voyage of the 'Columbia,'" *Voyages of the "Columbia" to the Northwest Coast, 1787-1790 and 1790-1793*, ed. Frederic W. Howay, Massachusetts Historical Society Collections, Volume 79 (Boston, 1941), pp. 361-438.

8. See, for an account of Old State House designed by Charles Bullfinch and completed in 1796, Florence L. Marcy Crofut, *Guide to the History and the Historic Sites of Connecticut* (New Haven, 1937), I, 288-292.

9. Probably a hill or ridge in Hartford and not the town, Rocky Hill, which is about 9 miles from Hartford. See Rev. William Deloss Love, *The Colonial History of Hartford* (Hartford, 1914), p. 139; see also John Warner Barber, *Connecticut Historical Collections*, 2nd ed. (New Haven, 1836), pp. 39-40.

10. Jean-Jacques Rousseau, "Réponse de Jean-Jacques Rousseau au Roi de Pologne (duc de Lorraine)," *Oeuvres complètes* (Paris, 1832), I, 70.

11. Jonathan Trumbull (1740-1809), Governor of the State of Connecticut (1797-1809); Rochefoucault-Liancourt visited Trumbull and had a similar impression of him; see Liancourt, *Travels*, I, 516. John Trumbull, his brother (1756-1843); for circumstances of their acquaintance see Niemcewicz, *Pamiętniki* (Warsaw), II, 225, 226.

12. Niemcewicz may have been referring to the "State Armory" at the southern end of the village of Windham near Lebanon; the iron forge at Norwich is well known; see Barber, *Connecticut*, pp. 292, 447.

13. Jedidiah Huntington (1743-1818); Brevetted Major General (1783).

14. Daniel Lathrop Coit (1754-1833); these elms have been celebrated in verse; see Mary E. Perkins, *Old Houses of the Antient Town of Norwich* (Norwich, 1895), pp. 162, 164.

15. See *Connecticut*, American Guide Series (Cambridge, 1938), pp. 271-272; see also Barber, *Connecticut*, pp. 294-298.

16. *Słownik geograficzny* (Warsaw, 1884) does not identify any place in Podlasie, a district east of Warsaw, with the name of Łosie. There are towns named Łosie in mountainous districts of Poland.

17. We have found no evidence to support this conclusion. Wansey makes a similar observation but offers a different and more plausible comment, "It is nothing unusual in America for army officers to keep taverns. . . . During the American war, a man's promotion was not measured so much by his rank or fortune, as by his zeal and assiduity in the service of his country, and it was a cheap way of rewarding him for his services." Henry Wansey, *An Excursion to the United States of North America in the Summer of 1794* (Salisbury, 1798), pp. 18-19; Washington's own rule for the selection of officers laid supreme emphasis on ability; see letter quoted by Jared Sparks, *The Life of George Washington* (Boston, 1843), p. 210.

18. Niemcewicz was in error. Roger Williams (c. 1604-1684) arrived in Boston from England in 1631. A sentence of banishment was passed by the Massachusetts General Court in 1635. He left in January 1636.

19. Weybosset Bridge; see Morse, *The American Geography*, p. 342.

20. "A ship of 950 tons, for the East India trade, was lately built in this town, and fitted for the sea," Morse, *The American Geography*, p. 345.

21. Rhode Island College, founded in 1764 in Warren, moved to Providence in 1770; its first building there was University Hall. Its name was changed on the 6th of September 1804 to Brown University as a result of a $5,000 gift from Nicholas Brown, Jr. See William Howe Tolman, *History of Higher Education in Rhode Island* (Washington, 1894), passim.

22. John Innes Clark [Clarke?] and Nightingale were wealthy merchants of Providence; see William B. Weeden, *Early Rhode Island* (New York, 1910), pp. 246, 324. Liancourt was entertained by Mr. Clark; see his *Travels*, I, 507-508.

23. See Brissot, *New Travels*, pp. 143-144, for generalizations which substantiate these criticisms. Liancourt appears less deserving of this rebuke. His information could well have been obtained from those he met. He visited the town on two occasions; Liancourt, *Travels*, I, 497-498, 504-507, II, 141, 143, 146; first published *Voyage dans les Etats-Unis d'Amérique fait en 1795, 1796 et 1797*, 8 vols. (Paris, 1798). Volney does not discuss Providence; see his *Tableau du climat et du sol des Etats-Unis d'Amérique*, 2 vols. in 1 (Paris, 1803).

24. "The village of Block Island . . . which is seldom called by its legal name of New Shoreham;" see *Rhode Island, a Guide to the Smallest State*, American Guide Series (Cambridge, 1937), p. 437.

25. Nathanael Greene married Catherine Littlefield of Block Island, 20 July 1774; see George Washington Greene, *The Life of Nathanael Greene* (New York, 1871), I, 73.

26. Most probably Goat Island; see United States Geological Survey, Newport, Rhode Island quadrangle, 1957; see also *Rhode Island*, p. 237.

27. George Gibbs, II (1735-1803); see George Gibbs, *The Gibbs Family of Rhode Island and Some Related Families* (New York, 1933), pp. 11-18; perhaps William Hunter (1774-1849), Senator from Rhode Island (1811-1821), *Biographical Directory of the American Congress, 1774-1949* (Washington, D.C., 1950); see also *Bulletin of the Newport Historical Society*, no. 61 (1927) 1, 2.

28. In 1786 some Narragansetts from Rhode Island emigrated to Brotherton, a tract of land held in trust for the Brotherton tribe on Oneida territory about 14 miles south of present day Utica, New York. The Oneidas had invited them to reside there. See Pomroy Jones, *Annals and Recollections of Oneida County* (Rome, New York, 1851), pp. 890-893; the treaty with the Oneidas of 22 September 1788, "contained an important provision sanctioning the arrangements previously made by the Oneidas in behalf of the expatriated Indians of New England and others of the Algonkin group who had settled on their land;" see Francis S. Drake, *The Indian Tribes of the United States* (Philadelphia, 1884), II, 289. The Oneidas of the Six Nations are of Iroquois stock whereas the Rhode Island Indians were Algonquins. There was therefore no direct blood relationship.

29. John Stewart (1749-1822); see *Encyclopaedia Britannica*, 11th ed. s.v. "Stewart, John."

30. 29 May 1790. Niemcewicz may have been unduly harsh. For a consideration of Rhode Island's concerns regarding the effect of joining the Union see

Frank Greene Bates, *Rhode Island and the Formation of the Union* (New York, 1898), p. 209 and passim.

31. For an account of packet boats and their uniqueness to America see Brissot, *New Travels,* pp. 150-151.

32. The bridge built at Howland's Ferry is described by D. B. Warden, *Description des Etats-Unis de Amérique Septentrionale,* tr. anon. (Paris, 1820), I, 534; see also *Rhode Island,* p. 416. In 1796 Liancourt wrote, "I have learned here that the bridge which had been erected last year over the East-Passage . . . was carried away last winter by the floods," *Travels,* II, 147.

33. Niemcewicz's earlier statement that he crossed to Tiverton implies a curious route for the stage from Newport to Bristol.

34. King Philip, famous Wampanoag chieftain (c. 1639-1676), was surprised by treachery and killed at the foot of Mount Hope in Bristol.

35. King Krakus and Queen Wanda, legendary prehistoric figures of the Cracow region.

36. See *Naval Documents . . . February 1797-October 1798,* pp. 146, 147; for anecdotal account of the building of the "General Greene," see also George Champlin Mason, *Reminiscences of Newport* (Newport, 1884), pp. 130-137.

37. Washington Bridge or India Bridge, a wooden bridge across the Seekonk River at India Point with a wooden statue of George Washington, built here in 1793 by John Brown. The bridge was washed away in 1807; see *King's Pocket Book of Providence,* ed. Moses King (Cambridge, 1882). John Brown (1736-1803). This foundry called "Furnace Hope" belonged to Brown; see *D.A.B.* s.v. "Brown, John"; see also for comments on Brown's house, etc., Liancourt, *Travels,* I, 508.

38. "Several mills have been erected upon these falls . . . have taken very much from the beauty and grandeur of the scene; which would otherwise have been indescribably charming and romantic," Morse, *The American Geography,* p. 346.

39. Catherine Gray kept a boarding house at 68 State Street. *The Boston Directory* (Boston, 1798), p. 55.

40. The Commencement at Harvard University was held 18 July 1798.

41. West Boston Bridge was chartered in 1792 and opened to the public November 23, 1793. Justin Winsor, *Memorial History of Boston, 1630-1880* (Boston, 1880-82), IV, 26. See also view of bridge in Robert Gilmor, "Memorandums made in a Tour to the Eastern States in 1797 with Views from Pen-sketches by the Author," *Boston Public Library Bulletin,* XI (1893), 72 reproduced here.

42. Puritan spirit seems an appropriate translation of the Polish word *prezbyterianizm* used by Niemcewicz here.

43. John Coffin Jones, merchant with a house on Hanover St., *The Boston Directory* (1789); see also *New England Historical and Genealogical Register,* XXX (1876), 235. Patrick Jeffrey (d. 1812) was the third husband of Lady Mary Hayley, sister of John Wilkes; see John Alman, *The Correspondence of the Late John Wilkes* (London, 1805), I, 4-5; see also Mary Caroline Crawford, *Old Boston Days and Ways* (Boston, 1909), pp. 288-294; see also *D.N.B.* for Francis, Lord Jeffrey, his nephew.

44. Charles Jarvis (1748-1807).

45. "More lasting than bronze." Horace, *Odes,* III, 30, line 1; *op. cit.* For a description and illustration of the monument see William W. Wheildon, *Sentry, or Beacon Hill* (Boston, 1877), pp. 65-76.

46. Samuel Nicholson (1743-1811). For confirmation of the presence of all three ships in Boston at this time see *Naval Documents . . . February 1797-October 1798*, pp. 209, 211, 215, 220, 222, 232, 236.

47. John Barry (1745-1803). The rank of Commodore accorded to Barry by Niemcewicz was applied to Captains commanding squadrons, although it did not legally exist until 1862; see *D.A.B.* s.v. "Barry, John."

48. Thomas Gage (1721-1787), the last royal governor of Massachusetts, major general 1761; Sir Henry Clinton (c. 1738-1795) fought in the battle of Bunker Hill and became Commander-in-chief in North America (1778); Sir Robert Pigot, Bart. (1720-1796), Major General (1777) commanded his regiment (the 38th) in the battle of Bunker Hill; Lord Hugh Percy (1742-1817), Lieutenant General (1777) fought in the American Revolution (1774-1777).

49. Gordon, *The History of the Independence*, II, 39-53. Ramsay, *The History of the Revolution*, I, 201-206.

50. Joseph Warren (1741-1775); see Liancourt, *Travels*, I, 478; for contemporary view of monument see Gilmor, "Memorandums," pp. 72-92.

51. John Duballet listed as a merchant in *The Boston Directory*, 1789.

52. "Le 1er verre de vin qui se buvait était à la Sainté du Pape, dont les Enfants Spirituels consomment beaucoup de poisson salé," see *Souvenirs d'Édouard de Mondésir*, ed. Gilbert Chinard (Baltimore, 1942), pp. 32-33.

53. It is generally agreed that the Empress of China out of New York (1784) was the first American vessel to trade at Canton; for account of early vessels out of Massachusetts see Samuel Eliot Morison, *Maritime History of Massachusetts* (Boston, 1921), pp. 44-45.

54. We have not found reference either to the import from England of this cloth or to its use in trade with Patagonia. John Boit's Log records the purchase of Sea Otter skins from North American Indians in exchange for blue cloth; see *Voyages of the "Columbia,"* p. 370.

55. In the text Niemcewicz transliterated chebec or xebec adding the Polish genitive ending, thus szebeki; his application to the Delaware of the name of a Mediterranean craft used by the Barbary corsairs was probably prompted by her recent exploit in capturing the La Croyable; see also Jefferson's use of the term as a synonym for "tender," *The Autobiography of Thomas Jefferson*, introd. Dumas Malone (Capricorn Books: New York, 1959), p. 77.

56. Adam Duncan (1731-1804), Viscount Duncan of Camperdown (1797), Admiral (1795); John Jervis (1735-1823), Earl of St. Vincent (1797), Vice-Admiral (1793), renowned for their victories off Camperdown and St. Vincent against the Dutch and Spanish respectively.

57. Complete stand—fully rigged; see *Shorter Oxford Dictionary*, 3rd edition (Oxford, 1944), s.v. "stand."

58. John Harrison (1693-1776), English horologist and inventor.

59. Boston Tea Party, 16 December 1773, Griffins' Wharf; Captain Thomas Preston at the Boston Massacre, 5 March 1770.

60. For description of Franklin Urn, Franklin Place (1792) and Franklin's birthplace see Nathaniel B. Shurtleff, *A Topographical and Historical Description of Boston*, 3rd. ed. (Boston, 1891), pp. 383, 615-625.

61. This series under the title *Bibliotheca Fratrum Polonorum* containing the writings of early Socinians was first published in Amsterdam in 1656-1692.

62. There is no evidence to substantiate Niemcewicz's identification of this copy as by Copley. In 1789 John Trumbull (1756-1841) gave to Harvard Col-

lege a copy of the Van Dyck Bentivoglio. This painting was copied, very probably by John Trumbull himself, from a copy painted by John Smibert (1688-1751). It appears reasonable to suppose that Niemcewicz may have seen the Trumbull gift. Alan Burroughs, ed., *Harvard Portraits* (Cambridge, Massachusetts, 1936), pp. 17-18. Copley has been called the Van Dyck of New England; see Howard Mumford Jones, *America and French Culture* (Chapel Hill, N.C., 1927), p. 316.

63. None of the Indian artifacts which Niemcewicz saw are now extant, nor is there any record of their disposition. I am grateful to Dr. John O. Brew of the Peabody Museum for this information. Niemcewicz's general description tallies very well, however, with that of known Massachusetts Indian artifacts. See Charles C. Willoughby, *Antiquities of the New England Indians* (Cambridge, 1935), pp. 161-166. Orrery of Joseph Pope, see Justin Winsor, *Memorial History of Boston,* (Boston, 1880-82), IV, 500-502; see also for presence of orrery in Niemcewicz's school at the time of his attendance, Stanisław Kot, *Historja wychowania* (Lwów, 1934), II, 49.

64. Leonard Jarvis; see, for his holdings and life in Cambridge, Lucius R. Page, *History of Cambridge, Massachusetts, 1630-1877* (Boston, 1877), pp. 173, 174, 176-178.

65. Mrs. Spooner was probably the wife of William Spooner, physician; see *The Boston Directory* (1798).

66. The action of *Paul et Virginie* (1789) by Bernardin de St. Pierre takes place in the Ile de France.

67. See Morse, *The American Geography*, p. 324.

68. "Accursed hunger for gold." Virgil, *Aeneid*, III, 57; *op. cit.*

69. Essex Bridge; see Morse, *The American Geography*, p. 324; builder Lemuel Cox (1736-1806), *D.A.B.* s.v. "Cox, Lemuel."

70. The Merrimack; see *Naval Documents . . . February 1797-October 1798,* pp. 525-526.

71. The Essex-Merrimack Bridge and Deer Island; for contemporary print and description see John James Currier, *Ould Newbury* (Boston, 1896), pp. 592-599; see also Morse, *The American Geography*, p. 324.

72. Compare "The first discovery made by the English of any part of New Hampshire, was in 1614 by Captain John Smith, who ranged the shore from Penobscot to Cape Cod; and in this rout, discovered the river Pascataqua. On his return to England, he published a description of the country, with a map of the coast, which he presented to Prince Charles, who gave it the name of New England," Morse, *The American Geography*, p. 305.

73. This could be any one of several related Sheafes living in Portsmouth; see Charles W. Brewster, *Rambles about Portsmouth*, 2nd series (Portsmouth, 1869), pp. 126-132.

74. Although the first ridge of hills west of the sea were called the Blue Hills (Morse, p. 291), Niemcewicz was probably speaking of the distant "blue" mountains to the west and north which belong to the Appalachian Chain, as do the Blue Ridge Mountains of Virginia.

75. Betula papyrifera: Paper birch; for discussion of European counterparts see Arthur Harmount Graves, *Illustrated Guide to Trees and Shrubs* (Wallingford, Conn., 1952), p. 68, n. 1.

76. The Piscataqua Bridge connecting Newington and Durham was about six and a half miles from Portsmouth, 2,362 feet in length with a chord of 444'6";

see Nathaniel Adams, *Annals of Portsmouth* (Portsmouth, 1825), pp. 306-308; see also for contemporary view, Gilmor, "Memorandums," p. 72; for discussion of Thomas Thompson and this bridge, and for anecdotes about tavern on island, see Mary P. Thompson, *Landmarks in Ancient Dover, New Hampshire* (Durham, 1892), pp. 193-194.

77. Zostera marina: Grass wrack, Eel-grass; see Gray, *Manual*, p. 565.

78. See Captain George Henry Preble, U.S.N., "Vessels of War Built at Portsmouth, New Hampshire, 1690-1868," *The New England Historical and Genealogical Register*, XXII (1868), 393-394.

78a. "In the summer season men often wore calico morning gowns at all times of the day in the street as well as at home," Elisabeth McClellan, *Historic Dress in America 1607-1800* (Philadelphia, 1904), p. 315; see Alice Morse Earle, *Two Centuries of Costume in America* (New York, 1903), II, 429-443.

79. Edmond Charles Edouard Genêt (1763-1834); M. Toscan, Vice-consul for New Hampshire, see *Fleet's Register and Pocket Almanac* (Boston, 1798).

80. Concord did not become the state capital until 1808. Phillips Exeter Academy, founded and endowed by John Phillips, incorporated in 1781 and opened 1783.

81. See Gilmor, "Memorandums," p. 72.

82. See *Naval Documents . . . February 1797-October 1798*, pp. 56, 158, 516.

83. Captain Daniel McNeil (1748-1833) was to command the Portsmouth; for this and pay for personnel see *Naval Documents . . . February 1797-October 1798*, pp. 7, 368, 399; see also *D.A.B.* s.v. "McNeil, Daniel."

84. See account *Columbia Centinel* (Boston), 4 August 1798.

85. See advertisement for deserters in *Columbia Centinel*, 25 July 1798, repeated 25 August 1798.

NOTES TO CHAPTER VII

1. The word "drabiasty" now drabiniasty used by Niemcewicz in the original Polish describes a special farm wagon with ladder-like sides. Here he must be referring to the American stage waggon; for description and illustration of such a waggon, see Weld, *Travels*, I, 27; Niemcewicz translated his French *wagon* into *drabiasty wóz*; see Niemcewicz, "Wiadomość o Washingtonie," *Dzieła*, XI, 62.

2. This was probably a member of the pioneer publishing family in Western Massachusetts, William Butler (1763-1831?) and Simeon Butler (1770-1847); see *Appleton's Cyclopedia of American Biography* s.v. "Butler, Simeon"; see also Solomon Clark, *Antiquities, Historicals and Graduates of Northampton* (Northampton, 1882), pp. 184-187.

3. Buttonwood tree: sycamore (platanus occidentalis).

4. Isaiah Thomas (1750-1831), famous printer, publisher and bookseller of America described by Brissot as the Didot of America; see *New Travels*, pp. 122-123.

5. Niemcewicz refers here to his publishing activities during the Four Year Diet with *Gazeta Narodowa i Obca;* see Dihm, *Niemcewicz jako polityk i publi-*

cysta, pp. 98-126; see also Anna Goriaczko, *Gazeta Narodowa i Obca* (Wrocław, 1953).

6. For an account of this enterprise see *D.A.B.* s.v. "Earle, Pliny" (1762-1832).

7. James Swan (1754-1830); for Monroe's description of Swan as, "a corrupt unprincipled rascal . . . had a monopoly of trade of both countries [America and France]," see *The Writings of James Monroe (1794-1795),* ed. Stanislaus Murray Hamilton (New York, 1899), II, 65 n. 1, 313-314; see also Colonel Swan, *Causes qui se sont opposées aux progrès du commerce entre la France et les Etats Unis avec les moyens de l'accélerer* (Paris, 1790).

8. *Sianożęci:* "Grassland that is annually mown for hay, . . . is the proper signification of the word 'meadow' in New England"; see Ralph H. Brown, *Mirror for Americans,* pp. 187, 291 n. 20.

9. See Morse, *Geography,* p. 313.

10. John Coffin (1765-1838), loyalist born in Boston, a member of the Legislative Assembly of New Brunswick; see *The Encyclopedia of Canada* s.v. "Coffin, John."

11. New Lebanon was not officially separated from Canaan until 1818; see John Homer French, *Gazeteer of the State of New York* (Syracuse, 1860), pp. 243, 248.

12. Probably the families of William or James Constable and Nicholas Gouverneur, wealthy New York merchants and bankers; see *The Memorial History of the City of New York,* ed. James Grant Wilson (New York, 1893), III, 66, 151, 152.

13. Cf. account of Liancourt, *Travels,* I, 389-394; see also Edward Deming Andrews, *The People called Shakers. A Search for the Perfect Society* (New York, 1953); *idem., A Gift to be Simple, Songs, Dances and Rituals of the American Shakers* (New York, 1940).

14. Silkweed: milkweed, Asclepias; see Gray, *Manual,* p. 339.

15. "They danced naked, while 'Mother Ann' went in among the men smiting ————— and dancing with them;" see the testimony of an apostate, William J. Haskett, *Shakerism Unmasked or the History of the Shakers* (Pittsfield, 1828), p. 43 and passim.

16. Text changed; cf. "Si fractus inlabatur orbis, / impavidum ferient ruinae." "Were the vault of heaven to break and fall upon him, its ruins would smite him undismayed." Horace, *Odes,* III, 3, line 7-8; *op. cit.*

17. For a bibliography of sources concerning the problem of Dutch- and English-speaking groups see Evarts B. Greene and Richard B. Morris, *A Guide to the Principal Sources for Early American History (1600-1800) in the City of New York,* 2nd ed. (New York, 1953), p. 288; see also Morse, p. 380.

18. The Tontine City Tavern and Hotel; see Joel Munsell, *The Annals of Albany* (Albany, 1871), III, 147.

19. Thomas Dobson, *Encyclopaedia,* 18 vols. (Philadelphia, 1790-98).

20. Fort Stanwix, now Rome. The Western Inland Lock Navigation Company completed a canal connecting the navigable waters of the Mohawk River and Wood Creek, at Rome, in 1797. See Pomroy Jones, *Annals and Recollections of Oneida County* (Rome, 1851), p. 375.

21. Niemcewicz visited this region in 1805; see "Journey to Niagara, 1805," in Part II here; see also Liancourt, *Travels,* I, 361-362.

22. Niemcewicz visited this region; see "Journey to Niagara, 1805;" see also John Maude, *Visit to the Falls of Niagara in 1800* (London, 1826), pp. 43-45.

23. See account of trade by Liancourt, *Travels*, I, 367-370.

24. The 22nd session (1798-1799) of the New York State Legislature, 1st meeting 9-27 August 1798; see *Journal of the Assembly of the State of New York* (Albany, n.d.), pp. 3-7; see also detailed accounts of proceedings in *The Albany Gazette*, 10 August 1798 and *The Albany Centinel*, 10 August 1798.

25. John Bartow Prevost/Provost, representative from New York City; see *The New York Civil List from 1777-1855*, prep. Franklin B. Hough (Albany, 1855), p. 181; for correspondence on Prevost's appointment as Monroe's secretary see Monroe, *A View of the Executive*, pp. 256-257.

26. Angelica Schuyler Church, whom Niemcewicz met in Paris in 1787; see *Pamiętniki* (Warsaw), II, 227; see also Dumas Malone, *Jefferson and the Rights of Man* (Boston, 1951), p. 140; for controversy of Kościuszko with her husband, John Barker Church, see Miecislaus Haiman, *Kosciuszko in the American Revolution* (New York, 1943), pp. 56-68.

27. John Bradstreet (c. 1711-1774), Major General (1772), under whom Philip John Schuyler (1733-1804) served in 1756. He married Catherine Rensselaer (1734-1803) in 1755 and went to England in Bradstreet's interest (1761-1763?); see *D.A.B.* s.v. "Schuyler, Philip John."

28. William Pitt (1708-1788), "the Elder Pitt," Earl of Chatham.

29. Compare "Je songe quelle étoit autrefois cette ville / Si superbe en remparts, en héros si fertile," Racine, *Andromaque*, line 197.

30. See note 55, Chapter III; there is no mention of Rome in Thompson, *History of Vermont*.

31. Stephen Van Rensselaer (1764-1839), lieutenant governor of New York (1795-1801); for map of Rensselaerwyck see *The Documentary History of the State of New York*, ed. Edmund Bailey O'Callaghan (Albany, 1850), III, 916.

32. "Nothing is happy altogether." Horace, *Odes*, II, 16, lines 27-28; *op. cit.*

33. Salmacis, nymph of the fountain in Caria where Hermaphroditus bathed.

34. The expression used by Niemcewicz probably derives from the Ptolemaic designations, Arabia Petraea, "Stony Arabia"; Arabia Felix, "Fertile: Fortunate Arabia"; and Arabia Deserta, "Desert Arabia"; for use of term in this district see quotation from Captain John Schuyler in 1698: "The 27th of August we went from Albany and came to Stony Arabia," *Documents Relative to the Colonial History of the State of New-York*, ed. Edmund Bailey O'Callaghan (Albany, 1854), IV, 404.

35. Richard Montgomery (1736-1775), killed leading assault on Quebec (31 December 1775); his wife was Janet Livingston; for possible identification of Mr. Jones see Maude, *Visit to Falls of Niagara in 1800*, pp. 235, 240, 244, 245, 248, 249; see also correspondence between Chas. Jones and Robert R. Livingston in *Livingston Papers*, New-York Historical Society.

36. Praga, now a part of Warsaw, once a little town on the opposite side of Vistula; Mazowsze is the home province of Warsaw; Mother Warsenga—a peasant name for Warsaw

37. A common designation for sturgeon; see Maude, p. 25.

38. Lunenburg: Loonenburgh and Esperanza; since 1805, Athens; see French, *Gazeteer*, p. 331, n. 4; see also Maude, pp. 15, 272.

39. Compare account of Hudson in Morse, *The American Geography*, pp. 385-386.

40. Sir William Herschell discovered planet Uranus (1781) and later satellites of Uranus and Saturn.

41. Seweryn Rzewuski, one of the leaders of the Targowica Confederation 14 May 1792; for Niemcewicz's speech, 27 January 1792, about Seweryn Rzewuski's overriding ambition to regain the full power of his hetmanship, see Czartoryski, *Żywot*, pp. 281-286, esp. pp. 284-285.

42. For a detailed map of the property showing distribution of tenants, 1798, etc., of Chancellor Robert Livingston, see Charles Oscar Paullin, *Atlas of the Historical Geography of the United States* (Washington and New York, 1932), Pl. 53C, 53D; see also *Documentary History of New York*, III, 690, 834.

43. Cape Jasmine (Gardenia jasminoides Ellis).

44. The founder of this American family prominent in colonial and post-colonial periods, Robert Livingston (1654-1728), was born in Ancrum, Roxburgh-shire, Scotland, emigrated to America (1673).

45. Margaret Beekman (1724-1800), daughter and heiress of Colonel Henry Beekman, married Judge Robert R. Livingston (1708-1775); see Florence Van Rensselaer, *The Livingston Family in America and its Scottish Origins* (New York, 1949), pp. 87, 149.

46. Margaret Maria Livingston (1783-1818) married Robert L. Livingston (1775-1843) 10 June 1798; Elizabeth Stevens Livingston married Edward P. Livingston (1779-1843) 20 November 1799; see Van Rensselaer, *The Livingston Family*, pp. 114, 123; cf. Dangerfield, *Livingston*, pp. 281-282.

47. The Polish gentry theoretically democratic and with no indigenous titles such as Prince and Count had gradations of dignities, civil and military, about which a "titleomania" grew up from the time of the Saxon kings. See Brückner, *Dzieje*, III, 20; see also Fryderyk Schulz, *Podróże inflantczyka* (Warsaw, 1956), pp. 99-123.

48. John Armstrong (1758-1843), American army officer and statesman; his friendship with Kościuszko has been explored by Haiman through their letters in his books *Kosciuszko in the American Revolution* (New York, 1943), passim, and *Kosciuszko Leader and Exile* (New York, 1946), passim.

49. For a list of publications see *D.A.B.* s.v. "Armstrong, John."

50. Alida Livingston (m. 1789), sister of Chancellor Livingston; see Van Rensselaer, *The Livingston Family*, p. 101.

51. All five sisters of Robert L. Livingston are listed by Van Rensselaer, pp. 92-93.

52. Niemcewicz is referring to the Newburgh letters (1783), anonymous letters written to Congress demanding the arrears in pay for army officers.

53. See Haiman, *Kosciuszko Leader and Exile*, p. 67.

54. This is an accurate description in essentials of Kosciuszko's service in the American revolutionary war.

55. Kulik: Kulig. A group of gentry visit a neighbor, eat and drink everything there and then in turn he and his family join the group to go to another and so on. See description in Chrzanowski, *Historja*, pp. 461-463.

56. For a description of the Red Hook estate of John R. Livingston (1755-1851) see Thomas Streatfield Clarkson, *A Biographical History of Clermont or Livingston Manor* (Clermont, 1869), p. 169.

57. Unidentified.

58. Niemcewicz on his visit to Italy wrote a poem entitled: "Wiersze na wierzchołku góry Etny pisane. 1784," *Dzieła*, III, 62.

59. We have not been able to find evidence of this particular incident. The

newspapers in New York carried long articles calling for calm and pleading restraint about the Yellow Fever; see *Greenleaf's New Daily Advertiser, Argus,* 4 September 1798.

60. Benedict Arnold (1741-1801).

61. For a description of the chain at West Point and the other at Fort Montgomery see French, *Gazeteer,* p. 542, n. 6.

62. The excerpt translated by Niemcewicz is included in quotation marks and set off. The English is taken from the account in David Ramsay, *The History of the American Revolution* (Dublin, 1793), II, pp. 493-499.

63. For a history of this song see Winthrop Sargent, *The Life and Career of Major John André* (New York, 1902), pp. 524-526; see also Sonneck, *Bibliography,* p. 246.

64. "Major André . . . had commenced a correspondence with Mrs. Arnold in 1779 under the plea of supplying her with millinery . . . ," Gordon, *The History of the Independence,* III, 129; see *D.A.B.* s.v. "Arnold, Benedict" for Mrs. Arnold's complicity. Cf. James Thomas Flexner, *The Benedict Arnold Case,* Collier Books (New York, 1962).

65. Biała Cerkiew and Tulczyn were the names of estates of two of the leaders of the Targowica Confederation, Ksawery Branicki and Szczęsny Potocki, respectively.

66. Pietro Antonio Metastasio (1698-1782), a prolific poet whose dramas achieved great fame when set to music; *Demofoonte* was such a one.

67. George Clinton (1739-1812), governor of New York (1777-1795; 1801-1804).

68. Anthony Wayne (1745-1796) led the attack which surprised and captured the British garrison at Stony Point (16 July 1779).

69. Old name given to the Palisades, probably after Frederick Closter, early grantee of these lands; see *New Jersey,* American Guide Series (New York, 1939), pp. 436-437.

70. Frederick Philipse (1626-1702) acquired manorial estate in Upper Yonkers. His manor hall is preserved by New York State as a historical relic. See also Lorenzo Sabine, *The American Loyalists in the War of the Revolution* (Boston, 1847), pp. 537-539.

71. "It is a sin peculiar to man to hate his victim." Tacitus, *Agricola,* 42; see H. Mattingly, trans. *Tacitus on Britain and Germany,* The Penguin Classics (Harmondsworth, Middlesex, England, 1960).

72. Lewis Rivers, tailor, at whose home Niemcewicz and Kościuszko stayed when they came to Elizabeth in October 1797 and where Niemcewicz lived until his marriage in 1800. See letter of Kościuszko to Gates, 3 October 1797, *Gates Papers,* New-York Historical Society, Box 18, no. 53; see also Niemcewicz, *Pamiętniki* (Warsaw), II, 229-230, 237-238; cf. *Biog. Index,* N.J. Hist. Soc. s.v. "Rivers."

73. Niemcewicz repeats the incidents concerning Kościuszko in a letter to Jefferson 3 September 1798; see Władysław M. Kozłowski, "Niemcewicz en Amérique," *Revue de Littérature Comparée,* VIII (1928), 36-37; see also Haiman, *Kosciuszko Leader and Exile,* p. 83. For the polemics in Poland on Kościuszko's wounds see Tadeusz Korzon, *Biblioteka Warszawska* (1907), I, 399-402; *idem. Kwartalnik Historyczny,* XXII (1908), 469-473.

74. This listing is the so-called "Bill of Mortality"; see *Aurora and General Advertiser,* 5 November 1798 (Philadelphia).

NOTES TO CHAPTER VIII

1. Niemcewicz was very much attached to Maclure. In his Diary written many years later under date 17 March 1834 he recounts the events of Maclure's life with seeming nostalgia; see his *Pamiętniki, Dziennik pobytu za granicą*, ed. J. K. Żupański (Poznań, 1877), II, 281-282. Thomas Peter Smith (c. 1777-1802), pioneer American geologist and chemist. He left his mineral collection and diary to the American Philosophical Society. See "Old Minutes of the Society from 1743-1838," *Proceedings of the American Philosophical Society*, XXII (July, 1885), Part III, no. 119, 337; see also for biography, Wyndham Miles, *Journal of Chemical Education*, XXX (1953), 184.

2. Kalmia latifolia considered poisonous at that time; see Benjamin Smith Barton, *Collections for an Essay Towards a Materia Medica of the United States* (Philadelphia, 1798), p. 18. The minerals listed by Niemcewicz have been found here; see Charles E. Hall, *The Geology of Philadelphia County and of the Southern parts of Montgomery and Bucks*, Second Geological Survey of Pennsylvania, Report of Progress (Harrisburg, 1881), pp. 1-13.

3. Here as elsewhere Niemcewicz used the old Linnean classification; Spirea trifolium: Spiraea trifoliata Linnaeus; known as Indian Physic, Bowman's Root; see Barton, *Collections*, p. 27; now Gillenia trifoliata; see Asa Gray, *Manual of the Botany of the Northern United States*, 6th ed. (New York, 1889), p. 154. Cypripedium L., Lady's slipper; see Ida A. Keller and Stewardson Brown, *Handbook of the Flora of Philadelphia and Vicinity* (Philadelphia, 1905), pp. 107, 172.

4. Tradescantia, L.: Spiderwort; Agrostemma Githago, L.: Corn Cockle. See Keller and Brown, pp. 93, 138.

5. Rattlesnake-root: Prenanthes, subgenus Nabalus; Heracium venosum (Rattlesnake weed); Actea racemosa: Cimicifuga racemosa. See Keller and Brown, pp. 148, 311, 312; see also Witmer Stone, *The Plants of Southern New Jersey with Especial Reference to the Flora of the Pine Barrens*, Annual Report of the New Jersey State Museum 1910 (Trenton, 1911), p. 451.

6. Famous inn 20 miles from Philadelphia, at that time run by the Fahnstock family; see Julius F. Sachse, *The Wayside Inns on the Lancaster Roadside between Philadelphia and Lancaster* (Lancaster, 1912), pp. 21, 44 ff.

7. Euphorbiaceae Ipecacuanhae (spurge); see Stone, p. 528.

8. Little Timber Creek flows into the Delaware River and is the southern boundary of the present day Gloucester City, Camden County, New Jersey; see *Atlas of the State of New Jersey* (New York, 1905), p. 36; see also for settlement Thomas F. Gordon, *The History of New Jersey* (Trenton, 1834), p. 249.

9. Nitric of quick silver would in this context be mercurous nitrate. However, silver nitrate is now and was then used for testing the salinity of water.

10. Probably Magnolia virginiana or glauca; see Stone, p. 446. Magnolia auriculata: Magnolia Fraseri although with fragrant flowers is not reported by Stone; see however Nathaniel Lord Britton and Addison Brown, *An Illustrated Flora of the Northern United States, Canada and the British Possessions*, 2nd ed. (New York, 1947), II, 81; see also Henry A. Gleason, *The New Britton and Brown Illustrated Flora* (New York, 1952), II, 152.

11. Now known as Big Timber Creek; for description of area see Gordon, pp. 249-250.

12. Now Berlin; for anecdote on original name see *New Jersey*, American Guide Series (New York, 1939), p. 599.

13. Blue Anchor. There is now a town here of this name.

14. Sisyrinchium Bermudiana, Blue-eyed grass; see Stone, p. 360; Lysimachia (Loosestrife), Stone, p. 631; Galium (Bed straw) or perhaps confused with Diodia Virginiana; see Gray, p. 225; Lupinus, Lupine, Gray, p. 128; see also Stone, pp. 497, 703-704; Gleason, III, 278.

15. Probably at the head of Great Egg Harbor River near the present Mays Landing. This is not Egg Harbor City; see *New Jersey*, p. 597; see also Thomas Gordon, *A Map of the State of New Jersey* (1828).

16. Colonel Richard Wescoat (born 1733); see Arthur Dudley Pierce, *Iron in the Pines* (New Brunswick, New Jersey, 1957), pp. 184-187, 193.

17. Helonias asphodeloides, Linnaeus (Turkey Beard), see Stone, p. 340.

18. Pennypot, now disappeared, was at the confluence of Pennypot Creek and Great Egg Harbor River; see Gordon, *Map of New Jersey;* see also Gordon, *History of New Jersey*, p. 212.

19. See *Encyclopaedia Britannica*, 11th ed. s.v. "Rattlesnake."

20. Niemcewicz is probably alluding to the eating of bears' paws as a special dish in Poland; see Władysław Łoziński, *Życie polskie w dawnych wiekach* (Paris, n.d.), p. 158; for American Indian preference for the paws of the bear see Weld, *Travels*, II, 153.

21. The view that the functional purpose of the leaves was the conservation of water was adopted by Linnaeus and many others; see Francis Ernest Lloyd, *The Carnivorous Plants* (Waltham, Mass., 1942), p. 18; see pp. 17-39, for general account of observations leading to the recognition of Saracenia as a carnivorous plant.

22. Rhus venenata: Rhus vernix, Linnaeus; Poison Sumac; see Stone, p. 537.

23. Somers family for which the present Somers Point is named and whose most famous member was the American hero, Richard Somers; see *D.A.B.* s.v. "Somers, Richard." The Collector was either Constant Somers (1760-1797?) or Jesse Somers (1763-1858); see John E. Stillwell [Stillwell Genealogy] (New York, 1930), III, 257-258; see also John F. Hall, *The Daily Union History of Atlantic City and County* (Atlantic City, n.d.), p. 435. For Jesse Somers and the Somers Mansion as a national relic see Herbert N. Moffet and Lewis B. Cook, *A History of the Somers Mansion* (Somers Point, N.J., 1942), p. 13 and passim. The Somers' tenure was short; the office of Collector started in 1799 and the name does not appear in official records; see Public Documents 6th Congress, 1st Session [Oliver Wolcott], *Letter from the Secretary of the Treasury transmitting a Letter from the Comptroller accompanied with an Abstract of the Compensations of the Officers of the Customs for the Year 1798, issued 5 February 1800; and for the Year 1799 issued 10 March 1800;* see also A. W. Greely, *Public Documents of the First Fourteen Congresses. Papers relating to Early Congressional Documents* (Washington, 1900), pp. 264-265.

24. Gloucester County at that time comprised the present Atlantic County as well as Camden County.

25. Cactus opuntia, Linnaeus, Stone, p. 573; Opuntia, Prickly pear, Indian fig (Cactus Family); see Gray, p. 197.

26. Pelicans are in general not seen as far north as the New Jersey coast; Fish

hawks: ospreys; golets probably gulls; and plovers; see Roger Tory Peterson, *A Field Guide to the Birds* (Boston, 1947), pp. 12, 67, 123, 91.

27. Rubus: Bramble; see Gray, p. 154; Convolvulus Family, Gray, p. 367; Oenothera; Evening Primrose, Gray, p. 190; Cistaceae (Rock rose family), Gray, p. 76.

28. Uca pugilator: fiddler-crab. The body is ⅔ of an inch wide, the great claw is an attribute of the male; see O. W. Hyman, "Adventures in the Life of a Fiddler-Crab," *Annual Report of the Board of Regents of the Smithsonian Institution 1920* (Washington, D.C., 1922), pp. 443, 444.

29. Batsto; William Richards (1738-1823). For an account of this enterprise see Pierce, *Iron in the Pines*, pp. 117-134.

30. Limodorum tuberosum, Linnaeus (Grass pink), now Calopogon pulchellus; see Stone, p. 372; see also Gleason, I, 466.

31. Silene, Catchfly Campion, Stone, p. 437; Prunella vulgaris: self-heal, heal-all, common weed of cultivated ground, Stone, p. 6; Asclepias, milkweed, Stone, p. 647; Apocynum cannabium, Indian hemp, Stone, p. 646.

32. Itea Virginica, Stone, p. 472; Thalictrum dioicum (early meadow rue), Stone, p. 458; Epigaea, L., Ground laurel, trailing arbutus, Stone, p. 619.

33. The building was erected in 1792 by the Quakers; see *New Jersey*, American Guide Series, pp. 217-218; see also William E. Schermerhorn, *The History of Burlington, New Jersey* (Burlington, 1927), p. 214.

34. Early name of Camden, called after William Cooper and his enterprise, Cooper's Ferries; see *New Jersey*, American Guide Series, p. 228.

35. Niemcewicz had visited these forges on his arrival in America; see Chapter I. The new pagination here, follows the major time discontinuity and the passage in French now transferred to the appendix, q.v.

36. In 1740 the township of Morris was officially named; see *Encyclopaedia Britannica*, 11th ed. s.v. "Morristown."

37. Captain David Ford (d. 1835), *New Jersey Historical Society Proceedings*, VIII (1856-1859), 73.

38. Brzeskie (Brześciańskie), Niemcewicz's home county.

39. Mrs. Faesch, the wife of the elder Faesch, was related through her mother to the Kearney family; therefore Miss Carny's name is probably misspelled. *History of the First Presbyterian Church, Morristown, N.J.*, Part II, 1742-1885 (n.d.), pp. 69, 298; see also James Parker, *The Parker and Kearney Families of New Jersey* (Perth Amboy, 1925), p. 21. Dr. Darby was a physician in Perth Amboy; see *Diary of William Dunlap*, I, 338; for other doctors in this district with this name see Stephen Wickes, *History of Medicine in New Jersey and of its Medical Men* (Newark, 1879), pp. 224-225; see also Hatfield, *History of Elizabeth*, pp. 640-641.

40. Richard Brinkerhoff Faesch (1778-1820).

41. Possibly Captain Josiah Hall; see J. Percy Crayon, *Rockaway Records of Morris County, New Jersey Families* (Rockaway, 1902), pp. 211-216, 290.

42. *De L'Esprit des Lois* (Paris, 1820), I, 225, "Quand les sauvages de la Louisiane veullent avoir du fruit, ils coupent l'arbre au pied, et cueillent le fruit. Voilà le gouvernement despotique."

43. suslik: A spermophile, or ground squirrel (*Citellus citillus*) of northeastern Europe . . . has mottled grayish-brown fur. Niemcewicz was very interested in squirrels. For his description of their love life, see "Journey to Niagara, 1805," here reprinted in Part II; for sailing across Lake Erie on bits of bark see "Diary

of Second Visit," in Part III; cf. Weld, *Travels*, II, 45-46; for their use as the first metamorphosis in Niemcewicz's poem *Moje Przemiany* see Julian Krzyżanowski, *Wiadomości* (London), 22 June 1958.

44. For a discussion of the various types of pheasants, especially Bohemian, see *Encyclopaedia Britannica*, 11th ed. s.v. "Pheasant, Partridge."

NOTES TO "JOURNEY TO NIAGARA"

1. M. and Mme. Belasise, neighbors of Niemcewicz in Elizabeth, N.J. Belasise was the pseudonym used, during their ten years in America, by George Richard, 3rd Viscount Bolingbroke and 4th Viscount St. John, and Isabelle Charlotte Antoinette Sophia, Baroness Hompesch; see Introduction, n. 17 and Chapter V, n. 26.

2. The name for the present site of Passaic, N.J., in use until the middle of the 19th century; see *Encyclopaedia Britannica*, 11th ed. s.v. "Passaic."

3. Probably Gnaphalium obtusifolium, L. or G. polycephalum, Michx. (cudweed, fragrant, life everlasting), although only G. uliginosum, L. (Marsh cudweed), found on low ground is known as mouse's ear; A. Brown, *An Illustrated Flora of the Northern U. S., Canada and the British Possessions*, 2nd ed. (New York, 1947), III, 454-55; see also P. Kalm's description of a similar plant, *Travels into North America*, tr. J. R. Forster (Warrington, 1770), I, 130-31.

4. This is probably Captain John Hopper (1761-1819; see William S. Stryker, *Official Register of the Officers and Men of New Jersey in the Revolutionary War* (Trenton, N.J., 1872), pp. 35, 105, 395; Francis B. Heitman, *Historical Register of Officers of the Continental Army during the War of the Revolution*, new ed. (Washington, 1914), p. 300. His inn is identified as standing then in what is now Ho-Ho-Kus, N.J.; see Rosalie Fellows Bailey, *Pre-Revolutionary Dutch Houses and Families* (New York, 1936), Pt. II, p. 299; Sue F. Hudson, *Background of Ho-Ho-Kus History* (Ho-Ho-Kus, N.J., 1953), pp. 26, 29-32.

5. In the original manuscript the space occupied by the word *Ramapo* was left blank by Niemcewicz and the word written in, in pencil, in handwriting obviously not that of Niemcewicz. The geography of the region strongly suggests that the Ramapo is correct.

6. The folklore on rattlesnakes and the leaves of the Ash has been current since first mentioned by Pliny the Elder, Gaius Plinius Secundus (23-79 A.D.); see Pliny, *Historia Naturalis*, tr. J. Bostock and H. T. Riley (London, 1855-57), III, 366; L. M. Klauber, *Rattlesnakes, Their Habits, Life Histories and Influence on Mankind* (Berkeley and Los Angeles, 1956), II, 1231.

7. Profits of fifteen to twenty dollars an acre from the raising of hemp on the "sunken swamps and bog-meadows" of Orange County in use for twenty years are referred to by William Thompson, "Letter on the Cultivation of Hemp, Goshen, Nov. 30, 1803," *Transactions of the Society for the Promotion of Useful Arts in the State of New York* (Albany, 1807), II, 121, 125. See also for lack of success and difficulties of cultivation, E. L. Lord, "Industrial Experiments in British Colonies of North America," *Johns Hopkins University Studies in Hist. and Pol. Sci.*, Ex. Vol. XVII (1898), 84.

8. Springtown, now a hamlet of New Paltz; see J. H. French, *Gazeteer of the State of New York* (Syracuse, 1860), p. 665; David H. Burr, *An Atlas of the State*

of New York containing a Map of the State and of Several Counties (New York, 1829).

9. Sopos in original manuscript. An early local spelling of Esopus. The geography is in error; the Walkill river flows through this region.

10. There is no known river oak designation but this species is probably the swamp white oak, Quercus bicolor, Willd., recognized by F. A. Michaux and others as especially abundant in northern N.J. near N.Y.; see F. A. Michaux, *Histoire des Arbres Forestiers de l'Amérique Septentrionale* (Paris, 1810-13), II, 46; A. Gray, *Manual of Botany* (New York, 1889), p. 476; A. H. Graves, *Illustrated Guide to Trees and Shrubs* (Wallingford, Conn., 1952), pp. 81-2.

11. Benjamin S. Delameter, born in 1783, and Racheal Snyder, born in 1788, were married Jan. 29, 1805 in the Old Dutch Church of Kingston. Roswell Randall Hoes, ed. *Baptismal and Marriage Registers of the Old Dutch Church of Kingston* (New York, 1891), p. 678; Lafayette Delamater, *Descendants of Claude Le Maitre, 1652* (Albany, 1882), Appendix, p. 192.

12. Although Niemcewicz here used the French word sevrer, to wean, it seems probable from the context and from the fact that the child, Helena, was only two weeks old, having been born 22 September 1805 (*Ibid.*, p. 485), that he should have used the verb to suckle.

13. In the original manuscript in Niemcewicz appears to be using the word "mail" in its, now obsolete, English meaning of traveling bag, as otherwise the meaning of the French is obscure.

14. October 16, 1777.

15. For an account of such an immigration see Dr. M. Ellis, "The Yankee Invasion of New York, 1783-1850," *New York History*, XXXII (1951), 3-17.

16. Coeymans: written Queens in the French original, the error presumably arose from the similarity in pronunciation; see French, *Gazeteer*, p. 163.

17. Tontine Coffee House: Principal hotel in the city situated on State Street, founded in 1795; see *History of the County of Albany from 1609-1886* (New York, 1886), p. 651.

18. This map was either *Map of the State of New York,* published in Albany Oct. 16, 1802, by Simeon de Witt, Surveyor General of New York, showing the state as far west as the "pre-emption line," with an insert ½ scale showing the continuation of the whole state, or a contracted version showing the whole state published at New York in 1804 and reproduced here.

19. The name is more probably Vedder, a very common name in this district at this time. However, since the name Verder also occurs, though less frequently, we can not be certain; it is therefore not possible to locate the tavern exactly; see Jonathan Pearson, *Contributions for the Genealogies of the Descendants of the First Settlers of the Patent and City of Schenectady from 1662-1800* (Albany, 1873).

20. Mount Johnson, now Fort Johnson, where Sir William Johnson (1715-1774) lived from approximately 1743 to 1763 when he removed to Johnson Hall in Johnstown, N.Y.; see William Johnson, *Papers*, eds. J. Sullivan, A. C. Flick and W. M. Hamilton (Albany, 1921-53), I, xvii-xviii.

21. Joseph Brant (1742-1807), brother of Molly Brant, Sir William's Indian wife.

22. The Mohawks, however, were themselves one of the Six Nations.

23. The piaster referred to here is the Spanish dollar. The New York shilling, actually the "real," was worth twelve and a half cents, one-eighth part of the

Spanish dollar then in common use; see Neil Carothers, *Fractional Money, A History of the Small Coins and Fractional Paper Currency of the U.S.* (New York, 1930), pp. 34, 82. For a table showing value given to the shilling in various states at that time see François, duc de La Rochefoucauld-Liancourt, *Voyage dans les Etats Unis (1795-1797)* (Paris, 1799), I, xviii.

24. Twickenham, 12 miles from London, noted for its pleasant situation and the houses of famous people both royal and literary, Strawberry Hill, the residence of Horace Walpole, being one of the more interesting.

25. Turkish Oak may be Quercus cerris L. which is known as Turkey Oak; see Graves, *Illust. Guide to Trees*, p. 83. It may be Q. stellata Wang., Post Oak (Q. obtulsiloba Michx.) which Michaux says is called locally Turkey Oak because the sweet acorns attract this bird. He notes that the tree is not seen further north than the Palisades of the Hudson; see Michaux, II, 39.

26. Mr. Pride was licensed to keep a tavern in the Town of Caughnawaga, and the tavern was located between Tribes Hill and Fonda; see J. R. Simms, *The Frontiersman of New York* (Albany, 1883), I, p. 362. Mr. Edward Sheehan, County Archivist, The Montgomery County Historical Society, Amsterdam, N.Y., kindly substantiated this information.

27. A Josiah or Joseph Shepard kept a stage house at Canajoharie; see French, *Gazeteer*, p. 345, n. 11; Nelson Greene, ed. *History of the Mohawk Valley* (Chicago, 1925), II, 1217.

28. Palatine Bridge, present name of the community built at the site of the bridge erected in 1803 and attracting the attention of travelers; see T. Bigelow, *Journal of a Tour to Niagara Falls in the Year 1805* (Boston, 1876), p. 17, and Greene, *History*, II, 1224; see also C. Robb de Graff P. E. and Margaret de Graff, *Historical Map of Montgomery County* (1952).

29. Acer rubrum.

30. That is, the Little Falls on the Mohawk River, at the town of Little Falls, N.Y.

31. In the Census of 1800 Andrew Sobreski is listed as living in the Town of Palatine, Montgomery County, heading a family of four persons. Andrew Zabriskie served in the State Assembly Jan. 25 to April 15, 1814, representing the County of Montgomery; see *Census of 1800, Montgomery County, N.Y.,* Reprint (St. Johnsville, N.Y., 1934). For the origin and history of this name in America see Chapter I, n. 77.

32. John III Sobieski, King of Poland (1674-96), famous for his Vienna victory (1683) against the Turks .

33. From time to time Niemcewicz uses expressions in French which are translations from Polish and have no equivalent in French. Therefore *Capitaine de Cercle* is *Kapitan cyrkułu*, which in turn comes from *Kreishauptmann* or captain or prefect of the district.

34. Canal, one mile long, with five locks started in 1792 by the Western Inland Lock Navigation Co. and completed in the fall, 1795, was seen by the Duc de La Rochefoucauld-Liancourt in 1795 who said, "They have been working on it for three years and it is little advanced." See La Rochefoucauld-Liancourt, *Voyage*, II, 279-80; see also J. Morse, *The American Gazeteer* (Boston, 1797) s.v. "Mohawk River"; and Burr, *Atlas*, p. 17.

35. William Alexander, native of Schenectady, came about 1790 to Little Falls and died Jan. 13, 1813; see French, *Gazeteer*, p. 346, n. 6; G. A. Hardin and F. H. Willard, *History of Herkimer County* (Syracuse, 1893), pp. 248, 250.

36. Mme. Williams, wife of Jonathan Williams (1750-1815), née Mariamne Alexander; see *D.A.B.* s.v. "Williams, Jonathan."

37. Ephraim Snow came from Connecticut to Herkimer Village sometime before 1800. He lived and died there highly respected. He held office for one year, having been appointed Sheriff March 6, 1806; see Hardin and Willard, pp. 154, 221.

38. Niemcewicz appears to be joking here about the quality of the coffee. Palma Christi: Ricinus communis is the Castor Oil plant and there is no known use of this material for the adulteration of coffee. On the other hand this could be an error for Cichorium Intybus or chicory, an American weed the root of which is used as a coffee substitute. See W. H. Ukers, *All about Coffee* (New York, 1935), pp. 70, 258, 494; Bigelow, *Journal*, p. 17; V. P. Hedrick, *A History of Agriculture in the State of New York* (N.Y. State Agricultural Soc., 1933), p. 225.

39. The Holland Land Company (1796-1846). See P. D. Evans, *The Holland Land Company*, Buffalo Hist. Soc. Pubs., XXVIII (1924), O. Turner, *The Pioneer History of the Holland Purchase* (Buffalo, 1849).

40. Captain Arent Schuyler De Peyster, born April 4, 1779, intrepid sailor and discoverer of (Peyster) Ellice Islands. He married Catherine Macomb, sister of the American General Alexander Macomb, Feb. 8, 1804; see J. Watts De Peyster, *Miscellanies by an Officer (Colonel Arent Schuyler de Peyster, B.A.)* (1774-1813) (New York, 1888), Appendix, lxxiv-lxxx, clxxviii; see also Waldron Phoenix Belknap, Jr., *The De Peyster Genealogy* (Boston, 1956), p. 58.

41. Ga-ne-o-di-yo, or Ganio'dai'o, mis-spelled by Niemcewicz in the French text as Canadia, was a Seneca sachem who received his vision in 1800 and whose sermons were handed down by his disciple grandson So-she-o-wa; see H. J. Cookinham, *History of Oneida County* (Chicago, 1912), I, Part 1, 15-18; A. C. Parker, *The Code of Handsome Lake, The Seneca Prophet*, Educ. Dept. Bull., 163 (Albany: N. Y. State Museum, 1913), pp. 9-13, 27-81. In his letter to Mrs. Kossakowski, reprinted here, Niemcewicz stated that the brother of Ganio'dai'o was Ket Gallet; presumably he meant Red Jacket. This is not so. Ganio'dai'o's half-brother was Cornplanter: Gaiänt'waka; see Parker, pp. 23, 136-138.

42. Manitou or Manito: Algonquin Indian word for one of the powers or spirits that dominate the forces of nature.

43. The white pastor, to whom Niemcewicz referred, was very probably the Reverend Samuel Kirkland (1741-1808) who founded the Hamilton-Oneida Academy (1793) at Clinton for whites and Indians. The Academy later became Hamilton College (1812); see *D.A.B.* s.v. "Kirkland, Samuel."

44. Chief Skenandoah died in 1816 and was buried next to his friend Reverend Kirkland on the grounds of Hamilton College. See Pomroy Jones, *Annals and Records of Oneida County* (Rome, 1851), pp. 865-868.

45. Eagle Hill, altitude 1,252 ft.; see *U.S. Dept. of Int. Geological Survey, Manlius, N.Y. Quadrangle, Rev. 1957*.

46. Mr. Staniford opened a tavern in Eagleville 1½ miles east of Manlius. See Joshua V. H. Clark, *Onondaga* (Syracuse, 1849), II, 220.

47. Madison County was not created from Onondaga County until March 21, 1806; see French, *Gazeteer*, p. 390.

48. The Military Tract: a huge tract of land given to the soldiers who took part in the Revolutionary War. The final legislation was passed Feb. 25, 1789. The tract of land is in the Finger Lakes region of New York State; see A. C. Flick, ed., *History of the State of New York* (New York, 1933-37), IV, 21-22, V, Ap-

pendix Map for all purchases and reservations; see also O. Turner, *History of Pioneer Settlement of Phelps-Gorham's Purchase* (Rochester, 1852), Chapter on Military Tract.

49. Niemcewicz did not list the place-names in the original manuscript. For the lively controversy concerning these names see Charles Maar, "Origin of the Classical Place Names of Central New York," *New York State Hist. Assoc. Quart. Journal Proceedings,* XXIV (1926), 155-167; Flick, *History,* X, 314-319.

50. For another contemporary account of the salt works see Benjamin de Witt, *A Memoir on the Onondaga Salt Springs and Salt Manufactures in the State of New York,* Trans. of the Soc. for the Promotion of Agri. Arts and Manufact. in the State of N.Y. (Albany, 1801), I, 268-286; see also E. B. Tustin, "Development of the Salt Industry in New York," *New-York Hist. Soc. Quarterly,* XXXIII (1949), 40-46.

51. A widely accepted belief at that time. The phenomenon in male squirrels is caused by the botfly warble (cuterebra emasculator); see E. T. Seton, *Lives of Game Animals* (New York, 1929), IV, Part 1, 9, 10, 54 ff. I am indebted to Dr. Joseph Curtis Moore of The American Museum of Natural History, New York, who gave me this information.

52. *petit palais:* I have been unable to identify a game with this name. Mr. Albert Morehead, Games Editor, *The New York Times,* New York, has suggested (private communication) that "petit palais" may have been the local name for a variation of any of those many games which allowed two kinds of bets, "grand" and "petit," and in which the places on the board where the bets were laid were called "grand palais" and "petit palais" respectively. A possible alternative explanation would involve a mis-spelling of "palet"—quoits; see *Grande Encyclopedie sous la direction de Berthelot* s.v. "Palet: Jeu;" *Encyclopedie de Diderot* (editions Neufchatel, 1765) s.v. "Le jeu du Petit palet."

53. Morgan Lewis (1754-1844), Governor of New York, 1804-1807.

54. In the original French the phrase is written "des brames ou des gangarides." This is difficult to translate; the reference is probably to a fowl. The Brahmas, a large Asiatic breed of domestic fowl, is known to have been in America at that time. Further, there is a game bird, the ruffed grouse, whose cogener in France was the ganga. Ganga is a Catalan word used to describe the "gelinotte de Pyrénées." See Richard Parkinson, *A Tour in America in 1798-99-1800, exhibiting Sketches of Society and Manners and a Particular Account of the American System of Agriculture* (London, 1805), p. 299; see also A. Newton, *A Dictionary of Birds* (Cambridge, n.d.), p. 394; Kalm, *Travels,* I, 339; T. G. Pearson, *Birds of America* (New York, 1923), II, 17; *Grand Dictionnaire Universelle du XIX Siècle* (P. Larousse: Paris, 1865), VIII, 991.

55. Metheglin: a beverage made from honey and water, originally Welsh.

56. Famous honey from the district of Kowno, Lithuania; see Zygmunt Gloger, *Encyklopedia staropolska,* III, 219.

57. The American gray birch, Betula populifolia, Marsh., has its counterpart in the European birch, B. alba L., B. pendula Roth; see Graves, *Illustrated Guide,* pp. 66, 68; Michaux, *Histoire,* II, 140; *Drzewoznawstwo* (Warsaw, 1955), pp. 176-180.

58. An Indian by the name of John convicted of the murder in cold blood of Ezekiel Crane, Jr., in 1803 was sentenced to be hanged but asked to be shot instead; see French, *Gazeteer,* p. 200, n. 6.

59. John Nicholas (1756?-1819).

60. Sir William Pulteney (1729?-1805), born William Johnstone; see *Burke's Peerage and Baronetage*, 101st ed. (1956), p. 1198; *Gentlemen's Magazine*, LXXV (1805), Part 1, 587-588. In an association with John Hornby and Patrick Colquhoun known severally as The London Associates or Pulteney Associates, Sir William Pulteney bought in 1791 from William Temple Franklin, agent of Robert Morris, a large tract of land. This transaction was made through their agent Charles Williamson (1757-1808) because of an existing law whereby only American citizens could own land. The land extended between the Genesee River and Lake Geneva and south into Steuben County. See Appendix Map, Flick, *History*, V. For contemporary opinion by foreign visitors of Williamson see La Rochefoucauld-Liancourt, *Voyage*, I, 228-232; John Maude, *Visit to the Falls of Niagara in 1800* (London, 1826), p. 87. Williamson spent the money of his principals with a generous hand, not always to their liking; see H. I. Cowan, *Charles Williamson*, Roch. Hist. Soc. Pub. Series, XIX (Rochester, 1941), pp. 290-291.

61. Taylor's Hotel, so named when taken over by Taylor in 1803, was the principal hotel in Canandaigua and was known as The Hotel; see W. H. McIntosh, *History of Ontario County* (Philadelphia, 1876), p. 103.

62. General Amos Hall (1761?-1827) came from Guilford, Conn., and settled about one mile east of West Bloomfield. He was Deputy Marshall of the Census of 1790, State Senator 1809-13. He was commander of the American forces for a short time on the Niagara Frontier during the War of 1812; see McIntosh, *History*, p. 216; Bigelow, *Journal*, pp. 40-41; George S. Conover, *History of Ontario County* (Syracuse, 1893), pp. 368-369.

63. Hartford: In the original French manuscript this town was written "New Hartford" in error. Maude made the same error. The name was changed to Avon in 1808; see French, *Gazeteer*, p. 382; Maude, *Visit*, p. 102.

64. Niemcewicz was in error; the Holland Company's purchase was made from Robert Morris, who had bought the tract from Massachusetts. See Note 39 above.

65. This was probably Peter Vandeventer, who purchased land in Township 12, Range 5, Section 8, 9 under the rolls of The Holland Land Company for the year 1801. The first town meeting of Batavia was held in his tavern in 1803; see Turner, *Holland Purchase*, pp. 455, 520, 545; Crisfield Johnson, *Centennial History of Erie County* (Buffalo, 1876), pp. 29, 108, 111-112. Bigelow, *Journal*, pp. 45, 46, writes of Vandeventer and misspells his name as Vendevener.

66. Probably Louis Simond (1767-1831); see George C. Groce and David H. Wallace, *Dictionary of Artists in America 1564-1860* (New Haven, 1957), p. 580. In one of his books Louis Simond refers to his visit to Niagara; see Louis Simond, *Journal of a Tour and Residence in Great Britain during the Years 1810-1811* (New York, 1815), I, 217-219.

67. François Girardon (1628-1715), sculptor.

68. Elias Ransom (1762-1845) was born in Colchester, Conn., and came from Great Barrington, Mass. He lived in the first frame house west of Batavia at a place called Williamsville, 7 miles east of Buffalo, where he kept an inn in 1805; see Turner, *Holland Purchase*, pp. 421, 454; French, *Gazeteer*, pp. 282, 283, n. 1.

69. Farmer's Brother, famous Seneca chief, present at the Big Tree Treaty when the Indians ceded their rights prior to the Phelps-Gorham Purchase.

70. John Crow came to Buffalo in 1801-02 and built a frame addition to a log trading post and kept a tavern on Crow Street, which is now Exchange Street. The Mansion House replaced his tavern in 1806; see Johnson, *Centennial*, pp.

125, 127, 147; F. C. White, ed. *A Descriptive Work on Erie County* (Boston, 1898), pp. 126, 134, 140, 158.

71. Constantin François Chasseboeuf Volney, *View of the Climate and Soil of the United States of America,* tr. anon. (London, 1804), pp. 98-117.

72. Of the many poets who wrote about Niagara, Billardon de Sauvigny, Chateaubriand, Goldsmith and Thomas Moore may be listed. See Charles Mason Dow, *Anthology and Bibliography of Niagara Falls* (Albany, 1921), II, 695-697; Gilbert Chinard, *L'Amérique et le Rêve Exotique dans la Littérature Française au XVIIe et au XVIIIe Siècle* (Paris, 1934), pp. 405, 420, n. 1. Perhaps Niemcewicz did not know all these poets and their works. He did know Chateaubriand and almost certainly had read his work *Atala* which appeared in 1801; see Niemcewicz, *Pamiętniki,* II, 249; cf. Gilbert Chinard, *L'Exotisme Américain dans L'Oeuvre de Chateaubriand* (Paris, 1918), p. 244.

73. This is probably Col. Samuel Street (1775-1844) who married Abigail Hyde Ransom, daughter of Elias Ransom. He was the son of Nehemiah Street who had traded in furs in this region and whose widow settled with her children at Niagara Falls after his murder. See Turner, *Holland Purchase,* pp. 311, 416, 421; Henry and Marya Street, *Street Genealogy* (Exeter, N.H., 1895), pp. 55, 97.

74. Table Rock: A promontory on the Canadian side used to view the falls. A part collapsed in 1818 and again in 1850; see A. M. Grabau, *Paleontology and Geology of Niagara Region* (Albany, 1901), p. 13.

75. Cascate delle Marmore in Terni, Italy.

76. The Betonica family is not naturalized in America. The flower Niemcewicz may have seen was probably either the wood betony, pedicularis Canadensis L., or a flower of the family Stachys, hedge nettle; see N. L. Britton and Addison Brown, *Illustrated Flora of the Northern U.S. and Canada,* 2nd ed. (New York, 1947), III, 126, 128.

77. A flower of the Campanula family; see Britton and Brown, *Illustrated Flora,* III, 295; C. A. Zenkert, *The Flora of the Niagara Frontier Region* (Buffalo, 1934), p. 252.

78. Joseph-Geneviève, Comte de Puisaye (1755-1827), at the instigation of the English landed a small army of emigrees at Quiberon, arr. Lorient on the Brittany coast. There it was defeated by Hoche in 1795 and 711 of the prisoners were shot on the field of Brech because of the rule of the Convention. Puisaye left Canada in 1802 for England where he died. See *Grand Dictionnaire Universelle du XIX Siècle* (Larousse: Paris, 1865), XIII, 403, 539.

79. Robert Hamilton (1750-1809), merchant prince and legislative councilor; see *Encyclopaedia Canadiana* (Ottawa, 1957-58), V, 70

80. The schooner Speedy with Captain Paxton and all hands was lost off Presqu' Isle in Lake Ontario. Included among the passengers were Judge Cochrane and Solicitor General Gray. Testament of Mr. Roger Bates in *The Coventry Papers* kept in the Parliamentary Library, Ottawa; *Ontario Historical Society, Papers and Records,* VII (1906), 165-66.

81. Alexander Macdonell (1762-1842), was elected Speaker February 1st, 1805, of the Legislature of Upper Canada. See *Ontario Province Public Records and Archives,* 1911, Report 8. See also Legislative Minutes under date February 1805, and *Encycl. Canadiana,* VI, 255, for variant spelling.

82. Thomas Clark, Esq., agent of John Jacob Astor in Queenstown. See Turner, *Holland Purchase,* p. 586; Kenneth Wiggins Porter, *John Jacob Astor* (Cambridge, Mass., 1931), I, 260 nn. 29, 30, 412.

83. Thomas Douglas Selkirk (1771-1820), fifth earl.

84. Baldoon, named after a village in Scotland, in the County of Kent in Upper Canada where Lord Selkirk acquired 950 acres in 1803. Of the 100 colonists who went there in May 1804, 42 died; see George Bryce, *Life of Lord Selkirk* (Toronto, n.d.), Chapters V and VII.

NOTES TO "AMERICA REMEMBERED"

1. Niemcewicz wrote extensively of his Elizabeth Town neighbor Marolles in the diary of his return journey to Poland in 1807. He visited him in his castle Chissay, the former seat of Jean Dunois (c1403-1468), The Bastard of Orleans. As Marolles was the *mair* of the district, Niemcewicz discusses the function of this office in raising troops for Napoleon. He also saw many Russian prisoners working on the estate. See "Dziennik kieszonkowy J. U. Niemcewicza" [12 June 1807—9 November 1807], ed. Antonina Wellman-Zalewska, *Miscellanea z doby oświeciena*, Archiwum Literackie, V (Wrocław, 1960), pp. 475, 480-484. In his Memoirs Niemcewicz repeated this story but with some changes of detail. See Niemcewicz, *Pamiętniki* (Warsaw), II, 260-261. See also for an elaborate marriage contract (4 Sept. 1799) between Joseph Nicholas . . . Marolles and Rose Ann Budan (minor) daughter of Jacques Pierre Budan and Rosette Budan, *Essex County [N.J.] Deeds*, D 495-499. See also "Our dear, worthy Mrs. de Marolles has written that she rejoiced to find that you had left your dear Varsovie." Copy of MS. letter of Susan Ursin Niemcewicz to her husband 13 Nov. 1831 found at Skoki, now at Ursino, Elizabeth, N.J. For sale of house occupied by Mr. Kercado [Kirkadeau?] see *N.J. Journal*, 23 Jan. 1798. Du Buc was probably Abraham Du Buc de Marentile, whose name appears on a family tombstone in the cemetery of St. John's Episcopal Church in Elizabeth, N.J. Jovin was probably Jean Louis Jauvin; see *Essex County Records*, Mortgages C 278, D 174-175. Musron may be a misspelling of Masson to whom Niemcewicz referred later in his Memoirs as well as in his *Travels through America*, q.v. Chapter I, n. 68.

2. James Ricketts (1754-1826), Captain of the 60th Regiment of Royal Americans of the British Army, married Sarah Livingston (1755-1825), sister of Susan Livingston Kean. See Florence Van Rensselaer, *The Livingston Family in America* (New York, 1949), pp. 94-95. For extensive references to the Ricketts, Mrs. Kean and her first husband, John Kean, see Duc de Liancourt (La Rochefoucauld-Liancourt), *Journal de Voyage en Amérique et d'un Séjour à Philadelphie*, ed. Jean Marchand (Baltimore, 1940), passim; see also his *Travels through the United States of North America* . . . (London, 1799), I, 543-544. Of the well-known families referred to here, Niemcewicz was closely acquainted with Elias Jr., Elias Sr., William, Jane, Horatio and Cornelia Dayton, with Dr. Matthias Hampton Williamson (c1774-c1836) and with Colonel Aaron Ogden. Some of these names appeared on his marriage certificate and are mentioned in his will of 1807, copies of which are now in Ursino, N.J. Dr. Williamson treated Niemcewicz for fever; see *Pamiętniki*, II, 253. Colonel Ogden sponsored Niemcewicz's citizenship. For further details see *D.A.B.*; Edwin F. Hatfield, *History of Elizabeth, N.J.* (New York, 1868), passim, and his MSS. *Notes* in New-York Historical Society; *Charles Carrol Gardner Collection*: Rutgers University Library

Genealogical Holdings, New Brunswick, N.J.; *Biographical Index*, N.J. Historical Society. See also Chapter I, nn. 58, 59, 60.

3. Aleksandra Lubomirski Potocki with whose husband, Stanisław Kostka Potocki (1755-1821), Niemcewicz served on the Education Commission. A member of the highest aristocracy in Poland, she was a very close friend of Niemcewicz's. See *Pamiętniki* (Warsaw), I, II, passim. Mrs. Potocki led the list of subscribers for Niemcewicz's collected works. See his *Pism różnych wierszem i prozą* (Warsaw, 1805), II.

4. This letter properly identified as from Thomas Law to his brother (not to Niemcewicz) is included in Niemcewicz's publication on Washington; see his *Pism różnych* (Warsaw, 1803), I, 320; see also this Introduction, n. 35. A manuscript copy of the letter was in the Czartoryski Museum in Kraków and is printed in full in Haiman, *Poland and the American Revolutionary War*, p. 195.

5. Jean Victor Marie Moreau (1763-1813), a French Revolutionary and Napoleonic General banished to America in 1805 for taking part in a coup d'état against Napoleon. He was killed in the Siege of Dresden. Niemcewicz was present at his trial in Paris (1804) and gives an extensive account of it. See "Dziennik drugiej podróży do Ameryki," *Przegląd Lwowski*, V (1873), 589-591. See also *Pamiętniki*, II, 233-235. In Niemcewicz's inventory of his luggage he lists 84-year-old Tokay and essence of truffles, "a few drops [of which] give a delightful flavor to stews." For extensive account of Moreau's stay in America see Walter Barret [Joseph A. Scoville], *The Old Merchants of New York City* (New York, 1885), I, 337-347.

6. For Budan see note 1. Niemcewicz writes of an affectionate meeting in Paris, 9 Dec. 1833 with the Count d'Allemand, then living in Tours, his former neighbor in Elizabethtown; see *Pamiętniki Juliana Ursyna Niemcewicza. Dziennik pobytu za granicą od dnia 21 lipca 1831 r. do 20 maja 1841 r.*, II, 186.

7. Pierre Samuel Du Pont de Nemours (1739-1817), French economist, friend of Jefferson, was in America from 1799-1802. His two sons Victor Marie and Éleuthère founded the American branches of the family. He was invited by Prince Adam Kazimierz Czartoryski to Poland in 1774 and was secretary to the Educational Commission but left after three months. See *Pamiętniki*, II, 351 n. 5; see also Jean Fabre, *Stanislas-Auguste Poniatowski et L'Europe des Lumières* (Paris, 1952), pp. 278-279, 568 n. 21, 624 n. 47. The book of which Niemcewicz speaks is *Philosophie de l'univers*, 1st ed. (Paris, s.d.); 3rd ed. (Paris, 1799).

8. Peter Philip James Kean (1788-1828) had a deep and lasting affection for his stepfather. Some of his early letters to Niemcewicz and his biography of Niemcewicz are preserved at Ursino (the name given in his honor to "Liberty Hall" by his wife and stepson); they reflect their mutual respect and understanding. Peter Kean married Sarah Sabina Morris, daughter of General Jacob Morris of Otsego County, N.Y. On the death of Peter Kean (see his obituary in *New Jersey Journal* 7 October 1828) his widow married Looe/Love Baker (6 Jan. 1831, *Essex County Clerk Records*, B 214) and maintained a home at 19 Bond Street, New York, where Mrs. Susan Ursin Niemcewicz lived in her declining years. Mrs. Baker corresponded with Niemcewicz; some of her letters to him were found in Skoki, and copies are preserved in Ursino.

9. 2 July 1800, *Essex Cty. Clerk Records*, A 19:24. In the marriage contract recorded *Essex Cty. Deeds*, N 3.32 Mrs. Niemcewicz's brother Philip Peter Liv-

ingston (1740-1810) and her cousin John Rutherfurd (1760-1840) were parties of the third part.

10. William Dayton married Jane Tongrelou Chandler (c1767-1859), daughter of the Rev. Thomas Bradbury Chandler (Tory minister of St. John's Church; see Hatfield, p. 550). They were good friends of the Niemcewiczs, witnesses of their marriage contract, guests at their wedding, and were mentioned in Niemcewicz's will of 5 May 1807.

11. For the circumstances of the Clark sale see, "1 April 1800 Dr. Abraham Clark of Eliz. Town and wife to Aaron Ogden in trust for Susan Kean widow all that dwelling house and two lotts of land which said Dr. Clark purchased of Elias Boudinot bearing date twenty ninth of Sept. 1795 [*Essex Cty. Deeds*, D 242] 'on which the honorable Jonathan Dayton lived situated on the main street in Eliz. Town leading from the Court House to the Point,' " *Essex Cty. Deeds*, D 289. We have found no record of the purchase of the 18 acres of land. Niemcewicz wrote 18 morgs; a morg is 1.38 acres, but he probably used the word as the direct equivalent of an acre. Dr. Clark was the son of the Revolutionary patriot Abraham Clark (1726-1789); see Hatfield, pp. 586-587.

12. John Henry Hobart (1775-1830), deacon of the Protestant Episcopal Church, was pastor at New Brunswick, Hempstead and Trinity Church in New York. In 1816 he became the third Bishop of New York. See *Encyclopaedia Britannica*, 11th ed. s.v. "Hobart, John Henry;" see also Chapter I n. 60. The certificate of this marriage is preserved at Ursino and lists as witnesses with Hobart, E. B. Dayton, Aaron Ogden, W. Dayton, Jane Chandler (Mrs. Thomas Bradbury Chandler, d. 1801; see Hatfield, pp. 540, 551), E. C. Dayton, Mary G. Hobart, Jane T. Dayton and P. P. J. Kean.

13. Wilhelm Malcz (1795-1852). Niemcewicz bought a small estate called Rozkosz [Delight] near Warsaw from Princess Lubomirski in the twenties and lived there until his departure as Ambassador to England in 1831. His unpublished poem *Dumania w Ursynowie* reflects the happiness of his life there. See, for excerpts from this poem, Czartoryski, *Żywot*, pp. 203-210; *Wiek XIX. Sto lat myśli polskiej* (Warsaw, 1906), I, 311. See also *Pamiętniki* (Warsaw), II, 351-352.

14. Abraham Mann was buried in the cemetery of St. John's Church in Elizabeth, N.J. See *Gardner Collection* s.v. "Mann, Abraham;" see also "Death of Abram Mann in 81st year 9 Dec. 1837," *Biog. Index*, N.J. Hist. Soc.

15. See ". . . Whereas from the situation of the two windows of the back room of the before mentioned house which opens into yard of the said Horatio R. Dayton; they being liable to be obstructed by buildings erected contiguous to same, the said Abraham Clark promises and agrees to indemnify the said Susan Kean from all damages . . ." *Essex Cty. Deeds*, D 291. See also "Horatio R. Dayton, son of General Elias Dayton, married to Miss Cornelia R. Dayton (1782-1815), daughter of Dr. Jonathan J. Dayton, by Rev. Menzies Reyner 28 Jan. 1800," *Biog. Index*, N.J. Hist. Soc.

16. Tadeusz Matuszewicz (1765-1819), fellow member of the Four Year Diet and worker on the *Gazeta Narodowa i Obca*. He was Minister of the Treasury of the Grand Duchy of Warsaw as well as of the Congress Kingdom, translator of Horace, Virgil, Delille and Thomas à Kempis, and fellow member of the Society of the Friends of Learning.

NOTES TO "JOURNEY TO AMERICA.
DIARY OF SECOND VISIT"

1. The disastrous fire most generally referred to occurred in 1799, but large fires were of frequent occurrence. There was one in 1804 to which Niemcewicz may have referred. See *Virginia. A Guide to the Old Dominion State,* American Guide Series (New York, 1940), p. 243; see also for both 1799 and 1804 fires William S. Forrest, *Norfolk and Vicinity* . . . (Philadelphia, 1853), pp. 102, 111.

2. Since the provenance of the first published version (1873) of this diary rests on a copy made from a copy of the purported original, the names here as elsewhere are sometimes badly misspelled. See "M. Oster, commissary and commercial relations from the French Empire, 10 brewer St.," *The Norfolk Directory* . . . *also a Register* . . . *Town of Portsmouth* (Norfolk, 1806), p. 25. See for mention of this name and variation in spelling Moreau de Saint Méry, *Voyage aux États-Unis de L'Amérique, 1793-1798,* ed. Stewart L. Mims (New Haven, 1913), pp. 47, 250.

3. "Packet sailing between Norfolk and the following Ports: Baltimore . . . Schooner Eliza, Captain Ferguson;" see *Norfolk Directory,* p. 46.

4. See "The only remnant of the port which up to 1837 was a very important terminus on Elk river is (1940) the old French Town Tavern," *Maryland. A Guide to the Old Line State,* American Guide Series (New York, 1940), p. 360. See also for extensive contemporary (1794) account Moreau de Saint Méry, *Voyage,* pp. 94-95.

5. There was a French boarding house at the corner of Prune [Locust] St. and So. Fourth St. where Louis Phillipe had stayed; see Map insert, *Historic Philadelphia* . . . , Trans. Amer. Phil. Soc. XLIII, Part 1 (1953).

6. Marquis Carlos Maria Martinez de Irujo y Tacon de Casa Irujo (1765-1824). The spelling is somewhat similar to the established manuscript spelling of Niemcewicz. See Chapter II, p. 46.

7. Rembrandt and Rubens Peale on the ship Juliana, 5 weeks to London; see Charles Coleman Sellers, *Charles Willson Peale,* Memoirs of The American Philosophical Society, XXIII (1947), II, 148; this journey took from 4 July to 6 August 1802 according to Niemcewicz's MS. of this journey, since lost. See "Wiadomość o rękopisach pozostałych po J.U.N.," *Przegląd Poznański,* XXVI (1858), 43.

8. Maria Eliza Rickets, daughter of James Rickets and Sarah Livingston Rickets; see Van Rensselaer, *Livingston Family,* p. 120. Alexander James Dallas (1759-1817), American Administrator, admitted to the bar (1785), Secretary of Treasury (1814-1816); see *D.A.B.* s.v. "Dallas."

9. Maria Matilda Bingham and Comte Alexander de Tilly married in 1799, divorced in 1800; see Thompson Westcott, *The Historic Mansions and Buildings of Philadelphia* (Phila., 1877), p. 348. For Niemcewicz's meeting with this daughter in May 1834, then Mme. Blaisell, see his *Dziennik pobytu za granicą,* II, 349. See also Faÿ, *Revolutionary Spirit,* p. 457.

10. Jonathan Hampton, d. 31 Dec. 1803; he was perhaps a Judge of the Court of Common Pleas; see *Essex County Deeds,* D 249. See also "Statement of Guard-

ian," Elizabeth Gilmore executrix of will, *Essex County Surrogate Records,* Docket 606. The Hampton will was probated 7 Jan. 1804, *Superior Court of New Jersey* (Trenton), *Wills* File 10278 G. Mrs. Niemcewicz leased the house; she had the drawing room papered 25 Sept. 1804 in preparation for Niemcewicz's arrival; see "Statement of Guardian." I thank Professor Theodore Thayer for the suggestion that the man called "Stampton" in the printed Polish version of this material might be called "Hampton."

11. Perhaps Mrs. Barbara Dębinski Czacki, wife of Tadeusz Czacki (1765-1813), one of the leading exponents of the Polish Enlightenment. See *Polski słownik biografyczny* s.v. "Czacki, Tadeusz." Mrs. Barbara Czacki was a subscriber to Niemcewicz's work; see *Pism różnych,* II. Possibly Mrs. Maryanna Radziwiłł Krasiński, wife of Wincenty Krasiński (1783-1858), parents of one of Poland's great Romantic poets, Zygmunt Krasiński; cf. *Podróże po Ameryce,* p. 443; see also *Pamiętniki* (Warsaw), II, 358. The gifts were somewhat reduced by confiscation by the French customs authorities in Mayenne [Mainz]; see Niemcewicz, "Dziennik drugiej podróży do Ameryki," *Przegląd Lwowski,* V (1873), 449. Many of these gifts with an inventory kept by Niemcewicz are preserved at Ursino.

12. See *Pamiętniki* (Warsaw), II, 252. "Liberty Hall" was purchased by Peter Kean in trust for his mother Susan Ursin Niemcewicz 23 March 1811. See Chap. I n. 67. The sword and some other gifts do still decorate Ursino today.

13. "Riding through the little town after an absence of a year and a half it seemed to me that I had not been away even a day. For nothing had changed and the inhabitants were occupied with the same amusements to the extent that Mr. Mann who before my departure was planing shingles in front of Bily Dayton's house was today also sitting at this very place occupied with the same job as if during the past year and a half he had not gotten up from his chair." *Pamiętniki* (Warsaw), II, 252 (translated here from original MS. in the Bibliothèque Polonaise, Paris, which differs slightly from published version).

14. Lease was for one year commencing 1 April 1804 at a rent of 300 dollars; "It has therefore been unanimously concluded by all the relations of the s'd ward that it would much conduce to the benefit and advantage of the s'd ward to have all the real estate . . . converted into cash . . . and proceeds into stock . . . This opinion has been founded upon a full conviction of the rents . . . being entirely inadequate to support and educate the ward." See "Statement of Guardian Sworn 17 October 1804."

15. Betty was a Niemcewicz servant of long standing. After his departure in 1802 his wife's letter to him of 25 June, found in his home in Skoki, complained about her obstreperous behavior and wished her husband was there to control her.

16. See "By virtue of an order of the Orphans Court of the County of Essex for selling the lands of said minor for his maintenance and education she did advertise the lands to be sold on the 26th day of March 1805 at which time John Mayo having bid the sum of six thousand and fifty dollars for the house and lot of land . . . and no person bidding more the same were struck off to him." "Report of Elizabeth Gilmore, guardian, 1 April 1805," *Essex Cty. Surrogate Records,* Docket 606. John Mayo (1760-1818), Colonel in the State Militia of Virginia married Abigail DeHart, daughter of John DeHart of Elizabeth Town, a distinguished lawyer and a member of the first Continental Congress. Their eldest daughter Maria married General Winfield Scott in 1817. They occupied this house from time to time. See *Appleton's Cyclopaedia of American Biography* s.v.

"Mayo, Wm." See also Charles Winslow Elliot, *Winfield Scott. The Soldier and the Man* (New York, 1937), p. 213.

17. The term "canicular" is usually applied there, as here, to the summer season.

18. Niemcewicz's inventory preserved at Ursino lists, "Most excellent Lithuanian Flax seed, wheet, oats."

19. Sarah Eliza Julia Ann Kennedy (1801-1886), daughter of Sarah and James Ricketts, baptized 16 April 1802; see *Records of St. John's Episcopal Church, Elizabeth, N.J.* Typewritten MS. at New-York Historical Society. Julia Ricketts is the Julia née Ricketts Laurence who wrote the letter in defense of Lord and Lady Bolingbroke in *The New York Times*, 29 January 1877. See Introduction n. 17. See also Van Rensselaer, *Livingston Family*, p. 120.

20. Niemcewicz confused the maiden name of Mariamne née Alexander Williams with the married name of her two sisters. Letters found at Skoki make this clear. See *Pamiętniki*, II, 253. See also *D.A.B.* s.v. "Williams, Jonathan."

21. Jonathan Williams resigned in 1803 and accepted reappointment 19 April 1805. He founded the United States Military Philosophical Society of which Niemcewicz became a member 4 November 1805. Niemcewicz's membership certificate in this society is preserved at Ursino. He was very proud of this membership, listing it as one of his honors on the titles of his books. He was not, however, a consistent payer of dues as only one payment of 5 dollars in 1806 is credited to him. See MS. Records of this Society in New-York Historical Society.

22. Thomas Biddle married Christine Williams 12 February 1806, *Essex County Clerk Records*, Book A 50:78; see also Walter Livingston Cochrane Biddle, *Colonel Clement Biddle with a Genealogy of the Biddle Family* (Philadelphia, 1883), pp. 3-4.

23. "This certificate in my present sorry state is of great value to me and will continue to be so. For I travel about and stay here [France] with an American passport. Out of gratitude to Mr. Ogden I gave him a saber given to me in London by the excellent Mr. Kołaczkowski with the inscription: *Wiwat konstytucja 3 maja 1791*. And so this souvenir will remain in the New World. *Quae ora* [regio] *in terris nostris non plena laboris* [Virgil, *Aeneid*, I, 460. What tract on earth is now not full of our sorrow.]" This citizenship certificate dated June 1806 was searched in 1833 in Newark and a notarized copy was found amongst the papers in Skoki. There is a copy in Ursino. Niemcewicz speaks at length of Mr. Kołaczkowski in his *Pamiętniki* (Warsaw), I, 229, 230; II, 208, 256.

24. Lamus, from the German Lehmhaus, and here the diminutive. Usually a storehouse for preserving valuables from fire. In the old days they could be very elaborate buildings. See Zygmunt Gloger, *Encyclopedia staropolska* photo offset (Warsaw, 1958), II, 133-134. From Niemcewicz's letter to Mrs. Kossakowski translated here in which he speaks of receiving visitors and then bringing them into his house, his lamusik served as an outside study.

25. Margaret Rutgers (1773-1849), wife of Gerard Rutgers of Belleville, N.J. Her mother was Catherine Livingston, a sister of Mrs. Niemcewicz, who married Nicholas Bayard, Jr. See Van Rensselaer, *Livingston*, p. 94. See also *Gardner Collection*, Rutgers University Library. Gerard Rutgers (1765-1831) was commander of a company of the 2nd regiment of the Militia of New York. See MS. s.v. "Rutgers, Gerard" in New-York Historical Society; see also *Biog. Index*, N.J. Hist. Soc. There is considerable correspondence between her and the Niemcewiczs in Ursino.

26. Dominick Lynch (1754-1825); see Joseph Healey, "Four Gentlemen of

New York," *The Rosary*, LXXXII, no. 2 (Sept. 1932), 6. Thomas Barclay (1753-1830), see *New York Genealogical and Biographical Record*, IV (1873), 173. John Stevens (1749-1838), American inventor. For description of the Villa Stevens, present site of Stevens Institute in Hoboken, N.J., see Archibald Douglas Turnbull, *John Stevens: An American Record* (New York, 1928), p. 160.

27. Christopher Robert (c. 1749-1827); his three daughters were Elizabeth, Mary and Lucille; see *Essex Cty. Surrogate Records*, Wills Book D, Docket 3441; see also *Biog. Index*, N.J. Hist. Soc.

28. Margaret née Marshall Armstrong (1762-1827), wife of Colonel William Armstrong; see *Biog. Index*, N.J. Hist. Soc. See also *Essex Cty. Surrogate Records*, Wills Book D, Docket 3499. A charming book has been devoted to Mrs. Armstrong and her family, containing many letters concerning Niemcewicz and his American connections; see Margaret Armstrong, *Five Generations, Life and Letters of an American Family. 1750-1900* (New York, 1930). Margaret Armstrong is mentioned a great deal in correspondence found at Ursino and Skoki and she is also mentioned by Niemcewicz in his will. Mrs. Armstrong did not have a sister who was Mrs. Arnold.

29. George Izard (1776-1828), Major General (1814) during War of 1812. Attended Ecole du Génie in Metz. Married Mrs. Thomas Lee Shippen née Elizabeth C. Farley 6 June 1803. See *D.A.B.* s.v. "Izard, George."

30. This daughter is not listed in *Biddle Genealogy*. A tender letter (1807) from Christine Biddle to Mrs. Niemcewicz describes the sad circumstances of the death of the child; it is now found at Ursino.

31. The Academy was opened to the public in April 1807; see *The Pennsylvania Academy of the Fine Arts 1807-1870. Cumulative Record of Exhibition Catalogues*, ed. Anna Wells Rutledge, Memoirs of the American Philosophical Society, XXXVIII (Philadelphia, 1955), 2. In his will of 1807 Niemcewicz asked that the works of art he left to his wife go ultimately to the Academy. The fire of 1845 may have destroyed all records of his bequest as none of it remains.

32. There is one item of general interest in the will dated 5 May 1807. See "I give and bequeath to Princeton College Library all my medals, a Thermo lamp, a copy of Homer translated into the Polish language and two volumes of my works." All that remains from this bequest is a card copied from old records of acquisitions reading "Homerus, Iliada. Warszawie, 1800 2 V" and the two volumes of his works *Pism różnych* (1803-1805) with his inscription "To the college of New Jersey from the Author."

33. In a letter to Niemcewicz 19 July 1802, during his first absence, his wife had written, "Hatfield affected me greatly; he told me that you had been round to take leave of the Butchers, your goodness never omits to pay attention to the most menial person."

34. On the eve of a departure Niemcewicz liked to list in his diaries the names of the friends he was leaving. Compare "Dziennik drugiej podróży do Ameryki," *Przegląd Lwowski*, V (1873), 72. The Watts family is probably that of Robert Watts (1743-1814) who married Mary Alexander. Robert Watts and Robert Watts, Jr. (1784-1850), witnessed Niemcewicz's will. The Watts' Papers are in the New-York Historical Society. John Rutherfurd (1760-1840), Senator from New Jersey; see Livingston Rutherfurd, *Family Records and Events* (New York, 1894), p. 200 ff. Probably Alexander Macomb, "The Speculator"; see *Genealogy of Macomb Family*, MS. s.v. "Macomb, Robert" in New-York Hist. Soc.;

see also in *Genealogy* marriage of aunt of General Macomb to Colonel Francis von Pfister of the British Army; *Five Generations,* pp. 21, 54, 58, 319; *Essex Cty. Deeds,* D 256. Probably John Murray, Jr. (c. 1749-1819), and member of the Quaker merchant family; see [Scoville], *The Old Merchants of New York City,* pp. 292-301; see also Alice Colden Wadsworth, MS., *Notes on the Murray Family,* N.Y. Public Library. John Barker Church married Angelica Schuyler, an old friend of Niemcewicz; see *Travels through America,* Chap. VII n. 26. Bertram Peter Cruger, son of Nicholas Cruger of whom Niemcewicz wrote at length in his *Travels through America,* see Chap. I nn. 30, 31, 42, first married Catherine, daughter of John Barker Church and Angelica Schuyler Church, and later Mary, daughter of Robert and Mary Watts, *The New York Genealogical and Biographical Record,* VI (1875), 78.

APPENDICES

I

ON READING GIBBON

Interpolation from Manuscript Notebook
Numbered VIII

1 fev: 1799

[VIII. 13] Dans le pr[emier] volume de Gibbon Chapitre IX il y a une description abregée mais tirée entièrement de Tacite des moeurs des Germains. C'est une chose vraiment frappante que la ressemblance qu'on trouve entre les premiers habitants de l'Allemagne, et les sauvages de l'Amérique. Si on mettait d'un côté ce que Tacite dit des Germains et de l'autre ce que Charlevoix & autres rapportent des Indiens américains on dirait que tous deux ne parlent que du même peuple, quelques antiquaire iroit peut-être jusqu'à prouver que les Américains descendent des Germains, tandis que la conclusion la plus simple est que l'homme est partout le même. Des antipodes qui n'auront jamais entendu parler les uns les autres, si vous les placez sous les climats et le sol, en auront les mêmes passions, les mêmes habitudes et par conséquent les mêmes vertus, vices et le même degré de Civilisation, etc.

Dans le Chapitre suivant il eu parlé des barbares qui dans le 3me siècles inonderent l'Empire Romain. Les Goths vinrent des bords de la Baltique, ils traversirent toute la Prusse & la Pologne en traversant Le Pripet, arriverent en Ukraine du côté du Don de là passerent dans la Crimée où ayant renversé le petit Royaume de Bosphore, ils s'emparerent ils se servirent des petits vaisseaux qui y'étaient, pour se porter sur les Côtes de l'Asie, saccager Trebizonde, Athènes, etc. Il est à remarquer qu'après avoir piller et s'être enrichir [14] ils retournaient toujours à leurs établissements en Ukraine. Quoique c'était un ramas des peuples [illegible] venus de la Baltique, que des Scythes aujourd'hui Tartares, des bords de la mer noire et Caspienne, les historiques les appellent souvent des Jazyges [Iazyges]. Qui sait si ce ne

349

sont pas des Kozaks du Don & des Zaporoz, Kozak peut-être une corruption des Jazyges? Le Sit[e], l'amour du pillage, la manière de vivre,
le costume qu'on voit sur la colonne Trajane, tout parait justifier
cette conjecture.

Gibbon en parlant de peuples qui habitaient l'Allemagne, ainsi
qu'une grande partie de la Pologne cite Tacite qui faisait L'Enumér-
ation des différentes peuplades s'exprime ainsi sur les Arii occupant
la grande Pologne du côté de Brandebourg.

"*Ceterum Arii Super Vires quibus enumeratos paulo ante populos
antecedunt, truces, insitae feritati arte ac tempore lenocinantur, nigra
scuta, tincta Corpora, atras ad proelia noctes legunt; ipsaque formi-
dine atque umbra feralis exercitus terrorem inferunt, nullo hostium
sustinente, novum ac velut infernum a[d]spectum, nam primi in om-
nibus proeliis oculi vincuntur.*"

Cette peuplade était une branche de la grande nation de *Lygii*.

[François-Xavier de Charlevoix, *Histoire et description général de
la Nouvelle France, avec un Journal historique* (Paris, 1744); Tacitus
Germania, 43. The parallel drawn here by Niemcewicz is between the
treatment of the Indians by Charlevoix and of the Germans by Tacitus.
A similar comparison was made by Guizot of the treatment of the
North American Indians by James Fenimore Cooper and of the Germans by Tacitus; see Edward Gibbon, *The History of the Decline
and Fall of the Roman Empire*, ed. William Smith, 6 vols. (New
York, n.d.), I, 493, note a; see also François Guizot, *L'Histoire de la
Civilization en Europe* (Paris, 1828), I, 272. There is correspondence
which may pertain to this matter; see Czartoryski, *Żywot*, p. 354.]

II

GENERAL NOTES AND QUOTATIONS

From Cover Leaves of Notebooks Numbered II, IV, V, VII and VIII

Notebook No. II, inside front cover leaf:

President, Indiens Amboy.

Greenwood English gramer, at the end of which are two Essays of Rhetoric and Logic—Xenephon's Memorabilia of Socrates [Niemcewicz certainly read Franklin's autobiography. See, "While I was intent on improving my language, I met with an English grammar (I think it was Greenwood's), at the end of which there were two little sketches of the arts of rhetoric and logic, the latter finishing with a specimen of a dispute in the Socratic method; soon after I procur'd Xenephon's Memorable things of Socrates," *Autobiography of Benjamin Franklin*, ed. John Bigelow, Dolphin Books (Garden City, New York, n.d.), p. 78. Franklin was in error. The sketches, etc., are in Brightland's *Grammar;* see John Brightland, *A Grammar of the English Tongue: with the Arts of Logick, Rhetorick, Poetry, etc.,* 8th ed. (London, 1759); cf. Leonard W. Labaree, et al., ed. *The Papers of Benjamin Franklin* (New Haven, 1960), III, 410.]

To a heart formed for Friendship and affection, the Charms of Solitude are very shortlived. [unidentified]

L'espérance n'est qu'un Charlatan qui nous trompe sans cesse [Sebastien-Roch Nicolaus Chamfort (1740-1794), *Oeuvres Principales* (Paris, 1960), p. 28]

Quand on a été bien fatigué, bien tourmenté par sa propre sensibilité on s'apercoit qu'il faut vivre au jour le jour, oublier beaucoup, enfin, éponger la vie à mesure qu'elle s'écoule. Chamfort [cf. *ibid.*, p. 43.]

Notebook No. IV, inside front cover leaf:

In the South the Guayacum, and in the North Stylingia Silvatica
are the Indian specifics for pox. [Guaiacum; see *Encyclopaedia Bri-*
tannica, 11th ed. s.v. "Guaiacum." Stillingia sylvatica; see Benjamin
Smith Barton, *Collections for an Essay towards a Materia Medica,*
Part I, 2nd ed. (Philadelphia, 1801), pp. 32, 54]

Notebook V, outside back cover leaf:

Suskwehanna, my step. Departure. Life not mine, when they came
I did not die. *Court Houses.*

Notebook VII, inside front cover leaf:

O toi, qui m'a placé sur la terre, fais que j'y remplisse ma destina-
tion de la manière la plus conforme à la volonté sainte et la plus
convenable au bien de mes frères! [unidentified]

Notebook VIII, front cover leaf:

Spanheim de Usu Numismatum [Spanheim, Ezechiel, Freiherr von
(1629-1710), *Dissertationes de praestantia et usu numismatum an-*
tiquorum (Rome, 1664).]

Notebook VIII, inside front cover leaf:

Il est tel degré d'hypocrisie dont il n'y a plus de honte à être dupe
car il faudrait être pervers pour le soupçonner. [unidentified]

Le bonheur tient bien moins aux choses exterieures qu'à la disposition de l'Esprit aux Affections de l'âme. [unidentified]

Seneque le tragique a paru prédire la découverte de l'Amérique par
ces vers.

> . . . venient annis
> Secula ceris quibus oceanus
> Vincula rerum laxet, et ingens
> Pateat tellus etc. . . .

[Seneca, *Medea,* 1, 375]

Lineus—*The System of Vegetables with a copious explanation of all*
the Terms used in Botany, translated from a Thesis of Dr. Elms-
green with the Plat[e]s & references From the Philosophia Botanica
of Lineus by Leigh & Sotheby. To the families of Plants is prefixed
a Catalogue of the names of Plants & other Botanic Terms a work
of great labor in 2 vol. by Johnson. 16 Shil. [Johannes Elmgren,
Termini Botanici (Upsala, 1762);

> "Among the 'learned and ingenious' to whom
> acknowledgments are made in the Preface is
> 'that great master of the english [sic]

tongue Dr. Samuel Johnson for his advice in
the formation of the botanic language' "

see *Catalogue of the Works of Linnaeus in the British Museum,* 2nd
ed. (London, 1933), p. 49.]

Materia Medica Americana, p Marshall Humphrey and Barthen
[Humphry Marshall, *Arbustum Americanum: The American Grove*
(Philadelphia, 1785); Benjamin Smith Barton, *Collections for an
Essay towards a Materia Medica,* Part I (Philadelphia, 1798)]

Chimical Tests by J. F. A. Gottling proffessor in Jena. [Johann
Friedrich August Goettling, *Description of a portable chest of
Chemistry; or a complete collection of Chemical Tests . . . trans-
lated from the original German* (London, 1791)]
Notebook VIII, inside back cover leaf:
From 8 *Aug*[ust] to 3 *Oct*[ober] in 1798 2774 people died in Phila-
delphia from pestilential disease

in 1793 2 [died].

*The deaths in New York from the 1st day of Aug. to the 20 of
Oct. amounts to 1029 men 528 women and 346 childern Total 1903
of whom 1310 have died of the fever since the 1st of Sept before
that day we have no regural* [regular] *accounts of deaths by the
fever.*

Address of Libisz[ewski] in Havana *to the Care of St. Maria
Cuesta*

Spem vultu simulat, praemit altum Cord dolorem [Virgil, *Aeneid,*
I, 209.]

1 Decem[ber] 1799 The first snow fell in Eliz[abeth] T[own]

In difficillimis Rei publicae temporibus urbem non deserui, in pub-
licis nihil de publico delibavi, in desperatis nihil timui. [unidenti-
fied]

III

LISTS, EXPENSE ACCOUNTS AND CALCULATIONS

From Notebooks Numbered III, IV, V, VI, VII and VIII

Notebook No. III, back cover:

Breeches	3.
Neck handker[chiefs]	2.
Shirts	3.
Vestcot	1.
Stocking	2.
Pocket Hanker[chiefs]	3.
Night caps[?]	1.

Notebook No. IV, 42:

Expenses from Philad[elphia]
[8 May–15 June 1798]

	6D	S
Stage		
Board	2	4
in Baltimore	7	
Laundry		4
Stage and Dinner	6	
in Fed[eral] City, laundry	1	4
in Alexand[ria] and Great Falls	3	
Mount Vernon to the people [tips]	3	2
to the people [tips] Law	4	4
Stage to Fri[derick]	3	
Breakfast and dinner		5
	38	

354

[We note that here and elsewhere (except where noted) Niemce-wicz used a conversion factor of 8 shillings equivalent to 1 dollar. Polish was used except as shown.]

[Niemcewicz's expense accounts begin after the departure of Kości-uszko. The 6 dollars listed as the first item is given as 5 dollars in the text, III, 29.]

[Calculation of number of square feet in an acre]
An acre consists of 69 yards

$$69$$
$$\overline{621}$$

$$414$$

Three feet in $\overline{4761}$ square yards
    a yard 9
    $\overline{42,849}$ square feet

Notebook No. V, 12:

[c 15 June (overlap)—9 July]

Stage	3D	[S]
on the road	1	
Horse to Harper's Ferry	3	
in Harper	1	4
Horse		6
in the inn	4	
Stage to Lancaster	4	4
on the road	2	
in Lancaster	1	3
Stage to Philad[elphia]	4	
in the inn	1	
laundry	1	
Stage to Brun[swick]	4	
Lent to Virgisa[?]	3	
on the road	1	4
in Brunswick		4
in Elizab[eth]	1	2
in N[ew] York	3	4
Geog[raphy] book	1	4
	42	

Notebook No. V, 28:

[9 July—12 July]

	4[D]	[S]
For the boat		
in the inn and *stage*	2	
Item	1	4
in Hartford, inn	1	2
	8	6

Notebook No. V, 43:

[12 July—17 July]

	10D	[S]
For hiring the cabriolet in Hartford		
in Harwich [Norwich] in the inn		2
Stage to Providence and the inns	4	
in Providence	1	3
Boat to New Port	1	
	16	5

Notebook No. VI, 12:

[17 July—19 July]

	2D	Sh
In New Port, the inn and laundry		
To the shoemaker for repair		2
Stage	2	4
Dinner in Bristol		3
In Providence		6
Stage to Boston	3	
dinner		3
	9	2

Notebook No. VI, 36:

Expense
[19 July–31 July]

In Boston, the inn and laundry	7P	4
Stage back and forth to Ports-m[o]uth	8	
Eating, there and back	2	
In Portsm[o]uth, the inn and laundry	2	4
Ink in cans		3
	20	3

[One piaster equivalent to one dollar]

Notebook No. VI, 42:

Expense
[31 July–4 August]

Inn and laundry	2 Piasters	
Shoes	2	2
Waggon and expenses on the way	10	
	14 pia	2 Shil

Notebook No. VI, outside back cover leaf:

42		[15 June–9 July]
8	6	[9 July–12 July]
16	5	[12 July–17 July]
9	2	[17 July–19 July]
20	3	[19 July–31 July]
14	2	[31 July–4 August]
35	3	[4 August–?30 August]
146	5	
16		
162		
155		
317.		

[The first six figures here unidentified correspond to the sums of earlier expense accounts as shown; the seventh figure is the sum of the expenses from Notebook No. VII, 29.]

Notebook No. VII, 29:

[4 August–?30 August]

	[Dollars]	[Shillings]
In Lebanon	2	
Stage	1	
Powder, pomade and buckles	1	4
Hired horse	2	4
In the inn	5	
On the boat	2	4
In Clermont	2	
At Armstrong's—laundry		4
Boat	1	2
Sloop	1	
In New York dinners	1	
Hat	5	4
Boots	7	
Tobacco and soap		4
Laundry etc.	1	
Boat	1	1
	35D	3

Notebook No. VIII, 12:

Expense
[From September to 31 December]

	[Dollars]	[Shillings]
Bo[a]rding	9	
Laundry	1	
Fare and expenses in Brun[swick]	5	
Shoes	2	4
Powder		4
Bo[a]rding	9	
Book	2	
Laundry	3	
Paper and postage	1	
A negro	1	
	34	
Wood	4	4
Tarcie[?]	1	
Bo[a]rding	12	
Dentist	3	
Br[u]ns[wick]	3	
Bo[a]rding	12	
Laundry	2	
Postage	1	4
Powder and pomade etc.	1	
Wetstone	1	
Bo[a]rding	12	
Barton [?Materia medica]	1	2
Brunswick	3	
Christmas gift [for servants]	3	
	94	2
	year 1799	
in hand	140	
in gold	10	
	150	

Notebook No. VIII, 13:

Expenses in 1799

	[Dollars]	[Shillings]	
Laundry	2	3	2
Postage		4	
Fare to N[ew] Y[ork]	1	5	
Handkerchiefs	2	2	
Whist	2		
Pomade etc.		5	
Caramel		2	
Return fare	1	1	
For beer		2	
Bo[a]rding	15		
Boots	2		
Fare to Philadel[phia] and back	15	4	
Meterlo[?]	4		
Inn	3	4	
Boots	5	4	
Jacket etc.	6		
Alterations	1		
Ball	2		
Boots	2	4	
Wood	3	4	
Laundry	2		
Boy		3	
Boarding	15		
Laundry	1	4	
	91D	4	

[A conversion factor of 8 shillings to the dollar would give a sum of 90 dollars and 3 shillings; and of 7 shillings to the dollar 91 dollars and 2 shillings. The significance of the third column 2 after Laundry is unexplained.]

Notebook No. VIII, 14:

Avril

	[Dollars]	[Shillings]
Metterlo[?]	4	
Postage	1	
Laundry	2	
Powder and pomade		4
Libisz[ewski]	30	
Bo[a]rding	15	
Various	2	
Boarding	1 [squeezed in]	

May   Jun[e]

	[Dollars]	[Shillings]
Boarding	9	
Laundry	2	2
Stage to Phil[adelphia] and expenses on the way	6	4
Inn Phil[adelphia]	1	2
Microscope	2	
Metterlo[?]	2	
Paper	1	4
Knife		5
Metterlo[?]	8	
Landlord	2	
Boots	6	4
A sketchbook	2	
On the way	10	
Transportation		4
May Jun[e]	54	4 [54 1]
April	54	4 [55 4]
	109	
From September	185	
	294	

BIBLIOGRAPHY

BIBLIOGRAPHY

Akty powstania Kościuszki. Vol. III, eds. Włodzimierz Dzwonkowski, Emil Kipa and Roch Morcinek. Wrocław and Kraków: Zakład im. Ossolińskich. Wydawnictwo Polskiej Akademii Nauk, 1955.

Askenazy, Szymon. *Napoleon a Polska.* Vol. III. Warsaw and Kraków: Towarzystwo Wydawnicze w Warszawie, 1919.

————. "Przysięga Kościuszki," *Biblioteka Warszawska,* I (1912), 477-491.

————. *Thaddeus Kosciuszko.* London: The Polish Review Offices, 1917.

Aurora and General Advertiser (Philadelphia), 19 August 1797.

Baudouin de Courtenay, Romualda. *Nowe materyały do dziejów Kościuszki (Archiwum księcia Woroncowa).* Kraków: Fr. Kluczycki i Spółka, 1889.

Berent, Wacław. *Zmierzch wodzów.* Warsaw: Gebethner i Wolff, 1939.

————. *Zmierzch wodzów.* Rome: Polska YMCA przy AP., 1946.

Berndt, Margarethe. *J. Niemcewicz und K. Ryleev.* Berlin: Ernst Reuter, 1961.

Borowy, Wacław. *Studia i rozprawy.* 2 vols. Wrocław: Zakład Narodowy im. Ossolińskich, 1952.

————. *Kamienne rękawiczki.* Warsaw: Warszawski Instytut Literacki, 1932.

Brissot de Warville, J. P. *New Travels in the United States of America Performed in 1788,* trans. anon. London: J. S. Jordan, 1792.

Brückner, Aleksander. *Dzieje kultury polskiej.* 4 vols. Kraków: W. L. Anczyc i Spółka, 1931-1946.

————. *Dzieje literatury polskiej w zarysie.* 3rd ed. 2 vols. Warsaw: Bibljoteka Polska, 1921.

Brückner, Alexander. *Geschichte der polnischen Litteratur.* 2nd ed. Leipzig: C. F. Amelang, 1909.

Budka, Metchie J. E. "The American Notebooks of Julian Ursyn Niemcewicz. An Early Source of the Polish Ballad," *The Slavonic and East European Review* (Dec. 1964).

Bystroń, Jan Stanisław. *Literaci i grafomani z czasów Królestwa Kongresowego. 1815-1831.* Lwów: Książnica-Atlas [1938].

Cazenove, Theophile. *Cazenove Journal 1794,* ed. and trans. from the French by Rayner Wickersham Kelsey. (Haverford College Studies, Number 13) Haverford, Penna.: The Pennsylvania History Press, 1922.

Channing, Edward. *A History of the United States.* Vol. IV. New York: The Macmillan Co., 1920.

Chinard, Gilbert. *L'Exotisme Américain dans l'Oeuvre de Chateaubriand.* Paris: Librairie Hachette et Cie., 1918.

Chrzanowski, Ignacy. *Historja literatury niepodległej Polski (965-1795).* London: Interim Treasury Committee for Polish Questions, 1947.

————. *Literatura a Naród.* Lwów: Zakład Narodowy im. Ossolińskich, 1936.

————. "Władysław pod Warną Niemcewicza jako utwór tendencyjny," *Pamiętnik Literacki,* XIX (1921), 117-119.

————. *Z epoki romantyzmu.* Kraków: J. Czernecki, 1919.

Chrzanowski, Ignacy, Henryk Galle, Stanisław Krzemiński, eds. *Wiek XIX. Sto lat myśli polskiej.* Warsaw: Gebethner i Wolff, 1906.

Čiževskij, Dimitrij. *On Romanticism in Slavic Literature,* trans. D. S. Worth. The Hague: Mouton & Co., 1957.

Colbert, Edouard-Charles-Victurnien, comte de Maulevrier. *Voyage dans l'intérieur des Etats-Unis et au Canada,* with an introduction and notes by Gilbert Chinard. (Historical Documents, Institut Français de Washington) Baltimore: The Johns Hopkins Press, 1935.

Commager, Henry Steele. "Leadership in Eighteenth-Century America and Today," *Proceedings of the American Academy of Arts and Sciences,* XC, No. 4 (1961), 652-673.

Czartoryski, Adam. *Żywot J. U. Niemcewicza.* Berlin and Poznań. Biblioteka Polska w Paryżu, 1860.

Dihm, Jan. *Niemcewicz jako polityk i publicysta w czasie sejmu czteroletniego.* (Prace Historyczno-Literackie Nr. 29) Kraków: Kasa im. J. Mianowskiego, 1928.

————. "Nieznana powieść J. U. Niemcewicza," *Pamiętnik Literacki,* XXIX (1932), 207-216.

"Doprosy Kostiuskie, Niemceviču i dr. i ich pokazanja." *Čtenja v Imperatorskom Obščestvje Istorii i Drevnostej Rossiskich pri Moskovskom Universitetie,* Part IV (smes) (1866), 186-202.

Dunlap, William. *Diary of William Dunlap (1766-1839),* with an intro. by ed. Dorothy C. Barck. 3 vols. New York: New-York Historical Society, 1930.

Engeström, Lawrence. *Pamiętniki Wawrzyńca hr. Engeströma,* ed. and trans., Józef I. Kraszewski (Pamiętniki z ośmnastego wieku, XV). Poznań: J. K. Żupański, 1875.

Evans, A. W. W. *Memoir of Thaddeus Kosciuszko.* New York: Society of the Cincinnati, 1883.

Fabre, Jean. *Stanislas-Auguste Poniatowski et L'Europe des Lumières* (Publication de la Faculté des Lettres de l'Université de Strasbourg). Paris: Societé d'Edition, 1952.

Faÿ, Bernard. *Bibliographie critique des ouvrages français relatifs aux Etats-Unis (1770-1800).* Paris: Librairie Ancienne Edouard Champion, 1924.

————.*The Revolutionary Spirit in France and America,* trans. Ramon Guthrie. New York: Harcourt Brace & Company, 1927.

Gates Papers. New-York Historical Society Manuscript Collection.

Gibbon, Edward. *The History of the Decline and Fall of the Roman Empire,* with notes by Dean Milman, M. Guizot and Dr. William Smith. 6 vols. New York: Harper and Brothers, n.d.

Goriaczko, Anna. *Gazeta Narodowa i Obca* (Studia Historycznoliterackie, Vol. XII). Wrocław: Zakład im. Ossolińskich. Wydawnictwo Polskiej Akademii Nauk, 1953.

Gorjainov, S. M. *Zatočenie T. Kostiuški v Kreposti (1794-1795 g g.).* Moscow: Imperatorskoj Obščestvo Istorii i Drevnostej Rossijskich pri Moskovskom Universitetie, 1912.

Gubrynowicz, Bronisław. "W sprawie pamiętników i pism publicystycznych J. U. Niemcewicza," *Pamiętnik IV powszechnego zjazdu historyków polskich.* Lwów: 1925.

Haiman, Miecislaus. *Kosciuszko in the American Revolution.* New York: Polish Institute of Arts and Sciences in America, 1943.

————. *Kosciuszko Leader and Exile.* New York: Polish Institute of Arts and Sciences in America, 1946.

————. *Poland and the American Revolutionary War.* Chicago: The Polish Roman Catholic Union of America, 1932.

Handelsman, Marceli. *Adam Czartoryski.* 3 vols. Warsaw: Towarzystwo Naukowe Warszawskie, 1948-1950.

Handlin, Oscar, Arthur Meier Schlesinger, Samuel Eliot Morison, Frederick Merk, Arthur Meier Schlesinger, Jr., and Paul Herman Buck. *Harvard Guide to American History.* Cambridge, Mass.: The Belknap Press of Harvard University Press, 1955.

Historic Philadelphia. Transactions American Philosophical Society, XLIII, Part 1 (1953).

Jankowski, Władysław. "Geneza i dzieje 'Śpiewów historycznych' Niemcewicza," *Pamiętnik Literacki,* IX (1910), 52-71.

Jefferson, Thomas. *Notes on the State of Virginia,* ed. William Peden. Chapel Hill: The University of North Carolina Press, 1955.

Jones, Howard Mumford. *America and French Culture, 1770-1848*. Chapel Hill: The University of North Carolina Press, 1927.

Kaplan, Herbert H. *The First Partition of Poland*. New York: Columbia University Press, 1962.

Kleiner, Juljusz. "Krasicki jako przeciwnik literatury dworskiej," *Studja staropolskie. Księga ku czci Aleksandra Brücknera*. Kraków: Nakładem Krakowskiej Spółki Wydawniczej, 1928.

Korbut, Gabrjel. *Literatura polska*. 2nd ed. 4 vols. Warsaw: Kasa im. Mianowskiego, 1929-1931.

Korzon, Tadeusz. *Kosciuśzko biografia z dokumentów wysnuta*. 2nd ed. Kraków: Nakładem autora, 1906.

——. "Kwestya wyjazdu Kościuski z Ameryki," *Biblioteka Warszawska*, I (1907), 399-402.

Kościuszko, Tadeusz. "Listy do cesara Pawla I," *Russkaja Starina*, XXXIV (April 1882), 241-242.

Kot, Stanisław. *Historja wychowania*. Vol. II. Lwów: Państwowe Wydawnictwo Książek Szkolnych, 1934.

Kowalska, Aniela. "Nieznana karta publicystyki literackiej J. U. Niemcewicza," *Łódzkie Towarzystwo Naukowe. Sprawozdanie z Czynności i Posiedzeń*, XVII, No. 2 (1963), 1-12.

Kozłowski, Władysław M. (trans. and ed.) "A Visit to Mount Vernon a Century Ago," *The Century Magazine*, LXIII (Feb. 1902), 510-522.

——. "Pobyt Kościuszki i Niemcewicza w Ameryce w latach 1797 i 1798," *Biblioteka Warszawska*, IV (1906), 241-284.

——. "Niemcewicz en Amérique et sa correspondance inédite avec Jefferson (1797-1810)," *Revue de Littérature Comparée*, VIII (1928), 29-45.

——. "Niemcewicz u Niagary," *Bluszcz*, Nos. 28, 29 (1917), 210-211, 218-219.

——. "Rozstanie się Kościuszki z Niemcewiczem w Filadelfji," *Kwartalnik Historyczny*, XX (1906), 225-252.

Kożmian, Kajetan. *Pisma prozą*. Kraków: 1888.

Krasicki, Ignacy. *Pisma wybrane*. 4 vols., ed. Tadeusz Mikulski. Warsaw: Państwowy Instytut Wydawniczy, 1954.

Kraushar, Aleksander. *Towarzystwo Warszawskie Przyjaciól Nauk 1800-1832*. 4 vols. Kraków: Gebethner i Spółka, 1900-1906.

——. *Okruchy przeszłości*. Warsaw: Gebethner i Wolff, 1913.

——. "Rylejew i Niemcewicz," *Obrazy i wizerunki*. Warsaw: J. Fiszer, 1906.

Kridl, Manfred. *Literatura polska*. New York: Roy, 1945.

Krzyżanowski, Julian. "The 'Old King's Jester' Stańczyk," *Oxford Slavonic Papers*, VIII (1958), 49-65.

————. "J. U. Niemcewicz, w dwóchsetną rocznicę urodzin," *Wiado-mości*, XIII, no. 25 (London) (22 June 1958).

————. *W świecie romantycznym*. Kraków: Wydawnictwo Ludowe, 1961.

Krzyżanowski, Ludwik, ed. *Julian Ursyn Niemcewicz and America*. New York: The Polish Institute of Arts and Sciences in America, 1961.

Kunert, Ilse. *J. U. Niemcewicz: Śpiewy Historyczne. Geschichts-auf-fassung und -darstellung*. (Ph.D. dissert.) München: 1955.

La Rochefoucauld-Liancourt, duc de Liancourt. *Journal de Voyage en Amérique et d'un Séjour à Philadelphia 1 Octobre 1794-18 Avril 1795*, with an intro. and notes by Jean Marchand (Historical Doc-uments—Institut Français de Washington XII). Baltimore: The Johns Hopkins Press, 1940.

————. *Voyage dans les Etats-Unis d'Amérique Fait en 1795, 1796, et 1797*. 8 vols. Paris: Dupont, l'An VII [1799].

La Rochefoucault Liancourt, Duke de. *Travels through the United States of North America, the Country of the Iroquois and Upper Canada in the Years 1795, 1796 and 1797*, trans. H. Neuman, 2 vols. London: R. Philips, 1799.

Leśnodorski, Bogusław. *Polscy jakobini*. Warsaw: Książka i Wiedza, 1960.

Libiszowska, Zofia. *Opinia polska wobec rewolucji amerykańskiej w XVIII wieku*. Łódź: Zakład Narodowy im. Ossolińskich we Wroc-ławiu, 1962.

Linde, M. Samuel Bogumił. *Słownik języka polskiego*. 3rd ed., photo-offset. Warsaw: Państwowy Instytut Wydawniczy, 1951.

Lord, Robert Howard. *The Second Partition of Poland*. Cambridge, Mass.: Harvard University Press, 1915.

Maliszewski, Edward. *Bibljografja pamiętników polskich i Polski do-tyczących (druki i rękopisy)*. Warsaw: Towarzystwo Milośników Historji, 1928.

Maude, John. *Visit to the Falls of Niagara in 1800*. London: Longman, Rees, Orme, Brown & Green, 1826.

Michałski, Jerzy. *Z dziejów Towarzystwa Przyjaciół Nauk*. Warsaw: Towarzystwo Naukowe Warszawskie, 1953.

Miejska biblioteka publiczna im. Edwarda Raczyńskiego w Poznaniu. Poznań: 1959.

Mikulski, Tadeusz. *Ze studiów nad oświeceniem*. Warsaw: Państwowy Instytut Wydawniczy, 1956.

Moreau de Saint-Méry. *Voyage aux Etats-Unis de l'Amérique, 1793-1798*, ed. with intro. and notes Stewart L. Mims (Yale Historical

Publications, Manuscripts and Edited Texts) New Haven: Yale University Press, 1913.

Morse, Jedidiah. *The American Geography, or A View of the Present Situation of the United States of America . . . and in the West Indies, and of Europe, Asia and Africa.* New ed. with 25 maps. London: John Stockdale, 1794.

Niemcewicz, Julian Ursin. *Pamiętniki czasów moich,* ed. Karol Ursin Niemcewicz. Paris: Printed privately, 1848.

Niemcewicz, Julien Ursin. *Notes sur ma Captivité à Saint-Pétersbourg en 1794, 1795 et 1796,* ed. Charles Sienkiewicz. Paris: Bibliothèque Polonaise, 1843.

Niemcewicz, Julian Ursyn. *Dwaj panowie Sieciechowie,* ed. Jan Dihm (Biblioteka Narodowa, Series I, No. 135) Wrocław: Zakład Narodowy im. Ossolińskich, 1950.

———. "Dziennik kieszonkowy," ed. Antonina Wellman-Zalewska. *Miscellanea z doby oświecenia* (Archiwum Literackie, Vol. V) Wrocław: Zakład Narodowy im. Ossolińskich, 1960.

———. *Dzieła poetyczne wierszem i prozą.* 12 vols., ed. Jan Nep Bobrowicz. Leipzig: Breitkopf and Haertel, 1838-1840.

———. *Jan z Tęczyna,* ed. Jan Dihm (Biblioteka Narodowa, Series 1, No. 150) Wrocław: Zakład im. Ossolińskich, 1954.

———. "Journey to Niagara, 1805," trans. and ed. with notes Metchie J. E. Budka. *The New-York Historical Society Quarterly,* XLIV, no. 1 (1960), 73-113.

———. *O wolnem mularstwie w Polszcze,* ed. Józefa Wagnerówna. (Prace historyczno-literackie nr. 36) Kraków: Kasa im. J. Mianowskiego, 1930.

———. "List do pani [Katarzyny] Kossakowskiej (Lizabeth-Town w Ameryce d. 23 list. 1805)," ed. W. Tarnowski. *Archiwum Wroblewieckie.* Lwów (1883), pp. 24-30.

———. *Pamiętniki (1811-1820).* 2 vols., introd. Józef I. Kraszewski. Poznań: J. K. Żupański, 1871. [Memoir period actually 1809-1820]

———. *Pamiętniki czasów moich.* 2 vols., ed. Jan Dihm. Warsaw: Państwowy Instytut Wydawniczy, 1957.

———. *Pamiętniki. Dziennik pobytu za granicą od dnia 21 lipca 1831 r. do 20 maja 1841 r.,* Vol. I, 1831-1832, Vol. II, 1833-1834. Poznań: J. K. Żupański, 1876-1877.

———. *Pamiętniki Juliana Ursyna Niemcewicza 1804-1807. Dziennik drugiej podróży do Ameryki,* ed. anon. Lwów: K. Wild, 1873.

———. "Pamiętniki Juliana Ursyna Niemcewicza (Dziennik drugiej podróży do Ameryki) 1804-1807," *Przegląd Lwowski,* V, VI (1873).

————. *Pamiętnik o czasach Księztwa warszawskiego* (*1807-1809*), ed. Alexander Kraushar. Warsaw: Gebethner i Wolff, 1902.

————. "Pamiętniki z lat 1820-1829," ed. Wacław Zawadzki. *Pamiętniki dekabrystów*. Warsaw: Państwowy Instytut Wydawniczy, 1960.

————. *Pamiętniki z 1830-1831 roku*, ed. Maryan Antoni Kurpiel. Kraków: Akademja Umiejetności. Skład główny w księgarni G. Gebethnera i Spółki, 1909.

————. *Pism różnych wierszem i prozą.* 2 vols. Warsaw: Tadeusz Mostowski, 1803, 1805.

————. *Podróże po Ameryce 1797-1807*, with an introd. and notes, ed. Antonina Wellman-Zalewska, general ed. Emil Kipa. Warsaw: Zakład Narodowy im. Ossolińskich, 1959.

————. "Podróż Juliana Ursyna Niemcewicza z Petersburga do Ameryki w r. 1796 z francuskiego oryginalu na język polski przełożona," trans. anon., *Przegląd Poznański*, XXV (1858), 438-461.

————. *Powrót posła . . . oraz wybór bajek politycznych z epoki Sejmu Wielkiego.* 6th ed., ed. Stanisław Kot (Biblioteka Narodowa Series I, No. 4). Wrocław: Zakład Narodowy im. Ossolińskich, 1950.

————. "Rok 3333; czyli sen niesłychany," *Przegląd Poznański* XXVI (1858), 346-356. Reprinted as book, *Rok 3333; . . .* (Biblioteka im. Jana Jeleńskiego. Żywy pomnik z ofiar współziomsk ów no. 3). Warsaw: [Polak-Katolik], 1911.

————. *The American Diaries of Julian Ursyn Niemcewicz* (*1797-1799, 1805*), with an introd. and notes, trans. and ed. Metchie J. E. Budka (Ph.D. thesis, Harvard, 1962).

Niles, Hezekiah. *Principles and Acts of the Revolution in America.* Baltimore: W. O. Niles, 1822.

Odrowąż-Pieniążek, Janusz. "Materiały Niemcewiczowskie w Bibliotece Polskiej i w Muzeum Mickiewicza w Paryżu," *Miscellanea z lat 1800-1850* (Archiwum Literackie, Vol. VII). Wrocław: Zakład im. Ossolińskich, 1963.

————. "Un poèm canado-américain de J. U. Niemcewicz," *Études Slaves et Est-Européennes*, VII, 1, 2 (1962), 78-80.

"Old Minutes of the Society from 1743-1838," *Proceedings of the American Philosophical Society.* XXII, Part III, no. 119 (1885).

Palmer, R. R. *The Age of the Democratic Revolution. A Political History of Europe and America, 1760-1800.* 2 vols. Princeton: Princeton University Press, 1959, 1964.

Pigoń, Stanisław. *Z epoki Mickiewicza; studja i szkice.* Lwów: Zakład Narodowy im. Ossolińskich, 1922.

Płoszewski, Leon. "Pierwsza redakcja 'Spiewów historycznych' (z r. 1809)," *Pamiętnik Literacki,* XIV (1916), 276-288.

Potocki, Jan. *Podróż do Turek y Egyptu z przydanym dziennikiem podróży do Hollandyi podczas Rewolucyi 1787,* trans. J. U. Niemcewicz. Warsaw: 1789.

————. *Podróże:* [Podróż do Turek i Egiptu oraz "Podróż do Hollandii" wg. tłumaczenia J. U. Niemcewicza], ed. Leszek Kukulski. Warsaw: Czytelnik, 1959.

Prumbs, Zygmunt. "Tam, gdzie żył adjutant T. Kościuszki Julian Ursyn Niemcewicz," *Nowy Świat—The Polish Morning World* (New York), 19 June 1938.

Ramsay, David, M.D. *The History of the American People.* 2 vols. Dublin: William Jones, 1793.

Schulz, Friedrich. *Podróże inflantczyka z Rygi do Warszawy i po Polsce w latach 1791-1793,* ed. Wacław Zawadzki, trans. Józef Ignacy Kraszewski. Warsaw: Czytelnik, 1956.

Sidwa, Anne H. and Marion Moore Coleman. *Niemcewicz An Anniversary Tribute.* Cambridge Springs, Penna.: Alliance College, 1958.

Skałkowski, A[dam] M. *O kokardę legionów.* Lwów: Gubrynowicz i Syn, 1912.

————. *Z dziejów insurekcji 1794 r.* Warsaw: Gebethner i Wolff, 1926.

Smoleński, Władysław. *Przewrót umysłowy w Polsce wieku XVIII.* 2nd ed. Warsaw: Ministerstwo Wyznań Religijnych i Oświecenia Publicznego, 1923.

Sterne, Laurence. *A Sentimental Journey through France and Italy,* introd., Virginia Woolf (The World's Classics no. 333). London: Oxford University Press, 1957.

Tarnowski, Stanisław. *Historya literatury polskiej.* 2nd ed. 4 vols. Krakow: Spółka Wydawnicza Polska, 1904.

Terszakoveć, Mykhailo. *"Spiewy historyczne" J. U. Niemcewicza przedmiotem zabiegów dyplomatycznych.* Lwów: Zakład Narodowy im. Ossolińskich, 1930.

The Cambridge History of Poland from Augustus II to Pilsudski (*1697-1935*), eds. W. F. Reddaway, J. S. Penson, O. Halecki and R. Dyboski. Cambridge: Cambridge University Press, 1951.

Tretiak, Józef. *Finis Poloniae. Historja legendy maciejowickiej i jej rozwiązanie.* Kraków: Krakowska Spółka Wydawnicza, 1921.

Turner, Frederick J. *Correspondence of the French Ministers (1791-1797),* Vol. II of Annual Report of the American Historical Association for the Year 1903. Washington: Published as the Seventh Report of the Historical Manuscripts Commission, 1904.

Tyrowicz, Maryan. "Działalność publiczna J. U. Niemcewicza w latach 1807-1813," *Ateneum Wileńskie,* VII (1930), 263-292.

———. "Juljan Ursyn Niemcewicz w dobie Królestwa Kongresowego i nocy listopadowej," *Przegląd Współczesny,* IX (October, 1930), 94-106; (November, 1930), 230-255.

Van Rensselaer, Florence. *The Livingston Family in America.* New York: Printed privately, 1949.

Volney, C. F. *View of the Climate and Soil of the United States,* trans. anon. London: J. Johnson, 1804.

Vorobjev, G. A. "Razgovory Imperartora Pavla 1-go c Tadeusem Kostiuško v Peterburge," *Russkaja Starina,* CXXIV (1905), 392-396.

Węgierski, Tomasz Kajetan. "Z życia Węgierskiego, pamiętniki listy," ed. Stanisław Kossowski, *Przewodnik Naukowy i Literacki,* XXXVI (1908), 44 ff.

Weintraub, Wiktor. *Literature as Prophecy.* The Hague: Mouton & Co., 1959.

———. ed., *Wybór pism,* by Ignacy Krasicki. Jerusalem: Ministerstwo Wyznań Religijnych i Oświecenia Publicznego, 1944.

Weld, Jun., Isaac. *Travels through the States of North America and the Provinces of Upper and Lower Canada during the years 1795, 1796 and 1797.* 4th ed. 2 vols. London: John Stockdale, 1807.

"Wiadomość o rękopisach pozostałych po Julianie Niemcewiczu." *Przegląd Poznański,* XXVI (1858), 34-46.

Witkowski, Michał. "Misja J. U. Niemcewicza do Miechowa i Krakowa w r. 1831." *Miscellanea z okresu romantyzmu* (Archiwum Literackie, Vol. I). Wrocław: Zakład im. Ossolińskich Wydawnictwo Polskiej Akademii Nauk, 1956.

———. "Oczyma Niemcewicza," *Literacki przystanki nad Wartą.* Poznań: Wydawnictwo Poznańskie, 1962.

Wojciechowski, Konstanty. *Historja powieści w Polsce.* Lwów: Gubrynowicz i Syn, 1925.

Wojtkowski, Andrzej. *Edward Raczyński i jego dzieło.* Poznań: Bibljoteka Raczyńskich, 1929.

"Wykaz rękopismów pozostałych po J. U. Niemcewiczu," *Czas,* No. 164 (1866).

Załuska, Apolonja. *Poezja opisowa Delille'a w Polsce* (Prace Historyczno-Literackie, no. 44). Kraków: Kasa im. J. Mianowskiego, 1934.

Zbyszewski, Karol. *Niemcewicz od przodu i tyłu.* Warsaw: Roj, 1939.

Zgorzelski, Czesław. *Ballada polska* (Biblioteka Narodowa Series I, no. 177). Wrocław: Zakład Narodowy im. Ossolińskich, 1962.

INDEX

Index

Acknomak (ship), 291

Acquackanonck (Passaic, N.J.), 233

Adams, Mrs. John, description of, 29

Adams, John, anecdote on King of Prussia, 30; asks news of Kościuszko, 29; asks news of Lafayette, 29; death on same day as Jefferson, 269-270; reception for at New Brunswick, 29-30; refusal to attend Washington Ball, 44; tea at Whites, 30; Washington's opinion on, 107

Albani, Francesco, 212

Albany (N.Y.), Tontine Coffee House, 180, 237; trade of, 181; trade with New York City, 190; visited (August, 1798), 180-183; visited (1805), 237

Alexander, William, 241

Alexandria (Va.), 91-92

Alien and Sedition Bills, 68, 125

Amboy (N.J.), description of, 32; indolence of inhabitants, 32; loyalty to British, 32; proximity to New York City prevents commercial growth, 7-8

America, birds, variety in, 24, 73; bridges, profusion of, 160-161; carriages, like Turkish carriage from Moldavia, 216; homestead, cost of, 7; hunting, difficulty of, 11, for fox, 234; manufacturing in, 26, 155; militia, *see* Militia; nut trees, ways of picking, 229-230; pheasants, 24, 230; squirrels, 24, 230, 247, 283; way of life in little town, 272-273

American Diaries, dependence on Morse, *Geography*, xxxvi-xxxvii

American Navy, seaman's pay, 166; war preparations, 68

American Philosophical Society, xxviii, 48, 64, 65; election of Niemcewicz, 64

American Revolutionary War, Battle of Charleston (S.C.), 11; Battle of Long Island, 10; stupidity of British generals, 10, calculated, 211

American women, description of, 35, 54-55, 274; seduction, 275

Americans, age rapidly due to succulent meats and hot drinks, 64; antipathy toward foreigners, 71, 138; attitude toward riches, 64; bear, preference for eating whole, 218; behavior of young society, 21; beverages drunk, cider in winter, rum in summer, 6; calumniating Washington and Franklin, 268-269; dependence on English, 16; dinner menu, entertainment, 10; drunkenness, 216-217; eating habits, 111; equality in New Brunswick, 9; exaggeration of, 62, 155, 156; facility in conversation on politics, 191; favorite drink of, 110; fecundity of seaman, 154; horse stealing, 116; hunting, 11; jealousy, anecdote on tailor, 192; manner of dress, homespun clothes, 28, nightcaps and dressing gowns, 164; morality in married life, 21; not bloodthirsty, 53; not economical in decoration of